ARNOLD READERS IN HISTORY

TITLES IN THE *ARNOLD READERS IN HISTORY* SERIES

ALREADY PUBLISHED

THE ENGLISH CIVIL WAR
Edited by Richard Cust and Ann Hughes

THE FRENCH REVOLUTION IN SOCIAL AND POLITICAL PERSPECTIVE
Edited by Peter Jones

FORTHCOMING

BRITISH POLITICS AND SOCIETY 1906–1951
Edited by John Stevenson

GENDER AND HISTORY IN WESTERN EUROPE
Edited by Bob Shoemaker and Mary Vincent

THE IMPACT OF THE ENGLISH REFORMATION 1500–1640
Edited by Peter Marshall

THE ORIGINS OF THE SECOND WORLD WAR
Edited by Patrick Finney

THEORIES OF FASCISM
Edited by Roger Griffin

THE TUDOR MONARCHY
Edited by John Guy

WOMEN'S WORK: THE ENGLISH EXPERIENCE 1650–1914
Edited by Pamela Sharpe

THE ENGLISH CIVIL WAR

Edited by

RICHARD CUST

Senior Lecturer in Modern History,
University of Birmingham

and

ANN HUGHES

Professor of History, University of Keele

A member of the Hodder Headline Group
LONDON • NEW YORK • SYDNEY • AUCKLAND

First published in Great Britain 1997 by
Arnold, a member of the Hodder Headline Group,
338 Euston Road, London NW1 3BH
175 Fifth Avenue, New York, NY 10010

Distributed exclusively in the USA by
St Martin's Press, Inc.
175 Fifth Avenue, New York, NY 10010

British Library Cataloguing in Publication Data
A catalogue record for this book is available from the British Library

Library of Congress Cataloging-in-Publication Data
A catalog record for this book is available from the Library of Congress

ISBN 0 340 66199 2 (hb)
ISBN 0 340 63173 2 (pb)

Typeset in 10/12pt Sabon by J&L Composition Ltd, Filey, North Yorkshire
Printed and bound in Great Britain by J.W. Arrowsmith Ltd, Bristol

Contents

SECTION III SOCIETY AND CULTURE

Acknowledgements

We are grateful to all the contributors to this volume for permission to republish their work. More generally, we are indebted to them for the support and encouragement they have given in putting the volume together. All the articles here are reprinted whole, without cuts in either the text or the footnotes. The editors and publishers would like to thank the following for permission to use copyright material in this book: J.S.A. Adamson, 'The Baronial Context of the English Civil War', *Transactions of the Royal Historical Society*, Fifth Series, Volume 40 (1990), pp. 93–120. Reprinted by permission of the Royal Historical Society. Richard Cust, 'News and Politics in Early-Seventeenth Century England', *Past and Present*, Volume 112 (1986), pp. 60–90. Reprinted by permission of Oxford University Press. Clive Holmes, 'The County Community in Stuart Historiography', *Journal of British Studies*, 19 (1980), pp. 54–73. Reprinted by permission of the University of Chicago Press. Ann Hughes, 'The King, the Parliament and the Localities During the English Civil War', *Journal of British Studies*, 24 (1985), pp. 236–63. Reprinted by permission of the University of Chicago Press. Mark Kishlansky, 'The Emergence of Adversary Politics in the Long Parliament', *Journal of Modern History*, 49 (1977), pp. 617–40. Reprinted by permission of the University of Chicago Press. Peter Lake, 'Anti-Popery: The Structure of a Prejudice', in Richard Cust and Ann Hughes, eds, *Conflict in Early Stuart England* (1989), pp. 72–106. Reprinted by permission of Addison Wesley Longman. J.S. Morrill, 'The Religious Context of the English Civil War', *Transactions of the Royal Historical Society*, Fifth Series, Volume 34 (1984), pp. 155–78. Reprinted by permission of the Royal Historical Society. J.S. Morrill and J.D. Walter, 'Order and Disorder in the English Revolution', in A.J. Fletcher and J. Stevenson, eds, *Order and Disorder in Early Modern England* (1985), pp. 137–65. Reprinted by permission of the authors and Cambridge University Press. Conrad Russell, 'The British Problem and the English Civil War', *History*, 72 (1987), pp. 395–415; and 'Parliamentary History in Perspective, 1604–1629',

History, 61 (1976), pp. 1–27. Reprinted by permission of Blackwell Publishers. N.R.N. Tyacke, 'Puritanism, Arminianism and Counter-Revolution', in C.S.R. Russell, ed., *The Origins of the English Civil War* (1973), pp. 119–43. Reprinted by permission of Macmillan Press Ltd. David Underdown, 'The Chalk and the Cheese: Contrasts Among the English Clubmen', *Past and Present*, Volume 85 (1979) pp. 25–48. Reprinted by permission of the author and Oxford University Press. David Wootton, 'From Rebellion to Revolution: The Crisis of the Winter of 1642/3 and the Origins of Civil War Radicalism', *English Historical Review* (1990), pp. 654–69. Reprinted by permission of Addison Wesley Longman.

To the best of our knowledge all copyright holders of material reproduced in this book have been traced. Any rights not acknowledged here will be noted in subsequent printings if notice is given to the publisher.

List of abbreviations

Place of publication is London unless otherwise stated.

Add. MS	Additional Manuscript, British Library
AHR	*Agricultural History Review*
BL	British Library
Bodl. L	Bodleian Library, Oxford
BIHR	*Bulletin of the Institute of Historical Research*
BRO	Berkshire Record Office
CCC	*Calendar of the Proceedings of the Committee for Compounding*, ed. M.A.E. Green, 5 vols (London, 1889–92)
CCRO	Chester City Record Office
CD 1621	*Commons Debates in 1621*, 7 vols, eds W. Notestein, F.H. Relf and H. Simpson (New Haven, 1935)
CD 1625	*Debates in the House of Commons in 1625*, ed. S.R. Gardiner (Camden Soc., new ser., 6, 1873)
CD 1629	*Commons Debates for 1629*, eds W. Notestein and F.H. Relf (Minneapolis, 1921)
Chamberlain	*The Letters of John Chamberlain*, ed. N.E. McLure, 2 vols (Philadelphia, 1939)
Clarendon	Edward Hyde, earl of Clarendon, *The History of the Rebellion and Civil Wars in England*, ed. W.D. Macray, 6 vols (Oxford, 1888)
CJ	*Commons' Journals*
CSPD	*Calendar of State Papers Domestic*
CSP Ven.	*Calendar of State Papers Venetian*
C and T, Chas 1	*Court and Times of Charles 1*, ed. T. Birch, 2 vols (1848)

C and T, Jas 1	*Court and Times of James 1*, ed. T. Birch, 2 vols (1848)
CUL	Cambridge University Library
DNB	*Dictionary of National Biography*
Ec. HR	*Economic History Review*
Eg. MS	Egerton Manuscript, British Library
EHR	*English Historical Review*
FSL	Folger Shakespeare Library, Washington
Gardiner, *History*	S.R. Gardiner, *The History of England 1603–42*, 10 vols (1883–4)
Harl. MS	Harleian Manuscript, British Library
Hist.	*History*
HJ	*Historical Journal*
HLQ	*Huntington Library Quarterly*
HLRO	House of Lords Record Office
HMC	Historical Manuscripts Commission
Holles	*The Letters of John Holles 1587–1637*, ed. P.R. Seddon (Thoroton Soc. Rec. Ser., 31, 35, 36, 1975–87)
HR	*Historical Research*
JBS	*Journal of British Studies*
JEH	*Journal of Ecclesiastical History*
JMH	*Journal of Modern History*
KAO	Kent Archives Office
Laud	W. Laud, *The Works*, 6 vols (Oxford, 1853)
LJ	*Lords' Journal*
MH	*Midland History*
Neg.Post.	*An Apology for Socrates and Negotium Posterorum by Sir John Eliot*, ed. A.B. Grosart (1881)
NH	*Northern History*
NLS	National Library of Scotland
NLW	National Library of Wales
NRO	Northamptonshire Record Office
P&P	*Past and Present*
PD 1610	*Parliamentary Debates in 1610*, ed. S.R. Gardiner (Camden Soc., old ser., 81, 1862)
P in P 1610	*Proceedings in Parliament 1610*, ed. E.R. Foster, 2 vols (New Haven, 1966)
P in P 1628	*Proceedings in Parliament 1628*, eds R.C. Johnson, M.F. Keeler et al., 6 vols (New Haven, 1977–83)
PRO	Public Record Office
Proclamations	*Stuart Royal Proclamations*, eds P.L. Hughes and J.F. Larkin, 2 vols (Oxford, 1973–83)
Rushworth	J. Rushworth, *Historical Collections*, 7 vols (1659–1701)

Rymer	T. Rymer, *Foedera*, 20 vols (1704–35)
Scrin. Res.	*Scrinia Reserata: A Memorial offr'd to the great deservings of John Williams D.D.*, John Hacket, 2 parts (1692–3)
Somers Tracts	*Somers Tracts*, ed. Sir Walter Scott, 2nd edn, 13 vols (1809–15)
SP	State Papers
SRO	Scottish Record Office
ST	*State Trials*, eds W. Cobbett and T.B. Howell, 33 vols (1809–26). References are to column numbers.
Strafforde Letters	*The Earl of Strafforde's Letters and Dispatches*, ed. W. Knowler, 2 vols. (1729)
THES	*Times Higher Education Supplement*
TLS	*Times Literary Supplement*
TRHS	*Transactions of the Royal Historical Society*
Wentworth Papers	*The Wentworth Papers 1597–1628*, ed. J.P. Cooper (Camden Soc., 4th ser., 12, 1973)
VCH	*Victoria County History*

Dates are old style unless otherwise stated, except that the year is taken to begin on 1 January.

Introduction

Continuities and discontinuities in the English Civil War

A reader bringing together articles on both the origins and the course of the civil war now requires justifications unnecessary 20 or so years ago. In recent decades a variety of scholarship on the period, sometimes tagged 'revisionism', has made complicated a political story that was perhaps too simple, separating out different aspects of historical experience – economic, social, political, religious and cultural – which earlier work tended to connect together. Before 'revisionism', chronological and thematic coherence was provided by the concept of the 'English Revolution'. This was 'one of the decisive political episodes of modern times', a wide-ranging phenomenon which made England distinctive amongst early modern political systems.[1] It had its origins in the social, political and religious changes of the sixteenth century and was confirmed, in a subdued form, by the Revolution Settlement of 1689. The label connected events before 1642 with those of the civil war and after; it also brought together religious, political and social 'factors'. This is not to say that there was consensus amongst historians over how this revolution should be characterized or interpreted. Indeed there were fierce and bitter debates, especially over the connections between political and religious issues on the one hand, and social and economic developments on the other. For historians working in Marxist traditions, the revolution was both brought about by, and helped to facilitate, an emerging capitalist system in England; it was closely connected to the transformation of the English ruling elite from a traditional feudal rentier class into capitalist exploiters. It was, in short, a bourgeois revolution.[2] Alternatively, the 'Whigs' stressed the opposition to arbitrary monarchy fuelled by constitutional principle and self-confident Protestant or Puritan zeal, and focused on parliament, or more precisely on the house of commons. It was the Commons that, from Elizabeth's reign, came increasingly to oppose royal aspirations and ultimately organized successful military resistance to a tyrannical monarch.[3]

In Whig and Marxist accounts the parliamentary cause was progressive and dynamic, with the potential to spawn the political and religious radicalism of the later 1640s in the city of London and in parliament's New Model Army. Obviously the dramatic experiences of civil war itself were an important radicalizing influence, and all historians stressed how many, even most, parliamentarians drew back in horror at the prospect of regicide and republicanism, and abhorred religious liberty. In the framework of a successful 'bourgeois revolution', moreover, the defeat of radical popular demands, as well as of royal authoritarianism, was a crucial element. None the less, there was a fundamental sense in which the events of the 1640s were seen as part of a single process. Zealous Protestantism justified resistance to Charles and his bishops; it could also, logically, lead to religious separatism and calls for liberty of conscience. The defence of the laws and liberties of England against royal tyranny could encourage humbler men to call for political rights and a legal system that served their needs, such as the Levellers demanded in 1646–9. Parliamentarianism had popular appeal, to respectable householders of the 'middling sort', if not to poorer groups.

This view of the English Civil War as part of a wide-ranging revolution still survives as a patriotic English (not British) myth, insisting on the distinctiveness of England's history and traditions, especially in contrast to those of continental Europe.[4] It has, however, been subject to comprehensive challenge in much recent scholarship. Although Geoffrey Elton had already challenged the notion of a 'high road to civil war', the collection of essays edited by Conrad Russell on *The Origins of the English Civil War* had the most dramatic influence.[5] Russell side-stepped the current debates over Marxist interpretations and argued instead that it was now time to challenge the common ground between Marxists and Whigs: 'not only the belief in inevitability, but also the belief that the Parliamentarians, because they won, were "progressive", and in some way stood for the future'. Russell inaugurated a fracturing of the seamless chronology of the 1640s, insisting that the rebellion of 1641–2 and the 'revolution' of 1647–9 had to be distinguished. The causes of the second crisis could not be deduced from the origins of the first.[6] This marked the beginning of what has since been labelled 'revisionism'. This term is applied to historians who differ significantly amongst themselves, but it is generally taken to indicate some shared broad approaches, of which a complex chronological precision is one. The civil war, on this view, was by no means the culmination of some inevitable long-term process: in *The Revolt of the Provinces*, another key 'revisionist' text, John Morrill argued that 1640 and 1642 were distinct crises, with distinct causes.[7] Still more has the impact of civil war been separated from its origins: in the new Oxford History series, perhaps the standard 'mainstream' interpretation of English history, the seventeenth-century volumes are to be split in 1643, whereas in the older series the early Stuart volume ended and the later Stuarts began in 1660.

Furthermore, revisionist historians tend to make thematic distinctions where earlier scholars made links. There has been a clear move away from attempts to connect the outbreak of civil war to long-term processes of social change or to deep-rooted ideological divisions. For Kevin Sharpe, the task is to explain how civil war could possibly have occurred in a consensual political culture, where there was basic agreement on the fundamentals of politics.[8] For Russell, the civil war can be connected to long-term structural weaknesses in the English (or more properly the British) monarchy: a localist-minded political elite unwilling to shoulder the financial and bureaucratic burdens of effective royal government together with the contradictions within a Church of England which attempted to combine the evangelical impulses of Calvinism with the 'Anglican' stress on uniformity compounded the stresses of ruling over three very different kingdoms. The civil war was not exactly an 'accidental' conflict, for it emerged in a political system subject to serious practical strain. But it was a contingent product of the political weaknesses of Charles I in dealing with his multiple kingdoms, and especially of his ineptitude over religious issues.[9] Most revisionists deny that opposition to monarchy was 'progressive'; some have argued, or hinted, that if any development was 'forward looking' it was absolute monarchy. Consequently the parliamentarians of 1642 are usually seen as hesitant or conservative, aristocratic not democratic, except on some interpretations of their religious stance.[10] In this framework the radical experiments of the 1640s and 1650s are desperate anomalies, minority responses which need to be explained through the specific experiences of civil war and religious experimentation rather than through some underlying radical potential in English popular culture. Although rarely articulated fully, the 'revisionist' view of English society in general is as deferential, hierarchical, traditional and localist, in contrast to the views of Hill or Manning, who argued that exploitation and class conflict could breed subversive attitudes and movements.[11]

Chronological fissures are not confined to political history; developments in social and cultural history have also contributed to the isolation of many aspects of the 1640s and 1650s. Much important work on crime, sexual relationships, literacy, popular protest, even religious affiliations, deals with long-term trends, apparently little affected by civil war; other studies end in 1640, or only begin after 1660. Much of the most interesting social and cultural history has thus become rather de-politicized, while it is difficult to connect the years of revolution to fundamental cultural or social developments. The most common assumption has again been that the basic conservatism of most English people made them indifferent or antipathetic to the most startling radical developments of this period.[12] There are, of course, exceptions to these generalizations; the most important attempt at a social, cultural and political synthesis is that by David Underdown, whose work is included here (Chapter 11).[13]

The challenge to 'grand narratives', to the straightforward stories of the linear development of parliamentary democracy, religious freedom and economic prosperity in English history is not of course confined to the seventeenth century, although the debate on this period is as fierce as any. The last 20 years have been a confusing, but also an exhilarating time for both students and researchers. We cannot go back to earlier certainties, to the view of English history – which at some unexplored level is assumed to stand for British history also – represented by the statute of Oliver Cromwell outside the houses of parliament, as a pioneer of parliamentary democracy. The events of 1647–58 offer ample evidence of the ambiguous connections between Cromwell and parliaments, never mind parliamentary democracy; while the Lord General's part in the conquering of both Scotland and Ireland in the 1650s highlights very sharply the complexities of any true British history. The 350th anniversary of the signing of the National Covenant in 1988 was a purely Scottish commemoration; despite much recent academic work the experience of Ireland is often a deliberately half-forgotten, darker side of British history.

We can present in this volume only a small selection of the vast number of important articles and chapters published on the origins and course of the civil war. They are not necessarily the 'best'; even if we could have reached agreement on which these were, we have preferred to choose those that were and remain the most challenging and productive of debate. Neither have we tried to offer a representative or 'balanced' selection; at times only one 'side' of a controversy is presented, with readers left to provide the broader context through the guides to further reading. This Introduction offers reflections on the state of scholarly debate over the civil war rather than summaries of the articles; readers should remember that the editors are themselves partisans in the debates over this most controversial period of English history, by no means judicious or neutral by-standers.

We wish now to follow a series of themes or arguments through from the early seventeenth century to the 1640s. Despite the insistence on discontinuity in much revisionist writing, part of our intention here is to show how certain approaches do run through the whole period. The more radical events of the 1640s and 1650s do have roots in some aspects, at least, of early-seventeenth-century political culture or practice, as well as being a product of the experience of civil war itself.

Parliament and politics

Conrad Russell's critique of the 'Whig' view of parliaments (Chapter 1, below) was one of the most significant assaults on the old narrative of the origins of civil war. He denied that the early modern house of commons was an increasingly self-confident institution, more and more successful in opposing the crown's measures, especially through securing the redress of grievances before voting supply through taxation. In Thomas Cogswell's words, 'seventeenth-century parliaments, which were earlier seen as jogging down the Whiggish High Road to Civil War, are now instead viewed as slouching along the Low Road to Extinction'.[14] Russell's account of the relative weakness of parliament, developed in his influential book on the 1620s,[15] was based on a particular understanding of central–local relationships in the English state. Members of the house of commons could not mount a credible opposition to royal government because of their own, and their constituents', 'localist' attitudes. MPs were not willing to vote the taxation necessary to support the cost of government; more particularly they would not underwrite the costs of war, despite some ephemeral enthusiasm for the conflict with Spain in 1624. On Russell's account, developed at length by Kevin Sharpe in his major study of the personal rule,[16] a king who had called regular parliaments in the 1620s was driven to dispense with them in the 1630s after their failure to finance wars they ostensibly supported.

Both Russell and Sharpe have also stressed the desire for unity and harmony in early Stuart politics and denied the existence of any fundamental ideological cleavages between king and parliament that would have predisposed them to conflict. Within parliament there was no division into two sides of 'government' and 'opposition'. Parliament was primarily designed to do the 'king's business' and, as Mark Kishlansky argues in the article reprinted here (Chapter 2), the procedures to achieve this were consensual rather than oppositional: reasoned debate, unanimous decision-making and so on. In a study of the 'points of contact' within the English political system, Sharpe has argued that the basic disagreements in principle were found within the royal family and the court as well as within parliament and the country. Differences were, in any case, 'normal to political life'; tensions in England were no more serious than those found in any other political system. Where the system was breaking down was in the failure of communication between the landowners who governed the localities and the court and the privy council at the centre.[17]

These views on the structure and ideology of English politics and the nature of parliaments have proved controversial. At the level of political ideas, Johann Sommerville has argued that there were fundamental differences over issues such as the degree of consent that was required before the king could levy taxes, the extent to which his freedom of action was circumscribed by law and the scope of parliament's role as king's adviser and representative of the people. Spokesmen for the royal prerogative tended to advance an absolutist interpretation of such matters, arguing that ultimately the king was answerable only to God, while proponents of the common law and government by consent insisted that the king's powers were limited.[18] In practice much of the time these theoretical differences were glossed over; but when circumstances brought them to the surface, for example during the forced loan of 1626–7, they could cause bitter political conflict. These ideas were also linked to differing diagnoses of what happened when unity broke down and conflict occurred. On the royalist account, this could often be attributed to 'popular', democratic elements within the political system, encouraged by Puritans in the church, who were seeking to subvert the prerogative and destroy royal authority; for those advocating a more limited view of the king's powers, however, blame generally lay with 'evil counsellors' and supporters of absolutism, operating in tandem with papists and Arminians.[19] Some of these themes are reflected in an alternative account of the parliaments of the 1620s by Thomas Cogswell. He argues that MPs showed a considerable capacity for opposing the crown where they disagreed over policies and were skilled in using the weapon of withholding supply to extract concessions. In general, they were neither as ineffective nor as powerless as Russell implies: by delaying supply in 1624 they persuaded James to yield to their wishes over war with Spain and the treatment of Catholics, whilst the same tactic in 1628 finally forced a reluctant Charles to grant the Petition of Right. Moreover, experience of using this weapon during the 1620s gave the Commons immense political leverage during the crisis of 1640–2.[20]

Conrad Russell famously described early Stuart parliaments as 'irregularly recurring events', denying the existence of parliament as an institution.[21] There was, however, a radical discontinuity in the nature of parliament from 1641. The need to pay off the victorious Scots' army and the increasing disarray of royal government meant first that parliament was protected against dissolution by the king, and second that it gradually took over crucial aspects of government, from finance to religious reformation. The change was reflected in parliament's records: in 1641 the journals of both houses became 'bulky archives filled with routine business . . . which had previously gone to the Privy Council'.[22] It is reflected furthermore in the changing relationships of MPs to their constituents. Unease that men who had been sent to London as channels for provincial opinion were now presuming to give orders to their neighbours helped to strengthen royalist support in 1642; resentment at the role of Sir Robert Harley in Herefordshire is a well-known example.[23] There were corresponding changes in how MPs regarded their constituents. The Kentish gentleman Edward Partridge humbly solicited the support of the Sandwich corporation in a complicated Long Parliament election; but by November 1641 he was writing irritated letters about how the Commons preoccupation 'with the greate affaires of the kingdom' gave them no time to deal with religious disputes in the town, and in 1646 he was giving them orders about how to conduct a day of public humiliation.[24]

The implications of this change were made clear at the outbreak of civil war in the summer of 1642. Those MPs who had not joined the king were then faced with the need to establish the financial and military arrangements necessary to win the war. The demands of civil war transformed parliament, or at least the house of commons. The personal and informal groupings among MPs characteristic of earlier, ephemeral meetings, were necessarily replaced, for crucial minorities, by more stable, organized factions or groups in a permanent institution with executive responsibilities. Much energy was expended by historians in the 1960s and 1970s in defining these groups, identifying their members and tracing their transformation through the 1640s. Broadly, it was agreed that a relatively fluid split in the first years of war between the peace party, the war party and the middle group, gave way from 1645 to a starker division between 'Presbyterians' and 'Independents'; however, these last categories proved problematic because they could be used to describe both a political stance (where Presbyterians were those most anxious to dismantle the war-time administration and to make peace with the king) and a view on church government (where Presbyterians were those in favour of a coercive national church organized by classes and synods). It was possible to be a religious Presbyterian and a political Independent, to some historians' dismay.[25] As we shall see, below, English parliamentary divisions in the 1640s have also to be viewed within a broader 'British' perspective.

'Revisionist' historiography of parliament has been more concerned to discuss the origins than the course of civil war, with the major exception of Kishlansky's work on the crucial period 1645–7 (see Chapter 2, below). Here he explores the theme – also developed in his work on parliamentary elections – of the way in which politics was transformed by the civil war. Prior to 1640, the political process was characterized above all else by a hatred of division and a desire to promote harmony and consensus. But out of the upheavals of the war there emerged 'adversary politics', a system where division and conflict were accepted and the aim of political actors was to achieve a majority position for their party.[26] The crucial turning-point came immediately after the war when parliament was irrevocably divided by the quest for a peace settlement. Political practices developed to reflect this. With the Presbyterians making most of the running, earlier consensual procedures were abandoned: the power of committees was reduced, the number of divisions increased and party politics became institutionalized. However, in this there also lay the seeds of the Presbyterians' and parliament's downfall: for it was a sense that the Commons, in particular, had become the tool of faction, that prompted military intervention in the form of New Model Army's entry into London in August 1647.

The events of 1647 have been read very differently in the work of John Adamson. Here moves towards a projected settlement and the eventual army coup are seen as the result of a series of initiatives taken by senior members of the nobility, notably Lord Saye, Lord Wharton and the earl of Northumberland.[27] This builds on the arguments set out in the article reprinted here (Chapter 3), in which emphasis is placed on the medieval, baronial context of the civil war. Noblemen, such as the earl of Essex, were seen as the leading political actors in the conflict and the key to much of parliament's strategy lay in limiting the king's freedom of action by placing him under the supervision of a noble Protector and baronial council. This is an approach which emphatically contradicts the traditional 'progressive' interpretation of the civil war, but also presents a different perspective from the revisionists.[28] The stress on the Lords is in contrast to the parliamentary studies of Russell on the 1620s and Kishlansky on the 1640s. Despite their attacks on Whig notions of inevitable conflict, they shared the Whigs' preoccupation with the Commons rather than the Lords. Furthermore, Adamson's interpretation spans the 1642 divide, for his account of noble alliances and rivalries is intended as an explanation of the political divisions amongst parliamentarians as well as of the initial challenge to the king.

The British Problem

Russell's work on the 1620s had an English focus, but more recently he has inspired the important attempt to move beyond England to an examination of the multiple kingdoms of Charles I, king of Scotland and Ireland as well as England and Wales (see Chapter 4). The British context is another theme that crosses the 1642 barrier. It has clear relevance to the course of the civil wars in all three kingdoms, although as yet no full integration of English and British developments has been achieved for the 1640s, comparable to Russell's book on *The Fall of the British Monarchies*. Furthermore, on a British level 1642 is arguably less important a landmark than 1643, the year of the cessation of war in Ireland between the rebels and Charles's supporters, and of the Covenanters' entrance into the English Civil War on the side of parliament. It also challenges the view of the English Revolution as a distinctive event, one of the founding moments of the modern world. Russell, influenced by European historians such as Koenigsberger and Elliott, has sought to counteract two long-standing, tacit assumptions amongst English historians: first, that England's experience can be held to stand for Britain as a whole; and, second, that England/Britain was very different from rest of continental Europe. In support of the latter point, he restates a contemporary insight that the regal union of Scotland and England was very similar to that of Castile and Portugal, though we now know that it was destined to be much more resilient.[29] Russell also argues that a British perspective should make us sceptical about the validity of social or cultural explanations of the English Civil War, since the three kingdoms of England, Scotland and Ireland had contrasting social and economic structures and there were vast cultural differences between them.[30] For example, the Scots' rising rather than the English Civil War comes first both in time and in logic, for Scottish political culture made possible much more elaborate justifications of resistance.[31] What all three kingdoms did have in common, however, was that they were ruled over by Charles I. Charles's failures as a politician play a central role in Russell's explanations of the origins of rebellion in Scotland, Ireland and England.

A fully integrated British narrative for the 1640s and 1650s has not yet been attempted; however, attitudes to the Scots have long been regarded as an important influence on parliamentarian political stances in the 1640s. In the debate about 'parties' in the 1960s and 1970s, the Scots' alliance of 1643 was credited chiefly to the most militant English parliamentarians, with a crucial realignment occurring during the struggle to establish the New Model Army in the winter of 1644–5. Thereafter the Scots were allies of the moderate parliamentarians associated with Essex. English and Scots 'Presbyterians' shared a desire for settlement with the king, worked together for a religious reformation that would prevent the growth of sectarianism and were both increasingly suspicious of the influence of the New Model Army.[32] The influence of the Scots also aroused considerable hostility. The noble factions discussed by Adamson were divided, in part, by views on the Scots alliance (see Chapter 3, below), and unease at Scottish involvement and the exactions of the Scots army can be found far beyond high political arenas. For example, the journal of the 'Independent' sympathizer and London militia officer, Thomas Juxon, includes regular expressions of anti-Scottish sentiment, prompted in part by a reading of past history. He noted 'the general practize of auxilliari forces that come to assist another Nation who seldome leave what they have once possesd. England was conquered by the Saxons and Daines in that maner.'[33] In the parish listings of taxation and other exactions drawn up for parliament's accounts committees, the losses by the Scots' army were often listed separately, in meticulous resentful detail: in Warwickshire, for example, one small town claimed losses of over £500 when the Scots marched through in 1645.[34] These accounts may have been prompted from the centre: in the haggling over the Scots' demands for money before they would withdraw, the English parliament sought to set quarter and other exactions against the Scots claims. But they also reveal considerable anti-Scots feeling.[35]

Clearly attitudes to the Scots were an important influence on political alignments in England in the 1640s. This is not to say that they were *the* determining influence. Patterns of belief and allegiance on the parliament's side were too complex to allow the isolation of a single determinant or the construction of neat polarities, as the confusing recourse to the category 'Presbyterian/Independents' illustrates. But the Scots were undoubtedly significant, because of their presence in England and their claims to influence English policy, especially over religion. The same, however, cannot really be said for the Irish. For much of the 1640s Ireland was no more than an ominous side-show. It was not until the end of the English Civil War, when the question of how to deal with the continuing rebellion again became pressing, that Irish affairs once more seriously impinged on Westminster politics.

This raises important questions about the coherence of the 'British' framework. Much of the analysis remains decidedly Anglo-centric. Historians of Ireland and Scotland have pointed out that events in their two countries are still examined mainly for their impact on England;[36] whilst some uses of the 'British Problem' have recently been described as 'the continuation of revisionism by other means', because the conflict in England is explained with reference to 'outside', chiefly Scottish, influences exploited by a minority of disaffected English politicians.[37] For the most part, it has also been assumed that the direction of political events was determined by what happened in the kingdom of England. The exception to this is Russell's analysis of the interrelationships of the three kingdoms prior to 1642, which shows the Scots holding the initiative. But during the later 1640s and the 1650s the Scots are discussed in terms of English attitudes towards them, and it is English events that have clear priority. The Scots who made the running in the later 1630s are mostly seen as reacting to, or as victims of, English developments in the 1640s. The years between 1647 and 1651 provide a partial exception when English historians have had to take account of complex and variable Scots divisions, although again their significance is judged mainly in relation to the impact they had on English royalism. As Derek Hirst has recently emphasized for the 1650s, this approach is not simply a product of the Anglo-centricity of modern historians, but reflects seventeenth-century attitudes and contexts.[38] The mid-seventeenth century was a crucial period in the 'making of Britain' in terms of the dominance of the richer and more powerful English kingdom. It intensified the need, already obvious for more than a century, for Irish and Scots politicians to be involved with English events. The English themselves could be more ignorant or indifferent over Scotland itself. The anti-Scots feeling of men like Juxon or, for that matter, the approval of Scotland's church by Presbyterians, like the polemicist Thomas Edwards, was based on what the Scots were doing or might do for England. There was virtually no discussion of Scottish issues for their own sake.

To advance the analysis, we need more precision on what the British Problem is supposed to deal with or explain. Discussion of the origins of the English Civil War, or the war of the three kingdoms, as Nicholas Canny has stressed, assumes that high politics – the king's relationships with the great men of Scotland, Ireland and England – is all-important.[39] Social and economic developments need to be considered; so too do the complex issues of identity and state-building implicit in any study of early modern 'Britain'. A British framework involves not only looking at the practical difficulties of communication and patronage; it also entails the working out of the impact of the Protestant reformation in the three kingdoms. It has, for example, been argued there was a degree of cultural integration between English and Scots Protestant elites from the 1560s which underlay cooperation in the later 1630s and early 1640s, although it did not prevent increasing distance and conflict from the mid-1640s.[40] The implications of this sort of development need to be explored. Here we connect with another very influential current in recent explanations of the *English* war, the stress on religious divisions as a source of breakdown.

Religion

Although most historians agree that religion was important to the outbreak of the civil war, they differ profoundly over the precise nature of religious divisions, over how religion should be connected to political, cultural or social developments, and over how important religion was compared to these other 'factors'. There is no clear divide between revisionists and anti-revisionists: in the preface to his *Personal Rule*, Kevin Sharpe stresses that he disagrees 'substantially' with Conrad Russell over religion.[41] Debates over religion derive ultimately from different views on the implications of the Protestant reformation in England. S.R. Gardiner's discussion of a 'Puritan revolution' can be connected to a triumphalist account. Here zealous Protestantism gained widespread support amongst people from both elite and middling ranks in society; it encouraged a sturdy individualism and independence which naturally opposed royal authoritarianism. Furthermore Puritanism represented the future, albeit in unpredictable ways. The reformers of the early 1640s encouraged, often despite themselves, the burgeoning of radical separatist sects during the revolutionary decades, leading to the liberating expression of new ideas, brilliantly described in Christopher Hill's *The World Turned Upside Down*.[42] Protestant unity was decisively broken in the 1640s and had in the end to be ratified by the Toleration Act of 1689, to lasting Whig pride.

Nicholas Tyacke's 'Puritanism, Arminianism and counter-revolution' (Chapter 5, below), one of the most important articles of the last 30 years, attacked the assumption that Puritanism and revolution were naturally or automatically connected. Rather the link was created by circumstances. A broad agreement on predestinarian Calvinist theology amongst churchmen in the late Elizabethan and Jacobean church helped to minimize differences over ceremonial conformity or church government.

This agreement was shattered by Charles's support for a novel, avant-garde Arminian stance in theology and worship. Tyacke's essay provided a crucial underpinning for revisionist attacks on the view that parliamentary-Puritans were 'progressive'; indeed they could here be seen as conservative defenders of the status quo.

One straightforward account, not endorsed by Tyacke himself, is that a 'Calvinist consensus' in the 'Jacobethan church' was broken by the personal preferences of the king and his leading churchmen, Laud, Neile and Wren. Tyacke's work – or, more usually, simplified versions of it, for his views on both Puritanism and Arminianism have developed considerably since the article reprinted here – has been controversial. Sharpe, along with Peter White, has denied that the 1630s saw radical new initiatives in theology or religious policies generally. There is no proof, they claim, that Laud was an Arminian and, in Sharpe's view, his main aims were to preserve the order and unity of the church. In any case, on Julian Davies's account, church policies were driven by the king.[43] On the other hand, Peter Lake and Anthony Milton have developed rather than challenged Tyacke's account. Lake argues that the notion of a Calvinist consensus before the 1620s blurs the significant cleavages within English Protestantism over the nature of the Christian community and over the implications of religious doctrine for social and political life. It also prevents an understanding of the importance of anti-Puritanism in early-seventeenth-century England. In Lake's discussion, Charles's adoption of an anti-Calvinist church policy was not a contingent personal preference, but a logical response to a perceived threat from Puritan activism. Although the English church was not united under Elizabeth and James, the church policies of the 1630s did mark an unprecedentedly aggressive assault on many of the assumptions of English Protestantism. The assault was not only, or specifically, theological but involved church architecture, attitudes to preaching, and an approach to worship, summed up as 'Laudian style'.[44] Likewise Anthony Milton has argued that dominant churchmen of the 1630s were engaged in a deliberate tactical evasion of provocative issues, notably avoiding any commitment to Arminian theology. None the less, they endorsed and promoted distinctly different positions on the nature of the English church and its worship, and on its relationship with the Church of Rome.[45]

Some have taken Tyacke's early work to imply that it is impossible to distinguish 'Puritanism' as an ideology or a movement from the broader ranks of English Protestants.[46] Others have argued that the term 'Puritan', originally a polemical construction by hostile conservatives, has limited value as a description of real religious attitudes. Still others, such as Peter Lake or Tyacke himself in an important recent study, suggest there was none the less a positive Puritan identity based on a complex process of self-definition of the 'godly', often against the taunts and opposition of their opponents. The idea of a Puritan 'movement' surviving from the 1560s to the 1640s may be too simple, but continuities in attitudes and long-standing networks of patronage and support can, none the less, be traced.[47] Kevin Sharpe's sympathetic account of Charles's religious policies in the 1630s is also based on a more robust view of Puritanism – on a view, indeed, similar to the king's own. Here Puritanism was a potentially revolutionary, politically subversive creed, in England as in Scotland. It was by no means popular, particularly compared to festive or ceremonial cultures, but there was enough support for Puritanism and even separatism to prevent a dismissal of the king's fears as either paranoia or as an opportunistic justification for authoritarian political policies.[48]

Historians have generally paid more attention to Puritanism than to conformist Protestantism, because they have been more interested in parliamentarians and revolutionaries than in royalists. An influential body of revisionist work on the Reformation, however, has offered an interesting challenge to this emphasis. This revisionism stresses the vitality and accessibility of late-medieval Catholicism, and the consequent alienation and disruption brought through the imposition, by a minority, of a demanding, word-based reformed religion. For Christopher Haigh and John Morrill, Puritanism was not liberating or popular in the Gardiner model, but an off-putting, over-complex creed that offered little practical comfort to most of the population.[49] It was by no means the case that a clericalist, aggressive Laudianism was popular either, but some of its communal, ritualistic, and ceremonial aspects might have chimed in with local needs. Morrill, Judith Maltby and others have thus described a widespread positive commitment to a non-Puritan church of England by 1640. This was based on the hierarchical solidarity of the parish, bolstered by games and festivities as well as the ceremonies of the church, and on the rhythms of the Book of Common Prayer, with a regular pattern of worship through the year; hence the labels 'prayer-book' or 'parish' Anglicanism. This style of worship, suggests Morrill, was more accessible to the unlearned than a demanding, intellectual Puritan stress on doctrine and the preaching of the word. It taught a straightforward morality as the best pathway to salvation, thus offering a practical alternative to Calvinist determinism. Calvinist preaching, it is argued, offered little guidance to most people on how to live, for its determinism produced either despair or an arrogant certainty, both irrelevant to everyday life.[50] Furthermore, it became apparent in 1640–2, when episcopacy came under increasing attack from committed Puritans, that there was substantial support for a vision of the English church governed by non-Laudian bishops. Hence in their influential account of disorder during the revolutionary years (see Chapter 12, below), John Morrill and John Walter stress that both orthodox religious reformation and radical separatism were disruptive influences because of their unpopularity with most people in most local communities. Within this framework religious radicalism created upheaval in a negative fashion, through the reaction it provoked; religious radicals are clearly seen as a small minority. We have come a long way from the positively subversive popular radicals, the heirs to Christopher Hill's emancipatory Reformation of the 1640s.

For Morrill, zealous Puritanism, although a minority position, was crucial to the cleavages that produced the English Civil War, the 'last great war of religion' rather than the first world revolution (see Chapter 6 below). The gulf between Puritan reformation and adherence to an epis-copal church and the Book of Common Prayer was central to the forma-tion of royalist and parliamentarian parties in 1641–2, both at Westminster and in the provinces, as seen by the extensive petitioning for and against the bishops. Religion was the prime motivator of active participants in the civil war and the chief occasion of division, in contrast to debate over political and constitutional issues, over which Morrill feels compromise and agreement were possible.

Morrill's notion of a 'war of religion' distinguishes where others might make connections, particularly between 'religion' and 'politics'. In con-trast Peter Lake's discussion of anti-popery (Chapter 7 below) suggests this ideology, or combination of ideas and reactions, was one crucial way of bringing together religious and political aspects of life. Furthermore, where Morrill suggests that willing participants in the civil war were a small minority of zealots, particularly on the parliament's side, Lake argues that anti-popery, in some circumstances at least, was a means of enlarging the potential popularity of Puritanism.[51] Hostility towards Catholicism was embedded in mainstream English culture by the seven-teenth century, as seen for example in the annual commemorations of Queen Elizabeth's accession day or of the providential failure of the Gunpowder Plot.[52] For contemporaries, the pervasive, malign influence of popery was a means of explaining the failure of the highest hopes for reformation; contending against popery promoted activism at all levels from the immediate neighbourhood to the international confessional struggle. Anti-popery was thus flexible and complex; its impact could vary widely depending on context.

Localism

Alongside religion, local, particularly county, history has been an increas-ingly important framework for understanding both the origins and course of the civil war. The initial context for much local research was the historiographical *cause célèbre* of the 1950s and 1960s, 'the gentry con-troversy'. Counties provided a sample of landed society which made it possible to test the links between the economic attitudes and fortunes of gentlemen and their civil war allegiance: was parliamentarianism (or royalism) characteristic of prospering or declining gentry, of paternalists or entrepreneurs? In addition, county studies could be used to investigate the economic impact of the civil war on landed society.[53] A broader approach to county history, however, was pioneered by Alan Everitt; here the county was not simply a convenient laboratory for testing general theories, but a crucial organic community in its own right. The social and public life of the Tudor and Stuart gentry focused on the 'county community' rather than the nation; when a gentleman referred to his 'country' it was the locality that he meant. 'Localism' was the prism through which the demands of central government were experienced or interpreted; loyalty to the county community was the essential framework for understanding the political attitudes and activities of the gentry. On Everitt's account, the provincial gentry were uninterested in national issues, and reluctant to accept the demands of central authority if they were likely to disrupt local arrangements.[54]

This version of localism was crucial to Russell's account of the reasons for conflict in the parliaments of the 1620s (Chapter 1 below) and also Sharpe's account of the breakdown of the Personal Rule.[55] 'Localism' undermined the crown's efforts to raise the men and money needed to wage war, with particularly disastrous results in 1639–40 when it brought a collapse of the military effort against the Scots and widespread opposition to Charles's policies. This analysis has also been extended into the civil war in John Morrill's eloquent and influential synthesis of local history, *The Revolt of the Provinces*. 'Overcoming localism' was the key to success in fighting the war. Unprecedented resources of men and money had to be extracted from the localities and, in order to win, both sides resorted to arbitrary rule, riding roughshod over the legal procedures and traditions so important in provincial life. A 'parliamentary tyranny' was erected, far more formidable than anything attempted in the 1630s. Victory was hard-won; the sullen resentment of the provinces erupted in some areas in the second civil war of 1648, and formed a resilient obstacle to reform or even stability in the 1650s.[56]

These views have, however, proved controversial. A growing body of work, represented here by Clive Holmes's critique of the 'county community' (Chapter 8), has argued that local inhabitants were much less self-contained and inward looking than Everitt's approach suggested. Counties themselves were often divided by geography, farming regions and administrative boundaries; and the mental horizons of the gentry, in particular, were both narrower and broader than the county. Personal contacts, economic activity and their work as local governors were often concentrated in the immediate locality of their estates; but visits to London, education at the universities or Inns of Court and experience of working within a national legal system gave them ample experience of the world beyond the shire.[57] As Richard Cust's article (Chapter 9) demonstrates, they were also kept informed about national political developments through a well-developed news network. The earlier emphasis on 'localism' as the characteristic response of those living in the counties has been considerably revised. Holmes concludes that many local inhabitants 'were well informed and deeply concerned about national religious and constitutional issues . . . [and] participated in a national political culture'. This has been endorsed by work on local resistance to the forced loan and ship money which also reveals that political opinion in the shires was much less monolithic than had been assumed. The gentry, and freeholders and urban artisans as well, were often fundamentally divided over the political principles at stake.[58]

This critique of the 'localist' framework has been extended into the 1640s in Ann Hughes's article (Chapter 10). She argues that parliament was more successful in the civil war not because it was more 'tyrannical', but because it integrated its war effort more effectively with local concerns. The political structures and bureaucracy developed by the Long Parliament, and the longstanding practice of parliament receiving petitions and appeals from the localities, ensured that it had well-developed mechanisms for hearing grievances against military rule. Local concerns were aired and remedied much more readily than on the royalist side, where ultimate power was concentrated narrowly in the hands of the king and his leading advisors. This meant that parliament was often less 'efficient', as disputes between factions dragged on for months or even years; but this in itself tended to draw local interests more closely into the parliamentarian cause because they found themselves needing to demonstrate their loyalty to win their case. Local and national concerns were harmonized, with the result that parliament's war effort was more resilient than that of the king. Hughes also questions more broadly the concept of 'parliamentary tyranny', pointing to ways in which parliament's claims to serve the 'public' and its formalized legal structures limited the tendencies towards arbitrary rule.[59]

Society and culture

One of the main features of older, 'progressive' accounts of the English Revolution was the attempt to connect the political and religious upheavals of the mid-seventeenth century to overall patterns of social and economic change. Perhaps the most influential example of this approach has been the work of Christopher Hill, inspired by the classical Marxist notion that the seventeenth century was a crucial stage in the transition from a feudal to a capitalist society. His seminal work, *Society and Puritanism*, for example, explored the social implications of zealous Protestantism, developing a wide-ranging picture of the ways in which Puritan religious practices were adopted and adapted by the industrious middling sort of early Stuart England. Hill's impact can be seen, with significantly different emphasis, in the work of Brian Manning and Keith Wrightson. For both, Puritanism provided a means of creating a self-conscious identity for the 'middling sort'. For Manning, this was a form of assertive class consciousness, directed against the rich as much as the poor; whereas for Wrightson Puritanism marked more clearly the boundary between the respectable, godly, middling sort and the disorderly unrespectable poor. Furthermore, it offered parish elites an ideology of reformation invaluable in the late sixteenth and early seventeenth centuries, a period of economic change and uncertainty.[60] The influence of Hill's work can also be seen in Robert Brenner's *Merchants and Revolution*. This offers both a detailed analysis of the economic basis for political divisions in London and a more general account of the ways in which economic developments in England made possible elite independence of, and opposition to, the crown. However, Brenner's approach has been criticized by some as too 'materialist', making insufficient allowance for the influence of religion on allegiance.[61] This is typical of a more general suspicion of, and disillusion with, materialist accounts in recent work which have ensured that such broad analysis is now rarely attempted.

The most notable exception to this is David Underdown's ambitious attempt to connect the political conflicts of the civil war to a broad cultural and social cleavage, rooted in regional contrasts. He owes something to Hill's and Wrightson's understanding of the social implications of Puritanism, but Underdown has also attempted to identify the social context and appeal of a more festive, collective and 'traditional' culture associated with the parish-Anglicanism discussed in the section above on religion. Underdown's work forms an immensely important exception to the de-politicization of social history; his understanding of cultural conflict combines a powerful sense of the ambiguous and contested impact of the Reformation with a broader notion of the various potentialities of religious and social change. An individualistic, reforming Puritan culture emerged in some environments, whilst a more traditional, communal and hierarchical festive way of life was preserved in others.[62] Whereas Russell insists that 'rival social policies' played no part in the divisions between king and parliament, Underdown suggests that political allegiance can be linked to different patterns of social and economic change and to the cultural responses these provoke.[63] We present Underdown's views through an early piece focusing on the reactions of west-country villagers to the depredations of civil war in the 'Club movements' of 1645 (Chapter 11 below). Like much local history, Underdown stresses the disruption caused by troop movements, taxation and plunder; however, unlike some working in a localist tradition who regarded hostility to military exactions as a natural, undifferentiated reaction, Underdown argues that responses were more complex and variable; they need to be placed within a precise social, cultural and ideological context.

Underdown's full account of cultural conflict and allegiance, in *Revel, Riot and Rebellion*, has met with much criticism as well as admiration. Some historians reject the whole attempt to link cultural and ecological patterns as unacceptably determinist; others argue that both the cultural and the regional contrasts are too simply and too sharply drawn.[64] However, Underdown's broader arguments have gained more support, particularly the notions that popular allegiance was a crucial element in the course of the civil war and that allegiance varied and was not simply determined by elite coercion or by deference. For Underdown, in complex ways, the issues that divided king and parliament do have to be connected with problems of the relationships between elites and the ranks below them in a period of social change.

A discussion of similar issues, in a more clear-cut Marxist framework, is represented by Brian Manning's *The English People and the English Revolution*. It is these arguments which are addressed in Morrill and Walter's 'Order and disorder in the English Revolution', reprinted as Chapter 12 below. For Manning, social relationships were characterized essentially by class conflict between a ruling class of great landed proprietors and merchants, and the 'people', including the small landholders and masters, artisans and traders of the 'middling sort'. Social strains were intensifying as a traditional feudal society was increasingly affected by capitalist developments, such as fen-drainage, enclosure and concentrations of wealth in trade and industry. The rising tide of popular violence in the early 1640s prompted elite support for the king as the guarantor of social order, while class hostility was an important factor in the emergence, later in the decade, of both religious radicalism and of the Leveller political movement, which Manning characterizes as a movement of the 'people', especially the middling sort, against the dominance in law, politics and economics of the aristocracy and the rich.[65] Morrill and Walter's important piece is sceptical both of Manning's chronology and of his characterization of popular politics. The authors argue that popular unrest was comparatively limited during the civil war and deny that the middling sort were at the forefront of class hostility in the period. Over the previous century, social changes, such as the increasing respectability of the middling sort and the elaboration of a system of poor relief, had worked to lessen the incidence of broad, community-based social protests. In the 1640s, Morrill and Walter conclude, 'increased levels of disorder owed less to intra-communal strife than to the intrusion of "outsiders".' Religious reformers, sequestrators and troops provoked disorder, rather than intrinsic social divisions. Beyond this there is a scepticism about the validity of analysing the hierarchical and unequal world of seventeenth-century England as a class society where different social groups had sharply contrasting visions of acceptable social relations.[66] In contrast to Hill's *The World Turned Upside Down*, which focused on popular radicalism, Walter and Morrill argue that fundamental challenges to the social order were rare and stress the distance between popular grievances and radical movements.

Political culture, royalism and parliamentarianism

The sometimes bewildering variety of approaches to understanding the causes and course of the civil war is testimony to the fundamental issues at stake, issues which still cause political division today. In explaining how English men and women of all social ranks became involved in civil war, how should we connect the different aspects of human existence? What is the relative impact of material existence and practical, everyday affairs compared to beliefs about what the world is, or should be, like? Is it possible to disentangle the role of human decisions and actions, individual or collective, from the general or structural factors which influence and constrain human agency? Many of these distinctions are artificial, but it is hard to analyse developments without such separations.

Significant differences in the ways historians understand political culture in the first half of the seventeenth century are revealed, more or less overtly, in the essays reprinted here. They emerge around issues such as who was or was supposed to be involved in politics and what frameworks of ideas, what procedures were most important to the way in which political life was carried on. Richard Cust's account of news and politics (Chapter 9 below) raises these issues most directly. He explores the variety of means by which information about politics spread through provincial England before 1640, highlighting the verse libels and ballads, oral gossip and rumour which were accessible to the 'middling sort' and humbler people, as well as the more elaborate newsletters circulated amongst the gentry. The recent work of Cogswell and Bellany has reinforced Cust's stress on the importance of a well-informed public as part of the political framework in which, for example, the reputation of the duke of Buckingham or the government's capacity and resolve to fight a war, was pondered or opposed. Dagmar Freist is developing similar approaches for the 1640s.[67] Cust's work on the electorate and Cynthia Herrup's studies of the legal process also testify to the existence of a relatively broad, well-informed 'active citizenry' whose views and actions were at least partially independent of the influence of landed elites.[68] Underdown (Chapter 11 in this volume), and Morrill and Walter (Chapter 12), also stress the importance of popular political activity, although the latter do not connect popular attitudes so closely to national political divisions. In contrast, Adamson (Chapter 3) argues that the political process within a deferential aristocratic society centred essentially on relationships between the king and the nobility, who were able to rally large numbers of their social inferiors to their support. One third of the English nobility, notes Adamson, held some military command during the civil war.

Another important difference – often dividing revisionists and their critics – has been over the importance of consensus or conflict within political thinking. In this volume, Kishlansky (Chapter 2) denies the existence of fundamental divisions over the nature of political authority and argues that the drive towards consensus was at the heart of politics, while Morrill (Chapter 6) sees unbridgeable divisions in the religious sphere only. Lake (Chapter 7) in contrast, presents anti-popery as a vital adversarial contemporary framework, encompassing both religion and politics; and Cust (Chapter 9), argues that much of the news read or heard by men and women in early Stuart England presented political life in sharply polarized terms. These differences are also reflected in writing on early-seventeenth-century political theory. Johann Sommerville has pointed to sharp divergencies between absolutist and constitutional thinking on monarchy. Glenn Burgess, on the other hand, does not discern such contrasts: for him, 'all political societies are marked both by elements of consensus and by elements of conflict'. Under James, at least, political tensions were contained within 'a single intellectual system'; Charles, however, did not understand the conventions of political debate and 'spoke the wrong language', hence his policies aroused greater opposition than they deserved.[69]

These attempts to choose between consensus and conflict – between seeking to explain the civil war as a product of a consensual culture where agreement was seen as the norm and conflict abhorred, or, alternatively, as the inevitable upshot of sharp ideological cleavages – have dominated much of the recent debate on the causes of the civil war. However, as Lake and Sharpe have argued in an important recent essay, it is in many ways a false choice. The tendency has been for revisionists and their challengers simply to invert each other's arguments when they should recognize that political processes in seventeenth-century England could incorporate both a wish for consensus and a tendency to conflict. The languages and rhetorics out of which political and religious culture were formed were often relatively open-ended, and included a variety of codes and positions that could be adapted or combined creatively by different people in a variety of contexts.[70] On this reading, the period from the 1620s through to the 1650s saw the unveiling of a series of potentialities rather than the unfolding of inevitable developments.

The complex, sometimes contradictory, elements in political culture can be illustrated by looking at the development of parliamentarianism and royalism. Parliamentarianism in the 1640s was a godly cause, an aristocratic revolt and a constitutional movement, all at the same time.

Parliament was the representative of the people supporting legality against royal misdemeanours; it was the main hope of those who looked for godly reformation; and it was an arena where baronial ambitions could perhaps be fulfilled. These various elements interacted, sometimes in contradictory ways. Godliness helped to structure and make possible a certain type of aristocratic leadership, typified by the earl of Warwick or Lord Brooke, whose reputations were based on their patronage of true religion as well as on ancient lineage or extensive estates. But godliness could also make possible radical criticisms of the aristocracy and rejection of aristocratic leadership if it was incompatible with the cause. Adamson (Chapter 3 below) suggests that parliament's army became increasingly professional rather than baronial; but it was also a godly army of active and committed citizens, as its famous declarations stressed in 1647–8. 'We were not a mere mercenary Army, hired to serve any arbitrary power of a state; but called forth and conjured, by the several declarations of parliament to the defence of our own and the people's just rights and liberties.'[71]

Much recent historiography has taken traditional or conservative reactions on parliament's side for granted, as not really needing explanation. Radicalism, in contrast, was not a 'natural' outcome of English political culture, but a bizarre, minority position stimulated by the hardships and legal shortcuts of civil war. These assumptions, however, are brought into question by David Wootton's account of parliamentarian radicalization (see Chapter 13 in this volume). He presents the politics of the Levellers as one entirely logical reading of parliament's own propaganda in the early years of the war when it presented itself as the representative of the people, defending traditional and popular liberties.[72] And Cust's article on news (Chapter 9) shows that this propaganda was building in turn on earlier images of parliament and 'the country'. This is not to suggest that a comprehensive radical response to the civil war was inevitable; but it was one of a range of possible responses to contemporary understandings of the parliamentary cause. Again, the conservative reactions to military rule and religious change, described by Morrill and Walter (Chapter 12), were by no means automatic. Often they were new responses produced by the unprecedented impact of civil war. The 1640s prompted a functional and sentimental traditionalism as well as a radicalization; conservatism, like radicalism, always needs to be explained.[73]

On this basis, parliament's divisions in the 1640s and the conflicts of the 1650s can be seen as a struggle over the meaning of a complex parliamentary cause, often connected to rival understandings of the essential nature of English government.[74] Clearly the 1640s made a vital difference: the sufferings and sacrifices of civil war prompted anguished reflections on justice and legality; the unlooked-for collapse of the national church unleashed an unprecedented religious fragmentation, alarming to most but ultimately welcome to some; and the opening up of the press for reporting news or presenting arguments prompted startling speculations in circles broader than ever before, although precedents can be found in the 1620s and earlier. But there are many continuities, specific and general. In 1646–7, royalists alleged that the English and the Scots were claiming to deal with the king 'as if he were a child, a ward, or an ideot', a repeat of the policies of the parliamentary leadership of 1641, who were in turn drawing on medieval precedents, as discussed by Adamson (Chapter 3 below).[75] When Patrick Collinson stresses the republican nature of Elizabethan monarchy it is perhaps valid to stress how far the Rump, amongst other developments of the 'interregnum', was an expression of the collectivist potential of English government rather than an aberration.[76]

Similar complexities and contradictions are apparent in the interpretation of royalism. Hughes (Chapter 10) makes some attempt to grasp the sense of personal honour and loyalty that animated some followers of the king. More comprehensive recent work contributes to a picture of royalism almost as complex as the account of parliamentarianism already offered. Conrad Russell and D.L. Smith emphasize the constitutionalism and moderation of many royalists.[77] On the other hand, recent work by Anthony Milton on Sir Thomas Wentworth and by Ian Atherton on the ambitious Herefordshire politician Sir John Scudamore points to a more robust and authoritarian strand. Wentworth's dismissal of 'a saucy Magna Carta man' was a characteristic private indication of his anxieties about legal restrictions on prerogative power and of his absolutist attitudes.[78] A systematic and energetic hunt for 'news' loomed large in Scudamore's life, a salutary indication that the desire to be well-informed was as useful to an ambitious courtier as to the 'country' politicians discussed by Cust (in Chapter 9).[79]

A comprehensive analysis of recent cultural history and linguistically based scholarship suggested that for many periods historians were coming to neglect explanation in favour of detailed description; the 'hows' of history were more important than the 'whys'.[80] For the English Civil War, however, perhaps the opposite is true. Historians have concentrated on the causes of the war at the expense of attempts to understand how participants made sense of drastic upheaval, or how new forms of conceptualizing political actors and processes were developed. Here there is a great contrast with the most recent work on the French Revolution, which has had a distinct cultural focus, exploring the impact of print culture, the new political symbols and rituals in order to understand how change was possible and how it was experienced. If work on the English Civil War is to develop in this direction, then one of the things that is needed is a re-evaluation of the ways in which we use sources.

'Revisionist' scholarship has been very valuable in challenging or making more complex the 'grand narratives' of English history, the straightforward stories describing the rise of capitalism or the gradual, inevitable expansion of liberty and democracy; but in methodological terms its contribution has been less helpful. Usually a very sharp distinction has been made between manuscript and printed sources, and it is assumed that the former are of more value than inevitably biased pamphlet literature.[81] The polemical stance and rhetorical context of much source material has also been ignored in favour of more literal-minded readings. This approach can be both limiting and misleading. A sharp contrast between manuscript and contemporary printed sources cannot be assumed; rather it is neces- sary to elucidate the relationships between them in particular circum- stances. Political and religious debate in the 1640s, for example, involved a complex mixture of face-to-face oral discussion, manuscript circulation and printed text.[82] It has also to be recognized that the effects of political languages cannot be understood without regard to the context in which they were deployed. Critiques of Glenn Burgess's work on political theory have highlighted the need to distinguish public from private utterances, and have shown how ostensible appeals to moderation and consensus could themselves be instrumental, rhetorical ploys to discredit opponents and to gain advantage in bitter conflicts.[83] Beyond this, 'revisionism' has tended to encourage the study of sources simply for evidence of what happened, and not as 'an ingredient in the happening', as a historian of France urges.[84] The journal of Londoner Thomas Juxon, for example, has been much used as an eyewitness, manuscript account of city and parlia- mentarian divisions in the late 1640s. However, little attention has been paid to the fact that much of it is not about London at all: it covers military affairs all over England, and events in France, Poland, Germany and elsewhere. Thus it is not merely a source for what happened; it is an insight into how one well-placed, but not socially privileged, man attempted to make sense of the dangerous and dramatic times he lived in, using news-books, tracts, city and parliamentary gossip networks, as well as his own 'experience'.[85]

The sort of cultural analysis that has been made of the French Revolu- tion has also been discouraged by the assumption that the 1640s and 1650s were an aberration with little impact on, or relation to, more long-term aspects of English/British political culture. Political events have become disconnected from broader social and cultural frameworks, and culture and society have themselves become de-politicized. One of our basic aims in the selection and commentary for this volume has been to argue against this sort of discontinuity, and in the process suggest ways in which these developments might be re-connected, without losing sight of their com- plexity. Although we do not have the space here to explore the long-term impact of the English Civil War we would want to suggest that religious diversity and new forms of politicization were among the most significant outcomes.

Notes

1 Alex Callincos, in 'Symposium on Robert Brenner's *Merchants and Revolution*', *New Left Review*, 207 (Sept./Oct. 1994), pp. 124–33.

2 This is a simple summing up of a fertile and complex tradition: see C. Hill, *The English Revolution of 1640* (London, Lawrence and Wishart, 1940); *idem*, 'Recent Interpretations of the Civil War' in his *Puritanism and Revolution* (pbk edn, London, Panther History, 1986), pp. 13–40; *idem*, 'A Bourgeois Revolution?', in J.G.A. Pocock (ed.), *Three British Revolutions* (Princeton, NJ, Princeton University Press, 1980), pp. 3–20; Brian Manning, *The English People and the English Revolution* (1976).

3 Gardiner, *History*; *idem*, *A History of the Great Civil War 1642–1649*, 4 vols (London, Longman, 1893); J.E. Neale, *Elizabeth I and her Parliaments*, 2 vols (London, Jonathan Cape, 1957); W. Notestein, *The Winning of the Initiative by the House of Commons* (British Academy Lecture, 1924).

4 C.S.R. Russell, 'The Anglo-Scottish Union 1603–1643: A Success?', in A. Fletcher and P. Roberts (eds), *Religion, Culture and Society in Early Modern Britain: Essays in Honour of Patrick Collinson* (Cambridge, Cambridge University Press, 1994), pp. 238–56 insists that the 'Whig' view of history is an exclusionary English patriotic myth.

5 G.R. Elton, 'A High Road to Civil War?', in C.H. Carter (ed.), *From the Renaissance to the Counter Reformation* (London, Jonathan Cape, 1965), pp. 325–47; C.S.R. Russell (ed.), *The Origins of the English Civil War* (Basingstoke, Macmillan, 1973).

6 Russell, *Origins of the English Civil War*, pp. 2, 5.

7 J.S. Morrill, *The Revolt of the Provinces* (London, George Allen and Unwin, 1976), ch. 1; see also K. Sharpe, *The Personal Rule of Charles I* (London, Yale University Press, 1992), pp. 922–3 for another argument about the need for chronological precision, although Sharpe does see some continuities between 1640 and 1642.

8 K. Sharpe, 'A Commonwealth of Meanings: Languages, Analogies, Ideas and Politics', in *Politics and Ideas in Early Stuart England* (London, Pinter, 1989), pp. 63–71.

9 This combines aspects of Russell's analysis of the 1620s, in *Parliaments and English Politics 1621–1629* (Oxford, Oxford University Press, 1979), with his account of Charles I in 'The British Problem and the English Civil War, (Chapter 4 in this volume), *The Causes of the English Civil War* (Oxford, Oxford University Press, 1990) and *The Fall of the British Monarchies* (Oxford, Oxford University Press, 1991). It should be noted that in Russell's account of the 1620s the king is presented as a man placed in an impossible position by the refusal of members of parliament to provide him with an adequate revenue.

10 J.S. Morrill, 'The Religious Context of the English Civil War' (Chapter 6 in this volume) has argued for religious zeal as a dynamic, radicalizing force. On other views Puritan resistance is rather a response to an innovating avant-garde 'Arminianism': see N.R.N. Tyacke, 'Puritanism, Arminianism and Counter-Revolution' (Chapter 5 below).

11 Contrast J.S. Morrill and J. Walter, 'Order and Disorder in the English Revolution' (Chapter 12 below) with C. Hill, *The World Turned Upside Down* (London, Temple Smith, 1972) and Manning, *The English People and the English Revolution*.

12 See, for example, B. Sharp, *In Contempt of all Authority: Rural Artisans and*

Riot in the West of England (Berkeley, CA, University of California Press, 1980); Keith Lindley, *Fenland Riots and the English Revolution* (London, Heinemann Educational, 1982); M.J. Ingram, 'From Reformation to Toleration: Popular Religious Cultures in England, 1540–1690' in T. Harris (ed.), *Popular Culture in England, c.1500–1850* (Basingstoke, Macmillan, 1995), pp. 95–123 and the same volume generally; M. Spufford (ed.), *The World of Rural Dissenters, 1520–1725* (Cambridge, Cambridge University Press, 1995), especially her 'The Importance of Religion in the Sixteenth and Seventeenth Centuries', pp. 1–102; T. Watt, *Cheap Print and Popular Piety, 1550–1640* (Cambridge, Cambridge University Press, 1991).

13 D.E. Underdown, *Revel, Riot and Rebellion: Popular Politics and Culture in England, 1603–1660* (Oxford, Oxford University Press, 1985); see also C. Holmes, 'Drainers and Fenmen: the Problem of Popular Political Awareness in the Seventeenth Century', in A. Fletcher and J. Stevenson (eds), *Order and Disorder in Early Modern England* (Cambridge, Cambridge University Press, 1985), pp. 166–95; A.L. Hughes, 'Gender and Politics in Leveller Literature', in S.D. Amussen and M. Kishlansky (eds), *Political Culture and Cultural Politics in Early Modern England* (Manchester, Manchester University Press, 1995), pp. 162–88.

14 T.E. Cogswell, 'A Low Road to Extinction? Supply and Redress of Grievances in the Parliaments of the 1620s', *HJ*, 33 (1990), p. 285.

15 Russell, *Parliaments and English Politics*.

16 Sharpe, *The Personal Rule of Charles I*.

17 K. Sharpe, 'Crown, Parliament and Locality: Government and Communication in Early Stuart England', *EHR*, 399 (1986), pp. 321–50.

18 J.P. Sommerville, *Politics and Ideology in England, 1603–1640* (Harlow, Longman, 1986); *idem*, 'Ideology, Property and the Constitution', in R.P. Cust and A.L. Hughes (eds), *Conflict in Early Stuart England* (Harlow, Longman, 1989), pp. 47–71.

19 R.P. Cust, *The Forced Loan and English Politics, 1626–1628* (Oxford, Oxford University Press, 1987); *idem*, 'Charles I and a Draft Declaration for the 1628 Parliament', *HR*, 63 (1990), pp. 143–61; P.G. Lake, 'Anti-popery: the Structure of a Prejudice' (Chapter 7 below); R.P. Cust, 'News and Politics in Early-Seventeenth-Century England' (Chapter 9 in this volume).

20 Cogswell, 'Supply and Redress of Grievances in the Parliaments of the 1620s', pp. 283–303. For further criticisms of Russell's approach to the parliaments of the 1620s, see T.E. Cogswell, *The Blessed Revolution* (Cambridge, Cambridge University Press, 1989); *idem*, 'War and the Liberties of the Subject', in J.H. Hexter (ed.), *Parliament and Liberty from the Reign of Elizabeth to the English Civil War* (Stanford, CA, Stanford University Press, 1992), pp. 223–51; C. Thompson, 'Court Politics and Parliamentary Conflict in 1625', in Cust and Hughes (eds), *Conflict in Early Stuart England*, pp. 168–92; R.P. Cust, 'Charles I, the Privy Council and the Parliament of 1628', *TRHS*, 6th ser., 2 (1992), pp. 25–50.

21 C.S.R. Russell, 'The Nature of a Parliament in Early Stuart England', in Howard Tomlinson (ed.), *Before the English Civil War* (Basingstoke, Macmillan, 1983), p. 125.

22 Russell, 'The Nature of a Parliament in Early Stuart England', pp. 149–50; Russell, *The Fall of the British Monarchies*, p. 496.

23 Russell, 'The Nature of a Parliament in Early Stuart England', p. 125; J. Eales, *Puritans and Roundheads* (Cambridge, Cambridge University Press, 1990),

ch. 6; A.L. Hughes, *The Causes of the English Civil War* (Basingstoke, Macmillan, 1991), pp. 178–9.

24 D. Hirst, *The Representative of the People? Voters and Voting in England under the Early Stuarts* (Cambridge, Cambridge University Press, 1975), pp. 208–9; KAO, Sa./C1, fo. 70; Sa/ZB2/110.

25 The classic account of these issues is D.E. Underdown, *Pride's Purge: Politics in the Puritan Revolution* (Oxford, Oxford University Press, 1971): see also J.H. Hexter, *The Reign of King Pym* (Cambridge, MA, Harvard Studies, 1941) and his 'The Problem of the Presbyterian-Independents', *American Historical Review*, 44 (1938/9), pp. 29–49 which sparked a debate that continued into the 1970s in, for example, V. Pearl, 'Oliver St John and the "middle group" in the Long Parliament', *EHR*, 81 (1966), pp. 490–519.

26 M. Kishlansky, *Parliamentary Selection* (Cambridge, Cambridge University Press, 1986).

27 J.S.A. Adamson, 'The English Nobility and the Projected Settlement of 1647', *HJ*, 30 (1987), pp. 567–602. For debate about the sources and approaches used in this article, see M.A. Kishlansky, 'Saye what?' *HJ*, 33 (1990), pp. 917–37; J.S.A. Adamson, 'Politics and the Nobility in Civil-War England', *HJ*, 34 (1991), pp. 231–55; M.A. Kishlansky, 'Saye No More', *JBS*, 30 (1991), pp. 399–448. For further interpretations of the events of 1647 which differ from both Adamson and Kishlansky, see A. Woolrych, *Soldiers and Statesmen: The General Council of the Army and its Debates, 1647–8* (Oxford, Oxford University Press, 1987); I. Gentles, *The New Model Army in England, Ireland and Scotland, 1645–1653* (Oxford, Blackwell, 1992); R. Ashton, *The Second Civil War and its Origins, 1646–1648* (London, Yale University Press, 1994).

28 For further work on the baronial context of this period, see J.S.A. Adamson, 'Parliamentary Management, Men of Business and the House of Lords, 1640–9', in C. Jones (ed.), *A Pillar of the Constitution: The House of Lords in British Politics, 1640–1784* (London, Hambledon Press, 1989), pp. 21–50; *idem*, 'The *Vindiciae Veritatis* and the Political Creed of Viscount Saye and Sele', *HR*, 60 (1987), pp. 45–63.

29 Russell, 'The Anglo-Scottish Union', pp. 238–56. For European perspectives, see M. Greengrass (ed.), *Conquest and Coalescence: The Shaping of the State in Early Modern Europe* (London, Arnold, 1991); J.H. Elliott, 'A World of Composite Monarchies', *P&P*, 137 (1992), pp. 48–71. New collections on the British Problem emerge all the time; for two recent examples, see S.G. Ellis and S. Barber (eds), *Conquest and Union: Fashioning a British State, 1485–1725* (1995) and A.J. Grant and K.J. Stringer (eds), *Uniting the Kingdom? The Making of British History* (London, Routledge, 1995).

30 Although Nicholas Canny, 'The Attempted Anglicization of Ireland in the Seventeenth Century: An Exemplar of "British History"', in J.F. Merritt (ed.), *The Political World of Thomas Wentworth, Earl of Strafford, 1621–1641* (Cambridge, Cambridge University Press, 1996), p. 158, argues that Russell assumes social and economic conditions in the three kingdoms were similar or even identical.

31 See also Russell, *Fall of the British Monarchies*, pp. 525–6.

32 Underdown, *Pride's Purge*, chs 3–5.

33 Thomas Juxon's Journal, Dr Williams's Library, London, MS 24.50, fo. 101^r.

34 Ashton, *Counter Revolution*, pp. 304–9; A.L. Hughes, *Politics, Society and Civil War in Warwickshire, 1620–1660* (Cambridge, Cambridge University Press, 1987), p. 256.

35 Ashton, *Counter Revolution*, p. 315. On one of Juxon's calculations, indeed, the Scots owed the English money: Juxon's Journal, fo. 88[r].

36 Canny, 'The Attempted Anglicization of Ireland', especially pp. 157–8. As Canny points out, the terms Britain or British Isles are in themselves controversial for Ireland.

37 P.G. Lake, 'Retrospective: Wentworth's Political World in Revisionist and Post-revisionist Perspective', in Merritt (ed.), *The Political World of Thomas Wentworth*, especially p. 279.

38 D. Hirst, 'The English Republic and the Meaning of Britain', *JMH*, 66 (1994), pp. 451–86.

39 Canny, 'The Attempted Anglicization of Ireland', p. 158.

40 Jane Dawson, 'Anglo-Scottish Protestant Culture and Integration in Sixteenth-century Britain,' in Barber and Ellis (eds), *Conquest and Union*, pp. 87–114.

41 Sharpe, *Personal Rule*, p. xxiii.

42 Gardiner, *History*; *idem*, *The Great Civil War*. There is a rich literature on the religious radicals of the 1640s and 1650s, unfortunately not easy to anthologize; see, in particular, William Haller, *Liberty and Reformation* (New York, Columbia University Press, 1955); Hill, *The World Turned Upside Down*; B. Reay and J.F. Macgregor, *Radical Religion in the English Revolution* (Oxford, Oxford University Press, 1984).

43 For the main developments and revisions in Tyacke's work, see N.R.N. Tyacke, *Anti-Calvinists: The Rise of English Arminianism c. 1590–1640* (Oxford, Oxford University Press, 1987) and *idem*, *The Fortunes of English Puritanism 1603–1640* (Dr Williams's Library Lecture, 1990). Sharpe, *Personal Rule*, pp. 286–7; Julian Davies, *The Caroline Captivity of the Church: Charles I and the Remoulding of Anglicanism* (Oxford, Oxford University Press, 1992); Peter White, *Predestination, Policy and Polemic* (Cambridge, Cambridge University Press, 1992); *idem*, 'The *Via Media* of the Early Stuart Church', in K. Fincham (ed.), *The Early Stuart Church* (Basingstoke, Macmillan, 1993), pp. 211–30.

44 P.G. Lake, 'Calvinism and the English Church, 1570–1635', *P&P*, 114 (1987), pp. 32–76; *idem*, 'The Laudian Style: Order, Conformity and the Pursuit of Holiness in the 1630s', in Fincham (ed.), *The Early Stuart Church*, pp. 161–85; for anti-Puritanism see also *idem*, 'A Charitable Christian Hatred: the Godly and their Enemies in the 1630s', in C. Durston and J. Eales (eds), *The Culture of English Puritanism, 1560–1700* (Basingstoke, Macmillan, 1996), pp. 145–83; A.L. Hughes, 'Religion and Society in Stratford upon Avon, 1619–1638', *MH*, 19 (1994), pp. 58–84.

45 A. Milton, *Catholic and Reformed: The Roman and Protestant Church in English Protestant Thought, 1600–1640* (Cambridge, Cambridge University Press, 1995); *idem*, 'The Church of England, Rome and the True Church: the Demise of a Jacobean Consensus', in Fincham (ed.), *The Early Stuart Church*, pp. 187–210.

46 Russell, *Causes of the English Civil War*, pp. 88–108.

47 P. Collinson, *The Religion of Protestants: The Church in English Society, 1559–1625* (Oxford, Oxford University Press, 1982); P.G. Lake, 'Defining Puritanism – again?' in F. Bremer (ed.), *Puritanism: Transatlantic Perspectives on a Seventeenth-Century Anglo-American Faith* (Boston, MA, Massachusetts Historical Society, 1993), pp. 3–29; Tyacke, *The Fortunes of English Puritanism, 1603–1640*; J. Eales, 'A Road to Revolution: the Continuity of Puritanism, 1559–1642', in Durston and Eales (eds), *The Culture of Puritanism*, pp. 184–209. For Tyacke's stress on the revolutionary potential of Puritanism, see his 'The "Rise of Puritanism" and the Legalising of Dissent, 1571–1719', in O.P.

Grell, J.I. Israel and N.R.N. Tyacke (eds), *From Persecution to Toleration: The Glorious Revolution and Religion in England* (Oxford, Oxford University Press, 1991), pp. 17–28. For networks, see T. Webster, 'The Godly of Goshen Scattered: an Essex Clerical Conference in the 1620s and its Diaspora' (Cambridge University PhD, 1993); A.L. Hughes, 'Thomas Dugard and his Circle in the 1630s: A Parliamentary-Puritan Connection?', *HJ*, 29 (1986), pp. 779–93.

48 Sharpe, *Personal Rule*, chs 6 and 12.

49 C. Haigh, *English Reformations: Religion, Politics and Society under the Tudors* (Oxford, Oxford University Press, 1993), pp. 14–18, is the latest summing up of the 'revisionist' position; see also Eamon Duffy, *The Stripping of the Altars: Traditional Religion in England 1400–1580* (New Haven and London, Yale University Press, 1992). John Morrill has eloquently developed this perspective for the 1640s and 1650s, notably in 'The Church in England', in J.S. Morrill (ed.), *Reactions to the English Civil War* (Basingstoke, Macmillan, 1982), pp. 89–114.

50 J. Maltby, ' "By this book": Parishioners, the Prayer Book and the Established Church', in Fincham (ed.), *The Early Stuart Church*, pp. 115–37; Morrill, 'The Church in England', pp. 89–114; see also Watt, *Cheap Print and Popular Piety, 1550–1640*, a study of ballads, prints and chap books which argues that popular tastes were not attracted to zealous Calvinist positions.

51 See also P.G. Lake, 'Deeds against Nature: Cheap Print, Protestantism and Murder in Early-Seventeenth-Century England', in P.G. Lake and K. Sharpe (eds), *Culture and Politics in Early Stuart England* (Basingstoke, Macmillan, 1994), pp. 257–83, for a further attempt, using very different material, to challenge the view that Puritanism could not be popular.

52 D. Cressy, *Bonfires and Bells: National Memory and the Protestant Calendar in Elizabethan and Stuart England* (London, Weidenfeld, 1989).

53 J.T. Cliffe, *The Yorkshire Gentry* (London, Athlone Press, 1969); B.G. Blackwood, *The Lancashire Gentry and the Great Rebellion, 1640–1660* (Manchester, Chetham Soc., 1978); Hill, 'Recent Interpretations of the Civil War', pp. 13–40.

54 A. Everitt, *The Community of Kent and the Great Rebellion* (Leicester, Leicester University Press, 1966); *idem, The Local Community and the Great Rebellion* (Historical Association pamphlet, 1969). For discussion of some of the ambiguities of the term 'country' see R.P. Cust and A.L. Hughes, 'Introduction: After Revisionism', in Cust and Hughes (eds), *Conflict in Early Stuart England*, pp. 19–20.

55 K. Sharpe, 'The Personal Rule of Charles I' in Tomlinson (ed.), *Before the English Civil War*, pp. 67–78.

56 Morrill, *Revolt of the Provinces*, ch. 2, an argument also developed in R. Hutton, *The Royalist War Effort, 1642–1646*, (Harlow, Longman, 1982), and Ashton, *Counter Revolution*, ch. III.

57 See also A.L. Hughes, 'Warwickshire on the Eve of Civil War: A county Community?', *MH*, 7 (1982), pp. 42–72; *idem*, 'Local History and the Origins of the Civil War', in Cust and Hughes (eds), *Conflict in Early Stuart England*, pp. 224–53; R.P. Cust and P.G. Lake, 'Sir Richard Grosvenor and the Rhetoric of Magistracy', *BIHR*, 54 (1981), pp. 48–50.

58 Cust, *The Forced Loan*; K. Fincham, 'The Judges' Decision on Ship Money in February 1637: the Reaction of Kent', *BIHR*, 57 (1984), pp. 230–7; N. Jackson, 'The Collection of Ship Money in Northamptonshire, 1635–1640' (University of Birmingham M.Phil. thesis, 1987).

59 See also A.L. Hughes, 'Parliamentary Tyranny? Indemnity Proceedings and the Impact of Civil War: a Case Study from Warwickshire', *MH*, 9 (1986), pp. 49–78.

60 C. Hill, *Society and Puritanism in Pre-Revolutionary England* (London, Secker and Warburg, 1964); Manning, *The English People and the English Revolution*; *idem*, 'Puritanism and Democracy, 1640–1642', in D. Pennington and K. Thomas (eds), *Puritans and Revolutionaries* (Oxford, Oxford University Press, 1978), pp. 139–60; K. Wrightson, *English Society, 1580–1680* (London, Hutchinson, 1982); *idem*, 'Two Concepts of Order', in J. Brewer and J. Styles (eds), *An Ungovernable People* (London, Hutchinson, 1980), pp. 21–46.

61 R. Brenner, *Merchants and Revolution: Commercial Change, Political Conflict, and London's Overseas Traders, 1550–1653* (Cambridge, 1993); I. Gentles and J.S. Morrill, 'Symposium on Robert Brenner's *Merchants and Revolution*', pp. 103–112, 113–23.

62 Underdown, *Revel, Riot and Rebellion*.

63 See Russell, *Fall of the British Monarchies*, p. 363, n. 141, 'The similarity of the Parliament's plague orders to the Book of Orders . . . would seem to follow from the fact that both were largely the work of the earl of Manchester. This fact is a useful symbol to show that King and Parliament did not stand for rival social policies.'

64 J.S. Morrill, 'The Ecology of Allegiance in the English Civil War', in his *The Nature of the English Revolution* (Harlow, Longman, 1993), pp. 224–41; Hughes, 'Local History and the Origins of Civil War', pp. 224–53; B. Sharp, 'Rural Discontents and the English Revolution', in R.C. Richardson (ed.), *Town and Countryside in the English Revolution* (Manchester, Manchester University Press, 1992), pp. 251–72; M.J. Ingram, ' "Scolding women cucked or washed": a Crisis in Gender Relations in Early Modern England?', in G. Walker and J. Kermode (eds), *Women, Crime and the Courts in Early Modern England* (London, UCL Press, 1994), pp. 48–80. For a recent discussion which endorses the cultural aspects of Underdown's argument, see M. Stoyle, *Loyalty and Locality: Popular Allegiance in Devon During the English Civil War* (Exeter, Exeter University Press, 1994).

65 Manning, *The English People and the English Revolution*.

66 For this scepticism and broader discussion of 'class analysis', see K. Wrightson, 'Estates, Degrees and Sorts: Changing Perceptions of Society in Tudor and Stuart England', in P. Corfield (ed.), *History, Language and Class* (Oxford, Blackwell, 1991), pp. 30–52.

67 Cogswell, *The Blessed Revolution*; *idem*, 'Underground Verse and the Transformation of Early Stuart Political Culture', in Amussen and Kishlansky (eds), *Political Culture and Cultural Politics*, pp. 277–300; A. Bellany, ' "Rayling rhymes and vaunting verse": Libellous Politics in Early Stuart England', in Lake and Sharpe (eds), *Culture and Politics*, pp. 285–310; Dagmar Freist, 'The Formation of Opinion and the Communication Network in London, 1637 to *c*.1645' (Cambridge University PhD, 1992).

68 R.P. Cust, 'Politics and the Electorate in the 1620s', in Cust and Hughes (eds), *Conflict in Early Stuart England*, pp. 134–67; C.B. Herrup, 'The Counties and the Country: Some Thoughts on Seventeenth-century Historiography', *Social History*, 8 (1983), pp. 169–81.

69 Sommerville, *Ideology and Politics*; *idem*, 'Ideology, Property and the Constitution', pp 47–71; G. Burgess, *The Politics of the Ancient Constitution* (Basingstoke, Macmillan, 1992), p. 165. For an interesting review of Burgess, and other works, see J. Champion, *Parliamentary History*, 14 (1995), pp. 187–98.

70 P.G. Lake and K. Sharpe, 'Introduction', in Lake and Sharpe (eds), *Political Culture*, pp. 1–20; Lake, 'Wentworth's Political World', pp. 252–83. For an exploration of the uses and implications of these languages in the career of a leading politician, see R.P. Cust, 'Wentworth's "change of sides" in the 1620s', in Merritt (ed.), *The Political World of Thomas Wentworth*, pp. 63–80.

71 *A declaration, or Representation, from his Excellency, Sir Thomas Fairfax, And the Army under his command* (June, 1647) in W. Haller and G. Davies (eds), *The Leveller Tracts 1647–1653* (reprint Gloucester, Mass., 1964), p. 55.

72 See also Andrew Sharp, 'John Lilburne and the Long Parliament's *Book of Declarations*: a Radical's Exploitation of the Words of Authorities', *History of Political Thought*, 9 (1988); Hughes, 'Gender and Politics in Leveller Literature', pp. 162–88.

73 Underdown, *Revel, Riot and Rebellion*, chs 6–9; Morrill, 'The Church in England', pp. 89–114; Ashton, *Counter Revolution*.

74 Hughes, 'Parliamentary Tyranny?', pp. 49–78; *idem*, 'Gender and Politics', pp. 162–88; see also the debates on the recognition of Richard Cromwell as Lord Protector in the parliament of 1659, conducted in a historical framework going back to the Anglo-Saxons: J.T. Rutt, *The Diary of Thomas Burton*, 4 vols (London, 1828), III, 87–105, for a speech by Sir Arthur Haselrig beginning, 'Time was, this nation had seven kings . . .'.

75 Ashton, *Counter Revolution*, p. 313.

76 P. Collinson, 'The monarchical republic of Elizabeth I', *Bulletin of the John Rylands Library*, 69 (1987), pp. 394–424; for the Rump see S. Kelsey, *The Political Culture of the English Republic* (Manchester, Manchester University Press, forthcoming).

77 Russell, *Fall of the British Monarchies*; D.L. Smith, *Constitutional Royalism and the Search for Settlement, c.1640–1649* (Cambridge, Cambridge University Press, 1994).

78 A. Milton, 'Thomas Wentworth and the Political Thought of the Personal Rule', in Merritt (ed.), *Political World of Thomas Wentworth*, pp. 138–9, 153.

79 I. Atherton, 'John, First Viscount Scudamore (1601–1671): A Career at Court and in the Country' (Cambridge University PhD, 1993).

80 R. Samuel, 'Reading the Signs', *History Workshop*, 32 (1991), pp. 88–109; 33 (1992), pp. 220–51.

81 Cust and Hughes, 'After Revisionism', pp. 12–13.

82 A.L. Hughes, 'The Meanings of Religious Polemic', in Bremer (ed.), *Puritanism*, pp. 201–29.

83 Milton, 'Wentworth and Political Thought', pp. 151–2; P.G. Lake, 'The Moderate and Irenic Case for Religious War: Joseph Hall's *Via Media* in Context', in Amussen and Kishlansky (eds), *Political Culture*, pp. 55–83.

84 R. Darnton, 'Introduction', in R. Darnton and D. Roche (eds), *Revolution in Print: The Press in France 1775–1800* (Berkeley CA, University of California Press, 1989).

85 Dr Williams's Library, London, MS 24.50.

SECTION
I

POLITICS

1

Parliamentary history in perspective,
1604–1629

CONRAD RUSSELL

A historian is like a man who sits down to read a detective story after beginning with the last chapter. The clues pointing to the ultimate dénouement then appear to him in such embarrassing abundance that he wonders how anyone can ever have been in doubt about the ultimate outcome. Much of a historian's working life, then, is spent in drawing attention to those clues which point towards the solution which he knows ultimately emerged. Usually, this is a useful process, but there is one important difference between life and detective fiction: life is not a story written by the author who had decided on the ultimate solution before the story began. A historian must always run the risk of letting hindsight lead him to see the evidence out of perspective. Those who write the story remembering the ultimate conclusion may miss many of the twists and turns which gave it suspense along the way. They may even forget that the result ever was in suspense.

This risk is particularly tempting for historians who describe the years before revolutions. In particular, the study of English parliamentary history of the years 1604–29 has been so dominated by the knowledge that it preceded a civil war that it is dangerously easy to treat it as a mere preface, and not as a story in its own right. It is dangerously easy to believe, because the story ended with parliament in a position to challenge the king for supremacy, that it was bound to end in this way, and that it was the direction in which most of the evidence points. In particular, the use of the word 'opposition' to describe the type of criticism the crown faced during these parliaments can easily suggest that the criticisms uttered during these years were such as to lead on logically to civil war against the crown. This tendency to see the parliamentary history of the period as a sort of historical escalator appears in such remarks as Professor Moir's comment on the exclusion of Sir Thomas Parry from the Commons in 1614, that 'the development had begun which led ultimately to parliamentary control of the executive'. It appears in Professor Zaller's claim that 'there was no logical end to this cycle but a total assumption of sovereignty, and this was exactly the position to which parliament was led in the 1640s'.[1] By themselves, such striking juxtapositions are not necessarily wrong, though they may be seriously misleading. We enter on rather more questionable territory with the statement of Professor Zagorin that in the civil war the sons of Sir Robert Phelips and Sir Edwin Sandys, two prominent members of the Commons 'broke with family tradition to become royalists' in the Civil War.[2] They did nothing of the sort: their fathers had left them no tradition of fighting against the crown. The assumption that armed revolution against the crown was the logical conclusion of their fathers' speeches in the 1620s is one which is too big to be sustained by hindsight alone: it would have to be sustained by evidence, and there is a good deal of evidence which conflicts with it.[3]

This tendency to see the parliamentary history of the years 1604–29 as a 'high road to civil war' is sufficiently deeply entrenched to have survived a somewhat erratic preliminary bombardment from Professor Elton.[4] The traditional view now faces a flank attack from European historians. Professor Myers disputes the common assumption that European parliaments and estates were institutionally less well developed than the English.[5] Professor Koenigsberger, in a far-reaching study of '*Dominium Regale* or *Dominium Politicum et Regale*: Monarchies and Parliaments in Early Modern Europe', has now attempted a general examination of the reasons why parliaments and estates survived in some kingdoms and not in others. He does not find the answer in the institutional and procedural development which has been the dominant theme in most studies of the English parliament. If this were the main determining factor, it would be hard to account for the survival of the Scottish parliament, whose procedure left it as susceptible to manipulation by the king as any parliament in Europe. To Professor Koenigsberger, many of the forces which determined the survival or extinction of parliaments and estates appear unpredictable. Among unpredictable influences which helped to determine the outcome of events, he lays particular stress on two: the relations between the different states of multiple kingdoms, and the effects of outside intervention: 'such intervention', he says, 'would alter the relative strength of the internal forces to an extent which is, I believe, unpredictable, even if we were to use game theory or a computer'. To him, the causes of the survival of the English parliament appear not in its procedural advances in the early seventeenth century but in the effects of Scottish intervention in 1640 and Dutch intervention in 1688. 'Clearly', he concludes, 'at its most critical and dramatic moments, English history cannot be understood in terms of a closed political system'.[6]

In stating these arguments, Professor Koenigsberger has issued a challenge to historians of the English parliament which we cannot afford to ignore. This belief that the ultimate survival of the English parliaments was not inevitable, and that its survival was due to events occurring in and after 1640, and even more the belief that outside intervention could reverse a trend already in progress, entirely contradicts the ingrained assumption of English parliamentary historians that parliament, well before the civil war, was already set on a course which led to serious challenges to the crown and ultimately to political supremacy. Faced with so deep-seated a difference, we must go back to the evidence and ask who is right.

The conventional belief that the parliaments of 1604–29 were a 'high road to civil war' logically implies two further beliefs. One is the belief that parliament was a powerful institution; it is only if parliament is thought of as a great power in the state that it can be made to fill the role for which it is cast, of a potential challenger to the king for supreme power. The other logical necessity to the belief that this period was a high road to civil war is the belief that the parliaments of these years witnessed a constitutional struggle between two 'sides', government and opposition, or, in modern language, court and country.[7] Two sides are an essential condition of a civil war, and where there are not two sides, there cannot be a high road to civil war.

These two beliefs are logically implied in statements made by well-known historians, and these implications have gained the status of received opinions. 'Every schoolboy knows' that parliament was growing more powerful in the early Stuart period, and that it was divided into supporters of 'government' and 'opposition'. It is the contention of this article that these two beliefs are false. Before 1640, parliament was not powerful, and it did not contain an 'opposition'.

Since these two beliefs have become so firmly rooted in our collective historical consciousness, it is interesting to see how tentative our leading parliamentary historians have been in stating them. The greater reservations concern the belief that parliament, and particularly the House of Commons, possessed political power. In his Raleigh Lecture on *The Winning of the Initiative by the House of Commons* Wallace Notestein, the greatest parliamentary historian in this field, conveyed this belief in three phrases only. One was the statement that 'Tudor despotism contained within itself the seeds of its own decay; it was leading on to a more active House of Commons, certain *in time* to demand power'. The second was his conclusion that these years 'gave us . . . a new kind of Commons, that was *by and by* to make inevitable a new constitution'. Both these phrases contain a crucial chronological reservation. The third phrase in which Notestein conveyed a belief in the power of the house of commons was the crucial ambiguity of his title *'The Winning of the Initiative by the House of Commons'*. Notestein himself said that he was describing how the Commons 'gained the real initiative *in legislation*'.[8] That independent members gained the initiative in the legislative process in the house of commons is undeniable, but the small proportion of their bills which passed into law may leave us wondering whether the initiative in the legislative process in the house of commons deserves to be described without qualification as 'the initiative'.[9]

Notestein showed an almost equal caution in stating the other belief here discussed, that parliament was divided into 'government' and 'opposition'. It is true that he used these terms throughout, but, in two little noticed passages of reservation, he denied that the leaders he described were a deliberate opposition with constitutional aims. He said that they proceeded 'without purpose or intent but to do the next thing that came to hand'. Similarly, in saying that the leaders he described ceased to take their cue from privy councillors, he said 'Not that they were definitely out to change the constitution. Rather, as leaders of opposition, they were full of devices to overcome particular difficulties, and when these devices led on to new custom, they saw in it nothing out of the way'.[10] Others, unmindful of this qualification, have noticed numerous occasions on which members of both houses of parliament failed to function in a coherent 'government' and 'opposition' pattern, but they have developed a tendency to treat such examples which fail to fit their picture as illustrations of the moral obliquity of the characters they are discussing. T. L. Moir complained that the officials and courtiers in the Addled Parliament 'should have formed a cohesive group in the House', though he was well aware that they did not do so.[11] The note of moral condemnation is strongest in Professor Zagorin's discussion of Sir Thomas Wentworth: 'if he held any principles, his conduct was no less marked by mercenary self-interest and lack of scruple. These traits appeared fully in his political *volte-face*. This moral condemnation was missing from the comments of Wentworth's contemporaries. Bedford, who by 1640 did deserve the title of 'leader of the opposition', wrote to Wentworth after his elevation to the presidency of the Council of the North, not with a complaint that he had 'changed sides', but with an offer to help to get his nephew a barony. It is then possible to wonder whether Wentworth's offence was against the moral standards of his contemporaries, or against the tidiness of Professor Zagorin's argument.[12]

At the least, the hesitancy shown by historians of the calibre of Notestein in asserting these two propositions, that parliament was a power in the state, and that it was divided into government and opposition supporters should lead us to wonder whether the assumptions are not open to serious doubt. In any discussion of power, it is essential to remember that parliament had two houses. Both in legislation and in judicature, the efforts of the Commons stood no chance whatever of persuading the king without the support of the Lords. Without backing from among the Lords, even the most aggressive verbal noises in the Commons amounted to no more than political tantrums. So shrewd a manager of men as Buckingham was more concerned about his critics among the Lords than among the Commons. We remember that during the Parliament of 1621 Sir Edwin Sandys and John Selden were imprisoned but tend to forget the earl of Southampton. It should give us pause to find the Venetian Ambassador describing the imprisonment of the earl of Southampton and 'three or four others of no consideration'.[13]

The ability to obstruct conciliar legislation conferred much less power on either house of parliament in this period than it would have done in, for example, the 1530s. From the late Elizabethan period onwards, the desire of crown and council to legislate appears to have declined sharply, and the political importance of control of the legislative process declined with it. Opening speeches by the Lord Keeper often warned parliaments that they were not called for the making of new laws, for there were more than enough already. On those occasions when James told a parliament that one of the reasons for which it was called was the making of laws, he normally intended the statement as a concession.[14] He was not announcing a 'government' legislative programme, since he had no desire for one. He was saying members could spend their time on issues of their own choice. The legislative initiative, then, was of little importance if the crown had no great wish to legislate. There was only one piece of legislation particularly dear to the heart of James I which was obstructed by the house of commons, and that was the Union with Scotland. The Great Contract also failed to pass through the legislative process in 1610, but to describe the Great Contract as an example of an 'opposition' frustrating 'government' legislation would be misleading. Many of the strongest opponents of the Great Contract were inside the government, and their criticisms may have had as much to do with its failure as any parliamentary 'opposition'. There can only be an 'opposition' where there is a clear 'government' line, and the Great Contract was not such an issue. It is, then, misleading to use the failure of the Great Contract to illustrate the power of a parliamentary 'opposition'.

There was only one thing which could give parliament power in a situation in which the king did not wish to be persuaded, and that was control of supply. A monopoly of the power of extraordinary taxation was the only means by which parliament could, in a situation of conflict, hope to force its will on a reluctant crown. What use did parliament make of its power to give or withhold supply, and what were the effects of its use? Professor Koenigsberger, at the end of an exhaustive study of European parliaments and estates, concluded that 'it seems to be a fairly general rule that a parliament which failed to insist on the redress of grievances before supply had no chance of winning its struggle with the monarchy; i.e. a parliament must not agree to grant taxes before the king has met its demands'.[15] By this test, the English parliament before 1629 was heading for extinction. In 1606, they voted three subsidies and three fifteenths, recognizing the principle that parliamentary supply should be used to meet defects in the king's ordinary revenue. They did not use the supply as a lever to secure redress of their grievances, since they only presented the grievances the day before the subsidy, and accepted from James what, in his predecessor, would have been called an 'answer answerless'. A few of the grievances, such as the patent for logwood, were briefly redressed before springing up again, but most of them continued unchecked until the Long Parliament.[16] In 1610, a vote of one subsidy and one fifteenth was accompanied by a Petition of Grievances. It was proposed that the subsidy be presented before the grievances on the ground that 'there was no reason to defer our gift till he had answered our grievances for the word of a prince was not a small matter, and he had promised us a good and a gracious answer to our grievances'. The Commons decided to defer the subsidy till the grievances had been presented, but James's reply of July 10, saying the grievances could not be suddenly answered, cannot be described as 'redress'. Once again, the subsidy was voted, and the grievances remained unredressed. When Sir Henry Neville told James 'that in this one parliament they had already given four subsidies and seven fifteenths, which is more than ever was given by any parliament at any time, upon any occasion; and yet withal that they had no relief of their grievances',[17] he spoke no more than the plain truth. In the first parliament of King James, the ability to link subsidies with redress of grievances did not confer any significant bargaining power on parliament, because the attempt to use it for this purpose was not made. The attempt was contemplated, both then and later. The significant fact is that members who contemplated using this weapon so frequently decided not to do so.

In 1621, when parliament met after a seven-year interval,[18] members of the Commons were even farther from attempting to use supply as a means of extorting the redress of grievances. The drama of the attack on the patentees in 1621 has distracted attention from the ease with which the subsidies went through. The subject was introduced on 15 February, just over a fortnight after the opening of the parliament, and an important shift at once appeared in the nature of the bargain involved in a grant of subsidy. In the words of Pym's diary, 'this meeting was to be employed uppon the twoe poynts of suply and grievances, but the former consumed most part of tyme, for the subiect being gracious and acceptable many were desireous to have their part in it'. Instead of redress of grievances, the motive of giving was now alleged to be 'to procure from his Majestie the love and frequency of parliaments, to take from the world the opinion of ielousye betwixt the king and his Comons, from our enemyes the hope of our devision, from our selves those mischefes and grievances which the discontinuance of parliaments hath caused. As we expect ease from his Majesties grace, to doe that which may procure his grace'.[19] The bargain had indeed shifted: it was no longer redress of grievances in return for subsidies, but subsidies in return for the summons of future parliaments. So eager were the Commons to please in this matter that they did not even accept the very mild suggestion of Pym: 'not to hinder the subsidy; but yet to prepare some bills to go up with it'.[20] This is why the parliament of 1621

presented the extraordinary spectacle of a session in which the subsidy bill
was the only legislation passed. Sir Robert Phelips, at least, appreciated
the significance of what had happened: he later complained that 'we have
broken all former precedents, in giving two subsidies at the beginning of a
parliament'.[21] It seems that the dramas of the revived parliamentary
judicature, and of the foreign policy debate of the second session, have
blinded us to a sharp fall, in 1621, in the bargaining power control of the
subsidy conferred on the house of commons. Even the revived judicature,
as the cases of Floyd and Yelverton show, was procedure which could only
be made effective with the king's consent. At no time before 1640 did
impeachment deprive the king of a minister whom he was determined to
retain.

In 1624, once again, the subsidy was voted before grievances were
discussed. The Petition of Grievances of 1624 was presented so late in
the parliament and it received so little attention that the Commons were
constrained to present the identical petition of grievances again in the next
parliament. In 1625, it can at least be said that the Commons went through
the motions of requesting redress of grievances before supply, but it cannot
be said that they had much success in doing so. They did not even purport
to regard the answers as satisfactory, and resolved, on the motion of Sir
Edward Coke, to petition the king for a 'more full' answer.[22] Some of the
1625 grievances, such as the new imposition on the Turkey merchants and
the new imposition on wines, provided staple issues of complaint in the
Parliament of 1628. Others, such as the imposition of Newcastle coals and
the restraint of building, were echoes of the old petition of grievances of
1610. Nevertheless, the Commons duly voted two subsidies without
waiting for their 'more full' answer.

It is necessary here to correct two widely held misapprehensions. The
first is that the decision in 1624 to appropriate parliamentary supply to the
forthcoming war with Spain, and to allow it to be paid to treasurers
nominated by the house of commons, represented an exercise of the power
of the purse by the Commons. Appropriation of supply had occasionally
been discussed in 1610 and 1614 as a way of increasing the parliamentary
power of the purse, but in 1624 the initiative for the appropriation did not
come from the house of commons. Both the proposal for appropriation
and the proposal for the subsidy to be voted to treasurers nominated by the
house of commons were first stated in public by King James I himself, in
his speech to both Houses of 8 March, 1624. The proposal was next
repeated by Lord Treasurer Middlesex in the house of lords, and it was
only after this firm official encouragement that it was introduced into the
house of commons by Sir Benjamin Rudyerd on 11 March. Dr. J. N. Ball
was undoubtedly correct in saying that 'Rudyerd's detailed propositions
came directly from the King', and even in describing Rudyerd as acting, in
this speech, as a 'government spokesman'.[23] This appropriation, great

though its long-term constitutional significance may have been, was not the result of any pressure by the house of commons, but an offshoot of the complex balance of forces at court between those in favour of the war with Spain and those against it. Subsequent attempts to make these treasurers account to the house of commons, as the wording of the act demanded, were a total failure.

The other misapprehension is that the failure to grant an additional supply in the Oxford session of 1625 represented an important use of the power of the purse for purposes of political coercion. The 1625 parliament had already voted two subsidies, and Charles was attempting to induce it to vote a second grant of subsidies in one year. The voting of two grants of subsidy in one session and in one year was something likely to provoke popular discontent, especially during a serious attack of the plague, and there was reason in Sir Thomas Wentworth's statement that 'wee feare the granting thereof wilbe esteemed by his subiects noe faire acquittal of our duties towards them, or returne of ther trusts reposed in us'.[24] The surprising thing about the request for an additional subsidy in 1625 was not that it was refused, but that it was ever seriously entertained. A similar request in 1610 had been turned down out of hand. There was only one recent precedent for the making of two grants of subsidy in one year. That was the grant of an additional subsidy in the second session of 1621, which James had thrown away by a premature dissolution.

By themselves, these occasions on which supply was voted without redress of grievances need not prove a lack of parliamentary power: they might only prove a desire to be conciliatory. Such a desire was certainly present in 1621. It is only possible to test the extent of the power conferred on parliament by the right to withhold supply by looking at the rare occasions on which parliaments did attempt to use the withholding or delaying of supply as a bargaining counter to extort political concessions. In the reign of James I, there was only one such occasion: the Addled Parliament of 1614. The issue here involved was the issue of impositions, in which the house of commons stood alone. They lacked majority backing from the house of lords in attempting to force the crown to abandon its right to impose duties on merchandise without the consent of parliament. The issue was one of the utmost importance, involving the right of the crown to place additional customs duties on merchandise at its pleasure. The subsequent history of impositions shows that members of the Commons were not mistaken in the importance they attached to them. The issue was, moreover, being discussed in a second consecutive parliament. In 1610, the Commons had mustered all their debating talent on this issue. Thomas Wentworth, son of Peter Wentworth, quoted Fortescue, expressing the fear that this meant the end of England's status as *dominium politicum et regale*, a parliamentary monarchy. Yet, though all the legal resources of the Commons were involved in the assembly of a formidable collection of precedents, John Chamberlain proved justified in his forecast that those involved in impositions 'no doubt will maintain their doings, knowing that though men storm never so much yet *vanae sine viribus irae*'.[25] It is remarkable that the 1610 Parliament, when they were so rightly, and deeply, concerned about impositions, did not attempt to make supply conditional on their abandonment. Even in 1614, when the king threatened immediate dissolution if supply was not granted, a surprising number of members were prepared to vote supply without first insisting on the abandonment of impositions. By my count, the speakers in the final debate on whether to grant the king an immediate supply were 14 on each side. The king, then, lost his supply, not through a collective resolution of the Commons to deny it, but through the success of the opponents of supply in preventing the putting of the question. This issue, then, came to a showdown in spite of the reluctance of a number of distinguished house of commons men, including Thomas Wentworth (son of Peter Wentworth), Nicholas Fuller, James Whitelocke and Sir Maurice Berkeley, to make an issue of it.[26] When the issue did come to a showdown, there was never a moment's doubt what the result would be. The parliament was dissolved, leaving so sober a member as Sir Thomas Roe claiming that it was 'a dissolution, not of this, but of all Parliaments'.[27] Impositions continued to be levied without parliamentary consent until the civil war, and increased from the £70,000 a year of 1614 to £218,000 a year in the 1630s. In this, the only profound constitutional conflict of the reign of James I, the result had been such an overwhelming victory for the king that there can hardly be said to have been a contest.

It was another round of the same issue which produced the second attempt of the period to use the withholding of supply as a weapon of political persuasion, the withholding of Tonnage and Poundage in 1625. On 14 April, 1624, the luckless Solicitor General Heath had cited the Jacobean Tonnage and Poundage Act of 1604 as a justification of the levying of impositions.[28] This necessarily produced a determination in the parliamentary leaders to word the new Tonnage and Poundage Act which had to be passed in the first year of Charles I's reign in such a way that it could not be so cited. In the words of the anonymous diarist:

> The reasons that moved the house not to grant it for life, as it was King James his tyme, was for that the kinges Councell in the Parliament of 18 Jacobi [*recte* 1624] did picke out reasons out of that Act for the ptermitted customs and other impositions wch lay and were imposed on the subts. very grievous unto them, and they had not tyme to examine and redress them.[29]

Since the Tonnage and Poundage bill was being prepared during a hasty session designed to reach a speedy end to avoid the plague, there was no time for a carefully worded new grant which would have either excluded impositions, or based them, as the Long Parliament ultimately did, on parliamentary authority. A temporary bill, granting Tonnage and Poundage for one year, therefore appeared the obvious way round the difficulty. There was no intention to deny Tonnage and Poundage, merely to word the act in such a way that it should not appear to sanction impositions. This plan foundered on the refusal of the Lords to pass the bill for one year only. The Lords' rejection of the bill left Charles without legal authority for Tonnage and Poundage, even for the proposed interim period of a year. Once again, he continued to collect it regardless of any legal authority. Once again, law proved to be no substitute for power, and the parliamentary right to deny supply proved to be nothing but a boomerang against those who used it.

In spite of this failure, the next parliament again attempted to use the right to withhold supply as a political weapon. The issue this time was the second of the two serious constitutional crises of the period, the impeachment of the duke of Buckingham, to which the forced loan and the Petition of Right were sequels. On this issue, the balance of forces was as favourable to parliament as it was ever likely to be. It is probable that Buckingham's overt opponents enjoyed a majority in both houses, and not just in the Commons. They enjoyed widespread popular support in the country at large, and very powerful leadership within the privy council. The Commons had also, rather late in the day, developed an effective procedural device for linking supply with redress. The subsidies were voted in principle early in the parliament, and the subsidy bill was then delayed in committee while members waited to see what the king would do to meet their demands. In addition, denial of supply was now being used in wartime, when the king was desperately and urgently short of money. If the denial of supply was ever going to be a successful means of extorting concessions, this seemed the most promising occasion possible. Yet even in 1626, there seems to have been no possibility that Charles would allow the combined forces of parliament and privy councillors to coerce him into parting with Buckingham. It appears that Charles's delay in deciding to dissolve the parliament was more likely to have been due to hope that the Lords would acquit Buckingham, leaving the Commons isolated, than to any hesitation in his ultimate commitment to Buckingham.[30] It is noteworthy that the privy seals under which Charles ultimately raised the forced loan he used instead of the lost subsidies were dated several weeks before the parliament was dissolved.[31] The decision to raise a forced loan if the impeachment seemed likely to succeed had been taken, as a contingency plan, before it was clear to Charles that Buckingham could not count on an acquittal. And the forced loan, for all the protests it created, must be counted a success. The money came in, and the final yield was little less than the five subsidies Charles lost by dissolving parliament. The difference was scarcely worth the holding of a parliament. It is even

possible to exaggerate the universality of the protests the forced loan
created. In Hampshire, the collectors had to ask for instructions on how
to handle money from those who offered contributions before they had
been assessed.[32] Once again, the denial of supply had proved a political
boomerang, leading only to the injury of those who used it.

The fourth and last occasion on which the threat to withhold supply
was used was the Petition of Right, of 1628. On this occasion also, five
subsidies were voted in principle, early in the parliament, and the subsidy
bill was delayed in committee while members waited to see whether the
king would give his assent to the Petition of Right. As in 1626, the demand
came from both houses, and not just from the Commons. This time, it
appeared in the short term that the threat had been successful, since
Charles acceded to the Petition of Right. However, it is probable that he
only did so because he was confident of being able to evade its intention.
When he had it printed, shortly after the session was over, he had it printed
with his first answer attached. This first answer, in the opinion of most of
the Commons, was unsatisfactory because it did not effectively prohibit
forced loans or arbitrary imprisonment: it left Charles under no more legal
restriction than he had been under before. The evasion was of course
noticed in the parliamentary session of 1629, but members could do no
more than threaten to punish the king's printer.[33]

In the Petition of Right, members of parliament were faced with the
inadequacy of an attempt to bind the crown by law, without having the
power to execute that law. When the Petition of Right was cited in the
courts, judges tended to interpret it along the restrictive line of the king's
first answer, and Attorney General Heath in 1629 claimed that 'a petition
in parliament is not a law'.[34] Sir Thomas Wentworth had already pointed
out during the debates of 1628 that a legal restriction demanding that the
crown should show cause for an imprisonment did not prevent the crown
from citing a false cause, and searching the accused's papers before he
could get his *Habeas Corpus*. The rule of law was not a useful ideal unless
backed by the power to enforce that law.[35]

The conclusion appears irresistible that the withholding of supply was
not a powerful bargaining counter. At the end of the parliament of 1628,
the king still had impositions, Tonnage and Poundage, Buckingham, and,
as the event was to show, the powers of arbitrary taxation and arbitrary
imprisonment. Parliament's inability to sustain a constitutional struggle
with the crown appeared to have been clearly proved. The one challenge of
James's reign had achieved nothing, and three in four years at the beginning of Charles's reign had merely called parliament's survival into question. Hakewill could remark in passing that confirmation of statutes
against arbitrary imprisonment would be a useful restraint on the judges,
'especially if there be continuance of parliaments'. The fact that the
question was open now appeared too obvious to call for comment. Perhaps

the most perceptive comment was the advice of Rudyerd 'to use such a carriage as may uphold parliaments for though the power of them sinke not at once yet itt may moulder away'.[36] It seemed in 1628 that if parliament was to continue at all, it would be on the king's terms. It seems an irresistible conclusion that Chamberlain was right that parliament was '*sine viribus*' – without power.[37]

At first sight it does not appear to make sense that the denial of supply should achieve so little impact at a time when the king was so desperately short of money. Why, when the king was trying to scrape together every penny he could collect, should the threat to deny him supply have so little coercive force? One very obvious reason is that the sums of supply being offered were too small: they fell so far short of the king's needs that they were simply not worth bargaining for. The financial and administrative paralysis which had overtaken other sources of royal revenue had overtaken the parliamentary subsidy as well, and the parliamentary subsidy had suffered much more severely than most other forms of revenue. While other forms of revenue were losing value in real terms in face of inflation, the value of the parliamentary subsidy fell, not only in real terms, but even in money terms. The same overgrowth of patronage and favour which was choking other sources of revenue was working even more acutely on the parliamentary subsidy. As Delbridge remarked in 1625, 'commissioners tax men higher and lower, at their pleasure, not respecting taxations brought in by the taxation'. Assessment for the subsidy had become yet another way in which a man showed favour or disfavour to his neighbours. The yield of one subsidy, which had been £130,000 in the middle of Elizabeth's reign, fell by 1621 to £70,000 and by 1628 to £55,000. The depression of the 1620s, as well as administrative weakness, probably contributed to this decline. As early as 1604, parliament had included in a statute the blunt admission that they were unable to grant the king enough money. They granted James Tonnage and Poundage 'although the same doe or hereafter shall nothinge in effect countervaile the same your great charges, nor yet wee your saide poor Comons able fullie to gratifie your highness by any means'.[38] Yet it was the very same men whose collective power as members of parliament was being diminished by under-assessment of the subsidy who, in their local capacities, allowed it to continue.

One of the big mistakes we have made in the past is to suppose that granting too little supply was part of the same process as the withholding of supply. The supposition may be true for 1625, but it is not true for other parliaments. In 1624, when the supply granted was less than half of what was needed, there was no possible further concession for which members could have been holding out. Grants remained excessively small even at times when members were leaning over backwards to demonstrate their eagerness to vote supply.[39] It is perhaps possible to take members of the Commons at their word when they said that they could not vote more for

fear of the reactions of their constituents. 15 February, 1621, the day when
Pym recorded that members talked about supply and not grievances
because it was more pleasing to the king, was also the day when they
decided to abandon fifteenths, 'because they come for the most part out of
poor men's purses, whome it is unfit to chardge before we have given them
ease'. In November 1621, in debating the proposal for a second grant of
subsidy in one parliament, Crew said 'if there be two taxes in one year . . .
there must be two harvests, two springs and two autumns'. He then went
on to support the motion for an extra subsidy.[40] It was not only their
poorer constituents members wished to conciliate, but also their fellow-
gentlemen. It was again on the same day as this extra subsidy was voted
that Sir Edward Coke opposed a proposal for a property qualification of
£100 a year for knights of the shire, on the ground that this would be a way
to have them assessed at so much in the subsidy.[41] It is in debates such as
these that it is important to remember that members were not permanent
Westminster politicians, but men who lived most of their lives among the
people whose money they were being asked to grant. The need to conciliate the king and the need to conciliate the county community could
compete in an uncomfortable uneven balance. Sir Robert Phelips, speaking
on the subsidy in 1628, denied that he would 'wishe at this time a shewe or
face of contradicion', but also said that 'I apprehend it necessary to look
back from whence I come'.[42] Our knowledge of Phelips' career in Somerset
makes it possible to take Phelips at his word on both points. A similar
conflict is implied in Delbridge's apparently self-contradictory statement
in the debate that 'I speake not to lessen the guift but by comand from my
countrey',[43] It has long been known that members made these protesta-
tions about the reactions of their local communities to grants of supply,
but in the past it has been suspected that such speeches were no more than
polite excuses to cover up a reluctance to subsidize royal extravagance.
Some speeches, such as that of Samuel Lewkenor in 1610, clearly fit this
interpretation, but it is not sufficient by itself. Two points weigh heavily
against placing too much weight on this interpretation. One is members'
continued insistence on the poverty of the country on occasions, such as
the first subsidy debate of 1621, when they were not attempting to link
their own grievances to the subsidy. The other is the discovery of Dr. D.M.
Hirst, in his new work *The Representative of the People?* that, with
increasingly frequent contested elections, local communities were in a
strong position to exert pressure on their members of parliament, and
often carefully followed their actions at Westminster. Members were often
alarmed about the effects of such constituency reactions to their parliamentary activities. For example, Sir Richard Grosvenor, in the recess
debate of 1621, complained that 'we that goe home may be made subjects
of the peoples fury, if not of disgrace'.[44] Parliament's increasingly close
links with feeling in the country at large were doubtless a strength to it in

1642, when its popularity helped to enable it to raise an adequate army. But what was a source of strength in 1642 was only a source of weakness in the 1620s, since it helped to prevent parliament from voting the supply essential to its own continuance.

Another reason why the threat of withholding parliamentary supply may have had so little effect on a poverty-stricken king is that the concessions parliament hoped to obtain may sometimes have done more to diminish the royal revenue than its supply did to increase it. The clearest example of this point is impositions. At £70,000 a year, they were worth the equivalent of a parliamentary subsidy every year. James was entitled to the complaint he made in 1610: 'is it a fit matter to dispute of taking away 70,000 li. a year from me when you are to consider of supply and support for me? I have expounded my necessities myself and my Treasurer at large to you, and the first device and dispute is what to take from me'. His warning that if he continued to meet such behaviour 'I shall be the more unwilling to call you to parliament' made sound financial sense, and all the more financial sense because of James's shortage of money.[45] In 1614, James was asked to choose between impositions, at £70,000 a year, and a sum unlikely to exceed two subsidies, of £70,000 each, with no certainty that they would be followed by more. In terms of financial arithmetic, this choice was simple, and it is hard to see how an impoverished king could have made it otherwise than he did.

Many more minor grievances concerned the collection of royal revenue. Many of the patents attacked in 1606 and 1621 had been granted because existing methods of local government were entirely inadequate to collect the king's revenue. The highly unpopular alehouse patent, for example, was granted to meet a situation in which many people admitted that the traditional machinery of law enforcement, and therefore of revenue collection, had proved inadequate.[46] The greenwax patent, which was included in the 1606 petition of grievances, was granted because local officials, by returning false names and addresses to the Exchequer, had been making it almost impossible to collect fines imposed in courts.[47] Cranfield, opposing the monopolies bill in the house of lords in 1621, said it would take from the king £30,000 a year. Gardiner noted that 'either this must be a great exaggeration, or Cranfield must have taken into calculation means of revenue not usually classed among monopolies'. When it is remembered that to Coke, who was largely responsible for the monopolies bill, a monopoly was first and foremost a method of law enforcement by a private individual, rather than a restraint of trade, it seems that Gardiner's second hypothesis is the more probable. If Cranfield exaggerated, he still calculated the cost of abandoning patents at a lower figure than Lord Keeper Williams, who said that the king had abandoned 37 grievances, each equivalent to a subsidy. If, in 1621, concessions to parliament were being costed against supply in this way, it would be possible to read an ominous note into Cranfield's warning that he 'wished the Commons to handle the business so as they might make the king in love with the parliament'.[48]

The cost of using parliament as a source of supply would appear even higher if the cost of revoking unpopular grants to the king's servants were taken into account. The king's servants, however unpopular they might be, needed to be paid, and if they were not to be paid at the expense of the Exchequer, they had to be paid at the expense of the public. The overwhelming majority of complaints raised by the Jacobean house of commons concerned methods of rewarding royal servants, and therefore, if met, threatened to create a new drain on the Exchequer. Professor Aylmer's picture of fees to officials as a form of indirect taxation can perhaps be extended to other grants as well.[49] If such grievances as the duke of Lennox's patent for sealing stockings are seen as forms of indirect taxation, their survival in the face of parliamentary criticism becomes more intelligible. There are some signs that people in court circles were thinking in these terms. In 1624, James bluntly vetoed a bill which would have forbidden him to grant recusants' forfeited estates to private individuals, on the ground that it would prevent him from rewarding his servants. This, even if not the true reason, was one which would appear convincing to so well-informed a crown servant as Edward Nicholas.[50] In 1606, in attacking Brouncker's patent for issues of jurors, the Commons were concerning themselves with something which was both a necessary method of law enforcement and a way of rewarding a crown servant. The crown was receiving £1,000 a year from fines on defaulting jurors, a source of revenue which had previously been negligible, while Brouncker, the patentee, was receiving relief from a private debt without any cost to the Exchequer. Fanshawe, who was both an Exchequer official and a good house of commons man, pleaded with the Commons to leave this grant alone, for 'this patent', said he, 'is assigned to a gentleman for satisfaction of a great debt, who is undone if this grant be revoked'. By revoking this patent, the king would have lost his power to reward Brouncker unless out of the Exchequer, as well as his £1,000 a year, and it is not surprising that in 1621, when this patent was the subject of further complaint, the council decided that 'we conceave this to be absolutely in the kings owne powre as part of his casuall revenue'.[51] As early as 1601, at the conclusion of the monopolies debate, Sir Robert Cecil had bitterly listed all the faithful servants of the queen who must go without reward if the Commons' complaints were met.[52]

It was, then, possible to ask whether, in financial terms, parliaments were worth their cost. The mere prospect that they might assemble kept down the yield of some sources of revenue, such as the sale of baronetcies, which was once noted as something which could be worth – 'if they knew there would be no parliament' – £20,000.[53] It was more important that the prospect of future parliaments hindered the chances of expanding revenue from impositions. It also prevented the king from developing the precedent set in the imposition on Newcastle and Sunderland coals, and in the imposition (or composition, as the king's lawyers preferred to call it) of 4d. a quarter on malt. These were precedents which opened the door to an excise, as the house of commons were very well aware.[54] Why, then, did James remain so faithful to his promise to the parliament of 1610 that he would not further expand impositions without consulting parliament?[55]

It is necessary to ask whether the reasons for continuing parliaments were as much political as financial. Did James continue to summon parliaments, not so much for a relief for his financial necessities, which they were unable to give, as for what Professor Elton calls 'a point of contact'? Was James sincere, for example, in telling the parliament of 1621 that he wished it to search out the causes of the scarcity of money, 'which neither himself nor his council could find out'?[56] James's treatment of the patentees in 1621 suggests that his desire to be informed of the griefs of his subjects was sincere.[57] It was also convenient to have a body whose decisions had the unquestionable force of law. James did not have a big legislative programme, but, for example, if so important a crown creditor as Philip Burlamachi wished for the legal benefits of naturalization, it was, other things being equal, preferable to have the means available to satisfy him. The importance of statute as the ultimate source of law was not seriously threatened, but the urgent questions of James's reign were not so much about what the law should say, as about how it could be effectively executed.

It was also considered essential to be able to call a parliament at the beginning of a war. Again, the reasons for this were not only financial. It appears to have been widely believed that the symbolic gesture of unity involved in a successful parliament would do much to make foreign ambassadors believe the country was united in a war effort. In 1628, Sir Humphrey May was quite blunt on this point. He said: 'you cannot resolve too soone for ye kinge neyther can you indeede give enough. But lett our harts joyne. Let forrane states knowe wee are united. Wee have here in towne six embassadors and they every day aske after us'.[58] The point of contact provided by a parliament was probably also essential to the domestic organization of a successful war effort. Men who were to be asked to do their utmost for the prosecution of a war needed to be able to feel that their local grouses about the organization of the military effort could be heard in higher quarters. The history of the years 1625–28 proved that the king was no more able to fight a war with a parliament than without a parliament, but this was something which only the event could show. Up to 1625, the possibility of a future war could have appeared a strong argument against allowing parliament to drift into extinction. What the catastrophic failure of the war effort showed was that parliament, as well as the king, was too handicapped by the creeping paralysis which had afflicted English administration since the late Elizabethan period to make a substantial contribution to a war effort. To call for war while under-assessing the subsidy, and while attacking military rates and the deputy lieutenants, was a contradiction in terms. The war years at the beginning of Charles I's reign did not show a relationship between an advancing institution and a declining institution: they showed a relationship between two declining institutions, both overtaken by the functional breakdown of English administration, and the only question was which would reach the bottom first. Until the intervention of the Scots, in 1639–40, it appeared overwhelmingly probable that the answer would be parliament.

If parliament had so little coercive power, its members were dependent, not on coercion, but on persuasion. If parliament could not, by with-holding supply, force the king to do what it wished, its members all had to engage in a process of lobbying designed to persuade the king, of his own free will, to do what they wished. Persuasion, moreover, had to be addressed to the king. As Pym said in November 1621, 'herein lyes the principall part of our labour to winne the Kinge for hee is the first mover, from whence all prosperitye of this and other affayres of Parliament must be derived'.[59] There was no point in persuading the public at large, except in a situation in which riot or revolution might be contemplated.

If parliamentary critics of the crown were entirely dependent on persua-sion, it must give us pause before describing them as an 'opposition'. An opposition, as we know the term now, can hope to force changes of policy, either by changing the government, or by appealing so eloquently to the public that the government is forced to change its ground. In this sense, opposition as we know the term now was impossible. It is also a char-acteristic of an 'opposition' that it is united by some common body of beliefs, which it does not share with members of the government. This ideological gulf between 'government' and 'opposition' is impossible to find in parliament before 1640. There were many disagreements on policy, often profound ones, but these were divisions which split the council itself. On none of the great questions of the day did parliamentary leaders hold any opinions not shared by members of the council. Men who depend on persuasion to get their way, and who hold no beliefs incompatible with office, cannot be described as an 'opposition' without grossly misleading modern readers. Their relations with councillors were more like the rela-tions of modern back-bench M.P.s with the leaders of their own parties than the relations of government and opposition. This is why attempts to divide parliament into two 'sides' have proved so grossly misleading. Even the impeachment of Buckingham was not a confrontation between 'government' and 'opposition': it was a confrontation between two groups within the council, in which both sides enjoyed support within the Lords and the Commons, but the less influential group in the council enjoyed majority support in the Commons. Buckingham himself, whose judgement of men was better than his judgement of measures, regarded his most dangerous opponents as being Pembroke, the Lord Chamberlain, Abbot, the archbishop of Canterbury, Arundel, the Earl Marshall, and Williams, who had just been sacked from the Lord Keepership of the Great Seal.[60] To describe these men as 'leaders of the opposition' would be an absurdity. After the impeachment had failed, it was Pembroke, and not the leaders of the Commons, whom Buckingham felt the need to conciliate. The contract for a marriage between Buckingham's daughter and Pembroke's nephew and heir is dated 3 August, 1626, only a few weeks after the end of the parliament, and it reads comically like a marriage alliance ending a war between two great powers.[61] It was probably the withdrawal of Pembroke's support, rather than a hypothetical meeting of leaders of the Commons at Sir Robert Cotton's house,[62] which did most to prevent the renewal of the impeachment in the parliament of 1628. It is noteworthy that when Eliot's study was searched, during the impeachment of Buckingham, the only document known to have been taken away was a petition to Pembroke for the office of deputy lieutenant in Cornwall.[63] As Buckingham saw it, Eliot had not gone over from the government to the opposition, but had changed his court patron, from Buckingham to Pembroke. Even with the support of such powerful members of the government, the impeachment of Buckingham remained an attempt at persuasion, rather than at coercion. As Dr. Ball remarked, in adopting their 1626 Remonstrance, the Commons 'were implicitly admitting that without the willing support of the Crown, the impeachment of a powerful minister could not hope to succeed'.[64]

If persuasion was the object of the exercise, it was essential for parliamentary critics of current policies to act in alliance with friends in the Lords and in the council, whose efforts could be used to make their attempts at persuasion more effective. There were always members of the council who were willing to join in such exercises in persuasion, both behind the scenes and publicly, in parliament. That they did so does not mean that they had 'gone over to the opposition': it means they were discharging the duty of a councillor to give good counsel. In the days before the collective responsibility of the cabinet, the duty of a councillor was not to toe some mythical 'government' line. It was, in Queen Elizabeth's words to William Cecil, 'that without respect of my private will you will give me that counsel which you think best'. Like his Stuart successors, William Cecil interpreted these words as applying to counsel given in parliament, as well as outside it, and like his Stuart successors, he accepted that it remained his duty to give good counsel even if he therefore got into trouble with his sovereign.[65]

It was, then, no breach with tradition that in the Addled Parliament, it was Secretary Winwood who moved the motion for stricter enforcement of the recusancy laws. When he was seconded in this motion by the reputedly 'opposition' member Sir Dudley Digges, no unholy alliance between government and opposition had taken place. All that had happened was that two personal friends were speaking together for a cause in which they both believed.[66] In 1621, when Lionel Cranfield encouraged the attack on the referees who had granted the obnoxious patents, he may have been pursuing his own advantage.[67] He was, however, also doing his duty as a servant of the crown. His chief principle as a crown servant was that the king's money ought not to be wasted, and in attacking those who wasted it, he was not being false to the principles on which he acted as a member of the government.

Though Solicitor General Heath was not a member of the privy council, the king had few more loyal servants, and few more dependable parliamentary spokesmen. Yet there were numerous occasions on which Heath gave parliamentary counsel which ran counter to the king's immediate wishes. In the first session of 1621, he initiated the attacks on a number of the patents which were questioned. As a law officer of the crown, he was under no obligation to support methods of law enforcement he believed to be illegal or against the king's profit. In the foreign policy debates of the winter of 1621, Heath was one of the first members of the Commons to press for war with Spain to be prosecuted in the West Indies, and was the man who finally reassured the Commons that it was within the limits of propriety to petition the king on a matter of state. For this, Heath, like some Elizabethan councillors before him appears to have got into trouble, but he was doing no more than giving the king the advice which he, and a number of the king's other councillors and servants, believed was the best. In 1625, Heath explicitly supported both the attacks on the Arminian Richard Montagu, and the Commons' right to take cognizance of matters of religion. In all these cases, Heath probably enjoyed the backing of the powerful Pembroke-Abbot group within the privy council.[68]

There appear to have been no important issues of principle which divided members of the so-called opposition from their friends in the council. Those who wanted war with Spain enjoyed the backing of Pembroke, Carlisle and Holland. Those who wanted to see the end of Arminianism were led by George Abbot, archbishop of Canterbury. Those who wished to restrict the activities of informers enjoyed the public encouragement of the earl of Salisbury. The English gentry in the 1620s were not a divided society: all the important political disagreements were such that those on both sides could work together within the same council. Where there is not a divided society, there is not the fuel to sustain a division into two parties. All the leading members of parliament of the 1620s were legitimately entitled to hope for office. Since they could accept office without abandoning any of the principles for which they pressed while in parliament, those, like Wentworth and Digges, who accepted office, do not deserve any strictures for 'changing sides'. They saw no sides to change.[69] Cases like these should be regarded, not as the exception, but as the rule.

Sir Dudley Digges makes an excellent case-study for this point, since we possess a document of his which amounts to something approaching a political creed.[70] Every point in this document is consistent, both with his parliamentary record, and with the royal service into which he ultimately entered. The document is an undelivered letter to King Charles, written in the early months of 1625. One might suspect that such a document, clearly compiled in the hope of office, might not be entirely honest, but it covers almost all the beliefs he expressed in parliament, including his hostility to Buckingham. He expressed a desire to combat the growing greatness of the House of Austria, to increase the prosperity of England by expanding overseas trade, to reduce the commissions of the peace to manageable size, to ensure the efficient management of the king's revenue, the disparking of remote royal forests, the granting to the outports of the right to farm their own customs, and the employment of 'grave counsellors'. Buckingham might perhaps have taken alarm at Digges' determination to 'owne that obligacon only to yor owne royall chaire wthout other dependance', but there was nothing in it to prevent Charles from regarding him as what he later became, a faithful servant of the crown. The really conspicuous omission from this document is the lack of any suggestion for an increased place for the house of commons. Digges said he regarded it as a body which had grown too large and contained some factious spirits. In spite of this, he continued to regard it as the proper source of extraordinary supply (warning Charles in the process of the trouble he could expect over impositions and the Tonnage and Poundage bill of 1625), but he seems to have seen no other place for it. This was the man who was a manager of the impeachment of Buckingham and took a leading part in the passage of the Petition of Right. He took a leading part in the attack on the patents and the foreign policy debate in 1621, and did so while hoping for office. He was thought by Chamberlain to have much increased his chances of office by his conduct in the first session of that parliament.[71] He was a pupil and a friend of Archbishop Abbot,[72] and could have been a welcome recruit to the Abbot-Pembroke group on the council. It seems clear that he regarded parliament, not as somehting to be magnified in its own right, but as one possible place in which to pursue causes which were better pursued in office. To men such as Digges, a division between government and opposition was meaningless.[73] A division between 'ins' and 'outs' had meaning, but this affected, not his beliefs, but only the forum in which he pursued them.

Another issue conspicuously missing from the Digges memorandum is that of religion, and in this Digges may not have been entirely typical of his fellow-members. His persistent opposition to bills for scandalous ministers suggests that he was a long way from being a Puritan by any definition.

Other members, such as Rudyerd, felt a much deeper concern about the
issue of Arminianism than Digges did. Digges was merely against Arminianism: Rudyerd detested it. However, in the opening years of Charles I's
reign, even the strongest feelings about Arminianism were not enough to
produce a Court–Country or government–opposition polarization. So long
as many of Arminianism's most effective opponents were still in the
council, and had access to the king's ear, it was not yet necessary for
opponents of Arminianism to sever their court connections in order to
pursue their principles. So long as Abbot, Pembroke, Manchester and Sir
John Coke were about the court, there was no reason why their fellow-
critics of Arminianism should not be there too.[74] It was not until 1626 that
John Preston wrote to 'a gentleman in Northamptonshire and a noble
Lord' (possibly Knightley and Saye) to tell them that Buckingham could be
no further use to them.[75] To others with closer connections with Buckingham, such as Harley and Fleetwood, opposition to Arminianism and
support for Buckingham appeared compatible for a good deal longer.
Harley's hatred of Arminianism was never in doubt, but in the Parliament
of 1626, he still found it compatible with a defence of Buckingham.[76]
Arminianism was an issue capable of producing a polarization into two
sides, a pro- and anti-government, but it would be using hindsight to claim
that before the death of Buckingham it had already done so. Buckingham
was a man whose intentions were often surrounded by confusion, and even
after the York House Conference, his anti-Arminian dependents, such as
Harley and Fleetwood, could have believed that his support for Arminianism no more represented his last word than his support for Spain had done
in 1621.[77] It was of the essence of the attacks made on Arminianism by
Pym that he thought his views, and not those of the Arminians, were the
orthodox doctrines of the Church of England, and the idea that belief in
the orthodox doctrines of the Church of England turned a man into a
member of 'the opposition' was one which many people took a number of
years to absorb.

What has already been said should suggest that many members of
parliament were concerned to adopt a conciliatory approach to the crown,
but this belief is difficult to sustain from the record of parliamentary
proceedings. The reason for this difficulty is that the evidence for conciliation consists, not of what is in the record, but of what is not in the
record: on many issues, conciliation was best expressed by silence, and we
have all been too preoccupied with collecting the speeches of conflict to
notice the silences of conciliation. Yet, like Sherlock Holmes's dog in the
night time, they are significant when they are noticed. Fortunately, in some
cases, Sir Robert Phelips' irresistible urge to draw attention to his own
virtue enables us to say that the silences were deliberate, and not the result
of loss of interest.

The most deafening of these silences was on the issue of impositions, in the parliaments of 1621 and 1624. Impositions were an issue on which, as James Whitelocke had pointed out in 1610, silence could well be taken for consent, 'and therefore if we let this pass *sub silentio* all posterity is bound by it and this will be as great a record as can be against them'.[78] Yet in 1621, despite Chamberlain's fears,[79] the issue of impositions remained unmentioned until the arrival of the king's angry letter of 5 December, almost at the end of the parliament. Phelips then lamented '[we] have never meddled with impositions (though highly concerning the subjects' interest) to make this a Parliament only of union . . . What then the cause of this soul-killing letter from his Majesty'?[80] In 1624, one of the articles in the impeachment of Cranfield was the laying of additional impositions without the king's consent. Phelips and Sandys warned the Commons not to raise the general issue of impositions, 'lest we rush upon a rock which will endanger our hopes'.[81] If there are any two members of the Commons from whom silence on impositions is exceptionally significant, they are Phelips and Sandys, who were probably the two members most profoundly concerned about this issue. Until the parliament of 1629, there was a similarly deafening silence about the unparliamentary collection of Tonnage and Poundage. No member seems to have expected the king to stop collecting Tonnage and Poundage, and the subject was mentioned only in occasional discussion of bills to make the king's collection of it legal. The depth to which this acceptance of a *fait accompli* had gone is best shown by a revealing verbal gaffe by Sir Edward Coke in 1628. In the course of a debate on pirates, he complained bitterly that the king was not spending Tonnage and Poundage for the purposes for which it had been *given* (my italics).[82] Similarly, for most of the parliament of 1628, there was a deafening silence on the great issue of the previous parliament, the duke of Buckingham. This time it was Rich who drew attention to the silence. After discussing the precedent of 1297, he asked 'Do we desire anything so high, have we called in question any ministers, do we demand any punishment on ill officers? Those are the men indeed that go about to trench upon power'. There is some point in the conclusion of Sir Robert Phelips, in a public act of contrition for his previous silences over impositions, that 'moderation is of great use, the times considered, but a silent moderation is the destruction of great councells'.[83]

Similarly, we have probably overrated the willingness of the Commons to take up privilege issues, since the speeches of those who wished to take them up are recorded, and the silences of those who did not wish to take them up are rarely so explicitly recorded. We know about the attempts of Mallory to raise a privilege dispute about the imprisonment of Sir Edwin Sandys after the first session of 1621, but it is only from Pym's private diary that we can discover his conviction that that motion was at first 'well past over' by the House. Similarly, it is only from the surprised note '*quaere quaere*' in Sir Thomas Barrington's diary that we can tell that he shared Pym's misgivings about the introduction of this dispute.[84] In 1629, Barrington's views on the big privilege dispute about Tonnage and Poundage do not emerge from the public debates, and it is only from a private letter to his mother that we can tell that he thought the whole introduction of the topic to be distinctly ill-advised.[85] Pym and Barrington were both good house of commons men and they may have been very far from alone among good house of commons men in their belief that many privilege disputes were started which would have been better left alone.[86] It would be possible to multiply the list of silences by running through long lists of unredressed grievances passed over in silence by subsequent parliaments, but it is doubtful whether the process is necessary. The silences on the two big issues of Buckingham and impositions are enough to show that in the two big constitutional conflicts of the period, parliament accepted defeat.

We can, then, conclude that Professor Koenigsberger is right in ascribing the ultimate success of the English parliament to the effects of Scottish and Dutch intervention. This ultimate result was so far beyond parliament's reach in 1604 to 1629 that they were not even trying for it. In both of the two big constitutional conflicts members of the house of commons were not the initiators. In the first, over impositions, the issue appears to have blown up to the equal surprise of all the participants, James, Salisbury and the Commons. There is no reason to believe that there was any thought in Salisbury's head over impositions except the need to fill the Exchequer. In the second, over the impeachment of Buckingham, we should follow Buckingham himself in seeing the initiative as coming, not from members of the house of commons, but from within the privy council. Dr. Ball is undoubtedly correct in seeing the concern of those who managed the impeachment of Buckingham as being, not with long-term constitutional objectives about the power of parliament, but simply with the immediate political issue of getting rid of Buckingham.[87]

If parliament was not engaged in the pursuit of supreme power, and if its leading members were not divided from their friends among the council by any issue of principle which turned them into an opposition, then much of the history of parliament in this period needs to be re-written. If we abandon the two main analytical tools which have been used to tell the story, we must put something in their place. For even if we abandon the picture of a government and an opposition struggling for power, which was always an anachronistically Gladstonian picture of the parliaments of this period, the fact remains that they were not very happy parliaments. How unhappy they were is a question which will doubtless need re-examination. In particular, we will have to reassess how much these parliaments were occupied with conflicts, and how much with relatively uncontentious legislative business, but it would be straining the evidence beyond belief to picture them as models of harmony. What, then, was the trouble about?

Some of it must undoubtedly be laid at the door of King James I. James may not have been an anti-parliamentary ruler, as he appears in traditional accounts, but neither was he a particularly competent parliamentary manager. The misunderstandings of 1604, and of the second session of 1621, arose mainly from the perennial uncertainty about James's intentions.[88] To say that James was a much better king than Charles, and enjoyed much better relations with his parliaments, is not to say that he was a good king, or enjoyed good relations with his parliaments.

However, it is impossible to follow Professor Elton in laying all the blame on incompetent kingship.[89] The faults in English administration were more fundamental than can be blamed on any one man, and they were too apparent during the Elizabethan war with Spain to make it a tenable thesis that they were entirely caused by an incompetent king who had not yet come to the throne. Of all the general theses which have been propounded about the early seventeenth century, the one which most closely fits the parliamentary evidence is Professor Everitt's picture of a permanent tension between the centre and the localities.[90] This tension was apparent even before 1588. It was no fault of Jacobean kingship, but a standing institutional weakness, which made Lord Keeper Nicholas Bacon warn the Parliament of 1576 that if the J.P.s did not execute the laws more effectively, the queen would be 'driven cleane contrarie to her most gratious nature and inclination to appoint and assign private men for profitt and gaines sake, to see her penal laws to bee executed'.[91] This speech summarizes most of the issues that disturbed parliaments for the next half-century. To accept this is not to turn members of the Commons back into representatives of an embattled 'country'. It has become a truism that a successful career in local government, which was what many leading members wanted, required backing both at court and in the country.[92] The idea that it was necessary to dispense with either was a profound threat to the careers of such men as Wentworth or Phelips.

In this context, it is interesting to see what meaning members of the Commons attached to the word 'country'. In the debate on the summer recess of 1621, nine members of the Commons expressed agitation about the reactions of 'the country' if they came home without passing any bills. By 'the country', they did not mean themselves. They meant people they would have to meet when they went home, who appeared to them to need to be conciliated every bit as much as the king did. This need appeared to cause them irritation, as well as alarm. Coke complained that 'if we goe into the country and tell them the difference twixt a prorogation and adiournment, theay will not understand us. *Non est discrimen intelligendum inter illiteratos*'. Delbridge, member for Barnstaple, protested that 'I had rather never have gone home than goe home in this manner. I doe dislike it, I protest I thinke it will doe that hurt I wish I were in Heaven'. Edward Alford expressed alarm at the prospect of going home without passing the Bill of Informers, because 'the King hath commanded us to tell the country this bill should pass'. Sir Thomas Wentworth, who had promised the passage of this bill while speaking as a subsidy commissioner during the Easter recess, was probably quietly asking himself the same question.[93] It is interesting to note the unanimous belief of these speakers that what 'the country' wanted was not assertions of parliamentary privilege or discussions of foreign policy, but the passage of bills.

The issue of informers is a typical example of the tension which faced members of parliament as representatives of the centre in the localities, and representatives of the localities in the centre. In their local capacities, they were sensitive to their neighbours' hostility to informers, and wished them abolished. In their capacity as Westminster legislators, they knew that without the aid of informers, much of their legislation would be unenforceable. In 1604, 11 out of 17 penal statutes passed called on the services of informers. Even in 1624, Pym pointed out that while they were in the middle of passing a statute to exclude informers from the Westminster courts, they were simultaneously passing another to call on the further services of informers for the enforcement of the laws against recusants.[94] The need to reconcile their central and their local capacities constantly put members of parliament into this state of helpless conflict with themselves. They needed to conciliate the king, and they needed to conciliate their neighbours, and it was becoming increasingly impossible to do both. Sir John Eliot, in 1628, expressed their desire to conciliate both court and country in a characteristically vivid image:

> There are two townes in Kent that serve for sea markes, when you see them both beeing at sea, it is a signe you are safe, but if you see but one of them the mariners know they are in no good rode and are out of hart and fearing ship-wrack untill both bee discovered.[95]

Parliament was, in Professor Elton's phrase, the 'point of contact' between the centre and the localities. But in a situation of permanent tension between the centre and the localities, the point of contact becomes the point of friction. In this conflict, parliament was not the champion of one side: it was a collection of those whose interests did not permit them to let two sides develop. The conflict between the central government and the county communities was one in which almost every member of parliament had divided loyalties. The conflict between these divided loyalties was one of the most important reasons for their powerlessness. The conflict between 'court' and 'country' was not fought out between members of parliament and the king: it was fought out within the members' own minds.

Notes

1 T.L. Moir, *The Addled Parliament of 1614* (Oxford, 1958), p. 104: Robert Zaller, *The Parliament of 1621* (1971), p. 4. I would like to thank Dr. D.M. Hirst, Professor H.G. Koenigsberger, Dr. Ian Roy and Dr. N.R.N. Tyacke for reading and commenting on drafts of this article.

2 Perez Zagorin, *The Court and the Country* (1969), p. 335.

3 T.G. Barnes, 'County Politics and a Puritan Cause Célèbre: Somerset Church-ales 1633', *TRHS*, 5th Series, 9 (1959), pp. 103–23. Professor Barnes concludes: 'implicit in the churchales controversy is a warning to those who would search in the counties during the personal rule for the developments leading to civil war'. The years 1640 and 1641 clearly need separate discussion, yet even as late as this, we should remember, when reading the debates, that civil war was a defeat, not a victory, for those who took part in them. See Russell (ed.), *The Origins of the English Civil War* (1973), pp. 27–31.

4 G.R. Elton, 'A High Road to Civil War?', in *Essays in Honour of Garrett Mattingly*, ed. Charles H. Carter (1966), pp. 315 ff. It is unfortunate that Professor Elton concentrated so much of his argument on the *Apology of the Commons* of 1604. Whoever its authors may have been, the *Apology*, if read with care and without hindsight, can shed valuable light on the parliamentary session of 1604. Professor Elton's error in this article is in too easily reading the *Apology* in the light of the interpretation Gardiner placed upon it.

5 A.R. Myers, 'The Parliaments of Europe and the Age of the Estates', *Hist.*, 60, no. 198 (February 1975), pp. 18–20.

6 H.G. Koenigsberger, '*Dominium Regale* and *Dominium Politicum et Regale*: Monarchies and Parliaments in Early Modern Europe' (Inaugural Lecture delivered at King's College, London, on 25 February, 1975), pp. 25, 23. I am very grateful to Professor Koenigsberger for allowing me to read a typescript of this lecture before publication.

7 This article is not intended to dispute Professor Zagorin's contention that there was conflict between 'court' and 'country'. It is intended to dispute his contention that this was a conflict in which members of parliament were able or willing to choose sides, and especially his readiness to classify members of parliament as 'oppositionists'. See his list of 'oppositionists' on pp. 79–80. For a more detailed discussion of the weaknesses of Zagorin's argument, see G.R. Elton, 'The Unexplained Revolution', in *Studies in Tudor and Stuart Politics and Government* (Cambridge, 1974), II, pp. 183–9.

8 Wallace Notestein, *The Winning of the Initiative by the House of Commons* (1924), pp. 47–8, 54, 4 [my italics].

9 Notestein's picture of the winning of the legislative initiative provides a contrast, though not a conflict, with Pym's picture of the last parliaments of the 1620s as being 'like dying men *intestabiles*, incapable of making their wills, the good Acts that they were about': Rushworth, III, i, 21.

10 Notestein, *Winning of the Initiative*, pp. 4, 51.

11 Moir, *Addled Parliament*, p. 167.

12 Zagorin, pp. 57–8: *Wentworth Papers*, pp. 309–10. I am grateful to my pupil Mr. Richard Cust for an illuminating discussion of Wentworth's early career.

13 *CSP Ven., 1621–3*, p. 80.

14 G.R. Elton, 'Tudor Government: Points of Contact: Parliament', *TRHS*, 5th Series 24 (1974), p. 188: *Wentworth Papers*, pp. 63–4.

15 Koenigsberger, 'Monarchies and Parliaments', p. 25.

16 *The Parliamentary Diary of Robert Bowyer*, ed. D.H. Willson (Minneapolis, 1941), pp. 164–7. Gardiner, *History*, I, 299. For the text of the grievances, see *Bowyer*, pp. 153–6. One, the cost of passing sheriffs' accounts, was redressed by statute in 1624. On the principle of supply to meet ordinary expenditure, see the preamble of the Subsidy Act, *I Jac. I c. 26*.

17 *P in P 1610*, II, 145–8, 286, 338n. James's answer (*P in P 1610*, 273) can hardly be called satisfactory. For Sir Edwin Sandys' proposal to present the same list of grievances again in 1614, see. *CJ*, I, 465.

18 It is interesting that these years have never come to be known as the 'seven years of unparliamentary government'.

19 *CD 1621*, IV, 56, II, 84–91.

20 *CJ*, I, 550.

21 *CJ*, I, 658.

22 Queen's College, Oxford, Ms. 449, fo. 243a. I am grateful to Mr. Allen Croessmann for drawing my attention to this MS.; *CJ*, I, 802; *CD 1625*, pp. 37–41.

23 J.N. Ball, 'The Parliamentary Career of Sir John Eliot 1624–1629' (Cambridge PhD Thesis, 1953), pp. 40–1. I am grateful to Dr. Ball for lending me a copy of this thesis, which is, as he says (p. i) 'the first attempt except for studies of the Petition of Right and of Eliot's leadership in the Parliament of 1626, to rewrite any of the political history of the period 1624–9 both in the light of new materials and from a point of view outside the "Whig" tradition of English historiography'. *LJ*, iii, 250; *Lords' Debates in 1624 and 1626*, ed. S.R. Gardiner (Camden Society N.S. xxiv, 1879), p. 22; Add. Ms. 18, 597, fo. 70–2; HMC *Mar and Kellie (Suppl.)*, p. 195. It is recorded in an endorsement on the act itself that 'the grounds of this act proceeded originallie from the gratious proposition of his Matie. himself'. Judges' resolutions of 26 May 1624, *LJ*, iii, 408, and HLRO, original Acts, 21 Jac. I c. 33).

24 *Wentworth Papers*, p. 238. Wentworth said they should refuse a second grant, 'having regard unto our creditts and reputations'.

25 *P in P 1610*, II, 108 and n.

26 This calculation counts the six members who moved for a committee as neutrals.

27 *CJ*, I, 506.

28 Harvard, MS Eng. 980, fo. 229. I would like to thank Dr. Colin G.C. Tite for lending me a transcript of this MS.

29 Queen's College, MS 449, fo. 259.

30 Jess Stodart Flemion, 'The Dissolution of Parliament in 1626: A Revaluation', *EHR*, 87 (1972), pp. 784–90. PRO 31/3/63, pp. 57, 61, 63, 73, 79, 89, 99.

31 PRO, E.401/2442. The privy seals there mentioned are dated 1 May (Rutland), 12 May (Devon), 16 May (Herefordshire) and 19 May (Brecon). I am grateful to Mr. D.L. Thomas for this reference. The Bishop of Mende reported Charles's intention to raise money by 'extraordinary ways' on 23 May/2 June. PRO, 31/3/63, p. 79.

32 Robert Ashton, *The Crown and the Money Market* (Oxford, 1960), pp. 39, 41. The comparative figures were £264,000 for the forced loan, against £275,000 for the five subsidies of 1628. Hants. R.O., Jervoise MSS DD44/M 69/012 (Deputy Lieutenants to Conway) 8 December and 13 December, 1626.

33 Elizabeth Read Foster, 'Printing the Petition of Right', *HLQ* 38, 1 (Nov. 1974), pp. 81–3. *CD 1629*, pp. 54–6.

34 *ST*, III, 285, 1109, 1125: Rushworth, II, ii, 191 and 237–8. For a conspicuous exception, see Hutton's ship money judgement, Rushworth, II, ii, 164–5. The

act of parliament abolishing ship money enacted that the Petition of Right should be put in execution. *Statutes of the Realm 16 Car. 1 c. 14.*

35 *Wentworth Papers*, p. 293. See also the illuminating comments of Clare, *Wentworth Papers*, pp. 287–8.

36 BL, Stowe MS 366, fo. 124a, 115a.

37 Above, n. 25, and *Chamberlain*, II, 421 (19 Jan. 1622). Chamberlain's comment on the Protestation of December 1621 was *'vanae sine viribus irae,* and that there is noe disputing nor contesting with supreme authoritie'.

38 *CJ*, I, 803; A. Hassell Smith, *County and Court: Government and Politics in Norfolk 1558–1603* (1974), p. 115: *Statutes of the Realm 1 Jac. 1 c. 33.*

39 The argument in Russell (ed.), *The Origins of the English Civil War* (1973), p. 103, that members of the Commons did not realize the true cost of government, is true. On the other hand, the work of Dr. D.M. Hirst (*The Representative of the People?* (Cambridge, 1975)) makes it impossible to regard it as the whole truth, or even the most important part of the truth. I am very grateful to Dr. Hirst for allowing me to read this book before publication.

40 *CD 1621*, IV, 58, II, 466. Alford thought that three subsidies in one year called for three harvests, but also gave his voice in favour of an additional grant. *CD 1621*, VI, 208.

41 *CJ*, I, 649.

42 BL, Stowe MS 366, fo. 48 a–b.

43 BL, Stowe MS 366, fo. 44a.

44 *CD 1621*, III, 347.

45 *P in P 1610*, II, 105. See *P in P 1610*, II, 273 for James's promise on impositions.

46 *CD 1621*, IV, 326–31, VII, 312–22.

47 *Parliamentary Diary of Robert Bowyer*, pp. 126–7; *CD 1621*, VII, 372–6, IV, 31; *Wentworth Papers*, pp. 232–3; A. Hamilton Bryson (ed.), 'A Book of the Several Officers of the Exchequer', *Camden Miscellany*, 4th Series 14 (1975), p. 112.

48 *Debates in the House of Lords 1621*, ed. S.R. Gardiner (Camden Soc, 1st Series no. 103, 1870), p. 104 and n.: *CD 1621*, III, 416: *LJ*, iii, 168. Such redress of grievances as happened in 1621 was a consequence, not a cause of the voting of subsidies.

49 G.E. Aylmer, *The King's Servants* (1961), pp. 246–8.

50 *CSPD 1623–5*, vol. clxiv, no. 61. The real reason for the veto appears to have been French diplomatic pressure (PRO, 31/3/58, fos. 67a, 70b, 74a, 119, 122). The excuse was presumably chosen because contemporaries would find it convincing.

51 *CD 1621*, VII, 387–90: *Parliamentary Diary of Robert Bowyer*, p. 127.

52 Sir Symonds D'Ewes, *The Journals of All the Parliaments* (1682), p. 653.

53 Katherine Van Eerde, 'The Jacobean Baronets', *JMH*, 33 (1961), p. 140, see also p. 138.

54 *P in P 1610*, II, pp. 267–70. The anonymous diarist of 1625 remarked on this clause of the Petition of Grievances 'but note there is no answer to the laying an imposition on a native commodity'. Queen's College, MS 449, fo. 240b. For the debate on whether this was an imposition or a composition, and for Phelips' fear that it might lead to an excise, see *CD 1621*, II, 476 and n. 480–1. The value of this imposition to the king was estimated at £3,500 p. a. Diary of John Hawarde (Wilts. R. O. Ailesbury MSS), unfoliated *sub* 30 November, 1621.

55 *P in P 1610*, II, 273. James's fidelity to this promise was not total.

56 Elton, 'Points of Contact: Parliament', pp. 183–200; *CD 1621*, V, 429.

57 It is worth recalling James's statement, in his proclamation dissolving the parliament of 1621, that it had 'proceeded some months with such harmony

between us and our people as cannot be paralleled by any former time': J.R. Tanner, *Constitutional Documents of the Reign of James I 1603–1625* (reprinted Cambridge, 1960), p. 290.

58 BL, Stowe MS, 366, fo. 15a. For Sir Henry Neville's concern with the effect of parliaments on England's reputation abroad, see Moir, *Addled Parliament*, pp. 13–14. On the whole, the comments of foreign ambassadors do not bear out the widespread English belief that they were much concerned with events in parliament.

59 *CD 1621*, IV, 448.

60 *Strafforde Letters*, I, 28 (Ingram to Wentworth). The Bishop of Mende, the Queen's Almoner, regarded Arundel as the prime mover in the impeachment of Buckingham, and tried to lead him to believe he enjoyed the queen's support: PRO, 31/3/63, p. 73 (Mende to Richelieu).

61 Sheffield City Library, Elmhirst MSS 1351/4. Salvetti noted this contract on 21/31 July 1626, only just over a month after the dissolution of the parliament: HMC, *11th Report I*, p. 82.

62 J.N. Ball, 'Sir John Eliot', pp. 222–3. Dr. Ball has found no record of this meeting at Sir Robert Cotton's house, but believes the outlines of the story to be correct. On the importance of Pembroke's attitude to Buckingham in 1628, see also *CSPD 1627–8*, vol. xcii, no. 12 (Hippisley to Buckingham, 2 February, 1628). I am grateful to Mr. Paul Fowle for this reference.

63 *CSPD 1625–6*, vol. xviii, no. 68.

64 J.N.Ball, 'Sir John Eliot', p. 211.

65 Conyers Read, *Mr. Secretary Cecil* (1955), I, 119. For an example of how Burghley interpreted this injunction, see the story of his Interregnum Bill in J.E. Neale, *Queen Elizabeth I and Her Parliaments*, II (1957), pp. 45–8. Neale's comment that 'Stuart days were not far distant' can be read two ways. See also G.R. Elton, *Studies in Tudor and Stuart Politics and Government* (Cambridge, 1974), vol. II, p. 159.

66 *CJ*, I, 475.

67 *CD 1621*, V, 261, III, 227. Cranfield succeeded Mandeville, the referee he attacked with most vigour, as Lord Treasurer.

68 *CD 1621*, IV, 150, II, 155, VI, 21, V, 16, II, 123: *CJ*, I, 648, 657; *CJ*, I, 806. Heath's connections appear to have been with Buckingham, rather than Pembroke, but this only illustrates the fact that Buckingham's clients were rarely expected to function as a monolithic 'party'.

69 The only prominent members of parliament who could conceivably be regarded as excluded from office by their beliefs are Nicholas Fuller, Thomas Wentworth son of Peter, and possibly John Pym after the York House Conference. In all three cases, the obstacle was religious. Sir Roger Owen and Edward Alford were temperamentally unsuited to office, but they held no beliefs incompatible with it. On the range of opinions compatible with office, see G.E. Aylmer, *the King's Servants* (1961), pp. 351–6.

70 PRO, SP 16/19/107. This document is hard to reconcile with Zagorin's description of Digges as an 'oppositionist'. *Court and Country*, p. 79.

71 *Chamberlain*, II, 385–6, 389, 392.

72 Digges was not merely a fair-weather friend to Abbot. After Abbot's hunting accident, when other ambitious people were avoiding him, Digges rode post to pay him an immediate visit: *Chamberlain*, II, 394–5.

73 It is typical of the early Stuart structure of politics that in 1614 Digges, a supposedly 'opposition' member, was in charge of a 'government' bill for the

creation of county record offices: Moir, *Addled Parliament*, pp. 19, 203: *CJ*, I, 487.

74 N.R.N. Tyacke, 'Arminianism in England in Religion and Politics 1604 to 1640' (Oxford D.Phil. Thesis, 1969), pp. 134, 194.

75 I. Morgan, *Prince Charles's Puritan Chaplain* (1957), pp. 164–5.

76 HLRO, Diary of Sir Nathaniel Rich, fo. 37v: CUL, Diary of Bulstrode Whitelocke, MS Dd 12–20, fos. 59b, 58b, 40a.

77 Aylmer, *The King's Servants*, pp. 353–4, 374–9.

78 *P in P 1610*, II, 109.

79 Chamberlain's fear that the parliament of 1621 would be of little use because 'the prerogative is grown a *noli me tangere*' was a fear that the parliament would break over the issue of impositions. The allusion is presumably to Bishop Neile's '*noli me tangere*' speech about impositions, which had done so much to wreck the previous parliament. Chamberlain thought impositions, as well as patents, had become so grievous 'that of necessity they must be spoken of': *Chamberlain*, II, 313: Moir, *Addled Parliament*, p. 117.

80 *CJ*, I, 658. The picture of Phelips as being, not an opposition member, but a mediator between Somerset and the court is supported by the fact that one of his earliest political actions was to lend the crown £1,000 in 1613. His fellow-lenders, Burlamachi, Vanlore, Courteen and Sir Baptist Hickes, will hardly serve for a roll-call of leaders of the opposition: BL, Cotton MS Titus B iv, fo. 101b.

81 Harvard, MS Eng. 980, fo. 209, 221–2.

82 BL, Stowe MS 366, fo. 145b.

83 BL, Stowe MS 366, fos. 185b, 173b. Phelips' attempt to reopen old arguments over impositions was brusquely silenced by Rich's advice that they should pass it over, 'ascribing all that is past to councells of necessity'.

84 *CD 1621*, IV, 441, III, 410.

85 HMC, *7th Report, App*, p. 544.

86 See Phelips' remarks on the deliberate passing over of the 1614 imprisonments in 1621: *CJ*, I, 658. For a valuable attempt to place privilege issues in perspective, see D.M. Hirst, 'Elections and Privileges in the House of Commons in the Early Seventeenth Century', *HJ*, 18 (1975), pp. 851–62.

87 J.N. Ball, 'Sir John Eliot', pp. 143, 181. See also pp. 8, 18.

88 I hope to discuss the second session of 1621 elsewhere. On 1604, see the important article by N.R.N. Tyacke, 'Sir Robert Wroth and the Parliament of 1604', *BIHR* (1977), pp. 120–5, and HMC, *Salis* xvi, pp. 141–4.

89 Elton, *Tudor and Stuart Politics and Government*, II, pp. 161, 166.

90 Alan Everitt, *The Local Community and the Great Rebellion* (Historical Association, 1969), pp. 5–10. During such a conflict, the distinction of being the local community's representative at the centre was likely to be an uncomfortable one.

91 Hassell Smith, *Norfolk*, p. 124.

92 T.G. Barnes, *Somerset 1625–1640* (1961), pp. 289–90; Hassell Smith, *Norfolk*, pp. 42–3; *Wentworth Papers*, pp. 5, 7.

93 *CD 1621*, III, 325–406; *Wentworth Papers*, pp. 152–5. The nine members concerned were Sir Edwin Sandys, Sir Robert Phelips, Sir Samuel Sandys, Sir Edward Coke, Sir Dudley Digges, Neale, Alford, Sir Edward Montagu and Delbridge. They provide a representative cross-section of the speakers of the House. For an authoritative discussion of the relationship of M.P.s with their electorates, see Hirst, *The Representative of the People?*, *passim*.

94 Bodl. L., MS Tanner 392, fos. 1b, 34b. Hassell Smith, *Norfolk*, pp. 120–1.

95 BL, Stowe MS 366, fo. 74b.

2

The emergence of adversary politics in the Long Parliament

MARK KISHLANSKY

Groups, factions, parties: the perplexing categories of political organization. War party, peace party, middle group, Presbyterians, Independents,
Presbyterian-Independents, Royal Independents, revolutionaries, conformists, moderates, radicals, probable latent moderates, core radical/fringe
moderates: the astounding nomenclature of political participation. Since
Samuel Rawson Gardiner completed the first modern history of the politics
of the English Revolution, historians have struggled to define the nature
and composition of Long Parliament political alignments. For Gardiner, as
for his age, it was all straightforward enough. Politics was structured into
parties with contrasting ideologies, adherents of peace or war in the early
years and of Presbyterianism or Independency once the first civil war had
ended. Politicans who argued for peace were overwhelmingly Presbyterians, while those who urged all-out war were by and large Independents.
Ideology was an amalgam of religious and political beliefs, a tempera-
mental consistency which was maintained despite the increasing complexity of issues which confronted the men at Westminster. Thus Gardiner held
to two static notions of political participation: that the system by which
politics operated was an oppositional one and that those who composed
the contending camps did so on the basis of a single, consistent set of
principles – an ideology.

The forceful revisons of Gardiner's interpretation have been largely
successful in demonstrating the inadequacy of his political groupings,
but they have done little to test his assumptions about political structure
– his belief that parliamentary politics was oppositional politics. From
J.H. Hexter's 'middle group' to J.R. MacCormack's moderates and
radicals, a unitary concept of political structure has prevailed. Prosopo-
graphic research has succeeded only in eroding the solid phalanges that
Gardiner labeled party, shuffling individuals, clientage groups, and localist
connections from one category to another with such cheerful abandon that
Hexter, who initiated the inquiry, has been forced to conclude 'that politics
is a poker game with all the red cards wild.'[1] Despite continued taxonomic
confusion, however, the new emphasis upon fluid and amorphous political

An earlier version of this article was read at the annual meeting of the American Historical
Association, Washington, D.C., 1976.

groupings revives the possibility of a reexamination of the Long Parliament's underlying political structure.

By interchanging terms like 'group,' 'faction,' and 'party,' historians expressed their uncertainty about the coherence of the bodies they were describing. But all three labels, in their structural senses, furthered a uniform notion of oppositional politics. Even D.E. Underdown, who stressed the importance of unaligned and non-committed members when he questioned the existence of a coherent Independent party, ignored his own caveats. In the most sophisticated system for the classification of M.P.s yet devised, he left out of the three parties only those who could not be confidently labeled.[2] If, as A.B.Worden states, 'we can no longer think of the war and peace parties as parties in the modern sense,'[3] in what sense were they parties? What was the system of political organization; what was the concept of political behavior that encompassed both shifting groups and coherent parties?

An analysis of the structure of parliamentary politics must focus not upon the polarities against which members can be measured but upon the points of contact that made them common participants in a political system. The principles of the institution from which they operated must be scrutinized to reveal the shared precepts of political behavior. In the houses of parliament the primacy of reasoned debate and unanimous decision making reflects a concept of politics far different from the modern emphasis upon predetermined positions and contrariety. The rhetoric that eschewed faction and interest suggests not an adversary system of politics but a consensual one. Indeed, despite the stresses and strains of the early seventeenth century, consensus politics survived in the procedures and practices of the Long Parliament. Only gradually was parliamentary political structure transformed, undermined by political pressure groups and the rise of parties during four years of civil war. By 1647 the men at Westminster would witness the emergence of adversary politics.

I

To understand the structure of parliamentary politics, it is first necessary to realize that parliament was not simply the arena for political activity that it became in the 1640s but an institution with formal methods, procedures, and functions. Although much has been made of its legal aspects, its power to participate in the creation of statute law, parliament was in the first place an institution organized to do the king's business. In its primary role as a council, parliament might best be described as a sounding board, for it resonated the monarch's will among the estates of the realm. Like the sounding board, its function was to amplify and enhance, to offer counsel and reason to bolster that provided by the monarch's permanent advisers. It was no mere echo chamber, simply reverberating what was presented to it, no rubber stamp, to change the metaphor, but a body which added weight to the king's government, assenting to the king's laws and regulating the king's justice, creating legislation by confirming the judiciousness of the monarch's judgment. This was parliament's purpose, and its methods were devised to give full tone to the notes struck by the king. Thoughtful consideration and careful decision making characterized the parliamentary way. Its two guiding principles were the primacy of debate and the unanimity of resolution.

Free debate was the *sine qua non* of the parliamentary process, but free debate was not the equivalent of free speech. Propriety was its first restriction, especially in relation to the deference due to monarchical authority: members were to speak 'their consciences in matters proposed in the House but with all due respect to your majesty.'[4] This was illustrated not only by the imprisonment of overzealous M.P.s but even in Henry Marten's expulsion from the Commons in 1643 for suggesting that the royal family should not be placed in balance with the nation. More important, debate was limited to the business brought before the Houses. Parliament men were directed to speak only to the issues they had been summoned to hear; and extraneous concerns, like the queen's marriage or foreign policy in 1621, were beyond these bounds. Traditionally, Elizabeth answered the Speaker's ceremonial plea for freedom of speech with the explicit exclusion of religious matters. Before the session of 1621, James proclaimed against 'excessive lavish and licentious speech of matters of state.' Yet an index of forbidden subjects should not be hastily drawn, for other business would raise other issues; and what was beyond the purview of one parliament might be the focus of the next, as was seen in 1625. Within these limits unencumbered debate could still flourish, for debate was considered to be persuasive discussion: reasoned argument among men uncommitted to predetermined positions. Debate revealed the strengths and weaknesses of the measures presented to the Houses and initiated the committees which reshaped the bill in light of arguments offered by the speakers. Debate was designed to convince, not to conquer, and during debate the members of the socially stratified house of commons acted as equals. Great rhetoricians and cunning lawyers as well as aristocratic heirs were not to have an overbearing influence upon the House, and the rule that no member could speak twice to an issue was strictly enforced.[5]

As debate was designed to convince, it was also intended to perfect rather than to oppose the king's business. Indeed parliamentary practice left little place for opposition. A member who spoke against the body of a bill could not be named to the committee which considered it: 'For by being a committee it is supposed he liketh the bill for matter, but disliketh the form only, which is the office of committees to amend.' Such rules favored the passage of all bills and led to what one parliamentarian condemned as 'policies in Parliament.' 'Tis a common policy in Parliament if any man be against a bill but would not seem to be so, to speak for it and by way of objections to show such matter against it as may not be answered.'[6] The necessity for such circuitous techniques is one indication that opposition was not an integral part of parliamentary experience. This can also be seen in relations between the Houses, where it was a general rule that one House would not reject a bill presented to it by the other. Bills could be amended, although not to negate their intention; or they could be withdrawn, generally as the result of a conference between the Houses. 'If the two Houses cannot agree,' wrote William Hakewill, 'then sometimes the Lords, sometimes the Commons, require a meeting of some of each House, whereby information may be had of each others' mind for the preservation of a good correspondency between them, after which meeting for the most part, (though not always) either part agrees to the Bill in question.'[7] When the house of lords protested against the self-denying ordinance, this procedure was still followed. The Commons insisted that the peers' objections be submitted as amendments, but as they comprised a negation of the bill, the Lords were forced to substitute an ordinance of their own for that of the Commons.[8] In general, however, matters which aroused opposition or required excessive time or energy were 'allowed to sleep' by the Speakers or the members of the Houses who could refuse commitment. Rejection of a measure was uncommon and acceptance so routine that the Speaker would accumulate a half-dozen or more bills before presenting them, one after another, for final resolution.

The procedural prejudice in favor of the king's business is also exemplified by the method of putting questions. Although the speaker was at liberty to end debate by accepting a call for the question, he could only present a motion for the passage of a bill, never for its rejection. 'If upon the second reading of the bill, the[y] cry away with it, the speaker may not make that the question, but must put it to the question whether it shall be committed or no; if the greatest voice be no, the speaker must put the question for the engrossing, which is always denied, if it be denied a committee by a negative, but the speaker is notwithstanding to make the question so.'[9] Moreover, questions were put first in the affirmative, a factor which allowed undecided members to abstain when the negative vote was taken.

Unanimity rather than diversity was the goal of parliamentary procedure. The committee system was intended to deflect opposition, and committees were appointed after debate so that any exceptions raised there could be considered. It was the committee's prerogative to amend the bill, and this was another method of providing a compromise course when opposition or disinclination persisted. Committees were eager to achieve consensus, and, as Notestein observed of the committees in the parliamentary sessions of 1604–10, 'to gain agreements they would put forward amendments and provisos until the final form of the measure was burdened with exceptions.'[10] Once a bill was reported by the committee and returned to the House, its chances for unanimous approval could easily be determined, for any opposition to its final form had to be expressed before its engrossing. Then an effort might be made 'to have the question deferred till the next day or some longer time . . . especially if it be a matter they desire should either pass with unanimous consent or not at all.' Even after the vote was taken, moves might still be afoot to achieve unanimity: 'And if upon putting the question in the negative there be but one that is heard to say no it hath been seen that he being a man of special note hath been desired by the House to discover to them the reason of his differing in opinion from the whole House.'[11]

That parliamentary procedure eschewed opposition is not to say that none existed, but it is a reminder that opposition was not the normal course of affairs and that it explictly violated one of the Houses' underlying principles. Two striking illustrations of this point can be found among the descriptions of parliamentary procedure. In a chapter entitled 'Concerning Cases and Judgments Which Are Hard,' Hakewill relates how the most difficult judgments 'between the King and some nobleman' or a complicated legal case 'before the Chancellor' could be resolved by parliament. A committee of twenty-five Lords and Commoners was appointed to study the matter. If disagreement was present in that body, it would select half of its number to consider the case, and this declension was continued to its logical conclusion: 'If the King consent to three, these three may condescend to two, and may descend to another, and so at length his ordinance shall stand above the whole Parliament, and so condescend from twenty and five persons to one only person, unless the greater number will agree and ordain, at the length, one person, as is said, shall agree for all, who cannot disagree from himself.'[12]

The second example is found in an examination of the division, the house of commons' single institutionalized form of opposition. The division, like the poll in an election, enabled the Speaker to determine which side held a majority. Like the poll, it was rarely necessary, and it was generally related to private rather than public business. Two of its characteristics, however, are worth noting. Divisions occurred on issues seen to have a conservative and an innovative side. It was the innovators who were required to leave the House, a distinct disadvantage both because of the competition for seats and the strong conservative bent of the Commons' members. 'If the question be for the passing of a bill, those of the affirmative part do always go forth, and those of the negative part sit still (which privilege of sitting is given to them, because they are against innovation, which every new bill brings in though it be never so good in appearance).' The innovators had raised the issue, which in normal practice should not have come to the vote without the opposition to it being cleared or the entire matter deferred, and the onus was on them to prove the worthiness of their cause. If they did, however, those who had opposed them customarily withdrew from their seats, 'thereby to acknowledge their consent to it, and their error in being against it,' and together both sides reentered the House and presented the bill to the Speaker as the sense of the unified membership.[13] As opposition was rare, the methods of dealing with it were also unusual.

If, beginning in 1626, parliamentarians could not always act according to these ideals of consensus politics, and this became more difficult as substantive issues obtruded into the king's business, neither parliamentary procedure nor political practice was adopted to reflect a new relationship between king and parliament. As Conrad Russell has argued so poignantly, the fathers of the 1620s left their heirs 'no tradition of fighting against the crown.'[14] Nor was the mostly unsuccessful attempt to press redress *along with* supply an alternation of the role of parliament or a diminution of the prerogative of the monarch. Even the Petition of Right had clear procedural precedents and, like most of the Commons' petitions during James's reign, asked only for the preservation of long-established privileges against future encroachments; or, as the Apology of the Commons stated, 'the prerogatives of princes may easily and do daily grow; the privileges of the subject are for the most part at an everlasting stand.'[15] So much of the content of these issues centred upon conservation and preservation that they were (except for their occasional bad form) acceptable to the staunchest defenders of the king's prerogatives.[16] Sir John Eliot was a martyr only to some of his parliamentary colleagues; and the insistence upon privileges had clearly overstepped the bounds of propriety in 1629, when it was necessary to restrain the Speaker forcibly from dissolving parliament. The opposition which appeared in Charles's parliaments, however intense, was neither the precursor nor the equivalent of the parliamentarian cause. The initiative of the house of commons was not won – it was thrust upon an unwilling body by a monarch who believed that the king's parliament could not exist without him.

In actuality, the experiences of parliament throughout the early seventeenth century were an impractical guide to government without the monarch. 'Policy' initiated by parliament was devised (if it simply did not occur) to obstruct rather than to achieve. As the historian of the parliament of 1624 observes, 'In some cases the consensus among members was such that alternative proposals to those advocated by the crown could be put forth, but with rare exceptions, the coalescence of opinion in the Commons represented a negative rather than a positive approach toward government.'[17] Once Charles raised his standard, the focus of parliamentary opposition disappeared. A new and unprecedented set of procedures had to be mapped out so that a legislative council could operate as an executive assembly. These changes proceeded at an agonizingly slow pace, for once the rupture with the king was accomplished, most parliament men resisted any changes of a permanent character. More important, when parliament was forced to its own devices, it was the heritage of consensus rather than the brief flirtation with opposition which presented the building blocks for the parliamentary cause. Its diverse components, its initial zealousness, its religiosity, all were strengthened by reliance upon unencumbered debate and unified decision making. When, in July 1647, another Speaker of the house of commons was thrust into his chair to prevent an adjournment – this time by a mob rather than by members – a true transformation of political practice had been completed.

II

Another of the difficulties modern historians experience in describing seventeenth-century political structure derives from their use of the term 'party.' Contemporary commentators were not merely slip-shod when they employed the word, as today we bandy labels like 'left' and 'right wing'; rather, during the course of the seventeenth century the meaning of 'party' underwent an important transformation. During the early part of the century 'party' did not have a political sense – it simply meant a part of the whole. In its legal usage it was synonymous with a side, but only as an expression of a group or individual in a suit. Its military meaning, which first appeared during the war, denoted a group of soldiers, as in 'the Lord Goring's party.' In an organic political structure there was hardly much place for such a term, and it continued to express groupings in a neutral way throughout the war. Thus Whitelocke spoke of 'Cromwell's party,' Ludlow hailed the 'commonwealth party,' and Baillie reviled the 'party of worldly profane men'; when the war began the Royalists were called the 'King's party.'[18] Dozens of similar descriptions, usually preceded by the name of a leading 'grandee,' abounded, as did the less frequent but equally general identifications like the 'godly party.' In this sense, parties were not structures in the political system but groupings of politicians: the house of commons was never divided into Independents, lawyers, and worldly profane men except as Baillie viewed the opposition to the *jure divino* Presbyterian settlement. In modern parlance this meaning of 'party' is best equated with 'group,' because it is an identification of loose and transitory political configurations and an expression of an amorphous political system.

After the outbreak of war, 'party' began to lose its neutral connotations and came to be an expression of political practice. It is impossible to date such a change in meaning precisely, and the older sense was never wholly replaced, but by the mid-1640s another meaning of 'party' was clearly taking shape. It became synonymous with words that described political structure and practice, the three most usual being 'cabal,' 'faction,' and 'junto.' Baillie expressed the confusion of meanings when he wrote in 1646, 'There are here four or five juntoes, all of diverse and somewhat contrary cabals, but those who are little acquainted with the designs of any of them are the greatest, strongest, and honestest party.'[19] But D'Ewes, who recorded the proposal to censure Chillingworth in 1641 'for his scandalous speeches against this House, in saying there were parties or sides in the House of Commons,' began referring to an 'Independent party' by 1645.[20] 'The leading men or grandees first divided themselves into two factions, or juntoes of presbyterian and independent,' Clement Walker observed of this same period when writing in 1647.[21] In this sense, 'party' came to describe a new method of political action, one which implied a corruption of the old political system – more explicitly, the pursuit of self-interest against the common good. This is what Edmund Ludlow meant when he explained why he was ousted from his command of the Wiltshire forces: 'Observing me not fit to promote a faction and solely applying myself to advance the cause of the public, they combined against me.' This was what Whitelock meant when he exhorted his children, 'Learn my children of your father, so to carry yourselves in public business that you may be esteemed of all parties and believed that you follow your own conscience and no faction.'[22] In modern parlance this use of 'party' is best equated with faction, expressive of its pejorative connotations and of the personal rivalries that generated its appearance.

When contemporaries came to use terms like 'Presbyterian party' and 'Independent party,' they were thus assimilating two different meanings of the word, expressing both a segment of the whole and the corrupt methods employed by members of the groupings. By the end of the first civil war the political system had adopted this oppositional structure, which was first identified as faction, and political groupings had stabilized into coherent and durable bodies. The intervention of the army and its impeachment of its opponents accelerated this process, as did the subsequent events of the Revolution. The unitary parliamentary cause was fragmented into opposing political parties, with leadership, organization, ideology, and constituency – that is, the modern notion. In this sense 'party' again became a neutral term, for it expressed the oppositional political structure and its coherent organization. When memorialists spoke of the Presbyterian party or the Moderate party, they now meant not only a group of individuals but one with an explicit ideology opposed to another ideological grouping. Whether or not the development was lamented, 'party' lost its unsavory connotations and became a description of both organization and structure. The successive stages of political development were masked by the continuous use of a single word and by the fact that the new meaning of 'party' became its durable modern one. Preparty politics could only be defined in party terms, and since so many of the contemporary accounts of the revolution were written retrospectively, the political structure which emerged became the model of explanation for all preceding events. Parties, in the modern sense, did appear in the revolution, but the inconsistent use of the term made it seem that they had existed from the beginning of the war or, from Clarendon's account, even earlier.

This change in the meaning of 'party' is one element in the transformation of political practice which occurred during the course of the revolution. During the early years of the war, parliamentarians practiced consensus politics – decision making characterized by unencumbered debate and, wherever possible, unanimous resolution. It was a political scene dominated by 'the greatest, strongest, and honestest party' of men uncommitted to predetermined positions, swayed by debate, and used to compromise. This was the principle that Lucy Hutchinson defended when she exonerated those non-committed members who supported the 'Independent faction': 'The rest believed to adhere to them only out of faction, as if those who did not vaingloriously lay out themselves without necessity, but chose rather *to hear and vote*, had no understanding of right and wrong.'[23] 'To hear and vote' was the parliamentary way; to follow faction was its corruption. 'To resign a man's judgment to the opinion of another man's is but a silly trust and confidence,' Clement Walker declared, in an effort to persuade honest parliamentarians to desert the leaders of the juntoes.[24] Even Denzil Holles conceived of the political process in this fashion, claiming that in 1647 the Independents lost their support because they were 'now a known, engaged, faction.'[25]

Across the spectrum of political opinion a single concept of politics prevailed, even after it had fallen into disuse. Colonel Hutchinson, his wife declared, 'was as ready to hear as to give counsel, and never pertinacious in his will when his reason was convinced.' 'They knew him very little that could say he was of any faction, for he had a strength of judgement able to consider things himself and propound them to his conscience.'[26] 'Nothing should be done,' Cromwell told the agitators in July 1647, 'but with the best and most unanimous concurrence.'[27] The eleven members impeached by the army sounded the same theme, proclaiming 'that they detest the maintaining of a faction, or carrying on of any design other than the common good.'[28] Indeed, when the agitators presented the Agreement of the People at Putney, Cromwell objected to it on the grounds that predetermined propositions could not be debated as befitted a 'company of men that really would be guided by God.' 'But if any come to us tomorrow only to instruct us and teach us,' he warned the agitators, 'I refer to every sober spirited man to think of and determine how far that will consist with the liberty of a free deliberation or an end of satisfaction. I think it is such a preengagement that there is no need to talk of the thing.'[29] The search for God's guidance was an effort to humble individual will to the good of the public, and extraordinary fasts and humiliations were frequent during political crises.

III

Consensus decision making observed the traditional practices of the house of commons and maintained parliamentary unity. When the first important political difference between supporters of war and advocates of peace appeared in parliament, the contending proponents did not simply struggle for ascendancy. As neither side could be convinced of the opposite course, both policies were pursued. While new armies were erected, peace propositions were drafted. It was not a middle group but a middle way which John Pym mastered in the winter of 1643–44, and this preference for contradictory policies that would maintain unity endured beyond his death and even the succession of political crises of the following year. In the winters of both 1644–45 and 1645–46 peace propositions accompanied new military developments. The other great issue of the war's early years was handled in much the same manner. A committee of accommodation was appointed to find a middle ground in the religious dispute between Presbyterians and Independents. It was revived in 1645, and even the declaration of April 1646, after the passage of the Presbyterian establishment, promised toleration for tender consciences. Members of parliament who supported these opposing viewpoints were incorporated in committees, occasionally purposely balanced, and heard in debate. Not until 1646 would such practice alter.

Indeed until 1646 the house of commons was not separated into structures which represented differing political persuasions. The principles of consensus ensured that members who held strong views would participate in the processes of decision making. In the winter of 1644–45 war supporters took a central role in establishing the Uxbridge proposals and presenting them to the king, while peace supporters were no less active in the creation of the New Model Army. Both the terms of peace and the military reestablishment represented compromise courses; if, after three years of fighting, unanimity was no longer possible, moderation was. After Charles's refusal to accept Parliament's propositions, the war was directed by the Committee of Both Kingdoms, in which prominent advocates of peace like Sir Philip Stapleton were instrumental in devising strategy.[30] The New Model Army did not begin its campaign with battle at Naseby but with the siege of Oxford – yet another compromise.

But the transformation in the language of politics mirrored a more concrete change in political practice. By the summer of 1646, with the war ended and the peace to be established, the men at Westminster abandoned consensus decision making. The deliberative process, with its practiced speeches and persuasive debates, was entirely too cumbersome when confronted by the need for rapid policy formation and executive control which now appeared. Without the king or his armies to unify it and without the anticipation of the resumption of constitutional government to restrain it, the parliamentary cause shattered. The personal factions which sprang from individual animosities following the formation of the New Model Army and were nourished on the Savile affair and contentions over the role of the Scots matured into political parties. Their emergence as ideological bodies stressed, for the first time, permanent contrariety, leaving disputes to be resolved not by debate but by divisions of the house of commons into majority and minority opinions. This was not of itself innovative, for the two Houses had always conducted their business by votes on resolutions, but majoritarianism had never been as important as unanimity. The methods of consensus had relied upon the deliberative process, through debates and committees, to arrive at resolutions which expressed the sense of the whole House. With the use of divisions, the parties inverted this procedure, establishing a majority opinion through the resolution of the issue, and circumventing the process by which consensus was achieved.

The political power struggle which resulted in the rise of party politics first became permanent in the spring of 1646. Before then the groups and factions of parliament men, though at times openly hostile, had few issues upon which they could test their strength. Until the war had ended the factional leaders were in agreement on critical areas of policy. As Holles and Stapleton continued their support of Scottish interests, Vane and St. John raised money to maintain the Scottish army. While the war continued, all agreed that the Scots' presence was necessary. The preparations of the Newcastle propositions were also commonly supported. Although there were sharp differences over specifics, neither faction could claim control of the progress the proposals made once they reached the floor of the Commons. There they were slowed by votes over individual exceptions to the pardon and local issues which transcended factional contentions. Until settlement with the king was achieved, the maintenance of parliament's military might was also a shared objective. Even the church settlement, in its initial stages, was an issue over which the factional leaders studiously avoided clashes. Not until Holles became actively involved in the establishment of the diluted Presbyterianism favored by the majority within the Commons did the factions join issue over religion. Significantly, this occurred in the spring of 1646. In one sense, then, the emergence of the parties awaited the appearance of issues which in 1645 were still buffered from consideration by the war.

By no test of individuals or issues can it be demonstrated that party politics existed until the spring of 1646. Leadership in the house of commons continued to reflect local and administrative enterprise rather than party discipline. The debates over religion were chaired by Lawrence Whitacre, the devout but essentially apolitical parliamentary diarist. The peace propositions were coordinated by Sir Thomas Widdrington, an influential north country M.P. Scottish affairs were the particular preserve of the elder Vane, Robert Goodwin, and Sir William Armine. In these critical areas the factional leaders had not taken control of parliamentary affairs. To enforce discipline either faction might have held out the rewards of the impending settlement; but its uncertainty, the oscillating course of political decision making, and the existence of the 'Presbyterian-Independents' were all factors which conspired against party discipline.

By similar tests, fledgling political parties appeared in the spring of 1646. An increase in divisions and committees helped to solidify the positions of parliamentary leaders. While Denzil Holles and Sir Philip Stapleton continued to champion a lenient posture toward king and Scots, Sir Henry Vane, Jr., and Oliver St. John moved off from the center of the political stage. In their places, Sir Arthur Hasilrig and Sir John Evelyn of Wiltshire took the lead in advocating a sterner political position and opposition to the established Presbyterian church. The failure of the full House to find a settlement with the king strengthened the hands of the leaders of both organizations. Rewards and constraints, necessary to enforce discipline, appeared with the likelihood that only one of the parties would secure agreement with the king. As the ideological positions of the parties diverged, especially in relation to church government, interest groups within the City of London acted as constituencies for both. In the struggle for power these groups threw their support behind the parties, petitioning for the adoption of their policies and providing financial resources. No outside pressure was stronger than that applied by the city's government. In a series of petitions beginning in the summer of 1645, the city government successfully challenged the doctrine of parliamentary privilege until the two Houses could no longer claim that their debates were unencumbered and their decisions uninfluenced.[31]

As the idea of adversary politics developed, the party leaders adapted parliamentary procedures to reflect their conflict. The frequency of divisions in 1646, in contrast to their sporadic occurrence in the years of war, was indicative of two changes in parliamentary practice: that debates and committees were no longer able to disperse opposition and that the dynamics of adversary politics were continuously on display. Between January 1 and December 31, 1644, only thirty-four divisions occurred in the house of commons, seven of them during the controversy over the self-denying ordinance. In the following year just thirty-eight divisions were recorded. But during 1646 the members of the lower house found it necessary to divide on 102 occasions, eighty-eight of those in the last three-quarters of the year.[32] More important, while divisions during the early years of the war, with the important exception of self-denial, rarely dealt with fundamental matters of policy, those during 1646 touched every critical area of decision making. In the fall, immediately following the failure of the Newcastle negotiations, the proceedings of the house of commons were dominated by divisions: in sixteen sessions during

September, twelve divisions occurred; and in twenty-five sessions in October, there were thirteen divisions. The leaders of the emerging parties were finding it easier to count heads than to change hearts.

If the proliferation of divisions characterized the emergence of adversary politics – soon even the decimated house of lords would hold formal divisions among barely more than a dozen members – the decline of the nominated committee epitomized the erosion of consensus. Committees encompassing members of all political and religious persuasions had been the cornerstone of parliamentary practice throughout the war. They were appointed, in ever-increasing numbers, to debate the Commons' policy on the broad range of issues posed by the war. Thirteen members of parliament appeared on at least one-third of the ninety committees appointed in the first six months of 1646.[33] They consistently dominated small committees which were appointed to debate crucial decisions. In fact the increased frequency of naming committees of fewer than twenty members was one indication of the Commons' search for a method to devise and implement policy. In January 1646, for example, five of the ten members chosen to consider the Scots' plea to treat with the king were from the thirteen. In a thirteen-man committee appointed to prepare the bill for the peace propositions, seven were from this group of prominent committeemen.[34] Although this might be coincidental, the trend by which these men constituted a bare majority on small committees is marked throughout the spring. In February, ten of eighteen were appointed to prepare an answer to the king and five of ten to preserve parliamentary privileges on the revenue; in March, eight of sixteen to examine the French ambassador, ten of nineteen to consider a paper from the Scots, six of ten to invite the Prince of Wales to London, and five of seven to answer another letter from the king were all of the most active committeemen. In the two small committees appointed in April, the thirteen continued to hold majorities: six of eleven were appointed to communicate a breach of privilege to the Assembly of Divines and four of six to examine a letter from the army.[35]

But beginning in the summer of 1646 the role of the committees nominated from the floor of the House was severely attenuated. From the formation of the Derby House Committee in October, small committees charged with formulating parliamentary policy practically disappeared. In the first three months of 1647, of the twenty-five committees nominated, only two had fewer than fifteen members.[36] Even the important committee appointed on March 17 to examine the first charges against the army petition contained sixty-five members, incapacitated, perhaps deliberately, by its unmanageable size. Moreover, during these months committees were no longer appointed to consider the critical aspects of parliamentary policy. Instead, policy was coordinated at Derby House by a carefully packed standing committee managed by Denzil Holles. The symbolic irruptions in parliamentary procedure during these months, Ireton's famed challenge of Holles to a duel, and the inglorious flight of Holles and Stapleton from the floor of the Commons to avoid appearing on opposite sides of a division were hardly as revealing of the transformation of political practice as the fact that in each of these months the House held more divisions than it appointed committees.[37]

The rise of the division and the decline of the committee were the most spectacular but by no means the only changes in parliamentary practice which enabled the parties to dominate political affairs. In January 1646, contention in the House gave rise to a physical confrontation between Walter Long and Francis Allen. Long's temper might be considered a weathervane for tensions in the House, for during self-denial and the debates over the New Model he had assaulted William Cauley.[38] The vivid expression of Long's frustrations could also be seen in the development of questionable parliamentary procedures. On February 1 the House voted that the Speaker was required to inform the members immediately of the presence of messengers from the Lords who were to be admitted promptly into the House. On the same day the Commons found it necessary to revive the order that no new bills could be read after 12 P.M., when many members left the House for committee meetings.[39]

The problem of new business being introduced in the absence of members was complemented by the absence of members when unpopular business was debated in the House. As was seen on those occasions when division to put the question preceded votes on the issue, more members were willing to express opinions on the procedural than on the substantive question. On April 11, for instance, the House debated the petition presented by the Assembly of Divines which many M.P.s considered a breach of privilege. A division ensued on whether to put the question of privilege, and 191 members voted, the majority in favor. On the issue, however, only 164 members expressed opinions.[40] Accordingly, when the crucial vote to remove the king from Scottish custody was taken, Holles and Stapleton attempted to force the hand of those members who refused to commit themselves to any course of action. In an extraordinary motion, they requested that the doors of the Commons House be locked before any votes on the issue were taken. On this motion they were defeated by five votes in a total of 241. Their fears proved justified, as only 218 members voted on the first issue of substance and only 186 on the second. Characteristically, on an intervening motion to put a question 236 members responded by voting.[41] For the time being the leaders of the emerging parties could not force uncommitted members to choose.

These stresses on parliamentary procedure were followed by others. The introduction of a formal agenda began in September, succeeded almost immediately by the suspension of all private business.[42] At the beginning of October, after acrimonious debate over places and preferments, a move to set a ballot box in the lower house was narrowly defeated.[43] Strategies to adjourn or continue daily sessions became so complex that divisions on whether to bring in candles occurred four times during the late autumn. The last such occasion was unintentionally farcical, for the division to bring in candles took place in such darkness that the members could not be counted without the aid of the candles which they had not yet determined to bring in.[44]

IV

If parliamentary procedure and the language used to describe political practice underwent fundamental transformations in the latter half of 1646, so too did parliamentary policy. It was not until the winter that Holles and Stapleton emerged as leaders of an incontestable majority in parliament. The successful negotiation of Scottish withdrawal and English custody of the king resolved the fear of royal alliances and renewed fighting. Policy was now shaped by efforts to ameliorate the economic hardships of the war, to disband or reconstitute the armies, and to constrict the burden of taxation. Since the conclusion of fighting in June, Holles had proposed plans to dissolve the military establishment, reform parliamentary finances, and suppress the Irish rebellion. As his opponents had chosen to prepare for further war and continued taxation, once the tides had turned toward peace initiative passed to Holles. Unrestrained by the procedural safeguards that had enmeshed Pym and no longer controlled by the process of consensus, he was free to pursue a single-minded and coordinated political policy.

The strength of Holles's majority – composed not only of his party followers but of godly Presbyterians, conservative peers, and uncommitted country M.P.s as well – enabled him to attain incomparable power. By his preeminence in securing Scottish withdrawal and preparing the Irish invasion, Holles controlled important standing committees; by introducing legislation across a wide range of issues, he came to report and manage much of the Commons' business with the Lords; and by recasting the Derby House Committee into an executive body, Holles reigned over both the Irish invasion and the military disestablishment, an interconnection which brought the fate of the New Model into his hands. Besides his control of military affairs, personally reporting to the Commons important calculations on troop strengths and financing, Holles was the prime mover of the ordinance for the Great Seal, twice carrying votes to the Lords and once, with Stapleton and Browne, managing a conference. On January 9, 1647, he delivered proposals to the upper house for the regulation of the Admiralty and the Cinque Ports, replacing the usual naval administrative experts Sir Henry Vane, Jr., and Giles Green. When the Scots sent in their final requests prior to surrendering the king, it was Holles who reported the results of a conference with the Lords and who, some days later, drafted a letter of thanks to the earl of Leven. At the beginning of February he and Stapleton were added to the Goldsmiths' Hall Committee and became commissioners when the Committee was expanded. In seven divisions during the first quarter of the year in which he acted as teller, only one was carried against him, and that was on the relatively unimportant question of an appointment for a circuit judge.[45]

In attaining this predominance, Holles left his political opponents desperate. No longer could they expect their proposals to be considered by the full House, where an unsympathetic majority could stifle debate and carry divisions. Nor could they hope to influence the implementation of policy by appointment to the House's customary working committees. The accumulation of power by the Derby House Committee attenuated ordinary administration, and the few committees now called into being were either unmanageably large or carefully composed. The frustrations experienced by Hasilrig and Evelyn were complete. From January to the end of May 1647, Sir Arthur Hasilrig was a teller in fifteen parliamentary divisions, of which he was able to carry just one. Evelyn achieved only slightly better results, telling the majority in four of the fourteen contests which he counted, although two of these victories came when he appeared with members of Holles's party, Sir William Lewes and Sir Philip Stapleton.[46] Moreover, Hasilrig's and Evelyn's inability to influence even the most incidental political decisions was aggravated by Holles's willingness to turn parliamentary procedure to his advantage. Not only were temporary working committees replaced by permanent standing ones, but apolitical administrative committees were jettisoned in favor of the burgeoning Derby House Committee. Even the most undeniable privileges of the house of commons were set aside to further political programs, as when the Lords were permitted to initiate a finance bill or the city allowed to dictate the terms of its loan. The traditional inclusion of spokesmen of differing persuasions had given way to the rule of a tyrannical majority. 'The authority of Parliament,' wrote William White, M.P. for Pontefract, to Sir Thomas Fairfax, is 'that which is passed by a majority of votes however contrary to particular opinions.'[47] The transformation of the political process was as evident in White's need to define parliamentary authority to Fairfax as in the definition itself.

Holles's incontestable power and his inclination to use it without restraint was soon challenged. His plan to dissolve the New Model Army, through subscription for the Irish venture and disbandment without regard for the soldiers' material grievances, brought into focus questions of parliament's underlying authority. The rejection of the soldiers' right to petition for redress of grievances, far more than the grievances themselves, initiated a process of radicalization within the army that centered on parliament and its members. The belief of soldiers and citizens that members of the Houses pursued faction and interest encouraged the

growth of interest groups outside Westminster who claimed the right to
participate in political decision making as a counterweight to the influence
of faction and party in the Houses. In the army especially, parliamentary
policy was interpreted as the actions of only a part of the membership – 'a
design [by their enemies] to ruin and break this Army into pieces.'[48] Thus
was justified the impeachment of the eleven members and the subsequent
march on London. Anthony Nicoll was charged with bringing in twenty-
eight Cornish members 'on purpose to carry on the designs and practices
before mentioned and to make a faction in the said House.' Walter Long
was reviled as 'the Parliament driver' for acting as a whip, leading 'a
faction by votes.'[49] In every particular, the army sanctioned its own
participation in political activity by the unexpected and inappropriate
transformation of parliamentary practice. The confrontation between
parliament and the army in 1647 was not the inevitable resolution of
longstanding political and religious disputes but, rather, the result of the
growth of parties and the emergence of adversary politics.

'To speak a sad truth,' Sir William Waller reflected, when he reconstructed the events which led the army to march on London in July 1647,
'the destruction of the Parliament was from itself.' Like Holles and
Whitelocke, Waller attributed the decline of parliamentary authority to
its failure to suppress the army's incipient mutiny in March, when they
might have 'crushed the cockatrice in the egg.'[50] Their concession had
served only to increase the army's appetite for power and to encourage
its supporters at Westminster 'who prevailed but little, being a known,
engaged, faction.'[51] 'The Parliament fell neither bound nor fettered,'
Waller concluded, 'but betrayed by the insidious practices of its own
members.'[52] Neither in 1647 nor in later years, when these men penned
their apologetic memoirs, did they understand the change they had
wrought in political practice or the consequences that change had for
the system of government they had fought to defend. To them the
explanation for the army's actions in the summer of 1647 was singularly
clear: the army and their party in the house of commons had betrayed
their trust and their nation. As Holles sardonically stated, 'these are they
who fight for privilege of parliament, – who have made a covenant with
God and man so to do: and well they perform it; those they mislike must
be thrust out by head and shoulders; and such as remain, if they be not
obedient to them shall be served with the same sauce; And this is to
make a free Parliament.'[53]

Although the ways to achieve parliamentary freedom and privilege were
contested and the actions of the contenders plainly diminished parliament's authority, the ideal of parliamentary freedom remained unaltered.
Those like Holles who saw only hypocrisy and disingenuousness in the
conduct of their opponents could not perceive how the meaning of parliament and its authority had been transformed; those like the army who

were willing to bring force into the political process could not foresee that in their effort to preserve parliament they might destroy it. Just as the parliamentarians had engaged in war against the king for his own protection, so the army and the city assaulted parliament in its defense. 'All authority is fundamentally seated in the office,' the army declared, 'and but ministerially in the persons.'[54] The authority of parliament, therefore, had been corrupted by parliamentarians and the contaminating influence was manifest to all: the growth of party and interest. Party was antipathetic to the welfare of the nation; it was the advancement of the particular against the whole – the supersession of the public good. In the houses of parliament, parties, whether of malignants who served the ends of the king, recruiters who followed the whip of Walter Long and Anthony Nicoll, supporters of the army, or Holles's clique at Derby House, now predominated.

Constantly the army repeated its opposition to party and interest. 'We do not seek anything of advantage to ourselves, or any particular party whatever, to the prejudice of the whole,' they declared in June.[55] 'We have nothing to bargain for or to ask, either from his majesty or the Parliament for advantage to ourselves or any particular party or interest of our own,' they reiterated in July.[56] As the chain of events which began with the order for piecemeal disbandment moved to its inexorable conclusion, the army justified its extraordinary actions by its opposition to party politics: 'Those worthies who have formerly acted, and carried on things for public good, right and freedom, are now awed or overborn by a prevailing party of men, of other private interests, crept in, and that neither we, nor any other can expect right, freedom, or safety (as private men) or to have things acted in Parliament for public good while the same parties continue there in the same power, to abuse the name and authority of Parliaments, to serve and prosecute their private interests and passions.'[57]

Nor was the army alone in identifying party as a corrosive development in political practice. Holles claimed that the Independents discredited themselves in parliament by being 'a known, engaged, faction.'[58] Prynne argued, in defense of the eleven members, that the army's charge of impeachment was 'only to weaken the Presbyterian party so the Independents might overvote them';[59] while Waller thought the charges made reflected more upon parliament than upon the impeached members of which he was one: 'It resembled an arraignment of the House of Commons, supposing them so weak and corrupt as to be acted by particular interests.'[60] Even the vituperative Clement Walker, the bane of religious Independents, could diagnose the disease, publishing his remarkable backbencher's manifesto, *The Mystery of the Two Juntoes*, in June. The war, Walker reasoned, 'working upon the human frailty of the *speaking and leading* members of the Houses, caused them first to interweave their particular interests, and ambitions with the public welfare, and lastly, to prefer them before the public welfare.' He identified these usurpers as 'Grandees,' the leaders of the 'two factions or juntoes of Presbyterians and Independents.'[61]

It was fitting, then, that the struggle to preserve parliamentary privilege should be conducted by the army and the city through threats of force and violence. For parliament, either in 1646, when it surrendered to city divines and financiers, or in 1647, when it collapsed in the face of a militant army, had proven unable to preserve its institutional prerogatives. It was not coincidental that this confrontation should center upon opposition to parties and interests, upon the repudiation of the transformation that had occurred at Westminster. Although the apprentices could restore the eleven members and the army those who fled the mob's violence, neither could revive consensus. The decline of parliamentary authority – so much the result of the growth of adversary politics – also meant the eclipse of parliamentary legitimacy. This was never better expressed than by Sir Thomas Fairfax. When the king demanded of him 'by what authority he durst thus resist him and his Parliament,' Fairfax forthrightly replied, 'There was necessity.'[62]

The emergence of adversary politics had far-reaching consequences. In the short term it caused the military intervention which transformed civil war into revolution. If the erosion of monarchical authority had engendered the initial conflict, the collapse of parliamentary authority shaped its resolution. Eventually, the diminution of both allowed for constitutional recomposition. The revolution had one ineradicable result: it made parliament a political institution, a permanent and separate part of a system of government. Since Elizabeth I regularized its sessions, the two Houses had groped toward establishing conventions and procedures that would have changed a council into a legislature. Thirteen years of continuous sittings in the absence of executive authority accomplished this transformation.

In another sense, perhaps, adversary politics is an example of 'deep structure,' a reflection of meanings broader and deeper than its own dynamics. Consensus politics resolved conflict in an organic society in which power relationships were carefully ordered and oppositions appeared as physical confrontations to be brutally suppressed. Consensus served to maintain hierarchy by incorporation: allowing for factionalism within levels of the social structure but treating all other conflict as usurpation. Adversary politics reflected a divergence of interests, the separation of towers on San Gimignano, in Lawrence Stone's lucid metaphor.[63] It emerged in parliament as a set of procedures and practices necessary for executive action, but it appeared in the nation as sets of polarities: court and country, king and subject, Puritan and Anglican, Royalist and Parliamentarian. Despite the rhetoric which eschewed 'interest' and the practice which enforced moderation, the organic political nation had become pluralistic. Adversary politics was a means of legitimating interest and absorbing permanent contrariety. If another century would pass before it became systematized, its emergence was another legacy of the English Revolution.

Notes

1 J.H. Hexter, 'Presbyterians, Independents, or Puritans', *P&P*, 47 (1970), p. 135.
2 David Underdown, 'The Independents Reconsidered', *JBS*, 3, no. 2 (1964), pp. 57–84; and *Pride's Purge* (Oxford, 1971), pp. 366–90.
3 Blair Worden, *The Rump Parliament* (Cambridge, 1974), p. 6.
4 J.R. Tanner (ed.), *Constitutional Documents of the Reign of James I, A.D. 1603–25* (Cambridge, 1930), p. 222.
5 Elizabeth Read Foster, 'Petitions and the Petition of Right,' *JBS*, 14, no. 1 (1974), pp. 21–45; C.S. Sims (ed.) 'Policies in Parliament,' *HLQ*, 15 (1951), p. 51. There were, of course, occasional violations of this rule, but as late as 1644 D'Ewes still found them rare enough to be recorded in his journal (BL, Harl. MS 166, fo. 153).
6 Sims, 'Policies', pp. 51, 47.
7 William Hakewill, 'The Manner of Holding Parliaments' (London, 1641), unpaginated.
8 *LJ*, vii. 131, 134–45. In May 1646, when the Commons demanded the peers' reasons for the rejection of a bill, they expressed a similar practice: 'Such a negative answer they hold not to be usual in the proceedings of Parliament; for if one House may give a negative answer without any reasons offered, the other House may adhere without giving any reasons for the same; and so the Houses will have no clear understanding of the grounds of each others' resolutions' (LJ, viii. 314).
9 Sims, 'Policies', p. 50.
10 Wallace Notestein, *The House of Commons, 1604–10* (New Haven, Conn., 1971), p. 441.
11 C.S. Sims (ed.), 'The Speaker of the House of Commons'. *American Historical Review*, 45 (1939) p. 92.
12 Hakewill, 'The Manner of Holding Parliaments', unpaginated.
13 Sims, 'The Speaker of the House of Commons', p. 95.
14 Conrad Russell, 'Parliamentary History in Perspective, 1604–29'. See Chapter 1 above.
15 'The Apology of the Commons', in Tanner, *Constitutional Documents of the Reign of James I*, pp. 222–3.
16 This was equally true in 1640–41, when the initial movement for reform attracted widespread support which dissipated in the Grand Remonstrance controversy over an issue of form rather than substance.
17 Robert Ruigh, *The Parliament of 1624* (Cambridge, Mass., 1971), p. 92.
18 *Oxford English Dictionary* s.v. 'party'; Bulstrode Whitelocke, *Memorials of English Affairs*, 4 vols (London, 1853), ii. 146; Edmund Ludlow, *The Memoirs of Edmund Ludlow*, ed. C.H. Firth, 2 vols (Oxford, 1894), i. 141; Robert Baillie, *The Letters and Journals of Robert Baillie*, ed. David Laing, 3 vols (Edinburgh, 1841–42), ii. 336.
19 Baillie, ii. 410.

20 *D'Ewes*, ed. Wilson Coates (New Haven, Conn., 1942), p. 233. I owe this reference to C.S.R. Russell.

21 Clement Walker, 'The Mystery of the Two Juntoes,' in *Select Tracts Relating to the Civil Wars in England*, ed. F. Maseres (London, 1815), i. 333.

22 Ludlow, i. 147; Whitelocke, 'Annals,' BL, Add. MSS, 37, 344, fo. 4.

23 Lucy Hutchinson, *The Memoirs of Colonel Hutchinson* (London, 1973), p. 166; emphasis added.

24 Walker, p. 334.

25 Denzil Holles, 'Memoirs,' in Maseres (ed.), *Select Tracts Relating to the Civil Wars in England*, i. 250.

26 Hutchinson, *The Memoirs of Colonel Hutchinson*, pp. 7, 166.

27 C.H. Firth (ed.), *The Clarke Papers* (Camden Society Publications, 4 vols, London, 1891–1901), i. 178.

28 *The Parliamentary or Constitutional History of England* (hereafter cited as *O.P.H.*), 24 vols (London, 1751–62), xvi. 151.

29 A.S.P. Woodhouse, *Puritanism and Liberty* (London, 1938), p. 31.

30 *CSPD, 1644–45*, p. 488; D'Ewes, BL, Harleian MS 166, fo. 210; Whitacre, BL, Add. MS 31, 116, fo. 210.

31 See Mark Kishlansky, 'The Emergence of Radical Politics in the English Revolution' (Ph.D. diss., Brown University, 1977), ch. 7.

32 These totals are achieved by counting all divisions except those in which an initial division affirmatively determined whether a question would be put. Their inclusion would strengthen the point but dilute its significance.

33 The thirteen M.P.s who sat on at least thirty committees were Nathaniel Fiennes (41), Henry Marten (40), Denzil Holles (39), John Glynn (36), Edmund Prideaux (35), Sir Henry Vane, Jr. (34), Samuel Brown (34), Sir John Evelyn of Wiltshire (34), Sir Arthur Hasilrig (34), Bulstrode Whitelocke (32), Oliver St. John (31), Sir Philip Stapleton (31), and Francis Allen (31).

34 *CJ*, iv. 399, 423.

35 *CJ*, iv. 428, 444, 426, 478, 490, 518, 523.

36 *CJ*, v. 143, 151.

37 The debate over the appointment of commanders for the Irish expedition aroused such passion that 'Holles and Ireton [were] like to fight a duel' (Harington, BL, Add. MS 46, 374, fo. 53). The Commons ordered their reconciliation (*CJ*, v. 133). On May 27 the House divided on appointing Francis Rivett to a post in Wiltshire. Holles and Stapleton were present both at the debate and at the time the question was put. Neither appeared in the division, and the Speaker directed them to give their votes. Stapleton voted yea and Holles no (*CJ*, v. 187). In March there were ten divisions and seven committees; in April, twelve divisions and eight committees; and in May, fourteen divisions and ten committees.

38 *CJ*, iv. 400; Whitacre, fo. 253.

39 *CJ*, iv. 426.

40 *CJ*, iv. 506.

41 *CJ*, iv. 542.

42 *CJ*, iv. 672, 679, 688.

43 Whitacre, fo. 285; Harington, fo. 45.

44 *CJ*, v. 10.

45 *CJ*, v. 53, 60; *LJ*, viii. 655; *CJ*, v. 63, 73, 72, 76.

46 For Hasilrig, see *CJ*, v. 117; for Evelyn, see *CJ*, v. 57, 76, 99, 107.

47 Firth (ed.), *The Clarke Papers*, i. 103.

48 Henry Cary (ed.), *Memorials of the Great Civil War, 1642–52*, 2 vols (London, 1842), i. 203–4.
49 *O.P.H.* (n. 28 above), xvi. 89, 91.
50 Sir William Waller, *Vindication of the Character and Conduct of Sir William Waller* (London, 1793), p. 152.
51 Holles, 'Memoirs', p. 250.
52 Waller, *Vindication of the Character and Conduct of Sir William Waller*, p. 190.
53 Holles, 'Memoirs', p. 248.
54 Rushworth, *Historical Collections*, 8 vols (London, 1721), vi. 565.
55 Rushworth, *Historical Collections*, vi. 570.
56 *LJ*, ix. 323.
57 Rushworth, *Historical Collections*, vi. 586.
58 Holles, 'Memoirs', p. 250.
59 William Prynne, 'A Declaration of the Officers' and the Army's illegal Proceedings,' BL, Thomason Tracts E. 397 (8).
60 Waller, *Vindication of the Character and Conduct of Sir William Waller*, p. 176.
61 Walker, 'The Mystery of the Two Juntoes', p. 333.
62 *LJ*, ix. 273.
63 Lawrence Stone, 'Social Mobility in England, 1500–1700,' *P & P*, 33 (1966), p. 17.

3

The baronial context of the English Civil War

J.S.A. ADAMSON

When rebellion broke out in England in 1642, the political nation had been, for over a decade, obsessed with medieval precedent and its gothic past. Practices and institutions which had seemed defunct revived, during the 1630s, into new and sometimes controversial life. Trial by combat was reintroduced in appeal of treason in 1631,[1] and confirmed by the judges in 1637 as a legitimate legal procedure even in disputes of property;[2] in 1636 a bishop was appointed to the Lord Treasurership for the first time since the reign of Edward IV;[3] in 1639 England went to war without the summons of a parliament for the first time since 1323;[4] and the following year the Great Council of Peers met, for the first time since the reign of Henry VIII,[5] to deal with a revolt of the Scottish nobility. At court, the king was encouraging a gentleman of his Privy Chamber, Sir Francis Biondi, in his labours on a massive survey of the baronial struggles in England from Richard II to

The Alexander Prize Essay, read 19 May 1989.

Henry VII – a work which, when it appeared in 1641 as *The Civill Warres of England*, was shortly to be endowed with a profoundly ironic topicality.[6]

This essay is an attempt to understand how the contemporary fascination with precedent influenced English politics during a decade in which rebellion affected all three of Charles I's monarchies. It seeks to address two central questions: how did the contemporary preoccupation with medieval precedent affect the terms in which the aristocratic leadership in the civil war defined their conduct and comprehended their experience? And, in particular, how did the attempt to find historically validated solutions to the problem of the 'evil counsels' of Charles I – a problem which was itself defined in medievalised terms – affect the nobility's choice of political options in that decade of civil war?

The definition of the conflict in terms of a baronial war was not one confined to the particular outlook of the parliamentarian nobility. The king set up his standard at Nottingham, not against his parliament, but against the 'late rebellion of the Earl of Essex': so his August ultimatum to parliament declared; so royal pronouncements reiterated throughout 1643.[7] Whatever the truth of this as the *casus belli*, at the outset of the war Essex was widely regarded both as the leader and the personification of the parliamentarian cause.[8] Essex's ascendancy as parliamentarian commander-in-chief entailed a concentration, in the hands of a single individual, of political and military power within the kingdom which had not been seen since the early sixteenth century. It brought with it not only an aristocratic reaction against this over-mighty subject, but also, in its wake, a profound change in the English nobility's attitude to its military tradition – the tradition in which the power and obligations of the nobility were nowhere more honourably exemplified than in the profession of arms and in the command of armies in the field.

I

It is, of course, a commonplace that in early modern England history was the tutor of politics.[9] History provided the frame of reference within which the dilemmas of the present could be compared and contrasted with the experience of the past, and whence remedies and solutions could be sought. It was, affirmed Richard Greenway, the translator of Tacitus, 'as well as a guide, an image of mans present estate, [and] a true and lively patterne of things to come'.[10] Though classical reference forms a regular source of analogy in early seventeenth-century political discourse, (and comparisons between Charles I and Tiberius or Caligula were commonplace), it was not Livy and Tacitus who enjoyed the greatest literary vogue during the early years of the Long Parliament, but works recounting the baronial crises of fourteenth- and fifteenth-century England.

In the years 1640–9, publication on English medieval history reached a peak for the seventeenth century which was not to be approached again until the years of the Exclusion Crisis. With public interest heightened by the revolt of the Scottish nobility in 1639 – a revolt unequivocally baronial in organization, if religious in professed intent – publishers responded with a flood of histories, discourses and annals, chronicling the reigns from Henry III to the defeat of Richard III. This was the period of 'the civill warres of England', as the earl of Monmouth termed it in 1641.[11] Moreover, much of this body of publication was dedicated to, or undertaken by, the friends and clients of, those peers who were associated with the 'commonwealth party' in the house of lords during the early years of the Long Parliament, and subsequently with the parliamentarian cause: with Essex, Warwick, Pembroke and Saye. Nor should this be surprising; for it was these peers who, in advocating a restoration of the medieval great offices of state, stood most to gain from a revived, baronial view of the nobility's role as a counterpoise to the arbitrary powers of kings. In the three years between 1641 and 1643 there were no less than 15 large-scale histories of the period of the Wars of the Roses,[12] and a large number of shorter works and extracts from the Parliament Rolls.[13]

Parliament's *Nineteen Propositions* – the rejection of which was the immediate catalyst for its decision to raise an army[14] – were steeped in, and informed by, this heightened awareness of the medieval past. It was an awareness most strikingly evident in the provisions for the re-establishment of the ancient 'great officers of the kingdom': the Lord High Steward and the Constable of England. These were to be restored, not as ceremonial functionaries, appointed for specific occasions, but as permanent officers of the realm wielding the full range of powers enjoyed by (or attributed to) their medieval predecessors.[15] The *Nineteen Propositions* legislated for a revolution in government: a separation of the spheres of the king's household and the commonwealth's government. Repudiated was the system of government in which intimacy of attendance on the king, rather than noble birth and status within the commonwealth, determined the efficacy of a counsellor's advice;[16] in place of government by privy chamber or bedchamber was to be a baronial council, dominated by the magnates and great officers of state.[17] Its intended effect was, as the king correctly understood, 'to depose both our self and our posterity'.[18]

How was this virtual deposition to be achieved? The table of precedence listed in the *Propositions* is here highly significant. The first officers of the kingdom were to be the Lord High Steward of England, and the Lord High Constable – offices which had been claimed respectively, by the earl of Essex's step-grandfather, Leicester, and his father, the 2nd earl.[19] After these two revived medieval officers[20] ranked the Lord Chancellor, the Lord Treasurer, the Privy Seal, Earl Marshal, Lord Admiral, Warden of the Cinque Ports, Chief Governor of Ireland, Chancellor of the Exchequer, the Master of the Wards, and the two Secretaries of State. These officers, nominated by parliament, were to be the representatives of the 'common- wealth' within the council.[21] The king still had free nomination of the officers of his household – the Lord Great Chamberlain, the Steward and Chamberlain of the Household, and the other domestic officers; and these could still be sworn of the council. But as the council was to have a maximum number of 25, it was the 13 'officers of state' who, in any full council meeting, would always constitute a majority of one. Here was a reassertion of the role of the Lords Appellant[22] in checking monarchical power, their authority now founded not on the medieval power-base of retainers-in-arms, but on the legislative authority of a parliament in which the nobility and gentry cohered. From this perspective, parliament was, in Henry Parker's phrase, 'the admirable Councell of Aristocracy'.[23]

These propositions, sent from the Lords and later approved by the Commons, were carefully constructed to locate their radical redefinition of the powers of the crown within an ancient, and thus legitimizing, historical tradition. The figure of twenty-five, as the maximum for the new privy council, was hardly coincidental; it identified the new council with the tradition of the 'twenty-five persons from all the peers of the kingdom' described in the *Modus Tenendi Parliamentum*, the most widely circulated of all the medieval parliamentary texts in early Stuart England.[24]

Two questions here arise. What powers did the framers of the *Nineteen Propositions* intend the Steward and Constable to possess? And why was it that these offices, so prominent in the agenda of 1642, disappear from lists of officers of state in the parliamentary peace terms proposed after 1645? To the second of these questions I hope to suggest an answer later in this paper; first, let us take the question of their powers.

It was of course from amongst the authors of the propositions – from the circle of Northumberland, Essex, Saye,[25] Pembroke, Mandeville and Brooke – that the parliament was most likely to appoint such officers. (Indeed, Pembroke had been already nominated to the Lord Stewardship of the Household by the Commons in August 1641.)[26] Perhaps the clearest indication of their future intentions may be gleaned from a tract published in October 1642, a week before the battle of Edgehill, under the aegis of Essex and Mandeville. It has been possible to trace the manuscript from which this tract was printed, which was MS Titus CI in the Cottonian Library.[27] Cotton had scrupulously recorded the removal of manuscripts from his library – in particular the removal of a series of tracts in 1630, when the library was sealed on the orders of the Privy Council, by Mandeville's father, the Lord Privy Seal, the 1st earl of Manchester.[28] Amongst these papers, which included Fortescue's treatise 'de dominio politico et regali',[29] was this Titus manuscript, and a collection of anti- quarian tracts. Thereafter the Titus manuscript remained at Manchester

House and was not returned until after the civil war. Intended as a polemical work, it reflects the attitudes of Essex's and Mandeville's circle within the Lords to the authority and jurisdiction of the great officers of state.[30]

The treatise attributed to the Steward and Constable quasi-regal powers.[31] Citing a 'an old booke of Parchmine' once in the possession of Recorder William Fleetwood – the fourteenth-century *Treatise on the Steward* – the tract printed in 1642 argued that the Steward's jurisdiction was 'immediately after the *King*, to oversee and governe the whole Kingdome of *England*, and all the Offices of the Justice . . . in all times both of Peace and Warre'.[32] Yet that which spoke most pertinently to the circumstances of 1642 was the power of the Steward and Constable to prosecute the king's 'evill Counsellours'.[33] If, after admonishment, the king would not rid himself of any who was reputed 'amongst the people . . . to bee an evill Counsellour to the King', the two great officers of state possessed almost unlimited powers.

> Then for the Weale Publick it is lawfull for the Steward, Constable of *England*, noble men and other of the Commonaltie of the Realme, with Banner in the Kings name displayed to apprehend such Counsellour[s] as common enemie to the King and the Realme.[34]

Thus, when parliament sent its *Nineteen Propositions* to the king in the summer of 1642, the peers at Westminster had a clear perception of the nature and extent of the powers they were seeking to revive: by October 1642 (when this tract appeared), parliament's new Lord General, Essex, was already asserting his claim to the Constableship.[35]

In the context of October 1642, publication of the treatise on the medieval great officers[36] was part of a political campaign, directed by Essex, to confer upon himself protectoral rank and power. Giustiniani, the Venetian Ambassador (whose informants in the house of lords included Feilding and Holland), had reported in mid-September that Essex was resisting requests that he advance against the king because 'he is anxious to induce Parliament to declare him [High] Constable of England first, and to grant him despotic powers for conducting the war, as well as to negotiate and conclude the [agreement] with the king'.[37] It was as part of these attempts to define Essex's role in the war in terms of the Constableship that his allies published the tract on the great officers – including the translation of the medieval tract on the Steward – in the week before Essex encountered the king at Edgehill.

As the earl of Essex, likened to, and armed with the powers of, the High Constable, marched out with his army to do battle with an enemy characterised, in equally gothic terms, as the king's evil counsellors, the war of 1642 seemed to some at Westminster disconcertingly like a barons' war. Contributing powerfully to this perception was the manner in which the conflict had escalated over the summer, and the nobility's expectations as to how the contest was to be resolved once battle was joined.

II

Throughout the country, over the summer and autumn of 1642, rival peers vied with each other for control of the kingdom's arsenals and its places of military strength. Lord Brooke confronted the earl of Northampton in Warwickshire;[38] Lord Fairfax the earl of Cumberland in Yorkshire; Pembroke the marquess of Hertford in Wiltshire; peers – either as parliamentarian Lords Lieutenant or as royalist Commissioners of Array – sought to rally support and outmanoeuvre opponents in a series of trials of local strength. Public perceptions of the opening of the war were dominated, not simply by the clash of 'parliamentarian' and 'royalist', but by a series of localized aristocratic struggles for regional control. With a third of the English nobility leading armies in the field[39] – a figure comparable with the baronial conflicts of the fourteenth and fifteenth centuries – it was the battles of barons and viscounts, marquesses and earls, that dominated published (and contemporary private) accounts of the war. A contemporary diarist entered his account of Edgehill, not as a battle between king and parliament, but between 'the king and the Earle of Essex'.[40] In the pamphlets and newsbooks which related the fighting, the national conflict was particularised in titles such as *Lord Falkland's encounter with the Earl of Essex's Forces before Worcester,* or the *True relation of the late fight betweene the Earle of Manchesters Forces and the Marquesse of Newcastles Forces.*[41] Forces were referred to by the name of their aristocratic commanders even more often than as 'Cavaliers' or the 'Parliament's forces'. Lord Falkland crowed over his 'encounter with the Earle of Essex Forces before Worcester';[42] accounts of major battles, such as the first battle of Newbury in 1643, where the earls of Caernarvon and Sunderland and Lord Falkland met their deaths, inevitably stressed the combatants' rank and status, and the peers' personal engagement in battle. The way the war was conducted, and reported, in the years before the creation of the New Model Army in 1645, threw the military role of the nobility into high relief.

The opening of the civil war, then, suggested obvious parallels with the baronial conflicts of the past. These parallels were emphasized in the rhetoric in which parliamentary and royalist pronouncements were cast: in the royalist enemy characterised as 'evil counsellors', and in a parliamentarian party cast as the abettors of a 'rebellion of the earl of Essex'. Thus, even at the battle of Edgehill, the king could offer free pardon 'to both officers and soldiers', 'verily believing that many of his Subjects, who are now in actual Rebellion against him, are ignorant against whom they fight'.[43] In the conduct of the war, the perception of the conflict as a baronial war had its correlative in the chivalric code by which the fighting was engaged. Nowhere was this more strikingly apparent than in the issuing of challenges to personal combat and to trial by battle. Even before the battle of Edgehill, when royalist and parliamentarian forces had already mobilised in Warwickshire, Lord Brooke offered, to 'avoyde the profusion of bloud', that he and his royalist opponent, the earl of Northampton, 'might try the quarrell by the sword in single combat'.[44] According to Edward Howard, son of the royalist earl of Berkshire and an officer in the king's army, a similar scene was enacted by the earl of Lindsey, the king's commander in chief, in the opening stages of the battle of Edgehill. And early in 1643, the royalist earl of Newcastle challenged Lord Fairfax to trial by battle, self-consciously evoking 'the Examples of our Heroicke Ancestors'.[45]

The archaic formalities of the challenge to combat testify to a perception, shared by the principal participants, that the war was taking place within a tradition of aristocratic conflict – or, from the king's perspective, of aristocratic rebellion – a tradition which dictated the combatants' code of behaviour.[47] Clarendon, a hostile witness, was convinced that Essex's sense of chivalry would have prevented him from joining battle at Edgehill had he realised the king was present in the field.[48] To Essex, the adversary was not the person of the king, but his fellow privy councillors amongst the nobility who, he held, had persuaded the king to tyrannous courses of action.[49] It was to vindicate himself against these opponents, while observing the clause in his commission to preserve the safety of the king's person, that Essex returned to the expedient of trial by battle in July 1643. Then, in what was perhaps the most gothic moment of the civil war, parliament's commander-in-chief proposed that the war be determined by a single, set-piece battle, on condition that the king absented himself from the field.[50]

These challenges to combat cannot be understood outside the contemporary political and historical culture which informed the opening stages of the civil war. The *locus classicus* for the challenge to trial by battle was the challenge issued in 1398 by Henry of Lancaster to Richard II's 'evil counsellor', the duke of Norfolk – accounts of which were published on the eve of Essex's rebellion of 1601,[51] and again in 1641, 1642 and 1643. In most versions, the challenge to trial by battle was accompanied by an account of Bolingbroke's denunciation of the evil counsellors of Richard II. Sir John Hayward's version – republished in 1641, again in two further editions in 1642, and widely plagiarized – gives the essence of the charge. Bolingbroke launched

> into [a] complaint, how the King regarded not the Noble Princes of his bloud and Peeres of the Realme, and by extremities used to some, discouraged the rest from intermedling in any publique affaires; how

instead of these, hee was wholly governed by certaine new-found and new-fangled favorites, vulgar in birth, corrupt in qualities, having no sufficiency either of councell for peace, or of courage for warre.[52]

This was an indictment of the king's disregard for the counsels of his nobility which spoke directly to the framers of the *Nineteen Propositions*. Although it went through three editions during 1641–42, it had first appeared in 1599 under the patronage of the 2nd earl of Essex. Then it had been read as a thinly veiled attack on the dominance of Cecil.[53] When it was reprinted in 1642, on the eve of the second Essex rebellion, Henry of Lancaster's accusation had a similar contemporary force: as a protestation of the nobility's right to govern the counsels of the king.

So the challenges to combat issued by Brooke, Lindsay and Essex in the first years of the civil war were part of a political and chivalric culture in which the challenger identified himself with virtuous counsel, and with the nobility's 'just rights'. Only in this context do the opening moves of the battle of Edgehill, or Essex's offer of trial by battle in 1643, cease to be eccentric anachronisms and attain a coherence as part of a political culture which comprehends such diverse phenomena in Caroline England as the revival of trial by combat and the Great Council of Peers, the literary vogue for medieval history, and the proposals for the re-creation of the great medieval offices of state.

III

It is against this background that the figure of Essex needs to be reassessed: the soldier-turned-statesman whose role as protector of the commonwealth during the first half of the 1640s was to create so influential a precedent for Oliver Cromwell in the succeeding decade. It was natural in a kingdom habituated to personal monarchy that the alternative to government by Charles I should be thought of in terms of a figure endowed with quasi-monarchical powers. The appointment of a *custos regni*, such as had governed during the minority of Henry VI,[54] had been suggested as early as 1641.[55] Various forms of protectoral office – from the *custos regni* of 1641, the 1642 Captain-Generalship, and the Governorship of the King's Children of 1645 – were suggested, and tried, to fill the vacuum in the exercise of monarchical power. Essex's commission of appointment as commander-in-chief in 1642 created him Captain-General, an office linked with protectoral or vice-regal rank.[56] The king, for one, did not miss the significance of Essex's title: in a proclamation significantly entitled 'for the suppressing of the present Rebellion under the Command of Robert Earle of Essex', the king declared that Essex 'hath assumed unto himself those Titles [sc. the Captain-Generalship]', and begun to execute 'those Powers and Authorities which are inconsistable with Our Soveraignty'.[57]

Public protocol reinforced this identification of Essex's Captain-General-ship with constabular or protectoral rank. From his appointment as Captain-General, Essex (who stood in precedence after such ancient titles as those of the 10th earl of Northumberland or the 10th earl of Kent), assumed a status which out-ranked all the other peers in parliament. More-over, members of the house of commons were required to make the utterly baronial undertaking 'to live and die with the earl of Essex' in this cause.[58] From 11 August 1642, this oath to Essex became as much a test for member-ship of the house of commons as the oaths of allegiance and supremacy had been before the outbreak of the war.[59] The oath was, strictly, an oath of fealty. From Essex's point of view, as his later conduct demonstrated, the oath brought the Lords and Commons close to being his liege men.[60] '*Vive le Roy et Essex*, God save the king and Essex', Lord Robartes claimed in September 1642, would henceforth be the Commons' cry.[61] Lord Robartes's suggestion that Essex's name would be joined in the traditional royal acclamation – as '*Vive le Roy et Essex*' – takes on heightened significance when placed beside the protocol and civic ceremonial that attended the Captain-General.[62] Alone amongst the parliamentarian commanders before 1645 was Essex distinguished by the honorific title 'His Excellency'. Alone of the commanders during the civil war, Essex was permitted to stage 'triumphs': state entries into the City on his return from successful campaigns.[63]

Essex's entry into the City after Edgehill, in November 1642, was explicitly modelled on Charles I's royal entry in November of the previous year. Just as at the king's entry, Essex was received by the City dignitaries outside the City walls, where after speeches and homage from the City fathers, he entered London by Moorgate,[64] tracing the route to Guildhall, and then on to Whitehall, that had been followed by the king only twelve months before.[65] As on that occasion, the streets were thronged with spectators; and on his arrival at Westminster Essex was presented with formal addresses, congratulatory verses,[66] and a royal gift of £5,000 – actually paid – by the Commons.[67]

Much of the language used in the parliamentarian propaganda of 1642–3 describes Essex in terms of almost religious reverence.[68] Devout but simple souls in the garrison of Wallingford in 1643 placed credence in reports that Essex was the returned Saint John the Baptist.[69] And so unparalleled was Essex's place in history, Daniel Evance thought in 1646, that future patriotic Englishmen would even train their parrots to 'prate great Essex's name'.[70]

The civic pageantry attending Essex's second formal entry into the City in September 1643, after the Gloucester campaign, made his claim to vice-regal status still more bluntly. Essex was acclaimed by the City Militia forces at their formal review in Finsbury Fields.[71] This time, however, Essex did not go to Whitehall to receive the thanks of parliament.

In a carefully orchestrated and highly significant change of procedure, now it was the members of the two Houses and their Speakers who gave attendance in the presence chamber at Essex House – not the earl who attended the Houses at Westminster. At Essex House, the Speaker presented humble addresses before the victorious Lord General as before a king. After homage from the two Houses, 'the Mayor and Aldermen of London came in their scarlet gowns to him.' Whitelocke noted, 'and highly complemented him, as the protector of them and their fortunes'.[72] The only parallels for such homage from the two Houses were royal. And regal ceremonial on a scale of unparalleled magnificence and self-consciously archaic pomp attended Essex's funeral at Westminster Abbey in October 1646: the parliamentary contribution alone was £5,000.[73] The only comparable display in recent memory had been the royal funeral of James I in 1625.[74] No contemporary could have failed to notice the obvious political claim symbolized in these exhibitions of vice-regal status and power.

For such was the power which Essex claimed: the power of a medieval Constable, or the unlimited commission of a Roman dictator. In January 1643, three months after he had claimed the Constableship, Essex again declared – through his secretary, Henry Parker – the extent of the power he sought. 'As our dangers now are', wrote Parker, 'it would bee good for us to adde more power to the Earle of *Essex* . . . for till I see him lookt upon, and served as a temporary Dictator, and the bounds of his Commission to bee only this, *ne quid detrimenti capiat Respublica cavere*,[75] I shall never think the Parliaments safety sufficiently provided for'.[76] This classical political vocabulary encoded Essex's claims to protectoral, vice-regal authority, and became an increasingly important element in the Lord General's propaganda after the triumphal entry into London in September 1643. The Latin account of Essex's victories, issued with the authority of the house of lords in 1644 and directed to a European audience, spoke pointedly of Essex as 'Robertus, Supremus Imperator'.[77]

Regal ceremonial and a classical rhetoric of unlimited civil and military power did not pass without provoking a nervous reaction amongst Essex's erstwhile equals in the house of lords. Essex, no longer *primus inter pares*, but now recognizing no equal but the king, posed a classically baronial problem: that of the over-mighty peer attempting to dominate politics in an acephalous kingdom. As Essex's ascendancy brought in its train an aristocratic reaction against the extent of his authority, the nature of the problem recommended a series of equally baronial solutions. The first clear signs of misgivings had appeared after Essex's triumphant return to London in September 1643, when the two Houses and the City fathers had given attendance in person at Essex House. Within a week of that act of homage it had been proposed that the duke of Gloucester, the king's youngest son, then in the custody of parliament, should be appointed

'Constable of England by Ordinance of Parliament, and then Menage the warre in his Name'.[78]

The aristocratic reaction of that September was, however, nugatory in comparison to the furore of January 1644, when both houses of the royalist parliament at Oxford petitioned Essex to mediate a peace.[79] Presented to Essex on 30 January, the petition's form was as significant as its content. Unlike previous approaches to Essex on this subject, it was not simply a letter, but a formal address of the parliament, engrossed on parchment;[80] those who petitioned for his mediation included the Prince of Wales and the duke of York, and all the peers and commons of the Oxford Parliament. As with the Westminster Parliament's addresses at Essex House, the only precedents for such formal, engrossed addresses from the two houses of a parliament were submissions to a Protector or to a reigning king.[81]

For the Lord General's fellow peers at Westminster, acknowledgement of Essex's protectoral status by loyal parliamentarians was one thing; acknowledgement by a royalist parliament at Oxford quite another. Peers such as the earl of Northumberland and Viscount Saye and Sele, who themselves hoped to exercise a formative influence on the terms for peace, felt most acutely the threat of Essex's ascendancy. Their response was almost immediate. Two days after Essex received the Oxford parliament's supplication, Saye introduced into the house of lords a radical new bill intended to usurp Essex's supremacy of command.[82] Exploiting the Scots' hostility towards an English Captain-General who claimed jurisdiction over the deployment of their forces, Saye put forward his proposal to concentrate executive power in a Committee of *Both* Kingdoms, a powerful executive to be composed of a small contingent of English parliamentarians, meeting with the Commissioners of Scotland.[83] Henceforth, the Committee would be empowered 'to order and direct whatsoever doth or may concern the managing of the war' and 'whatever may concern the peace of his Majesty's dominions'[84] – the two areas of policy which Essex had sought to appropriate as his proprietary concerns.[85]

Yet one who had tasted such power was not so easily to be tamed. Throughout the campaigning season of 1644, Essex showed a lofty disregard to the new Committee's orders and remonstrations. His own political objectives remained as they had been in 1642: the rescuing of the king from his 'evil counsellors'; and pursuit of a negotiated peace, a peace which comprehended moderates at Oxford – such as Dorset and his own brother-in-law, Hertford – in the membership of a reformed privy council.[86] These political principles dictated his military strategy. So long as he could dominate the terms of the settlement as commander-in-chief, the purpose of war was not to inflict a crushing military defeat on the king's forces, but merely to secure a strategic superiority whereby both sides would not only have to reach a compromise, but have to reach a compromise in which Essex was architect of the peace.[87] Ironically, Essex's claim to vice-regal status rendered him far more acceptable to Charles I as a party to negotiation than the institution of parliament for which he had so adamant a contempt. In November 1643, shortly before the presentation of the Oxford Parliament's Address, Charles confided to the duke of Richmond that while he could never do business with a parliament, he would deal with Essex or with none at all.[88]

It was against this background that the king made a second overture for peace, in August 1644, again acknowledging Essex's role as mediator between himself and parliament. Addressing himself in terms almost of equality, Charles invited Essex to join forces with him to impose a settlement that guaranteed Essex's dominance of the future government. The king was scarcely exaggerating when he wrote: 'you have at this time in your power to redeeme your country and the crown, and to obleidge your King in the highest degree, . . . Such an oppertunitie as, perhaps, Noe subiect before you euer had, or after you shall haue'.[89] United, their power would be irresistible. And should anyone be so foolhardy as to oppose this alliance, the king added with characteristically sinister philanthropy, 'Wee will make them happie, by Godds blessing, euen against their wills'.[90]

It is here, at Lostwithiel in August 1644, that the origins of the Self-Denying Ordinance – the final phase of the aristocratic reaction against Essex in both Houses – are to be found. Essex's decision to advance into the west towards the king's army had been against the expressed instructions of the Committee of Both Kingdoms, to which Essex was now nominally subordinate.[91] Misgivings as to Essex's military objectives were now heightened by the prospect that he might accept Charles's offer and turn against the Scots.[92] 'This with other things', Saye declared in 1646, 'then laid the foundations in mens hearts of that resolution, which soon after was put in execution, to new Model the Army, and put the Command into other hands'.[93] To those who had been the promoters of the alliance with the Scots – to Saye, Northumberland, St John and the younger Vane – the disaster of Essex's army in the west-country was parliament's Cannae; but it was also a providential reprieve: had Essex been in a position of strength in August 1644 that would have guaranteed his personal bargaining position with the king, a conjunction of the boundlessly ambitious Essex and a king who had offered him 'all possible meanes of assurance to the publique and to his own perticular if he would consent vnto it'[94] seemed all too close and terrible a possibility.

So the problem posed at Westminster by Essex was not simply military; indeed, the memory of his brilliant victories at Gloucester the previous year had not yet been effaced. Essex posed a political problem: the baronial problem of a noble with a military power-base, claiming protectoral or constabular rank, exercising a corresponding authority, and heedless of the instructions even of parliament itself. It is in this context that the origins and effect of the military reforms of the winter of 1644–5 – the famous

Self-Denying Ordinance, the creation of the New Model Army, and the appointment of Sir Thomas Fairfax as Lord General – need to be re-examined.

The principal object of the Self-Denying Ordinance – the chief instrument of these reforms, removing members of both Houses from civil and military command – was widely perceived to be the dismissal of the earl of Essex.[95] As with the bill to establish the Committee of Both Kingdoms, one of the principal moving spirits behind this ordinance was Viscount Saye. On 9 December 1644, he moved in the Lords for the resolution for 'self-denial' – that all members of both Houses should give up the civil and military offices that had been conferred since the outbreak of the war; that day, almost certainly by prior arrangement, Zouch Tate, then chairman of the Committee for the Lord General's Army, moved the same motion in the house of commons.[96]

If the Self-Denying Ordinance and the replacement of Essex by Sir Thomas Fairfax as Lord General solved the military aspect of this problem, it did not solve the political problem caused by the protectoral status Essex had claimed, and been accorded, particularly within the capital. (Even in May 1646, more than a year after his enforced resignation as Captain-General, he was presiding at the general muster of the City forces as commander-in-chief, despite the absence of any statutory authority for such a role.)[97] The attempted solution to this aspect of the problem was a second piece of legislation – introduced at the same time as the Self-Denying bill, and clearly part of the same process of reform[98] – elevating the 10th earl of Northumberland to the Governorship of the King's Children, and giving him the status of Lord Protector in all but name. Northumberland, the senior peer attending the house of lords, was to have free choice of any of the royal residences;[99] was to have custody of the dukes of Gloucester and York, and Princess Elizabeth;[100] and he was to take precedence over all others peers – including, now, the deposed earl of Essex – in the protocol of the house of lords.

The vice-regal figure of Essex was to be supplanted by a figure, resident at St James's, of even more explicit vice-regal pretensions.[101] With the establishment of this court at St James's[102] came the revival of the Board of Green Cloth to oversee expenditure in Northumberland's state household,[103] and a spate of appointments to vacant household offices in which Northumberland's own household servants acquired offices in the reconstituted royal household at Whitehall and St James's. Northumberland's Gentleman of the Wardrobe, Lancelot Thorneton, for example, acquired the title of Clerk of the Robes and Wardrobe to the king in 1646.[104] The following year Northumberland spent the staggering sum of £3,077 on what his accountant modestly described as 'a rich Coach' – a magnificently ornamented coach drawn by six coach horses – nominally for the duke of

York, but used by Northumberland in his journeys from St James's Palace to the parliament.[105]

If the elevation of the earl of Northumberland represented the baronial solution to the problem of the status claimed by Essex, the intimate connexion between the political and military aspects of that solution was epitomized in the new prominence assumed by Robert Scawen, Northumberland's secretary and the steward of Syon House, as chairman of the Army Committee[106] – the standing committee charged with overseeing the financial and logistical supply of the army, and with maintaining relations with its new commander-in-chief, Sir Thomas Fairfax.[107] Not surprisingly, much of Scawen's work was undertaken from his master's houses: from Northumberland's state residence of St James's: [108] from his newly acquired Suffolk House;[109] or, as during the army negotiations of autumn 1647, from Syon House.[110] As the recent work of Dr Starkey has emphasised,[111] the functions of the 'household' and of the bureaucracy of the state were intimately linked in early modern England; to this the government erected by the nobility during the English civil war was no exception.

Thus the new-modelled army was not to provide Gardiner's janizaries of the 'puritan revolution'; nor was it – as has been argued – a balanced and essentially apolitical response to the military misfortunes of 1644.[112] Military disaster in the west, and Cromwell's suspiciously timely feud with the earl of Manchester,[113] provided the occasion for reform. But the palace coup of 1645 – the coup which installed Northumberland in St James's Palace and demoted Essex, the claimant of the Constableship, to the earls' benches in the house of lords – was merely the culmination of a conservative aristocratic reaction to the phenomenon of Essex which had its origins in the peers' first nervous reaction to the vice-regal status he had successfully claimed in his 'triumph' – the triumph of a self-styled 'Supremus Imperator' – back in September 1643. The makers of this coup in the Lords were, almost to a man, the scions of Tudor privy councillors: Salisbury, Nottingham, Howard, Pembroke, North; or those whose claim to be *consiliarii nati* was even more ancient: men such as Northumberland, Kent, Dacre and Saye. Their ideas for a blue-print for the future government were to find expression in Saye's projected settlement of 1647.[114]

The political and baronial causes of the coup affected both the choice of Essex's successor, and the terms upon which he assumed his command. Fairfax inherited Essex's honorific title as 'his Excellency'; but otherwise he entered upon an office radically transformed. There was to be no fealty sworn to the new commander-in-chief; no ceremonial entries into the capital at the conclusion of successful campaigns. Following on the towering and charismatic figure of Essex, invested with the mystique of Leicester and the martyred 2nd earl, Fairfax – the scholarly soldier, apparently lacking in either interest or acumen for politics – seemed an able and maleable choice. Indeed, after Essex, Fairfax's mediocrity in politics commended him to the Saye-Northumberland interest at Westminster no less than his distinction in the field. This recipient of Essex's military office was, moreover, a loyal upholder of the Percy interest in his native Yorkshire, and a friend of the earl of Northumberland – upon whom the political mantle snatched from Essex had so recently been cast.[115]

Nothing witnesses to the transformation of the status of the Lord Generalship so clearly as the change in the ceremonial and civic ritual that attended its two incumbents. Essex's formal entries into the City were characterised, as we have seen, by vice-regal ceremonial, second only to that which attended the king at his entry into the City in November 1641. Until Essex's removal from command in 1645, these entries were annual events.[116] Fairfax's treatment was otherwise. Up to Pride's Purge, the Lord General was permitted only one formal entry into the City. In August 1647, after the abortive 'Presbyterian' coup of July, he made a triumphal entry into the City at the head of his troops, returning the Speakers to the two Houses and the Saye-Northumberland peers, to whom in large measure he owed his command, to an unrivalled dominance of the house of lords. The symbolism of the procession was highly significant. Fairfax entered, not as Charles I and Essex had done, riding a charger – the formal equestrian entry of a Renaissance *triumphator* – but riding in a domestic coach, as the prelude to a magnificent cavalcade of the peers in their coaches, led by Northumberland in his magnificent new state coach.[117]

The political meaning of such a change in the civic ceremonial associated with the Lord Generalship was not lost on contemporaries. It was 'such a deep dissembled ceremony', observed one M.P., 'that no man but saw through it, and did beleeve, with reason, that the *Members* brought his Excellency to the Parliament, and not he them'.[118] When Essex received the thanks of parliament in 1643, the two Houses had waited on him in person at Essex House; when Fairfax received thanks from the Speakers, it was normally by post. Essex had at times seemed parliament's master; Fairfax, for the moment at least, seemed its employee – a circumstance which sharpened the point of Presbyterian taunts that the New Model was 'a mere mercenary army'.

Changed too were the conventions by which the war was to be fought. Gone were the self-conscious evocations of baronial wars: the challenges to combat, the oath 'to live and die' with the Lord General, the chivalric scruples over the safety of the person of the king. The new war of 1645 was to be professionalised and efficient, fought to victory by an able general, apparently innocent of political ambition – to a victory which left power with an oligarchic faction at Westminster, not with a Lord General with aspirations to constabular rank.

With a redefinition of the purpose of war went a repudiation of the two great military offices of state: the Stewardship and the Constableship, the two offices which had outranked all others in the propositions of 1642.

From the preparation of the Uxbridge Propositions, formulated contemporaneously with the military reforms over the winter of 1644–5, the Stewardship and Constableship were dropped from the list of the offices of state. Henceforth, the two senior officers of state would be the Chancellorship (already exercised as if in commission by the allies of the Saye-Northumberland group),[119] and the Lord Treasurership, to which Saye openly aspired.[120] Amongst the old nobility and their Commons allies at Westminster, the experience of what might be termed the baronial phase of civil war – during the years of 1642–4 – had provoked an oligarchic reaction. For this group at Westminster, their political power base was to be, even more emphatically than before, the control of place, patronage, and the effective working of their parliamentary 'interests' in the two Houses.

The redefinition of the political function of the army was embodied in the new commission to Fairfax as Lord General. Passed, against the staunch opposition of Essex's faction in the Lords,[121] the new commission omitted any reference to 'saving the safety of the King's person', which had been the touchstone of Essex's baronial conception of the war as a crusade against evil and papist counsellors. The war that was renewed in 1645 was to be fought, as Charles had long since perceived, to reduce him to the status of 'a Doge of Venice'.[122] The peers who effected the political coup of 1645 were fighting a war, in Lord Brooke's phrase, 'to reduce [the king] to a necessity of granting'.[123] There was more than a little truth in the charge of the royalist ballad-monger that

> You must have places and the Kingdomes sway,
> The King must be a Ward to your Lord *Say.*[124]

The power-base of the nobility that displaced Essex was not to be the ability to mediate a settlement through the dominance of personal military command (one of the traditional roles of the nobility), but through the command of a complex patronage machine, in parliament and in the bureaucracy of the state; through the triumph of an aristocratic oligarchy buttressed by an obedient and effective military force. Throughout the years 1646–7, it was the Saye-Northumberland group in the house of lords, and their allies in the Commons, who fought most doggedly to oppose the disbandment of the army they had themselves 'new-modelled'.[125] The ancient military power base of the nobility, personal command of armies in the field – a power base upon which Essex had effectively built in the early years of the war – was effectively dismantled in England after 1645.

During the 1650s it was also dismantled literally. The passing of the 'military age' of the nobility was starkly symbolized by the demolition and slighting of castles throughout the country, enforced during the years immediately after the second civil war.[126] Castles such as Basing, Raglan, Warwick and Belvoir – the fortified bastions of the medieval nobility – had proved to be of dangerously contemporary use in England's most recent experience of civil war.[127]

By the reign of Charles II, a radically different attitude to military power and military service held sway among the nobility. Peers continued to hold at least nominal posts of command; but more for the lucrative trade in commissions this afforded than for zeal for martial honour in the field. After the great causes of the early seventeenth century – the heroic campaigns of Maurice of Nassau or of Gustavus Adolphus – the prospect of service in Bombay or Tangiers simply did not have the same cachet.[128] When, in 1688, the nobility again found it necessary to depose a king, it imported a foreign army to do its work. In little more than a generation there had been a profound change in the nobility's attitude to military command.[129] In 1640, as in 1340, generalship of armies in the field had been seen as the natural concomitant of noble status; by 1700, it had become the forlorn last choice of the noble younger son too stupid to find another more lucrative career.

Of course there were exceptions. Eminent military command remained a route of entry into the peerage for General Monck as for General Haig. Even after the Restoration, a few peers of ancient lineage continued to make their careers in war. Aubrey de Vere, 20th earl of Oxford, was a professional soldier into the reign of William III.[130] But he was a lone survivor of that antediluvian generation which had gone in search of martial honour in the Low Countries before the civil war.[131] Dodo-like, he lumbered on to the opening of the eighteenth century; but with his death in 1703, his illustrious and indigent title became extinct. Yet the martial tradition he represented had long since predeceased him. And, in the feudal ceremonial of 1646, amid the regal pomp attending the obsequies of the Captain-General of England's last baronial war, it had had its fitting interment.

Notes

1 College of Arms, Arundel MS LIV (Procs. in the Court of Chivalry, 1631–2); Bodl. L., MS Additional c. 79 (notes of the trial of Lord Reay); P.H. Hardacre, 'The Earl Marshal, the Heralds, and the House of Commons, 1604–41', *International Review of Social History*, 2 (1957), pp. 106–25; HMC, *Mar and Kellie MSS* (1904), pp. 184–192.
2 CUL, Add. MS 7569 (misc. 17th cent. papers), fos. 41–3; *Claxton v. Lilburne*, printed in Rushworth (8 vols, 1680–1701), II, pp. 788–90.
3 William Juxon was appointed Lord Treasurer in 1636; the last bishop to hold the office was William Grey, bishop of Ely, who was Lord Treasurer 1469–70.
4 C.S.R. Russell, *The Fall of the British Monarchies* (Oxford, 1991).
5 Bodl. L., MS Tanner 91, fo. 187 (historical notes, c. 1640).
6 Sir Giovanni Francesco Biondi, *An History of the Civill Warres of England, betweene the two Houses of Lancaster and Yorke* (2 vols, 1641–6).

7 See the king's proclamation of 9 Aug. 1642; and his offer of pardon to the rebels at Edgehill, 24 Oct. 1642: *An exact collection of all remonstrances* ([Husbands's collection], 1643), pp. 503–7, 673; cf. the king's proclamation of 27 Oct. 1642, *An exact collection of all remonstrances*, pp. 675–7. *Two speeches spoken by the earl of Manchester, and Jo. Pym* ([13 Jan.] 1642[3]), p. 9.

8 Essex's role in the parliamentarian war effort is discussed below.

9 Cf. Barnabe Barnes, *Fovre books of office: enabling privat persons for the speciall seruice of all good princes* (1606), p. 168. Degory Whear, *Relectiones hyemales, de ratione et methodo legendi ultrasque historias* (Oxford, 1637). Whear was Pym's tutor at Oxford; and the first edition of the work, in 1625, was dedicated to William, 3rd earl of Pembroke: (1625 edn), sig. ¶ 2. See also, D.R. Woolf, 'Change and Continuity in English Historical Thought, c. 1590–1640' (unpublished D. Phil. thesis, University of Oxford, 1983); *idem*, 'The True Date and Authorship of Henry, Viscount Falkland's *History of the life, reigne, and death of King Edward II*', *Bodleian Library Record*, XII (1988), pp. 440–52; K. Sharpe, *Sir Robert Cotton* (Oxford, 1979). *English Historical Scholarship in the 16th and 17th centuries*, ed. Levi Fox (Publ. of the Dugdale Soc., Oxford, 1956). Pauline Croft, 'Annual Parliaments and the Long Parliament', *BIHR*, 59 (1986), 167. L.L. Peck, *Northampton: Patronage and Policy at the Court of James I* (1982), ch. 6.

10 The work's printer, Richard Whitaker, was associated with Saye's faction in the house of lords: for his relations with Saye, see V. Malvezzi, *Discourses upon Cornelius Tacitus* (1642), sig. A2, ep. ded. from Whitaker to Saye.

11 Biondi, *The Civill Warres of England*, title page and sig. a.2.

12 Esp. Sir Thomas More, *The Historie of the Pitifvll Life, and unfortunate death of Edward the fifth* (1641); Sir Robert Cotton, *A Short View of the Long Life and Reigne of Henry the Third* (1641); J[ohn] T[russell], *A Continuation of the Collection of the History of England . . . being a Compleat History of the begining and end of the Dissention betwixt the two houses of York and Lancaster* (1641); Sir Francis Bacon [Viscount St Alban], *The Historie of the reigne of King Henry the Seventh* (1641); Sir Richard Baker, *A chronicle of the kings of England* (1643); cf. George Buck, *The History of the Life and Reign of Richard the Third* (1646), dedicated to the earl of Pembroke, and reprinted in 1647.

13 Sir John Hayward, *The History of the Life and Raigne of Henry the Fourth* (1642), one of many works republished in the 1640s with its original (1599) dedication to the 2nd earl of Essex. Thomas Merke, bishop of Carlisle, *A Pious and Learned Speech delivered in the High Court of Parliament, 1 H[enry] 4* [1642] – a work reprinted during the Exclusion Crisis, and again in 1689 (Wing, M 1826–7, S 4868A). For extracts from the Parliament Rolls, see, e.g., *The Bloody Parliament in the Raigne of an unhappy Prince* ([9 Feb.] 1643), printing part of the Parliament Roll for 10 Ric. II. For the printing of the medieval tract of the Steward see, *Certaine Observations touching the two great Offices of Seneschalsey . . . and High-Constableship of England* (17 Oct. 1642). Bracton had been reprinted in 1640: Henricus de Bracton, *De Legibus et Consuetudinibus Angliae Libri Quinque* (1640).

14 *CJ*, ii, pp. 668–9; *LJ*, v, pp. 204–6. Cf. BL, Add. MS 33374 (Jones of Gellilyfdy papers), fos. 19v–20.

15 There had not been a regular High Steward of England (to be distinguished from the domestic office of Steward of the Household) since the death of the duke of Clarence at the battle of Beaugé in 1421: L.W. Vernon Harcourt, *His*

Grace the Steward and Trial of Peers (1907), p. 191. The nature of the powers the Lord Steward was intended to enjoy by the framers of the *XIX Propositions* is discussed below.

16 David Starkey, 'Court History in Perspective', in *idem* (ed.), *The English Court: from the Wars of the Roses to the Civil War* (1987), pp. 1–24.

17 *LJ*, v, pp. 97–9; S.R. Gardiner, *The Constitutional Documents of the Puritan Revolution 1625–1660* (3rd edn, Oxford, 1906), pp. 250–4.

18 Charles I, 'Answer to the *XIX Propositions*', printed in Rushworth, V, pp. 728–32. *LJ*, v. p. 97; Gardiner, *Constitutional Documents*, p. 251.

19 I am grateful to Professor Wallace MacCaffrey for a discussion of the 2nd earl of Essex's claim to the Constableship. In the late 1590s (when Essex made his claim to this office and the Earl Marshalship), as in 1642, it was an office which (possessing vice-regal powers) would have been of particular importance in the event of the monarch's death.

20 These two great offices were omitted from the table of precedence in Henry VIII's Act of Proclamations: 31 Hen. VIII, c. 8, § 4.

21 Gardiner, *Constitutional Documents*, p. 251 (*XIX Propositions*, § 2).

22 A. Tuck, *Crown and Nobility 1272–1461* (1985), pp. 191–8.

23 [Henry Parker], *Observations upon some of his Majesties late Answers and Expresses* (1642), p. 24. Parker's *Observations* were written in response to the king's *Answer to the XIX Propositions*. For Parker's links with the circle which drafted the propositions, see J.S.A. Adamson, 'The *Vindiciae Veritatis* and the political creed of Viscount Saye and Sele', *HR*, 60 (1987), pp. 60–1.

24 'Modus Tenendi Parliamentum', § xvii; printed in N. Pronay and J. Taylor, *Parliamentary Texts of the Later Middle Ages* (Oxford, 1980), p. 87; the text is common to both the 'A' and 'B' recensions of the Latin *Modus*. For the earl of Arundel's copy, College of Arms, Arundel MS XLI. A copy of the *Modus* is the first item listed as having been found in Saye's study when it was searched for seditious and subversive papers at the conclusion of the Short Parliament: Bodl. L., MS Tanner 88*, fo. 115. As most legally literate members of the Long Parliament would have been aware, these twenty-five, summoned by the Steward, the Constable and the Earl Marshal, had power to deal with political crises – where 'there is discord between the king and some magnates', or where there was a division within the peerage ('Modus', ed. Pronay and Taylor, 87). Similar passages attributing particular significance to twenty-five men chosen from the parliament appear in the medieval *Treatise on the Steward*, versions of which were almost as widely circulated as the *Modus* itself: BL, Cotton MS Vespasian B VII, fo. 100 (for other copies, bound with the *Modus*: Cotton MS Nero CI, fos. 1–5^V; Landsdowne MS 522, fos. 6^V–7^V). Other treatises on the Steward, Marshal and Constable frequently accompanied copies of the *Modus*: BL, Cotton MS Domitian A XVIII, fos. 15^V–22 (*Modus*), fos. 23–35 ('Officium Marescalli et Constabularii Anglie'). BL, Add. MS 32097 (William Lambarde's copies of 15th century treatises), fos. 13–21. Harcourt, *Steward*, pp. 164–7; Pronay and Taylor, *Parliamentary Texts*, p. 27n.

25 SRO, Hamilton MS, GD 406/1/1658: Saye to Hamilton, 3 June 1642: the reason for Saye's omission from the drafting committee was that he was suffering from 'a feavorish distemper' and was not well enough to attend the House; as his letter to Hamilton indicates, the propositions clearly expressed his own aspirations for the settlement of the kingdom.

26 Christ Church Muniment Room, Oxford, Nicholas Box (Evelyn collection): earl of Pembroke to Edward Nicholas, 29 Nov. 1641. *LJ*, iv, p. 355.

27 BL, Cotton MS Titus CI; the 'emperor system' for the classification of the

Cottonian Library was not introduced until after Cotton's death in 1631, though it appears to have been operative by 1639: C.G.C. Tite, 'The Early Catalogues of the Cottonian Library', *British Library Journal*, 6 (1980), p. 148.

28 BL, Harl. MS 6018 (1621 catalogue of the Cotton Lib.), fos. 178, 184: the volume is listed as 'A booke of collections of many things concerning the office of the steward, Constable, and especially the Marshall of England' (fo. 184).

29 BL, Harl. MS 6018, fo. 184.

30 BL, Cotton MS Titus CI. These papers, presented to the Society of Antiquaries, were almost certainly the source of the copies made for the earl of Northumberland (Alnwick Castle, Northumberland MSS 541–2). For Hakewill's employment in antiquarian research by the earl of Northumberland during the early 1640s, see KAO, De L'Isle MS U 1475/A 98 (Northumberland's general account for 1640; a stray from the Alnwick archives). The notes on 'The Office and Jurisdiction of the Constable and Marshall of England' [c. 1640s], drawn from 'Mr [Francis] Thynns Collectio[n]' (Bodl. L., MS Tanner 91, fos. 186–9) derive from a later copy of the treatises in Cotton MS Titus CI.

31 BL, Cotton MS Titus CI (Antiquaries' tracts), fos. 26–32; printed as *Certaine Observations tovching the two great Offices of the Seneschalsey . . . and High Constableship of England* (17 Oct. 1642). It was printed for Laurence Chapman, a stationer later associated with the publication of the *Scotish Dove*.

32 *Certaine Observations*, sig. B[r–v].

33 *Certaine Observations*, sig. B2.

34 *Certaine Observations*, sig. B2[v].

35 Christ Church Muniment Room, Oxford, Nicholas Box (Evelyn collection): Pembroke to Nicholas, 29 Nov. 1641. There was little doubt as to who would be the incumbents of the offices. The earl of Pembroke, whose household vied in size and splendour with the royal court, had been nominated by the Commons to the Lord Stewardship as early as August 1641: *LJ*, iv, p. 355. On the size of Pembroke's household see [George] Sedgwicke, autobiographical narrative, printed in J. Nicholson and R. Burn, *History and Antiquities of the counties of Westmorland and Cumberland* (2 vols, 1777), i, p. 296: '[Pembroke's] family [sc. household] in London was for the most part about 80, in the country double that number'. Sedgewicke was Pembroke's man-of-business at London and one-time assistant to Michael Oldisworth as secretary to the earl. Pembroke's palace at Wilton was conceived on a scale larger than any building attempted by any monarch since Henry VIII.

36 Cf. BL, Cotton MS Vespasian C XIVB, fos. 98–101[v]. The treatise published by Mandeville and Essex was possibly one of a series prepared for Essex's father in 1597, when the 2nd earl was pressing his claim to the Constable's office, by the antiquary, Francis Thynne; cf. Peck, *Northampton*, p. 241n. It is possible that Robert Bowyer's collection of notes on 'Honor and Armes', made in 1598, which examined at length the powers of the Constableship, was prepared in connexion with this claim: BL, Add. MS 12191 (Bowyer's notes), fos. 117–125. In advancing his claim to the Constableship in 1642, Essex was aided by the common identification, advanced in official and unofficial polemic alike, between the crusade against Charles I's evil counsellors, and the attacks on Edward II's favourite, Piers Gaveston, and the parliamentary assault on the evil counsellors of Richard II in 1388. The association first gained currency during the attack on Strafford in 1641: see 'The Earle of Strafford Characterized', [March] 1641: Strafford's favour with the king was thought to 'have beene purchased and bought from the peoples affections at a higher price then all the

Privadoes of Edw. the Second, or Rich[ard] the 2[n]d, for that this onely man [Strafford] hath cost and lost the King and Kingdome more trasure and loyalty then Pierce of Gaveston, the Two Spencers, and Marques of Dublin [in 1387–8] did ever cost their masters, being put together'. Bodl. L., MS Rawlinson D 924 (misc. papers), fo. 139[V]. This letter seems to have been widely circulated in MS; for a contemporary copy see KAO, Foulis MS U 1886/L 26. The Lords' committee that drafted the resolution declaring in 1642 that the king intended to make war on parliament, accompanied their votes with extracts from the Parliament Rolls of 11 Richard II (justifying the Constable's proceedings against evil counsellors), and 1 Henry IV (confirming Richard's deposition): *LJ*, v, pp. 76–7. The committee which drafted these resolutions consisted of Northumberland, Essex, Mandeville, Saye, Brooke, Holland, Leicester and Paget. It was Northumberland who characteristically, on 16 May 1642, reported to the House that before proceeding further in answering the king's messages, precedents should be searched. *LJ*, v, p. 66.

37 Giustiniani to the Doge and Senate, 18 Sept. 1642: *CSP Ven.*, 1642–3 (1925), p. 154.

38 Thomas Johnsons, *Some speciall passages from Warwickshire* ([Aug.] 1642), 1–5 (BL, E 109/3).

39 J.B. Crummett, 'The Lay Peers in Parliament, 1640–44' (D. Phil. dissertation, Manchester, 1972), appendix XIV.

40 Bodl. L., MS Rawlinson D 141 ('Certaine memorable accidents', anon.), p. 47.

41 *A true relation* (1643), relates a fight which took place on 11 Oct. 1643.

42 *A letter sent from the Lord Falkland . . . vnto the . . . earle of Cvmberland* (York, 30 Sept. 1642), sig. A2.

43 Proclamation, 23 Oct. 1642: *The Parliamentary or Constitutional History of England* (24 vols 1751–62), xi, 471 (hereafter, *Old. Parl. Hist.*). The proclamation was intended to be read by the Clarencieux herald before Essex's army on the day of the battle.

44 Bodl. L., MS Eng. Hist. e.240, 35–6; printed as 'The Genealogie, Life and Death of the Right Honourable Robert Lord Brooke', ed. P. Styles, *Miscellany I* (Publications of the Dugdale Society, Oxford, 1977), p. 178. The 'Genealogie' was written in 1644 by Thomas Spencer, a chaplain who had served in the household of the 2nd Lord Brooke. See also the contemporary account of the incident in *Englands losse and lamentation occasioned by the death of . . . Lord Brooke* ([9 Mar.] 1642[3]), sig. A2[V].

45 Edward Howard, *Carololoiades, or, the Rebellion of Forty One* (1689), p. 37. (I owe this reference to Mr John Sutton.) *A Declaration of . . . the Earle of Newcastle* ([?] Feb. 1642[3]), p. 9. The challenge was, in effect, a formal accusation of treason, a process that had been employed before the king himself at the trial by battle of Lord Reay in 1631, a trial at which Lindsey presided as High Constable of England. This gave particular significance to the king's choice of Lindsay as commander-in-chief, as Lindsey's adversary at Edgehill in Oct. 1642, Essex, had claimed the Constableship only the month before. Essex was to be opposed by an earl of equal distinction who had already held, on the *king's* terms, the very office which Essex was seeking to claim. For Reay's trial, College of Arms, Arundel MS LIV (Procs. in the Court of Chivalry, 1631–2); Bodl. L., MS Additional c. 79. Cf. Also, Sir George Clark, *War and Society in the Seventeenth Century* (Cambridge, 1958), ch. 2 'The Analogy of the Duel'.

46 *Old. Parl. Hist.*, xi. 471.

47 Challenges to combat were not, however, confined to officer peers. For a challenge from Sir William Balfour's son to a royalist officer in Col. Lunsford's

regiment: *A copy of a letter from his Excellencie, Robert Earle of Essex* ([Sept.] 1642), pp. 2–3 (BL, 100.b.22). John Lilburne, an officer in Essex's army who also thought of the war in profoundly historical terms, issued a challenge to the royalist court martial which condemned him in November 1642. Demanding a sword, Lilburne challenged Prince Rupert and the earls Rivers and North-ampton, 'telling them he desired to die in single opposition, man to man, with any there'. Lilburne knew the precedents well: his father, Richard Lilburne, had caused consternation to Justice Berkeley at the Durham sessions in 1638, when he arrived with a champion 'in Array', 'who cast his Gantlet into the Court', to offer trial by battle with a Durham neighbour with whom he had a long-standing property dispute. Rushworth, ii, 788–90; for the back-ground to the case: P. Gregg, *Free-born John: a Biography of John Lilburne* (1961; 1986 edn), pp. 72–3.

48 Edward Hyde, earl of Clarendon, *The History of the Rebellion*, ed. W.D. Macray (6 vols, Oxford, 1888), ii, 355–6 (Bk vi, § 79n). Propaganda issued on Essex's behalf throughout the war repeatedly emphasised his chivalric behaviour: see, for example, *The earle of Essex his desires to the Parliament* (13 Aug. 1642), p. 3.

49 Cf. William Bridge, *A sermon preached unto the voluntiers of the City of Norwich* (30 Jan. 1642[3]), pp. 17–18.

50 Essex to Speaker Lenthall, 9 July 1643: printed in W.B. Devereux, *Lives and Letters of the Devereux, Earls of Essex* (2 vols, 1853), ii. 367–9. V.F. Snow, *Essex the Rebel* (Lincoln, Nebr., 1970), pp. 371–2.

51 On Hayward and the circle of the 2nd earl of Essex, M.E. James, 'At the crossroads of the Political Culture: the Essex Revolt, 1601', in *idem, Society, Politics and Culture: Studies in Early Modern England* (Cambridge, 1986), pp. 418–23.

52 Sir John Hayward, *The History of the Life and Raigne of Henry the Fourth* (1642 edn), pp. 90–6.

53 James, 'At the Crossroads of the Political Culture', p. 420. Cecil claimed Hayward's history was intended to make 'this time seem like that of Henry IV, to be reformed by him [Essex] as by Henry IV' (James, 'At the Crossroads of the Political Culture', citing *CSPD, 1598–1601*, p. 555).

54 J.S. Roskell, 'The Office and Dignity of Protector of England, with Special Reference to its Origins', *EHR*, 68 (1953), p. 194.

55 PRO, SP81/51/2, fo. 215: the elder Sir Henry Vane thought that a *custos regni* would be appointed before the king's departure for Scotland in the summer of 1641.

56 The two most famous of his predecessors in the office were Lord Protector Somerset (created 'Locumtenens [Regis] ac Capitaneus Generalis pro Guerris et Bellis' in 1548) and, in the 1580s, the earl of Leicester – with whose supposed monarchical ambitions Essex was frequently associated. Thomas and Leonard Digges, *An Arithmetical Warlike Treatise named Stratiotikos* (1590), sig. Aij (ep. ded. to Leicester), and ch. xxiii: 'The Lord General', esp. pp. 305, 307, 315; the first edition appeared in 1579. Roskell, 'The Office and Dignity of Protector', p. 229.

57 *An exact collection* (1643), p. 504 (proclamation of 9 Aug. 1642); *Stuart Royal Proclamations Vol. II: Royal Proclamations of King Charles I, 1625–1646*, ed. James F. Larkin (Oxford, 1983), p. 791.

58 *CJ*, ii, 668–9; *LJ*, v, 206, 208.

59 *CJ*, ii, 715 for the resolution; for examples of the oath being tendered to M.P.s, *CJ*, ii, 741, 743, 755–6, 765, 767, 774, 784, 787, 802, 810, 822, 832, 874.

60 When relations between the Lord General and parliament became strained, Essex was quick to remind the Commons of their solemn undertaking to adhere to him as leader and protector of the parliamentary cause. The terms of the oath to Essex were frequently reiterated in parliamentarian propaganda, particularly after such crises as Waller's plot, in June 1643: *A Declaration of the Lords and Commons . . . setting forth the Several Plots* ([5 June] 1643), 16 (BL, E 105/5).

61 *The Resolution of . . . the Earle of Essex his Excellence* ([9 Sept.] 1642), 2–4, 5 (BL, 100 b. 21).

62 Robert Codrington, *The Life and Death of the illustrious Robert, Earle of Essex* (1646), 14; on the traditional royal processional route through the City, D.M. Bergeron, *English Civic Pageantry 1558–1642* (1971), pp. 118–21; and *idem*, 'Charles I's Royal Entries into London', *Guildhall Miscellany*, iii (1970), pp. 91–7. Corporation of London R.O., MS 86.5 (Accounts of extraordinary disbursements of the Chamber, c. 1640–60).

63 Codrington, *Life of Essex*, p. 38.

64 For the king's entry in 1641, *The Subjects Happinesse, and the Citizens Joy* (1641), sig. A2; *Ovatio Carolina* (1641); Robert Withington, *English Pageantry: An Historical Outline* (2 vols, Cambridge, Mass., 1918–20), i. 238–9. For Essex's triumphal entries of 1642–4, the place of meeting outside the walls was either Finsbury Fields or Moorfields.

65 Devereux, ii. 360; *LJ*, v, 441.

66 For the presentation of congratulatory verses as part of Charles I's formal entry in 1641: Withington, *English Pageantry*, i. 238–9.

67 *A Continuation of Certaine Speciall and Remarkable Passages* (4–11 Nov. 1642), 4 (BL, E 127/3); for the payments, BL, Add. MS 5497 (Parliamentary papers, 1642–9), fo. 56r–v. Compare the gift presented to Charles I in November 1641: Corporation of London R.O., City Cash Book 1/4, fo. 146v–8.

68 The congratulatory ode which marked Essex's and Warwick's return to London in November 1642 claimed that henceforth 'children shall rejoyce/In their first language, and the common voyce/Shall be to chaunt soft Hymnes and pleasant layes/To Noble Essex and brave Warwicks praise'. *London's Ioyfull Gratulation and Thankfull Remembrance for their Safeties* ([11 Nov.] 1642), 7 (BL E127/1).

69 *The Journal of Sir Samuel Luke*, ed. I.G. Philip (3 vols, Oxfordshire Rec. Soc., 1950–3), i. 76.

70 Daniel Evance, *Justa Honoraria: or, Funeral Rites in honour to the Great Memorial* (1646), 14. John Wild thought that if Essex had died in ancient Rome, he would have been deified: J. W[ild], *An Elegie upon the Earle of Essex's Funerall* ([29 Oct.] 1642), BL, E359/11.

71 *Merc. Civicus*, no. 18 (21–28 Sept. 1643), 141; Bodl. L., MS Rawl. D. 141, 'Certaine memorable accidents', 150–1. On this occasion the troops were reported to have declared their undertaking to serve Essex personally 'when soever his Excellence (their Heroick Generall) should command their service': Codrington, *Life of Essex*, p. 38; for the attendance of the Lord Mayor and aldermen at Temple Bar: Codrington, *Life of Essex*, p. 38. See also, G.A. Raikes, *The History of the Honourable Artillery Company* (2 vols, 1878–9), i. 128.

72 Mount Stuart, Rothesay (Isle of Bute), MS 196 D. 13 (Diary of Bulstrode Whitelocke), fo. 63^V; most of this account is also to be found in BL, Add. MS 37343 (Whitelocke's Annals), fos. 275^V–6. The capitalization of 'Protector' is, perhaps, revealing. The wearing of scarlet gowns by the Lord Mayor and

alderman was also the traditional form of apparel for the reception of the king: John Taylor, *Englands Comfort, and London Ioy* (1641).

73 *LJ*, viii, 490, 507, 508, 533, 540–2.

74 PRO, LC 2/6 (Lord Chamberlain's dept., accounts of James I's funeral), fo. iv. The total cost of James's funeral was £16,520 – a total which included the cost of hanging the interiors of the principal royal houses near London with mourning cloth, and providing mourning clothes for the members of the royal household. Essex's funeral was on a par – in terms both of cost and magnificence – with the royal funerals of the early seventeenth century. On the importance of Essex's funeral, see the perceptive remarks of Miss Sheila Lambert, 'The Opening of the Long Parliament', *HJ*, 27, (1984), pp. 286–7.

75 This was the so-called 'ultimate decree' of the Roman Senate: cf. Cicero, *Pro Nilone*, XXVI. 70.

76 [Henry Parker], *The Contra-replicant, his Complaint to His Majestie* [31 Jan. 1643], 19. Cf. Richard Vines, *The Hearse of the Renowned . . . Robert, Earle of Essex* ([29 Oct.] 1646), 30–1: 'You . . . looked out for a *Dictator*', Richard Vines reminded both Houses in Essex's funeral sermon, 'and happily pitcht your eye and choyce upon this man'; (delivered 22 Oct. 1646).

77 *Descriptio rerum guestarum in expeditione, quam suscepit illustrissimus heros, Robertus Comes Essexiae, Supremus Imperator* ([14 April] 1643 [*recte* 1644]), title page; Sir Philip Stapilton, the commander of Essex's body-guard was termed the Tribune of the Praetorian Guard, the imperial bodyguard: *Descriptio rerum guestarum in expeditione*, 5. The Lords' order for its publication is dated 1 November 1643: *Descriptio rerum guestarum in expeditione*, sig. E[1]. For the English original, see *A true relation of the late expedition* (1643), BL, E 70/10.

78 KAO, Sackville MS U 269/C267/19: the earl of Bath to the countess of Bath, 1 Oct. 1643.

79 Text printed in *Old Parl. Hist.*, xiii. 59–61, 73–77; for Essex's reply, addressed to the earl of Forth, 30 Jan. 1644: Devereux, ii. 390. *The Copy of his Excellency the Earle of Forth's letter to the Earle of Essex* (Oxford, 7 March 1644), 1–5.

80 BL, Add. MS 37343 (Whitelocke's Annals), fo. 286r–v. Whitelocke, who claimed to have been consulted by Essex for advice as to how to reply, described the document as 'a parchment rowle' (BL Add. MS 37343 (Whitelocke's Annals), fo. 286^r).

81 Devereux, ii. 390.

82 For the text of this first bill: *CJ*, iii, 504; printed in Gardiner, *Constitutional Documents*, pp. 273–4; the bill pointedly gives the earl of Northumberland precedence (as a 10th earl) over Essex, who should otherwise have outranked all other peers as Captain-General. For Essex's precedence, BL, Add. 37343 (Whitelocke's Annals), fo. 285v. The establishment of the committee is discussed in W. Notestein, 'The Establishment of the Committee of Both Kingdoms', *American Historical Review*, 17 (1911–12), pp. 477–95, where the authorship of the bill is ascribed to the younger Vane (p. 482). Notestein offers no evidence to support this assertion; and there is no reason to suppose that Saye, who introduced the bill, was not also its draftsman. *LJ*, vi, 405; *CJ*, iii, 384; *Merc. Aulicus* 7th week (11–17 Feb. 1644), 828 (BL, E 35/27).

83 BL, Add. MS 37343 (Whitelocke's Annals), fo. 287^V: the English contingent was to consist of 7 lords and 14 members of the Commons, to be 'a joint Councell'. The question of the committee's size was controversial; 'the fewnes of the number', Whitelocke observed, 'distasted many who were left out'. The nobility was disproportionately well represented on the committee, for although

the English contingent was composed according to the usual ratio for parliamentary committees (two Commons to one peer), peers predominated amongst the Scottish Commissioners; the effect at meetings was to make the overall ratio of peers to Commons much closer to one-to-one than one-to-two. The proposal for such a joint committee first emerged in Saye's circle in a positional paper drafted by Saye's nephew, Henry Parker, in the summer of 1642. Its publication, in a limited edition of 50 copies, was paid for by Sir John Danvers; and the proposal was presented to the marquess of Hamilton in June 1642. See H[enry] P[arker], *The Generall Junto, or the Councell of Union* (1642), and Thomason's MS note to his copy, BL, 669 fo. 18/1; and Sir John Danvers to Hamilton, 1 July 1642: SRO, Hamilton MS GD 406/1/1700.

84 *CJ*, iii, 504. BL, Harl. MS166 (D'Ewes's diary), fo. 7.

85 The Committee of Both Kingdoms supplanted the authority of the (exclusively English) Committee of Safety, a Committee which was staffed by Essex's household men, and which acted as an extension of his commissariat. PRO, SP 28/261–262 (Cttee of Safety papers); many of these papers are in the hand of Henry Parker, who doubled as secretary to the Committee of Safety and secretary to the earl of Essex. Denzell Holles and Sir John Meyrick, two of Essex's staunchest supporters in the Commons, were conspicuously absent from the ranks of the new Committee of Both Kingdoms, even though they had formerly served on the Committee of Safety. For the lame duck existence of the Committee of Safety after February 1644, see PRO (Kew), WO 47/1 (Ordnance Office, entry bk of orders 1644–5), 8, 14, 26, 35; Holles continued to attend the Committee of Safety's meetings throughout 1644: e.g., Ordnance Office, entry bk of orders 1644–5, 35, 40, 57.

86 BL, Add. MS 18980 (Prince Rupert corr., 1642–3), fo. 60: Sir Edward Nicholas to Prince Rupert, 11 May 1643. William Salt Library, Stafford, Salt MS 509: Essex to Prince Rupert, 22 June 1643. (I owe this last reference to Dr David Smith, of Selwyn College, Cambridge.)

87 Cf. the peace initiative proposed by Essex after his triumphant return from the Gloucester campaign in September 1643, when his political stock was at its highest. Through his secretary, Henry Parker, Essex advocated the disbandment of both armies, and a readmission of moderate royalist councillors (such as his brother-in-law, Hertford), to the parliamentary deliberations on the settlement of the kingdom: [Henry Parker], *The Oath of Pacification: or a forme of Religious Accommodation* (1643), 22, 29–30.

88 Leeds Castle, Kent, Fairfax MS, unfol.: duke of Richmond and Lennox to Rupert, 12 Nov. [1643].

89 BL, Add. MS 27402 (Misc. historical papers), fo. 79: Charles to Essex, from Liskeard, 6 Aug. 1644.

90 BL, Add. MS 27402 (Misc. historical papers), fo. 79: Charles to Essex, from Liskeard, 6 Aug. 1644; cf. Prince Maurice and others to Essex, 8 Aug. 1644: Devon R.O., Seymour MS 1392 M/L 16/1644/54.

91 *CJ*, iii, 504.

92 BL, Add. MS 27402 (Misc. historical papers), fo. 80. The bearer of the king's letter, John Richard, explained to Essex that the offer was made for '[the] common end of preseruing this Kingdom from a Conquest by the Scotts, and from vtter ruine and desolation'. John Richard would have been familiar to Essex as he was in the household of the earl's brother-in-law, the marquess of Hertford, and seems to have acted as Hertford's man-of-business at London: Longleat, Seymour Papers, Box V, fo. 30.

93 [Viscount Saye and Sele], *Vindiciae Veritatis* (1654), p. 52.

94 BL, Add. MS 27402 (Misc. historical papers), fo. 80: summary by John Richard of what was said at the presentation of the king's offer to Essex, 7 Aug. 1644.

95 Essex, *A Paper Delivered into the Lords House . . . at the offering up of his Commission* (1645), p. 3 [*recte* 5].

96 John Vicars, *Magnalia Dei Anglicana. Or Englands Parliamentary-Chronicle* (1646), pp. 74–5; for Saye's involvement in the management of the legislation, *ibid.*, 130, and [Saye], *Vindiciae Veritatis*, p. 53. *CJ*, iii, 718.

97 Bodl. L., MS Clarendon 28, fo. 40[V]: newsletter, 21 May 1646.

98 Vicars, *Magnalia Dei Anglicana*, 127–30. The conference on Fairfax's officer-list, approval of which made the creation of the New Model almost inevitable, was on 18 March 1645; Northumberland's appointment was approved by the Lords on the same day. Bodl. L., MS Tanner 60, fo. 86 (report on the custody of the king's children); PRO, SP 16/511/62. *LJ*, vii, 277, 317.

99 PRO (Kew), AO 1/2429/79 (Surveyor of the Works, decl. acc., 1647–8). Northumberland chose to reside in St James's Palace; his apartments were at the west end of the queen's chapel. *CJ*, iv. 270.

100 Bodl. L., MS Tanner 60, fo. 86. HLRO, M[ain] P[apers] 14/4/45, fo. 80; *CJ*, iv. 270.

101 Alnwick Castle, Northumberland MSO. I. 2(f): Northumberland to Hugh Potter, 23 Dec. 1646; Northumberland MS O. I. 2(g): the earl to Potter, 22 Dec. 1646. PRO, SP 16/513, fo. 64 (notes made by Northumberland, *c.* 7 Feb. 1646).

102 *The History of the King's Works*, (ed.) H.M. Colvin, iv (1982), 241–252; v (1976), fig. 21 (facing 247), for a plan of the palace. The palace had been extensively ornamented by Charles I: the king's collection of antique sculpture was housed there, and Van Dyck's 1633 equestrian portrait of Charles I hung at the end of the gallery.

103 PRO, SP 16/539/300 (investigation into the accounts of Cornelius Holland, Clerk of the Green Cloth to the Prince, 2 Aug. 1645); PRO, SP 16/515/84.

104 Petworth House, Sussex, MS 629; PRO, SP 28/251/1, fo. 343v. *LJ*, viii, 663, 680.

105 Alnwick Castle, Northumberland MS U. I. 6, Gen. acc. 1646–7: 'for a rich Coach and sett of Coachhorses'. A royalist writer who saw the coach in April 1647 described it as a costly 'French Embrodered Coach [with] 6 excellent Coach horses'; it was also used by the royal children for drives in Hyde Park: Bodl. L., MS Clarendon 29, fo. 165.

106 PRO (Kew), WO 47/1 (Ordnance Office, entry bk of orders 1644–5), 245 (order signed by Scawen); for Scawen's activities in general see, *ibid.*, 211–345. Claydon House, Bucks., Verney MS: Henry Verney to Sir Ralph Verney, 17 April 1645. For Essex's reconciliation with the Scots – perhaps the most remarkable *volte face* associated with the coup – see, HLRO, Willcocks MS 1: Essex to Manchester, 23 March 1645; and Dr Williams's Lib., MS 24.50 (Juxon diary), fo. 37[V].

107 PRO (Kew), WO 47/1 (Ordnance Office), 211–345. The committee was occasionally referred to as the Committee for the Army and Contracts (WO 47/1, 291). Scawen gradualy supplanted Zouche Tate (chairman of the other army committee in January 1645), who was in ailing health: *CJ*, iv, 26. As usual in the parliamentarian bureaucracy, the most effective members of the administrative committees were the nobility's men-of-business. Thomas Pury senior, who occasionally deputised for Scawen as chairman of the committee, was a client of (and later executor to) the earl of Pembroke, and intimately connected with the Saye-Northumberland interest which had pushed through

these political and military reforms. For Pury, see also PRO, SP 28/257 (Army Cttee papers), unfol.; SP 28/28/4, fo. 309; SP 16/514, fo. 15; for his connection with Pembroke: Sheffield Central Lib., Elmhirst MS 1352/11; Elmhirst MS 1360, fo. 6; with Salisbury: Hatfield, A. 44/8; he gave evidence on behalf of Nathaniel Fiennes at his trial in 1644: W. Prynne and C. Walker, *A true and full relation of the prosecution . . . of Nathaniel Fiennes* (1644), sig. Aa2^V. Pury also served on the vestry of the parish of St Martin-in-the-Fields, a body that was stacked with the clients of the parish's chief inhabitants, Northumberland, Pembroke and Salisbury: Westminster Public Lib., MS F 2517, fo. 22.

108 PRO (Kew), AO 1/2429/79 (Surveyor of the Works, decl. acc., 1647–8).

109 Bodl. L., MS Tanner 60, fo. 214: Scawen to Sir John Potts, from Suffolk House (later renamed Northumberland House), 17 July 1645. For Scawen's powers of patronage as chairman of the committee: Silvanus Taylor to Scawen, 12 June 1645: PRO, SP 28/30/4, fo. 389.

110 *CJ*, v, 298: Pury served as his second in the Commons: *CJ*, v, 308. See also Scawen's accounts for the parliamentary commissioners to the army, 8 June–29 Sept. 1647: PRO, E 351/1275 (Pipe Office, decl. acc.).

111 Starkey, 'Court History in Perspective', pp. 1–24.

112 Cf. M.A. Kishlansky, *The Rise of the New Model Army* (Cambridge, 1979), pp. 26–51.

113 PRO, SP 16/503, fos. 140–182: depositions related to Cromwell's accusations against the earl of Manchester; Dr Williams's Library, MS 24.50 (Juxon diary), fos. 24^V, 27v–28, 31, 33. *Mercurius Britanicus*, no. 52 (30 Sept.–7 Oct. 1644); *Mercurius Britanicus*, no. 60 (2–9 Dec. 1644): *CJ*, iii, 703–4.

114 *LJ*, vii, 276–7; 297. I am grateful to Professor Hugh Trevor-Roper for a discussion on this point. J.S.A. Adamson, 'The English Nobility and the Projected Settlement of 1647', *HJ*, 30 (1987), pp. 567–602.

115 Leeds Castle, Kent, Fairfax MS, unfol.: Northumberland to Ferdinando, Lord Fairfax, 9 Dec. 1644 (from York House). 'I am informed by my officers in the North', Northumberland wrote, '[that] your Lo[rdshi]p is pleased to afford them your countenance and protection vpon all occations in my businesses.' For the strength of Northumberland's ties with the Fairfaxes, see also: Alnwick Castle, Northumberland MS O. I. 2(f): Northumberland to Hugh Potter, 14 Jan. 1645; for their long standing: Christ Church, Oxford, Muniment Room, Nobility Letters (Evelyn coll.) I, fo. 99: 1st Lord Fairfax to Northumberland, 26 Jan. [no year, but 1630s]. For Sir Thomas Fairfax's consultations at Syon House, on 31 July 1647, before the army's march on London: *A narrative by John Ashburnham of his attendance on King Charles the First* (2 vols, 1830), ii. 92; *The Memoirs of Edmund Ludlow*, ed. C.H. Firth (2 vols, Oxford, 1894), i. 162; Hatfield, Accounts, Box L/1.

116 Even after Essex's disastrous western campaign of 1644, his return to London was attended by considerable ceremonial. He made a formal entry on 27 Sept. accompanied by two regiments, and was met by the sheriffs of the City and a delegation of chief citizens: L.C. Nagel, 'The Militia of London, 1640–9' (Ph.D. dissertation, University of London, 1982), p. 206.

117 Bodl. L., MS Clarendon 30, fo. 32: Sir Edward Forde to [Lord Hopton?], 9 Aug. 1647; *Perfect Occurrences of Every Daie Iournall*, no. 52 (6–13 Aug. 1647), 210–11 (BL, E 518/17). Almost to a man, the peers who comprised that procession were the same group that had effected the deposition of Essex and military reforms of 1645.

118 G.S. [Giles Strangeways?], *A Letter from an Ejected Member of the House of Commons to Sir Jo: Evelyn* (16 Aug. 1648), p. 11.

119 HLRO, MP 10/11/45, fo. 38; *CJ*, iv, 477, 599, 634. PRO (Kew), AO 1/361/15. See also the draft in Northumberland's hand of a proposed list of Commissioners of the Great Seal: HLRO, MP 24/12/46, fo. 78; *LJ*, viii, 626. For the earl of Kent's activities as Commissioner of the Great Seal, see Bedfordshire R.O., Lucas MS L29/27/1. After the death of the earl of Bolingbroke in 1646, the earl of Salisbury joined Kent as the other peer in commission, further strengthening the influence of the Saye-Northumberland group: HLRO, MP 3/7/46; *LJ*, viii, 410.

120 Bodl. L., MS dep. C. 170 (Nalson papers xvi), fos. 181ᵛ, 193. KAO, De L'Isle MS, U 1475/C114/21: Sir John Temple to the earl of Leicester, 22 July 1641.

121 *LJ*, vii, 277; Kishlansky, *New Model Army* p. 47.

122 SRO, Hamilton MS GD 406/1/10492: Charles I to Hamilton, 25 June 1638. Bodl. L., MS Clarendon 34, fo. 17.

123 Lord Brooke, *Two Speeches made in the House of Peers* (1642/3), 6 (BL, E84/35).

124 *Sampsons Foxes Agreed to Fire a Kingdom* (Oxford, [22 June] 1644), 7 (BL, E 52/6).

125 See especially the Lords' divisions of 4 March 1647 and 27 May 1647: *LJ*, ix, 56–7, 207; Worcester College, Oxford, Clarke MS XLI, fo. 137: [Gilbert Mabbot?] to Fairfax, [27 May 1647, or shortly thereafter].

126 M.W. Thompson, *The Decline of the Castle* (Cambridge, 1987), pp. 138–57, and appendix 3, 'Parliamentary demolition, proposed or executed, 1642–60', pp. 179–85.

127 Their destruction is recorded in detail in PRO, E 317 (Commonwealth, surveys).

128 John Childs, *The Army of Charles II* (1976), pp. 19, 23, 28–46, 115–51.

129 During the 1620s and '30s, it was claimed, a generation of the peerage had sought service in foreign wars – against Spain in the Low Countries, and in the campaigns of the Thirty Years War – seeking the martial glory which was seen as the proper complement of the noble estate. 'At that time', Essex's biographer, Robert Codrington, wrote in 1646, 'the Netherland . . . was the Schoole of honour for the Nobility of England in the service of Armes.' Codrington, *Life of Essex*, pp. 8–9.

130 Arthur Collins, *Historical Collections of the Noble Families* (1752), pp. 276–82. His cousin, the 18th earl, had been Essex's companion-in-arms against Spínola in the 1620s. CUL, Add. MS 33 (Arthur Wilson's 'Observations'), fos. 9ᵛ–10.

131 Collins, *Historical Collections*, pp. 276–7.

4

The British Problem and the English Civil War

CONRAD RUSSELL

The study of the English Civil War has so far created more problems than it has solved. The tendency of much recent research has been to show England before the Bishops' Wars as a society not sufficiently divided or polarized to make the war easily explicable. Professor Elton, indeed, has been moved to say that 'some of us wonder whether there really was a civil war since its famous causes have all disappeared'.[1]

It is perhaps a consolation, if not a help, to find that this sense of bewilderment at the civil war was shared by some of those who lived through it. Sir Thomas Knyvett, in 1644, wondered whether 'the best excuse that can be made for us, must be a fit of lunacy'. In June 1642, Lord Wharton, an active enough parliamentarian to be in a position to know, wrote to the Chief Justice Bankes, who was with the king at York, to ask what they were quarrelling about. He said those he knew at Westminster were not disloyal, and those who were with the king at York 'wish and drive at an accommodation'. 'How is itt then, hath all this kingdome noe person prudent enough according to theyr affections to prevent the ruine coming upon us; or is itt want of industry, or is itt the wantonness of some few interested or unprovided people to pull downe more in one day, then the rest can build upp in yeares? Or is itt a judgement upon us immediately from the hand of God, for which no naturall or politique reason can be given?'[2]

Since the last of Wharton's explanations is not open to us, or at least not in our professional capacity, we are bound to supply a logical answer to his question. It does not help that both the types of explanation favoured over the past 40 years, based on long-term constitutional conflict and on long-term social change respectively, appear to have suffered irretrievable breakdown: we have to begin all over again.[3] There seem to be four possible ways of attempting the task.

This is a revised and expanded version of an inaugural lecture delivered at University College, London, on 7 March 1985. I would like to thank Peter Donald for numerous discussions of Scottish matters, and also my Yale pupils, notably Martin Flaherty, David Venderbush and Jim Wilson, who helped to stimulate my interest in matters British. The research for this article was done with assistance from the Small Grants Fund of the British Academy.

One would be to say that we have not found long-term causes of the civil war because there were none to find: that the war was the result of a short-term failure to solve a political crisis, together with the need to supply retrospective justification for actions taken in the heat of the moment. I am supposed in some quarters to have adopted this position already, and have been credited in one recent publication with having 'abolished the long-term causes of the Civil War'.[4] This report, like that of Mark Twain's death, is grossly exaggerated. Unlike some colleagues, I see no *a priori* impossiblity in this type of explanation, but it remains highly improbable. It should be adopted, if at all, only on the application of Sherlock Holmes's law: 'when you have eliminated everything else, what remains, however improbable, must be the truth'. Since we are very far from having eliminated everything else, this approach remains premature.

A second approach, which I would associate with Peter Lake, Richard Cust and Ken Fincham,[5] would argue that the appearance of an undivided society is deceptive, and rests on the fact that a high proportion of our surviving sources were either addressed to the privy council, or written in fear of an accident to the posts. This approach contains much truth: it appears that in this period the private letter is often a less free-spoken medium than the parliamentary speech, but it will take some time for us to be sure how much truth it contains. It is clear that there were significant divisions of opinion in England before the Bishop's Wars, and it seems clear that the effect of the Bishop's Wars was to exacerbate divisions which did exist, rather than to create others which did not. Yet it remains permissible to wonder how long these divisions, like fault-lines in rocks, might have remained latent if not subjected to the hammer-blows of outside intervention.

The third approach, which this article is designed to investigate, would argue that we have not found the causes of the English Civil War because the question involves trying to discover the whole of the explanation by examining a part of the problem. The English Civil War is regularly discussed as if it were a unique event, but it was not: between 1639 and 1642, Charles I faced armed resistance in all three of his kingdoms. In England and Ireland, civil war and resistance were simultaneous, but in Scotland five years elapsed between resistance in 1639 and civil war in 1644. This seems to be, not because Scotland was a less divided society than England or Ireland, but because the king of Scots, while resident in London, had so little power and patronage that he found the gathering of a party more uphill work in Scotland than in either of his other kingdoms. Charles appears to have regarded the absence of civil war in Scotland in 1639 as a political failure of his own, and his judgement deserves to be taken seriously.[6]

The tendency of dissidents in each kingdom to try to make common cause with sympathisers in the others ensured that the English, Scottish and Irish troubles could not remain three isolated problems: they triggered off a period of repeated intervention by the three kingdoms in each other's affairs, including Scottish intervention in Ireland in 1642, Scottish intervention in England in 1640, 1643, 1648 and 1651, and on a smaller scale, Irish intervention in England in 1643. This list is accompanied by a list of might-have-beens of which Strafford's supposed threat to use the Irish army is the most famous. Though the might-have-beens are not facts, the political hopes and fears they engendered are facts, and often influenced people's conduct. This period of acute British instability came to an end only with the English conquest of Scotland and Ireland in 1649–51.

When three kingdoms under one ruler all take to armed resistance within three years, it seems sensible to investigate the possibility that their actions may have had some common causes. We will not find them in constitutional development, for their constitutional structures were profoundly different. We will not find them in their social systems, for they were even more different: a social history of Britain in the early seventeenth century would be a stark impossibility. However, there are two obvious types of cause which are common to all three kingdoms. One is that they were all ruled by Charles I. It is perhaps fair to paraphrase Lady Bracknell, and so say that 'to lose one kingdom might happen to any king, but to lose three savours of carelessness'.

The other thing all three kingdoms have in common is that they are all parts of a multiple monarchy of three kingdoms. We now know, thanks to a large body of work, that the relations between multiple kingdoms were among the main causes of instability in continental Europe, and Professors Elliott and Koenigsberger have been asking for some time whether the rule which applies across the Channel also applies in Britain.[7] This article is intended to suggest that the answer to their question is 'yes'.

Thanks to them and many others, we now know a good deal about the normal flashpoints in multiple monarchies. They include resentment at the king's absence and about the disposing of offices, the sharing of costs of war and the choice of foreign policy, problems of trade and colonies, and the problems of foreign intervention. All these causes of difficulty were present in Britain. It is particularly interesting that Secretary Coke, probably in 1627–28, drew up a plan for a British version of Olivares' union of arms, and that the Scots in 1641 were demanding the right to trade with English colonies.[8] Yet these issues are surprisingly peripheral: it is possible to find them if we look for them, but only in Anglo-Irish relations between 1625 and 1629 does one of them (in this case the cost of war) become a central theme.[9] The absence of wars for much of the period between 1603 and 1640, and the overwhelming preponderance of the English revenue over those of Scotland and Ireland both contribute to this comparative silence.

This leaves only one of the normal causes of trouble within multiple kingdoms, that caused by religion. This one issue alone accounted for almost all the difficulties between the kingdoms of Britain between 1637 and 1642, and it caused enough trouble to leave very little room for any others. Some of the trouble seems to have arisen from the fact that religion for Charles, like arms for Olivares, was the issue on which he chose to press for greater uniformity. In Britain, as in the Spanish monarchy, it is the issue on which the centre demanded uniformity on which the liberties and privileges of the outlying kingdoms are most loudly asserted.

The rare cases in Europe of multiple kingdoms with different religions do not suggest that the British reaction is disproportionate. One case is that of France and Béarn, where Louis XIII, discovering, to his dismay, that he was king of the Protestant kingdom of Béarn (part of Henri IV's old kingdom of Navarre), decided to invade it and suppress it, even at the risk of war with Spain.[10] The most famous case of multiple kingdoms with different religions is that of Spain and the Netherlands, and that produced disturbances on the same scale as the British. Britain, moreover, offered the peculiar and illogical combination of difference of religions with a theory of authority in two kingdoms (or, as Charles believed, in three) vesting authority in the king as supreme head of the church. A British king who presided over different religions thus offered a built-in challenge to his own authority, something which Charles I was never likely to accept with equanimity. Though there are other cases in Europe in which one king presided over two religions, I am aware of none in which a single king presided over three. Moreover, Britain appears to be a unique case of multiple kingdoms all of which were internally divided in religion, and in all of which there existed a powerful group which preferred the religion of one of the others to their own. Perhaps the problem we ought to be trying to solve is not why this situation produced an explosion under Charles, but how James succeeded in presiding over it for 23 years without one.

The capacity of religion to cause political trouble in the seventeenth century did not just arise from the actions of zealots, though there were plenty of those. It was more serious than this. Respectable conventional or governmental opinion accepted that it was its duty to enforce truth, and to repress error. The case for religious unity was such a conventional cliché that, as the Scottish Commissioners in London put it, it was accepted by 'sound . . . politicians'. It was the sound politicians' intellectual assent to many of the zealots' propositions which led them into actions which caused trouble. In the Scots Commissioners' words 'we doe all know and professe that religion is not only the mean to serve God and to save our owne soules, but it is also the base and foundation of kingdomes and estates, and the strongest band to tye the subjects to their prince in true loyalty'.[11] Conversely, as they said, 'the greatest zeal in different religions, the greater division'. They even invoked Bede's account of the Synod of Whitby to support the proposition that it was unwise to allow the existence of different religions within the same island. In this, if in little else, the Covenanters agreed with Charles I.

Charles, at some date not later than 1633, and possibly as early as 1626,[12] decided to drop a match into this powder-keg by setting out to achieve one uniform order of religion within the three kingdoms. The task was the more necessary for the fact that Charles's interpretation of the English religious settlement, and especially of the 39 Articles, made the gap between the three churches appear considerably wider than it had done under James. Under James, it had been as true in a British as in an English context that Calvinist doctrine served for a 'common and ameliorating bond'[13] between those who disagreed about many other things. When Charles broke this 'common and ameliorating bond' between the churches, he not only widened the gap between them, but also offered a handle to his critics. It became possible for them to challenge Charles, as Pym did, through praise for the Irish Articles of 1615, or, as Peter Smart of Durham did, by publishing material highly critical of English authorities in Edinburgh.[14] It was, perhaps, essential to the survival of Charles's and Laud's Arminian innovations in England that Scotland and Ireland should cease to provide anti-Arminian Englishmen with a much more attractive alternative model. It was perhaps for this reason that Charles seems to have employed Laud as a sort of Secretary for ecclesiastical affairs for all three kingdoms. As early as 1634, Laud complained to Wentworth that 'I was fain to write nine letters yesterday into Scotland: I think you have a plot to see whether I will be *universalis episcopus*, that you and your brethren may take occasion to call me Antichrist'.[15] This attempt to make the three kingdoms uniform in order to protect Charles's changes in England was bound, to heighten theological resistance, to provoke fears that they were being dragged at English chariot wheels, being made, as Baillie put it, 'ane pendicle of the dioces of York',[16] and to encourage those Englishmen who resisted Charles's changes to rely on Scotland and Ireland for assistance in doing likewise.

Laud and Wentworth were both committed to this policy of uniformity between the kingdoms, which Wentworth even carried to the length of recommending that Scotland be governed by the English Privy Council as a dependency of England. Yet they both feared that, in his zeal to implement this policy, Charles did not see how difficult it was. In 1634, Wentworth wrote to Laud that 'the reducing of this kingdom (Ireland) to a conformity in religion with the church of England is no doubt deeply set in his Majesty's pious and prudent heart, as well in perfect zeal to the service of the Almighty as out of other weighty reasons of state and government' but, he added, in a typical Wentworth phrase, to do so without adequate preparation 'were as a man going to warfare without munition or arms'.[17] It is a warning to which Charles should have paid attention.

In trying to impose a uniform religion on Britain, Charles had to work through three very different legal and constitutional systems. Scotland was not in any way legally dependent on England, and it was of some importance to many Scots that in 1603 the king of Scots had inherited England, and not vice versa. The English Privy Council had no *locus standi* on Scottish matters, and even in 1639, between the Bishops' Wars, the earl of Northumberland, who was a member of the Council Committee for Scottish affairs, was reduced to complaining that he knew no more of Scottish affairs than if he were at Constantinople.[18] The Committee for Scottish Affairs could advise on how, or whether, to use English military force to enforce the king's Scottish policy, but if any of them believed the policy itself to be mistaken, they had no authority to say so. Scotland had its own privy council, its own parliament, and its own law. The Scottish privy council could govern so long as it was allowed an effective form of devolution, but whenever the king of Scots chose to form policy from London, his Scottish council found it was not easy to advise him from Edinburgh. Scotland also had its own form of church government. It had bishops, but what authority they might have, and how that authority might be related to that of a General Assembly, were to an extent matters of opinion. There was a widespread Scottish sentiment which held that the only ultimate source of lawful authority was the General Assembly, what Alexander Henderson called the 'representative kirk of this kingdom'. For such men as Laud, who protested during the Glasgow Assembly that 'for a national assembly, never did the church of Christ see the like', such theories were more than offensive: they were incomprehensible.[19] A pure Ullmanite ascending theory of power was equally beyond the comprehension of Charles, who believed, with little obvious justification, that he was supreme head of the Church of Scotland.[20] At the Pacification of Berwick, the Covenanters were faced with the task of explaining to Charles that he did not have a negative voice in a General Assembly as he did in an English parliament, and he simply did not understand what they were talking about.[21] Moreover, Charles was offended by Scottish liturgical practice, as well as by Scottish doctrine and discipline. In 1633 when he went to Edinburgh to be crowned (eight years late) he insisted on using the English liturgy wherever he worshipped. In the *Large Declaration* of 1639, after he had officially abandoned the new Service Book, he complained of the 'diversitie, nay deformitie, which was used in Scotland, where no set or publike form of prayer was used, but preachers and readers and ignorant schoolmasters prayed in the church, sometimes so ignorantly as it was a shame to all religion to have the Majestie of God so barbarously spoken unto, sometimes so seditiously that their prayers were plaine libels, girding at sovereigntie and authoritie; or lyes stuffed with all the false reports in the kingdome'.[22] It perhaps highlights the difficulty in communication which difference of religion might cause that the way the Scots would have expressed the same point was that they did not have a reading ministry.

Ireland, by contrast, was not an independent kingdom, but, like Massachusetts or Virginia, a semi-autonomous dependency of the English Crown. Under the king, the Dublin administration was headed by a lord lieutenant, lord deputy or lord justices (the title varying according to the status of the holder). He and his Irish privy council were answerable to the English privy council, which could, and sometimes did, discuss Irish affairs. There was also an Irish parliament though the operation of Poynings' Law firmly subordinated it to the English privy council. The English parliament, before 1640, was not normally regarded as having any standing in Ireland: in British terms, the English parliament was as much a local assembly as the Cortes of Castile.[23] In religion, there was an established Protestant Church of Ireland, run by Archbishop Ussher along lines acceptable to St John or Brereton, and to many of the increasing numbers of Scots settled in Ulster. Outside the Church of Ireland, the Catholic majority, handicapped by a formidable series of legal disabilities, enjoyed an intermittently Nelsonian blind eye.

Irish affairs also suffered from a threefold division of race. The New English, Protestants who usually controlled the government in Dublin, were English settlers who had arrived since the Reformation. For them, the key problem was always how to stop Ireland being Irish, an aim which became more and more closely identified with Protestantism and with a policy of plantation. The 'mere' or native Irish were excluded from the political nation, though with an apparantly increasing number of exceptions. The pigs in the middle of Irish politics were the Old English, descendants of pre-Reformation English settlers, and often either Catholics or church-papists. The key to the Old English creed seems to have been the belief that it was possible to be a gentleman first, and a Catholic second. As owners of a third of the profitable land in Ireland, they felt increasingly threatened by the policy of plantation. The earl of Ormond, threatened by one such scheme, commented that he was the first Englishman to be treated as if he were Irish.[24] He was not the last: in 1641, one of the rebels marked the great watershed in Irish history by describing them as the 'new Irish'.[25]

It is no wonder that the complexity of these arrangements enmeshed Charles in many things for which the simplicity of his original plans had left no room. It is also important that though there was a privy council for each kingdom, there was no institutional equivalent of the Spanish council of state, which could advise on issues affecting all three. Laud and Wentworth, or on occasion Hamilton and Lennox, might give British counsel, but only when the king asked for it. On most British issues, Charles, like the classic medieval tyrant, was without counsellors.

Charles's attempt at British uniformity was begun in Ireland, where some sharp political infighting between Lord Deputy Wentworth and Archbishop Ussher appears to have ended in a draw.[26] He was nearly 'surprised' by an attempt by Ussher's friends to secure confirmation of the Calvinist Irish Articles of 1615, but managed to secure Irish confirmation for the English 39 Articles. The attempt to set up an Irish High Commission was successful, and the attempt to impose new Irish canons produced a long battle between Ussher and Bishop Bramhall, Laud's chief Irish ally. Taken together with Laud's remark that there was no need to introduce the English liturgy because the Irish had it already, the programme sounds remarkably like the one which was tried out in Scotland from 1635 onwards.

It may have been the need to compromise with Irish resistance which moved Charles and Laud to act with so little consultation in Scotland. They consulted some of the Scottish bishops, who belonged to that faction in Scotland which welcomed moves towards uniformity with England. The use of proclamation, however, bypassed all the normal machinery of consultation. The Scottish canons appeared almost without warning, and though the new Prayer Book was expected, when ministers were commanded to buy it and use it, there were no copies available and none of them had yet seen it. The attempt to produce the Scottish Prayer Book as a *fait accompli*, however, cannot be regarded as a success.

It is fortunately unnecessary to recount the narrative of Scottish resistance to the Prayer Book: for the moment, it is the British implications which concern us. Two stories will perhaps help to illustrate them. Both tell of Covenanter conversations with the king's commissioner the marquess of Hamilton. In one, the Covenanters explained that the Reformation of England was 'verrie farr inferior to the Reformatione of Scotland'.[27] This was an idea Charles could not allow to get loose in England. It also helps to explain why the Scots, who had had to admit to junior partner status in so much, clung so obstinately to the belief in the superiority of their Reformation, and so helps to explain their policy in England in 1640–41, when the boot was on the other foot. The other story describes how Hamilton told the Covenanters that his instructions allowed him to remove the Scottish canons and Prayer Book, but not to condemn anything in them 'which might reflect against any public order or any thing practiced, or allowed by my Lord of Canterburie and his followers in England or elsewhere'.[28] This story illustrates, both one of Charles's reasons for sticking to his guns, and the likely consequence for England of a Covenanter victory. The Covenanters' response, according to Baillie, was to insist that the doctrines be condemned because so many in their own church held them. Superb organisation and the King's absence enabled the Covenanters to claim to be much more representative of Scottish opinion than in private they ever believed themselves to be. We can see here the possibility of the anti-Covenanter opening which became crucial to Charles's Scottish policy in 1641 and beyond.

Charles first planned to invade Scotland with an Irish force under the earl of Antrim, head of that clan who were Macdonnells in Ireland and Macdonalds in Scotland.[29] In doing so, Charles turned Argyll and his clan into devout Covenanters, since Antrim's chief motive had been to secure possession of lands in dispute between him and the Covenanters. As Baillie reflected, the ways of Providence were indeed strange.[30]

Charles finally decided to play his trump card of English intervention, and, to cut a long story short, lost at the battle of Newburn, on 28 August 1640. This was the day on which the apple was eaten: for some 14 years from Newburn onwards, the kingdoms were involved in each other's affairs with a daily urgency which had not been seen since the days of Edward I and Robert and Edward Bruce. When Hamilton told the Covenanters, shortly before war began, that if Charles turned to English intervention, he doubted if he would ever see peace in this kingdom again,[31] he spoke little more than the truth: he was executed in 1648 for leading a Scottish intervention in England on behalf of Charles I.

There is no sense, in an article of this type, in attempting a blow by blow narrative of the period from Newburn to the civil war. It seems more sensible to examine the ways in which the affairs of one kingdom impinged on those of others.

The first way was by direct control, exemplified by the Scots in the 12 months after Newburn. They had an occupying army in Northumberland and Durham, while their commissioners negotiated a peace treaty in London. It was the Scots who dictated that Charles should call an English parliament, since they refused to negotiate with any commissioners who were not appointed by king and parliament, or to accept any treaty not confirmed by an English parliament.[32] As Secretary Vane said in reporting this demand to Secretary Windebank, 'by this you may judge of the rest'. It was thus Scottish intervention which created an English parliament, and which made a crucial contribution, by involving it in the treaty negotiations, towards giving it a share in executive power. It was also the Scots, by deliberately prolonging the treaty for the sake of their English friends, who made the first contribution to turning it into a Long Parliament.

The second way in which the kingdoms influenced each other was by direct copying. The Queries of the Irish Parliament appear to be a copying of the Petition of Right,[33] while their attempt in 1641, to impeach their Lord Chancellor, the Lord Chief Justice, Bishop Bramhall and the Laudian Provost of Trinity College, Dublin, was surely an imitation of what the English parliament was busy doing to Strafford. The committee they sent to negotiate with Charles in 1641 was empowered to act as a recess committee if there were a dissolution.[34] This was a Scottish idea, copied by the Irish and only subsequently by the English. The oath of Association of the Irish rebels in 1641, beginning 'I A.B. doe in the presence of Almightie God', is a copy of the English Protestation of May 1641, with a few intriguing alterations. The oath is taken in the presence of all the angels and saints, as well as Almighty God, the qualification 'lawful' is omitted from the things they engage to do in defence of religion, and the word 'Protestant' is at all points replaced by 'Catholic'.[35] Perhaps the Irish Rebellion was the greatest copying of them all. One of its leaders, arrested at the beginning of the rebellion, was asked what he was trying to do, and replied: 'to imitate Scotland, who got a privilege by that course'.[36] In England, the Triennial Act followed, at the Scots' suggestion, a Scottish Act to the same effect,[37] and the proposals of 1641–42 that the parliament should choose the great officers, were consciously borrowed from the Scottish settlement of September 1641.[38]

It is also possible to regard the Scots' drive to impose Scottish uniformity on England as a copying of what the king had been doing to them. Baillie said that they had 'good hopes to get bishops' ceremonies and all away and that conformitie which the king has been vexing himself and us to obtaine betwixt his dominions, to obtaine it now, and by it a most hearty nation of the kingdomes'.[39] It was also the Scots, first and foremost, who insisted on the death of Strafford, whom they regarded as the one Englishman unwilling to accept the verdict of Newburn as final. As the Scots painstakingly explained, using arguments almost comically like those used by Charles in 1639, they could not guarantee their own domestic security except by imposing profound changes on the domestic politics and religion of England.[40] They found, as Charles had done before them, that such attempts created considerable resentment.[41] It was these efforts by the Scots, and notably their paper of 24 February, which prevented Pym and his allies from reaching a peaceful settlement with the king, since a settlement which did not remove the Scottish army would be no settlement, and not worth reaching.

The existence of three kingdoms also created opportunities to fish in troubled waters, and these opportunities were much used. Any group who lost a round in their own kingdom could always make common cause with their sympathisers in another, and call in another kingdom to redress the balance of their own. The Scottish Arminians, who were very heavily dependent on English backing, were the first to learn this lesson, and only time prevented them from holding all the best bishoprics and deaneries in Scotland. The English parliament learned it second, and the Irish parliament, relying on the English parliament for its remonstrance against Strafford, learned it third, but it was perhaps Charles who learned it most thoroughly. In May 1641, after the failure of the Army Plot, Secretary Vane expected Charles to settle with his English parliament, 'there being in truth no other [course] left'.[42] In saying this, Vane merely revealed his ignorance of Charles's Scottish policies. Since 3 March 1641,

Charles had been committed to a growing intrigue with Montrose which was designed to create a Scottish party to counterbalance the one at the disposal of his opponents, or (as in the event happened) to induce the Covenanters to withdraw from England before he could succeed in this attempt.[43]

Charles' opportunity came from growing hostility to the Covenanters inside Scotland. One of the major surprises of this work has been finding how strong this sentiment was. In the spring of 1641, it had reached the point at which the liturgy against which the Scots were fighting was being used inside the Scottish army.[44] Other things, such as Montrose's increasing jealousy of the power of Argyll, are the sort of thing which is part of the price of power. So are Scottish resentment at such things as the prohibition of salmon fishing on the Sabbath, or the occasion on which Baillie denounced his patron from the pulpit because at a wedding there was among the lords 'more drink than needed'.[45] The stages of Charles's intrigues with anti-Covenanter Scots are obscure, stretching through the plot of Napier, Keir and Blackhall,[46] the Incident in October 1641, and an abortive plan of May 1642 to secure Scottish intervention against the English parliament.[47] The consistent theme underlying the details is Charles's desire to build a party of anti-Covenanter Scots, and to use that party to redress the balance of English politics. The schemes he began in 1641 were the ones he pursued until he pulled them off in 1648, and lost his head for it. The point which is immediately relevant to the origins of the English Civil War is that it was Charles's hope of breaking the Anglo-Scottish alliance which encouraged him to believe that Vane was wrong in insisting that he must settle with his English subjects. It is worth remembering that in September 1641, Charles did succeed in breaking the Anglo-Scottish alliance, and it was only the outbreak of the Irish Rebellion which kept the English parliament in being from then on.

The existence of three kingdoms also provided dissidents with an alternative model, and thereby contributed to polarising the politics of all three. The English godly, who for so long had had to be content with half a loaf, found that having a Scottish army to press their demands had an intoxicating effect. When Burges, at the opening of the Long Parliament, preached on the delivery of Israel from Babylon by an army coming from the north, it was impossible to mistake his meaning.[48] As Baillie put it, 'God is making here a new world', and the reaction of many of the English godly was 'gramercies, good Scot'.[49] The opportunity encouraged D'Ewes to hold forth on the proposition that the English and the Scots were one nation, except for the Hebrideans, who were Irish, and to propose the setting up of a committee for the abolishing of superstition.[50] When the Root and Branch Bill passed in the Commons, Nehemiah Wallington commented 'Babylon is fallen, is fallen'.[51]

The polarizing effect of such utterances was because these men's hopes were other men's fears, and the fears tended to be expressed in the form of appeals to anti-Scottish sentiment. The Scots gave a particularly good opportunity for this when they asked for a euphemistically named 'Brotherly Assistance' of £300,000. Hyde's friend Thomas Triplett, who was pouring a stream of anti-Scottish sentiment into Hyde's ear from Newburn onwards, reported a rumour that the money for the Brotherly Assistance was to be raised by fining Alderman Abell the wine monopolist, 'and so lett Abel pay Cain'.[52] Gervase Holles, in the house of commons, said the Scots might be our younger brothers, but, like Jacob, they were stealing our birthright – an image liable to boomerang on him.[53] The earl of Bristol, the chief English negotiator, was surely not choosing his words at random when he described the Brotherly Assistance as a 'viaticum' for the Scots.[54] This anti-Scottish feeling grew steadily through the summer of 1641, and the emotions which led to civil war were very near the surface when Sir Robert Harley reported that Sir William Widdrington had been overheard saying that he looked forward to the day when any member calling the Scots 'brethren' would be called to the bar.[55]

The Scots' paper of 24 February 1641 demanding the Presbyterianising of England and the death of Strafford, gave this body of feeling its opportunity for organised expression. The debate on this paper on 27 February, according to D'Ewes, 'raised one of the greatest distempers in the House that ever I saw in it'.[56] This debate marks the appearance of two-party politics in the Commons. The study of this and other debates bearing on the Scots shows that who spoke for and who against the Scots provides a better predictor of allegiance in the civil war than any other issue, even Root and Branch or the Militia Ordinance. This fact is surely not purely coincidental. Charles was perhaps justified in accusing the Scottish negotiations in London of trying 'to stir up his people of England, and make a division between him and his subjects'.[57] Whether or not they tried, they certainly succeeded.

In the relationship between the three kingdoms, any rapprochement between two of them had a billiard-ball effect on the third, and for most of the first half of 1641, it was Ireland which came out third. The Scottish parliamentary alliance aimed, in the ominous phrase of the petition of the 12 peers, at 'the uniting of *both* your realms against the common enemies of the reformed religion'.[58] Ireland was a likely victim of any such unity. We are fortunate to have an early Irish reaction to this anti-popish drive. John Barry, an Irish Officer in the King's English army, reported that the parliament had taken orders to cashier all popish officers, 'and among the rest myself. They call out bitterly against us, and begin to banish us out of town, and remove us from court: what will become of us, I know not, but we are in an ill taking at present.' Barry resented the imputation of disloyalty: 'Sir, I was never factious in religion, nor shall ever seeke the ruine of any because he is not of my opinion'.[59] For him and many like him, the imputation was to become a self-fulfilling prophecy.

Barry was one of those who saw in the increasing co-operation between the English parliament and the Scots an opportunity for increasing co-operation between the Old English and the king. In the spring of 1641, Charles was negotiating with an Irish parliamentary committee at the same time as he was negotiating with the Scots, and their demands were to an extent alternatives. The main thing the Irish committee wanted was confirmation of the Graces, a set of royal concessions of the 1620s of which the key one was itself copied from England. It would have applied to Ireland the English Concealment Act of 1624, making 60 years' possession of an estate a valid title to it. In England, this merely stopped an unscrupulous way of raising money. In Ireland, it would have had the much more far-reaching effect of putting a stop to the policy of plantation. For this reason, it caused great alarm to the government in Dublin. When Charles confirmed the Graces, on 3 April 1641, he forged an alliance with the old English, but he also forged another, between the lords justices in Dublin and the English parliament.

During 1641, many Irishmen came to realise that the greatest threat to their liberties came, not from the English king, but from the English parliament. When the parliament had set out to impeach Strafford for his conduct as Lord Deputy of Ireland without having any jurisdiction in Ireland they set out on a slippery slope. At first, they were very cautious, dealing with Irish petitioners by recommending, requesting and referring, but such caution could not last.[60] They were finally pushed over the edge by a series of cases of which the most important was that of Henry Stewart, the Don Pacifico of the British Civil Wars. Henry Stewart was an Ulster Scot, imprisoned by Wentworth for refusing to take an oath renouncing the Scottish Covenant, and the Scottish negotiatiors were demanding that those who imprisoned him should be punished. As a result, the English house of lords summoned the whole of the Irish privy council to appear before them as delinquents. This was too much, and the Irish privy council and parliament immediately protested.[61]

In denying that Ireland was subject to the English parliament, the Irish were up against the Scots, who repeatedly assumed that it was. They also had to eat a number of their own words, dating from the anti-Strafford phase in which the Irish parliament had been busy claiming the liberties of Englishmen, and trying to make common cause with the English parliament. Like many later Whigs, they hoped that the English parliament gave more weight to its rhetoric about law and liberty than to its rhetoric about anti-popery, and they realised their mistake too late. If they faced subjection to an English parliament in which they were not represented, they would be reduced to the unambiguous status of a colony, and with a parliament as anti-popish as the English, the prospect was not inviting. In December 1641, when the Old English decided to throw in their lot with the Irish rebels, they accused the lords justices of having conspired 'to make this realm totally subordinate to the jurisdiction of the Parliament of England'. They said it was their aim 'to preserve the freedom of this kingdom without dependency of the Parliament or State of England'.[62] Thus, the Irish Rebellion was a reaction to changes in the power structure in England, brought about by Scottish intervention, which in turn had been provoked by attempts to impose English religion on the Scots, lest the Scots might set an evil example to English dissidents. There can be no better illustration of the fact that this subject does indeed have an Athanasian complexity.

This article has been intended to test two different, but not incompatible hypotheses. One is the hypothesis that when there are rebellions in three highly disparate kingdoms, one possible cause is the king who provides the most conspicuous common factor between them. This case appears to contain much truth. It is not given to historians to make controlled experiments, but the study of Charles I in a Scottish, an English and an Irish context is perhaps less remote from a controlled experiment than most things we are able to do. Variables, of course, are not eliminated, and it is particularly important that the Charles who handled the English crisis had already handled and suffered from the Scottish. Yet the man who appears in all three stories is perhaps more totally the same than, in such different situations, he should have been. The same convictions, the same imaginative blind spots, and the same defects in political methods, show up in all three situations. One constant characteristic is Charles's refusal to accept that he was bound by the limits of political possibility. His determination, during 1638, to force the Scots to give up the Covenant appears to have been immune to any advice that this was something he simply could not do. As Traquair reported to Hamilton in July 1638:

> I find nothinge sticke with his majestie so much as the covenant, he have drunk in [sic] this opinion, that monarchie and it can not stand together; and knowing the impossibilitie of haveinge it renderit upp, you may easily conjecture what will ensue if the king continue but a few days more of that mynd . . . If I was wearied in Scotland, my heart is broke heir, since I can see no possibilitie to satisfie our masters honor, so deeply doth he conseave himself interessed, as the country from ruine.

When Hamilton, in September 1638, advised Charles how to gain a party for the Glasgow Assembly, 'his answer was, that the remedy was worse than the disease'.[63] This is surely the same man who believed, in January 1641, that he could enjoy the services of Pym as Chancellor of the

Exchequer together with those of Juxon as archbishop of York.[64] The king emerges, not only as a man who had difficulty in recognising the limits of the possible, but also as one who, when he did recognise them, was liable to conclude that peace could have too high a price. This is the same king who told Hamilton, in December 1642, that, win or lose, he would make no more concessions in the English Civil War, and would rather live a glorious king, or die a patient martyr.[65] He is perhaps an example of E.M. Forster's Law, that the tragedy of life is that one gets what one wants.

He also emerges in the Scottish and English stories as a man with a real allergy to Puritanism in all its forms. In many places, this prevented him from facing facts. His repeated promises to the Scots that there would be no 'innovation' in religion seem to have been made in all sincerity, and in blissful ignorance that they appeared to many of his honest subjects to contradict the policies he was then pursuing.[66] This is the same king who emerges from the tangled story of the English Arminians and the 39 Articles. This allergy also seems to be the main explanation for his obstinate, and apparently sincere, insistence that the Scottish troubles were not about religion at all, since he was unable to absorb that many Scots sincerely believed him guilty of innovation.[67] This blindness to the force of puritanical conviction does not seem to have made it easy for him to handle a force whose very existence he was incapable of admitting.

Charles also emerges as a king subject to the political failing of saying 'never', and then retreating, thereby encouraging his subjects to believe that they could always press him harder, and he would retreat further. From the Petition of Right to the execution of Strafford, this habit handicapped Charles in England, and it is equally apparent in his handling of the Scottish service book. It was the earl of Nithsdale, not the most conciliatory of his Scottish advisers, who reproved him for this habit: 'it would have been better to refuse them at the first, and better to grant what they ask with a seasoning to resent, then still to give ground'. As Hamilton explained after the Pacification of Berwick, this habit made life very difficult for Charles's servants. 'Those particulars which I have so often sworne and said your matie would never condiscend to, will now be granted, therefore they will give no credit to what I shall say ther after, but will still hope and believe, that all ther desires will be given way to'.[68]

It was a political style which tended to advertise the fact that concessions were made unwillingly and under duress. In instructing Traquair for the 1639 Scottish parliament, he commented on the act for abolishing episcopacy: 'we consent to this act only for the peace of the land, and in our own judgement hold it neither convenient nor fitting'. He then told Traquair to publish this opinion. At the same time, he reassured the archbishop of St Andrews that 'you may rest secure, that tho perhaps we doe [erased] may [inserted] give way for the present, to that which will be prejudiciall both to the church and our government, yett we shall not leave thinking in time how to remedy both'. In September 1640, Loudoun commented that the king's actions 'beget a suspition that his matie doth not yet intend a reall peace'.[69] It is not surprising that Pym and Saye should have come to share this suspicion, and should have formed a desire to institutionalise Charles's concessions so thoroughly that he would be unable to reserve them. There is no reason to suppose Pym and Saye paid as much attention to the history of the Irish Graces as they did to that of the Scottish bishops, but had they done so, the story could only have strengthened a belief that Charles's concessions had to be bound in chains.[70] We are dealing with a king who invited resistance in all of his three kingdoms, and got what he was asking for.

Yet this stress on blame for Charles will not serve to eliminate the other major theme of this article, that the relationship between the three kingdoms itself, and not merely its mishandling, was a major cause of instability in all three of them. That Charles's English regime was in the event brought down through military defeat at the hands of the Scots is a point too obvious to need labouring. What perhaps needs saying is that this is not the intervention of a random factor like a stroke of lightning, but the results of a long-term difficulty in securing religious unity between Charles's three kingdoms. Charles's decision to impose the Scottish liturgy was not taken out of the blue, and 'folly' is not a sufficient explanation for it. It was the result of a long-standing conviction, known to Wentworth and Laud by 1634, that there must be a closer union in religion between Charles's dominions. The underlying thinking emerges in Laud's insistence, in 1633, that English *and Scottish* soldiers and merchants in the Netherlands should be compelled to use the English liturgy, or in his otherwise Utopian objective of sending a bishop to New England.[71]

It is clear that Charles was well aware that his Scottish policy had English implications. To take one example among many, in 1639, he would agree to Traquair, as commissioner, assenting to an act of the Scottish parliament declaring episcopacy contrary to the constitutions of the kirk of Scotland, but not to one calling it 'unlawful':

> If I doe acknowledge or consent that episcopacie is unlafull in the kirk of Scotland, though as you may have sett it downe in your consenting to the act, the word unlafull may seem to have only a relation to the constitt, of that kirke, yet the construction there of doth runn so doubtfull, as that it may too probably be inferred, that the same callin is acknowledged by us to be unlafull in any churches of our dominions.[72]

The political realism of a concern for unity in religion between the three kingdoms is perhaps best illustrated by the fact that Charles shared it with the Scottish Covenanters, with Pym and with James. The political danger of the objective is also illustrated by the fact that Charles shared it with all these people, and by the fact that no two of them were pursuing unity in the same religious position. The inherent difficulty of the situation has perhaps been masked by James's success in pursuing union in religion between the kingdoms so slowly, and so much by stealth, that Dr Galloway has even been moved to question whether he had the objective at all.[73] James's pursuit of episcopacy in Scotland was conducted by so many small stages, over such a long period of time, that there was no one moment at which it was obvious that its opponents should stand and fight. The process of reconciling moderate Presbyterian ministers to episcopacy stage by stage looks remarkably like the policy of separating moderates and extremists described for England by Dr Fincham and Dr Lake.[74]

Taken by itself, or even together with the Five Articles of Perth, James's commitment to Scottish episcopacy need not show that he was working towards unity between the three kingdoms. It looks much more likely that James had the objective when his commitment to Scottish episcopacy is taken beside his commitment to Calvinist doctrine for England and Ireland. From 1603 onwards, many Scots recognised an adherence to Calvinist doctrine as an essential ground for unity between the churches,[75] and James's policy seems to have been to build up a church with Scottish doctrine and English government. The choice of George Abbot to consecrate his Scottish bishops puts his policy in a nutshell.[76]

The difference between James and Charles, then, was not in the objective of unity between the three kingdoms, but in the theological position from which they pursued that objective. Charles pursued it from a position which markedly increased the number of influential Englishmen who preferred the Scottish model to their own. Also, Charles did not pursue unity, as James had done, by shifting each kingdom a little bit towards the others, but by shifting Scotland and Ireland towards that interpretation of the English settlement which, of all others, made it most remote from the Scottish and Irish churches. Charles's Arminian stance may have been barely sustainable as an English one, but it was certainly beyond the bounds of the possible as a British one.

It was by involving the Scots in English politics that Charles created that vital ingredient of a major political crisis, a serious rival power centre to himself. Over and over again, the Scots, by changing the bounds of the possible in England, drew Charles's critics to attempt what they would not otherwise have risked. The petition of the 12 peers, for example, had been discussed between Englishmen and Covenanters for a year before it surfaced.[77] It is not a coincidence that it ultimately did surface when the Scots crossed the Tweed, and was immediately reported to Edinburgh.[78] Indeed, Hamilton had warned Charles, as early as June 1638, of the opportunity a Scottish war would give his English critics:

the conquering totally of this kingdome will be a difficult worke, though ye were sertain of what assistants ingland can give you, but it

faires me that they will not be so forwardt in this as they ought, nay
that there are some malitious spereites amongst them thatt no souner
will your bake be turned, bot they will be redie to dou as we have
doun heir, which I will never call by a nother name than rebellioun.[79]

For such 'malitious spirits', for whom Burges and Marshall may serve as
fair examples, and for those to whom they preached, Scottish intervention
in England could serve 'in working up their hearts to that indispensable
pitch of heavenly resolution, sincerely to strike through a religious and
invoiable covenant with their God'.[80] It was Scottish intervention which
turned the programme of 'further reformation' for which the Long
Parliament Fast preachers were spokesmen, into practical politics.

Yet, by the very act of turning 'godly reformation' into practical politics,
the Scots also presented Charles with an opportunity to recruit an English
party. It is no coincidence that Falkland and Sir Frederick Cornwallis long
before they were royalist MPs had been anti-Scottish volunteers in the First
Bishops' War,[81] for it was anti-Scottish feeling, and fear of the 'further
reformation' the Scots brought with them, which provided the cement
between Charles and his new royalist allies of 1641. Falkland probably
spoke for them all when he commented on the Scots' Brotherly Assistance
that it was an English proverb not to look a given horse in the mouth, and
he wished it were a Scottish one too.[82]

In this situation, Charles reacted with more than usual shrewdness. He
appreciated that it was the Scots who conferred power on his English
opponents, and from the beginning of the Long Parliament onwards, his
strategy was designed to divide Pym and his group from their Scottish
allies. For the first few months of 1641, Charles's terms for settlement, the
preservation of episcopacy and the life of Strafford, were precisely those
which would have the effect of separating the English parliamentarians
from their Scottish allies. From March 1641 onwards, he pursued the same
objective by another method, and aimed, by Scottish concessions, to
remove the Scots from English politics. In the autumn of 1641, when he
exacted promises of non-intervention in English affairs from Argyll and
Loudoun as part of his Scottish settlement, he appeared to have
succeeded.[83]

It was at this point that the Irish Rebellion drove Charles back onto the
mercy of his English parliament. The Irish Rebellion, like the Bishops'
Wars, is regularly discussed as if it were a random intervention of an
outside factor, like a stroke of lightning. In fact, it was not. It was the
very measures taken to draw England and Scotland together which had
forced England and Ireland apart.[84] It was demonstrated that one of the
most Athanasian characteristics of the British Problem was the way in
which avoidance of one error led straight to the perpetration of another.
For the second time, it was failure to handle the British Problem success-

fully which led Charles to failure in England. Perhaps the point on which we should really be pondering is that it took five years of continuous British crisis to drive the English body politic to the point of civil war. This might perhaps suggest that, in spite of all the strains to which it had been subjected, the English social fabric of 1637 was still very tough indeed.[85]

It is part of the Athanasian quality of this subject that Charles's kingdom provided three independent stories, as well as one combined one, and it is worth asking what were the peculiarities of each kingdom as they emerge from comparison. The order in which the kingdoms resisted Charles was Scotland, Ireland, England, and it seems that this may represent more than a chronological progression. Though the Irish troubles proved after 1649 to be more long-lasting, there are more senses than one in which the Scottish troubles may be regarded as the *primum mobile* of the British. The Scots from the beginning showed none of that extreme hesitancy at the idea of resistance which characterised the English. Through Knox and Buchanan they could draw freely on a tradition of resistance theory, which was subject to none of the taboos which inhibited it in England. With their ascending theory of power in a kirk which was 'ane perfect republic'[86] they were better equipped than the English with a rival ideology to that of Charles I. Over and over again the key measures and ideas of the English parliament, the Triennial Act, the notion of treason against the realm, or the election of the great officers in parliament, turn out to have been anticipated in Scotland.

By contrast, the peculiarity of England is that, of Charles's three kingdoms, it was the one in which the king gathered the largest party. Since it was the kingdom in which Charles lived and the source of nine-tenths of his revenues, it is not surprising that he found it the easiest kingdom in which to gather support. Moreover, it was for his vision of the Church of England that Charles offended the Scots, and it is not surprising that the Church of England, like the Tory party after it, found more support in England than in the rest of Britain. The gravity of the English Civil War, when it came, was that it resulted from an even division of opinion: in no other kingdom did Charles muster the support of nearly half the kingdom. England experienced trouble, not because it was the most revolutionary of Charles's kingdoms, but because it was the least. Baillie was quite entitled to his observation that 'a gloom of the King's brow would disperse this feeble people, for any thing yet we see, if the terror of God and us afrayed not their enemies, if help from God and us did not continue their courage'.[87]

Notes

1 G.R. Elton, 'English National Selfconsciousness and the Parliament in the Sixteenth Century' in *Nationalismus in Vorindustrieller Zeit*, Herausgegeben von Otto Dann (München, 1986), p. 79.

2 B. Schofield (ed.), *The Knyvett Letters* (Norfolk Record Society, 1949, XX), p. 133. I would like to thank Miss Ann Brophy for this reference. G. Bankes, *Corfe Castle* (1853), pp. 132–3.

3 This was written before the publication of J.P. Sommerville, *Politics and Ideology in England 1603–40* (1986). The book has not caused me to change this judgment, but it has convinced me that it needs more defence than can be offered here.

4 Christopher Haigh, *The Reign of Elizabeth I* (1985), p. 19.

5 Peter Lake, 'The Collection of Ship Money in Cheshire', *NH*, 17 (1981), p. 71. Kenneth Fincham, 'The Judges' Decision on Ship Money in 1637: the Reaction of Kent', *BIHR*, 57 (1984), pp. 230–6. R.P. Cust, *The Forced Loan and English Politics 1626–1628* (1987).

6 *CSPD 1639*, vol. CCCCXVII, nos. 3, 26, 65; Vol. CCCCXVIII, no. 50.

7 J.H. Elliott, 'The King and the Catalans', *Cambridge Historical Journal*, 1953. H.G. Koenigsberger, *Dominium Regale and Dominium Politicum et Regale: Monarchies and Parliaments in Early Modern Europe* (London, 1975).

8 PRO, SP 16/527/44: BL, Stowe MS 187, fos. 51a, 57b.

9 Aidan Clarke, *The Old English in Ireland* (1966), pp. 28–60. *Strafforde Letters*, I, 238.

10 J. Russell Major, *Representative Government in Early Modern France* (New Haven, 1980), pp. 449, 474.

11 NLS, Advocates' MS 33.4.6, fos. 142a–146b.

12 *Proclamations*, II, 90–3. I would like to thank Dr N.R.N. Tyacke for this reference. *Strafforde Letters*, I, 187. I would like to thank Martin Flaherty for this reference.

13 C. Russell (ed.), *The Origins of the English Civil War* (1973), p. 121.

14 *P in P 1628*, IV, 261, III, 515; *CD 1625*, p. 181. Peter Smart, *The Vanities and Downfall of the Present Churches* (Edinburgh, 1628). I am grateful to Dr Tyacke for drawing my attention to the significance in this context of the citations of the Irish Articles against Charles's Arminian tendencies.

15 *Strafforde Letters*, I, 271. Laud was making fun of the 'Jonnisms' he associated with Wentworth's supposedly 'Puritan' upbringing in Cambridge.

16 Robert Baillie [hereafter Baillie], *Letters and Journals*, ed. D. Laing (Bannatyne Club, Edinburgh, 1841), I, 2 (further references are to Vol. I unless otherwise stated). Also Nicholas Tyacke, *Anti-Calvinists* (Oxford, 1987), pp. 230–4.

17 David Stevenson, *The Scottish Revolution* (Newton Abbot, 1973), p. 100 (*Strafforde Letters*, II, 190–2); *Strafforde Letters*, I. 187. I would like to thank Martin Flaherty for this reference.

18 HMC, *De L'Isle and Dudley*, VI, 366, KAO, U 1475 C.85/2.

19 John Leslie, Earl of Rothes [hereafter Rothes], *A Relation of Proceedings Concerning the Affairs of The Kirk of Scotland from August 1637 to July 1638*, ed. James Nairne (Bannatyne Club, Edinburgh, 1830), pp. 45–6, 5. SRO, GD 406/1 Hamilton MSS no. 547.

20 For the claim to the royal supremacy in Scotland, see the Scottish canons, Laud, V, 586. For Laud's belief that such authority was inherent in all sovereign princes, as it had been in the Kings of Judah, see Baillie, II, Appendix p. 434.

For a rare attempt to justify Charles's claim in Scottish law and practice, see John Rylands Library, Crawford MSS 14/3/35, probably dating from the Pacification of Berwick. I am grateful to the earl of Crawford and Balcarres for permission to use these MSS, and to Dr J.S.A. Adamson for bringing them to my attention. For the case Charles appears to have been discussing, see B. Galloway, *The Union of England and Scotland 1603–1608* (Edinburgh, 1986), p. 87. See also *Proclamations*, II, 91.

21 SRO, Hamilton MSS M. 1/80. For the case for believing the supremacy was *jure divino*, and not founded on the municipal laws of any kingdom, see PRO, SP 16/288/88.

22 Gordon Donaldson, *The Making of the Scottish Prayer Book of 1637* (Edinburgh, 1954), pp. 42–3. *A Large Declaration* (1640), pp. 20, 16.

23 This was the conventional view, but in *Calvin's Case* it had been argued that the parliament of England could bind Ireland by express words: Coke, *Seventh Report*, 17. For the conventional view, stated by the earl of Leicester, probably when about to take up appointment as Lord Deputy, see KAO, De L'Isle and Dudley MSS, Z 47. I am grateful to Blair Worden for drawing my attention to this uncalendared portion of the collection and to Viscount De L'Isle and Dudley for permission to quote from his family papers.

24 *New Irish History*, edited by T.W. Moody, F.X. Martin and F.T. Byrne (Oxford, 1976), III, 242.

25 Aidan Clarke, 'Ireland and the "General Crisis"', *P & P* 1970, p. 81.

26 *Strafforde Letters* I, 212, 298, 329. I would like to thank Martin Flaherty for these references.

27 Rothes, p. 144.

28 Baillie, p. 120.

29 The suggestion of using Antrim appears to have originated with Hamilton. SRO, Hamilton MSS, 10,488, Hamilton to Charles, 15 June 1638.

30 Baillie, pp. 192–4.

31 Rothes, p. 137.

32 PRO, SP 16/466/36, 467/5; BL, Harl MS 457, fos. 3b, 4a, 6b, 8a.

33 PRO, SP 63/260/7.1; *C.J. Ireland*, I, 174ff.

34 *C.J. Ireland*, I, 165.

35 Bodl. L., MS Carte 2, fo. 137b.

36 *LJ*, iv, 415.

37 BL, Stowe MS 187, ff. 9b, 41a. PRO, SP 16/471/22 shows the Scots pressing for such an Act in England, in order that any future disputes between the kingdoms should be considered in parliament.

38 H.B. Wheatley (ed.), *Diary of John Evelyn* (1906), IV, 95, 97, 98.

39 Baillie, 278.

40 NLS, Advocates' MSS 3.4.6, fos. 145–6; David Stevenson, *The Scottish Revolution* (Newton Abbot, 1973), pp. 218–21. The Scots' paper of 24 February is in BL, Stowe MS 187, fos. 38–9, and Thomason Tracts 669 f. 3(4). It is worth remarking that the MS version is in Scottish spelling, and the printed version in English spelling.

41 *LJ*, iv, 216; BL, Harl MS 6424, fo. 55a. NLS, Advocates' MSS 33.4.6, fos. 130, 133. Edinburgh University Library, Ms Dc 4.16, fos. 93a–94a.

42 PRO, SP 16/480/20.

43 NLS, Wodrow MS fos. 65, 65a, 72a–b. For the hardening line towards the Scottish Commissioners in London which accompanied this switch, *see LJ*, iv, 175.

44 NLS, Advocates' MSS 33.4.6, fos. 119a, 121b.

45 Baillie, II, 6–7, 34–5.

46 Gardiner, *History*, IX, 395–98. NLS, Wodrow Ms fos. 65, nos. 12, 17.

47 This abortive plan was perhaps more important in Charles's strategy in 1642 than has been appreciated. See Gardiner, *History*, X, 203, and Stevenson, *Scottish Revolution*, pp. 248–49. See also *RPCS*, VIII, 255–63, 264–65, *Letters of Henrietta Maria*, ed. M.A.E. Green (1853), pp. 53, 60, SRO, Hamilton MSS 1653, 1723, 1753, 1760, HMC, *Buccleuch*, I, 298, and East Riding RO, Hotham MSS DD/HO/1/4.

48 C. Burges, *The First Sermon* (1641), p. 6.

49 Baillie, p. 283. The poem to which Baillie refers is in *Diary of John Rous*, edited by M.A.E. Green, Camden Society, (1886), cxvi, 110–11, and NLS, Advocates' MSS 33.1.1, XIII, no. 69.

50 W. Notestein (ed.), *Journal of Sir Symonds D'Ewes* (New Haven, 1923), p. 320, BL, Harl. MS 163, fo. 10a.

51 Nehemiah Wallington, *Historical Notices*, edited by Rosamond Ann Webb, I, 171. His text, *Rev* 18.2, describes the downfall of the Beast. See also Paul S. Seaver, *Wallington's World* (Stanford, 1985), p. 164.

52 Bodl. L., MS Clarendon 10, no. 1514.

53 Yale University Beinecke Library, Osborn Shelves b 197, fo. 40b.

54 Maija Jansson (ed.), *Two Diaries of the Long Parliament* (Gloucester, 1984), p. 18.

55 BL, Harl MS 163, fo. 696b.

56 *D'Ewes* edited by Notestein, p. 418; *Two Diaries of the Long Parliament*, pp. 12–13.

57 NLS, Advocates' MSS 33.4.6, fos. 129a. See also NLS, Wodrow MS Quarto 25, fo. 117b, describing how the Scottish preachers in London were ordinarily invited to preach publicly to great auditors, and Surrey RO (Guildford), Bray MSS 52/2/19(8), Nicholas to Charles, 8 August 1641, reminding Charles 'what invoncenience pmitting the Scots comrs. to be in towne and treate hath beene to yet mats. affaires, and what a disturbance their daily presence did give to ye government'. I am grateful to Dr J.S.A. Adamson for drawing my attention to this important group of Nicholas Papers.

58 PRO, SP 16/465/16 [my italics].

59 HMC, *Egmont*, I, 122.

60 *D'Ewes* edited by Notestein, pp. 3, 100–2, 224; PRO, SP 63/258/51, 53, 68.

61 HLRO, House of Lords Main Papers, 9, 17, 30 July 1641. For an attempt by the Irish bishops to involve the English parliament in Irish affairs, see PRO, SP 63/274/44.

62 J.T. Gilbert, *History of the Irish Confederation* (Dublin, 1882), I, 251, 289.

63 SRO, Hamilton MSS 718, 719.

64 HMC, *De L'Isle and Dudley*, VI, 366; KAO, U 1475 C 114/7.

65 SRO, Hamilton MSS 167.

66 *CSPD 1639*, Vol. ccccxviii, no. 50; *RPCS*, VIII, 3–4; Rothes, pp. 98–9; Baillie, pp. 25, 43.

67 *A Large Declaration* (1640), pp. 1–16.

68 SRO, Hamilton MSS 883, 948.

69 SRO, Hamilton MSS 1031, 1030, 1218.

70 See my article, 'The British Background to the Irish Rebellion', *HR* 61 (1988).

71 Laud, VI, i, 23; H.R. Trevor-Roper, *Archbishop Laud* (1940), pp. 157–62. See also Gardiner, *History*, VIII, 167.

72 SRO, Hamilton MSS 1031.

73 Galloway, *The Union*, pp. 86–9.

74 Kenneth Fincham and Peter Lake, 'The Ecclesiastical Policy of King James I', *JBS* (1985, 24), pp. 169–207. W.R. Foster, *The Church Before the Covenants* (Edinburgh and London, 1975), pp. 12, 16, 18, 20, 22, 26, 29.

75 Galloway, *The Union*, pp. 6, 43; Foster, p. 2.

76 Foster, p. 29.

77 SRO, Hamilton MSS 985. The story emerged from a rash Covenanter boast to Traquair, and was relayed by Traquair to London.

78 NLS, Advocates' MSS 33.1.1, no. 28. I am grateful to Dr T.I. Rae for drawing my attention to this Ms. The Petition of the 12 Peers was reported together with the City petition, which was prepared jointly with it. For a text of the City Petition, see Yale University Beinecke Library, Osborn Shelves b. 197, fo. 9ᵛ.

79 SRO, Hamilton MSS 327.1.

80 C. Burges, *The First Sermon*, Ep. Ded.

81 *CSPD 1639*, Vol. ccccxvii, nos. 85, 92.

82 Bodl. L. MS Rawlinson D. 1099, fo. 22b.

83 SRO, Hamilton MSS 1585, 1586.

84 See my article, 'The British Background to the Irish Rebellion', pp. 166–82.

85 For a very different route to a similar conclusion, see John Morrill and J.D. Walter, 'Order and Disorder in the English Revolution', Chapter 12 below.

86 The phrase is from *Reasons for a Generall Assemblie* (Edinburgh?, 1638), STC 22,054 Sig B.1.

87 Baillie, p. 283.

SECTION

II

RELIGION

5

Puritanism, Arminianism and counter-revolution

NICHOLAS TYACKE

I

Historians of the English Civil War all agree that Puritanism had a role to play in its origins. Beyond this however agreement ceases. For some, particularly the Marxists, Puritanism was the ideology of the newly emergent middle classes or *bourgeoisie*, as they are sometimes called. Puritan ideas, it is argued, complemented and encouraged the capitalist activities of 'progressive' gentry, merchants and artisans alike. On the assumption, again made by those most under the influence of Marxism, that the English Civil War was a 'bourgeois revolution' the Puritans are naturally to be found fighting against King Charles and his old-world followers. An alternative and widely held interpretation sees Puritanism as a religious fifth column within the Church of England, and one whose numbers dramatically increased during the first decades of the seventeenth century; by the early 1640s, with the collapse of the central government and its repressive system of church courts, the Puritans were thus able to take over at least in the religious sphere. These two schools of thought, the Marxist and the fifth-columnist, are best represented by the writings respectively of Dr. Christopher Hill and Professor William Haller.

In the following essay however a different view will be put forward, to the effect that religion became an issue in the civil war crisis due primarily to the rise to power of Arminianism in the 1620s. The essence of Arminianism was a belief in God's universal grace and the freewill of all men to obtain salvation. Therefore Arminians rejected the teaching of Calvinism that the world was divided into elect and reprobate whom God had arbitrarily predestinated, the one to Heaven and the other to Hell. It is difficult for us to grasp how great a revolution this involved for a society as steeped in Calvinist theology as was England before the civil war. But whether or not we agree with the arguments of Christopher Hill, it is clear that the Puritan ideas to which he ascribes so much importance for the development of modern, capitalist society are in the main predestinarian ones. Similarly with Haller's thesis concerning the growth of Puritanism, the message preached with such success from Puritan pulpits was rooted in the Calvinist theology of grace.[1]

At the beginning of the seventeenth century, a majority of the clergy from the archbishop of Canterbury downwards were Calvinists in doctrine, and the same was probably true of the more educated laity. So Puritanism in this Calvinist sense was not then seen as a political threat. Only when predestinarian teaching came to be outlawed by the leaders of the established church, as was the case under Archbishop William Laud, would its exponents find themselves in opposition to the government. Any doubts that the Church of England was doctrinally Calvinist, before Laud took control, can be resolved by reading the extant doctoral theses in divinity maintained at Oxford University from the 1580s to the 1620s. There, year after year predestinarian teaching was formally endorsed, and its opposite denied. The following are a representative selection of such theses, translated from the original Latin and listed in chronological order: 'No one who is elect can perish' (1582); 'God of his own volition will repudiate some people' (1596); 'According to the eternal predestination of God some are ordained to life and others to death' (1597); 'Man's spiritual will is not itself capable of achieving true good' (1602); 'The saints cannot fall from grace' (1608); 'Is grace sufficient for salvation granted to all men? No.' (1612); 'Does man's will only play a passive role in his initial conversion? Yes' (1618); 'Is faith and the righteousness of faith the exclusive property of the elect? Yes' (1619); and 'Has original sin utterly extinguished free will in Adam and his posterity? Yes' (1622). The licensed publications of the English press tell the same Calvinist story, albeit in a more popular vein, as do many religious preambles to wills where the testator confidently affirms belief in his divine election. A good example of this type of Calvinist will is that made by Lord Treasurer Dorset, who died in 1608; George Abbot, future archbishop of Canterbury, was so impressed by Dorset's claim to be an elect saint that he quoted the will verbatim when preaching his funeral sermon in Westminster Abbey. Calvinism at the time was clearly establishment orthodoxy, and contemporaries would have found any suggestion that Calvinists were Puritans completely incomprehensible.[2]

Puritanism around the year 1600, and for more than two decades subsequently, was thought of in terms either of a refusal to conform with the religious rites and ceremonies of the English Church, or as a presbyterian rejection of church government by bishops. At that date conformists and nonconformists, episcopalians and presbyterians all had in common Calvinist predestinarian ideas. Here however we come to the crux of the matter, for Calvinism also helped to reconcile the differences between them. Thus the late Elizabethan archbishop of Canterbury, John Whitgift, who was a Calvinist in doctrine, regarded Puritan nonconformity in a different light from that of the Arminian Archbishop Laud. This did not stop Whitgift as archbishop from attacking nonconformists, especially with Queen Elizabeth hard on his heels, but it did impose important limits on the extent of his persecution. Before the advent of Laud, nonconformists and even presbyterians were never regarded as being totally beyond the pale; they were seen instead as aberrant brethren deserving of some indulgence. Symbolic of the pre-Laudian state of affairs is that in the 1560s Whitgift had been a nonconformist and Thomas Cartwright, the later presbyterian, a candidate for an Irish archbishopric and, despite a long history of public controversy between them, they ended up on good terms in the 1590s. Calvinist doctrine provided a common and ameliorating bond that was only to be destroyed by the rise of Arminianism. As a result of this destruction, during the 1620s, Puritanism came to be redefined in terms which included the very Calvinism that previously had linked non-conformists to the leaders of the established church, and the nonconformist element in the former Calvinist partnership was driven into an unprecedented radicalism. The Arminians and their patron King Charles were undoubtedly the religious revolutionaries in the first instance. Opposed to them were the Calvinists, initially conservative and counter-revolutionary, of whom the typical lay representative was John Pym. These are the developments which we must now consider in detail. First however something more needs saying about the definition of a Puritan.[3]

One possibility would be to define Puritanism in terms of Calvinist predestinarian teachings, and certainly many modern writers agree in labelling this body of ideas as in some sense Puritan. We have already noted that such labelling involves the paradox of making Archbishop Whitgift and most of his fellow bishops into Puritans. Doctrinal Calvinism does not however explain why Elizabethan Protestants became nonconformists, presbyterians, and sometimes separatists. Here what seems to have been critical was a difference in attitude to the authority of the Bible as a religious model, although the distinction is by no means clear cut. Indeed the point needs making that it is extremely artificial to start drawing hard and fast lines between Puritans and 'Anglicans' in the Elizabethan and Jacobean periods. There are far too many cases which defy categorisation. For example in a sermon collection published in 1585, Archbishop Sandys of York asserted that 'in the scriptures . . . is contained all that is good, and all that which God requireth or accepteth of', and that this was no empty claim is clear from his will, dated two years later, where he wrote 'concerning rites and ceremonies by political constitutions authorised amongst us, . . . in the church reformed, and in all this time of the gospel (wherein the seed of the scripture hath so long been sown), they may better be disused by little and little'. Despite these declared views Archbishop Sandys himself conformed, and was prepared on occasion to prosecute in the church courts those who did not. At the other extreme however the separatist leader Henry Barrow, writing in 1591, justified his separation from the Church of England on the grounds that 'every part of the

Scripture is alike true, inspired of God, given to our direction and instruction in all things'.[4]

But if Calvinism did not cause Puritan nonconformity there was as we have said a willingness among predestinarians to tolerate such aberrations, or at least not to regard them in a very serious light. This can be illustrated by a visitation sermon preached in 1605 about 'the lawful use of things indifferent'. The author was a doctrinal Calvinist, Sebastian Benefield, who later as Lady Margaret professor of divinity at Oxford became well known for his attacks on Arminian heresy. In his sermon of 1605 he took as his model St. Paul, who became 'all things to all men' that he might 'by all means save some', and placed ceremonial conformity firmly in the context of the elect's calling to salvation by the sowing of 'the immortal seed of the word of God'. Preaching he described as the human means 'whereby the foreknown of God from all eternity, and the predestinated to life of God's pure favour, are effectually called from the state of servitude to liberty'. This task of preaching took priority over any conscientious scruples about wearing surplices and the like, and it was the duty of a minister to conform rather than be silenced. On the other hand, although Benefield did not explicitly make the point, those in authority logically should exercise great restraint in applying ultimate sanctions against nonconformists lest their evangelising services be lost. Another doctrinal Calvinist whose writings exhibit an even more marked ambiguity than do Benefield's as regards nonconformity, was Samuel Gardiner. His theology can readily be deduced from a series of surviving sermons which he preached in 1611 on the subject of God's eternal predestination. Earlier, in 1605, he had published a work in dialogue form concerning 'the rites and ceremonies of the Church of England,' in the course of which the conformist admits to his opponent that 'if the laws had not been in these cases already made, I should never, for my own part, wish to have them made.' But for the present ceremonies were to be tolerated until 'it shall seem good by higher powers, they may as superfluous or little profitable, grow out of use.' The views of Benefield and Gardiner are highly relevant for understanding official attitudes to Puritan nonconformity before the time of Laud, because both men became chaplains to George Abbot, archbishop of Canterbury from 1611 to 1633. Abbot, a committed predestinarian, was chided by King James in 1613 for advancing 'one of the puritans' arguments', when he maintained that 'Scripture doth directly or by consequence contain in it sufficient matter to decide all controversies, especially in things appertaining to the church.' This links Abbot with Archbishop Sandys, who, as we have seen, believed that the rites and ceremonies of the Church of England needed further reformation.[5]

In the light of such evidence it should already be apparent that the first decades of the seventeenth century in England did not witness any straightforward contest between an 'Anglican' hierarchy on the one hand

and the serried ranks of Puritanism on the other. This becomes even clearer if we take the case of William Perkins, whom Christopher Hill has described as 'the dominant influence in Puritan thought for the forty years after his death' in 1602. His funeral sermon was preached by James Montagu, shortly to become dean of the chapel royal and subsequently bishop of Winchester, and the chief critic of Perkin's works was answered in print by Bishop Robert Abbot of Salisbury, whose intellectual position was identical to that of his brother the archbishop. While this blurring of religious differences seems characteristic of the period, a further complicating factor was the religious standpoint of the monarch, as supreme head of the English Church. James I was much more sympathetic to Calvinist doctrine than his predecessor Elizabeth, and to that extent those Puritan nonconformists were correct who hoped for better things on the queen's death in 1603. The proof of the king's Calvinist affinities was conveniently published as a pamphlet in 1626, by Francis Rous, who was the step-brother of John Pym and an outspoken parliamentary critic of Arminianism. Two examples of this royal Calvinism must suffice. In 1604 James was officially quoted as saying that 'predestination and election dependeth not upon any qualities, actions or works of man, which be mutable, but upon God his eternal and immutable decree and purpose.' Similarly in 1619 he wrote that 'God draws by his effectual grace, out of that attainted and corrupt mass [mankind], whom he pleaseth for the work of his mercy, leaving the rest to their own ways which all lead to perdition.' Yet having demonstrated James's Calvinism, and therefore the existence of a common and potentially reconciling bond with Puritan nonconformists, one is faced with the problem of his celebrated outbursts against Puritans – as for instance when he described them in March 1604 as a 'sect unable to be suffered in any well-governed commonwealth', and the deprivations for nonconformity which occurred during his first years on the throne. The explanation, however, would seem to lie in *raison d'état*, as that was interpreted by the king. His exposure in Scotland at an early age to Calvinist theology had left him favourably disposed towards its teachings, yet his experience there of religious rebellion had also made him politically suspicious of anything remotely akin to presbyterianism. Whereas for Elizabeth political considerations had complemented her religious antipathies, with James there was thus something of a conflict. The preface to the 1603 edition of his book *Basilicon Doron*, where James withdrew some earlier unflattering comments about Puritans, has often been seen as propaganda aimed at smoothing the path of his succession to the English throne. But the same sentiments recur, notably in some royal remarks paraphrased by Robert Cecil during a Star Chamber speech in 1605. 'For the puritans . . . [the King] would go half way to meet them, and he loved and reverenced many of them, and if they would leave their [nonconformist] opinions, there were some of them he would prefer to the best bishoprics that were void.' King James himself put the dichotomy more succinctly in July of the previous year. 'To discreet men I say, they shall obtain their desires by grace, but to all I profess, they shall extort nothing by violence.'[6]

These distinctions would be rather academic had James's fear of Puritan nonconformity continued to dominate him as much as it did during the earliest years of his English reign. Increasingly however, a countervailing political factor emerged in the shape of an intensified fear of Catholicism. This was particularly the case between 1608 and 1615, a period in which the king himself wrote as many as three works on the subject of the oath of allegiance. The latter was a modified form of the supremacy oath, enacted by statute during the aftermath of Gunpowder Plot in an attempt to isolate politically disloyal Catholics. Any chance of success which the scheme might have had was effectively wrecked by strong papal opposition and an ensuing pamphlet war. Almost inevitably Puritanism benefited from this redirection of government energies. Religious differences among the various royal champions who entered the lists were subsumed in a cloud of zeal against the common papist enemy. Catholic charges that Puritans differed on doctrinal grounds from the established church were publicly denied even by emergent Arminians like Bishop Andrewes, and there was a widespread campaign to ban the use of the term Puritan completely. Suggestive also is the fact that from 1611 until 1618 no work directed specifically against Puritanism, either in its nonconformist or presbyterian guises, is recorded in the Stationers' Registers as being licensed for the press.[7]

In part symptomatic of the altered climate was George Abbot's own promotion to Canterbury in 1611. The Jesuit Father Coffin wrote of the new primate as 'a brutal and fierce man, and a sworn enemy of the very name of Catholic'. Certainly his elevation occurred during a two-year period which witnessed a third of all the Catholic martyrdoms under James. The supposition that these events were linked is further strengthened by the terms in which the appointment of Toby Matthew to the archbishopric of York had been canvassed back in 1606. Already at that date there was alarm in government circles over conditions in the north, as an area 'overpestered with popery and not with puritanism'. Cecil was urged to promote the appointment of 'a painful and preaching successor' to Archbishop Hutton and one 'industrious against papists'. Policy however was often inextricably interwoven with patronage; just as Cecil was Matthew's patron, so Abbot had been recommended as archbishop by the current royal favourite Dunbar. Abbot, as Dunbar's chaplain, had been instrumental in helping reconcile the Scottish Church to episcopacy, and his Puritan proclivities almost certainly contributed to the success of that enterprise. Compared with his Protestant predecessors at Canterbury, Abbot in his general outlook seems most to have resembled Edmund

Grindal. The latter has recently been described by Professor Collinson as
'one of the very few Elizabethan bishops who enjoyed the full approval of
the protestant governing class and the equal confidence of all but a small
embittered minority of the godly preaching ministers.'[8]

By contrast, the archiepiscopal predecessor whom Abbot least
resembled was the man he immediately succeeded. This was Richard
Bancroft, whose policies more than those of any other churchman prior
to the Arminian Laud drove Puritan nonconformists to extremes.
Bancroft's loathing of Puritanism amounted almost to paranoia, and his
espionage methods threatened to make real the Puritan conspiracy which
originated largely as a figment of his own imagination. He was also among
the first Protestant churchmen in England to disassociate himself from the
predestinarian teachings of Calvinism, and therefore lacked the restraining
influence of a theology shared with his nonconformist opponents. Fortunately, from the point of view of political stability, Bancroft's extremism
was kept in check by King James. Indeed the appointment of Bancroft to
Canterbury in 1604 was a Jacobean anomaly; his Elizabethan record of
severity against Puritans apparently recommended him as the man of the
hour, when nonconformist clergy, backed by gentry support, seemed to
pose a serious political threat. As archbishop, Bancroft had from the start
been a rather isolated figure. Those who succeeded him in the bishopric of
London, a post which administratively ranked second only to Canterbury,
were all Calvinists during his lifetime. One of them, Richard Vaughan,
who was bishop of London from 1604 to 1607, became well known for his
tolerance of Puritan deviation from the strict letter of the law. Moreover in
1608 Bancroft was forced to acquiesce in the publication of an official
Calvinist commentary on The Thirty-Nine Articles – the Church of
England's confession of faith. After his death in 1610 Calvinist dominance
became even more marked, and the combined religious and political atmosphere generally favoured a *modus vivendi* with Puritan nonconformity. In
addition to government attacks on Catholicism, which distracted attention
from disagreements among Protestants, the chief posts in the church were
filled by men whose views at many important points merged with those of
their nonconformist brethren. Both Archbishop Abbot and John King,
bishop of London from 1611 to 1621, had been lecturers in the 1590s,
and the former expressed the hope during a parliamentary debate in 1610
that he would die in the pulpit. They were also sabbatarians, Abbot
successfully intervening in 1618 to preserve the Puritan Sunday from the
threat of the royal Declaration of Sports. A third very powerful Jacobean
cleric was Bishop James Montagu of Winchester, editor of King James's
collected works and a privy councillor. He had been the first master of
Sidney Sussex College in Cambridge where he had not enforced conformity, and we have noted his connexion with the 'Puritan' theologian
William Perkins. His brother, Sir Edward Montagu, had been a prominent

spokesman on behalf of nonconformist Puritans during the parliament of 1604. All three bishops were Calvinists, Montagu assuming a watching brief for doctrinal orthodoxy at Cambridge and Abbot placing his brother Robert and his chaplain Benefield, respectively in the Regius and Lady Margaret chairs of divinity at Oxford. At the same time, with royal fears of Catholicism still in the ascendant, these churchmen had the support of the new favourite Buckingham. Archbishop Abbot was on sufficiently familiar terms in 1616 to call him 'my George', being dubbed 'father' in return, and Montagu, who died in 1618, described Buckingham in his will as 'the most faithful friend that ever I had'. In Montagu's view the period since the accession of King James in 1603 had on the whole been one of 'harmony' with the Puritans.[9]

This impression of comparative calm receives some statistical confirmation from a recent study of Puritan lecturers in London by Dr. Seaver. Between 1604 and 1606 out of twenty identifiable Puritan lecturers only six came before the church courts, and of these six only one was permanently suspended from preaching. From 1607 to 1609 the pattern was 'much the same'. During the second decade of the seventeenth century prosecutions for nonconformity were even fewer and Seaver conjectures that 'at a time when controversy was at a minimum, when no great issues divided public opinion . . . some puritanically inclined ministers might have found little cause for militancy and small reason not to conform'. A situation similar to that in London existed in the northern province, under Archbishop Toby Matthew, where citations for nonconformity were rare despite the existence of many potential offenders. According to Dr. Marchant's account of Puritanism in the diocese of York, a 'general policy of toleration' prevailed there until the late 1620s. Matthew was a Calvinist and employed at least one moderate nonconformist, John Favour, as his chaplain, as well as being an indefatigable preacher himself. With archbishops like Matthew and Abbot in command, Puritanism presented no real problem.[10]

There was however an element of uncertainty in the situation, since much could depend on the vagaries of international politics and the shifting sands of court favour. Just as the oath of allegiance controversy, and its associated anti-Catholic attitudes, had worked to the benefit of Puritan nonconformity, so with plans for marrying Prince Charles to a Catholic Spanish infanta the process seemed about to go into reverse. By 1618 there was talk of tolerating Catholicism, as a condition of the Spanish marriage. The concomitant of this would be a slump in demand for polemic against the popish Antichrist, and tighter government control over the diversity of Protestant practice. That this threat did not materialise was mainly due to a political crisis in the Low Countries, which was deemed to affect England's foreign policy interests. In the United Provinces, Oldenbarnveldt and Prince Maurice were engaged in a struggle for power, and had enlisted on their respective sides the rival Dutch church parties of Arminian and Calvinist. King James, for reasons which included theology, supported Maurice and the Calvinists, and in late 1618 sent a delegation, under Bishop Carleton of Llandaff, to participate in an international synod at Dort. This gathering proceeded to condemn the Arminian theology of grace, and affirm its Calvinist converse, and was an event which has never received the emphasis it deserves from students of English religious history. For the Calvinist doctrines at issue in the United Provinces were fundamental to English Puritanism before the civil war, in a way that ceremonies and discipline were not. Calvinist predestinarian teaching was, as we have indicated, a crucial common assumption, shared by a majority of the hierarchy and virtually all its nonconformist opponents, during the Elizabethan and Jacobean periods. Indeed it is not too much to say that for many people in the early seventeenth century the basic issue as between Protestantism and Catholicism was that of divine determinism versus human freewill. Calvinist affinities between the bishops and their critics lent substance to claims that rites and ceremonies were matters of indifference. Accordingly the assertion of predestinarian Calvinism made by the Synod of Dort, with English delegates participating and its published proceedings dedicated to King James, served to emphasise afresh the theology binding conformist and nonconformist together, and the limits which that common bond imposed on persecution.

Hindsight is often the curse of the historian, and none more so in attempting to reconstruct the religious history of the pre-civil war era. The battle lines of 1640–2 were not drawn by the early 1620s in this any more than other spheres. The parliaments of 1621 and 1624 were remarkable for a dearth of religious grievances. 'Godly reformation' was limited to allegations of corrupt practices by certain ecclesiastical officials, and requests that the recusancy laws be more strictly enforced. Among the clergy an appeal from Bermuda in 1617 by the presbyterian Lewis Hughes, to avoid persecution by emigration, fell on deaf ears. Moreover in 1621 Hughes's own form of catechism concerning 'public exercises of religion', as well as a tract on strict sabbath observance, were licensed for publication by one of Archbishop Abbot's chaplains. When therefore the Spanish marriage negotiations finally collapsed in 1624 it was natural for the favourite Buckingham to cultivate closer relations with John Preston, at that date 'leader of Puritan party', again to quote Chrisopher Hill. Two years before, Buckingham had secured for Preston the mastership of Emmanuel College, Cambridge, and now held out promises of further preferment. Preston was a Calvinist conformist and the Cambridge protégé of John Davenant, who had been a delegate to the Synod of Dort and was now bishop of Salisbury. Far from being an untypical eccentric, Davenant was in the mainstream of Calvinist episcopalianism, and that Preston also found favour was of a piece with Jacobean religious developments. Indeed

Preston might well have ended up adorning the episcopal bench. This was the context in which John Pym, during the parliament of 1621, rejected 'that odious and factious name of puritans' which a fellow member had tried to fasten on the promoters of a bill for the better observance of Sunday. Pym thought that the speech was especially reprehensible in that it tended to 'divide us amongst our selves . . . or at least would make the world believe we were divided'. As it turned out however Preston died in the ecclesiastical wilderness in 1628, and a doctrinal revolution took place within the established church which shattered the Jacobean dispensation. The two events were intimately connected, for during the 1620s the Calvinist heritage was overthrown and with it the prerequisite of English Protestant unity. The result was a polarisation of extremes unknown since the Reformation, and one which rendered earlier compromises unworkable. It is this triumph of Arminianism, and its divisive consequences, which we must now consider.[11]

II

England in the early seventeenth century was doctrinally a part of Calvinist Europe, and it is within this ambience that the teachings of the Dutch theologian Arminius at Leyden have to be seen. During the first decade of the century, Arminius elaborated a critique of doctrinal Calvinism so systematic as to give his name to an international movement, namely Arminianism. He was concerned to refute the teachings on divine grace associated with the followers of Calvin, but he spoke as a member of the fully reformed and presbyterian Dutch Church, whereas his doctrinal equivalents in England were part of a different ecclesiastical tradition. There the most notable survivor of the English Reformation, apart from episcopacy, was the Prayer Book which, as its critics were pleased to point out, was an adapted version of the old Catholic mass book. Consequently Arminianism in England emerged with an additional, sacramental dimension to that in the United Provinces. Arminius was read with approval by anti-Calvinists in England but adapted to the local situation. English Arminians came to balance their rejection of the arbitrary grace of predestination with a new found source of grace freely available in the sacraments, which Calvinists had belittled. Hence the preoccupation under Archbishop Laud with altars and private confession before receiving communion, as well as a belief in the absolute necessity of baptism.

By the 1620s the Church of England had been Calvinist in doctrine for approximately sixty years. There had however always been a minority of dissidents, who led a more-or-less clandestine existence; in so far as these had a collective designation in the Elizabethan period they were known as 'Lutherans', after the second-generation followers of Luther who had rejected Calvinist predestinarian teaching. Not until Bancroft did the

English 'Lutherans' find a champion holding high office and, as we have noted, not even he was strong enough to swim against the Calvinist tide. But after Bancroft's death in 1610 other lesser figures emerged to lead what it now becomes proper to call the Arminian party within the Church of England. The most powerful member of this early Arminian leadership was Bishop Richard Neile, although it also included Bishops Andrewes, Buckeridge and Overall; Laud was still a relatively obscure figure, dependent on Neile's patronage. They were not allowed to air their Arminian views in print, but managed to register them in a variety of covert ways. For example, in 1617, Neile, on his translation to the bishopric of Durham, had the communion table transformed into an altar at the east end of the cathedral and supported Laud in a like action the same year at Gloucester, where the latter was dean. A few years later Overall and Andrewes can be found advocating the novel practice of private confession before receiving the communion. As Laud was to say, during the 1630s, 'the altar is the greatest place of God's residence upon earth, greater than the pulpit; for there 'tis *Hoc est corpus meum*, This is my body; but in the other it is at most but *Hoc est verbum meum*, This is my word.' Such a view involved the replacement of preaching as the normal vehicle of saving grace, and one restricted in its application to the elect saints, by sacraments which conferred grace indiscriminately; baptism of all infants, without qualification, began the process of salvation, and this was to be followed by the regular receiving of communion as a result of which all partakers, provided they confessed past sins, were renewed in grace. This flank attack on predestinarian Calvinism has misled historians into thinking that the Dutch and English Arminian movements were unconnected. In fact both Arminian parties considered themselves to be engaged in a mutual duel with Calvinism; as early as 1605 the views of Arminius were being cited with approval by anti-Calvinists in Cambridge, and the Dutch Arminians can be found from 1613 until the eve of the Synod of Dort appealing for help to Arminian bishops like Andrewes and Overall. But the latter were powerless to intervene in the United Provinces, engaged as they were in their own English struggle for survival.

If the situation was ever to alter in favour of the English Arminians, their best hope lay in trying to capture the mind of the king or at least that of the royal favourite. This was the course on which they embarked, during the aftermath of the Synod of Dort. Neile was the chief intermediary between the Arminians and King James, while Laud came to play an equivalent role in Buckingham's entourage. Apart from direct theological argument in favour of Arminianism, one powerful lever was to suggest that Calvinist conformists were Puritans at heart and as such politically subversive, or again that predestinarian Calvinism lent itself to so much popular misunderstanding that its widespread propagation inevitably led to religious conflict. By 1624 arguments of this kind seem to have affected adversely James's attitude towards Calvinism. Fear of approaching death may also have helped sap his confidence in deterministic teaching, for should doubt as to whether one was an elect saint ever become unbearable, there was always the Arminian possibility of denying that the predestinarian scheme was true. As regards Buckingham, opportunism was the most effective argument for his listening sympathetically to the Arminians. In 1624 he was identified with war against Spain, and was temporarily the hero of the parliamentary and ultra-Protestant camp. Buckingham was well aware however that the situation could rapidly change and a need arise for new allies. His willingness to support the Arminian Laud, while at the same time patronising the 'Puritan' Preston, was part of a double insurance policy for the future.

It was in this more hopeful atmosphere that the Arminian party decided on a test case. This took the form of publishing a book in 1624, by the Arminian Richard Montagu, which while ostensibly answering Roman Catholic criticisms of the Church of England also rejected predestinarian Calvinism, on the ground that this was no part of the teaching enshrined in the Thirty-Nine Articles. The interpretation of these articles was and still is debatable, but not only were Bishop Neile and his chaplains able to get Montagu's book, the *New Gag*, past the censor; they also managed to prevent its subsequent suppression. In terms of previous Arminian experience in England this was a dramatic breakthrough. Outraged Calvinist clergy appealed to parliament; John Pym took up their cause in the house of commons, and Archbishop Abbot made representations to King James. The only result was a royal request that Richard Montagu clarify his views by writing a second book. Yet it soon became clear that the final arbiter of England's theological fate would be the heir to the throne, Prince Charles. Prior to his accession some observers considered Charles to be inclined towards Puritanism, but those closer to him, among them the Arminian Mathew Wren, claimed the reverse was true and that on this score his reign would contrast with James's. Wren's prediction was to prove abundantly true, for King Charles became the architect of an Arminian revolution which had at most been dimly foreshadowed in the last year of his father's reign. As the house of commons was to complain in 1629: 'some prelates, near the King, having gotten the chief administration of ecclesiastical affairs under his Majesty, have discountenanced and hindered the preferment of those that are orthodox [i.e. Calvinist], and favoured such as are contrary.'[12]

The suddenness of James's death in March 1625 seems to have taken most people by surprise. Buckingham survived as royal favourite, but it was now Charles who increasingly made the religious pace. The new king had never apparently been a Calvinist; certainly a decisive bias in favour of Arminianism became clear during the first few months of his reign. Calvinist bishops were excluded from the royal counsels, and in July 1625 the

Arminian Richard Montagu was placed under Charles's personal protection. In February of the following year Buckingham, clearly acting with the
approval of Charles, chaired a debate at York House on the subject of
Montagu's writings, in the course of which he made plain his Arminian
sympathies. The Arminian Bishop Buckeridge was pitted against the
Calvinist Bishop Morton, and during their exchanges the question arose
as to how predestinarian doctrine could be reconciled with Prayer Book
teaching on the sacraments of baptism and communion. 'What,' exclaimed
Morton, 'will you have the grace of God tied to sacraments?' Buckeridge's
seconder, Dean White of Carlisle, replied that all baptised infants were
'made the sons of god by adoption', and Buckingham told Morton that he
'disparaged his own ministry, and did . . . debase the sacrament'. White
further argued that the Synod of Dort, by limiting Christ's redemption to
the elect, had overthrown the sacrament of communion; he asked how on
such predestinarian assumptions could ministers 'say to all communicants
whatsoever, "The body of our Lord which was given for thee", as we are
bound to say? Let the opinion of the Dortists be admitted, and the tenth
person in the Church shall not have been redeemed.' This clash of interpretation underlines the sacramental emphasis of the English Arminian
rejection of Calvinism, whereby the Prayer Book was thrown into the
scales against the Calvinist interpretation of the Thirty-Nine Articles
which had been so prevalent in Elizabethan and Jacobean times.[13]

The York House conference was however far from being a mere wrangle
among theologians. It had been called at the request of Viscount Saye and
the earl of Warwick, who were two of the government's most prominent
critics and subsequently leaders of the parliamentary party in the Civil
War. Moreover Bishop Morton's seconder at the conference was the
'Puritan' John Preston, and their ability to collaborate in this fashion
exemplified the sixty-year-old shared Calvinist assumptions which were
now at risk. Immediately after the conference, the Arminian John Cosin
was reporting that the king 'swears his perpetual patronage of our cause',
and the rebuff that Calvinism received at York House was the signal for the
house of commons to begin impeachment proceedings against Buckingham
for alleged gross mismanagement of the government. The fiction was
maintained by the opposition that Buckingham's policies were distinct
from those of the crown, but this became increasingly unconvincing especially as regards religion. In June 1626 Buckingham was foisted on
Cambridge University as chancellor, and all predestinarian teaching was
forthwith forbidden. This was backed up by a royal proclamation which
effectively outlawed Calvinism on a national basis. The London and
Cambridge printing presses rapidly succumbed. At Oxford University
however under the chancellorship of the Calvinist third earl of Pembroke
predestinarian views were preached and printed for another two years. But
even Oxford yielded when in late 1628 Charles reissued the Thirty-Nine

Articles with a prefatory declaration which insisted on their 'literal and grammatical' sense and commanded 'that all further curious search be laid aside, and these disputes shut up in God's promises, as they be generally set forth to us in holy scrptures'. As Prideaux the Oxford Regius Professor of divinity put it, 'we are concluded under an anathema to stand to the Synod of Dort against the Arminians'.[14]

Reaction in parliament to this Arminianisation of the Church of England became increasingly strident, and the situation was made worse by the readiness of the Arminians to brand their Calvinist opponents as Puritans. We know from Laud's diary that in 1626 he had been promised the succession to Canterbury, and from this date he comes into prominence as the chief religious spokesman of the government. His sermon at the opening of Charles's second parliament in February 1626 was remarkable for its aggressive tone. He conjured up the vision of a presbyterian conspiracy, aiming at the overthrow of church and state. 'They, whoever they be, that would overthrow *sedes ecclesia*, the seats of ecclesiastical government, will not spare (if ever they get power) to have a pluck at the throne of David. And there is not a man that is for parity, all fellows in the Church, but he is not for monarchy in the State'. The reply of Pym and numerous other Calvinist members of the house of commons was that on the contrary they were the true orthodox loyalists and that the new Arminian religion was both heterodox and the means of introducing Roman Catholicism into England. Some went further and claimed that the denouement would be the murder of the king at the hands of Jesuit-inspired plotters. They took particular exception to Richard Montagu's use of the term Puritan – a use shared by Laud who in 1624 had written on the subject of 'doctrinal Puritanism'. A Commons committee reported in 1625 that Montagu 'saith there are Puritans in heart' and that 'bishops may be Puritans'; since Montagu also defined predestinarian Calvinists as Puritans, the committee were quite correct to conclude that 'by his opinion we may be all Puritans'. More generally the Commons appealed to recent history in justification of their Calvinist exposition of English religion.[15]

Arminianism was of course only one among a number of reasons for the breakdown of relations between Charles and his parliaments in the late 1620s, but some idea of its relative importance is conveyed by the last parliament before the Personal Rule, that of 1628–9. The first session was largely taken up with the Petition of Right, in an attempt to prevent any future resort by the crown to forced loans, but the second session saw Arminianism as an issue taking precedence over other questions; charges of heterodoxy were levelled at Neile and Laud, who had both been made privy councillors in early 1627, and it was claimed the path of ecclesiastical preferment was blocked to all but men of their persuasion. The debate on Arminianism was opened on 26 January 1629 by Francis Rous. The issue he said was 'right of religion . . . and this right, in the name of this nation,

I this day claim, and desire that there may be a deep and serious consideration of the violation of it'. The violations, he thought, reduced to two, consisting of both a growth of Catholicism and Arminianism, the latter being 'an error that maketh the grace of God lackey it after the will of man, that maketh the sheep to keep the shepherd, that maketh mortal seed of an immortal God'. Moreover he claimed that the two phenomena were biologically connected, 'for an Arminian is the spawn of a Papist', and it was now high time for the Commons to covenant together in defence of true religion. Arminianism and the more mundane subject of tonnage and poundage were the main items of the session until it was forcibly terminated on 2 March. Rous and all the other contributors to the debate on religion, with one Arminian exception, spoke as Calvinist episcopalians. The rise of Arminianism was seen as a function of clerical pretentiousness, but was not yet considered to discredit the episcopal order as such. Indeed Sir John Eliot, speaking of Richard Montagu who had been consecrated a bishop in August 1628, said 'I reverence the order, I honour not the man'. But this reverence was subject to the continued existence of other bishops 'that openly show their hearts to the Truth'.[16]

John Pym was not given to the rhetoric of Eliot and Rous, but he more than any other M.P. inspired the Commons' case against Arminianism. From 1624 to 1629 he can be found chairing committees, delivering reports, and preparing impeachment charges on the Arminian question. Like many of his fellow M.P.s, Pym had imbibed Calvinism both in the home and at university. For them cynical calculations of the kind made by Buckingham were not a primary motive, nor in most cases did their religious stance disguise materialistic hopes of stripping the church of its remaining wealth. Nevertheless speeches on the floor of the house of commons were not made *in vacuo*, and it is therefore particularly interesting to penetrate where possible behind the public image. While this cannot on present material be done for Pym, considerable evidence has survived for Oliver St. John who was to inherit the leadership of the Long Parliament on Pym's death in 1643. St. John, who was about fourteen years younger than Pym, had been a pupil of Preston at Cambridge, and there still exists a religious commonplace book which he kept during the 1620s and early 1630s. This allows for a reconstruction of his beliefs before the civil war experience intervened, and an illuminating portrait emerges. He appears quite prepared to accept the order of episcopacy and has no objection to ceremonial conformity, in both cases quoting with approval the views of Bishop Davenant. Especially noticeable however is his dominating concern with predestinarian theology, Calvinist views being listed at length and their opposites labelled as 'heterodox'. Although he seems to agree with William Prynne's hostile views on the subject of bowing at the name of Jesus, so did Archbishop Abbot. The only other signs of Puritanism are some doubts about whether clergymen might hold civil office, and strong diapproval of men growing their hair long or any similar marks of what St. John calls 'effeminacy'.[17]

All the indications are that Pym's brand of Puritanism was much the same as that of St. John. This is supported by a mass of material relating to the fourth earl of Bedford, who was both St. John's employer and Pym's close associate. The evidence, again consisting of commonplace books, has only recently become available to historians and investigation is not yet complete. Like St. John, Bedford appears to be a firm Calvinist and much exercised about the predestinarian controversy. At the same time he does not think of himself as a Puritan, whom at one point he dismisses as a person who 'will eat his red herring on Christmas day, and his roast beef on Good Friday'. He sees Arminianism leading logically to Catholicism, writing of the former as 'the little thief put into the window of the church to unlock the door', and cites Bishop Williams against the altar-wise position of the communion table. Unfortunately such entries cannot be dated as accurately as those from St. John, and the *terminus ad quem* is Bedford's death from smallpox in 1641. Thus it is not clear from how long before the Long Parliament dates his dislike of lordly bishops. He writes, or quotes from some anonymous authority, that 'lordship [was] forbidden to the apostles, Matth. 20.25, therefore dars't thou assume it?' But he also notes that when the Hussites thrust out bishops there was left 'neither bishop nor earl'. His general social conservatism and concern to preserve the aristocratic order are revealed in a number of passages, as for instance when considering the rise of favourites or quoting Viscount Saye on the ambitions of plebeians. Bedford perhaps carried the greatest weight among the leaders of the opposition to Charles I. His religious views seem to have been fairly typical of the opposition leadership as a whole, although Saye, his son Nathaniel Fiennes, and Lord Brooke all held more radical beliefs. Their families, who tended to intermarry, sometimes had formidable Calvinist matriarchs in the background like Elizabeth Clinton, countess of Lincoln. It was she who campaigned against the upper class practice of putting children out to wet nurses on the ground, among others, that the infant might be 'one of God's very elect . . . to whom to be a nursing mother, is a queen's honour'. Her son, the fourth earl of Lincoln, was also a pupil of the 'Puritan' Preston at Cambridge, and married a daughter of Viscount Saye. He distinguished himself by raising troops to fight for the recovery of the Palatinate, and in 1626 refused to contribute to the forced loan. Not very surprisingly he ended by siding against the king in the civil war. Another Calvinist bluestocking, this time from the upper gentry, was Lady Mary Vere, wife of the hero of the siege of Mannheim and instrumental in securing the archbishopric of Armagh for James Ussher in 1624. Ussher was a close friend of some of the leading Puritan nonconformists, and his scheme for limited episcopacy put forward in the first months of the Long Parliament looked briefly like proving an acceptable compromise.

With the subsequent destruction of the hierarchy he was appointed, at the instigation of St. John, lecturer at Lincoln's Inn. Indeed the 'godly bishop' long remained a legitimate Puritan aspiration.[18]

Among the clergy in the late 1620s, as with the laity, the hallmark of opposition to the Arminian policy of the government was still Calvinist episcopalianism. Puritan nonconformity although subsumed within this Calvinist episcopalianism was not the question at issue. As for presbyterianism, it was a negligible element in the situation, being confined to a handful of survivors from Elizabethan days. Nevertheless, it has been argued by Christopher Hill that English Puritanism in the first decades of the seventeenth century was taking on a new and looser institutional form, along the lines of congregationalism *within* episcopacy. In so far as this was the case, it still implies a compatibility of religious approach prior to the Arminian 1630s. The continued failure however of Calvinist episcopalianism to withstand the pressures of Arminianism was bound in the longer term to result in its being discredited as a viable church system. Charles's decision in 1629 to rule without parliament brought that time nearer, for it meant there was now no court of Calvinist appeal left. In 1630 died the third earl of Pembroke, who had been the most influential Calvinist among the king's privy councillors. He was moreover succeeded as chancellor of Oxford by Laud, who since 1628 had been controlling the London printing press as bishop of London. The York primacy had been filled with a succession of Arminians since the Calvinist Matthew's death in 1628, and from 1632 was occupied by Neile. At Canterbury the Calvinist Abbot, in disgrace ever since refusing to license a sermon in support of forced loans in 1627, lingered on until 1633 when he was succeeded by Laud. By this process the court increasingly isolated itself from Calvinist opinion in the country. Arminian doctrines were now freely published while Calvinism languished in silence. An instance of the lengths to which propaganda went is supplied by the 1633 edition of the standard Latin–English Dictionary, compiled by Francis Holyoke. Published at Oxford and dedicated to Laud, this new edition contained for the first time the word *Praedestinatiani*, who were defined as 'a kind of heretics that held fatal predestination of every particular matter person or action, and that all things came to passe, and fell out necessarily; especially touching the salvation and damnation of particular men'. While Calvinists would regard this as misrepresenting their views, the definition was clearly aimed at them. This is confirmed by its citation in a book of 1635 by the Arminian Edmund Reeve, called *The Communion Catechisme Expounded*. Dedicating the work to Bishop Wright of Coventry and Lichfield, he claimed Bishops Overall and Buckeridge as his mentors. The exposition, which grew from the needs of his congregation at Hayes in Middlesex, contains an explicit refutation of predestinarian Calvinism and is a typical product of the decade.

Theory went hand in hand with practice. In November 1633, three months after Laud became archbishop of Canterbury, King Charles by act of privy council established the precedent that all parochial churches should follow the by then general cathedral practice of placing communion tables altar-wise at the east end of chancels. We have already had cause to comment on the sacramental undermining by English Arminians of the Calvinist theology of grace, and on the basis of this privy council ruling Arminianism during the 1630s was made manifest throughout every parish in England, the sacrament of the altar becoming henceforth a propitiation for the sins of all partakers. These were the years too which saw an unprecedented onslaught on the lecturing movement, the *cause célèbre* being the dissolution of the Feoffees for Impropriations in 1633. The Feoffees were a trust, administered by a group of clergy, lawyers and merchants, and set up in an attempt to improve the level of clerical incomes. Laud, supported by Charles, claimed that a plot was involved to destroy episcopal jurisdiction. This sinister interpretation was not however shared by bishops like Morton, who in 1630 can be found recommending an impoverished curate to the charity of the Feoffees. Morton was, as we have seen, a Calvinist, and did not agree with Laud's dictum that the altar took precedence over the pulpit. The attitude of the hierarchy to lecturers was in fact largely a matter of theological perspective. From a Calvinist standpoint preaching, whether by a beneficed incumbent or a lecturer, was the chief means of salvation. Only an episcopate dominated by Arminians could contemplate with equanimity, and indeed pleasure, a diminution in the number of sermons preached. Similarly Arminian bishops had little compunction in silencing nonconforming lecturers, whereas their Calvinist predecessors had so far as possible avoided this extreme.[19]

This change in attitude was not confined to the treatment of lecturers, but extended to nonconformity in general, and not only did the breaking of the Calvinist theological bond lead to the stricter enforcement of conformity: nonconformity itself acquired a much wider definition. Nonconformist offences now included expounding the Thirty-Nine Articles in a Calvinist sense or any form of predestinarian preaching, objecting to the new ceremonies associated with the transformation of communion tables into altars, and refusal to implement the Declaration of Sports which was reissued by Charles in 1633. The surviving Calvinist bishops found themselves in an alien world, and were distrusted by their colleagues; the Arminian Laud went so far as to put a spy on the tail of the Calvinist Morton. We have already noted that the English Arminians redefined Puritanism so as to include doctrinal Calvinism and this elicited from Bishop Davenant of Salisbury the anguished complaint: 'Why that should now be esteemed Puritan doctrine, which those held who have done our Church the greatest service in beating down Puritanism, or why men should be restrained from teaching that doctrine hereafter, which hitherto has been generally and publicly maintained, (wiser men perhaps may) but I cannot understand.' When however in 1633 the Calvinist Davenant, who was also a sabbatarian, had to discipline the recorder of Salisbury, Henry Sherfield, for destroying an allegedly idolatrous window in a church, doubts were expressed by his cathedral dean as to whether he would take a sufficiently firm line. Hardly surprisingly the 1630s as a whole saw a great increase in the number of prosecutions for Puritanism, an indirect measure of this being the large scale emigration to New England. In addition to creating widespread resentment of the episcopal hierarchy, these persecuting activities generated a Puritan militancy which in the early 1640s was to erupt in the shape of presbyterianism and congregationalism.[20]

Arminian clerics also revealed themselves as very hostile to lay intervention in church matters. This was partly because parliament had proved so antagonistic, and they were in any case completely dependent on royal protection, but there was also a novel sacerdotal element in their teaching whereby the priestly replaced the preaching function. Evidence exists to suggest that one of the factors involved here was a desire to compensate for a sense of social inferiority. Certainly the Calvinist bishops had better blood relations with the gentry and aldermanic classes than did their Arminian successors, and there was some substance to Lord Brooke's derogatory remarks in 1641 about low-born prelates. At the same time the reassertion of sacramental grace lent itself to the view that clerics were almost a caste apart, but because of their magical not their preaching roles. Indeed many English Arminians consciously regarded themselves as engaged in a counter-reforming movement dedicated to undoing the Protestant damage of the Reformation.

While English Arminianism did not automatically result in the theoretical advancement of royal absolutism in the secular sphere, the injunction 'render unto Caesar' might seem a fitting counterpart to the idea of a holy priesthood with consecrated property rights. The Calvinist oposition however conveniently forgot that during the debates on the Petition of Right the Arminian Bishop Harsnett had spoken out in defence of the subject's liberties, and instead they remembered the stance of Archbishop Abbot, in condemning the arguments of Sibthorpe and Mainwaring for unparliamentary taxation. Indeed as early as the 1590s Abbot had taught that 'God is better pleased, when good things shall be commanded, first by the highest in place, and then after it shall be added, by the Lords spiritual and temporal, and by the assent of the commons. And Princes which are gracious do never grieve at this, and wise men do love that style, when all is not appropriated to one, but there is a kind of parting.' Yet a decade or so earlier Archbishop Sandys, a man of similar theological colour to Abbot, had preached that taxation was a tribute due to the king and not a gift freely given. Thus there was an element of accident in the Arminian and royalist partnership. But in practice the religious policy of King Charles meant that during the Personal Rule absolutism and Arminianism became closely identified in the popular mind.[21]

On the future parliamentarian side there did however exist a positive link with Calvinism, concerning the right of political resistance. Calvinists held no monopoly of such views, but among Protestants they had developed the most explicit body of teaching on the subject. In England by far the most important vehicle of their thought was the Genevan annotated version of the Bible, which among other things had a predestinarian catechism bound up with it. Not always entirely consistent and stopping considerably short of an outright doctrine of tyrannicide, the Genevan commentators were prepared to admit the legitimacy of resistance to magistrates in certain circumstances, especially when the issue was religion. Their medium was Biblical history, notably that contained in the Old Testament, and the use they made of it led King James to insist that the new Authorised translation of the Bible should contain no marginalia at all, apart from variant readings and cross-references. Illustrative of the political tendency of the Genevan annotations is that Ecclesiastes, viii. 3. had been glossed as 'withdraw not thy self lightly from the obedience of thy prince,' and the famous opening verse of Romans xiii, 'Let every soul be subject unto the higher powers . . .' was described as relating to a 'private man', thus in principle leaving inferior magistrates free to act against erring superiors.[22]

Despite the existence of an official rival from 1611 onwards, the Genevan Bible long retained its popularity, being printed latterly in the Low Countries with the fictitious date 1599 on its title page. In origin the Genevan version was the work of a group of Marian exiles. They had included Goodman and Knox, who were both authors of works advocating the right of armed defence, particularly against heretical and persecuting rulers. Although the product of a specific exilic situation, ideas of this type survived the turn of the century, by which date however they were usually confined to discussions about continental Protestantism. Thus in 1603 Robert Abbot, brother of the future archbishop, dedicated a book to King James which contained a defence of both Dutch and French Protestant rebels. At the same time there existed a competing body of passive-resistance theory, against which the only regular antidote was the Genevan Bible. With the subsequent rise of English Arminianism, Calvinist ideas of resistance took on new domestic relevance; as early as 1632 a Puritan lecturer, Nathaniel Barnard, dared to make the connection in a sermon. After the actual outbreak of hostilities, one of those to be found defending the parliamentary cause on religious grounds was Stephen Marshall, who has been described as 'the most famous political parson of the Revolution'.

Eschewing legal arguments, Marshall cited Biblical precedent and among more recent authorities Bishop Abbot.[23]

Perhaps even without a rebellion in Scotland the finances of the Personal Rule would have foundered on their own inadequacies, and a parliament have had to be summoned. What however until recently has largely gone unnoticed, is the part played in the Scottish disturbances by Arminianism. The Scots at this time are usually thought of as intransigent presbyterians for whom Charles's attempt to impose an English-style prayer book was simply an excuse to throw off the whole episcopalian system. But it has been pointed out that many of the members of the Glasgow Assembly, which in 1638 abolished bishops, had never known a fully presbyterian church. Moreover someone like Robert Baillie, who is traditionally thought of as a presbyterian diehard, was even at that date not prepared to deny that a form of episcopacy had scriptural warrant. Arminianism however appears to have been the deciding factor. The Glasgow Assembly explicitly modelled itself on the Synod of Dort and listened to a series of harangues on the Arminian question. What really seems to have rankled was not so much the office of bishop but that the hierarchy were mostly Arminians. Again and again this charge features in the indictments, and heterodox teaching on predestination clearly is meant. The dual association with unpopular royalist policies in the secular field and with Arminianism in the religious meant that episcopacy went down even faster in Scotland than it was to in England where the system was more indigenous.[24]

The Short Parliament of 1640, called to subsidise the suppression of the Scottish rebellion, did not last long enough for the religious question fully to come out in the open, although 'innovations in matters of religion' were high on Pym's list of grievances. The fact that after the dissolution of parliament the convocation of clergy continued in session and proceeded to enact a series of canons which included a strong statement of royal absolutism, all fostered a mounting hostility to the episcopate. Nor was the example of Scotland lost on the English opposition, and increasingly too a presbyterian model in religion became the price of Scottish support. When the Long Parliament assembled later in the year more radical pressures were brought to bear by the London populace, and the Root and Branch Petition of December, which called for the abolition of bishops, in part represented such interests. Even here however it was the woeful results of episcopacy, with Arminianism taking a prominent place, that were stressed rather than the essential unlawfulness of the order. Moreover, Calvinists like Archbishop Ussher and Bishop Morton meeting in committee during March 1641 with Puritan ministers such as Marshall and Calamy looked like agreeing on a common reformist platform. But the basic Arminian intransigence of King Charles, combined with the sheer speed of events, made religious compromises of this kind unworkable. Conciliation was overtaken by the drift to war.[25]

As an old man looking back on the civil war at the end of the century, Philip fourth Lord Wharton, who had fought against the king, claimed that 'a hundred to one of the Calvinists . . . joined the parliamentarians'. The process which had brought this alleged situation about was highly complex, and even Wharton would not have seriously maintained that all they were fighting about was Calvinism. At the same time the propaganda put out by parliamentary army officers in the early stages of the war does suggest a high degree of religious motivation. This declaration of sentiments took the visual form of battle standards flown by the captains of each cavalry troop, who incidentally all claimed to be gentlemen. While Magna Carta and a blood-stained head, probably Strafford's, were occasionally chosen as symbols, the dominating motif was the Bible with accompanying slogans such as 'Verbum Dei', 'Sacra Scriptura' and 'Jehova Nisi'. Also depicted were bishops tumbling from their thrones with the caption 'Antichrist Must Down', a lethal rain of arrows labelled 'Contra Impios' and cloud-wreathed anchors illustrating the assertion 'Only in Heaven'. Comparable propaganda on the Royalist side was of a much more secular kind, displaying the insignia of monarchy or satirising the 'round-head' opposition. One popular emblem was a pack of hounds all barking 'Pym'. Revealingly, Charles described his opponents as consisting mainly of 'Brownists, Anabaptists and Atheists'. Such was the gulf of misunderstanding that had opened up between the Arminian king and his Calvinist subjects.[26]

In terms of English Protestant history the charge in 1640 that King Charles and Archbishop Laud were religious innovators is irrefutable. The reaction provoked however by the Arminian revolution was of such violence that it could be transformed with relative ease into a call for 'root and branch' remedies, and presbyterianism emerged as the cure of Arminian disease. Thus what had begun as a counter-revolution itself became radicalised.

Notes

1 C. Hill, *Society and Puritanism in Pre-Revolutionary England* (1964); W. Haller, *The Rise of Puritanism* (New York, 1938). Since this article was first published the author has considerably revised and developed his views on both Arminianism and Puritanism: see N.R.N. Tyacke, *Anti-Calvinists: The Rise of English Arminianism, c. 1590–1640* (Oxford, 1987 and 1990 edn with foreword) and *idem*, *The Fortunes of English Puritanism 1603–1640* (Dr Williams's Library Lecture, 1990). For specific changes to the accounts of both Bancroft and Pym given in this essay see Tyacke, *Anti-Calvinists*.

2 A. Clark (ed.), *Register of the University of Oxford* (1887–9), ii, pt. 1 pp. 194–217; G. Abbot, *A Sermon preached at Westminster* (1608), pp. 19–20.

3 H.C. Porter, *Reformation and Reaction in Tudor Cambridge* (Cambridge 1958), pp. 365–75; P. Collinson, 'The "nott conformytye" of the Young John Whitgift', *JEH*, 15 (1964), pp. 192–200; A.F. Scott Pearson, *Thomas Cartwright and Elizabethan Puritanism, 1535–1603* (Cambridge 1925), pp. 22–3, 396.

4 J. Ayre (ed.), *The Sermons of Edwin Sandys* (Cambridge 1842) pp. 223, 448; R.A. Marchant, *The Puritans and the Church Courts in the Diocese of York, 1560–1642* (1960), pp. 18–21; L. Carlson (ed.), *The Writings of Henry Barrow, 1590–1591* (1966), p. 62.

5 S. Benefield, *A Sermon preached at Wotton Under Edge* (Oxford, 1613); S. Gardiner, *A Dialogue* (1605), sigs. E3v, B4r; W. Scott (ed.), *Somers Tracts* (1809), ii, pp. 307–8, 311.

6 C. Hill, *Puritanism and Revolution* (1958), pp. 216, 238; R. Abbot, *A Defence of the Reformed Catholic of W. Perkins* (1611); F. Rous, *Testis Veritatis* (1626), pp. 2–3; C.H. McIlwain (ed.), *The Political Works of James I* (Cambridge, Mass. 1918), p. 274; W.P. Baildon (ed.), *Les Reportes . . . in Camera Stellata, 1593 to 1609* (1894), p. 191; J.P. Kenyon (ed.), *The Stuart Constitution* (Cambridge, 1966), p. 41.

7 L. Andrewes, *Responsio* (1610), p. 123; T.G. Crippen (ed.), 'Of the Name of Puritans', *Trans. Congregational Hist. Soc.*, vi (1913–15), p. 83; E. Arber (ed.), *A Transcript of Registers of the Company of Stationers, 1554–1640* (1875–94), iii.

8 H. Foley, *Records of the English Province of the Society of Jesus* (1877–83), i, p. 70; M. Tierney (ed.), *Dodd's Church History* (1839–43) iv, pp. 179–80; HMC, *Salisbury* xviii, p. 21; A.G.R. Smith, *The Government of Elizabethan England* (1967), p. 65; P. Collinson, *The Elizabethan Puritan Movement* (1967), p. 159.

9 R. Bancroft, *Dangerous Positions and Proceedings . . . under pretence of Reformation* (1593); M. Knappen (ed.), *Two Elizabethan Diaries* (Chicago, 1933); p. 32; T. Rogers, *The Faith, Doctrine, and Religion professed and protected in . . . England* (Cambridge, 1607/8); *P in P 1610*, ii, p. 78; G. Goodman, *The Court of James I* (1839), ii pp. 160–1; P. Hembry, *The Bishops of Bath and Wells* (1967), p. 211; *The Works of [King] James* (1616), sig. e. For much of the information in this and succeeding paragraphs, see Tyacke, *Anti-Calvinists*.

10 P. Seaver, *The Puritan Lectureships . . . 1560–1662* (Stanford 1970), pp. 224–9; Marchant, *Puritans and Church Courts* p. 43.

11 Manchester MSS (formerly at PRO), Hughes to Nathaniel Rich, 19 May 1617; L. Hughes, *A Plain and True Relation of . . . the Summer Islands* (1621); Hill, *Puritanism and Revolution*, p. 146; I. Morgan, *Prince Charles's Puritan Chaplain* (1957); *CD 1621*, iv, p. 63.

12 *CD 1629*, p. 100.

13 J. Sansom (ed.), *The Works of John Cosin* (Oxford 1843–55), ii, pp. 61–4.

14 Sansom (ed.), *The Works of John Cosin*, ii, p. 74; Kenyon, *Stuart Constitution*, pp. 154–5; S.R. Gardiner, *The Constitutional Documents of the Puritan Revolution, 1625–1660* (repr. Oxford 1962), p. 76.

15 Kenyon, *Stuart Constitution*, pp. 153–4; S.R. Gardiner (ed.), *Debates in the House of Commons for 1625* (Camden Soc., N.S. vi, 1873), p. 49.

16 *CD 1629*, pp. 12–15, 27.

17 BL, Add. MSS 25, 285. I owe my knowledge of this volume to Dr. V. Pearl.

18 Bedford MSS xi, 96, 100, 158, 248, 1236, 1293; W. Fiennes, Viscount Saye, *Two Speeches* (1641), pp. 13–14; N. Fiennes, *A Speech . . . concerning Bishops*

(1641); R. Greville, Lord Brooke, *A Discourse opening the Nature of . . . Episcopacy* (1641). E. Clinton, *Countess of Lincoln's Nurserie* (1622), p. 17; *Complete Peerage* (1929), vii, pp. 696–7; Morgan, *Puritan Chaplain*, p. 43; D. Underdown, *Pride's Purge* (Oxford, 1971), p. 20.

19 Gardiner, *Constitutional Documents*, pp. 103–5; I.M. Calder, *Activities of the Puritan Faction . . . 1625–1633* (1957), p. xxii.

20 R. Howell, *Newcastle-upon-Tyne and the Puritan Revolution* (Oxford, 1966), p. 112; CSPD 1631–3, p. 571.

21 *C and T Chas. I*, i, p. 347; G. Abbot, *An Exposition on the Prophet Jonah* (1613), pp. 436–7; *The Sermons of Edwin Sandys*, p. 199.

22 *The Geneva Bible* (facsimile of first edition, Wisconsin, 1969).

23 R. Abbot, *Antichristi Demonstratio* (1603), pp. 92–3; S. Marshall, *Copy of a Letter* (1643), pp. 11, 20; H.R. Trevor-Roper (ed.), *Essays in British History* (1965), p. 89.

24 M.C. Kitshoff, 'Aspects of Arminianism in Scotland', unpublished M.Th. thesis (St. Andrews 1968).

25 Kenyon, *Stuart Constitution*, pp. 167–8, 172, 198; W.A. Shaw, *History of the English Church . . . 1640–60* (1900), i, pp. 65–76.

26 G.F.T. Jones, *Saw-Pit Wharton* (Sydney 1967), p. 50; Dr. Williams's Library, Modern Folios 12.7; BL, Add. MSS 5247, and Harl. MSS 986; *Old Parliamentary History* (1760–3), xi, p. 435.

6

The religious context of the English Civil War

JOHN MORRILL

Lengthy reports survive of speeches by several members of the Long Parliament for 9 November 1640, at the end of the first week of the session. The future royalist militant, George Lord Digby is reported to have begun his address by saying that:

> you have received now a solemn account from most of the shires of England of the several Grievances and Oppressions they sustain, and nothing as yet from Dorsetshire: Sir I would not have you think that I serve for a Land of Goshen, and that we live there in sunshine, whilst darkness and plagues overspread the rest of the land . . . [1]

The future royalist moderate Sir John Culpepper is reported to have begun: 'I stand not up with a Petition in my hand, I have it in my mouth', and he enumerated the grievances of his shire beginning with 'the great increase of papists' and the 'obtruding and countenancing of divers new ceremonies in matters of religion'.[2] The future parliamentarian moderate, Harbottle

Grimston, said that 'these petitions which have been read, they are all remonstrances of the general and universal grievances and distempers that are now in the state and Government of the Church and Commonwealth.'[3] The future parliamentarian radical Sir John Wray said:

All in this renowned senate, I am confident, is fully fixed upon the true Reformation of all Disorders and Innovations in Church or Religion, and upon the well uniting and close rejoining of the poor dislocated Great Britain. For, let me tell you Mr Speaker, that God be thanked, it is but out of joint and may be well set by the skilful chyrurgeons of this Honourable House.[4]

In November 1640 there was apparent unity of purpose amongst the members of the Long Parliament. Fortified by petitions signed by their county establishments at Michaelmas Quarter Sessions or at the county court on election day, they arrived determined to take the once-for-all opportunity which had presented itself to set things right. For this parliament met in unique circumstances. The military defeat of the king by his Scottish subjects and the latter's occupation of north-east England guaranteed that this would be no addled parliament as in the spring, for the Scots had made it clear that they would not go home without reparations voted by the English parliament, a parliament which could make that supply dependent upon the redress of grievance. There was no expectation of civil war, nor even of constitutional aggression. As Sheila Lambert says:

the opening of the parliament following the traditional pattern: the earl of Essex carrying the cap of state in the opening procession. The proceedings of Parliament during the first few weeks were entirely in accordance with the precedents of the early Stuart Parliaments.[5]

But while the *form* of the parliament was familiar enough, and while the expectation was that the remedy of grievance would follow established practice, the mood and context of the parliament were unprecedented. This is most obviously seen in the contrast between the rhetoric and the agenda of the Long Parliament in its early weeks and those of the Short Parliament. When the latter had assembled, the king had retained the initiative, the freedom to dissolve them at will and resume the Personal Rule. He could reach an understanding with them and continue his war with Scotland, or he could make painful concessions to the Scots and be rid of parliament, or he could be tempted to seek an understanding with Philip IV and the Pope and to resume both the Personal Rule and the Bishops' War. Conscious that the initiative lay with the king, both houses set their sights low.[6] In the autumn, the king had lost effective freedom, and the managers of the parliament set their sights high.

It is true that one crucial dimension to the history of the Long Parliament is the working out of factional rivalries and the struggle for office.

But while this forms a necessary dimension of any rounded account of the collapse of royal authority, it does not offer a sufficient explanation – any more than it does of the parliamentary clashes of the 1620s.[7]

My argument will be that there was in 1640 an ideological crisis as well as a functional crisis. But I wish to argue that, however jumbled together they were in the hectic early days of the Long Parliament, there were three quite distinct and separable perceptions of misgovernment or modes of opposition – what will be called the *localist*, the *legal-constitutionalist*, and the *religious*. One man could hold two or three of them; but many did not do so. It was possible for an individual to see links between royal secular and religious misgovernment, but not necessary or usual for him to do so. Too often in the past we have assumed that those who opposed most vigorously the Caroline religious experiment would also be in the forefront of the protest against forced loans or ship money. There are notable examples of those who did oppose both (though the link is stronger in the case of the forced loans) and who saw a connection between them. But there were many more who were prominent in their protest against either fiscal feudalism or Laudianism and who risked their careers and their liberty in protesting against one of them, but who fell in with the other. Many notable puritans paid ship money without protest, and some were even effective ship money sheriffs; many notable protesters against secular misgovernment proved to be loyal defenders of the established church in 1641–2.

The argument of the paper will be that the localist and the legal-constitutionalist perceptions of misgovernment lacked the momentum, the passion, to bring about the kind of civil war which England experienced after 1642. It was the force of religion that drove minorities to fight, and forced majorities to make reluctant choices.

The localist perception of misgovernment need not detain us. Recent work drawing attention to localism has much to teach us about the nature of the civil war, but little to tell us about why civil war broke out.[8] It will probably be widely accepted that the decline of other *loci* of political and social action – the baronial household, the liberty and franchise etc – and the expansion of the duties and responsibilities of royal commissions of which the sphere of operations was the shire, and the development of distinctive and valued patterns of local government (unique administrative arrangements, customary procedures etc.) made the county a focus of loyalty and identity. The leading families in each county had a greater or lesser degree of attachment to their 'county community'. Not all gentry put the coats-of-arms of the families of their shire around the ceiling bosses of their great halls, but many did so. It is not claimed that this made for a cosy world of purring, contented squires, enjoying one another's company and getting cross only when the crown made demands on them. Quite the contrary. The social and political institutions of the county were arenas within which rivalries were worked out, disputes arbitrated, prestige and honour won and lost. Frequently the institutions of the county were respected or powerful enough to resolve such issues. But often they were not so, and appeals downward to the electorate or upward to the court were necessary extensions of the system. It was precisely the ability to arbitrate between rival groups or individuals within particular counties and boroughs or between rival counties and boroughs which gave privy councillors or courtiers their chance to ensure that the price of their arbitration was obedience to the crown's wishes.

There was a dual allegiance, and therefore alarm, anger, frustration when those dual allegiances were in conflict. This occurred with the collapse of the delicate patronage system in the 1620s, when powerful groups in many counties found that they had no friends at court, or none able to help them against the power of Buckingham, and it also occurred with the intrusive drive for 'unity through uniformity' in the 1630s.[9] Local traditions and customs were challenged, local men set aside, more demanded and less conceded than hitherto. Some of Charles's fiscal expedients – ship money for example – exacerbated or resurrected jurisdictional disputes, led to charges of unfairness and arbitrariness of distribution. Some articulated their protest in legal and constitutional terms; many more saw it as a source of needless local disputes and conflict.[10] By 1640 there was a widespread demand for a return to the older forms of local self-determination. Such a mood can be found in the addresses brought up by MPs, or reaching them from their constituents in the early months of the Long Parliament.[11] This perception – a strongly held but ultimately mild perception of arbitrary government, of innovation and externally induced disruption – helps to explain the mood of the electorate in 1640 and of the pressure for reform in 1641. But it does not explain the pressure for war in 1642. Localism in the 1630s or in 1640 leads naturally into neutralism in 1642. Indeed Anthony Fletcher has argued that what has been taken as neutralism in 1642 is in fact an advanced form of localism, with leading magistrates and others seeking either to keep both sides out of their shire, or seeking to minimise the level of commitment to one side or the other for the preservation of the local peace.[12] That mentality which continued to see war as an unmitigated disaster, which could not decide between a loyalty to both king and parliament, is vital to an understanding of the *nature* of the war and of its outcome, but not to the explanation of its outbreak.

Derek Hirst and others have reminded us that there was more to the debates of the 1610s, 1620s and 1630s than a factional struggle for power and a dislike of centralising tendencies imposed on the crown by the need to finance itself.[13] There were major and deeply-held differences of opinion and belief about the nature and extent of the royal prerogative, about the accountability of the king's servants, and even (for some) about the origins and nature of kingly power. Such disagreements are natural in all sophisticated political cultures, and to identify such differences is not to identify the source of inevitable political collapse. Many of the issues were keenly felt, but everyone most of the time did accept that there were clear and unquestioned ways of expressing dissent: in and through parliament, in petitions to the king-in-council, *in extremis* by passive disobedience. What is remarkable about early Stuart England is the absence of political violence: virtually no treason trials, no rebellions, a decreasing and localised incidence of riot, no brigandage.[14] The English Civil War certainly did not grow out of a gradual and inexorable collapse in the state's ability to compel obedience. Those who preached passive obedience to the catholics in the late sixteenth and first decade of the seventeenth century could not, or at any rate did not, bring themselves to contemplate the right violently to resist wicked kings. This was in part because of the intellectual bonds in which they had wrapped themselves, but it was also in part because the area of constitutional dissent and alarm was still limited. What bound them together was far greater than what divided them. We must beware of two tendencies: to overlook the undebated common ground which united the political nation; and the habit of lumping together every complaint on every issue raised by any critic of royal policy and then to assume that anyone who articulated any of them accepted all of them. There is clear evidence that by 1640 very large numbers of men, in the gentry and beyond, had a limited but clear and firm belief in a partial royal tyranny. The king, albeit as a consequence of wicked counsel, was misusing his powers. But let us be clear what we mean. There was no criticism of monarchy itself; there was no criticism of the long-term development of the early modern state; there was no demand for fundamental change in the nature of royal power. The complaints were very specifically about the misgovernment of a single man, Charles I, and about the misuse of agreed powers, not about the attempt to usurp fresh powers. The king was not accused of trying to make law outside parliament, nor of claiming new prerogatives of emergency powers. What was widely asserted and believed was that the king was using approved powers in inappropriate circumstances, powers which he possessed *pro bono publico*, for the public welfare, *pro bono suo*, for his own benefit. He was most criticised for raising emergency taxation in non-emergency situations, for allowing private individuals to profit from the use of powers reserved to the king himself, and for corruption of justice.

This limited perception of royal tyranny produced a grim determination in the members of the Long Parliament to secure remedy and guarantees against the abuse of power. Yet the tale told by the journals of the Houses and the diaries of MPs is not one of headlong constitutional action, but of sluggishness and hesitancy.[15] In contrast to the debates on religion, the rhetoric of the constitutional debates was conservative,

restorative. Whatever the actual cumulative effect of the remedial legislation of 1641, the declared purpose, and, as far as we can determine, the
undeclared purpose, of those who devised, spoke to, and approved those
reforms was to maintain the rights and liberties of the subject by amputat-
ing diseased limbs of government, pruning back those emergency powers
which had been so readily subverted for corrupt purposes, in order to
preserve the essence of the ancient and established political order. There
was no will to new model the constitution, to reform it root and branch,
let alone to create parliamentary sovereignty.[16] It was the failings of
Charles I, not of the political system, which had to be rectified. In all
the political debates down to and beyond the Grand Remonstrance, nothing was presented as a grievance which predated the accession of Charles I.
The constitutional problem was a problem with a particular monarch. In
contrast, an increasing number of ecclesiastical reformers argued for a
fundamental reform of the church. The Elizabethan settlement was to be
dismantled and reconstituted.

The most puzzling aspect of the Long Parliament's first session is the
lack of urgency about legislative remedies. Although early speakers laid out
an agenda for reform, little attempt was made to enshrine that programme
in statute until after the execution of Strafford in May 1641. By that time,
it is true, the Triennial Act and the Act which gave the Long Parliament
control over its own dissolution had been enacted. But the substantive
attack on the conciliar and prerogative courts, and the statutory pruning
of royal emergency powers, only passed through the Houses in the summer
months. This may reveal supreme self-confidence in the inability of the
king to wriggle free, but to defer conclusive action until long after that
parliamentary session had become the longest in history may also indicate
that concern over the remedies were less obsessive than is often supposed.

By contrast, the attack on evil counsellors was immediate and effective.
Within a few weeks, most leading privy councillors and principal officers
of state were in the Tower, in exile or in disgrace. Less than half those who
attended meetings of the council in the second half of 1641 had been
members of it in November 1640.[17] But while the king's principal advisers
were hounded from office, there was no wider harrying of those responsible for civil misgovernment. In addition to the councillors, six judges
were impeached but allowed to preside over their courts while on bail,[18]
and there was a fitful pursuit of monopolists.[19] But there it ended. Those
lords lieutenant who had vigorously supported unpopular royal policies,
those who had exceeded their powers during the Bishops' Wars, those
zealous ship money sheriffs, were exempt from investigation and penalty.[20]
There was no call for the removal or persecution of those who enforced the
forest laws or knighthood fines; no weeding out of JPs who had openly and
brazenly extolled royal policies. We will see how stark is the contrast
between this and the Long Parliament's pursuit of churchmen.

The legal-constitutionalist perception of misgovernment was thus one of a limited tyranny, and it led to an unhurried and largely uncontroversial programme of remedial legislation consciously intended to restore a lost balance, to conserve the ancient constitution. There was no recognition either that the old system was unworkable or intrinsically tyrannical, or that the remedial legislation was making it unworkable or intrinsically unstable. There was no intellectual ferment in the period November 1640 to August 1641 creating new theories of government and new constitutional imperatives. If the king's behaviour left many unsatisfied with the achievements of the first session, there was no new rhetoric of popular or parliamentary sovereignty spurring members on to self-confident constitutional demands. All this is in stark contrast to the progress of religious concerns.

Unlike some recent commentators, I believe that it is almost impossible to overestimate the damage caused by the Laudians. I see no reason to doubt that most 'hotter sort of protestants' were integrated into the Jacobean church and state. Puritan magistrates and churchwardens abound, and can be found arguing for and working for an evangelical drive to instruct the ignorant, and an alliance of minister and magistrate to impose godly discipline. There was no incompatibility between serving God and the Crown. Such men found comfort in St John's letter to the true believers in Laodicea, a church pure in doctrine but not in worship, in which he urged them to work for reform from within. They yearned for a new Constantine, a godly prince who would put the power of the state at the service of the church. The godly magistrate and parish notable yearned for more to do rather than for less. They saw James I and even more Charles I as *abdicating* their responsibilities under God to promote true religion. But while they saw James I as moving too slowly but in the right direction, they found in Charles I a negligent king who was oblivious to the threat of popery at home, abroad, and within the church of which he was supreme governor.[21]

It remains uncertain how and how far Laud's doctrine of grace departed sharply from the spectrum of predestinarian views maintained by successive generations of bishops and theologians since 1559.[22] Certainly his ecclesiology does not appear to make sense except as the expression of a belief that man, morally and intellectually depraved, could only be reconciled to God and brought to sustain a saving faith by and through the sacramental grace mediated to him by the church.[23] Be that as it may, the programme of Charles and Laud was profoundly offensive to most lay and much clerical opinion. It rested upon a narrow and literal enforcement of the observances and practices of the book of common prayer and early injunctions of the Elizabethan church.[24] This prohibited the penumbra of observances and practices which had grown up around the prayer book, which for many represented the kernel of their witness, as the prayer book ceremonies represented the husk. This penumbra did not constitute a challenge to the church until Laud chose to make it one, by a narrow reading of the prayer book which treated its forms and rubrics not only as necessary, but as sufficient.[25] The heavy task Charles and Laud gave themselves, of bringing conformity to religion and of bringing sinful man to a due regard for the things of God mediated through His church, rested upon a profound clericism. The church had to be freed to evangelise, to convert, to impose order, and had to be freed from the cloying, stifling, corrupting intrusions upon its wealth and jurisdiction which had grown up over the previous century: the invasion by 'common law cormorants'; the secularisation of church lands and assets; lay appropriations and impropriations; and so on. In all of his kingdoms, Charles and Laud set out to restore the autonomy of the church.[26] Whatever they thought they were doing, by 1640 their programme had aroused disenchantment amongst its committed and its critical members, a disenchantment which gave rise to a debate more passionate than the debate on the constitution. In November 1640, Wentworth was the most feared man in England; but Laud was the most detested – 'the sty of all pestilential filth', according to Harbottle Grimston, 'like a busie angry wasp, his sting is in the tayl of everything'.[27]

The religious perception of misgovernment differed from the localist and the legal-constitutionalist perception first in its intensity. It spilled over into everything in the early weeks of the Long Parliament.[28] It saturates the language of the petitions to parliament; it crops up with greater regularity and persistence in the business of both Houses than do secular grievances.[29] The first positive achievement carried through was the annulment of the canons[30] of convocation approved during the spring of 1640 (canons which gave full force to the Laudian programme).[31] But the religious perception is more complex than the others. It too, at the outset, was in part a perception of tyranny. Laud was accused of promoting false doctrine which lent support to the king's arbitrary actions; and of abusing his own jurisdiction and that of other courts to impose unlawful observance and to silence 'professors' of the true religion.[32] But this was not simply a matter of the arbitrary use of power. Indeed, the scale of religious persecution under Laud was in fact quite limited: there were fewer deprivations and suspensions in the 1630s than in most other decades since the Reformation.[33] It was not his persecutions which caused most outrage. The religious perception was paradoxically also one of royal weakness, abdication, failure to halt the advance or popery. The attack on the bishops was built around their usurpation of the royal supremacy.[34] There were long debates in early 1641 about whether the bishops who had promoted the canons and prosecuted Bastwick were guilty of treason or *praemunire*, of derogating from the king's title and dignity.[35] In the words of Laud's impeachment:

'the said archbishop claims the king's ecclesiastical jurisdiction as incident to his episcopal office . . . and doth deny the same to be derived from the Crown of England.'[36] Laud had a plausible defence to the charge, but his own words in High Commission in the case of Sir Giles Allington[37] and the alleged words of John Cosin, that 'the king had no more power over the church than the man who rubs my horse's heels',[38] leave us in little doubt why his defence was unheeded. One of the most heated exchanges in the early months of the Long Parliament was over a report of a sermon by Dr Chaffin at the metropolitical visitation of Salisbury. Chaffin, referring to Laud as 'our little Aaron', had compared him favourably with 'the blessed archbishop Arundel'. He may have had in mind Arundel's silencing of preaching and harrying of Lollards, but d'Ewes was quick to remind the house that Arundel had been impeached for treason in 1397 for usurping the king's regality, dignity and crown.[39] Laud's usurpation had been intended to weaken the church: 'these are the men that should have fed Christ's flock, but they are the wolves that have devoured them'.[40] As Lord Falkland put it, they sought 'to introduce an English, though not a Roman, popery'.[41]

The remedies to the constitutional ills of the 1630s were widely agreed, leisurely pursued, based upon a conservative rhetoric. From the outset, the reform of the church was more contentious, more impulsive, and more divisive, because there quickly emerged a radical rhetoric which many could not accept. It is true that Laud and Laudianism were quickly swept away and without dissent. But within eight weeks of the opening of parliament, the Houses were subjected to a pulpit oratory and to a petitioning campaign that called not for the restoration of the pre-Laudian order, not for the conserving of the 'pure religion of Elizabeth and James', but for the abolition of the entire ecclesiastical order and its reconstitution along pure biblical lines. Edward Calamy called upon parliament to 'reform the reformation', and Stephen Marshall called upon them to 'throw to the moals and the bats every rag that hath not God's stamp upon it'.[42]

In the late 1620s, most critics of Arminianism spoke as defenders of the established church against novelty and innovation; even in late 1640 the number who appear to have anticipated the need to overturn the church of Elizabeth was small.[43] But whereas the events of 1641 reinforced constitutional conservatism, they polarised the religious views of members of both Houses. In part, this resulted from their response to the sermons, the tracts, the lobbying. In part, it was a response to Scottish pressure.[44] But in large part it was a response to the level of ecclesiastical corruption revealed by the Houses' enquiries.

The attack on churchmen was far wider than the attack on the laity. In addition to the thirteen bishops impeached in December 1640, and the overlapping group of twelve impeached in December 1641, there was a steady stream of complaints against individual ministers, especially from within London, East Anglia and the Midlands. The Commons sent more than twenty such complaints to committees by the end of November 1640 and a steady flow thereafter.[45] In those early weeks they also undertook long reviews of the trials of Burton, Bastwick, Prynne, Leighton and Lilburne, set aside their conviction and sentence, and awarded them damages against their persecutors. This was far more aggressive than anything done for the victims of secular tyranny.[46] In those early weeks when more than twenty clerics were hounded, only two civil officers, a sheriff and an under-sheriff, were investigated.[47] By the summer of 1641 the Commons were happily depriving ministers of their freehold, banning them from future preferment, imprisoning them in the Tower or elsewhere, or otherwise punishing them for ceremonialism or preaching up Laudianism. Those ecclesiastics responsible for ordering the parish of Waddesdon in Buckinghamshire to repair its organ and pay for an organist found themselves covering all the consequent costs by order of the Lower House.[48] As early as January 1641, the Commons declared that the judges in High Commission had acted *ultra vires* in ordering the parishioners of St Bartholomew's London to pay the wages of the parish clerk; they themselves acted *ultra vires* in setting aside the order and requiring the judges to pay the parishioners' fines and costs.[49] Such highhandedness soon produced a reaction amongst the members themselves. A study of the 700 and more cases taken on appeal by the house of lords in the early 1640s leads to the same conclusion. Far more and worse abuses of ecclesiastical authority were revealed than of secular authority. The Lords were far more resolute in the pursuit of ecclesiastical officials than of secular ones.[50]

At the very time that the Houses expressed alarm at the abuses within the church, the Commons were willing to wink at breaches of ecclesiastical law. In June 1641, 'mechanicall' lay preachers were called before the House but merely gently reprimanded and protected from the rigours of the law;[51] rather later, the JPs of Monmouthshire were ordered not to prosecute those who absented themselves from their parish churches in order to hear sermons elsewhere;[52] in a bitter ten-hour debate in early September 1641 the Commons issued instructions to local governors to take the law into their own hands to demolish 'innovations', and rejected an amendment which would have 'provided a remedy against such as did vilify and contemn the common prayer book'.[53]

The point is that by the end of the first session of the Long Parliament, not only had a militancy of rhetoric and action led to a militancy of conduct in religion different in kind from that generated by the constitutional debate; but that militancy had led to a decisive shift in perception amongst many MPs who had begun the parliament looking for a pruning and cleansing exercise in the church similar to that enacted for the state, but who now saw that the established church had to be abolished, reconstituted. For many, the existing order had been shown to be intrinsically unstable. For reasons of prudence, and for reasons of Providence (God's judgment appearing upon the order as well as upon the individuals who composed it), episcopacy had to be destroyed. Many accepted the necessity, fewer *embraced* the necessity, seeing it as the breaking of the mould, the opportunity of renewal and of the millennium. Yet the same militancy which had forged this new religious radicalism produced a reaction which created, or at any rate crystallised, a theoretical and practical defence of non-Laudian episcopacy and of the Anglicanism of the prayer book and of the Thirty Nine articles. The debates on church government in the spring and summer of 1641, culminating in the resolutions of the Commons in the final days of the session, witnessed a gradual polarisation of the members.[54] By the time of the recess there was no royalist party; but there was an anglican party.

The constitutional reform of 1641 was largely uncontroversial and created no major division, generated no major public debate. The perceived tyranny of the 1630s was remedied. No issue left over from the past remained on the agenda in late 1641. The renewed constitutional concern arose from the king's fresh misbehaviour. It is, of course, true that in 1642 questions of trust generated new constitutional demands which proved non-negotiable and which became the *occasions* of civil war. A review of the Militia Ordinance and the Nineteen Propositions, however, must keep in mind a number of easily forgotten points.[55]

The first is that parliament's defence of its actions remains basically conservative. A reading of the exchanges over the Militia Ordinance, over the king's attempt on Hull, over the Nineteen Propositions, leaves little doubt that the moves towards war were reluctantly taken. No such self-doubt can be found amongst those who pushed forward towards godly reformation in 1642, as iconoclasts, as the protectors of illegal gathered churches, as campaigners for presbyterianism. A reading of the debates, at least up to the battle of Edgehill, tells not of a radical group leading a quailing majority gently onwards, but of a leadership picking its way through a minefield, full of self-doubt, seeing the hazards of turning back as worse than the perils of pursuing their passage.[56] This impression is reinforced in two further ways. First the logic of events forced the Houses to make claims and then to justify them:[57] that is, the claims to exercise unprecedented control over the militia and the executive were not the inexorable working out of a clarified constitutionalism, but were desperate rationalisations of pragmatic responses to a king increasingly seen as deranged and incapable of governing, no longer a tyrant but a man incapable of discharging his trust. Secondly, the new claims made by the Houses were advanced piecemeal and tentatively. The so-called 'legislative' ordinances of 1642 were in fact astonishingly hesitant and half-hearted.

The most aggressive and assertive were those which dealt with religion, as that of June 1641 which extended local governors' powers to collect recusancy fines and amended the legal definition of recusancy.[58] In early August 1642, by contrast, parliament desperately needed money to raise an army to defend itself. The sixth and last of the Long Parliament's acts for the collection of tonnage and poundage had lapsed and there was no prospect of the royal assent to another one. Yet the Houses could not bring themselves to claim the right to vote themselves taxation. They appealed to all those liable to pay customs, asking them voluntarily to hand over their dues to parliament's treasurers, promising them a fifteen per cent discount and threatening refusers that when king and parliament once more worked in harmony, retroactive legislation would contain a clause 'for the forfeiture of the value of all such goods as shall not be duly entered'.[59] Similarly the Militia Ordinance possessed no legal force. The Houses specifically laid down that no action at law could follow from non-compliance. As d'Ewes said, the form of the ordinance was moral and not legal, telling the people how they ought to look to their own defence, not requiring them to do so.[60]

Most importantly, the constitutional issues of 1642 were means to an end, not ends in themselves. They were a controversial means to protect the uncontroversial settlement of 1641 and to deal with a king no longer trusted to keep his word. I shall argue below that that lack of trust grew out of a religious perception.

Finally, the Militia Ordinance and the Nineteen Propositions may have been the *occasion* of armed conflict, may have provided the non-negotiable issues which required men to take sides, but they were not the issues which determined which side most men would be on. This is a point which is particularly true of the provinces, as I shall argue at the end of the paper.

Once more, in 1642, a comparison of the constitutional and religious dynamics is suggestive. The presses remained remarkably silent on the theoretical issues underpinning consitutional issues. As Michael Mendle has written, there was 'no public debate on the major constitutional questions until mid 1642'.[61] Yet there was a vast and growing literature on the nature of the church and of episcopacy. The contribution of Lord Brooke, of John Milton, of the Smectymnuans and of others against episcopacy, and of Joseph Hall, James Ussher, Sir Thomas Aston and others in its defence is well-known, but they constitute only a tithe of the works which poured out on the subject.[62] Even the most important constitutional developments were swamped by literature on religious ones; in January 1642 four times as many pamphlets were devoted to the impeachment of the bishops as to the attempt on the Five Members.[63] The great issues of church government were fully rehearsed in print for months before the substantive debates on the issue. Recent studies of a number of MPs, including Sir Robert Harley, Sir John Wray, Sir William

Brereton and Sir Thomas Barrington, all show a dramatic process of radicalisation, a conversion to the necessity of root and branch reform.[64] That radicalisation grew out of a considered review of the possibilities; it grew out of a fundamental reappraisal and a belief in the need for a fresh start. As we have just seen, majorities in the Commons if not in the Lords consistently grasped the nettle of acting to promote and to protect those who challenged not merely Laudian innovation, but the very basis of the established church. Finally, the demand for a godly reformation was an end in itself, a vision. As Jacqueline Levy has recently written of the Harleys: '[They] viewed the civil war primarily as a war to establish true religion, in defiance of a catholic-inspired plot against church and state'.[65] She here points, as others have recently done, to the widespread belief in a Popish Plot about the king's person, which was seen as the only credible explanation of his behaviour.[66] It was not claimed that Charles I was a papist; but it was believed that he had ceased to be responsible for his actions, had ceased to govern. It was, in modern parlance, as though he had been got at by the Moonies, had been brainwashed, programmed; or in a metaphor more appropriate to the seventeenth century, that he had been insidiously and deliberately poisoned, so that he had gradually become disoriented, distracted. The Nineteen Propositions were designed for such a circumstance: not to deal with a tyrant or a despot, but with a deranged king, one who needed to be rescued from the contagion of popery, to be shielded and deprogrammed, to be decontaminated. The historical precedents to be pursued were those of the senile Edward III or the catatonic Henry VI, not the wicked Edward II or Richard II.[67]

The principal elements of the Popish Plot are well-known: the penetration of the court and household by known and suspected Catholics; the activities of papal envoys; the ascendency of the queen over the king; the use and projected use in 1639 and 1640 of Highland and Irish Catholic troops alongside an English army containing many catholic officers, all to be subsidised by Rome and Madrid, the ostensible purpose of which was to impose Charles's religious preferences upon the protestant church of Scotland. No wonder the papist threat to the state was seen to parallel the infiltration and subversion of the English church. While lay papists schemed to take over the state, the church was to be fatally weakened by the activities of the episcopal wolfpack.[68]

Yet not everyone shared this belief in the popish plot; or more importantly, not everyone continued to see it as the principal danger. This was partly the result of the excesses of those who most fully believed in it, and was partly the result of the wildly inconsistent signals sent out by the king. On the one hand, he was, or seemed to be, implicated in the Army Plots, the Incident, the Attempt on the Five Members, and, in the midst of all these, and most damagingly, the Irish Rebellion.[69] Those who knew of Charles's negotiations with the earl of Antrim in 1639 had little reason to

doubt the authenticity of the warrant which Catholic rebel leaders produced to vindicate their rising.[70] Yet Charles also projected another image
of himself. He accepted all the remedies for grievance put to him; he
pointedly and heartlessly abandoned Laud and his policies and promoted
to the episcopate moderate men, or at any rate men who were Laud's
enemies. [71] And he publicly associated himself with the slogans and values
of non-Laudian Anglicanism.[72] Just as Pym and his colleagues were increasingly obsessed[73] by the stranglehold of popery at court and beyond, so the
reinvigorated Anglicans became preoccupied with the indulgence given by
the Commons to fanatic preachers, to unlawful religious assemblies, to
mass picketing. The very measures which religious perceptions led a majority of the Commons to adopt as a defensive means to the end of safe-
guarding themselves and the nation from the threat of popery led an
increasing minority to back away. Fresh constitutional priorities were evaluated from the perspective of increasingly polarised religious assessments.

Talk of 'popery' is not a form of 'white noise', a constant fuzzy background in the rhetoric and argument of the time against which significant
changes in secular thought were taking place. This has been a fundamental
error in the intellectual historians of the English Revolution. This falsifies
the passionate belief, the passionate belief that is the ground of action, that
England was in the process of being subjected to the forces of Antichrist,
that the prospects were of anarchy, chaos, the dissolution of government
and liberties; and the equally passionate belief that disobedience to the
king, carried to the point of violent resistance, could only lead to chaos
and anarchy; and to the conviction of most men that both dangers were
equally real, a conviction which led to panic and a yearning for settlement.

There is a steady but inexorable shift from the muffled fears in the early
months of the Long Parliament to the outpourings of apprehension of
imminent Armageddon to be found in the declarations of 1642; from Mr
Thomas's call, during a debate on cathedral chapters in 1641, for the
abolition of church music:

> For I do find in my reading that anno 666, the year that was designed
> and computed for the coming of Antichrist, Vitalian, bishop of
> Rome, brought to the church singing of service and the use of
> organs;[74]

and from Sir John Wray's introduction of the Protestation as being

> first . . . to preserve our religion entire and pure without the least
> compound of superstition or idolatry; next to defend the defender of
> the faith, his royal Crown and Dignity. . . thus doing, Mr Speaker,
> and making Jerusalem our chiefest Joy, we shall be a blessed nation;[75]

from these to the exchanges of 1642, with Pym speaking of evil counsellors, who like 'diseases of the brain are most dangerous', and of a plot to

destroy all liberties, privileges and the rule of law.[76] Gone were the accusations of a tendency to arbitrary government; in their place is the language of anarchy and destruction, brought about by those whose 'devilish purpose was the better destruction of the true reformed religion'.[77]

If we read the sequence of parliamentary defences of its actions in 1642[78] to find out *to what end* they acted, rather than *by what right*, we find the same primacy of religious argument.

William Lamont's brilliant reconstruction of Richard Baxter's account of his decision to resist the king's authority lays emphasis on the king's responsibility for the Irish Rebellion and his abdication of the duty to protect his subjects from the forces of Antichrist. It was not royal tyranny but royal abdication which forced the people to look to their own defence.[79] At a stroke, decades of intellectualising about how subjects were bound to obey wicked kings as scourges sent by God were set aside; and at a stroke we can see how the constitutional issues of 1642 differed from those of 1640. The issue in 1642 was not the king's past tyranny; it was his present moral and political incapacity. This was precisely the argument of the Declaration of Lords and Commons sent to the north (11 July 1642)[80] and of the Declaration for Taking Up Arms (2 August 1642).[81] It is also the increasingly dominant theme in the work of Henry Parker, whose thought evolved under the impact of providentialist argument and a growing recognition that the king's will had been seduced by 'those execrable instruments which steal the king's heart from us, but they think the religion of protestants too tame and the nation of the English insensible to injuries'.[82] In the *Contra-Replicant*, for example, Charles was portrayed not as a tyrant but as a man helpless to prevent lawyers, corrupt clergy or soldiers from 'spoyling above the general law'.[83]

In 1640 and 1641 there is and was no way to distinguish 'moderate' and 'radical' constitutionalism. Future royalists like Hyde, Falkland, Dering and even George Digby, were no less 'hardline' than future parliamentarians like Pym, Selden and d'Ewes. What distinguished them was the gradual unfolding of the religious debate and the religiously-conditioned response to a new constitutional situation which was only indirectly related to the debates of 1640. None of those who defended the pre-Laudian church order in the debates of mid 1641 subsequently became a parliamentarian; few of those who demanded a fresh start supported the king. Defence of the established order, shorn of recent innovations, was partly a social perception: the defence of hierarchy in society and government. But it also owed much to affection for the practice and rhythms of a church of which they were third- or fourth-generation members; and to the claims for the superiority of the 'catholic and reformed' church as set forth by its apologists following Jewel and Hooker.[84]

The party which withdrew from Westminster during the winter of 1641–2 and during the spring of 1642 was the Anglican party. Those who remained were more or less unanimous in approving the Militia Ordinance, and the final form of the Nineteen Propositions, but they were far from unanimous on the need to wage war to implement them. While sources for religious commitment at that juncture are hard to come by, it seems likely that what distinguished those willing to raise armies to impose the new guarantees on the king, from those who voted against the escalation of the conflict, was the level of commitment to the godly cause. Robert Harley, William Brereton, Alexander Rigby are examples of men who had modest records of standing up to secular misgovernment; but all were men who were fired by the vision not simply of ecclesiastical reconstruction, but of building a godly commonwealth. By contrast, many of those with an impeccable record of standing up to legal and constitutional misgovernment but whose commitment to ecclesiastical reform was more cool, prudential, erastian, got cold feet in 1642. They felt that they had no choice but to stay at Westminster and to work for fresh guarantees of the constitutional settlement, but they could not bring themselves to support the means which alone could in fact achieve these guarantees. No one who reads the works of d'Ewes, Selden, Rudyard or Whitelocke can have much doubt that constitutionalism, however deeply felt, was inadequate as a ground for militant action. They would be parliamentarians in the war; but they did not will that war.[85]

Pressure of space has led me to an uncharacteristic concentration on the centre rather than on the provinces. What follows is the merest sketch of how the points made above can help to make as much sense of the provinces as of Westminster politics. MPs were too much in the limelight, too much on the spot, too much in the know, to be able to avoid making decisions which typecast them and limited their options. In the provinces, decisions were more easily hedged, fudged, deferred. It is quite clear that a majority of the gentry and of all social groups, whether they had a preference or not between king and parliament, had an absolute preference for peace, and the attempts of individuals and of county establishments to prevent or to limit the coming of the war to their communities are well enough known. Localism in 1640 led naturally to neutralism in 1642.[86]

Anthony Fletcher's study of the petitioning campaigns of 1640–2 is very telling. In the autumn of 1640, all three 'perceptions of misgovernment' can be found in the petitions, jostling side by side and sometimes inconsistently. By late 1641 and the first half of 1642, petitions on constitutional issues were beginning to show a lack of comprehension of developments at the centre. Fletcher discusses the petitions sent up by thirty eight counties and characterises them as containing paeans of praise for the achievements of the parliament in putting an end to arbitrary government; but he also argues that while 'at Westminster there was a sense of outright confrontation with the Crown . . . this is entirely absent in the provinces'. While some petitions showed an interest in the Militia Ordinance and a desire for regular musters, this was purely defensive and grew out of a concern with papist risings and local order. They remain suffused with a loyalty to Charles as well as to parliament.[87]

More dramatic still was the wave of petitions in the summer of 1642 which called for peace and accommodation and which refused to acknowledge the non-negotiability of the differences between Charles and the Houses. There was no great wave of petitions for and against the Nineteen Propositions, no great debate on its constitutional claims. Contemporaries took rather less interest than have historians in the exchanges of Culpepper and Parker.

Yet at the same time the religious issues were being stirred, the source of division and polarisation. The wave of anti-episcopal petitions in the spring of 1641 was followed by widespread iconoclasm, by 'swarms of conventicles' and by anti-catholic mobs, all winked at and countenanced by some in authority. Throughout the provinces this led, just as it did in parliament, to a reaction in favour of the established order, to movements to defend episcopacy and the prayer book. More than half the counties sent up petitions in the period pleading for the established church.[88] The bitterness of the language of the religious petitions of 1642 contrasts with the yearning for settlement and the increasingly forlorn pleading for peace which comes out of the constitutional petitions. Yet again, we find that the dynamism of religious argument contrasts with a shrinking away from constitutional choices.

The civil war broke out because small minorities thrust themselves forward, volunteered, took to arms. Neither the militia nor the array were the instruments of war. It was individual captains and colonels, recruiting their own companies and regiments who created the armies that went to war.[89] Many of the rank and file volunteered, doubtless because they expected a short campaign in the slack season after the harvest or to escape the trade slump in London. But many, especially amongst the officers, were motivated by a cause. And here for the last time, we find the familiar contrast. In Cheshire the royalist activists in 1642, who created the war effort and dragged the reluctant county establishment into the war, were led by Sir Thomas Aston, campaigner against ship money and for episcopacy; and the parliamentarian war effort was led by Sir William Brereton, constitutional quietist and sponsor of the anti-episcopal petition.[90] In Herefordshire Jacqueline Levy finds that 'religious issues lay at the heart of divided opinion . . . contemporaries were writing of "parties" in connection with episcopacy as early as January 1641'. She finds in 1642 reluctance to divide over the militia, but an increasing polarisation over the religious issues.[91] A similar conclusion was reached by Liam Hunt in his recent study of Essex.[92] If we go back to other county studies and distinguish between the issues which required men to make choices, and the grounds upon which they made their choices, I believe we will find that only where there was strong and distinctive and developed religious commitments will we find militancy. There were no constitutional militants.

On 10 September 1642 the Houses told the Scottish General Assembly that 'their chiefest aim' was 'the Truth and Purity of the Reformed Religion, not only against Popery but against all other superstitious sects and innovations whatsoever'.[93] Have we been so confused into seeking parallels between the British Crisis of the 1640s and the wave of rebellions on the Continent (brought on by war and the centralising imperatives of war), or between the English Revolution and the events of 1789 and 1917, that we have missed an obvious point? The English Civil War was not the first European revolution: it was the last of the Wars of Religion.

Notes

1 Rushworth, iv. 30.
2 Rushworth, iv. 33.
3 Rushworth, iv. 34.
4 Rushworth, iv. 40.
5 S. Lambert, 'The Opening of the Long Parliament', *HJ*, 27 (1984) pp. 265–88.
6 Existing impressions of the Short Parliament will be transformed by the availability of the very full parliamentary diary of Sir Thomas Aston. I am grateful to Judith Maltby for allowing me to see her full transcript of this very important diary which she is preparing for publication. It is the property of Mr Howard Talbot.
7 E.g. B.S. Manning, 'The Aristocracy and the Downfall of Charles I', in *Politics, Religion and the English Civil War*, ed. B.S. Manning (Manchester 1973), pp. 37–82; C. Roberts, 'The Earl of Bedford and the Coming of the English Revolution', *JMH*, 49 (1977); P. Christianson, 'The Peers, the People and Parliamentary Management in the First Six Months of the Long Parliament', *JMH*, 49 (1977); Lambert, 'Opening of Long Parliament'.
8 The critique by Clive Holmes, 'The County Community in Stuart Historiography' (Chapter 8, below) lists the main corpus of recent work. What follows is based on that corpus, bearing Holmes' strictures in mind.
9 For a recent survey of work on Caroline 'patronage' and 'faction' see K. Sharpe, 'Faction at the Early Stuart Court' *HT*, 33 (1983), pp. 39–46. The last phrase is from Ivan Roots, 'The Central Government and the Local Community' in *The English Revolution 1600–1660*, ed. E.W. Ives (1968), p. 42.
10 J.S. Morrill, *The Revolt of the Provinces* (1976), pp. 24–30, 144–50; Holmes, 'County Community'.
11 E.g. Morrill, *Revolt*, pp. 147–52.
12 A. Fletcher, *The Outbreak of the English Civil War* (1981), pp. 369–406.
13 D. Hirst, 'Revisionism Revised: Early Stuart 'Parliamentary History – The Place of Principle', *P & P*, 92 (1981), is the most cogent of many recent critiques of the 'revisionist' approach.
14 See J.S. Morrill and J.D. Walter, 'Order and Disorder in the English Revolution' (Chapter 12 in this volume).
15 Lambert, 'Opening of the Long Parliament'. Her account of the slowness of the

Houses to take up legislative redress of grievance is very telling. But I cannot agree with her that this is evidence of a house deeply divided over the need for such redress from the outset.

16 This is based principally upon a reading of the following: Rushworth, iv. *passim*; J. Nalson, *An Impartial Collection of the great affairs of State from the beginning of the Scotch Rebellion in the year 1639* (2 vols, 1682–3), *passim*; and the parliamentary journal of Sir Simonds d'Ewes (BL, Harl. MS 163–5, for which the period up to March 1641 and for the period November 1641 to March 1642 have been published in three separate volumes).

17 Fourteen of the thirty (reconstructed from the facsimile edition of the Privy Council Registers, PRO, PC 2/52–54).

18 W.J. Jones, *Politics and The Bench* (1972), pp. 137–43, 199–214; *Somers Tracts*, iv. 130, 300–8; Rushworth, v. 318–44.

19 *The Journal of Sir Simonds d'Ewes from the Beginning of the Long Parliament to the Opening of the Trial of the Earl of Strafford*, ed. W. Notestein (New Haven, 1923), pp. 19–20 and *passim*.

20 A committee was set up to investigate complaints against Lords Lieutenant and their deputies, but it appears never to have reported (Rushworth, iv. 98–9).

21 This paragraph and the succeeding ones are a synthesis of much reading in primary and secondary sources. The most influential of the latter include Professor P. Collinson's *The Religion of Protestants* (Oxford, 1982), *Godly People* (1983), especially chapters 4, 6, 20, and his Birkbeck lectures in Cambridge of Lent 1981 (as yet unpublished).

22 N.R.N. Tyacke, 'Arminianism in England in Religion and Politics', University of Oxford D.Phil. thesis (1968), and cf. P. White, 'The Rise of Arminianism Reconsidered' *P&P*, 101 (1983), pp. 34–54. The best work on Laud's own thought remains W.H. Hutton, *William Laud* (1895).

23 See also his statement, in reply to Lord Saye and Sele, that 'almost all of them (the Puritans) say that God from all eternity reprobates by far the greater part of mankind to eternal fire, without any eye to their sins. Which opinion my very soul abominates.' Laud, vi. 133.

24 K. Sharpe, 'Archbishop Laud', *HT*, 33 (1983) is correct to see Laud as consciously a 'traditionalist'; but by all evaluations, except Laud's own, he was stressing and imposing (often neglected) aspects of the Elizabethan church at the expense of other traditions and much established practice.

25 This view owes much to the ideas of Patrick Collinson in his Birkbeck lectures.

26 For key letters and instructions of Laud in relation to these issues, see Laud, v. 321, 324, 337, 345, 351, 355, 361, and vi. 310, 330, 332, 338, 341.

27 Rushworth, iv. 122–3.

28 It is not true, as has been often asserted, that the managers of the parliament sought to keep contentious ecclesiastical issues out of the Houses until after the secular reforms were achieved. See, for example, the willingness to escalate religious issues in *CJ*, ii. 25, 26–7, 35, 41, 52, 54, 71 etc; *d'Ewes*, ed. Notestein, pp. 4, 5, 16, 17, 18, 22, 24–5, etc.

29 For a full discussion of this, see J.S. Morrill, 'The Attack on the Church of England in the Long Parliament' in D. Beales and G. Best (eds), *History, Society and the Churches* (1985).

30 *Synodalia: A Collection of Articles of Religion, Canons and proceedings in Convocation in the Province of Canterbury*, ed. E. Cardwell (2 vols, Oxford, 1842), i. 380–406.

31 *CJ*, ii. 30–33, 41–52; *d'Ewes*, ed. Notestein, 21, 70–2, 125, 149, 152–7.

32 Rushworth, iv. 196.

33 Hutton, *Laud*, pp. 98–102.
34 W. Lamont, *Marginal Prynne* (1963), pp. 11–27; W. Lamont, *Godly Rule* (1969), pp. 44–52.
35 *d'Ewes*, ed. Notestein, pp. 70–2, 152–163, 427–8.
36 Rushworth, iv. 197.
37 Quoted in Hutton, *Laud*, p. 103.
38 Rushworth, iv. 210.
39 For the impeachment articles brought against Arundel in 1397, see *Select Documents of English Constitutional History 1307–1485*, eds S.B. Chrimes and A.L. Brown (1961), pp. 170–1. Arundel was impeached for issuing commissions 'en prejudice du roy et overtement encontre sa regalie, sa dignite, et sa corone'. For the debate, see *d'Ewes*, ed. Notestein, pp. 276, 419–420.
40 Rushworth, iv. 122.
41 Lucius Cary, Viscount Falkland, *A Speech Made to the House of Commons Concerning episcopacy* (1641), 4. For a discussion, see M.L. Schwartz, 'Lay Anglicanism and the Crisis of the English Church in the Early Seventeenth Century', *Albion*, 14 (1982), pp. 1–5.
42 E. Calamy, *England's Looking Glass* (22 December 1641), p. 48; S. Marshall, *A Sermon Before the House of Commons* (17 November 1640), p. 40. It should be said that the Fast Sermons as a whole displayed an indifference amounting to contempt for secular injustices, and focused with increasing clarity on the prospects for building a New Jerusalem. I am grateful to Mr S. Baskerville for his comments on this question.
43 W.M. Abbott, 'The Issue of Episcopacy in the Long Parliament' (Univ. of Oxford D. Phil. thesis, 1981), ch. 2.
44 C.L. Hamilton, 'The Basis of Scottish Efforts to Create a Reformed Church in England 1640/1', *Church Hist. 30* (1961), pp. 171–8; P. Crawford, *Denzil, First Lord Holles* (1979), pp. 42–51.
45 *CJ*, ii. 24–40; *d'Ewes*, ed. Notestein, pp. 4–40, *passim*.
46 *CJ*, ii. 24, 52, 102, 124, 134; *d'Ewes*, ed. Notestein, pp. 4, 17, 130, 172–4, 232–3, 240–9, 386, 400–1, 424–9.
47 *CJ*, ii. 23, 32.
48 *d'Ewes*, ed. Notestein, p. 306.
49 *d'Ewes*, ed. Notestein, pp. 281–2.
50 J. Hart, 'The House of Lords and the Reformation of Justice 1640–3' (Univ. of Cambridge Ph.D. thesis, 1985, ch. 3).
51 BL, Harl. MS 163 fos. 662, 669.
52 *The Private Journals of the Long Parliament 3 January to 5 March 1642*, eds W.H. Coates, A.S. Young, V.F. Snow (New Haven, 1982), pp. 302–3.
53 BL. Harl. MS 164, fos. 887–90, 895, 914; and for the rumbling battle over the declaration in the autumn, *The Journal of Sir Simonds d'Ewes from the First Recess of the Long Parliament to the withdrawal of King Charles from London*, ed. W.H. Coates (New Haven, 1942), pp. 1–66.
54 W.A. Shaw, *A History of the English Church during the Civil War and Under the Commonwealth* (2 vols, 1900), i. 1–121; Abbott, 'Episcopacy', *passim*.
55 The following is based not simply on the documents themselves (for which see *Constitutional Documents of the Puritan Revolution*, ed. S.R. Gardiner (3rd edn, Oxford, 1906), pp. 245–7, 249–54), but also on the debates which arose from them (see *Private Journals*, eds Coates *et al.*, pp. 291–5, 313–15, 334–50, 544–50; BL, Harl. MS 163, fos. 427–8; Rushworth, iv. 516–50, 691–735.
56 I recognise that this is a highly contestable view. Might not the prospective leaders of the parliamentary cause have deliberately played down their

radicalism for tactical reasons, for fear of alienating moderate opinion and losing the initiative? This is the very influential view of J.H. Hexter, *The Reign of King Pym* (New Haven, 1940), pp. 1–30 and *passim*. I prefer the view expressed here because (i) they displayed no such reticence on religious matters despite the fact that it cost them moderate support (ii) their private thoughts appear to reflect their public statements (iii) their rhetorical reticence led to a reticence of action which threatened the success of the military operations.

57 E.g. L. Schwoerer, '"The Fittest Subject for a King's Quarrel": an Essay on the Militia Controversy', *JBS*, 11 (1971); R. Tuck, '"The Ancient Law of Freedom": John Selden and the Civil War', in *Reactions to the English Civil War*, ed. J.S. Morrill (1982), pp. 137–64.

58 BL. Harl. MS 164, fos. 858, 876; *LJ*, iv 384–7; Fletcher, *Outbreak*, pp. 76–7.

59 *Acts and Ordinances of the Interregnum*, eds C.H. Firth and R.S. Rait (3 vols, 1911), i. 16–20.

60 Gardiner, *Constitutional Documents*, p. 247; BL, Harl. MS 163, fo. 247, viz. 'That all men ought to obey the ordinance it is not thereby implied that an ordinance of parliament hath the same vertue and efficacie that an Act hath . . . by those words that they ought to obey, is intended that . . . every man ought voluntarily, willingly and cheerfully to obey.'

61 M. Mendle, 'Politics and Political Thought, 1640–1642', in *Origins of the English Civil War*, ed. C. Russell (1973), pp. 219–46; idem, 'Mixed Government, the Estates, and the Bishops' (Washington Univ., St Louis, Ph.D. thesis, 1977), pp. 396–432; G.K. Fortescue, *Catalogue of the Thomason Tracts* (2 vols, 1908), pp. 1–116.

62 The best discussion is probably in *The Prose Works of John Milton* (8 vols, 1953–82), vol. i, ed. D.M. Wolfe, pp. 48–151; Fletcher, *Outbreak*, pp. 91–124 and *passim*.

63 Fortescue, *Thomason*, i. 57–73; similarly in March 1642 there was more discussion of the prayer book than of the militia (*ibid.*, 86–97).

64 J. Levy, 'Perceptions and Beliefs: The Harleys of Brampton Bryan and the Origins and Outbreak of the Civil War' (Univ. of London Ph.D. thesis, 1983), *passim*; R.N. Dore, 'The Early Life of Sir William Brereton', *Trans. Lancs and Cheshire Antiq. Soc.*, 63 (1954) 1–26; J.S. Morrill, 'Puritans and the Church in the Diocese of Chester', *NH*, 12 (1975), pp. 151–5; W. Hunt, *The Puritan Moment* (Cambridge, Mass., 1983).

65 Levy, 'Harleys', 175.

66 C. Hibbard, *Charles I and the Popish Plot* (Chapel Hill, 1983), *passim*; G. Albion, *Charles I and the Court of Rome* (1935), *passim*; W. Lamont, *Richard Baxter and the Millennium* (1979), pp. 76–123; M. Finlayson, *Historians, Puritanism and the English Revolution* (Toronto, 1983), pp. 79–119; Fletcher, *Outbreak, passim*.

67 I owe this point to conversations with Conrad Russell and to ideas contained in his unpublished paper 'The Causes of the English Civil War'. The notion that the king had been 'poisoned' is a common one, but more specific was the declaration of the Houses that they proceeded as though the king was suffering from nonage, natural disability or captivity (BL, Thomason Tract E241(1), pp. 207–8). Dr Ian Roy tells me that Sir Ralph Verney's (hitherto undeciphered) notes on the debate of 28 February 1642 show MPs considered the king in the position of a suicidal maniac, from whom the power of the sword must be removed. *Verney Papers: Notes of Proceedings in the Long Parliament by Sir Ralph Verney* (Camden 1st series, 31, 1845), p. 184. I am very grateful to Dr Roy for this reference.

68 See n. 66; also D. Stevenson, *Alasdair MacColla and the Highland Problem of the Seventeenth Century* (Edinburgh, 1981), chapter 1; J.H. Elliott, 'The Year of the Three Ambassadors', in *History and Imagination*, eds H. Lloyd-Jones, V. Pearl, A.B. Worden (1981).

69 Hibbard, *Popish Plot, passim.*

70 D. Stevenson, *Scottish Covenanters and Irish Confederates* (Belfast, 1981), pp. 43–65; A. Clarke, 'The Genesis of the Ulster Rising of 1641' in *Plantation to Partition*, ed. P. Roebuck (Belfast, 1981), pp. 40–61; Lamont, *Baxter*, pp. 77–87, 116–9, 230–2.

71 J.S. Morrill, 'The Church in England 1642–9' in *Reactions*, ed. Morrill, pp. 98–100; P. King, 'The Episcopate during the English Civil War' *EHR*, 83 (1968), pp. 526–30.

72 B.H.G. Wormald, *Clarendon* (Cambridge, 1951), p. 18; *Bibliotheca Lindesiana: A Bibliography of Royal Proclamations of Tudor and Stuart Sovereigns*, ed. R.R. Steele (2 vols, Oxford, 1910), i, 295.

73 There was a generalised anxiety about the growth of popery in and around the Court from the beginning of Charles' reign, but few saw it as the principal hazard until the events of 1641. For John Pym's precociousness in this respect, see C. Russell, 'The Parliamentary career of John Pym, 1621–1629', in *The English Commonwealth*, eds P. Clark, A.G.R. Smith, N.R.N. Tyacke (Leicester, 1979).

74 Rushworth, iv. 287.

75 Rushworth, iv. 240–1.

76 *LJ*, iv. 540–3.

77 *LJ*, iv. 512.

78 Rushworth, iv. 398–421 (since the pagination is awry at this point, 385–415 being used twice, this reference is to 398–415 and then 385–421), 516–50, 565–601, 691–739. A good starting point is 'the Declaration of Causes and Remedies' (*CJ*, ii. 443–6, reprinted in *Private Journals*, eds Coates *et al.*, pp. 543–50).

79 Lamont, *Baxter*, pp. 88–98.

80 *LJ*, v. 201–2.

81 *LJ*, v. 257–60.

82 H. Parker, *Observations on His Majesties late Answers and Addresses* (1642), p. 15.

83 H. Parker, *The Contra-Replicant His Complaint to his Majestie* (1642). See also his comments on the 'absolute and unlimitable power of the king's sword and sceptre' controlled by the Queen who is in turn controlled by 'the Romish vice-god' (Parker, *The Contra-Replicant*, pp. 10–15). Parker's thought was dramatically affected by the Irish Rebellion. My reading of Parker has been enormously helped by discussions with Howard Moss, and by supervising his admirable B.A. dissertation.

84 Fletcher, *Outbreak, passim*; Morrill, *Revolt*, pp. 46–50; Morrill, 'Church in England', pp. 89–114; J. Maltby, 'Approaches to the Study of Religious Conformity in Late Elizabethan and Early Stuart England' (University of Cambridge Ph.D. thesis, 1991). For the growing articulation of the case for episcopacy within the Commons, see the debates on the Grand Remonstrance (the most heated exchanges before the final vote all concerned the church) in *d'Ewes*, ed. Coates, pp. 117, 149–52, 165–6.

85 Innumerable works could be cited here. See for example, Fletcher, *Outbreak*, pp. 228–82; Gardiner, *History*, x. 152–219; Hexter, *King Pym*, pp. 1–30; Rushworth, iv. 754–5; B. Whitelocke, *Memorials of the English Affairs* (4 vols, Oxford, 1853), i. 148–90; R. Spalding, *The Improbable Puritan* (1979), pp. 78–97.

86 Fletcher, *Outbreak*, pp. 369–406.
87 Fletcher, *Outbreak*, pp. 191–227, 369–407. See how well this account fits the sequence of petitions in Kent, as discussed in A.S.P. Woods, *Prelude to Civil War* (Salisbury, 1981), pp. 30–62, 95–119, 141–4, 153–7.
88 Sir Thomas Aston, *A Collection of Sundry Petitions* (1642); Fletcher, *Outbreak*, pp. 283–96.
89 R. Hutton, *The Royalist War Effort* (1981), pp. 22–32.
90 J.S. Morrill, *Cheshire 1630–1660* (Oxford, 1974), pp. 31–74.
91 J. Levy, 'Harleys', chs 4–6.
92 Hunt, *Puritan Moment*, pp. 235–313, especially 311–12.
93 *LJ*, v. 348–50.

7

Anti-popery: the structure of a prejudice

PETER LAKE

I

Religion is back in fashion as an explanation for the English Civil War. This might seem unsurprising given the currency, until relatively recently, of the notion of the 'Puritan Revolution'. We are surely dealing here only with another revolution of the wheel of historiographical fortune of the sort produced by the institutionalized need for novelty of interpretation amongst professional historians. However, the interpretation now in vogue does not focus on the purposive, radical, even revolutionary ideology which earlier commentators liked to ascribe to the 'Puritans', but rather on the irrational passions and prejudices stirred up by the threat of 'popery'.

To take a few examples; Anthony Fletcher has written of two myths clouding contemporaries' perceptions and effectively concealing the enormous areas of common ideological ground still shared by the king and his opponents. The most pervasive and persuasive of these myths, according to Fletcher, was that of a popish plot to subvert the civil and religious liberties of England and it was the prevalence of this view that enabled parliament to mobilize support so effectively against the king. William Lamont has emphasized the sheer oddness and irrationality of anti-popery. Kevin Sharpe can only explain the extreme reaction of many Englishmen to the activities of William Laud (who, for Sharpe, was a simple Whitgiftian disciple of order and uniformity) by seeing it as a function of the irrational anti-popery of the period. John Morrill, too, locates the roots of conflict in the fanaticism of two relatively small group of religious engagés. His account can, at least, accommodate a positive role for the Puritan drive for further reformation; Michael Finlayson has, however, effectively collapsed Puritanism into anti-popery. For Finlayson Puritanism is a mere chimera, produced by modern historians fixated on the so-called 'English revolution' and consequently in desperate search for an appropriately revolutionary ideology. As for anti-popery, it was a cloud of unknowing through which contemporaries blundered into civil war. As such it can be considered as a wholly irrational and unitary 'thing' which merely has to be identified rather than analysed or explained.[1]

This emphasis on religious passion and anti-popish fear fits very neatly within recent trends in 'revisionist' writing on the causes of the civil war. For, if everyone wanted accommodation, if there were no major differences of secular ideology dividing contemporaries, if radical Puritanism was an illusion and religious innovation was a preserve of the Arminian right rather than the Puritan left, and if the majority of even the ruling class were more concerned with local than national issues, then the revisionists' greatest need was for a positive explanation of conflict.[2]

I want here to provide a framework for re-evaluating the religious component in the political crisis of the early seventeenth century, not by resurrecting a view of Puritanism as a revolutionary ideology (although, as Conrad Russell observed in 1973,[3] it was fulfilling that role by the early 1640s), but rather by examining the phenomenon of anti-popery. I want to see it as, at least in England, the most obvious and important example of that process of binary opposition, inversion or the argument from contraries which, we are increasingly being told, played so central a part in both the learned and popular culture of early modern Europe.[4] Certainly to many, if not most, educated Protestant English people of the period popery was an anti-religion, a perfectly symmetrical negative image of true Christianity. Anti-Christ was an agent of Satan, sent in to the Church to corrupt and take it over from within. He was not an overt enemy like the Turk, but rather rose by stealth and deception, pretending piety and reverence while in fact inverting and perverting the values of true religion. For the Cambridge Puritan divine William Fulke popery was tantamount to devil worship, while for the conformist John Bridges it represented a more serious threat to the true Church than the pagans, the Jews or the Turk.[5]

Since the Protestant analysis of popish anti-Christianity proceeded through a series of binary oppositions, every negative characteristic imputed to Rome implied a positive cultural, political or religious value which Protestants claimed as their own exclusive property. Thus the Protestants' negative image of popery can tell us a great deal about their positive image of themselves. What follows is an attempt to read off from their negative image of Rome the Protestants' own self image and then to present anti-popery as a 'rational response' to situations in which values central to that self image came under threat.[6] Whether the Protestant image of popery was accurate is therefore a question of no significance for the present enquiry. Clearly anti-popery was not an early exercise in the study of comparative religion. It was, however, a way of dividing up the world between positive and negative characteristics, a symbolic means of labelling and expelling trends and tendencies which seemed to those doing the labelling, at least, to threaten the integrity of a Protestant England.

II

The Protestant rejection of Rome was based fundamentally on a brutal dichotomy between the authority of man and the authority of God, the claims of the Church and the dictates of scripture, the creature and the creator. For Protestants popery had allowed merely human authorities, traditions and practices to take over the Church. The most obvious of these was the pope's usurpation of Christ's role as head of the Church.

Once established, the authority of the pope was used to set up and confirm in the Church a whole series of ceremonies, forms of worship and beliefs which were of entirely human origin. Crucial to the Protestant analysis of the falseness of these practices and beliefs was the concept of idolatry. That the worship of the one true God had been supplanted and subverted by the worship of his creatures was evident in the papists' reverence for the worship of idols and images, their use of the saints as intercessors and their virtual deification of the Virgin Mary. Perhaps the central example of this tendency toward idolatry was the doctrine of transubstantiation which sanctioned what Protestants contemptuously referred to as the 'bread worship' associated with the Catholic mass.[7]

Christ's sacrifice on the cross was no longer at the centre of popish belief and practice; the papists had substituted the doctrine of justification by works for one of justification by faith. Their insistence on the importance of religious works of human devising as a means to achieve salvation established hypocrisy as a central characteristic of popery. The guilt of virtually any sin could be assuaged and salvation attained through some form of external religious observance or act of clerical absolution.[8] Here Protestant treatments of popish attitudes to sex provide a useful encapsulation of the inverted, hall-of-mirrors quality that pervaded much anti-popish writing. For William Perkins the Catholic attempt to confer on celibacy a peculiarly exalted religious significance was a prime example of the pope's usurped and tyrannical claim to be able to set aside and alter at will the laws of God and nature, which had, after all, established marriage as an honourable estate. By so doing, of course, the papists forced many men and women into chaste lives for which they had no calling, with predictable results. Indeed, for many Protestants buggery became an archetypically popish sin, not only because of its proverbially monastic provenance but also because, since it involved the abuse of natural faculties and impulses for unnatural ends, it perfectly symbolized the wider idolatry at the heart of popish religion. Again the Protestants made great play with the papists' notorious laxity towards heterosexual promiscuity, citing here the stews of Rome and the papal revenues produced by licensing them.[9]

The capacity of the clergy to extract a profit from the vicious cycle of hypocrisy and guilt which such beliefs produced provided the Protestants with a convincing sociological explanation for the rise of Popery. But if the prevalence of popery was based on the greed and vainglory of the clergy it was also founded on the ignorance and credulity of the laity. The surface glitter of popish ceremonies and images were all intended to appeal to 'the heart of carnal man, bewitching it with great glistering of the painted harlot'. Popery was a religion based on illusion and trickery. The mass itself was compared to conjuring or magic, as were the false miracles and powers of exorcism claimed for saints and the priesthood respectively. Crucial popish doctrines were also designed expressly to appeal to the corrupt common sense and self love of the natural man. Justification by works was 'an opinion settled in nature'; human self-love and presumption were fostered by the doctrine of free will and merit.[10]

Popery was, therefore, an anti-religion, whose rise in the Church and popular appeal the Protestants explained by the accuracy with which it reflected and played upon the weaknesses and corruptions of man's fallen nature. The differences between this anti-religion and true religion were described by Protestants in terms of a whole series of opposites or contraries; one was carnal, the other spiritual, one inward, the other outward and so on. Here I want to concentrate on the contrasts they drew between tyranny and liberty and light and darkness. The tyranny of popery consisted most obviously in the pope's usurped claim to be the head of the Church. Through the exercise of that claim he trampled on the rights and liberties not only of other bishops and patriarchs but also those of Christian princes.[11] However, the tyranny of the pope was not limited to the 'high politics' of Church government. It consisted also in the spiritual oppression inherent in popish religion, whereby the spiritual rights and liberties of ordinary believers were subverted and destroyed. Their sense of a full and free redemption in Christ was undercut by the popish stress on works; in consequence their consciences were oppressed by the vain human traditions and laws laid upon them by the pope and his clergy.[12]

Of course, this tyranny could not exist without the ignorance of the laity. The papists realized that their hold over the laity would not survive exposure to the clear light of the gospel and had in consequence always opposed the spread of 'good letters' amongst the learned and scriptural knowledge amongst the people. According to Perkins and others the papists really did believe that ignorance was the mother of devotion. Thus the division between popish tyranny and Christian liberty led straight into that between popish darkness and the light of the gospel.[13] For Protestants the Reformation was a gradual process of enlightenment which, started by the likes of Wycliffe and Huss, culminated in the activities of the reformers of the sixteenth century and, in England, in the establishment of the gospel under Elizabeth. Protestants assumed that once the clear light of the gospel had been revealed to the people via the press and the pulpit it would inevitably cut a swathe through the clouds of ignorance and superstition left behind by popery.[14]

Thus Protestants claimed that while popery, through magic, symbols, false miracles and seeming common sense, appealed to the lower, carnal and corrupt side of human nature, their own religion sought to free all Christians from this world of illusion and inversion through the propagation of the unvarnished word. Obviously Protestant confidence in the power of the word was based primarily on the status of scripture as the divinely inspired word of God (and on God's promise that the action of the spirit would attend upon the exposition of his word from the pulpit). But there was also a sense in which Protestants regarded their faith as more rational, more internally coherent than popery. William Perkins, for one, was quite happy to prove that popery was self-contradictory. Transubstantiation was a nonsense, he wrote, involving as it did the simultaneous presence of Christ's body in heaven and in the bread and wine. Also contradictory were claims that man was saved by grace and then works and that sin was remitted by Christ only to be punished subsequently in purgatory.[15] The mindless acceptance of beliefs and practices merely because they had been held for centuries was also seen by Thomas Scott (the author of *Vox Populi*) and others as a defining mark of popish darkness. Faced with popish appeals to custom and tradition, Matthew Hutton, the future archbishop of York, replied that 'custom without truth is but old error'. In a culture which, we are often told, was dominated by the claims of custom and tradition the reformation of the Church gave contemporaries at least one prominent example of the reordering of established institutions and value systems according to the dictates of abstract criteria, rationally applied.[16]

Thus the whole Protestant view of popery not only associated it with a ritual-based vision of ignorance, superstition and unthinking traditionalism but it also appropriated for Protestantism an essentially word-based vision of rationality, enlightenment and knowledge. This opinion combined with the repudiation of popish tyranny both secular and spiritual revealed a strain of populism running through the centre of the Protestant image of Rome. Since true reformation could only be brought about as each individual came to a proper understanding and possession of his spiritual liberties and duties as a Christian, Protestant enlightenment was, almost by definition, popular enlightenment. In John Foxe's account of the struggle between the true and false Churches, underground groups of humble believers had kept the true Church alive while the ecclesiastical hierarchy of priests and bishops, aided by the princes of this world, had proved the leading agents of persecution.[17]

The logical culmination of this populist strand was reached in Presbyterianism. Presbyterians saw the rule of one minister over another as a direct emanation of the pope's tyrannical rule over the Church; popery had removed not only the spiritual liberties of ordinary believers but also their civil liberties as Church members. For Thomas Cartwright the right to a say in the election of Church governors and in the conduct of Church government was one of the liberties bought on the cross by Christ for all Christians and subsequently removed by the rise of Antichrist.[18]

Despite such trends and tendencies it would be absurd to see the political legacy of anti-popery as unequivocally populist. After all Foxe himself had made it clear that a central element in the supposed tyranny of Antichrist was his usurpation of the just rights of Christian princes. Moreover, the resumption of those rights had a crucial role to play in the expulsion of Antichrist from the Church. While John Bridges denounced the power of the pope as absolute and therefore tyrannical he did not understand that tyranny to flow from denial of the rights of ordinary believers or ministers to a consent-giving say in ecclesiastical government. Rather it resided, firstly, in the pope's denial of Christian princes' just and God-given powers over the church and secondly in his claim to be able to dissolve and alter the dictates of both natural and divine law.

According to Bridges the powers lawfully exercised by sovereign Christian princes were limited, but only by the dictates of natural and divine law not by the consent of their lay or clerical subjects. In this way conformist writers like Bridges were able to denounce the pope's power as absolute and therefore tyrannical without at the same time committing themselves to a view of political power inherently limited by the ruler's obligation to seek the consent of the ruled. Rather for them tyranny was to be avoided by the subjection of the ruler's will to the laws of God and nature; a subjection to which the pope would not submit.

In part in reaction to the papists' claim about the power of the pope to depose princes and in part in reaction against Presbyterian opinions that had similar implications for religious and secular authority, conformist divines came more and more to emphasize the sovereign powers of Christian princes. Popish tyranny was thus to be avoided not by the retrieval of any popular liberties but by the vindication of the rights of sovereign Christian princes as ecclesiastical governors. In so far as such writers retained any vision of the Reformation as an open-ended process of change, a genuinely popular movement, they limited that vision to the spiritual sphere of individual conversion and collective growth in grace. For them the institutional consequences of the Reformation consisted solely of the prince's resumption of his or her powers over the Church and the use of those powers to re-establish right doctrine. Of course, consent by both the laity and the clergy was presented even by the most drily conformist writers as a good thing. In practice, they claimed, English monarchs did govern the Church with the consent and co-operation of their (orthodox) subjects. However, the real difference between monarchic and papal power lay not in the consent of either the clergy or the laity but rather in the monarch's submission to natural and divine law.[19]

For these writers the extra-human origins of popery conferred an aura of eschatological significance on any régime that successfully contrived to resist it. The success of Elizabeth and James in expelling the pope, restoring the gospel, resisting the assaults of foreign princes and preserving England from the confessional strife which engulfed so many other countries all seemed to prove God's providential care for the English. They certainly provided many conformist defenders of the status quo with powerful arguments against Puritan attacks on the popish remnants within the English Church.[20]

To this can be added another central characteristic of popery in the eyes of English Protestants – it was foreign, involving allegiance to a foreign ruler (the pope) and acceptance of his right to excommunicate and depose Christian princes. The experiences of Elizabeth's reign served to associate popery indelibly with the aggression of foreign popish powers, particularly Spain. Precisely the same process of inversion and name-calling was applied by Protestants to the Spanish as had been used against the papists, a process which culminated, by the second half of Elizabeth's reign, in the so-called 'black legend' of Spanish cruelty and tyranny. Associated as it was with foreign powers, popery appeared to Protestants to be a solvent of the ties of political loyalty. In making that point Protestants tended to emphasize the populist theories of power which Catholic authors advanced to vindicate the rights of subjects to resist and remove heretical rulers. Politically, therefore, the legacy of anti-popery was decidedly ambiguous. Concern with the popish threat could prompt the development of authoritarian as well as of populist readings of the powers of the English crown and of the nature of authority in the English church.[21]

The legacy of anti-popery was also polemically ambiguous. In the debates between different strands of English Protestant opinion, Presbyterians used popery to emphasize the need to extend the process of reformation from the sphere of doctrine to that of discipline. Conformists invoked it to underwrite the essential soundness of the régime which had stood so long in the breach against Rome. Moderate Puritans and conformists both used it to play down the significance of the internal divisions among English Protestants in the face of the 'common adversary' and to stress the value, as a bulwark of order and obedience, of evangelical Calvinist preaching, even by nonconformists and erstwhile presbyterians.[22]

However, the ambiguity of anti-popery operated at deeper levels than the conscious polemical and political manipulations of contemporaries. Arguably the power of anti-popery as a source of ideological leverage and explanatory power was based on the capacity of the image of popery to express, contain and, to an extent, control the anxieties and tensions at the very centre of the experience and outlook of English Protestants. In part, the roots of those anxieties were obvious enough. There really was a popish threat to the autonomy of Protestant England for much of Elizabeth's reign. Under James the war with Spain ended, but as Tom Cogswell has pointed out, if the alarm over the Spanish Match is added to the traditional list which stretches from the Armada, through the gunpowder plot, the various invasion scares of the 1620s and the Irish revolt, then every generation of English people between the 1580s and the 1640s had personal experience of a popish assault on English independence.[23]

However, the anxieties which lay behind anti-popery had other, less obvious cultural roots. Kai Ericson in his seminal study of the witch craze in New England has argued that the production of such threatening ideal types of deviance and 'otherness' should be located within moments when the moral and cultural boundaries of groups or societies shift or are placed under threat. Clearly the reformation itself was just such a major shift. John Bossy has recently written of the sixteenth century as a period dominated by the emergence of an austerely word-and-doctrine-based view of true religion. In the English context the Protestant image of popery was perhaps the most important ideological means produced for explaining and controlling the strains associated with the transition to that word-based vision of true religion.[24] The image of popery as the natural religion for the fallen man drew on at least three elements within the situation of English Protestants. Firstly it explained and labelled as popish and undesirable the continuing appeal of ritual and symbol and visual imagery in a society still drenched in all three. Secondly it spoke to and helped to account for the pronounced religious conservatism of the English provinces;[25] and thirdly it keyed in with the Protestants' own very pessimistic view of human nature after the fall.

It has become increasingly obvious of late that the cultural struggles upon which English Protestants embarked at the Reformation lasted well into the seventeenth century.[26] This ensured that many of the anxieties about the potential popularity of 'popery', characterized in terms of what had become the inherently popish attributes of sin, sexual licence, superstition and the mindless acceptance of custom, retained their relevance for committed Protestants well into the seventeenth century. That relevance could only be heightened by the continued political threat from foreign popish powers and, increasingly under James and Charles, from popish influence at court. Insofar as this situation might rationally be taken to induce anxiety in Protestants, anti-popery allowed them to label, externalize and hence to act upon that anxiety and, to an extent, therefore, to quell it.

Another parallel explanation for the prevalence and appeal of anti-popery in this period may be found in the political system and its ideology of consensus decision-making. The early seventeenth century was a period of increasing political conflict in parliament. While revisionist scholars like Conrad Russell have demonstrated that the parties to that conflict are not best seen as a monolithic government and opposition it remains the case that the parliamentary history of the early seventeenth century was hardly a story of untroubled agreement and co-operation between crown and parliament. And yet revisionists like Russell and Mark Kishlansky have convincingly argued that despite these difficulties the practical and ideological assumptions of contemporaries remained dominated by the need for agreement between the king and his subjects. Parliament, it seems, drew its prominence in the world view of contemporaries from its supposed capacity to bring about such unanimity and harmony. In view of all this the political history of the period must have come as something of a shock and a disappointment to contemporary observers.[27] Such a basic failure on the part of the political system to produce the goods for which it was supposedly designed called not only for disappointment, it called also for explanation.

Whether the failure of the ruling class assembled in parliament to meet the financial needs of the crown was due to ideological principle or penny-pinching localism or some mixture of the two, the fact remains that as the crown resorted to new and unparliamentary sources of revenue what Dr Sommerville has revealed as two mutually exclusive views of political authority were brought increasingly into conflict. It is perhaps worth reminding ourselves that there was an ideological as well as a financial logic which led from impositions to the forced loan and then to ship-money. Given the relationship in contemporary thought between liberty and property it was inevitable that, however great the impulse towards ideological agreement, the functional breakdown delineated by Professor Russell would bring with it ideological conflict. At the level of theoretical argument, as Johann Sommerville has shown, there was precious little room for compromise and yet the workings of the political system and the assumptions of contemporaries were still predicated on the need for agreement and the existence of ideological consensus.[28]

At this point the spectre of popery and popish conspiracy came to the rescue. For the popish threat provided an unimpeachably 'other', foreign and corrupt origin and explanation for conflict, to which those elements in the political system deemed noisome or divisive could be assimilated, while yet leaving the basic structure of the English political system and Church pure and unsullied. As the political crisis of the period deepened during the 1620s the extent of the ideological differences dividing contemporaries came to be reflected in the development of an alternative conspiracy theory, this time centring on the threat of Puritanism.

We will return to that development below. For the present it is sufficient to note the way in which the Protestant image of popery allowed a number of disparate phenomena to be associated to form a unitary thing or force. That force could then be located within a certain eschatological framework, which, by explaining where popery came from, accounted for its awful more-than-human power, but did so in a way that made it quite clear that in the end Antichrist would fall and the gospel triumph. Viewed in this way, the world took on the shape of a progressive and therefore ultimately predictable struggle between Christ and Antichrist, and thus became the ground for the collective action of Protestants, who had been called together positively by their common apprehension of the truths of right doctrine and negatively by their common opposition to the threat of Rome. Popery thus became a unifying 'other' in the presence of which all those not directly implicated in the problem (popery) became part of the solution (non-popery).[29] In this way Protestants, who had started Elizabeth's reign as a minority (probably a small minority) had been able to produce an image of England as inherently Protestant because Protestantism's opposite, popery, was inherently foreign.

Until recently that image of England was associated with the notion of 'the elect nation', but as a number of scholars have recently pointed out, the whole idea of an elect nation was a theological nonsense for Protestants. While it was certain that ultimately Antichrist would lose and Christ would win, it was still an open question whether England would triumph with Christ or be destroyed with Antichrist. The answer depended on whether the English responded to God's commands expounded to them from the pulpit. If they did, God would protect them from the papists; if they did not he would surely use the papists as a stick with which to chastise his erring flock. Both here and in their vision of popery as appealing to those elements in human nature and contemporary society of which they most disapproved, committed Protestants were in grave danger of producing a perfectly circular argument. Elements in their objective situation were taken up and interpreted by Protestants as confirming central strands in their own view of the world, and in the process they produced an ideal type of deviance and evil against which all true Protestants should unite. This image was then employed as an ideological tool with which to label and repress the very impulses from which it was supposed to draw its strength and appeal. Thus what was an inherently purposive and dynamic vision of popery could be employed to underwrite an equally purposive and dynamic vision of further reformation, since only an active campaign against those things upon which popery fed could keep popery at bay.[30]

Whether the notion of further reformation thus canvassed was limited to the active propagation of the gospel and the repression of sin, or whether it was taken to include broader political and ecclesiastical initiatives, either way it is tempting to observe, paraphrasing Sartre's remark about anti-semitism, that if popery had not existed Protestants and, in particular Puritans, would have had to invent it.[31] Indeed, in one sense in the various images of popery that was precisely what they were doing. And yet popery did exist and intermittently throughout the period seemed to call into question the very existence of a Protestant England.

Among the committed minority the continuous cultural threats to Protestant values (compounded by the activities of recusants and missionary priests) were enough to keep the anti-popish pot boiling. However, at the popular level, as the researches of Dr Clifton have shown, anti-popery was crisis-related,[32] representing a symbolic means of dealing with an inherently foreign popish threat and latterly of expressing and controlling worries about internal divisions in terms of such a threat. While the anti-popish spasm lasted, the most committed Protestants were offered an opportunity to lead bodies of opinion far broader than those normally deemed Puritan. That, of course, was one of the things that happened between 1640 and 1642. In order to understand a little more of how and why that happened we need to turn to a more detailed analysis of the relationship between religious ideology and politics in early-seventeenth-century England.

III

From fairly early on in James' reign there were those about the king, including relative moderates like Ellesmere, who saw the crown's parliamentary difficulties as stemming from 'popular spirits' in the Commons who sought to reduce the power of the crown by playing up to the people. After the collapse of the 1610 parliament James blamed the Commons in the most acrimonious terms. By 1621 he was complaining of various 'firey and popular spirits' who had debated 'publicly of matters far above their reach and capacity tending to the high dishonour and breach of prerogative royal'.[33]

Conformist writers under Elizabeth had habitually associated a populist threat to monarchy with Puritanism. It was, however, possible to be worried about popularity and not to equate it with Puritanism. Ellesmere, for one, was a Calvinist with many moderate Puritan clients. However, it seems clear that for James the two concepts were integrally linked. Certainly in 1621 his complaints were centred on parliament's treatment of the Spanish match and the issue of the marriage of his son, the motivations for which were largely religious.[34] By 1626 an anonymous author was explaining the assault on Buckingham in parliament as the work of popular spirits in the Commons who sought 'the debasing of this free monarchy'. Amongst the malcontents likely to support such a conspiracy the author numbered Puritans and sectaries. Moreover, he located the origins of this movement in the Presbyterian programme first canvassed in 1584. Here he was consciously keying into a rhetoric of anti-Puritanism which had been established in the 1590s during the campaign against Presbyterianism when it had been argued that, since the Presbyterian platform gave the people a considerable role in the election of ministers and the government of the Church, Puritanism was an inherently populist and thus subversive movement.

William Laud in his sermon before the 1626 parliament made this connection newly explicit, in the course of an assault on what he took to be a Presbyterian plot against authority in Church and state. Such sentiments bulked large in the printed works of Richard Montague in which he repeatedly attempted to persuade King James of the evils of English Calvinism and of the need formally to realign the theological position of the Church of England *vis à vis* the church of Rome.[35]

The agitation over the Spanish match reactivated James' fears of a Puritan plot against monarchy. A similar concern about a populist threat influenced Charles' decision to dissolve the 1626 parliament as Richard Cust has shown. Such fears, felt by both James and Charles, clearly presented the Arminians, with their vision of a populist Puritan conspiracy against all constituted authority, with a window of polemical opportunity. This they exploited to good effect at the end of one reign and the beginning of the next. However, men like Montague and Laud were moved by more than a desire to curry favour with the king; their vision of Puritan popularity was integrally related to their own positive image of what constituted true religion. According to Howson, Laud and Buckeridge the errors of Calvinism (labelled by the Arminians as distinctively and definitively Puritan) were contrary to all civil government in the common-wealth as well as 'preaching and external ministry in the church'.[36]

Why was Calvinism taken to be incompatible with good government? As a religion of the word it was thought to stir up the lower orders by giving them a spurious interest in matters above and beyond them. In particular the Arminians took the doctrine of predestination, so central to Puritan practical divinity and the spiritual experience of the godly, to lead either to desperation or still worse to presumption. The habitual division between the godly and the ungodly, and the equation of those two groups with the elect and the reprobate, which was taken to typify Puritan piety was regarded by Arminians as inherently divisive and likely to lead to all sorts of anti-nomian excess and political disorder on the part of the godly, whose spurious claims to a status based on 'grace' undercut existing hierarchies of political office, birth or property. To shut up all the worship of God in the hearing of sermons was fatally to underestimate the value of outward ceremony, public prayer and the sacraments in the life of the Church. To this almost idolatrous addiction to sermons could be attributed the appallingly disordered state of many English parishes. Here, as elsewhere, the misguided enthusiasms of the Puritans fitted all too closely with the natural parsimony and anti-clericalism of the laity. The resulting chaos produced an irreverence not only towards God but also towards all constituted authority and where there was irreverence overt disobedience could not be far behind. Over against the Calvinist or Puritan emphasis on preaching the Arminians sought to elevate the role of worship – the solemn administration of the sacraments and public prayer – in the life of the Church. It was this predilection which prompted the liturgical experiments and innovations, the changes in the internal arrangements and decorations of many churches, to which their opponents objected so strongly in the late 1620s and 1630s. Not only did the Arminians take all this to be conducive to the beauty of holiness in the Church, they also believed that it would lead to greater respect for authority and obedience in secular affairs. Beliefs such as these underlay Laud's sermon to parliament in 1626 and his speeches at the show trials of the 1630s.[37]

Many commentators have got this far in their analysis of Laudian rhetoric, but of late they have tended to cut their argument short, to observe how misguided, even irrational, were Laudian fears of Puritan Calvinism.[38] Certainly Presbyterianism, either as a movement or even an expressed preference, was conspicuous by its absence from the Jacobean Church. This presented few difficulties for the Laudians, who, more convinced than recent historians of the existence of a distinctively Puritan strain of divinity, were quite happy to see in it the cunning of a subversive movement driven underground, waiting its chance under a thin veneer of formal and totally insincere conformity. In response to this view modern scholars have been quick to point out that Calvinism was little short of the received orthodoxy of the high Elizabethan and Jacobean Churches and that its carriers among both laity and clergy were essentially conservative pillars of the establishment in Church, state and locality. Certainly, it would be absurd, with the Laudian avant garde, to see men like George Abbot as crypto-Presbyterian or Puritan incendiaries or semi-republican enemies of monarchy. And yet there was a kernel of truth in the Laudian case. The whole cult of the godly prince and magistrate, to which nearly all Calvinists subscribed, was deeply ambiguous. Certainly it involved the exaltation of royal power but only within an eschatological schema predicated on the pope's identity as Antichrist and the Prince's opposition to popery. Thus when Sir Richard Grosvenor sang the praises of the English king as 'the immediate vice-gerent of God', subject to no rival or superior jurisdication in this world, he did so in the context of the struggle with Rome.[39]

What happened, however, if the Prince failed to live up to his divinely appointed role as the champion of the gospel and the hammer of the papists? As doubts about the religious reliability of Charles I grew during the 1620s even relatively radical spirits like Henry Burton responded by simply increasing the stakes and assuring Charles that, of course, he must and would fulfil his role as a godly prince in the final struggle between Christ and Antichrist, which Burton felt sure would arrive during Charles I's reign. Yet by 1628 Burton was warning Charles not to slide from godly rule into its opposite, tyranny, and by 1636 he was expressing the sarcastic hope that the people would not conclude from Charles' actions that 'this king hath no regard to his sacred vows'. The logical culmination of this train of thought was reached in 1641 when Richard Baxter, convinced that Charles was implicated in the Irish rebellion, concluded that in effect the king had abdicated and thus become subject to legitimate resistance.[40] Of course in the second and third decades of the century such ultimate decisions were a long way off. Yet, given the tightly defined view of what constituted popery to which men like Archbishop Abbot subscribed,[41] and the context of confessional strife within which European diplomacy was increasingly being conducted, the role of the godly prince, at least as defined by many of his subjects, placed very considerable constraints on James' freedom of manoeuvre.

As Conrad Russell and a number of foreign ambassadors of the 1630s have all pointed out, during the sixteenth century various English monarchs had changed the religion of the nation more or less at will. James I was, however, unable even to arrange the marriage of his son to the Infanta without rousing a storm of protest from his subjects. Orchestrated by Calvinist bishops like Abbot and moderate and not so moderate Puritans like John Preston and Thomas Scott, the rise of a stolidly Protestant and rabidly anti-papal public opinion thus represented a real limitation on the crown's autonomy.[42] No monarch, who was not a Calvinist zealot, could be expected to welcome this intrusion on his or her traditional prerogatives. From that perspective the Laudian rhetoric which equated Calvinism with Puritanism and Puritanism with popularity and subversion must have taken on a new credibility.

IV

Of course from the outside looking in things appeared rather different. From the outset James's ecclesiastical policy had involved the representation at court of a wider range of religious opinions than had ever made it into the inner circles of the Elizabethan régime. In particular James admitted crypto-Catholics like the earl of Northampton to positions of real influence. Even amongst members of the establishment the activities of those men caused dismay; Archbishops Bancroft and Abbot both complained about the presence of papists and crypto-papists on the privy council. Nor was this alarm limited to the court; in 1614 Sir Peter Bucke was hauled before Star Chamber for claiming that Northampton and other court Catholics had petitioned the king for a formal toleration for their co-religionists. Dark hints about Northampton's religious opinions appeared in some satirical poems by Thomas Scott, published in 1616. Commenting on news of the Overbury murder the Cheshire gentleman William Davenport noted that 'it is plain that my Lord of Northampton had he now been living would have had his head in shrewd hazard for he was a most dangerous traitor'. If Dr Peck is right that Northampton was innocent of any plot to addle the addled parliament then the fact that he was immediately blamed by the populace for its failure takes on renewed significance. Clearly by 1614 popular perceptions of politics cast Northampton in the role of evil counsellor; a role rendered conceptually necessary by the need to account for parliament's failure – of which the addled parliament provides so spectacular an example – to bring the king and his subjects together. It was a role for which Northampton's known crypto-popery fitted him all too well.[43]

Of course it was the Spanish match that really sparked widespread worry about undue popish influence at court and that associated the notion of evil counsel with popery. Davenport passed smoothly from an interest in the spectacular scandal of the Overbury murder to concern over Spanish schemes to undermine English religion through a match with the prince.[44]

Some observers, perhaps more politically sophisticated than Davenport, developed a dichotomy between court and country of the classic sort. The court, argued Thomas Scott, as the ultimate source of power and wealth could not but attract ambitious, self-seeking men as well as foreign papists and ambassadors like Gondomar. The country, however, being relatively free from such influences remained uncorrupt, Protestant, patriotic. In order, therefore, to keep things within bounds, the virtue of the country had to be brought into contact with the actual or potential corruption of the court. The obvious way to do that was through parliament.

Parliament's importance thus rested on its status as a genuinely representative institution. For pamphleteers such as Scott and country gentlemen such as Sir Richard Grosvenor that status could best be guaranteed if each freeholder stood up and cast his vote according to the dictates of conscience, true religion and the common good. Since such strictures applied even to uncontested elections their significance would appear to have been as much symbolic as practical. Nevertheless, they represented the direct application to politics of the evangelical Protestant or Puritan view that if England were to stand before God as a genuinely godly commonwealth each individual believer had to internalize fully and act on the ground of his or her salvation. This applied with particular force to the need to oppose the mystifications and spiritual tyranny of Antichrist. Such notions must, therefore, have seemed particularly apposite to both

Scott and Grosvenor, whose crucial concern was indeed the need to counteract the influence of foreigners and papists at the centre of power.[45]

In all this we can see central elements in contemporary moderate Puritan or evangelical Calvinist thought becoming enmeshed with native traditions of representative government, centred on parliament, and concepts of active citizenship based on essentially classical models which members of the ruling class had encountered during their years at university. Again, it is not going too far to see the basic paradigm for all the lesser oppositions between good and evil counsel, the public and the private good, through which many contemporaries looked at politics, in the master opposition between Christ and Antichrist, popery and true religion. For, as we have seen, the Protestant image of popery contained within itself all those other oppositions and inversions, and popery as the ultimate model of false order was an awful warning of what would happen if the process of decay and corruption were not halted and the pursuit of the public good and true religion not placed above merely private concerns and gratifications. There was, of course, a basic structural similarity between the Protestant view of the effects of popery on the Church and, say, Sir Edward Coke's view of the effects of corruption on the commonwealth. In both cases a sinister force, based on the corruption of human nature, spread gradually through what had started out as a perfectly stable and sound institutional structure, until it was utterly subverted and undermined.[46]

Of course, it might be possible to write off the likes of Scott, if not of Grosvenor, as unrepresentative firebrands but for the fact that nearly all the central elements in Scott's religio-political outlook were shared by as central a member of the establishment as George Abbot. With Scott, Abbot saw popery as a genuinely international threat. He was consistently worried by the influence of papists and crypto-papists at court and passionately opposed to the Spanish match. Again like Scott, Abbot saw parliament as a crucial means to bridle the influence of popery at court, enforce the recusancy laws at home and provide money for war abroad. In moments of crisis, again like Scott, although not so openly, Abbot was quite capable of appealing to wider bodies of Protestant opinion in order to put pressure on the king.

There were, of course, differences between the two men, differences summed up by their diametrically opposed estimations of the United Provinces. Where for Scott the Low Countries were the epitome of the godly commonwealth and England's natural allies against popish Spain, Abbot was more suspicious. He particularly disliked the popular structure of their government in Church and state and blamed it, along with the Low Countries' venal tolerance of other religions, for the prevalence of Arminianism there. This seemingly small difference of opinion shows two very different attitudes towards popularity and hierarchy in Church and state in general, and episcopacy in particular.[47] Twenty years later such nuances often made the difference between siding with the king or parliament. In the 1620s however, such definitive choices were a long way off and Scott and Abbot remained on essentially the same side, particularly as the rise of Arminianism raised the spectre of a crypto-popish fifth column taking over the Church from within.[48]

To committed Calvinists that was precisely what Arminianism looked like and not without reason. Arminian rejection of the central Calvinist doctrines of assurance and perseverance opened the way to what the godly regarded as a popish doubtfulness on the issue of personal salvation and an equally popish reliance on human works to merit salvation. Arminian deprecation of the sermon and revaluation of the role of ritual and outward reverence in the life of the Church also raised the spectre of popery, as did their agnosticism on the hitherto axiomatic identification of the pope as Antichrist. Add to that the undoubted prominence of Laud and Neile in the counsels of the King when the decision to resort to the forced loan was taken and their continuance in royal favour after the Parliament of 1628 and the grounds for implicating the Arminians in a popish plot against the secular and religious liberties of England become clear.

Whether one dates the emergence of Arminianism as a major issue in parliament relatively early in the 1620s or, with Professor Russell, somewhat later, it remains the case that by the end of the decade innovation in religion had become associated with an assault on the subjects' liberties.[49] That was no mere accident, a product of the contingent adoption by Charles I of an Arminian ecclesiastical policy, but rather the culmination of a longstanding ideological tension between the populist aspects of the English Protestant tradition and the desire in some circles to control and, indeed, even to suppress such tendencies. Thus Arminian religious opinions came to be associated with a jaundiced view of parliament and strongly absolutist accounts of royal power. This association was based on more than the politique consideration that parliament, left to its own devices, would have impeached the likes of Richard Montague or Roger Mainwaring. The link between the two positions, while scarcely rooted in the logical structure of Arminian theology itself, was founded on the polemical situation within which English Arminianism was formed and thus on the populist Puritan threat against which the Arminians felt themselves to be in reaction and the political values of hierarchy and obedience inscribed within Arminian piety itself.

On the other side, central elements in the Protestant image of popery rendered it an ideal polemical tool against a régime widely held to be adopting 'new counsels', antipathetic to the rights and liberties of the English. Men like Archbishop Abbot had long assumed that parliament could be relied upon to oppose popery and that in the struggle against crypto-popish influence at court an appeal both through and outside parliament to wider bodies of opinion was a useful card to play.[50] Thus it was natural to assume that papists would oppose parliament and equally natural, if there seemed to be a move afoot to suppress parliaments, to look for popish involvement. Here practical politics intersected with Protestant theory, since, as we have seen, the arbitrary, unlimited and thus tyrannical power of the pope was seen as the result of a gradual erosion of the liberties of all Christians – an erosion parallel to that supposedly taking place in Church and state in England during the 1620s and 1630s.

Thus by the end of the 1620s there were two structurally similar but mutually exclusive conspiracy theories, both of which purported to explain the political difficulties of the period. The one was centred on a populist Puritan plot to undermine monarchy, the other on a popish plot to overthrow English religion and law. Both theories offered a way out of the political impasse of 1629 by providing an explanation of conflict in terms of the activities of relatively small groups of ideologically motivated men. Thus the integrity of the political system as a whole was left untouched and each side, by labelling the other as intrusive and un-English subverters of a settled system of government, was able automatically to legitimate its own position as the guardian of English good government. As Professor Russell has suggested, the failure to achieve or maintain political and religious unity could push contemporaries into a sort of collective anxiety fit, for which the conspiracy theory might provide a very effective placebo. And yet, as Dr Sommerville has shown, there were two mutually exclusive visions of the English political system current among contemporaries. By adopting either the popish or the Puritan conspiracy as an explanation for conflict contemporaries were hence doing more than deciding between more or less interchangeable models of deviance; they were choosing between two very different sets of political, cultural and religious values.[51]

V

These two parallel but mutually exclusive conspiracy theories provided the conceptual framework through which many contemporaries viewed the events of the 1630s and early 1640s. It was precisely in terms of an international Calvinist conspiracy against monarchy that the papal agent George Con and Archbishop Laud described the Scots revolt to Charles I. Both Dr Hibbard and more recently Richard Cust have concluded that Charles himself viewed events through these same ideological spectacles. Conversely, the researches of John Fielding have revealed fears of a popish plot centred on the court current in the provinces as early as 1637. It was precisely on such fears that Pym and the other leaders of the Long Parliament intended their propaganda to play.[52]

Of course, the whole notion of a popish conspiracy offered considerable advantages to the parliamentary leadership. It provided a compelling explanation of the course of events from the 1620s until the outbreak of the war; an explanation which allowed them to put the blame for the political crisis squarely on the court and to excoriate the king's policies and advisers without directly attacking his person. A variant of the evil-counsellor argument, it had the advantage of not being limited to any one adviser or faction. Since popery was a principle of evil, with roots in foreign conspiracy and papal influence, it was infinitely extendable, retaining its explanatory force long after the fall of individual favourites like Laud or Strafford.[53]

Popery was not only able to perform this function within the political élite, it also struck a sympathetic chord among the populace. Riots, anti-popish panics and petitioning campaigns testified to popular concern over the issue, as the researches of Manning, Clifton and Hunt have all shown.[54] But how were these popular feelings related to the coherent ideological positions outlined in the first half of this essay? Of late we may have been seduced into taking too adversarial a view of the relationship between Puritanism and popular culture. It is certainly true that, when it suited them, Puritan ministers could use a brutally clear-cut division between the godly and the ungodly. Yet, as Eamonn Duffy has recently pointed out, they did so within a set of practical assumptions that left room for far more subtle distinctions between the different types or degrees of Christian profession. The ministers' use of the simple godly/ungodly dichotomy might best be understood, therefore, as a rhetorical device, designed to convince all those in some sense within the Church of how stark the choice that lay before them was and how seriously their duties as Christians had to be taken if they were to make good their membership of Christ's body and be saved. Many of the structures of thought and feeling employed by the ministers in this process may not have been so very different from those of their parishioners. Michael McDonald has suggested that popular views of illness and affliction as products of a cosmic struggle between light and darkness had much in common with the Puritan view of a world caught in struggle between God and Satan, Christ and Antichrist. Clive Holmes has made a related point, seeing Puritan and educated Protestant views of witchcraft as feeding off and attempting to control and organize more popular manichaean, even animist ways of looking at the world.[55]

As we have seen, anti-popery operated through precisely the same sort of binary oppositions and inversions as those underlying the attitudes to healing and witchcraft analysed by McDonald and Holmes. In particular, popish religious practices – the mass, miracles, exorcisms – were assimilated, via the pope's identity with Antichrist, to Satan. Like witches' maleficium, popish miracles and exorcisms were either simple tricks and illusions, or else, if they had any substance in reality, they were a product of Satan's complete mastery over second causes and natural forces, employed to deceive the human eye and lead the simple or the unwary to spiritual destruction. Perhaps, therefore, popular anti-popery was the product of Puritan or educated Protestant attempts to organize and enlist for their own purposes deep-rooted popular traditions and ways of looking at the world.[56]

Certainly Dr Clifton's analysis of the structure of the normal anti-popish scare indicates similarities and parallels between these popular 'performances' and the élite 'scripts' analysed above. Panics were normally started by the suspicious antics, often reported by children, of strangers and outsiders, whose actions were seen as part of a popish, often an Irish popish, plot. Clifton attributes to the intense localism of the period this suspicion of people from outside the immediate community or neighbourhood boundary, but then goes on to note that such panics were clustered around the political crises between 1640 and 1642. That the panics and national political crises coincided so closely might be used for purposes other than the demonstration of the strength of localism. Rather it surely provides further evidence of provincial and popular sensitivity to national political events and the intense worry such crises could generate. Richard Cust's recent findings on the circulation of political news and rumour among the classes beneath the gentry would seem to substantiate this view and further to illustrate the way in which the passage of news and rumour at a number of social levels was gradually creating a genuinely national political consciousness in this period.[57]

In fact the role of strangers in many anti-popish panics fits rather well with what we know of anti-popery at higher social levels and in the propaganda of the Long Parliament. There popery worked as a unifying 'other', an inherently un-English or alien force whose intrusive influence within the English Church and political system brought disagreement and conflict in its wake. The role of strangers, often taken to be Irish, in popular panics, dramatized that otherness and the resulting panic expressed, directed and thus helped to control anxiety generated by political events at the centre. The result was cathartically unifying local action, the structures of thought and feeling underlying which were essentially the same as those that underlay the polemics of the most educated and sophisticated of contemporaries.

The popular violence and iconoclasm which accompanied some of these panics, as they have been described by Professor Manning and Dr Hunt, were scarcely the products of indiscriminate hooliganism. Rather, they were directed at what were taken to be ritually impure or threatening objects – either the possessions of known papists or the altar rails and images introduced into parish churches under Laudian rule and commonly associated with popery. As Hunt has shown, men and ministers who surely deserve the appellation Puritan were centrally involved in identifying those targets as popish and therefore objectionable. Nonetheless, it remains (at least) questionable whether all those involved in these disturbances would, under normal circumstances, have numbered themselves or been numbered by others among the godly. John Ayly, who, as Jim Sharpe has shown, played a central role in the destruction of the altar-rails at Kelvedon, was a persistent offender in the local courts of a sort unlikely to have found a welcome in Puritan circles.[58]

That popular disturbances included both Puritan leadership and non-Puritan support illustrates rather neatly the relationship between Puritanism and anti-popery. For while anti-popery had never been anything like a Puritan monopoly, Puritanism had always enjoyed a peculiarly symbiotic relationship with popery. Popery, with its alleged preference for human as against divine authority in the Church, had always had a special part to play in the Puritan campaign to base the government and structure of the Church directly on the warrant of scripture and the divine authority it embodied. If Puritans were peculiarly sensitive to popish backsliding in matters of doctrine and ceremony, then the obverse side of that sensitivity had always been a rigorous concern for the personal and collective godliness and orthodoxy of the Christian community. The positive side of the rhetoric of Antichristian corruption was thus the rhetoric of edification and spiritual building. Moderate Puritans had always held that edification could take place within the rather imperfect structures of the national Church. But as the Laudian dominance of the Church, which Puritans regarded as the vanguard for popery, reduced those structures from morally neutral products of human reason and authority to corrupt, popish remnants (or innovations) Puritans came once again to associate edification with the total restructuring of church government, along austerely scriptural lines. That position had, of course, underlain Elizabethan Presbyterianism and by the late 1620s the process of regression to that earlier position had already started amongst the real radicals. Alexander Leighton in 1628, and then, through the 1630s, Burton, Bastwick and Prynne, all turned their backs on episcopacy and espoused the cause of ecclesiastical reform. By the early 1640s others were joining them in droves.[59]

How far such avant-garde notions of further reformation commanded a genuinely popular following is open to question. While the example of the London artisan Nehemiah Wallington shows that relatively humble men could and did espouse that cause with vigour, we can hardly assume that the likes of John Ayly and his friends were proto-Presbyterians.[60] Yet the fact remains that the political and polemical circumstances of the late 1630s and early 1640s conspired to allow Puritans to lead bodies of opinion which in normal times could scarcely be called Puritan. In short, the 'fused group' of the godly, whose unity was based on a common apprehension of the truths of right doctrine and on a recognition of one another as properly godly saints of God, had been placed at the head of the 'serial group' of the non-popish, whose unity derived only from a common opposition to popery.[61] Since the grounds for and intensity of their opposition to popery might vary considerably from group to group and individual to individual this community of the non-popish was inherently likely to be short-lived. Any attempt to convert it into a politico-religious force over the long term would surely founder on those differences. And yet, as Anthony Fletcher has pointed out, in 1642 it was the short term which counted.

Once the war had started, both sides erected structures of command and coercion that were able to withstand the reduction, if not the disappearance of the popular passions of 1642.[62] They needed to, for during the 1640s and 1650s the coalition which had been created by applying the rhetoric of Antichrist to the Laudian church and the Caroline court gradually fell apart. Its popular support was eaten away, on the right, by the austerities of Puritan worship, the impact of civil war and the reformation of manners. On the left, the coalition fell victim to the inherently fissiparous nature of the Puritan search for first a scriptural and then a spiritual authenticity of belief and practice. This first disrupted the unity of the godly and then, by enlisting some of the hitherto unregenerate populace to the cause of spiritual enthusiasm, created a brand new cause for moral panic in the sects and the Quakers.[63] In the process, contemporaries, like Prynne, alarmed by the drift of events, developed new ideal types of deviance and spiritual degeneracy to control the forces and anxieties unleashed by these changes. It should not surprise us, in these circumstances, to find the old anti-type of popery put to new uses; as phenomena as disparate as the regicide and the rise of the Quakers were attributed to some Jesuit plot to divide and rule.[64] Along with many other fixed points on the polemical map of pre-war politics, anti-popery was transformed by the turmoil of the interregnum and thus made available as a free-floating term of opprobrium. Even so, that should not blind us to the fact that before 1642 popery had a limited meaning to contemporaries as a polemical signifier or label, defined by its place in a longstanding ideological code.

It has been argued here that that code was itself a product of a dialectical process. Populist elements in the conventional Protestant image of true religion and the struggle against popish tyranny and ignorance prompted a political, theological and cultural reaction which reached its apogee in the Laudian church and the Caroline court. The seemingly popish nature of that reaction in turn strengthened the radical populist strain in English protestantism which it was designed to suppress. In the resulting turmoil anti-popery did not simply determine political attitudes, still less allegiances in the civil war. It was and always had been more than possible, with Archbishop Abbot or Lord Montague, to oppose both popery and popularity.[65] During the 1630s, however, to many outside the court the threat from the former must have seemed rather greater than that from the latter. But once the many-headed monster was loosed in massed demonstrations and petitions, once the principles of hierarchy and degree, enshrined in episcopacy, were called into question, things might look very different. For many, the choice between the king and parliament may have devolved into a choice between popery or a populist Puritanism as the greater threat to order. Certainly much of the propaganda put out by the king and parliament seems to have been predicated on that assumption.[66] And yet in that choice we have travelled a long way from an irrational panic or knee-jerk response to a non-existent popish threat. Rather, we are confronted with a choice between two competing sets of social and political, as well as religious, priorities and values.

That choice may not often have been approached in a spirit of rational detachment, but that need not surprise us given what was at stake. Certainly anti-popery appealed to people's emotions. It did so because it incorporated deeply held beliefs and values and it helped to dramatize and exorcize the fears and anxieties produced when those values came under threat. But that, surely, is what political ideologies do, and it is from their capacity to do it that they derive their ability to motivate and mobilize large numbers of people. It is, of course, always tempting to overestimate the 'rational' element in our own choices and to write off the ideologies of others as irrational. It is particularly easy when, as in the case of anti-popery, most of the carriers of that ideology are either dead or in Northern Ireland. If, however, we wish to understand a central strand in the political and religious history of seventeenth-century England it is a temptation we must resist.

Notes

1 A.J. Fletcher, *The Outbreak of the English Civil War* (London, 1981), pp. 407–19; K. Sharpe, 'Archbishop Laud', *HT*, 33 (1983) pp. 26–30; M. Finlayson, *Historians, Puritanism and the English Revolution* (Toronto, 1983), *passim*; J.S. Morrill, 'The Religious Context of the English Civil War', see above chapter 6; for Professor Lamont's opinion see his review of Caroline Hibbard's *Charles I and the Popish Plot* (Chapel Hill, 1983) in the *London Review of Books* (21 July–3 Aug. 1983).

2 This paragraph represents a perhaps rather crude pastiche of the views put forward in C.S.R. Russell, *Parliaments and English Politics, 1621–9* (Oxford, 1979) and J.S. Morrill, *The Revolt of the Provinces* (London, 1976).

3 C.S.R. Russell, *The Origins of the English Civil War* (London, 1973), pp. 24–6.

4 See S. Clark, 'Inversion, Misrule and the Meaning of Witchcraft', *P&P*, 87 (1980). Also see P. Burke, *Popular Culture in Early Modern Europe* (London, 1978), esp. pp. 185–91. For the use of inversion in popular religious propaganda see R.W. Scribner, *For the Sake of the Simple Folk* (Cambridge, 1981).

5 On the currency of the belief that the pope was Antichrist see C. Hill, *Antichrist in the Seventeenth Century* (Oxford, 1971). By far the best discussion of the

theological issues involved is R.J. Bauckham, *Tudor Apocalypse* (Abingdon, 1978). For popery as devil worship see W. Fulke, *The Text of the New Testament* (Cambridge, 1589), p. 881; 'they that worship Antichrist worship the devil not in their intent (for Antichrist boasteth himself to be God) but because they worship him who hath the power of the devil and serveth the devil in deceiving the world'. On popery as worse than paganism, Islam or Judaism see J. Bridges, *The Supremacy of Christian Princes* (London, 1573), pp. 952–3; on Antichrist's gradual rise to power in the church see W. Whitaker, *An Answer to the Ten Reasons of Campion the Jesuit*, translated from the original Latin by Richard Stock (London, 1606), p. 172. On the deceit involved, see Whitaker, *A Disputation of Holy Scripture* (Cambridge, 1849), pp. 20–1.

6 What follows is based on a variety of sources, but especial attention has been paid to one particular genre – the true confessions of Catholic renegades, converted or reconverted to Protestantism. Designed for a fairly low-brow audience, these pamphlets represent rather crude exercises in inversion and thus afford a view of the stock Protestant attitudes to Rome. This procedure has been borrowed from Dr Robin Clifton. See his article in Russell (ed.), *Origins of the English Civil War*, pp. 148–9. The renegade tracts used here are J. Gee, *The Foot out of the Snare* (London, 1624); Thomas Abernathy *Abjuration of Popery* (Edinburgh, 1638); J. Wadsworth, *The English Spanish Pilgrim* (London, 1630); R. Sheldon, *The Motives of Richard Sheldon Priest for his Just, Voluntary and Free Renunciation of Communion with the Bishop of Rome* (London, 1612) and *A Survey of the Miracles of the Church of Rome* (London, 1616).

7 Idolatry was central to the Protestant vision of popish corruption. Perhaps the basic text is the homily on idolatry in *Certain Sermons Appointed by the Queen's Majesty* (Cambridge, 1850), pp. 167–272. Also see Bridges, *Supremacy*, pp. 476–495; Sheldon, *A Survey*, p. 76, for the notion of 'bread worship', pp. 91–3; Sheldon, *The Motives of Richard Sheldon*, pp. 80–1, 85. On papists as idolators, *Works of Richard Sibbes*, ed. A.B. Grosart, 7 vols (1862–4), II, pp. 379–81; W. Perkins, *Works* (Cambridge, 1626) I, pp. 400, 676–94.

8 W. Whitaker, *Ad Nicolai Sanderi Demonstrationes . . .* (London, 1538), pp. 112–14; for Bridges the papists' doctrines of salvation by works not faith infringed the liberty and glory of God and led to popish doubtfulness; it stood, in fact, as a type for their wider preference for human rather than divine authority. See his *A Sermon Preached at Paul's Cross on the Monday in Whitsun Week, 1571* (London, 1573), pp. 36–7; also see Perkins, *Works*, I, 397–8. On hypocrisy based on the priestly power of absolution, see Gee, *Snare*, pp. 9–10; Wadsworth, *The English Spanish Pilgrim*, p. 28; Sheldon, *A Survey*, pp. 51–3.

9 Perkins, *Works*, I, p. 401; on sexual looseness as a peculiarly popish trait particularly in 'monkish cells' see Bridges, *Supremacy*, pp. 302–3; Sheldon, *A Survey*, pp. 17, 51–3, 134–7, 141, 192; Sheldon, *The Motives of Richard Sheldon*, pp. 85, 151, 155–6, 159.

10 According to Bridges in his Paul's Cross sermon (9), the papists had invented purgatory 'for lucre'; Gee, *Snare*, pp. 49–53; Sheldon, *A Survey*, pp. 51–2; Sheldon, *The Motives of Richard Sheldon*, pp. 77–83; Perkins, *Works*, I, p. 401. For the quotation about the carnal man, see W. Clarke, *An Answer to a Jesuit* (London, 1580), sig, B8; see also Sibbes, *Works*, IV, p. 357; on popish magic and enchantment, see Gee, *Snare*, pp. 41, 49–53, 62, 72; Wadsworth, *The English/Spanish Pilgrim*, pp. 76–7; see also Reginald Scott, *The Discovery of Witchcraft* (Wakefield, 1973), pp. 365–80; on the fit between popish doctrine

and corrupt human nature, see Perkins, *Works*, I, pp. 398–9; T. Scott, *The Highways of God and the King* (London, 1623), pp. 13–15; John Bridges agreed that the papists' rejection of the orthodox Calvinist doctrine of predestination showed typical popish presumption in making the will of God (expressed in election) subject to the will of man (expressed in the presence or absence of human merit) and thus appealed to human vainglory. *A Sermon*, 30–1, 36–7, 76–7, 81. See also Bridges, *Supremacy*, p. 517.

11 Bridges saw the presumption inherent in popish attitudes to justification and election as typical of a wider presumption which expressed itself in the usurpation of God's power over the Church and an aspiration 'to be equal to kings'. *A Sermon*, pp. 37, 127–30. For the pope's tyranny, defined as the denial or usurpation of the prince's powers, see Bridges, *Supremacy*, pp. 65, 228, 592, 765; see also T. Bilson, *The True Difference between Christian Subjection and UnChristian Rebellion* (Oxford, 1585), pp. 68, 349, 437; Perkins, *Works*, I, p. 399; Sheldon, *A Survey*, p. 186; Sheldon, *The Motives of Richard Sheldon*, 'To the Christian Reader'. The pope's claim to supremacy and infallibility in the church and his power to depose princes were at the centre of Sheldon's reasons for turning against Rome.

12 Bridges, *Supremacy*, pp. 455–7, where the papists' oppression of the church with superstitious ceremonies is compared to that of the pharisees. Also see p. 476 and Sheldon, *The Motives of Richard Sheldon*, p. 140; the tyranny of the pope is here defined in terms of the deprivation of the people of a saving knowledge of scripture.

13 Bridges, *Supremacy*, pp. 160–70, describes popery as a clerical conspiracy to keep the prince and people in ignorance; p. 396 notes the refusal of the papists to explain the sacrament to the people through the reading of scripture. Perkins, *Works*, I, p. 399; Gee, *Snare*, p. 84, describes the papists as 'blind guides and lovers of darkness more than the light' who (pp. 36–7, 41) used a 'foreign idol gull composed of palpable fiction and diabolical fascination, whose enchanted chalice of heathenish drugs and Lamian superstition hath the power of . . . Medea's cup to metamorpise men into bayards and asses' in order to 'gull, terrify and amaze the simple, ignorant people' into 'admiration of their priesthood, the sanctity of their attire and the divine potency of their sacrifice'. Richard Sheldon likewise saw the papists' reliance on false miracles to convert the people as rooted in the paucity of scriptural backing for their faith (*A Survey*, preface to the reader). They were 'children of darkness' who deal 'covertly and will not come to the light because they fear reproving'. The glory of the mass in particular was based on popular ignorance, as was the rise to power of the pope. See Sheldon, *The Motives of Richard Sheldon*, pp. 65–6, 129–31, 140.

14 For John Foxe see N.V. Olsen, *John Foxe and the Elizabethan Church*, (Berkeley, 1973) and for the eschatological framework within which these attitudes were developed, see Bauckham, *Tudor Apocalypse*. For the belief that 'as ice melteth at the rays of the clear sun' so popish error would be dispelled by the gospel, see Bridges, *Supremacy*, p. 459. Such optimism was not confined to conformists; a group of puritan ministers gathered together in 1589 concluded that the downfall of Antichrist, prophesied in scripture, was already taking place 'in the hearts and consciences of men' through the preaching of the word. (See Cambridge University Library, MSS Hh. VI 10, fo. 21 f.) Even Josias Nichols who, as a parish minister of long standing, knew the difficulties of converting ignorant papists and atheists, was convinced that where a learned minister was assiduous in 'preaching and private conferring' with the people

the gospel would triumph; a point he made by comparing the progress of the relatively well-taught south with the ignorance and popery of the untutored north. See J. Nichols, *The Plea of the Innocent* (1602), pp. 219–25. As I have observed elsewhere, the Protestant attitude to popery contained a nice balance between optimism and pessimism. Isolated quotation of the pessimistic statements of Protestants about the prospects of the gospel cannot be used to 'prove' the 'failure' of protestant evangelism.

15 Thus Protestant criticisms of popery revolved around the juxtaposition of the merely human authority of the Church and the divine authority of scripture. For a very clear statement of that position, see Whitaker, *Disputation of Holy Scripture*, pp. 415, 440–50; for popery as contradictory see Perkins, *Works*, I, pp. 402–4; to this can be added the constant Protestant allegations that the appeal of popery consisted in magic, enchantment, illusion, all of which contributed to a vision of popery as 'irrational'. See note 13 above for references.

16 Matthew Hutton, *A Sermon Preached at York before Henry Huntingdon* (London, 1579), fos. 4^r–6^r; Thomas Scott, *The Highways of God and the King*, p. 13.

17 This summarizes the argument of Jane Facey, 'John Foxe and the defence of the English church' in M. Dowling and P. Lake (eds), *Protestantism and the National Church* (London, 1987).

18 J. Whitgift, *The Works of John Whitgift* (Cambridge, Parker Society, 1851–53), I, pp. 405–6.

19 See Facey, 'John Foxe' and J. Bridges, *Supremacy*, pp. 657, 784, 806.

20 J. Bridges, *A defence of the government established in the church of England for ecclesiastical matters* (London, 1587), pp. 763, 765. Such arguments were not limited to conformists and anti-Presbyterian polemicists like Bridges. Robert Some, an erstwhile puritan, made the same points against the separatists. See R. Some, *A godly treatise containing and deciding certain questions moved of late in London and other places touching the ministry, sacraments . . .* (London, 1588), pp. 17–18 and *A defence of such points in Robert Some's last treatise as Mr Penry hath dealt against* (London, 1588), pp. 58–9.

21 On popish disloyalty, see Bridges, *Supremacy*, pp. 70–1, 74; Bilson, *The True Difference*, pp. 101, 109; Thomas Scott (the elder), *Christ's Politician and Saloman's Puritan* (London, 1616), pp. 24–5; Wadsworth, *The English-Spanish Pilgrim*, pp. 72–3; Sheldon, *A Survey*, p. 267 for the 'abominable regicides, rebellions, treasons, civil commotions, prophanations of churches, ruin of kingdoms' produced by popery; for the identification of Spanish monarchy and tyranny as the equivalent and concomitant of the tyranny in the Church of the pope, see Thomas Scott, *Vox populi or news from Spain*, sig. A3–B3; for the black legend, see W. Maltby, *The Black Legend in England* (Durham, NC, 1971), *passim*. For popish theories of resistance, see P. Holmes, *Resistance and Compromise* (Cambridge, 1982); for the increasingly absolutist response of English polemicists to this challenge, see J. Sommerville 'Jacobean political thought and the controversy over the oath of allegiance' (Ph.D thesis, University of Cambridge, 1981).

22 For moderate puritans, see P. Lake, *Moderate Puritans and the Elizabethan Church* (Cambridge, 1982), pp. 55–76; also see Nichols, *The Plea of the Innocent*, pp. 148–87; for moderate conformists, see P. Lake, 'Matthew Hutton: a Puritan Bishop?', *Hist.* 64 (1979) and Bridges, *A Defence*, pp. 172, 1336. Hard line conformists, however, sought to assimilate Presbyterian clericalism to that of the papists, see R. Bancroft, *Dangerous Positions* (London, 1593), pp. 2–3.

For the Presbyterian use of the popish threat and the notion of the discipline as the natural culmination in the realm of outward government of a reformation already complete in terms of doctrine see, for instance, *An humble motion with submission unto the right honourable lords of her majesty's privy council* (1590) sig. C4^v and F3^r. On the argument that Protestant preaching, even by Puritans, was a bastion of order in the face of popular irreligion and popery, see D. Zaret, *The Heavenly Contract* (Chicago, 1985), pp. 81–9.

23 See T.E. Cogswell, 'England and the Spanish Match', in R.P. Cust and A.L. Hughes (eds), *Conflict in Early Stuart England* (1989), pp. 107–33 and C. Hibbard, *Charles I and the Popish Plot* (Chapel Hill, 1983).

24 K. Erikson, *Wayward Puritans* (New York, 1966); J. Bossy, *Christianity in the West, 1400–1700* (Oxford, 1985); for another anti-type, developed to express and control anxiety about certain types of belief and behaviour, see M.C.W. Hunter, 'The Problem of Atheism in Early Modern England', *TRHS*, 5th ser., 35 (1985). Interestingly some contemporaries lumped papists and atheists together as threats to the cause of true religion, see, for instance, Nichols, *The Plea of the Innocent*, pp. 218–22.

25 On popular conservatism, see C. Haigh, 'The Continuity of Catholicism in the English Reformation', *P&P*, 93, (1981); see also C. Hill, 'Puritans and the Dark Corners of the Land', *TRHS*, 5th ser., 13 (1962).

26 For the introduction of the 'reformation of manners' as an organizing concept in the study of English Protestantism and society, see C. Hill, *Society and Puritanism in Pre-revolutionary England* (London, 1964); for more recent repetitions and refinements of Hill's position, see K. Wrightson, *English Society, 1580–1680* (London, 1982), esp. chs 6 and 7, and D. Underdown, *Revel, Riot and Rebellion* (Oxford, 1985).

27 Russell, *Parliaments and English Politics*, esp. ch. 1; see also M. Kishlansky, 'The Emergence of Adversary Politics in the Long Parliament', (chapter 2 above); see also his *Parliamentary Selection* (Cambridge, 1986).

28 J.P. Sommerville, *Politics and Ideology in England, 1603–40* (London, 1985); Russell, *Parliaments and English Politics*, pp. 49–53, 64–84.

29 P. Lake, 'The Significance of the Elizabethan Identification of the Pope as Antichrist', *JEH*, 31 (1980); 'William Bradshaw, Antichrist and the Community of the Godly', *JEH*, 36 (1985).

30 On the 'elect nation', see Bauckham, *Tudor Apocalypse*, pp. 70–3, 86–8.

31 J-P. Sartre, *Anti-semite and Jew*, transl. G.J. Becker (New York, 1948).

32 R. Clifton, 'Fear of Popery', in Russell (ed.), *The Origins of the English Civil War*; and 'The Popular Fear of Catholics during the English Revolution', *P&P*, 52 (1971).

33 L.A. Knafla, *Law and Politics in Jacobean England* (Cambridge, 1977), pp. 186, 254–62; HMC, *Report on the Mss of the Marquess of Salisbury (at Hatfield House)*, vol. 21 (1970), p. 266; J.R. Tanner, *Constitutional Documents of the Reign of James I* (London, 1930), p. 279. I owe these last two references to the kindness of Richard Cust.

34 Knafla, *Law and Politics*, pp. 54–5; K.C. Fincham and P. Lake, 'The Ecclesiastical Policy of James I', *JBS*, 24 (1985).

35 'To his sacred majesty ab ignoto' in *Cabala sive scrinia sacra* 3rd edn (London, 1691) pp. 255–7; Laud, I, pp. 63–89, esp. pp. 82–3; R. Montague, *A Gagg for the New Gospel? No: a New Gagg for an Old Goose* (London, 1624) and *Appello Caesarem* (London, 1625). For detailed reference see note 37 below. For Elizabethan anti-Puritan and anti-Presbyterian polemic see my *Puritans*

and Anglicans? Presbyterianism and English Conformist Thought from Whitgift to Hooker (London, 1987).

36 Laud, VI, pp. 244–6, Laud, John Howson and John Buckeridge to Buckingham, 2 Aug. 1625; see also Laud, VI, p. 249, Montaigne, Neile, Andrewes, Buckeridge and Laud to Buckingham, 16 Jan. 1626; on the role of the fear of popularity in the genesis of the forced loan, see Richard Cust, *The Forced Loan and English Politics, 1626–1628* (Oxford, 1987), pp. 13–30, 39–51.

37 For the identification of the doctrine of predestination with Puritanism and of Puritanism with popularity and Presbyterianism, see Montague, *Appello Caesarem*, pp. 7, 23, 39, 42, 43, 60, 72, 111, 114, 118, 182, 213, 320; for the equation of order and reverence in the Church with order and reverence in the state and the argument that the word-based Puritan style of religion was inherently irreverent and disordered, see M. Wren, *A sermon preached before the king's majesty on Sunday 17 February last at Whitehall*, (Cambridge, 1627); see also Isaac Bargrave, *A sermon preached before King Charles March 27, 1627* (London, 1627) *passim* and esp. pp. 4–5, 14; Laud, I, pp. 63–89; for Laud's conviction that there was a populist Puritan plot on foot during the 1630s, see S. Foster, *Notes from the Caroline Underground* (Hamden, Conn., 1978), and for the same assumptions applied on the local level by Robert Sibthorpe, see V. Stater, 'The Lord Lieutenancy on the Eve of the Civil Wars: The Impressment of George Plowright' *HJ*, 29 (1986). For Laudian changes in the internal arrangements of churches in Cambridge and the opposition it aroused, see D. Hoyle, 'A Commons Investigation of Arminianism and Popery in Cambridge on the Eve of the Civil War', *HJ*, 29 (1986).

38 See, for instance, Russell, *Parliaments and English Politics*, pp. 26–34 or P. Collinson, *The Religion of Protestants* (Oxford, 1982), *passim*. Such claims are, of course, in many ways quite justified and certainly to be preferred to the assumption of an inherent Puritan radicalism.

39 R. Cust and P. Lake, 'Sir Richard Grosvenor and the Rhetoric of Magistracy', *BIHR*, 54 (1981).

40 For Burton, see B.S. Capp, 'The Political Dimension of Apocalyptic Thought', in C.A. Patrides (ed.), *The Apocalypse in English Renaissance Thought and Literature* (Manchester, 1984). For Baxter, see W. Lamont, *Richard Baxter and the Millenium* (London, 1979), pp. 76–119.

41 K.C. Fincham, 'Archbishop Abbot and the Defence of Protestant Orthodoxy', *HR* 61 (1988), pp. 36–64. I should like to thank Dr Fincham for letting me see this article in advance of publication.

42 Fincham, 'Archbishop Abbot'; P. Lake, 'Constitutional Consensus and Puritan Opposition in the 1620s: Thomas Scott and the Spanish Match', *HJ*, 25 (1982); for John Preston, see C. Hill, 'The Political Sermons of John Preston', in *Puritanism and Revolution* (London, 1958) and I. Morgan, *Prince Charles' Puritan Chaplain* (London, 1957). See Cogswell, 'England and the Spanish Match'.

43 Fincham and Lake, 'Ecclesiastical Policy of James I'; P. Clark, *English Provincial Society from the Reformation to the Revolution: Religion, Politics and Society in Kent, 1500–1640* (London, 1977), p. 316; T. Scott, *Philomythologie* (London, 1622); CCRO, CR 63/2/19, fo. 9^r; L.L. Peck, *Northampton* (London, 1982), p. 210.

44 R.P. Cust, 'News and Politics in Early Seventeenth Century England' (chapter 9 below); CCRO, CR 63/2/19, fos. 2^r–14^v for the Overbury scandal; fos. 14^v–18^r, on the fate of Raleigh; fos. 24^r–25^v, 27^v–28^r, 35^r for the Spanish match; fos. 43^r–59^v

for the impeachment of Buckingham. Throughout, Davenport associated evil counsel with popish plotting.

45 Lake, 'Thomas Scott' and Cust and Lake, 'Sir Richard Grosvenor'. See also R.P. Cust, 'Politics and the Electorate in the 1620s', in Cust and Hughes (eds), *Conflict in Early Stuart England*.

46 S. White, *Sir Edward Coke and the Grievances of the Commonweal*, (Manchester, 1979), pp. 38–9; Lake, 'Thomas Scott'.

47 Lake, 'Thomas Scott'; Fincham, 'George Abbot'; for Abbot's dislike of the Low Countries, see PRO, SP 105/95, fos. 4^v–5^r, Abbot to Dudley Carleton, March 22, 1617/18; for Scott's very different estimation of the Dutch, see in particular his *The Belgic Pismire* (1622).

48 It is perhaps worth noting that there was a conceptually necessary vacancy in the attitudes of many contemporaries for crypto-popish evil counsellors, a vacancy which the Arminians were exceptionally well qualified to fill. See note 44 above. As early as 1616 Richard Sheldon had complained of the activities of 'hypocrite clergy . . . which being neither hot nor cold God doth cast out of his mouth and would God this church had or could spew them out'. (See Sheldon, *A Survey*, 'Preface to the reader').

49 Russell, *Parliaments and English Politics*, pp. 406–8; N.R.N. Tyacke, *Anti-Calvinists* (Oxford, 1987). See also Dr. Tyacke's review of Caroline Hibbard's *Charles I and the Popish Plot* in *Albion*, 16 (1984), pp. 49–50.

50 Fincham, 'George Abbot'.

51 Russell, 'Arguments for Religious Unity in England, 1530–1650', *JEH*, 28 (1967); 'The Parliamentary Career of John Pym, 1621–29', in P. Clark, A.G.R. Smith and N.R.N. Tyacke (eds), *The English Commonwealth* (Leicester, 1979); Sommerville, *Politics and Ideology*.

52 Hibbard, *Charles I and the Popish Plot*, p. 95; Cust, *The Forced Loan*, ch. i, conclusion. John Fielding, 'Opposition to the Personal Rule of Charles I: the Diary of Robert Woodford', *HJ*, 31 (1988), pp. 769–88. I should like to thank John Fielding for letting me read and cite his paper on Woodford and Richard Cust for showing me an unpublished paper on the role of the fear of popularity in Charles' relations with parliament both in the 1620s and in 1640.

53 S.R. Gardiner, *Constitutional Documents of the Puritan Revolution* (Oxford, 1951), pp. 206–7, 216.

54 B. Manning, *The English People and the English Revolution* (London, 1976), pp. 33–59; W. Hunt, *The Puritan Moment* (Cambridge, Mass., 1983), ch. 11; R. Clifton, 'Fear of Popery' and 'The Popular Fear of Popery'.

55 M. McDonald, 'Religion, Social Change and Psychological Healing in England, 1600–1800', in W.J. Sheils (ed.), *Studies in Church History*, vol. 19, 1982; C. Holmes, 'Popular Culture? Witches, Magistrates and Divines in Early Modern England', in S. Kaplan (ed.), *Understanding Popular Culture* (New York, 1985); E. Duffy, 'The Godly and the Multitude in Stuart England', *Seventeenth Century*, 1 (1986).

56 Sheldon, *Survey*, pp. 39–40; see also W. Whitaker, *Praelectiones . . . de ecclesia* (Cambridge, 1599), p. 348 and *Ad Nicolai Sanderi demonstrationes*, pp. 168–171.

57 R. Clifton, 'Fear of Popery' and 'The Popular Fear of Popery'; Cust, 'News and Politics'.

58 Manning, *English People*, pp. 189–96; and Hunt, *Puritan Moment*, ch. 11; J. Sharpe, 'Crime and Delinquency in an Essex Parish', in J.S. Cockburn, *Crime in England, 1550–1800* (London, 1977).

59 P. Lake, 'Identification of the Pope as Antichrist'; P. Christianson, *Reformers*

and Babylon (Toronto, 1977), chs 4 and 5; see also Capp, 'The Political Dimension of Apocalyptic Thought' and W. Lamont, *Marginal Prynne* (London, 1963), pp. 11–84.

60 P. Seaver, *Wallington's World* (London, 1985), ch. 6; that there were also respectable supporters of 'further reformation' amongst Ayly's Essex neighbours is clear from J. Sharpe, 'Scandalous and Malignant Priests in Essex; the Impact of Grassroots Puritanism', C. Jones, M. Newitt and S. Roberts (eds), *Politics and People in Revolutionary England* (Oxford, 1986).

61 J-P. Sartre, in his *Critique of Dialectical Reason*, distinguished fused groups, those united by a common world-view or political or emotional project from serial groups, those united only by their relation to an external object (like the members of a bus queue, united only by their relation to the approaching bus). Opposition to popery clearly evoked stronger emotions than waiting for a bus and yet the community of the non-popish scarcely fulfilled the criteria of the fused group. The different conceptions of and attitudes to the popish threat operative in the early 1640s prevented that common sediment of agreement from providing the basis for a genuinely fused group, united by a positive religio-political programme and a common core of spiritual experience.

62 Fletcher, *Outbreak of the English Civil War*, Conclusion; R. Hutton, *The Royalist War Effort* (London, 1982), pp. 201–3; A. Hughes, 'The King, the Parliament and the Localities during the English Civil War' (Chapter 10 in this volume).

63 J.S. Morrill (ed.), *Reactions to the English Civil War* (London, 1982), pp. 89–114; for the splintering effect on the left see C. Hill, *The World Turned Upside Down* (London, 1972); and F. McGregor and B. Reay (eds), *Radical Religion in the English Revolution* (Oxford, 1984).

64 On the emergence of the stereotype of the quaker as populist incendiary and anti-nomian threat to order, see B. Reay, *The Quakers and the English Revolution* (London, 1985), ch. 5; see also J.C. Davis *Fear, Myth and History; the Ranters and the Historians* (Cambridge, 1986), which argues that the ranters were, in effect, a polemical invention, produced to label and control the threat posed to order by the sectarian left. For the role of the reworked version of the popish threat in all this see W. Lamont, *Marginal Prynne*, ch. 6 and *Richard Baxter*, pp. 109–13. See also I. Thackray, 'Zion Undermined; the Protestant Belief in the Popish Plot during the English Interregnum', *History Workshop Journal*, 18 (1984) and S.A. Kent, 'The Papist Charges against the Interregnum Quakers', *Journal of Religious History*, 2 (1982–3).

65 For Montague see Esther Cope, *The Life of a Public Man: Edward, First Baron Montagu of Boughton, 1562–1644* (Philadelphia, 1981).

66 Manning, *English People*, pp. 59–83, 249–58; D. Hirst, 'The Defection of Sir Edward Dering', *HJ*, 15 (1972); B.H.G. Wormald, *Clarendon; Politics, History and Religion* (Cambridge, 1952). For an example of the royalist propaganda, predicated on the existence of a populist Puritan and Presbyterian threat to order see Sir Thomas Aston, *Remonstrance against Presbytery* (London, 1641).

SECTION III

SOCIETY AND CULTURE

8

The county community in Stuart historiography

CLIVE HOLMES

The 1635 ship money writ elicited a 'common feeling of dissatisfaction' throughout England. It was the general belief that the tax contravened 'fundamental law,' and that in its imposition Charles 'had deliberately treated the nation as a stranger to his counsels, and that if his claim to levy money by his own authority were once admitted, the door would be open to other demands of which it was impossible to foresee the limits.' Contrast this account by S.R. Gardiner with a more recent analysis of the response to ship money provided by J.S. Morrill, a scholar who has acknowledged a substantial intellectual debt to Alan Everitt, the progenitor and leading exponent of the concept of the 'county community' in seventeenth-century England. 'The King's right to levy the rate was rarely questioned in the provinces. Ship money was hated for its costliness and its disruptive effects on the social and political calm of the communities . . . Above all,' the levy was detested because 'it exemplified the government's insensitivity toward sentiment and belief.'[1]

In these divergent accounts, a fundamental difference emerges between the traditional school of England historians and the county community school of local historians. For Gardiner, seventeenth-century Englishmen were fully aware of and vitally concerned about the actions of their national rulers, actions they evaluated against the touchstone of constitutional principle. Everitt and Morrill insist, by contrast, that even the gentry were 'surprisingly ill informed' about 'wider political issues'; they were 'simply not concerned with affairs of state.' Rather, their political horizons were circumscribed by the boundaries of their shires – their 'county commonwealths,' their 'countries.' In an England that can be described as 'a union of partially independent county-states,' localism flourished, and local concerns took precedence over national issues.[2]

Many of the suggestions advanced by Everitt and his colleagues present valid challenges to Gardiner's account of the political milieu, with its predominant emphasis upon central institutions. We may agree that

This paper was originally presented at the Middle Atlantic regional meeting of the Conference on British Studies in November 1977. I am grateful to David Underdown, the commentator, and to J.H. Hexter, Derek Hirst, Linda Levy Peck, and Lawrence Stone for their criticisms.

provincial life exhibited considerable diversity and that the county was the focus of a degree of emotional attachment. It is equally clear that the political and administrative framework of seventeenth-century England allowed local agents to delay the execution of, and even to pervert or neglect, the injunctions of Westminster. It can be argued, however, that the further stage of analysis developed by Everitt, stressing the preeminence of local allegiance and the gentry's ignorance of and lack of concern for national issues, goes beyond the evidence, and that this undue emphasis upon the localism of the county community has occasioned other mis-understandings of Stuart politics and society. It has resulted in a neglect of popular attitudes and aspirations; in a failure to recognize ideological divisions, as against superficial rivalries for local status and prestige among the county gentry; in the establishment of a crude and unsym-pathetic account of the national government as a monolithic 'other' informed by no understanding of the constraints under which that govern-ment developed and administered its policies.

The argument for the existence of an introverted, isolationist local unit rests, in part, upon analysis of certain incidents in the period. Yet more fundamental than this element of *conjuncture* is the analysis of the *struc-ture* of provincial society. The insularity of the county community is ostensibly demonstrated by investigations both of the social and cultural milieu in which the gentry moved, and of their role in the burgeoning agencies of local government, the development of which recognized, inter-acted with, and enhanced the pattern of social relationships. It is this structural argument of the county community school that is questioned in this essay. The argument is sustained by an overemphasis on those elements that appear to suggest local autonomy and by a neglect of evidence to the contrary.

Provincial society

Everitt investigates the social and cultural experience of the county gentry in terms of a few crucial variables: the patterns of gentry marriage, particularly the extent of intracounty alliances; the relative antiquity of the gentry within the shire; the sources of their wealth; the ties of friend-ship and hospitality among them. He argues that the insularity of the county community of Kent stemmed from the local gentry's roots in their native soil (both in terms of their involvement in agricultural production and the antiquity of their families' settlement upon their estates), and from the web of cousinage, spun by endogamy, that conjoined them.[3]

With respect to antiquity of settlement, it is not the case that it neces-sarily bred an introverted conservatism. The medieval pedigrees of the Essex Barringtons and the Suffolk Barnardistons were impeccable, yet both families were deeply involved, through the Providence Island company and the New England venture of Winthrop and his associates, in the international schemes of the godly brotherhood. Conversely, Sir David Foulis, proposing opposition to the 1632 knighthood composition, rhapsodized the traditional concern of 'true Yorkshiremen . . . for their rights and liberties': Sir David was one of the hungry Scots who had crossed the border with King James and had built up his Yorkshire estates on the profits of court office.[4]

Not only is the supposed correlation between ancient lineage and the strength of localist sentiment unproven, but Everitt, arguing from his paradigm example of Kent, is too ready to suppose that antiquity of gentry settlement was the national norm. Lawrence Stone's comment, 'The gentry of Kent are the only stable landed community we know of,' may have to be expanded to include Cheshire and Lancashire, yet it is clear that Kent is far from typical.[5] The social profiles of many counties, some, like Dorset and Lincolnshire, remote from London, appear closer to those of Northamptonshire and Suffolk, where Everitt has himself suggested that the recent settlement of the gentry, and their business and marital ties beyond the county boundary, would make for a less introverted political culture.[6]

We should also reconsider the statistical analysis of marriage alliances that Everitt provides. More than two-thirds of the eight-hundred-odd Kentish gentlemen in 1640 'married among their neighbours.' Yet of this group only a few participated actively in the shire as a social or political unit. The bulk of them were lesser gentry, whose 'sphere was the parish rather than the county,' as Everitt writes. They were rooted on their tiny estates; they married in their immediate neighbourhoods: these facts would support, not a sense of county community identity, but a more limited local affiliation. It is the experience of the major gentry families, the governors of the shire, that is more relevant to the county community hypothesis. Here we are still confronted with diversity – just under 60 percent of the leading Kentish and Lancashire families married within their county as against 30 percent in Essex and Hertfordshire – but, in general, the proportions reveal social relations that are not so absolutely county centred.[7]

But what is the social consequence of the fact of the preponderance of intracounty marriage? That any significance can be attributed to the flat percentages of endogamy, or to the daisy chains of kinship beloved by prosopographers, turns ultimately upon demonstrating that family relationships involved real social interaction. In this respect the study of Sussex by Anthony Fletcher represents a major improvement over the works of those scholars who, from bare statistics, leaped to conclusions concerning the introversion of county society.[8] From a study of the names of those invited to dinners, hunting parties, and important rites of passage; of the recipients of gifts and legacies; of those nominated as the overseers and executors of wills, Fletcher concludes that 'the tight circle of intimate friendship . . . ran within the wider circles of blood.' His meticulous study of the patterns of friendship centring upon Sir Thomas Pelham of Halland is exemplary: yet, typically, while Fletcher stresses the importance of Pelham's alliances for 'the dynamics of county affairs,' connections that 'encouraged the introversion and strengthened the cohesiveness of the gentry community,' he does not give equal attention to the social or political significance of the knight's extracounty relationships. In the 1620s Pelham 'regularly' visited relatives in Hertfordshire and Cheshire; he also traveled to Brocklesby in northern Lincolnshire, where a cadet branch of the Sussex Pelhams had settled and made good. A junior member of that family, Henry, who shuttled between his London practice and Lincolnshire, was Sir Thomas' legal advisor.[9] With the Lincolnshire Pelhams, there is the opportunity to study the social characteristics of another exogamous marriage. The lawyer Henry's elder brother, Sir William, married a daughter of Lord Conway. It is not remarkable to find Sir William Pelham engaging in a friendly correspondence with his father-in-law, the secretary of state: such court ties had obvious utility if one sought, as did Sir William, to secure the punishment of a particularly scandalous local cleric or to avoid the shrievalty.[10] More surprising are the close ties that developed, as a function of the Conway match, between the Lincolnshire family and the Herefordshire Harleys – for Lady Pelham and Lady Brilliana Harley were sisters. Social visits and a regular correspondence were maintained. Edward Harley, an undergraduate at Oxford, was enjoined by his mother to watch over his freshman Pelham cousin: 'be . . . kinde to him.' The ties survived the death of Lady Pelham, and were more than purely social. Lady Brilliana recommended a favoured godly minister upon learning of the availability of a Lincolnshire living in Pelham's gift, and maintained a constant, and ultimately critical, concern for Sir William's political affiliations.[11]

The intellectual and political awareness of the major gentry was frequently enhanced by kinship ties with families from other counties. Two other elements in their social experience, which are neglected or dismissed by Everitt and his disciples, also broadened their horizons; their education and their contacts with London.

The former, gentry educational patterns, at least admits of some statistical analysis. J.H. Gleason has demonstrated that in 1562 two-thirds of the 'working group' of justices of the peace in his six sample counties had never been enrolled in a university or one of the Inns of Court; by 1636, while the number of justices of the peace in those counties had virtually doubled, only 16 percent lacked a formal eduction. The statistics are not at issue; their significance is another matter. Gleason writes of the changing educational pattern as constituting a major 'cultural revolution'; W.K. Jordan believed that educational endowments were 'a most important solvent of the parochialism which marked the English society at the outside of our long period.[12] Yet for Everitt the gentry's 'brief years' of formal education were 'an interlude, principally designed to fit them out for their functions in their own county'; while Morrill insists that we must not 'over-emphasise the educational sophistication of the country gentlemen,' and that their training produced merely 'a veneer of polite learning.' Victor Morgan has argued that the ties formed by Cambridge colleges to certain regions, through closed fellowships and endowments, nourished local particularism. For him, the attempt to link the influx of the gentry into institutions of higher learning with the rise of a national political consciousness and culture is nothing but 'a Whiggish conception stalking in modish statistical garb.'[13]

Yet this bizarre spectre is not easily laid. Morgan's arguments entail a conflation of the experience of the undergraduate scions of the gentry with that of the impoverished postulants for the ministry who were dependent on the beneficence of the college; and upon overemphasizing both the universality of local ties of the colleges and the role of the latter as the preeminent focus of university life. In his membership, for purposes of philosophical discussion and biblical exegesis, of 'an honest club of scholars, of his own, and other colleges,' Thomas Wadsworth was maintaining a tradition that extended back to Bilney's White Horse group.[14] Questionable for Cambridge, Morgan's formulation cannot be transposed to the seventeenth-century Inns of Court. While each inn had some 'regional bias,' that affiliation was so broad that it can hardly be viewed as reinforcing local particularism: like Shallow's drinking companions, the Lincoln's Inn students who were bound in a 'chain of amity' with Thomas Egerton were from widely dispersed areas. Nor was the inn the sole locus of its members' social contacts: the proximity of city opportunities and temptations guaranteed that. When William Welby of Gedney, a student at Grey's Inn, determined to undertake an action guaranteeing immortal fame (in fact, an assault on a Lambeth house of ill repute) none of his fellow roisterers was from either his home county or his inn.[15]

The institutions of higher learning performed a 'melting-pot' function, not only by expanding the potential range of social contacts of their alumni, but by broadening their intellectual horizons. The new educational system produced gentlemen-scholars, who, while their field of action may have been their locality, could articulate their local experience and concerns, organize and explain them, and generalize from them within the framework of a common intellectual system. Sir Thomas Aston wrote his *Remonstrance against Presbytery* in response to the activities of the Puritans in Cheshire after 1640, which, he feared, would lead to the collapse of public order and the subversion of social hierarchy in the county. Yet his arguments are buttressed by citations from the classics, the Fathers, eminent continental divines, popish casuists, the protagonists in late sixteenth-century debate on ecclesiastical government, and a slew of legal authorities from Bracton through Coke.[16] Scot's *Discoverie of Witchcraft* or Spelman's *History of Sacrilege* can be analyzed in similar terms: intellectual edifices stemming from the problems faced by, respectively, a Kentish J.P. and a Norfolk landowner. We should note that these gentlemen-scholars, whatever their local affiliations, formed a national intellectual coterie.[17] But a more important point in general social terms is that they anticipated that their arguments would be comprehended and appreciated by their fellow magistrates and landowners, who shared their training, if not their scholarly devotion. Reginald Scot's erudition was formidable (the book is prefaced by a table of the twenty-three English and 214 continental authorities employed in the work), while, as he wrote, the 'groundwork of my booke is laid' in 'divinitie and philosophie'; yet he believed that his gentry reader would be 'very sufficiently informed' in those subjects. Sir Thomas Barrington's purchases for his library suggest that his Cambridge and Grey's Inn education was far more than a 'veneer.'[18] A common educational pattern produced a common language of intellectual discourse and, thus, a common gentry culture.

Discussions of the influence of London upon the experience of the gentry lack even a common ground in statistics. Hence debate has consisted of vigorous exchanges of counter-examples: Fuller 'could call London "the inn-general of the gentry . . . of this nation" ' – yet Clarendon's mother 'spent the whole of her life in the county of Wiltshire.' The available evidence, including that of the expansion of appropriate housing facilities within London, suggests the increased resort of country gentry to the city, though it does not enable us to determine how general the practice had become.[19] Everitt has argued both that a journey to London was still exceptional for the gentry, and that the majority of those gentlemen who did visit the capital did so in circumstances – the pursuit of 'some wearisome lawsuit' – hardly likely to endear the place to them. Yet even infrequent visits on legal business had the effect of broadening social contacts and horizons. The tangled legal affairs of his family brought the Norfolk magistrate, Thomas Knyvett, to London almost annually in the 1620s and 1630s. In his letters to his wife, he expressed sentiments of disgust with this 'ungodly town' and his desire to be home 'in thy armes,' sentiments very similar to those of Henry Oxinden of which Everitt makes much.[20] Yet the London experience was important to Knyvett's perceptions and social contacts. He attended the court, and retailed its gossip to his wife; he sent back fabrics and other items of 'conspicuous consumption' and comments upon, and patterns for, the latest fashions. During his stays in London, remote kinship ties were transmuted into meaningful friendships: Knyvett boarded with 'my cousin Elsing' (the grandson of Knyvett's great-uncle's wife by her first marrriage) and dined frequently with John Hampden's mother, an equally distant relative. The contacts of these well-placed kinsmen were actively employed when, in 1643–45, Knyvett stood in danger of sequestration for his role in the abortive Lowestoft rising; later, in perhaps more typical circumstances, Henry Elsyng and Lady Hampden sought to assist Knyvett when he was contemplating remarriage. A 'wearisome lawsuit' had certainly expanded Knyvett's social circle beyond the boundaries of Norfolk.[21]

A variant aspect of the influence of a 'wearisome lawsuit' in broadening political horizons emerges in the correspondence of Lord Montagu. In the winter of 1626–27 Montagu was involved in a number of suits, and received regular reports on their convoluted progress from two of his estate agents and his solicitor in the city; but they also detailed the progress of the forced loan in London and the home counties; the king's anger at the judges' refusal to subscribe; the triumphant popular reception accorded those Londoners who resisted the demand 'so stoutly.' Stone has emphasized the degree to which 'public confidence in government' was diminished by the lurid gossip of the court purveyed by professional newsletter writers in London. But this luxury product was less important in heightening the political awareness of the gentry than was the correspondence of city lawyers, ministers, and merchants, retailing information to their country clients and cousins. The quantity and the quality of news available in the localities is apparent in the diary of the Suffolk clergyman, John Rous. Rous seldom travelled far from his home at Brandon; he certainly did not move in the circles of the county elite; yet, by collecting ballads, reading *corantoes* and royal proclamations, and, chiefly, by conversing with his fellow clerics and the minor gentry of the locality, some of whom were in regular correspondence with London, he kept well abreast of national affairs and constitutional arguments.[22]

Elements in the social milieu in which major gentry families participated necessarily entailed their involvement in relationships and attitudes that were not enclosed by their county boundaries. Exogamous marriage, participation in a common educational system, and intercourse with London ensured that their horizons were not narrowly local. A similar conclusion follows from a study of the second element in their experience that Everitt isolates as a foundation of the county community; the gentry's involvement in local government in a period marked by 'the growth of county administration, the development of county institutions.'[23]

Local government

While ever more gentlemen were enrolled in the commission of the peace and were responsible for the execution of an ever expanding series of enactments, it is a broad leap from these facts to the argument of a growth of *county* institutions. Gatherings of the full body of the county magistracy for collective action were comparatively infrequent. A magistrate's administrative and police activities focused upon the area in the immediate vicinity of his estate and upon the monthly 'petty sessions' formalized by the Book of Orders. Quarter-sessions was seldom a county event – certainly not 'a kind of local parliament.'[24] Even in Essex, a county where the judicial system was centralized, on average only 25 percent of the working group of J.P.s attended each Chelmsford quarter-sessions. A similar proportion attended in Somerset, a fifth in Cheshire; but in both these counties each of the four quarter-sessions was held in a different town, and many of the J.P.s would only attend the session held nearest their homes. Decentralization went further, and the concept of a 'local parliament' appears to be even less applicable in those shires where each of the four courts were held in separate towns for distinct divisions of the county; in Sussex, by the 1630s, the benches of the eastern and western parts of the county were effectively quite separate, lacking any 'regular opportunity to discuss and argue out administrative and political problems'; a similar situation appertained in Lincolnshire, which by the 1660s, was fragmented into eight divisions, each with its distinct series of quarter-sessions served by a discrete group of J.P.s.[25] So the bulk of the gentry's administrative experience was forged in units smaller than the county, and it could be argued that these smaller divisions became the cynosures of their loyalties. J.P.s frequently challenged their colleagues on the county bench over demands, chiefly the apportionment of taxation, that were thought to be inequitable or otherwise contrary to the interests of their immediate locality. And they might even refer to the latter as their 'country' – that term Everitt considered quasi-sacramental. In 1638 Sir Edward Hussey was praised by a fellow J.P. for his concern for 'the good of . . . the country'; but 'the country' in this case was Kesteven, unfairly rated by a Holland sheriff.[25]

This essay is not trying to insert yet more 'closed corporate communities' – the community of the division, perhaps, of the lathe, of the wapentake – into a landscape already cluttered with such entities. Yet it needs to be emphasized that the bulk of the gentry's administrative activities were undertaken in these limited areas, not the county.

There were gatherings attended by the magistracy of an entire county, but these were Janus-faced. At the assizes, at general meetings for the execution of special royal commissions, and at county elections – at each the county elite was reminded of its involvement in a national polity.

In Lincolnshire or Sussex, where a fully decentralized system of magistracy had developed, the county's administrative unity was regularly asserted only at the Lent and summer assizes; in a shire like Essex, too, the politico-administrative existence of the county community received a fuller expression by virtue of the higher attendance of the gentry elite at the assizes. The latter was an important social occasion, and general attendance ensured that matters of common concern to the local gentry, such as candidacies for a forthcoming election, would be discussed. Moreover, in the 1620s, in some counties, the magistrates sought to realize Bacon's ideal, that the assizes should be a place where 'the distastes and griefs of the people' could be represented to the government, by developing formal mechanisms, either petitions from the bench or grand jury presentments, to bring grievances to the judges' attention. Thus the assizes provided the fullest expression of the corporate existence of the county community and a forum where its collective sense could be articulated. It is in these respects that Everitt argues that the assizes 'resemble a kind of informal county "parliament".'[27]

The assizes *were* an important county gathering, but they also emphasized the local magistracy's responsibility to, and dependence upon, a centralized system of government and law. Some of the aura of royal majesty inhered in the assize judges, and was symbolically represented by the ceremonial panoply of their visitations upon which they insisted so pertinaciously – hence the lordly refusal of the judges at Gloucester assizes to accept the ministrations of ecclesiastics of lower rank than the prebendaries of the cathedral. The local J.P.s acknowledged the superior prestige and authority of the assize judges, not only in such little incidents as the fine of one hundred pounds, which the Worcestershire bench levied on a parish after Sir Robert Hyde had complained of the disgusting state of their highway upon which his lordship was obliged to travel, but, more significantly, in their readiness to enlist the judges to back them in the day-to-day business of local government. So, as T.G. Barnes has shown, administrative orders, which would have had equal legal validity had they been made at quarter-sessions, were issued under the aegis of the judges of assize in the belief that 'the judge's position was such that his order would be more decisive, more quickly obeyed, less readily contemned.'[28]

The judges' prestige was a function, in part, of their reputation as legal luminaries; in part, of their intimate contacts with the executive. In both respects they played a significant role in articulating the local magistracy into a national system of government.

As 'oracles of the law,' the judges' expertise provided valued assistance and instruction to the J.P.s. Abstruse technicalities beyond the capacities of the local bench – the exact definition of burglary, the distinction between treasonable and seditious words, the correct form of an indictment, whether a man who married the grandmother of a child maintained by the parish was to be 'accounted as a Grandfather within the statute' – were resolved by the judges in their decision in specific cases, or in answer to a question propounded formally by the county magistrates or informally by an individual J.P., perhaps over dinner in relation to a set of hypothetical facts. If a case or inquiry raised legal issues of any magnitude, the judges could debate it with their colleagues at Westminster and then issue a general ruling that would be promulgated at the assizes: so the 1624 licensing regulations or the 1633 'Resolutions of the Judges of Assize' concerning the Poor Law. This continuing legal education of the J.P.s might involve some harsh lessons; verbal castigation and heavy fines were visited upon those who failed to observe proper legal forms and procedures.[29]

The system, whereby the local magistrates were controlled and informed by professional jurists, did ensure, to quote Barnes again 'that the expanse of the common law . . . would remain common.' It is worth insisting upon this. The institutional arrangements of local adminstration varied from shire to shire; the 'conventions and customs to meet local needs,' which Morrill emphasizes, might develop with respect to matters where the relevant legislation gave the J.P.s discretionary powers. But in fundamentals, the English county communities were governed by a common law.[30]

The other element in the status and respect accorded to the judges by the local gentry was a function of their role as spokesmen for the government. They were the overseers of the various royal programmes for the more efficient execution of criminal justice and of administrative law. In their formal charges at the commencement of the assizes they apprised the local gentry of the current law enforcement, administrative, religious, and political priorities of the crown. And in the 1630s, they also preached the constitutional theory designed to legitimize those priorities. In 1635, the judges of assize were instructed 'to let the people know . . . with what Alacrity and Cheerfulness they. . . are bound in duty to contribute' to ship money, and in 1637, to promulgate the extra-judicial opinion upholding the king's right to demand the levy. The judgment in Hampden's case received similar official publicity: Finch, having treated his audiences at the assizes to a paraphrase of his high-flying exchequer chamber opinion, then 'inveighed against and threatened all such as refused to pay.' Political propaganda could inform not only the judges' charges, but their case decisions. At Gloucester assizes in 1636, it emerged that Richard Legge, suing a bailiff for an assault stemming from the latter's taking a distress for ship money, had originally refused to pay 'because it was not granted by Parliament.' Baron Davenport directed the jury to find against the plaintiff, and informed Legge, 'in great passion,' that 'the King was not to call a Parliament to give him satisfaction.'[31]

The response to this official propaganda was not always the loyal acquiescence intended by the government. The effect of the extra-judicial opinion that Charles solicited in February 1637 was undercut by the proliferation of rumours that some judges had only signed under considerable pressure. In 1638, Croke's powerful dissent in Hampden's case seems to have been more effective in mobilizing opinion than the majority decision; it was widely circulated, and invoked by the recalcitrant in Cheshire, Somerset, Nottingham, and Yorkshire. Indeed, judicial pronouncements could be counterproductive: Baron Weston's charge at Maidstone assizes gave focus to Sir Roger Twysden's previously inchoate doubts as to the legality of the writ.[32]

These facts do not square easily with Morrill's assertions, cited at the beginning of this paper, that ship money was not resented for any generally perceived lack of 'constitutional propriety,' but because the government's cavalier disregard for the customary arrangements governing tax assessments categorically demonstrated its 'insensitivity to localist sentiment.'[33] The dissonance between the facts and Morrill's assertions points to a second major flaw in the county community interpretation of early Stuart history. Concentrating its attentions exclusively upon the locality, the county community school provides inadequate accounts of the ideals and performance of the central government.[34] So, in his account of the history of the ship money levy, Morrill fails to recognize that a decisive element in the situation was the government's ability to police and to silence overt opposition.

Morrill insists that issues of constitutional principle did not lie behind the battery of complaints against ship money on 'administrative grounds': the latter were not 'a cover for deeper political designs.' Yet the local rating disputes were invariably generated by men closely associated with groups that had opposed the various royal fiscal expedients of the 1620s on grounds of constitutional principle. In Somerset, Sir Robert Phelips and Sir Henry Berkeley, who had excoriated the dangerous precedent of the 1627 ship money demand, led the attack upon the 1635 assessment of the county. In Lincolnshire in 1635, a number of men refused to pay their rates, claiming shrieval corruption and peculation; the list was headed by the loan refusers, Sir John Wray and the earl of Lincoln. Wray and another loan refuser, Sir Anthony Irby, men noted for 'their backwardness and crossness to . . . Royall prerogative, treading a parliament way,' were then in the forefront of the local investigation of the sheriff's manifold abuses.[35] Covert opposition, disingenuous sniping about the equity of the rates, was a preferred tactic. Why? Because the crown would crush overt opposition, and men did not court martyrdom.

In 1636, the earl of Warwick led resistance to the levy in Essex. Pressing the king to summon parliament, he told Charles to his face that the Essex men would not tolerate such 'notable prejudices as ship money,' or surrender 'the liberties of the realm.' The king was unmoved: deposition from office was threatened against recalcitrant magistrates; sixty refusers were arraigned in the exchequer; *quo warranto* proceedings were begun to test Warwick's right to appoint the hundred bailiffs who had refused to aid the sheriff. Under pressure, Warwick retreated. In 1637, he was still the spokesman for the county's opposition – but he now attributed Essex's backwardness to the inequities of the sheriff's rate. So too, Sir Simonds D'Ewes, who had expressed (in the secure privacy of his journal) the opinion that ship money 'was absolutely against law, and an utter oppression of the subject's liberty,' later, as sheriff, replied to government demands for expedition, not with high-sounding principles, but with evasive excuses about the poverty of Suffolk and administrative problems.[36]

Opposition could come into the open in 1639–40 when the council, overwhelmed with the manifold problems of the Bishops' Wars, lacked the leisure to supervise the system adequately. Its threats, very real to Warwick and his Essex cohorts in 1636, lacked bite and were neglected both by local officers, also weighed down with the additional burdens of war, and by taxpayers. Awareness of the situation at the centre is fundamental to an understanding of the development of local reactions.

A similar criticism, of a lack of concern for the changing priorities of the government, can be leveled at Fletcher when, contrasting the dismal returns upon the earlier royal fiscal expedients with the success of the forced loan in Sussex, he attributes the latter to the government's agreement that the shire might employ the bulk of the money to defray its vast outlay for billeting.[37] Yet in other counties, which lacked such powerful local stimuli to generosity, the high returns upon the loan were as marked and as unprecedented. The general success enjoyed by the loan was because it was *forced*, because the government dedicated itself (a dedication that, the Venetian ambassador complained, paralyzed all other business) to crushing opposition.[38] The employment of the subsidy book for assessment, the skillfully designed machinery of intimidation embodied in the secret instructions, the perambulating privy councillors, the fate of the recalcitrant, all demonstrate the government's determination. It is impossible to explain either the productivity of the forced loan or the collapse of the ship money collection in 1639–40 in terms of purely local considerations; in both cases the pressure that the central government was prepared, or was able, to exert is a critical determinant.

Discussion of the forced loan introduces the second category of general gatherings of the county magistracy. The meetings to execute special royal commissions, particularly those designed to extract extra-parliamentary revenues, were also amphibious, both county and national in their orientation. And at these, as at the assizes, 'wider political issues,' national concerns, were raised.

The attempts in 1614 and 1622 to raise benevolences had been (typically) lethargically administered by James's government, while the rhetoric of the request was low key – an emphasis on the dangerous international situation, plus a slap at parliament for its irresponsible failure to supply the king's wants adequately. In consequence, in most counties, the J.P.s instructed to organize the collection procrastinated or entered pleas of poverty before finally forwarding a derisory sum to the treasury. But some county elites responded not only with tight fists but with principled constitutional objections; typical was Devon's 1614 'scruple' that 'exceeding prejudice . . . may

come to posterity by such a president.'[39] Charles's initial demand in 1626 was
far more aggressively phrased. The J.P.s were to summon the populace, dilate
upon the international crisis, remind their audience of parliament's intention
(foiled by 'the disordered passions of some members') to grant four subsidies
and three fifteenths, and solicit the money as a gift: the king concluded that
his benign request was a signal favour since 'noe ordinary Rules can prescribe law to necessitie;' the 'very subsistence of the whole' was at stake 'and
might justly warrant us, if out of our royal prerogative and power we should
take any waie more extraordinary or lesse indifferent.'[40]

Only in three counties did the ominous, scarcely-veiled threats of the
royal missive result in even a sum equivalent to a single subsidy being
contributed. The J.P.s of twelve counties sent answers couched in virtually
the same form and phraseology as that of Hertfordshire, the first to reply:

> They are most willinge to contribute for the defence of the Kingdome
> and for the supply of his Majesty's wants . . . in a Parlementary
> manner even beyond their habilities

– But they would not fork out money *this* way.[41]

Rebuffed, Charles withdrew the request for a gift, but within a month
had devised a scheme for the loan of a sum equivalent to five subsidies
from the subsidymen. Again the constitutional issue was presented starkly
to the local gentry who, as before, were ordered to organize the collection:
'necessity (which makes laws to itself) puts him upon this course,' the king
asserted; he was 'enforced by necessity. . . to which noe ordinary rules of
law can be prescribed.'[42]

'Necessity. . . to which noe ordinary rules of law can be prescribed: ' the
county elites witnessed the consequences of the king's constitutional doctrine at first hand in their localities. Privy councillors attended the initial
county meetings and were swift to demonstrate 'that his Majesty wanteth
no good meanes to chastise . . . refractorie humors.' Local magistrates
who refused to assist in the collection or pay the sums demanded were
summoned before the privy council, harangued, and, if they remained
obdurate, imprisoned. Lesser men 'who will not serve him with their
purses . . . must serve . . . with their persons, and be enrolled among
those forces wherewith he purposeth to assist the King of Denmarke, or
otherwise must looke to have soldiers lodged upon them.'[43]

It did not require the tract *To all true-hearted Englishmen*, which was
dispersed at some of the county meetings,[44] to educate the gentry on the
'wider political issues' of the forced loan; royal pronouncements and royal
actions were very sufficient. In 1626–27 county-wide assemblies of the
local magistracy were confronted starkly with major issues of constitutional principle. We cannot suppose that the development of 'county
institutions' produced only closed political horizons and an introverted,
self-centred localism.

Consideration of the fiscal expedients attempted by James and his son raises another questionable characteristic of the county community school: a refusal to recognize the possibility of ideological division within the shires. The latter are suffused in a roseate aura of mutual love, charity, and unity. So Everitt compares the Kentish gentry to an extended family, its internal peace unruffled save by superficial squabbles over local precedence until, from 1642, Sir Anthony Weldon and his clique of power-hungry and unprincipled outsiders shattered the idyll.[45] Yet many county elites were bitterly divided in their response to the forced loan as they were to be again by distraint of knighthood and ship money. Some gentlemen preferred prison to payment. Some, such as Sir Robert Phelips, avoided contamination by a well-timed visit to London. Others conformed to the extent of subscription and initial participation in the collection process, but once government supervision relaxed, as the council became enmeshed in the logistical problems of the Rhe expedition, deliberately avoided further involvement. In Holland, the entire responsibility for raising the loan devolved upon two commissioners, who sardonically noted that the 'others, purchance, have justifiable excuse,'[46] Yet certain men accepted the royal claims embodied in the forced loan instructions, or in the justification offered for the 1627 ship money – 'the defence of a Kingdome . . . are not tyed to ordinarie and continued presidents.' In Lincolnshire, Lord Castleton, active in the execution of the forced loan and then of the knighthood composition, wrote that 'we must obey necessity: ' Sir Edward Rodney and the Somerset D.L.s acted in response to 'inevitable necessity' and 'because we heard of the King's absolute power at Westminister.'[47]

In parliament in 1628 Phelips, reflecting on the work of the deputy lieutenants in billeting, raising coat and conduct money, and enforcing the loan, denounced the 'decemvirate in every county.' The suggestion that every shire contained a clique absolutely committed to the court and to its novel constitutional doctrine is clearly an exaggeration. The extraordinarily complex patterns of affiliation and response to central demands in Yorkshire, as a function of the feud between Saville and Wentworth, each with his 'bande of reyters' among the gentry, and Phelips' own fluctuating allegiances, are warning enough that personal ambition for court preferment or local precedence could deflect and diffuse issues of principle.[48] Yet in many counties the court-country dichotomy is more analytically useful than a romantic evocation of an organic gentry community – in Northamptonshire, in Lincolnshire, in Cornwall, where a group of gentlemen not only worked actively to forward the forced loan, but agreed to oppose Sir John Eliot's candidacy for the 1628 shire election 'lest his majesty suspect our fidelity.'[49]

The county election is the third ambivalent institution in which the entire county elite was involved, which affirmed its corporate identity, and yet necessarily reminded the gentry of their participation in a national polity.

James frequently addressed the Commons as though members were errand-boys for their particular constituencies. M.P.s, especially during debates on taxation, voiced a similar self-image in their concern for the 'blame' ('fury' even) that their impoverished constituents would visit upon them if subsidies were voted without redress of grievances.[50] Yet other concepts of parliament's function and powers jostled and interacted with the belief that it was 'an aggregation of local informers . . . [and] . . . a group of messengers.'[51] Parliament was 'the great watch of the Kingdom,' the 'Counsell of the land;' M.P.s were 'publique [men] vested for the commonwealth's service.' In March 1628 Eliot classified the various capacities in which an M.P. might function.

> I speak . . . not for myself, that's too narrow . . . It is not for the country for which I serve. It is not for us all and the country which we represent, but for the ancient glory of the ancient laws of England.[52]

The Commons frequently acted, in accordance with Eliot's ranking, as though their responsibilities extended beyond their own bailiwicks. In 1628, the House, 'tender of the liberty of the subject,' was not deterred from censuring a Lincolnshire deputy lieutenant by the speeches in his favour by the knights of the shire.[53]

M.P.s might think in terms of their overriding duty to the nation, but what of those who elected them? The practice whereby the county court, at the conclusion of the election, presented a formal statement of local grievances to the knights of the shire to be forwarded to Westminster, might suggest, as do grand jury presentments at assizes, a conception of the county community as an independent political entity with its own peculiar concerns. Yet, as Hirst has shown, such petitions might deal directly with national issues, not merely their local repercussions. Similarly, in their speeches, M.P.s attributed national interests, some fairly sophisticated, to their constituents – an active concern for the privileges of parliament, for example. This was more than a rhetorical convention: Wentworth's local speech in justification of the 1621 subsidy dwells more upon parliament's concern for 'the happiness of the whole Kingdome,' and M.P.s 'duties towards our greatt mother, the commonwealthe' than upon any specific benefits that had accrued to Yorkshire.[54]

The growing reluctance of the counties to elect 'courtiers' is a relevant consideration here. Wentworth's argument in 1621 that immediate local interests, 'the Causes of our Countye,' might be advanced most effectively by a representative with access to, or enjoying the favour of, the executive, was duplicated in 1626 by John Winthrop, and in 1628 by the Cornish deputy lieutenants. Yet, as the Suffolk gentry responded to Winthrop while the privy councillor, Sir Robert Naunton, was 'abell to doe us good,' his connections with the court disqualified him:

> He was tyed in so partickiuler an obligation to his majesty as if ther was occasion to speke for the Cuntry he wold be silent, and in Generall they wolde give no voise to anye cortier espetially at this time of all others.[55]

With the alienation of the 'political nation' from the Stuart court, concern for the representation in parliament of the interests of the coun-try/county shaded into one for those of the country/commonwealth. Early in 1641, a member of the Norfolk elite wrote to the knight of that shire:

> it gives no smale content unto us in the Countrye to be assured of such constant Patriots as yourselfe, that will persevere faythfully in the defense of Churche and Commonwealth.[56]

This emphasis upon representation by 'Patriots' dedicated to 'Churche and Commonwealth' ensured that the county court was more than a political expression of a self-centred county community.

An examination of the attitudes of the electorate suggests another doubtful element in Everitt's analysis of seventeenth-century politics. He adheres to a patriarchal, organic model of social organization that is misleadingly elitist. Everitt's account of the March 1640 Kentish election rivals Sir Lewis Namier in its insistence upon the politics of deference:

> First the Knight . . . who set out to rule the county secured the support of the countryside around his own manor house. Then his kinsmen among the greater gentry obtained the allegiance of their own labourers, tenants and neighbours. Finally each major family secured the adherence of those groups of minor gentry whose social influence depended on their place in these galaxies of greater gentry. In this way the whole community of the county gradually gathered into a series of rival family connection.

Everitt describes the organization of the March 1642 Kentish petition and the 1648 revolt in similar terms.[57] This conception of a society conjoined in organic hierarchy may explain the ambiguous use of the term county community that pervades Everitt's writings. The structural analysis designed to explain the social basis of the community is concerned exclusively with the local gentry: it is argued that their marriage alliances, their administrative experience, were rooted in the county and explain their devotion to its interests. Yet the expression county community is employed as a synonym for the entire population of the shire. This is legitimate, however, if we can assume that the significant attitudes, ideals, and concerns of the inhabitants of Kent are essentially identical with those of the gentry elite.

But we cannot make that assumption. A number of studies have shown that, while the organization of gentry alliances and the dragooning of tenants played a major part in electoral strategies in Kent in the 1620s and again in 1640, there was an independent electorate to be wooed, an electorate vitally concerned with the candidates' religious zeal and their political affiliations. The role of the independent freeholders was even greater in other shires in 1640; in Gloucestershire only slick shrieval legerdemain prevented the voters, encouraged by a 'pack of either deprived, silenced or puritanically affected' ministers, from upsetting the cosy arrangements of the local worthies.[58]

Unless the existence of groups of peasants and craftsmen who were perfectly capable of forming political opinions, and of expressing them forcibly in action, independent of the gentry, is recognized, events during the early stages of the civil war in many areas – Somerset, the West Riding – are inexplicable.[59] Nor can it be argued that such popular intervention was purely a consequence of the unprecedented conditions of 1642–43. Derek Hirst has demonstrated the existence of an electorate that was far from passive and deferential in a number of county contests in the 1620s;[60] and, in the pattern of opposition to royal fiscal demands in that and the following decade, the independent concerns of elements of the populace also emerges. Of course, opposition *per se* is no indicator of independence: the consistent hostility that the inhabitants of Hatfield Broadoak offered to Charles' fiscal project was certainly not unrelated to the machinations of their Barrington landlords. Yet we cannot invariably invoke seigneurial influence. The clothing towns of the Stour valley, backward in the forced loan, backward in the collection of ship money, refusing to erect altars or follow Laudian ritual, lacked a resident gentry.[61] So, too, did the fens of South Holland. Yet of the seventy-two men who absolutely refused to pay the forced loan in Lincolnshire, more than two-thirds came from Holland, and in the summer of 1627 the collectors of that division faced a barrage of excuses – pleading poverty or inequitable assessment – to a far greater extent than their counterparts in Lindsey or Kesteven were subjected. Popular opposition to ship money in 1635 was concentrated in the region, and in the next year the local officers were refusing to aid the sheriff, one saying that 'he had rather answere afore the Lords of the Counsell then distreine his neighbors.'[62] A model of a 'one-class society,' to which the county community school leans, cannot explain the behaviour of the fenmen during the personal rule, of the Gloucestershire freeholders in 1640, of the men of the West Riding upon the outbreak of war.

The central concern in this paper has been to challenge the analysis of the social structure of the county and of the institutions of local government within it made by the county community school. The social experience of the gentry, particularly their formal education and their involvement with the national capital, London, ensured that their horizons were not narrowly local. In their participation in local administration, the gentry were continuously reminded that England was a centralized polity, governed by a common law, and they were frequently obliged to confront major constitutional issues directly. Other aspects of the work of Everitt and his colleagues have also been questioned: the insufficient attention to the quality of the central government's intervention; the romantic image of communal corporatism; the failure to recognize the political aspirations and concerns of classes other than the gentry. Seventeenth-century England was more than 'a union of partially independent county-states.' Many of its inhabitants, particularly the gentry, were well informed and deeply concerned about national religious and constitutional issues. They participated in a national political culture.

Notes

1 Gardiner, *History*, viii. 85; J.S.Morrill, *The Revolt of the Provinces* (London, 1976), pp. 24–9.
2 The quotations are taken from Morrill, *Revolt*, p. 22; Alan Everitt, *The Local Community and the Great Rebellion* (London, 1969), p. 8; Everitt, *Change in the Provinces* (Leicester, 1969), pp. 47, 48. In fairness, it should be remarked that both Everitt and Morrill disclaim any intention of arguing that 'provincialism excluded concern for general . . . political or constitutional issues' (Morrill's phrase). Yet Everitt believes that localism 'was normally . . . more powerful' than any national consciousness, while in his narrative, Morrill consistently downgrades national concerns (Everitt, *Local Community*, p. 5; Morrill, *Revolt*, p. 14).
3 This account is distilled from Everitt's *The Community of Kent and the Great Rebellion* (Leicester, 1966).
4 See Clive Holmes, *The Eastern Association in the English Civil War* (Cambridge, 1974), pp. 28–9; J.T. Cliffe, *The Yorkshire Gentry* (London, 1969), pp. 300–1.
5 Lawrence Stone, 'English Land Sales, 1540–1640: a Reply to Mr. Russell' in *Ec.H.R.*, 2nd series, 25 (1972), p. 121 note 6, and the sources cited there. For Cheshire, see J.S. Morrill, *Cheshire 1630–1660: County Government and Society during the English Revolution* (Oxford, 1974), pp. 2–4; for Lancashire, B.G. Blackwood, 'The Cavalier and Roundhead Gentry of Lancashire' in *Transactions of the Lancashire and Cheshire Antiquarian Society*, 77 (1967), p. 83; for Dorset, J.P. Ferris, 'The Gentry of Dorset on the Eve of the Civil War' in *Genealogists' Magazine*, 15, no.3 (1965), pp. 104–8. In Lincolnshire I find that only 17 percent of the gentry could claim pre-Tudor lineage.
6 Everitt, *Local Community*, pp. 21–2; Everitt, *Suffolk and the Great Rebellion* (Ipswich, 1960), pp. 17–22.
7 For Kent, see Everitt, *Community of Kent*, pp. 42–3, 328; for Lancashire, B.G. Blackwood, 'The Marriages of the Lancashire Gentry on the Eve of the Civil War' in *Genealogists' Magazine*, 16, no. 7 (1970), pp. 321–8; for Essex and Hertfordshire, Holmes, *Association*, pp. 13, 229.
8 Anthony Fletcher, *A County Community in Peace and War: Sussex 1600–1660* (London, 1975), pp. 44–53.

9 Fletcher, *County Community*, p. 53.

10 PRO, SP 14/162/58; 16/514/29.

11 T.T. Lewis (ed.) *The Letters of Lady Brilliana Harley* (London, 1854), pp. 9, 27, 30, 32, 59, 68, 81, 107, 130, 161.

12 J.H. Gleason, *The Justices of the Peace in England 1558–1640* (Oxford, 1969), pp. 83–95; W.K. Jordan, *Philanthropy in England, 1480–1660* (London, 1959), p. 361.

13 Everitt, *Local Community*, p. 6; Morrill, *Revolt*, pp. 23–4; Victor Morgan, 'Cambridge University and "the Country", 1560–1640' in Lawrence Stone (ed.), *The University and Society* (Princeton, 1974), vol. 1, pp. 183–245; quotation from p. 185.

14 H.C. Porter, *Reformation and Reaction in Tudor Cambridge* (Cambridge, 1958), pp. 45–6, 269–71.

15 W.R. Prest, *The Inns of Court under Elizabeth I and the Early Stuarts* (Totowa, 1972), pp. 32–40; for Egerton, see L.A. Knafla, *Law and Politics in Jacobean England* (Cambridge, 1977), pp. 48–9; for Welby, W.P. Baildon (ed.), *Les Reportes del Cases in Camera Stellata 1593–1609* (London, 1894), p. 315.

16 Thomas Aston, *A Remonstrance against Presbytery* (London, 1641), *passim*; for the local background to this work, see Morrill, *Cheshire*, pp. 45–53.

17 D.C. Douglas, *English Scholars 1660–1730* (London, 1951), pp. 30–7, analyzes the fruitful scholarly interaction of Spelman (Norfolk), Dugdale (Warwickshire), and Dodsworth (Yorkshire).

18 Reginald Scot, *The Discoverie of Witchcraft* (Totowa, 1973), p. xvi; Mary E. Bohannon, 'A London Bookseller's Bill, 1635–1639' in *The Library*, 4th series, 18 (1937–38), pp. 417–46.

19 Quotations are from Lawrence Stone, *The Crisis of the Aristocracy* (Oxford, 1964), p. 388 and Everitt, *Local Community*, p. 6; Stone (*Crisis of the Aristocracy*, pp. 385–98) provides a general review of the evidence for the attraction of London. In *English Provincial Society from the Reformation to the Revolution* (London, 1977), pp. 209, 447, Peter Clark argues that the Kentish gentry had closer ties with London than Everitt supposes; for the Yorkshire gentry, see Cliffe, *Yorkshire Gentry*, pp. 21–3.

20 Everitt, *Community of Kent*, p. 44.

21 B. Scofield (ed.), *The Knyvett Letters, 1620–1644* (Norwich, 1949), *passim*.

22 HMC, *Buccleuch*, vol. 3, pp. 307–14; Lawrence Stone, *The Causes of the English Civil War* (London, 1972), p. 91; M.A.E. Green (ed.), *The Diary of John Rous* (London, 1856), *passim*.

23 Everitt, *Local Community*, p. 6.

24 Stone, *Causes*, p. 95.

25 For Essex, see Joel Samaha, *Law and Order in Historical Perspective* (New York, 1974), pp. 81–3 and App. IV; for Somerset, T.G. Barnes, *Somerset 1625–1640* (Oxford, 1961), pp. 68–70; for Cheshire, Morrill, *Cheshire*, pp. 9, 16; for Sussex, Fletcher, *County Community*, pp. 134–6, 243.

26 PRO, SP 16/380/60. For similar local divisions within a county, see Clark, *English Provincial Society*, pp. 256–7, 311 (the paradigm county, Kent) and G.F.C. Foster, 'The North Riding Justices and their Sessions, 1603–1625' in *NH*, 10 (1975), pp. 110–11, 115, 118.

27 Everitt, *Kent*, p. 95 note 2. For Bacon's comment, see J.S. Cockburn, *A History of the English Assizes, 1558–1714* (Cambridge, 1972), p. 173; for examples of such presentments, see Derek Hirst, 'Court, Country and Politics before 1629' in Kevin Sharpe (ed.), *Faction and Parliament* (Oxford, 1978), pp. 134–5.

28 T.G. Barnes (ed.), *Somerset Assize Orders, 1629–1640* (Frome, 1959), p. xxix.

For the Gloucestershire and Worcestershire examples, see W.B. Willcox, *Gloucestershire: A Study in Local Government 1590–1640* (London, 1940), p. 43; R.D. Hunt (ed.), 'Henry Townshend's "Notes of the Office of a Justice of the Peace" 1661–63' in *Worcestershire Historical Miscellany*, II (Leeds, 1967), p. 109.

29 For these examples, see Hunt (ed.), 'Townshend's Notes,' pp. 83, 85, 86–87, 88, 90, 93, 94, 95, 109, 117; *The English Reports* (Edinburgh, 1907), vol. 80 (2 Bulstrode), 345, 348–9, 349–50, 351–2, 355–6; vol. 123 (Hutton), 99.

30 Barnes (ed.), *Somerset Assize Orders*, p. xxvii; Morrill, *Revolt*, p. 22. See also Cockburn, *English Assizes*, pp. 168–72.

31 Rushworth, *Historical Collections* (London, 1680), vol. 2, pp. 294–8, 352–6; vol. 3, pp. 985–9; William Oldys and Thomas Park (eds), *The Harleian Miscellany* (London, 1810), vol. 5, p. 568; *Articles of Accusation exhibited by the Commons . . . against Sir John Bramston* (1641), pp. 32–3.

32 *Articles of Accusation exhibited by the Commons . . . against Sir John Bramston*, pp. 5–6; Barnes, *Somerset*, p. 228 note 48; Elaine Marcotte, 'Shrieval Administration of Ship Money in Cheshire, 1637' in *Bulletin of the John Rylands Library*, 58 (1975–6), p. 159; *CSPD, 1637–38*, p. 443; Cliffe, *Yorkshire Gentry*, p. 309; F.W. Jessup, *Sir Roger Twysden, 1597–1672* (London, 1965), pp. 37–8.

33 Morrill, *Revolt*, pp. 24–9. Robert Ashton, *The English Civil War: Conservatism and Revolution 1603–1649* (London, 1978), pp. 63–6, also emphasizes the localist aspect of the opposition to ship money.

34 See Derek Hirst's recent articles 'The Privy Council and Problems of Enforcement in the 1620s' in *JBS*, 18 (1978), pp. 46–8; and 'Court, Country and Politics' in Sharpe (ed.), *Faction*, pp. 105–37.

35 Barnes, *Somerset*, pp. 216–7; PRO, SP 16/315/121; 331/26; 336/78.

36 V.A. Rowe, 'Robert, Second Earl of Warwick, and the Payment of Ship Money in Essex' in *Transactions of the Essex Archaeological Society*, 3rd series, vol. 1, part 2 (1962), pp. 160–3; J.O. Halliwell (ed.), *The Autobiography and Correspondence of Sir Simonds D'Ewes* (London, 1845), vol. 2, pp. 129–36.

37 Fletcher, *County Community*, pp. 195–6, 212.

38 Hirst, 'Privy Council,' pp. 52–3.

39 *APC, 1613–14*, pp. 491–3, 557–8, 628–31, 649–50, 655–6; *APC 1621–23*, pp. 176–8; James Spedding (ed.), *The Works of Francis Bacon* (London, 1869), vol. 5, pp. 81–3, 132–4; *CSPD 1621–23*, p. 393.

40 PRO, SP 16/31/30, 31.

41 PRO, SP 16/33/8; *CSPD 1625–26*, pp. 397, 398, 399, 404, 406, 407, 410, 413, 419, 424, 425, 428, 435.

42 PRO, SP 16/25/75, *Instructions which his Majesty's commissioners for the loan of the money . . . are exactly and effectually to observe and follow* (London, 1626), *passim*.

43 *APC 1627*, pp. 23–4.

44 PRO, SP 16/54/82; *C and T., Chas. I. i.* 202.

45 Everitt, *Kent*, pp. 52–3, 117–18.

46 PRO SP 16/71/50. Ashton (*English Civil War*, p. 47) has also emphasized that 'the Commission of the Peace was by no means monolithic in its attitude to royal centralising processes.'

47 PRO SP 16/60/31; *P in P 1628*, ii. 254.

48 *P in P 1628*, ii. 69; *Wentworth Papers* pp. 5, 314; Cliffe, *Yorkshire Gentry*, pp. 282–306; Barnes, *Somerset*, pp. 281–98; Ashton, *English Civil War*, p. 66.

49 *P in P 1628*, ii. 33. See also Harold Hulme, *The Life of Sir John Eliot* (London, 1957), pp. 173–81.

50 See Derek Hirst, *The Representative of the People?* (Cambridge, 1975), pp. 166–77. The debates on March 19–20, 1624 concerning the subsidy provide the fullest example of this habit of thought (Houghton Library, Harvard, English Ms. 980, pp. 123–39, 143–9: I am extremely grateful to the Yale Center for Parliamentary History for allowing me to use their transcripts of the manuscript diaries for the parliaments of 1624 and 1626).

51 E.R. Foster, 'The Procedure of the House of Commons against Patents and Monopolies, 1621–1624' in W.A. Aiken and B.D. Henning (eds), *Conflict in Stuart England* (New York, 1960), pp. 59–85, especially pp. 61–2.

52 *CD 1621*, ii. 353–54; iii 30; CUL, Ms Dd 12 22fo. 17v; *P in P 1628*, ii. 57.

53 *P in P 1628*, iii. 355, 356, 359, 360.

54 See Hirst, *Representative*, pp. 164–6, 175; (Sir Edward Nicholas), *Proceedings and Debates in the House of Commons in 1620* (Oxford, 1766), pp. 296, 343, 352; *Wentworth Papers*, pp. 152–7.

55 G.W. Robinson (ed.), *The Winthrop Papers*, vol. 1 (Boston, 1929), pp. 324–6. See also Hirst, *Representative*, pp. 143; 175.

56 Bodl. L., Tanner, Ms 66, fo. 65.

57 Everitt, *Kent*, p. 83: see also pp. 48, 70, 98, 240–59.

58 J.H. Plumb, 'The Growth of the Electorate in England from 1600 to 1715' *P & P*, 45 (1969), pp. 105–6; Clark, *Provincial Society*, pp. 385–6; J.K. Gruenfelder, 'The Elections to the Short Parliament, 1640' in R.H. Reinmuth (ed.), *Early Stuart Studies* (Minneapolis, 1970), pp. 209–10, 223–4.

59 David Underdown, *Somerset in the Civil War and Interregnum* (Newton Abbot, 1973), pp. 38–41; Brian Manning, *The English People and the English Revolution* (London, 1979), pp. 210–15.

60 Hirst, *Representative*, pp. 144-7; see also the analysis of the 1620s elections in Kent by K.B. Sommers in her unpublished Yale University doctoral dissertation, 'Court, Country and Parliament: Electoral Influence in Five English Counties, 1586–1640' (1978), pp. 239–47.

61 PRO, SP 16/350/54.

62 PRO, SP 16/56/39; 58/110; 73/45; 78/8; 357/96 VIII; *CSPD 1637*, p. 104.

9

News and politics in early-seventeenth-century England

RICHARD CUST

One of the more problematic issues currently being discussed by early seventeenth-century historians relates to the impact of news. Although few attempts have been made to address this directly, it is central to an understanding of political attitudes, particularly in the localities. It has implications for debates about the awareness and independence of electors and the role of the 'county community'; and at a more refined level it affects our judgement of the place of principle in politics and the extent to which its processes were perceived as adversarial.[1] News is of considerable importance, and yet historians have been unable to agree about its impact.

Most would accept that the volume of political news was increasing during the early seventeenth century; but the consequences of this are uncertain. Those writing within the Whig tradition have argued for a relatively direct connection between this increase and a heightening of political conflict. Hence Zagorin has linked interest in current affairs and the appearance of the first newspapers to division between 'court' and 'country'; and Stone has cited the earl of Newcastle's advice to Charles II, that to avoid the unrest of his father's reign he should suppress newsletter-writers.[2] These views have, however, been treated with scepticism by a more recent generation of historians, whose research into local archives has revealed only limited evidence of such influences at work. Hirst, after examining numerous elections and detailing the methods by which parliamentary events were published in the shires, has stressed none the less that 'nowhere prior to the 1630s was there a consistent record of political arousal on the part of the electorate'. Morrill has emphasized that, although there was plenty of material in circulation, much of it 'treated great affairs of state in a surprisingly trivial manner', leaving the reader confused rather than enlightened, 'knowing a good deal that was distasteful and unpleasant about the Court, but knowing and understanding less about the real constitutional issues'. And, drawing on this work, Russell has argued that the pressures exerted by constituents on their M.P.s related

I am grateful to Ann Hughes, Jacqueline Levy, Tom Cogswell, Peter Lake, Conrad Russell and Christopher Thompson for commenting on drafts of this article. A version of it was read at the Anglo-American conference, July 1984. I am grateful to those present for their comments, in particular John Morrill, Malcolm Smuts and Margaret Spufford.

mainly to local concerns such as taxation.[3] These conclusions have, however, been challenged in turn: Holmes and Hughes, on the basis of their local research, suggest links between the gentry's receipt of news and their understanding of broad issues of principle; Hill has pointed to ways in which the general awareness of constituents created pressures for M.P.s; and Hirst himself has shown that voters were often able to differentiate candidates for election in terms of broad political alignments.[4] Moreover, in a detailed account of the outbreak of civil war, Fletcher has continually highlighted the effects of the news. Not only did it keep the localities informed about national events and encourage widespread discussion, it also gave rise to a series of petitioning campaigns which revealed both the sophistication of local élites and their concern to influence politics at the centre.[5]

Fletcher's work, in particular, invites a reassessment of the role of news, and this is the main purpose of this article. It will first of all look at how news circulated to the shires, in order to assess its volume and likely audience; then investigate its content, and the ways in which it was presented and perceived; and finally suggest some of its effects for the formation of political attitudes and ideas. The discussion will draw mainly on evidence of domestic politics during the 1620s; but it will be argued that the conclusions apply more widely, to reflect a series of general developments in the period before 1640.

I

Prior to the 1640s the printing of domestic news was tightly controlled by the privy council. The corantoes which appeared at this time – and which have attracted considerable attention as the forerunners of the newspaper – dealt only with foreign affairs, and were generally careful to avoid controversial topics lest they forfeit their licences.[6] In spite of this, however, a good deal of sensitive material still came into circulation. Some of it was printed abroad – usually in the United Provinces or Germany – and then imported; but most was written in England and circulated in manuscript, either as newsletters or what were known as 'separates'. These took the form of transcripts or detailed reports of proceedings in parliament, state trials, advice to the crown, diplomatic negotiations, military campaigns and so on. Together with newsletters they generally avoided conciliar restrictions, and from the 1580s onwards these two sources provided the basis for an expanding network of news.[7]

Originally the newsletter had been largely unformalized, consisting simply of news items sandwiched between personal and business correspondence in letters to friends or relations. This sort of communication continued – and probably remained the most common method for conveying written news – but alongside it there developed the 'pure newsletters', given over wholly to news, both domestic and foreign. These 'pure newsletters' were the forerunners of the internal news-sheets of the 1640s and were in many cases being produced by an emerging class of semi-professional journalists who ranged from well-connected men of affairs, such as John Chamberlain, to the sort of anonymous hack caricatured in Ben Jonson's 1620 play, *News from the New World*:

> a factor of news for all the shires of England, I do write my thousand letters a week ordinary, sometimes twelve hundred, and maintain the business at some charge both to hold up my reputation with mine own ministers in town, and my friends of correspondence in the country. I have friends of all ranks and of all religions, for which I keep an answering catalogue of dispatch, wherein I have my puritan news, my protestant news and my pontifical news.[8]

It is possible to learn a good deal about some of the more prominent members of this group, and their networks of correspondence reveal much about the way provincial readers were kept in touch with public affairs. Sir John Scudamore in Herefordshire, for example, paid £20 a year for the services of John Pory, who was at various times a geographer, overseas adventurer and M.P., and who numbered among his contacts Archbishop Abbot, Sir Dudley Carleton, the earl of Warwick and two leading Warwickshire gentlemen, Sir Thomas Lucy and Sir Thomas Puckering.[9] Another acquaintance of Pory's – Joseph Mead, the Cambridge theologian – provided a comparable service for the Suffolk gentleman, Sir Martin Stuteville, keeping him up to date by sending as many as four letters a week, collected from various London correspondents.[10]

As the newsletter developed and altered its form so too did the 'separate'. From providing an occasional account of a really notable public event in the late sixteenth century, it had been extended to cover almost anything which attracted the public interest; in particular, it provided the means for circulating the first public account of events in parliament, the Proceedings and Debates for 1628.[11] Moreover, unlike the newsletter, which was by nature ephemeral and frequently open to correction, the 'separate' was regarded as an authoritative record, and as such was copied into commonplace books and preserved in library collections.[12] Indeed there was a considerable overlap between manuscripts produced in this form and the printed work. Books and pamphlets which were prohibited or in short supply – such as Sir Walter Ralegh's *The Prerogative of Parliaments* or Thomas Scott's *Vox Populi* – were frequently copied by hand and then made available through the channels used for distributing 'separates'.[13]

As the market expanded, techniques of production evolved rapidly. A seller of 'separates', like the antiquarian, Ralph Starkey, could employ a whole team of scriveners and copyists and produce detailed accounts of newsworthy occurrences within a few days. This sort of organization helped to keep prices down, and for much of the period they were running at levels comparable to printed works: in 1628, for example, items relating to the parliament were selling for between 6d. and 2s.; and in 1637 Sir Richard Grosvenor was buying 'separates' for between 2s. and 3s., while paying 2s. and 2s. 6d. for printed sermons. There was also competition to reproduce material as cheaply as possible, with London scriveners under-cutting each other in selling transcripts of Justice Croke's ship-money judgement.[14] This all ensured a very considerable volume of production. It has been estimated by Notestein and Relf that by 1629 between fifty and seventy-five copies of parliamentary 'separates' were being produced; how-ever, given the fact that the amount surviving can only be a fraction of the original output, this looks like a large underestimate. By this date many corporation archives, as well as most of the substantial gentry collections, contain at least some of this sort of material; and it was possible for a less wealthy individual – such as William Davenport of Bramhall in Cheshire – to transcribe 'separates' circulating among his neighbours.[15] The numbers of copies made of popular items, then, must have run into hundreds, if not thousands.

In spite of this rapid expansion of written material, however, it seems that the commonest method of passing on news remained word of mouth. This was in keeping with the habits of a society which was still only partially literate and in which the opportunities for oral exchange were growing with the development of internal trade and increasing resort to London. It also avoided some of the hazards attached to writing down news which was controversial.[16] By its very nature, of course, much of the evidence for this has been lost to the historian; none the less, what was said can still sometimes be traced. Mead recorded conversations which he had had with travellers passing through Cambridge, and Pory referred to gossip and hearsay as the basis for his reports. The most revealing source, however, is a 'news-diary' kept by John Rous, a Suffolk clergyman who spent most of his life in his immediate locality.[17] On one occasion he mentions journeying to London, and on another going abroad to Geneva, but apart from this he rarely seems to have travelled beyond East Anglia. His social contacts were similiarly restricted. There is no mention of direct contact with his eminent cousins, the Rouses of Henham, or with other leading gentry of the area, and he appears to have passed most of his time in the company of fellow clergymen, minor gentry and literate yeomen.[18] His diary, therefore, can be taken to indicate the news available to a well-informed, but essentially provincial, observer.

Most of this came in the form of gossip. Rous mentions receiving the odd newsletter and coranto from London, and journeying to Thetford to read proclamations pinned to the corner-post of the Bell inn; but the source he most frequently indicates is local talk, variously described as 'some say', 'it is commonly said', 'great talk', 'it was tould us', 'a rumour there was', 'country intelligence', and, most often, simply as 'ut dicitur'. Occasionally he was more specific and elaborated on the sources of news: on one occasion it was a conversation with a shopkeeper on the way to Wickham market; on another, a visit to the minister at Feltwell in Norfolk; and on a third, the report given out by Sir Roger Townsend returning home during a recess of parliament. In spite of this diversity, however, the content of the material was very similar to the reports in newsletters or 'separates'. Thus 'country intelligence' in June 1626 was speculation about the causes of dissolving parliament; the 'news held currant' in February 1627 was of national resistance to the forced loan; and Townsend's report was of parliament's determination to proceed against the duke of Buckingham in 1628.[19] In fact much of this oral news has the appearance of being derived from written sources, as well as vice versa.

This overlap is again apparent in the last of the principal agencies of news, the verses and ballads recited in alehouses and other places where people met to socialize. Of all the media considered, this is the most problematic, since it is very hard to discover the origin of these verses or their intended audience. There is some evidence indicating that they were performed in public: for example, a Star Chamber trial in 1627 involving two Middlesex fiddlers arrested for performing a libellous ballad about Buckingham; or the comment made about Thomas Cotton of Colchester in the 1630s, that he was accustomed to reading out the latest news on market-day with locals flocking around him 'as people use where ballads are sung'. There are also occasional references by Rous and others which suggest that the verses they recorded originated with the 'vulgar multitude' and reflected their opinions.[20] However, it is hard to know whether all popular verses fell into this category or whether some were perhaps intended for a more educated audience. What, for example, would a gentleman-collector such as William Davenport have made of the verses which he recorded on the parliament of 1621?

> The[y] saye Sejanus doth bestowe
> What ever office doth befalle
> But tis well knowen it is not soe
> For he is soundlye paide for all . . .
>
> When Charles hath gott the Spanishe gyrle
> The Purytans will scowle and brawle
> Then Digebye shall be made an Earle
> And the Spanishe gould shall paye for all . . .
>
> When the Banquettinge howse is finisht quite
> Then James Sir Kingoe wee will calle
> And poet Ben brave maskes shall wryte
> And the subsidie shall pay for all . . .

> Sir Giles is much displeased with the Kinge
> That he a Parliament did calle
> But my hoste and hostyces both doe singe
> The daye is come to paye for all . . .
>
> When Yelverton shalbe released
> And Buckinghame begin to falle
> Then will the Commons be well pleased
> Which daye hath lounge beene wishte of all.[21]

The references to Sejanus and to Digby, Jonson and Yelverton suggest that these were intended for a relatively knowledgeable and sophisticated audience. On the other hand, the generally derisory tone of all the references, from the king across the board to opponents of his Spanish policy, seems to preclude any serious political purpose. Probably Davenport would have looked on them as akin to the early political cartoons which appeared at this time, an amusing and graphic way of presenting political common-places.[22] However, he did not always treat them as casually as this might imply. Alongside one rhyme, relating to Mr. Hoskins – who was imprisoned for disrupting the 1614 Parliament – he took care to note that 'men more to blame . . . more preferr'd' included 'Lord Howard Chamb., Lo. Somersett et multis aliis'.[23]

Perhaps the most satisfactory conclusion one can offer is that verses of this sort often appear to have operated on at least two levels. They served to entertain and interest the literate contemporaries who collected them; but at the same time they provided a means of disseminating news and opinion to the illiterate and semi-literate, employing a familiar form derived from the ballad traditions of popular culture.[24] This dual function was illustrated in a set of verses produced late in 1627 after the duke of Buckingham's return from the disastrous expedition to the Ile de Rhé. Rous recorded these with some distaste as an example of the depths of vulgar muck-raking; but, at the same time, they indicate the more subtle side of popular news:

> And arte returnde againe with all they faultes
> Thou greate commander of the All goe naughts?
> And lefte the Isle behind thee: what's the matter?
> Did winter make thy chappes beginne to chatter? . . .
> Or didste thou sodenly remove thy station
> For jealous fear of Holland's supplantation?
> Or wast for want of wenches? or didst feare
> The King thou absent durst wrong'd Bristoll heare? . . .
> Or didst thou hasten headlong to prevent
> A fruitlesse hope of needfull parliament?
> All these, no question, with a restles motion

Vexted thy besotted soule as that blacke potion
Tortured the noble Scotte, whose manes will tell
Thy swolne ambition made his carcase swell . . .
Could not thy mother's masses nor her crosses
Nor sorceries prevent those fatal losses? . . .
Could not thy zealous Cambridge pupill's prayers
Composed of Brownist and Arminian ayres
Confound thy foes? . . . [25]

The imagery employed here bordered on the scatological and porno-
graphic, and there was a tendency for such material to fit political figures
into popular stereotypes, such as the good lord or evil counsellor.[26] None
the less, these verses do still present a view of politics which was relatively
sophisticated, both in its frame of reference and its underlying assumptions. The allusions to Buckingham's chancellorship of Cambridge and the
activities of his Arminian clients, to his supposed complicity in the murder
of King James and the duke of Hamilton and to his persecution of the earl
of Bristol all reflected complaints made against him during the 1626
parliament; and the mention of the earl of Holland and the countess of
Buckingham's reputation for popery implied a knowledge of events at
court.[27] Whether the inclusion of these references means that the alehouse
audience was entirely familiar with national politics, however, must
remain an open question. These verses had a whole series of different
aspects and operated according to the perceptions of those who heard
them or wrote them down. The political allusions would probably have
been picked up first and foremost by the educated connoisseur, while the
less-refined imagery may have had greater impact in a public performance.
None the less, we should beware of drawing too clear a distinction. In this
context, it is significant that such material was being presented at all, and
this suggests that the separation often made between popular and élite
culture was in practice sometimes non-existent. Here, at least, the literate
and the illiterate shared the same medium.[28]

This is important when it comes to assessing the impact of news. The
implication is that this was not confined exclusively to the educated, but
also had the potential to shape attitudes among the lower orders. The
means by which news was transmitted varied considerably and that which
was available at a popular level was generally less accurate and less refined;
however, in terms of content and direction the different sorts of news were
broadly similar. Developments in its circulation, then, were coming to
affect a broad social spectrum.

This was particularly the case after 1620, from which date there is a
marked increase in the survival of newsletters and 'separates', reflecting
public interest in the Thirty Years War, negotiations for the Spanish match
and renewed meetings of parliament.[29] As a result those with access to

written news came to be presented with an increasingly detailed insight
into current affairs, much of it provided by semi-professional journalists
with a reputation for accurate reporting.[30] At the same time those who
relied primarily on oral sources were being offered a broader and richer
range of material, often supplemented from the written news. Inevitably
all of this had important consequences for politics, and it is possible to
explore some of these by looking more closely at the content.

II

One of the more obvious effects of the news was that it helped to further a
sense of the integration of local and national. This was, of course, a
complex process, related to a wide variety of cultural, social and institutional influences; but it was one in which news appears to have played a
significant part.[31] Its impact was enhanced by the way in which newsgathering centred on St. Paul's Walk and the Exchange in London. According to Francis Osborne, looking back to his youth in the early seventeenth
century:

> it was the fashion of these times . . . for the principal gentry, lords,
> courtiers and men of all professions . . . to meet in Paul's Church by
> eleven and walk in the middle aisle till twelve, and after dinner from
> three to six, during which times some discoursed of business, others
> of news. Now in regard of the universal commerce there happened
> little that did not first and last arrive here . . . [32]

Provincial centres acted, to some extent, in a similar fashion, but none
could compete with London for the scope and detail of its reports. Hence
Mead in Cambridge occasionally picked up titbits which corrected or
expanded on his news from London, but by and large it was this that he
sent on to Stuteville; while the surviving reports which Sir John Wynn
received in North Wales come almost entirely from relatives in the capital.
Indeed the gossip of the 'Paul's Walkers' was reproduced so widely and so
precisely that one can find the same mistakes being repeated as far afield as
Cambridge and Devon.[33]

The news from London was, however, not simply London news. Rather
the city tended to serve as a melting-pot for information from all parts of
the country. Whenever there was a significant occurrence in the shires,
news of it was likely to reach the capital: in November 1625 Lord Vaux's
refusal to surrender his arms in Northamptonshire was a talking point for
several London newsletter-writers; Owen Wynn told his father, Sir John,
that the Merionethshire election was the talk of the town in February 1626;
and in 1631 John Pory was asking his Warwickshire correspondents,
Puckering and Lucy, to send him information on the riots in the Forest
of Dean.[34] This material was then worked together and retransmitted to

the shires as part of a connected sequence of events, generally set alongside what was happening at the centre. It was this process which encouraged contemporaries to view local events in a wider perspective, and something of this can be seen in the 'news-diary' of Walter Yonge.

Yonge lived at Colyton in Devon and, although a J.P. and linked with John White's Dorchester Company, during the 1620s he rarely travelled beyond his immediate locality.[35] His diary was therefore basically a record of local events, but it was one spiced and given perspective by the letters and reports which he frequently received from friends in London. These helped Yonge to bring out the national significance of what was happening in his shire: for example, when describing the efforts to train the militia in 1626 he was able to record first of all that the scheme had been adopted nationally, and then the details of the sergeant sent to Colyton; when he talked of his county's refusal to pay ship money in February 1628 he did so in the context of a postponement of parliament; and when discussing the forced loan he first described its launching nationally, then the response within his county, and finally the sufferings of his neighbour and friend, Sir Walter Earle, involved in the Five Knights Case.[36] These examples, and others, demonstrate the sort of mental link which Yonge was accustomed to making, and in this he appears to have been typical of his contemporaries. In a similar vein, Rous related billeting within his shire to preparationsfor the Ile de Rhé expedition; while both Joseph Mead and the earl of Clare, another prolific writer of newsletters, described local parliamentary elections in 1628 in terms which suggested that they were part of a concerted protest against the court.[37] Centralized newsgathering, then, helped to shape the attitudes of the recipients of news. In a different way it also had a considerable impact on those involved in making the news.

One of the consequences of the growth in the volume of material was to make the activities of national politicians highly visible to a wide public. The implications of this for parliament have been explored by Hirst and Russell. They have shown how the growing practice of reporting back to constituents and providing 'separates' of parliamentary proceedings led M.P.s to become more accountable and at the same time enabled them to shape local opinion. This brought credit for individuals whose actions were favourably reported and also enhanced the reputation of parliament as a whole;[38] however, such processes were not confined exclusively to parliament. Events outside were coming to be treated in almost as much detail with reports of council meetings, diplomatic negotiations, court intrigue and almost anything else which captured public attention. This exposed politicians to what must often have been an uncomfortable scrutiny; at the same time, however, it presented them with opportunities which they were quick to recognize and exploit.

Something of this can be seen from the way in which privy councillors were ready to 'leak' information in what appears to have been a quite calculated fashion. It was surely no accident that between 1626 and 1628, during discussions over the forced loan and the resummoning of parliament, particular names appeared in the news again and again. The council was split down the middle over these issues and for some members there was considerable advantage to be gained from making their views known more widely. Lord Keeper Coventry, for example, who was continually reported as the leading spokesman against the king's policy of rule without parliament, earned considerable popular esteem as 'a good patriot . . . and a martir'; while Buckingham took every opportunity to present himself to the people as 'first adviser' for a parliament, 'by which', as Sir Robert Cotton commented, 'he may remain not only secure from any further quarrel with them, but merit a happy memory amongst them of a zealous patriot'.[39] Politicians were prepared to go to considerable lengths to use the news to their advantage, and this could have consequences not only for their own reputations, but also for the opinions and responses of the public. The efforts of Coventry and other councillors may well have served as an encouragement to those county justices who drafted protests against the king's attempts to forestall the 1628 Parliament with a levy of ship money.[40] Similarly, earlier in the 1620s the circulation of a speech against the Spanish match – purporting to have been delivered in council by Archbishop Abbot – was thought to have damaged its prospects. At the time Secretary Calvert tried to repair this by getting Abbot to disown the speech publicly; but the archbishop – in spite of acknowledging in private that it was a fabrication – refused to co-operate. He seems to have recognized that there was much to be gained from allowing its circulation in his name, since, as one contemporary newsmonger observed:

> if he be the author he did well and seriously at the last to succour his honor and reputacon which had suffered some censure as if he had growen cold and was carryed along upon the streame of the tyme; and if he speake it not, yet the copies being scattered into many hands, there wilbe somewhat of that will stick.[41]

This was a good illustration of the dual aspect of this sort of news; in exposing politicians to the public gaze it also gave them the chance to present their views to a wide audience. This could be extremely significant not only for privy councillors and courtiers, but also for M.P.s, leading clerics, local governors, forced-loan refusers and almost anyone else who came on to the public stage. As a result by the 1620s, if not before, the circulation of news had become an integral part of the political process, something which politicians had to make allowances for, and which they appreciated could substantially affect public attitudes.

Perhaps the most significant consequence of all this, however, lay not in the degree of exposure which it gave to national politicians, but rather in the effects it had on perceptions of their actions. These were intimately related to the fact that newsletters, 'separates' and oral reports tended to present an image of politics which was at considerable variance with contemporary rhetoric. Naturally enough, they focused on the events which made the headlines and treated their readers to a succession of dramatic incidents: court scandals, state trials, disputes in parliament, attacks on the duke and almost anything else of unusual interest. In the process, evidence of everyday agreement and co-operation tended to be ignored.[42] Hence the papists got into newsletters not when they were being submissive or loyal to the crown, but when – like Lord Vaux – they seemed to threaten national security. Similarly, the billeting of soldiers was ignored during the three years in which it proceeded comparatively peaceably, and reached the newsletters only when it became a matter of political controversy, early in 1628. Then it was the subject of a series of grossly exaggerated reports suggesting, among other things, that soldiers had set fire to Banbury and massacred local inhabitants in Witham.[43] All this was, perhaps, much as one would expect; however, it is worth considering its effect on political attitudes.

Recent historiography has tended to stress that these were dominated by the continual drive towards consensus. Kishlansky has argued that the debates and procedure of parliament were designed to secure agreement between crown and subject; and Russell and Judson have shown that the predominant emphasis of parliamentary rhetoric was on unity. The same appears to have been true locally. Addresses made at quarter sessions, assizes or meetings of subsidy assessors repeatedly harped on the need for co-operation.[44] This was understandable, and to some extent necessary, given the ambiguities and scope for disagreement inherent in the political ideas of the period. Nevertheless it should be recognized that this was not the only view of politics presented to the political nation. There was also the image in the news, with its characteristic stress on conflict.

This would seem to have operated at several levels. On the most general, it helped to erode the impression of harmony and consensus conveyed in the rhetoric. One does not have to look very far in the news material to appreciate the extent to which this focused on the dramatic constitutional clashes rather than the mundane evidence of agreement. Just as parliamentary diarists, according to Russell, omitted much of the consensual rhetoric, so newsletter reports tended to concentrate on the conflict: in 1621 it was the misdeeds of monopolists and the imprisonment of M.P.s; in 1625 arguments over supply and the treatment of recusants; in 1626 the proceedings against Buckingham; and in 1628 the grievances of the subject and the struggle for the Petition of Right.[45] Similarly, one can frequently find evidence of the king himself being implicated in such conflicts, rather than being raised above them as tended to be assumed in the rhetoric. Hence in May 1626 Mead was recording that Charles had taken all Buckingham's charges on his own head and informed the Commons that 'he would make them know he was their King'; as a result it was generally thought 'that the last parliament of King Charles his reign will end within this week'. A few months later he was describing the king as 'utterly disliking' the idea of a parliament, declaring to the council that he did 'abominate that name'.[46] Such unflattering references to the king were by no means untypical, and the widespread dissemination of a portrait so much at odds with the contemporary ideal inevitably undermined the prestige of the crown and confidence in the status quo.[47]

This process was advanced a stage further by a second aspect of much of this news, the way in which it presented politics as a process involving division, struggle and the need to opppose disruptive influences. A good deal of this material was slanted against the court and tended to support a 'country' or 'oppositionist' line, that the source of political problems lay with those close to the king; however, not all of it was of this type. A small amount, at least, could be taken to imply that the cause of difficulties lay elsewhere, among elements such as the Puritans or the 'popular multitude'. The precise implications of the news could vary a good deal, according to the origins of a report or the nature of events being described. None the less, what the majority of this material had in common was a continuing stress on conflict which counterbalanced the emphasis on consensus to be found in much of the rhetoric. This point can be pursued further; before doing this, however, it is necessary to say something about the ways in which contemporaries explained political conflict, in particular the notoriously ambiguous division between 'court' and 'country'.

III

Much of the difficulty associated with the terms 'court' and 'country' can be traced back to the failure of contemporaries to uncouple their different senses. Strictly speaking, these should be separated out and their use to denote a place or source of occupation distinguished from their use in describing sets of values attached to a particular image. The problem is that by the early seventeenth century there was an increasing tendency to link the meanings together and imply that they were normally to be connected: in other words, because someone belonged to the court it was suggested that therefore they were hostile to the interests of the subject, or vice versa. Of course, as Russell, Hirst and others have demonstrated, such notions were only partially based on the 'real' situation. Some of the most powerful images of 'country' virtue and 'court' corruption derived from the the writings of those connected with the court, such as Ben Jonson or Sir Walter Ralegh; while the policy of intervention in Europe, associated with the Protestant 'country', found some of its most vociferous exponents at court, and the prerogative policies linked with the 'court' were accepted and enforced by country gentlemen.[48] In 'real' terms there was no necessary connection between place and outlook; however, it is arguable that in relation to the development of ideas this was not wholly the point. The belief that such a connection existed was gaining ground none the less. Zagorin has traced the increasing use of 'court' and 'country' in the political language of the late sixteenth and early seventeenth centuries, and Stone has described the vices and virtues which had come to be associated with each. This was a development of some significance since, as Pocock has shown, shifts in the language used to described politics frequently disclose shifts in the assumptions underpinning the political process.[49] In other words, the increasing use of 'court' and 'country' would seem to indicate a growing tendency to view politics in terms of conflict, between two sides. The process by which such a view emerged was, of course, long and complex, and rather too involved to be discussed here; however, a perceptive commentary on its internal dynamics has been provided by Lake, in his discussion of the writings of Thomas Scott, the Puritan pamphleteer.[50]

Scott used the terms to represent two ideological poles which he saw as existing in the world of politics. These poles in turn were taken to reflect more fundamental spiritual divisions between good and evil, Christ and Antichrist. Hence the 'country' assumed all the attributes of the pure and the virtuous, and became in essence a vision of a godly commonwealth such as might exist if England was reformed along Protestant lines; while the 'court' was its direct antithesis, representing corruption and wickedness and taking the form of a nation undermined by popery and the self-seeking greed of favourites. For Scott these two entities existed in a state of constant conflict within what was fundamentally a balanced and harmonious political system. The 'court' and all it stood for was continually trying to upset this balance, whereas the 'country' was entrusted with the task of restoring it and repairing the damage. This was normally to be done through a meeting of parliament, where the purifying influence of the 'country' was first of all conferred on M.P.s through free elections, and then brought to bear at the centre when they transacted business with the king. Scott, then, had a view of politics which accepted the desirability of harmony between king and subject, but at the same time identified elements at work which were upsetting this. Hence, while acknowledging that the ultimate goal was consensus, he recognized that the best way to achieve this was by promoting a dynamic tension, in which the evil of the 'court' was constantly being purged and exorcized by the purity of the 'country'. This is of considerable significance, as there is a danger of assuming that because contemporary rhetoric placed such stress on the need for harmony, ideological conflict was almost a conceptual impossibility. Scott showed how the two could exist side by side.[51]

In articulating such views he was probably in a minority, representing the more godly and radical of those who criticized the crown's policies.

Most would probably not have gone as far as Scott or expressed themselves in quite the terms described here. None the less, many of the same basic assumptions – about the way in which politics worked and the elements responsible for upsetting the balance – were shared across a broad spectrum of opinion. They can be seen reflected, for example, in the parliamentary speeches of Sir Edward Coke, which increasingly stressed the responsibilty of the 'court' for the ills of the commonwealth; or in the addresses to Cheshire freeholders made by Sir Richard Grosvenor, which identified popery close to the source of power as the main threat to stability; or even in the actions of some of the electorate, who, in counties like Yorkshire and Suffolk, were prepared to reject candidates out of hand if they believed them to have links with the court.[52] Political disruption was coming increasingly to be blamed on the 'court'; however, as has been stressed, this was not the only element to which contemporaries attached responsibility. There was also a significant body of opinion, both at court and in the provinces, which saw problems as emanating elsewhere, among anti-monarchical tendencies inherent in Puritanism and the views of the lower orders. One of the clearest public expressions of these ideas was provided in a series of tracts and sermons published to justify the king's policy of prerogative rule between 1626 and 1628.[53]

The authors of these works shared a common belief that the maintenance of the king's authority was the central guarantee of harmony and the preservation of social order. Other entities, such as parliament or the law, were seen as having a role to play in this, but it was one clearly subordinated to the divinely ordained monarch, whose position was analogous to that of a patriarch within the family. Inside this framework the cement which held society together was the principle of obedience to commands from above. Any group or individual who denied this could be seen not only as failing in the first duty of a subject, but also threatening the very foundation of hierarchy and order. Hence those taxpayers who refused to pay the forced loan could be castigated as rebels and supporters of resistance theory; Puritans who refused to conform could be seen as seeking 'parity' in both church and state; and M.P.s who spoke out in defence of their privileges or who criticized royal ministers could be regarded as attacking the prerogative and responding to the expectations of the 'popular multitude'. Such fundamental threats called for drastic remedies, and in these circumstances politics came to be presented in terms of a confrontation between the forces of order and disorder. Once again, then, conflict was envisaged as an important part of the process. The role accorded to it here was less dynamic than within the 'court'/'country' model, and its existence was seen as a sign of breakdown and failure rather than as a positive contribution to the maintenance of harmony; none the less, there was still a very similar emphasis on the need to struggle to overcome disruptive elements.

As has been stressed, these two sets of ideas represented relatively extreme positions on the political spectrum. The middle ground still lay somewhere in between, based on a consensus which had been established during the reign of Elizabeth. However, one of the features of the early seventeenth century was the way in which this middle ground was progressively eroded as a consequence of political difficulties and tensions. In the process the terms and concepts described above came to be used more and more frequently, and this in turn further undermined consensus.[54] The root cause of this development can be traced back to political conflicts, in particular the problems of the late 1620s; however, it can also be linked, at least in part, to the way in which these were represented and publicized, and with such considerations we are back with the news.

IV

Perhaps the most effective way of investigating the impact of news is to look in detail at compilations of news items made by contemporaries. Through examining their processes of selection and comment it should be possible to see something of how they reacted to the material which they received. These compilations are generally of two sorts: either collections of 'separates' and newsletters, such as that made by Davenport; or what can best be described as 'news-diaries', of the sort kept by Rous and Yonge. The 'separate' collections generally contain full transcriptions of particular documents with little or no comment; the diaries, on the other hand, show extensive evidence of their author's involvement, with summaries and abbreviations of news often accompanied by remarks as to its implications and significance.

The perspective of diarists varied considerably: Yonge was evidently a committed Protestant, concerned particularly with recording the struggles of the godly; Rous attempted to remain more detached and compile an impartial account of contemporary events; while Simonds D'Ewes, in a cipher diary which he kept as a law student in London, described his aim to 'set downe each particular day's passages of my owne life which were most memorable'.[55] These variations, however, had little effect on the basic subject-matter. All three diarists appear to have derived the major part of their information from a common stock of London news, similar to that contained in less selective collections such as Mead's letters to Stuteville. This is significant because it allows us to observe the effects of similar material on individuals of different viewpoints.

Before looking at diaries, however, it is appropriate to say something about 'separate' collections. Of these, perhaps the most informative is that kept by William Davenport. Like Rous and Yonge, he was an individual firmly rooted in his locality: he rarely visited London, had no contact with prominent figures at court and no noticeable inclination towards godliness.

He also appears to have received most of his information from news items circulating among his neighbours, which he borrowed and copied out.[56] His collection therefore again provides an insight into what was available to the interested provincial observer. As Morrill has argued, much of this consisted of court scandal, which doubtless reinforced the 'country' view of a corrupt and popist presence around the king; however, a good deal of the material went further, presenting an altogether sharper and more detailed insight. The items relating to popery, for example, included a newsletter recounting a treasonous plot involving the earl of Somerset and the Catholic nobility, which Davenport noted was 'accordinge to the truest reporte'. The records of the Spanish match included Abbot's supposed council speech, a letter purporting to be from the king of Spain – informing Gondomar that the match was simply a ploy to keep James out of the Thirty Years War – and a copy of the famous letter from Thomas Alured to Buckingham, urging him to persuade the king to follow parliament's advice against the match.[57] The fullest reports of all related to parliament, and prominent among these – and occupying some twenty closely written folios – was news of the impeachment proceedings of 1626. This included the charges made by Dr. Turner and the earl of Bristol, speeches by Sir John Eliot and Sir William Walter and, more surprisingly, a copy of the Common's final Remonstrance, which the king had attempted to remove from circulation. The last section of this summed up the view presented in much of the material:

> wee proteste to your Majestie and the whole world that, untill this great person shalbe removed from the intermedlinge with the great affairs off state, wee are out off hope off any good success; and doe feare that any monie we shall, or can, give will throughe his mis-imployment, be tourned rather to the hurt and prejudice to this youre Kingdome then otherwise.[58]

As a whole the collection was dominated by reports which would have supported the arguments being put forward by Coke or Grosvenor or Thomas Scott, and in contrast there was very little evidence for the 'court' side of the story. Davenport occasionally took copies of the king's or lord keeper's speeches, and transcribed Buckingham's reply to his charges; but taken together these amounted to no more than eight of his first sixty-five folios. The nearest that his material came to suggesting that political problems emanated outside the 'court' were a few disparaging references to Puritans – along the lines of that cited earlier in the verses relating to the 1621 Parliament – and a copy of the king's letter to the Commons in 1626, accusing them of blatant irresponsiblity in failing to provide subsidies at a time of national emergency.[59] This sort of imbalance appears to have been typical of newsletter and 'separate' collections as a whole. Apart from the occasional leak by an individual, the council made little attempt to exploit either of these media. It preferred instead to rely on the official channels of proclamation and printed treatise.[60] This meant that those who depended for their view of politics on the sort of material copied by Davenport were generally presented with a version heavily biased against the 'court'. The question remains, however, what impact would this have had on their attitudes?

On Morrill's reading of the material, this would have been relatively limited. He has concluded that Davenport:

> resented royal policies, but he does not appear to have articulated this resentment within a radical frame of reference or into any intellectualised or idealised mould whatsoever. It is a crucial distinction which separates him, and I suspect a majority of his peers, from men like Pym and Hampden, who claimed to be able to understand royal policies and sought to promote a coherent system of government and ideas.[61]

There is evidently a good deal in this. Davenport was certainly no Puritan, he had no firsthand experience of national politics and probably enjoyed no more than a smattering of legal knowledge by which to judge the constitutional precedents being established in the period. Evidently, then, one would not expect him to be able to match the insights of an experienced 'parliament man' such as Pym. However, having said this, it is also arguable that to offer such considerations as a yardstick of political comprehension is rather artificial. There was in fact a wide range of issues on which the broader assumptions maintained by someone like Pym were borne out in the material copied by Davenport; and perhaps it is this sort of overlap that we should be looking for. After all, Davenport may well have been unable to appreciate the precise importance of extensions in the prerogative, but this did not preclude him from identifying corrupt courtiers and overweening favourites as responsible for the mismanagement of government. Similarly, while he may not have held strongly Protestant opinons, his collection must still have suggested that papists and Spaniards close to the seat of power were a threat to the security of the kingdom. And if he comprehended these things, then he had grasped some of the central notions in which Pym and others traded when they spoke in the Commons or appealed for support outside.[62] A more plausible conclusion, then, might be that, although Davenport's view of politics was relatively unrefined, nevertheless it contained some of the main features of an emergent 'country' ideology, in particular the stress of parliament's role in struggling against those elements which sought to disrupt. Unfortunately, in the case of Davenport it is extremely difficult to test such a verdict since his own comments on the material were too cursory to yield any clear impression. Like most contemporaries, he felt more at home recording the news than commenting on it; however, this was not always the case, and if we turn to the 'news-diaries' it is possible to see the news being both recorded and discussed.

In some cases the impact would appear to have been relatively straight-forward. A good example is provided by a 'news-diary' covering the period from 1625 to 1627. The identity of the author has remained a mystery, beyond the fact that he was sympathetic to the godly, strongly critical of the crown, and had obvious connections with Cambridge University and the neighbouring counties of Cambridgeshire and Northamptonshire.[63] Nevertheless his comments clearly indicate the way in which regular news of national events could confirm an individual in an 'oppositionist' viewpoint. The stories he recorded were invariably of the more dramatic and sensational sort, ranging from rumours of Catholic plots and omens of catastrophe to a lengthy account of parliament's attempts to impeach Buckingham and reports of the various revenges which the duke exacted on his enemies. Amid all this, there was little space for the gentler procedures evolved for securing consensus, and this was reflected in the diarist's comments. For example, in 1625 Mr. Glanville's criticisms of Buckingham were described as 'speaking for the country against the King'; while in 1626 bishops and peers were categorized according to whether or not they appeared to side with the duke, with those opposing him being described as 'courageous' or 'of the best'. Politics was generally presented as a process involving conflict, and this was nowhere more apparent than in the references to the king. Once again what is striking is the way in which Charles was brought into the analysis and assumed to be personally responsible for many of the actions hostile to the subject. Thus he was depicted as protecting the crypto-Catholic Bishop Goodman from his own convocation, dispatching loan ships to help the Catholic king of France against the Huguenots, persecuting members of the nobility who defied the court and above all, continually defending the interests of Buckingham, to which end he was instrumental in dissolving the 1626 parliament 'to the grief of all good subjects'. These critical comments culminated in a particularly robust condemnation of the forced loan: 'The King now sets afoot his royall subsidy which, if it be yielded to, it wilbe the greatest conquest since William the Conqueror'.[64] Remarks like this were very much at odds with the presumption of the king's virtue which normally dominated the rhetoric. None the less, they represented a reasonable reflection on the record of events set down by the diarist. At work here there was, of course, a very complex interaction between the nature of the events themselves, the ways of presenting them defined by the medium and the diarist's own preconceptions; and the precise weight of each is difficult to determine. However, the end result was clear enough, and this was to present the 'court' as the most disruptive element within the political order, and conflict as the logical consequence of the need to provide a remedy.

A similar impression is to be gained from the rather different sort of diary kept by John Rous. Rous's approach to politics was altogether more conservative, and in many respects he stood in the middle ground of contemporary opinion. He claimed that 'I would alwaies speake the best of that our Kinge and State did, and thinke the best too, till I had good groundes'; and in keeping with this he laid stress on material which demonstrated the hoped-for unity between king and subject, such as the king's confirmation of the subject's liberties in his answer to the Petition of Right or the loyal celebrations which greeted the birth of his heir in 1630. He was also careful to record material which presented the 'court' version of events, copying out a set of verses by Richard Corbet which associated Puritanism with resistance theory, and referring on several occasions to the king's account of his actions in 1629 entitled *His Majestie's Declaration of the Causes Which Moved Him to Dissolve the Last Parliament*. This material was reflected in some of his comments: he expressed apprehension at the unruly behaviour of M.P.s or the over-zealous way in which Puritans condemned Arminianism; and he was particularly worried by the 'vulgar multitude', who tended always 'to speake the worst of state businesses and to nourish discontente as if there were a false carriage in all these things'.[65] Notwithstanding all this, however, there are unmistakable signs that Rous's thoughts were moving more and more in the direction suggested by the bulk of his news, towards accepting a 'country' analysis of the problems of the day.

The first indications of this are visible in the late 1620s. Rous's reports describe in considerable detail the apprehension among his neighbours as the king appeared to be embarking on a policy of prerogative government in partnership with Buckingham and a group of Arminian clerics. During the 1626 Parliament he recorded how the exclusion of the local knight of the shire, Sir Edward Coke, and the imprisonment of the Norfolk magnate, the earl of Arundel, caused 'much griefe in the country' and led to a fear that these actions were 'making way . . . for the utter bringing under of parliament power and the jealousie betwixt the King's prerogative and the freedom of the country'. In 1627 he described the reaction to the Rhé expedition among local villagers, one of them, a Mr. Paine, speaking 'distastefully of the voyage and then of the warre with France which he would make our King the cause of for not establishing the queene in her joynture'; and another, Mr. Howlett, reciting 'ould discontents for the parliament being crossed, expenses, hazard of ships, etc.'. Rous did his best to defend the king's actions and was moved to observe that:

I sawe hereby that which I had seen often before, viz: Men be disposed to speake the worst of state businesses, and to nourish discontente as if there were a false carriage in all these things, which if it were so, what would a false hearte rather see than an insurrection? a way whereunto these men prepare.

However, he himself was not immune to such doubts. These came to a head at the time of the 1629 Parliament. The apparent success of the Petition of Right was seen by many at the time as a vindication of the basic unity between king and subject; but Rous was more pessimistic, and worried particularly about the influence of those around the king. Eventually it was this which seems to have prompted him to make a long and revealing confession:

> I have all this while . . . laboured to make the best construction of all, that the subjecte might be satisfyed, least discontents should burst out to our adversarie's rejoicing; yea I have yeelded reasons for carriage of state busines . . . for the necessityes of greate supplies to the King, for the great affayres on foote. I knowe the error of the vulgar which is to judge of all things by the event and therefore to speake according to our harde successe . . . but when I heare any alledging that the whole parliament feareth some miscarrying by trechery . . . then is my mouth stopped which otherwise hath beene free to speake my reach on the King's behalfe.

Rous's fears on this score may well have been strengthened by the events of the 1630s – since on several occasions he noted the disturbing influence of Henrietta Maria – but in general his comments are too brief to present a clear picture. However, by 1642 there is little doubt that he had come to share the views of John Pym and his associates that the source of the current difficulties was a 'malignant party' close to the king. 'I conceive', he recorded:

> (as the Parliament) that His Majestie is abused and I conceive of the Malignant Party. . . as of cheators, that desire to be believed till they have fully gulled the foole they have in handling . . . Some yet call Parliament side Roundheads, who be themselves, in requitall, called Malignants . . . but what title they deserve let themselves judge, who hate reformation and wold bring in tyrannie.

In these circumstances he also seems to have believed that, although peace and harmony were obviously desirable, this was unlikely to be achieved without some sort of armed struggle.[66] From a different perspective, then, his diary confirms what has already been argued, that the publicity given to clashes at the centre, and the way these were presented in the news, contributed to undermining faith in the established order.

Much the same can be seen from a third example, the diary of Walter Yonge. As a trained lawyer and friend of the parliamentarian Sir Walter Earle, Yonge was better equipped than many to appreciate the subtleties and nuances of politics at the centre; yet this did not prevent him from seeing alignments in relatively clear-cut terms. At some stage, towards the end of James's reign, he began noting what he called 'the Plagues of England', each of which was indicated by a number or symbol in the margin of his diary.[67] The earlier examples of these consisted of obvious material threats such as the spread of disease, bad weather or trade recession; however, as the reign progressed he began to draw attention to problems of a more political nature: the Spanish match and attempts to grant toleration to Catholics, purges of J.P.s with Puritan sympathies, the premature dissolution of the 1621 Parliament and the unparliamentary benevolence of 1622. Yonge came to abandon this habit of recording 'Plagues' soon after the accession of Charles, and one of the last to be noted was the billeting of soldiers after the return from Cadiz.[68] None the less, he continued to comment on the news and noted, with equal concern, what he seems to have regarded as a related series of developments: the extravagance and waste of money at court, the corruption of those entrusted with supplying naval expeditions, and the frequency with which those questioned in parliament for misdemeanours were promptly released and promoted by the king. This seems to have led him increasingly to view national politics in terms of two sides, one of which represented the interests of the subject and one of which clearly did not. This much is suggested in a note he made alongside a copy of one of Wentworth's speeches in the 1628 Parliament, describing him as a 'Turnecoate'; and it emerges even more clearly from the way in which he labelled each of the judges in Hampden's case as either 'pro patria' or 'pro rege'.[69] The comment on Wentworth may have been added later but, taken together with the news items he recorded, both descriptions surely gave an indication of the direction in which his attitudes were moving and demonstrated that he was increasingly accustomed to thinking in terms of 'adversarial politics'. In this sense he was far from unique. His diary is, perhaps, distinctive in that it gives a relatively long perspective on the development of such a view, showing how a staunch Protestant could move from a concern with external events and enemies abroad to a whole series of problems closer to home; but in most other respects it supports the impression gained elsewhere, that news encouraged contemporaries to view politics in terms of conflict.

V

This article has argued, in line with the Whig view, that news contributed to a process of political polarization in the early seventeenth century. In particular, it has been emphasized that the image of politics presented in the news was very different from that contained in contemporary rhetoric: it suggested that conflict and struggle were as much a feature of the process as the deference and willingness to compromise implied in clichés about unity. However, the effects of news should not be exaggerated. While it undoubtedly helped to shape political opinion, the link between this opinion and political action was by no means straightforward.

At the most obvious level it can be observed that those who received news hostile to the 'court' did not automatically become opponents of the crown. News was not the only influence which shaped their view of politics, and the way this view was applied in any given situation depended on the character and circumstances of the individual involved. Hence the fact that in 1642 William Davenport, far from siding with parliament, was at best neutral and on some accounts a royalist, should not be taken to deny the significance of news. Davenport's actions were probably influenced in part by recent royalist propaganda, which appropriated to the crown some of the virtues earlier associated with the 'country'; but they were also a function of external pressures and his own perceptions of immediate and long-term advantage.[70]

In relation to this it should also be noted that political awareness of the sort engendered by the news did not necessarily lead to open discussion of political issues. There were various constraints operating to inhibit such discussion, particularly at a local level. Some of these were imposed by the privy council whose policing discouraged not only public criticism of its actions, but also such statements in private correspondence, which was liable to be intercepted and examined.[71] Others developed out of the widespread concern to promote political harmony. Opinions differed as to precisely how this was to be attained, but many accepted that open expression of political grievances should be confined to parliament. Any attempt to channel these through the institutions of local government was liable to be regarded as disruptive both by the council and by local magnates; and the only obvious local platform for such matters was the parliamentary election, where much depended on the existence of a contest and the attitudes of leading protagonists.[72] Hence, at a provincial level, the interest shown in political news rarely translated into public debate. Letter-writers and local politicians – at least before 1640 – tended to reserve their opinions for the relative security of private conversation or an entry in their 'news-diary'.[73] This helps to explain why local historians have uncovered only limited evidence of such concerns.

The direct impact of news, then, should not be overestimated. Nevertheless its importance in shaping and developing political opinion remained considerable. This had been true in earlier periods when episodes such as the Pilgrimage of Grace demonstrated the effects of news and rumour.[74] However, by the early seventeeth century it had developed certain traits which enhanced its significance. One of the most notable of these was the way in which news had come to be centralized and directed through London, thus highlighting events which affected the whole nation, such as a meeting of parliament. This enabled politicians to manipulate and mobilize public opinion to a much greater extent than had been possible previously, which in turn helped to develop such manipulation as a deliberate political strategy. Thus, during the 1620s, politicians who opposed the Spanish match and the forced loan were able to organize campaigns of resistance which existed independently of parliament and the court; and the technique of appealing directly to public opinion was used to particular effect in the Grand Remonstrance of 1641.[75] Another notable development was the increase in the distribution of national news to the 'middling sort' and the lower orders. The effects of this are difficult to measure, but it is at least clear – from the descriptions given by Rous and others – that the literate yeomen, who comprised the bulk of county freeholders, were now capable of discussing national politics with considerable sophistication. Moreover they often appear to have done so in terms which omitted the consensual phraseology and polite restraint of their social superiors. This helps to explain a tendency which has been noted elsewhere, for the lower orders to view politics in terms of radical and clear-cut distinctions.[76]

As this last example indicates, the precise effects of news are often barely discernible or recoverable amid the various influences shaping political opinion. None the less, on the evidence presented here it is reasonable to conclude that news did contribute to a process of polarization. And it is finally worth noting that in this, as in many other aspects of the period, the instincts and judgements of S.R. Gardiner remain a reliable guide. One of the sources to which he attached most weight in assessing the development of public opinion was the printed collection of Mead's newsletters.[77] This article suggests that he was right to do so.

Notes

1 D. Hirst, *The Representative of the People?* (Cambridge, 1975), pp. 132–88; C. Hill, 'Parliament and People in Seventeenth-Century England', *P&P*, 92 (Aug. 1981), pp. 100–24; A. Fletcher and C. Hill, 'Debate: Parliament and People in Seventeenth-Century England', *P&P*, 98 (Feb. 1983), pp. 151–8; J.S. Morrill, *The Revolt of the Provinces* (London, 1976), pp. 13–31; C. Holmes, 'The County Community in Stuart Historiography' (Chapter 8 in this volume); D. Hirst, 'Revisionism Revised: Two Perspectives on Early Stuart Parliamentary History: The Place of Principle', *P & P*, 92 (Aug. 1981), pp. 79–99; J.H. Hexter, 'Power Struggle, Parliament and Liberty in Early Stuart England', *JMH*, 50 (1978), pp. 24–30.

2 P. Zagorin, *The Court and the Country* (London, 1969), pp. 106–8; L. Stone, *The Causes of the English Revolution, 1529–1642* (London, 1972), p. 91.

3 Hirst, *Representative of the People?*, p. 145; Morrill, *Revolt of the Provinces*, pp. 22–3; C.S.R. Russell, *Parliaments and English Politics, 1621–1629* (Oxford, 1979), pp. 78–9, 164–84, 233–4, 249–51.

4 Holmes, 'County Community in Stuart Historiography', pp. 61, 65–7; A.L. Hughes, 'Warwickshire on the Eve of the Civil War: "A County Community"?', *MH*, 7 (1982), pp. 56–9; Hill, 'Parliament and People in Seventeenth-Century England', pp. 115-18; D. Hirst, 'Court, Country and Politics before 1629', in K. Sharpe (ed.), *Faction and Parliament* (Oxford, 1978), pp. 134–7.

5 A. Fletcher, *The Outbreak of the English Civil War* (London, 1981), pp. xxv–xxx, 191–227.

6 J. Frank, *The Beginnings of the English Newspaper, 1620–1660* (Cambridge, Mass., 1961), pp. 5–7, 14.

7 S.L. Adams, 'Captain Thomas Gainsford, the *Vox Spiritus* and the *Vox Populi*', *BIHR*, 49 (1976), pp. 141–4; *CD 1629*, pp. xx–xli; F.J. Levy, 'How Information Spread among the Gentry, 1550–1640', *JBS*, 21 (1982), pp. 20–4.

8 Holmes, 'County Community in Stuart Historiography', p. 61; G. Cranfield, *The Press and Society* (London, 1978), pp. 5–10; W. Notestein, *Four Worthies* (London, 1956), pp. 29–119; *The Works of Ben Jonson*, ed. F. Cunningham and W. Gifford, 9 vols (London, 1875), vii, p. 336.

9 W.S. Powell, *John Pory, 1572–1636* (Chapel Hill, 1977), pp. 55–8. Scudamore also employed at least eight other correspondents during the 1620s and 1630s, including Amerigo Salvetti, the Tuscan envoy, Sir John Finett, the master of ceremonies at court, and Ralph Starkey, a London antiquary: PRO, C. 115/M. 25–37, N. 1–8 (I am grateful to Kevin Sharpe for drawing my attention to this collection).

10 BL, Harleian MSS. 389, 390.

11 *P in P 1628*, I, pp. 4–20; Russell, *Parliaments and English Politics*, p. 389.

12 *The Diary of Walter Yonge*, ed. G. Roberts (Camden Soc., 1st ser., xli, London, 1848), *passim*; BL, Harleian MS. 7010, fo. 212^r (I am grateful to Ann Hughes for this reference); J.S. Morrill, 'William Davenport and the "Silent Majority" of Early Stuart England', *Jl. Chester Archaeol. Soc.*, lviii (1975), pp. 118–21; Eaton Hall, Cheshire (hereafter E.H.), Grosvenor MS., no. 53; HMC, *Third Report, Appendix* (London, 1872), pp. 210–16. For a discussion of the factual accuracy of 'separates', see *P in P*, I, pp. 9–14.

13 *Wentworth Papers*, p. 266; Adams, 'Captain Thomas Gainsford', p. 144 n.; BL Add. MS 28640, fos. 92–100.

14 PRO, C. 115/N. 4; *Companion to Arber*, ed. W.W. Greg (Oxford, 1967), pp. 176–8; *CD 1629*, pp. xxxiii–xxxiv; E.H., Grosvenor MS., no. 45, pp. 143–50; A.L. Hughes, 'Politics, War and Society in Warwickshire, *c.* 1620–1650' (Univ. of Liverpool Ph.D. thesis, 1980), pp. 153–5.

15 *CD 1629*, pp. xxxi–xxxii; Hirst, *Representative of the People?*, pp. 179–80; Hughes, 'Warwickshire on the Eve of the Civil War'. p. 121; P. Clark *English Provincial Society from the Reformation to the Revolution: Religion, Politics and Society in Kent, 1500–1640* (Hassocks, 1977), pp. 219–20; Morrill, 'William Davenport', pp. 118–21. For 'separate' collections belonging to Davenport's Cheshire neighbours, see John Rylands Lib., Manchester, Leigh of Lyme MS., unfoliated; Chetham Lib., Manchester, MS. A. 6.8, A. 6.17, and Eng. MS. 293; CCRO, C.R. 63/2/21.

16 K. Wrightson, *English Society, 1580–1680* (London, 1982), pp. 193–9; A.M. Everitt, *Change in the Provinces* (Leicester, 1969), pp. 21–6, 38–43; M. Spufford, *Small Books and Pleasant Histories* (London, 1981; repr. Cambridge, 1985), pp. 111–26; *Letters of John Holles, 1587–1637*, ed. P.R. Seddon, 2 vols (Thoroton Soc., record ser., xxxi, xxxv, Nottingham, 1975–83), II, p. 314; N.L.W., Wynn of Gwydir MSS, 1389, 1391.

17 *C and T, Chas I*, I, pp. 164, 190, 207; Powell, *John Pory*, pp. 56–7; *The Diary of*

John Rous, ed. M.A. Everett Green (Camden Soc., 1st ser., lxvi, London, 1856).

18 *Diary of John Rous*, pp. v–x, 10–12, 31, 44–5.
19 *Diary of John Rous*, pp. 2–3, 5, 8, 10–11, 14–18, 31–3, 47; BL, Add. MS 28640, fo. 102 (this is a commonplace book belonging to Rous).
20 BL, Add. MS 48057, fo. 54; W.A. Hunt, *The Puritan Moment* (Cambridge, Mass., 1983), pp. 261–2; *Diary of John Rous*, pp. 18–22; *Poems and Songs Relating to George Villiers, Duke of Buckingham*, ed. F.W. Fairholt (Percy Soc., xxix, London, 1850), p. 6. The libellous ballad about Buckingham had the refrain 'The cleane, contrary way' (*Poems and Songs Relating to George Villiers, Duke of Buckingham*, pp. 10–13).
21 CCRO, C.R. 63/2/19, fos: 26^v–27^r.
22 See, for example, BL, Satirical Prints, no. 91 (1621), 'The Description of Giles Mompesson Late Knight, Censured by Parliament'.
23 CCRO, C.R. 63/2/19, fo. 3^v.
24 P. Burke, *Popular Culture in Early Modern Europe* (London, 1978), pp. 91–148; M.E. James, *Family, Lineage and Civil Society* (Oxford, 1975), pp. 78–80.
25 *Diary of John Rous*, pp. 18–22; *Poems and Songs Relating to George Villiers, Duke of Buckingham*, pp. 19–24. There are several different versions of this popular rhyme; I have quoted from the fullest of those I have found. For other versions, see CCRO, C.R. 63/2/19, fos. 62^v–64^r; PRO, H.C.A. 30/854 (I am grateful to David Hebb for this reference).
26 Burke, *Popular Culture in Early Modern Europe*, pp. 150–5.
27 Gardiner, *History*, VI, pp. 59–121; Russell, *Parliaments and English Politics*, pp. 260–322.
28 Wrightson stresses the 'widening fissure between polite and plebeian culture', but also draws attention to the overlap in certain areas: Wrightson, *English Society*, pp. 182–221.
29 Levy, 'How Information Spread', p. 23; Clark, *English Provincial Society from the Reformation to the Revolution*, p. 219. For further examples, see the letter collections of Sir John Wynn of Gwydir or the Leighs of Lyme Park, which indicate the regular receipt of news from 1620 onwards but not before: N.L.W., Wynn of Gwydir MSS., *passim*; John Rylands Lib., Leigh of Lyme MSS., *passim*.
30 Levy, 'How Information Spread', p. 22; Notestein, *Four Worthies*, p. 31 n.
31 Holmes, 'County Community in Stuart Historiography', pp. 62–5; R. Ashton, *The English Civil War* (London, 1978), p. 70; Clark, *English Provincial Society from the Reformation to the Revolution*, pp. 216–20; V. Morgan, 'The Cartographic Image of 'the Country' in Early-Modern England', *TRHS*, 5th ser., XXIX (1979), pp. 129–54.
32 Notestein, *Four Worthies*, p. 31 n; Pearl, 'London Puritans and Scotch Fifth Columnists: A Mid-Seventeenth Century Phenomenon', in A.E.J. Hollaender and W. Kellaway (eds), *Studies in London History* (London, 1969), p. 317, and the picture of the Exchange facing p. 316.
33 *C and T, Chas I*, I, pp. 134, 143, 190; N.L.W., Wynn of Gwydir MSS., 889–1445; *Diary of Walter Yonge*, pp. 94–5.
34 PRO, S.P. 16/10/16; *C and T, Chas I*, I, pp. 55–6; N.L.W., Wynn of Gwydir MS., 1389; *C and T., Chas I*, II, pp. 106–11 (I am grateful to Ann Hughes for this reference).
35 M.F. Keeler, *The Long Parliament* (Proc. Amer. Phil. Soc., XXXVI, Philadelphia, 1954), p. 404; *Diary of Walter Yonge*, *passim*.
36 *Diary of Walter Yonge*, pp. 90, 98–100, 109–11.

37 *Diary of John Rous*, p. 14; BL, Harleian MS. 390, fo. 356^v; *Letters of John Holles*, II, pp. 376–7; Nottingham Univ. Lib., Ne.C. 15404, p. 210.

38 Hirst, *Representative of the People?*, pp. 178–81; Russell, *Parliaments and English Politics*, pp. 19–22, 388–9.

39 R.P. Cust, 'Charles I, the Privy Council and the Forced Loan', *JBS*, 24 (1985), pp. 208–35; *Letters of John Holles*, II, p. 345; *Diary of John Rous*, p. 3; HMC, *Report on the MSS of the Duke of Buccleuch and Queensberry*, 3 vols (London, 1899–1926), III, p. 312; *C and T, Chas I*, I, pp. 164, 208; Rushworth, I, p. 472.

40 R.P. Cust, 'The Forced Loan and English Politics, 1626–1628' (Univ. of London Ph.D. thesis, 1983), pp. 112–15.

41 P.A. Welsby, *George Abbot: The Unwanted Archbishop* (London, 1962), pp. 108–10; PRO, S.P. 16/150/54–7; BRO, Reading, Trumbull MS., xvii, pp. 101–2 (I am grateful to Tom Cogswell for this reference). Copies of Abbot's speech are to be found in Rous's and Davenport's commonplace books; BL, Add. MS. 28640, fo. 112; CCRO, C.R. 63/2/19, fo. 35^r.

42 For a discussion of this tendency in reports of parliament, see C.S.R. Russell, 'Parliamentary History in Perspective, 1604–1629' (Chapter 1 above).

43 *C and T, Chas I*, I, pp. 56, 58, 251, 328, 331; G.E. Aylmer, 'St. Patrick's Day, 1628, in Witham, Essex', *P & P*, no. 61 (Nov. 1973), pp. 139–48.

44 M. Kishlansky, 'The Emergence of Adversary Politics in the Long Parliament' (Chapter 2 in this volume); Russell, *Parliaments and English Politics*, pp. 53–4; M. Judson, *The Crisis of the Constitution* (New Brunswick, 1949), pp. 1–107; R.P. Cust and P.G. Lake, 'Sir Richard Grosvenor and the Rhetoric of Magistracy', *BIHR*, LIV (1981), pp. 46–8; *Wentworth Papers*, pp. 152–5.

45 Russell, *Parliaments and English Politics*, p. xix; *C and T, Jas I*, II, pp. 234–84; *C and T, Chas I*, I, pp. 40, 86–104, 346–64. Newsletters sometimes included dramatic detail which was omitted from the diaries: Hill, 'Parliament and People in Seventeenth-Century England', p. 111.

46 *C and T, Chas I*, I, p. 104; BL, Harleian MS., 390, fo. 132.

47 *Diary of John Rous*, pp. 2–3; Trinity Coll. Lib., Cambridge (hereafter TCLC), MS. 0.7.3, fo. 4^v (I am grateful to Maija Cole for this reference).

48 Russell, *Parliaments and English Politics*, pp. 5–26; Hirst, 'Court, Country and Politics', pp. 33–7; L. Stone, *The Crisis of the Aristocracy, 1558–1641* (Oxford, 1965), pp. 392–4; Cust, 'Forced Loan and English Politics', pp. 376–91.

49 Zagorin, *Court and Country*, pp. 33–9; Stone, *Causes of the English Revolution*, pp. 105–8; J.G.A. Pocock, *Politics, Language and Time* (London, 1972), pp. 3–41.

50 P.G. Lake, 'Constitutional Consensus and Puritan Opposition in the 1620s: Thomas Scott and the Spanish Match', *HJ*, 25 (1982), pp. 805–25.

51 This paragraph is based on Lake's 'Constitutional Consensus and Puritan Opposition in the 1620s'. I am greatly indebted to this, and to more general discussions with the author.

52 S.D. White, *Sir Edward Coke and the Grievances of the Commonwealth* (Manchester, 1979), pp. 18–23, 187–276; Cust and Lake, 'Sir Richard Grosvenor', pp. 40–53; Hirst, 'Court, Country and Politics', p. 136; *Strafforde Letters*, I, pp. 10–13; Hexter, 'Power Struggle, Parliament and Liberty', pp. 27–8; *Winthrop Papers*, 5 vols (Massachusetts Hist. Soc., Cambridge, Mass., 1929–47), I, pp. 324–6.

53 C. Hill, 'The Many Headed Monster', in his *Change and Continuity in Seventeenth-Century England* (London, 1974), pp. 181–204; Laud, I, pp. 63–90; Matthew Wren, *A Sermon Preached before the King's Majestie on Sunday 17th of February last, at Whitehall* (Cambridge, 1627, S.T.C. 26015) (I am

grateful to Johann Somerville for drawing my attention to this); Robert Sibthorpe, *Apostolike Obedience* (London, 1627, S.T.C. 22525·5); Isaac Bargrave, *A Sermon Preached before King Charles, March 27th 1627: Being the Anniversary of His Majestie's Inauguration* (London, 1627, S.T.C. 1414); Roger Manwaring, *Religion and Allegiance* (London, 1627, S.T.C. 17751). These sermons are discussed at greater length in Cust, 'Forced Loan and English Politics, pp. 31–3, 83–9.

54 Cust, 'Forced Loan and English Politics', pp. 406–14; Hirst, 'Court, Country and Politics', pp. 133–7.

55 *Diary of Walter Yonge, passim*; *Diary of John Rous*, pp. x-xi, 109 (see also his comments on Scott's *Vox populi*: BL, Add. MS. 28640, fo. 100); *The Diary of Sir Simonds D'Ewes, 1622–1624*, ed. E. Bourcier (Publications de la Sorbonne, v, Paris, 1974), p. 38.

56 Morrill, 'William Davenport', pp. 115–17, 121.

57 Morrill, 'William Davenport', pp. 118–19; CCRO, C.R. 63/2/19, fos. 24ʳ–25ᵛ, 35ᵛ, 36ᵛ.

58 CCRO, C.R. 63/2/19, fos. 41ᵛ, 43ʳ–45ʳ, 56ᵛ–57ᵛ.

59 CCRO, C.R. 63/2/19, 19ᵛ, 27ʳ, 37ʳ–38ᵛ, 45ᵛ, 51ᵛ, 52ᵛ–56ʳ, 60ᵛ–61ᵛ.

60 It is significant that in 1621 the council failed to follow up a suggestion by Pory and others, that they be licensed to print a 'gazette of weekly occurants', intended 'to establish a speedy . . . way whereby to dispense into the veynes of the whole body of a state such matter as may best temper it . . . to the disposition of the head and principall members': Powell, *John Pory*, pp. 52–3. The council's approach reflected the distaste expressed by both James and Charles at the prospect of popular discussion of political affairs: *Proclamations*, I, pp. 495–6, 519–21; BRO, Trumbull Misc. MS., XVIII, 82, 104, and XXV, unfol. For an important departure from the normal approach, in which Buckingham and Charles appear to have employed the theatre to explain their opposition to the Spanish match, see T.E. Cogswell, 'Thomas Middleton and the Court, 1624: *A Game at Chess* in Context', *HLQ*, 47 (1984), pp. 273–88.

61 Morrill, 'William Davenport', p. 122.

62 Morrill, 'William Davenport', pp. 115–17; Morrill, *Revolt of the Provinces*, pp. 23–4; C.S.R. Russell, 'The Parliamentary Career of John Pym, 1621–1629', in P. Clark, A.G.R. Smith and N.R.N. Tyacke (eds), *The English Commonwealth, 1547–1640* (Leicester, 1979), pp. 147–65; A.L. Hughes, 'The Civil War and the Provinces', in C. Hill, A.L. Hughes, A. Laurence and A.L. Morton, *The Revolution and its Impact: Seventeenth-Century England: A Changing Culture, 1618–1689* (Open Univ., Milton Keynes, 1981), pp. 15–18.

63 TCLC, MS. 0.7.3, fos. 3–10.

64 TCLC, MS. 0.7.3, fos. 3–4, 5ʳ, 7ᵛ, 8ᵛ.

65 *Diary of John Rous*, pp. 4–6, 12, 19, 36–9, 40–1, 43.

66 *Diary of John Rous*, pp. 2–19, 49–50, 123–5, 131; Fletcher, *Outbreak of the English Civil War*, pp. 42–90, 125–57.

67 Keeler, *Long Parliament*, p. 404; *Diary of Walter Yonge*, pp. xxvii–xxxii, 82 n., 109–10. The 'Plagues' are not always indicated in the printed edition of Yonge's diary. I have therefore used the original manuscript: BL, Add. MS. 28032.

68 BL, Add. MS. 28032, fos. 9ᵛ, 10ᵛ, 12ᵛ, 13ᵛ, 23ʳ–24ᵛ, 29ᵛ–30ʳ, 31ʳ, 32ʳ, 36ʳ, 37ʳ⁻ᵛ, 39ʳ–40ᵛ, 42ᵛ–43ᵛ, 46ʳ–51ʳ, 54ᵛ, 64ʳ.

69 *Diary of Walter Yonge*, pp. 89, 98, 115; BL, Add. MS. 35331, fos. 11ᵛ, 68ᵛ.

70 Morrill, 'William Davenport', pp. 122–7; J. Daley, 'The Implications of Royalist Politics, 1642–1646', *HJ*, 27 (1984), pp. 745–55.

71 D. Hirst, 'The Privy Council and Problems of Enforcement in the 1620s', *JBS*,

18 (1978), pp. 50–1; Holmes, 'County Community in Stuart Historiography', pp. 65–6; *Calendar of the Correspondence of the Smyth Family of Ashton Court, 1548–1642*, ed. J.H. Bettey (Bristol Rec. Soc., XXXV, Gloucester, 1982), pp. 93–4 (I am grateful to James Robertson for this reference). Most contemporary letter-writers adhered to the advice given by the earl of Clare to his son, never to 'put yourself into any man's curtesy under the witnes of your own hand, especially to be a critike in state matters': *Letters of John Holles*, ed. Seddon, II, p. 314.

72 G.R. Elton, 'Tudor Government: The Points of Contact: I, Parliament', *TRHS*, 5th ser., 24 (1974), pp. 183–200; Hirst, 'Court, Country and Politics', pp. 131–3; Hirst, *Representative of the People?*, pp. 109–53. There was widespread acquiescence in the dictum of Sir Thomas Wentworth, 'never to contend with the Prerogative out of Parliament': *Strafforde Letters*, I, pp. 34–5. Grand-jury presentments were sometimes used as a means of publicizing broad political grievances, particularly during the 1630s; but this could result in recriminations against those involved: E.S. Cope, 'Politics without Parliament: The Dispute about Muster Master's Fees in Shropshire in the 1630s', *HLQ*, 45 (1982), pp. 271–84; T.G. Barnes, *Somerset, 1625–1640* (London, 1961), p. 226.

73 For a striking example of the breadth and sophistication of private discussions, see K. Fincham, 'The Judges' Decision on Ship Money in February 1637: The Reaction in Kent', *BIHR*, 57 (1984), pp. 230–7. After 1640 the situation was transformed by the collapse of council controls, and encouragement to express political opinions coming from the centre: Fletcher, *Outbreak of the English Civil War, passim*.

74 C.S.L. Davies, 'The Pilgrimage of Grace Reconsidered', *P & P* 41 (Dec. 1968), pp. 62, 69–74. For the role of news and rumour more generally in this period, see G.R. Elton, *Policy and Police* (Cambridge, 1972), pp. 46–170.

75 L.B. Wright, 'Propaganda against James I's "Appeasement of Spain"', *HLQ*, 6 (1942–3), pp. 149–72; Cust, 'Forced Loan and English Politics', pp. 265–92, 361–71; Fletcher, *Outbreak of the English Civil War*, pp. 81–90, 145–51.

76 D. Hirst, 'Unanimity in the Commons, Aristocratic Intrigues, and the Origins of the English Civil War', *JMH*, 50 (1978), pp. 59–60; Hill, 'Parliament and People in Seventeenth-Century England', pp. 115–18.

77 Gardiner, *History*, VI, pp. 131, 150, 154–8.

10

The king, the parliament and the localities during the English Civil War

ANN HUGHES

Debate over the nature of central-local relationships has played an important part in recent discussion of the origins and course of the English Civil War. It is an oversimplification, but not a caricature, to say that two distinct sets of views are current. The first, and in many ways the most consistent and coherent, arguments are those found in the work of the local historians who have developed the idea of the county community as the most important focus for the activities of the provincial gentry and, in more general form, in Morrill's *The Revolt of the Provinces* and Hutton's *The Royalist War Effort*.[1] In this work a clear separation is seen between local and national issues or preoccupations. The majority of the county gentry, and still more the ranks below them, were ill informed about national developments and concerned with the activites of central government mainly as they affected the stability of their local communities. Only a small minority of activists were genuinely committed to the royalist or the parliamentarian side of the civil war; the most characteristic provincial response to the divisions of 1642 was reluctance to become involved as shown both in widespread neutralism among individuals and in collective attempts at local pacification. Gradually the whole of England was drawn, willy-nilly, into the war, but allegiance was determined largely by contingent military factors: the proximity of London or of the king's army or the relative effectiveness of the small numbers of local partisans.[2] The war itself, in this framework, is a story of the ways in which activists on either side extracted the necessary resources of men and money from largely antagonistic or apathetic local communities. As Hutton has vividly remarked, 'It is becoming obvious that there were two civil wars, the formal struggle between the rival partisans, and the struggle between those partisans and the bulk of the population, whose support they attempted to enlist for their war effort.'[3] Here the local communities are perceived as

The author would like to thank Anthony Fletcher, Ian Gentles, Clive Holmes, John Morrill, Richard Cust, Peter Lake, and Colin Phillips. This article was first presented at the Anglo-American Conference in July 1983. Later versions were given to the Manchester Historical Association and to students at Birmingham University and Leicester University. It is intended as a contribution to the ongoing debate over localism and the causes of the English Revolution rather than as a fixed argument.

the victims of the two national war machines, but certainly not as passive victims. Everitt, Hutton, Morrill, and others have all emphasized that it was indeed a struggle to mobilize local resources for the war, a struggle in which the committed were opposed continually by dogged provincial cussedness and occasionally by armed resistance, as in the club risings or in the 'revolt of the provinces' – the second civil war of 1648.[4] As a whole, this body of work provides a neat and comprehensive explanation of the period: it offers a model of central–local relationships in which the central and the local are seen as fairly distinct and usually antagonistic spheres; it comprehends the course of the war as well as the outbreak; and finally, in the work of Morrill in particular, it contributes to an explanation of why the parliamentarians won. Parliament's victory is attributed to its greater success in *overcoming localism* and thus mobilizing the resources needed to defeat the king. Parliament's war machine, its 'administrative and legal tyranny,' was more ruthless and arbitrary than anything the royalists were able to construct.[5]

There remain, however, reasons for scepticism about this framework. In the first place, the model of central–local relationships on which it is based has been challenged. The work of Holmes, besides my own on Warwickshire, has suggested that the 'county community' did not necessarily form a discrete and all-important arena for the social and political activities of the local gentry.[6] In these and similar studies the local and the national are not portrayed as separate or conflicting spheres. Rather, the close and complex integration of central and local interests within a national culture and a national administrative and political structure is emphasized. Alone among the major states of early modern Europe, England had a uniform legal system, crucially dependent at many points on local implementation. Through the royal court, the privy council and parliament there were many avenues through which local factional struggles could become bound up with national politics.[7] One of the most important ways by which the integration of the central and the local was achieved, in the 1620s and again in 1640–42, was through the workings of the house of commons. M.P.s were of course dependent on various kinds of local influence for their place in this national body and were, as Hirst has shown, frequently regarded as the representatives of their constituents. In this role they began by seeking redress for local grievances, but often their similar experiences became generalized into national political positions. An excellent illustration of the way in which parliament facilitated the complex interaction between local and national concerns has been provided by Fletcher's account of the petitioning campaigns in the early years of the Long Parliament. The ritual presentation of a petition to parliament was a vivid embodiment of the links between centre and localities; the petitioning process could act both as a means by which provincial opinion could be educated by more sophisticated Westminster politicians and as an opportunity for local people to influence national developments.[8]

Here is is proposed that this second body of work provides a more convincing account of the general nature of central–local relationships in early modern England and a more balanced view of the degree of potential political or ideological commitment at the outbreak of the civil war. Fletcher, for example, concluded in his comprehensive study of the outbreak, 'It is hard to believe, in view of everything that has been said in this book about the interaction of Westminster and the localities since November 1640, that many well informed men were pure neutrals at heart,' although he is careful to emphasize that a variety of more pragmatic considerations could influence actual behaviour.[9] The argument of this article is thus set within the second framework, a framework of intimate integration and interaction between the centre and the localities, with provincial communities not held to be automatically unwilling to become involved in the national divisions of the 1640s (which is not to say that there was great eagerness to join an armed conflict). It is clear, however, that this 'integrationist' framework has not yet attained the overall coherence of the interpretation founded on a stronger notion of the 'county community,' and some of the difficulties must be touched on before alternative approaches are suggested.

One obvious problem in the integrationist approach is that historians working within this framework have concentrated either on the pre-civil war period or, for the 1640s, on parallels and interconnections between local struggles and national political divisions on the parliamentarian side alone.[10] Very little work on royalist areas has been done by historians sceptical about the county community or about automatic tensions between local and national interests. Consequently, the coherence and the comparative dimension of Hutton's or Morrill's work have been lacking. Some of the work on parliamentarians has tended to deny any independent integrity to local preoccupations and has been too ready to collapse local struggles into preconceived national political divisions. Most important, there has been no general challenge to the extractive and coercive model of the relationship between local communities and the two sides in the civil war. Indeed, whatever their general views of local–central interactions in this period, most historians have accepted this model, agreeing that parliament's greater success in overcoming localism was a major contribution to its victory.[11]

This conclusion would seem to be the weakest element in all discussions of central–local relationships during the civil war. In the work of historians who have challenged the idea of the 'county community' it seems illogical to argue on the one hand that a close and consistent interrelationship between the centre and the provinces was an essential characteristic of the English political system before 1642 but on the other hand that parliament's success was due to its drastic reorienting of this accustomed balance. This logical problem is only overcome by underestimating the vitality of local loyalties and defining localism as an essentially negative impulse. There are equally serious drawbacks in the work of historians who do give a more prominent role to localist concerns, for the explanation of parliament's victory relies heavily, in the analysis of Morrill especially, on a very high opinion of the efficiency and ruthlessness of the parliamentary 'tyranny' erected in the 1640s. But the view that the task facing royalists or parliamentarians was simply to enforce their commands on an unwilling local population is surely inappropriate in the context of an early modern state, particularly a state as bureaucratically weak as seventeenth-century England. Early modern states lacked the resources to coerce their populations indefinitely; their political processes were based rather on negotiation and cooperation, particularly between central government and local elites. The armies raised during the civil war were not formidable enough to alter these processes completely, especially given the problems of political legitimacy faced by both sides after the cleavage of 1642.[12]

Further problems about the view that localism needed to be overcome are raised by the increasing amount of work done on royalist organization during the war. Roy's conclusion – 'the more closely the royalist army is studied, the less certain it becomes that the outcome of the civil war was inevitable' – has been endorsed by later research. Wanklyn, like Roy, has denied that parliament's resources were overwhelmingly superior, while Hutton has demonstrated a hitherto unrealized capacity for efficient mobilization by the royalist war machine. Frequently, however, we are now left with an attenuated and ultimately unsatisfactory explanation of parliament's success. Hutton and Wanklyn have suggested that parliament's virutally unchallenged control of war-free East Anglia gave its cause a sounder basis than royalist supremacy in the war-torn north and west could provide and that finally the royalists lost because they were beaten at Marston Moor and Naseby, defeats attributed largely to contingent tactical and strategic factors.[13] Clearly military factors cannot be ignored, but nonetheless such conclusions raise other, political, questions. Why did parliament secure a war-free area at the start of the war, leaving the king with the battleground – particularly given the research showing more royalist than parliamentarian support among senior gentry in many regions? Why was the royalist war effort so much less resilient, so much worse equipped to deal with the aftermath of failure in major battles, compared with parliament's survival during the difficulties of 1643?

Hence it is necessary to accept some of the premises of the 'county community' historians about the strength and vitality of localism but to reflect, or even reverse, their conclusion on the outcome of the war. Overcoming localism was not the key to victory in the civil war. Rather, in a political system characterized above all by an inextricable intertwining of local and national concerns, the political basis for victory involved the harnessing of local interests, cooperation with, not a challenge to, localism, and the maintenance of the maximum of harmony between the local and the national. Parliament, for a variety of structural, institutional, and ideological reasons, was better able to work with localism than was the king; and the parliamentarian war effort, much more than the royalist, was sufficiently open and flexible to react to local conflicts in an integrative and creative manner. Paradoxically, local disputes, particularly in vulnerable frontier areas, could often work to parliament's ultimate advantage, whereas, on the royalist side, local infighting more frequently had a negative and destructive effect.[14] This was in no sense an accidental or contingent aspect of the two movements. On the contrary, contrasts in the relationships between the centre and the localities on either side reveal crucial divisions over the nature of politics and the state; indeed, an examination of these contrasts may provide one of the best means of comprehending the differences between royalism and parliamentarianism.[15]

It is worth beginning the more focused discussion with general contrasts between the ways localist sentiments and local military priorities could be accommodated within the overall character of parliamentarianism and royalism. It has now been clearly established for the sixteenth and early seventeenth centuries that the representation of local interests and the bringing together of provincial and central concerns were at the heart of a parliament's function and purpose. Through the presentation of petitions, the raising of grievances, and the passing of legislation, parliament blended together the overlapping and ambiguous notions of the 'country,' ranging from neighbourhood to commonwealth.[16] In 1642, it was natural and automatic for parliamentarians to combine local moves to control the county militias with the raising of a field army; the militia ordinance was successfully implemented in 1642 in twice as many counties as saw the execution of the royalist commission of array.[17] Throughout the civil war there were as many parliamentarian troops in local garrisons and on local service as there were in national armies.[18]

The character of royalism has been less well studied, but an obvious point is that the individual loyalty to a personal monarchy, which was an important element in royalist allegiance, was often difficult to reconcile with localist ties. This sense of personal duty to Charles permeates all royalist proclamations and declarations; it is found in the rhetoric of moderates, who saw royalism as the best bulwark for settled religion and legality and who were often localist by inclination, as well as among the more extreme 'genuine' royalists of Hutton's recent analysis of the royalist party. In a proclamation from York in June 1642, Charles declared: 'We require all our good subjects to take notice of the law (which is in print and full force) that their allegiance is due unto the natural person of their prince, and not to his crown or kingdom distinct from his natural capacity. . . they are bound to be true and faithful not to the king only as king, but to our person as King Charles and to bear us truth and faith of life and member and earthly honour.' The Shropshire gentry resolved in August 1642 'to adventure our lives and fortunes in the defence of his royal and sacred person, and honour the true Protestant religion, the just privileges of parliament, and the known laws and liberties of the subjects.' The Oxford Parliament declared in April 1644 that the king's 'natural person is not to be divided from his kingly office' and that 'our natural allegiance, and the oaths of allegiance and supremacy do bind us and all his other subjects to loyalty and allegiance to his natural person.'[19] This loyalty to Charles the man, repudiated by parliamentarians in their declarations and activities in 1642, helps to explain the widespread tendency of royalist activists to gravitate to the court or to the king's main army in the early stages of the war rather than persevering in attempts to secure control of their localities.[20] In Warwickshire and Lancashire, the absence of several prominent royalists along with the forces they had raised gave parliamentarians the opportunity for greater success than their support among the leading gentry at least justified. While Gloucestershire volunteers attended the raising of Charles's standard at Nottingham, parliament's militia ordinance was executed in the county as the best means of securing local peace. By the time the royalists were able to mount a military campaign in the county, the crucial garrison of Gloucester had been established, with outside help. In Wiltshire, also, parliamentarians won initial control, through peaceful and localist operation of the militia ordinance; subsequent royalist success was dependent on military strength and lacked a sound political foundation.[21] This lack of care for local concerns early in the war helps to explain why royalists failed to establish unchallenged control in many areas but were left with a contested battleground as their base. Throughout the war the most committed royalists of Cumberland and Westmoreland fought outside their counties, leaving only Sir Philip Musgrave to argue for a more dynamic stand at home. Newman has attributed the failure of the earl of Derby in Lancashire to the draining of his resources by the main royalist armies and has argued that the royalist north was not inevitably lost after Marston Moor, although it was once the decision was taken to withdraw the surviving northern cavalry from Yorkshire.[22] Attempts to give more weight to local military needs on the royalist side were halfhearted or too late. In the spring of 1644 the Oxford Parliament promoted volunteer auxiliaries for local defense, but these seem to have been established in three areas only. From late 1644 into the spring of 1645, local gentry in the west and west midlands campaigned through the 'association' movement, for gentry controlled local forces. Earlier in the war such a movement might have functioned in a creative and reciprocal manner whereby local gentry performed effective and genuine military service for the king in return for redress of grievances against the regular royalist forces. As it was, the associations floundered among the increasing war weariness of royalist areas and were destroyed by the club men.[23]

It was part of the common-sense and institutional routine of parliamentarianism that individual local M.P.s or committees supervised the levying of taxation or considered grievances in their native areas. In the course of the war, these local men themselves often came to override localist susceptibilities, but there was always a sense that local interests were being or might be taken into account. Some royalist commanders do seem to have juggled successfully with local civilian grievances and military priorities for a while: Hopton in Cornwall early in the war and Astley at Reading in 1644 are examples.[24] But the major royalist sources abound with hints that local concerns were in tension with loyalty to the king, that royalism 'went against the grain of localism.'[25] What was obvious within parliamentariansim had to be explained on the royalist side as when proposals for Anglesey and Caernarvon emphasized the need for governors to 'be native and of esteem and interest in the country' to counteract the influence of 'well-allied' parliamentarians.[26] Sir Edward Nicholas's famous complaint, 'Albeit I am a Wiltshire man yet I was never thought worthy to be trusted or acquainted with the proceedings for the west country,' is underlined by the modern historian of royalism in that county.[27] The experience of the Northern Horse is the classic example in practice and in rhetoric of the difficulties of combining localism and royalism. Removed by Rupert after Marston Moor, the two cavalry brigades spent many weeks on a 'melancholy pilgrimage' through the northwest and Wales. Their own locality had been abandoned by the Royalists apart from one or two garrisons, but as strangers the Northern Horse met with little welcome on their travels, facing attacks by local people and obstructions from other commanders. In January 1645 their own leaders expressed their feelings at this usage in a poignant appeal to Rupert to be allowed home to relieve Pontefract and Carlisle: [28]

> I beseech your Highness to lay it to heart of what countrymen the King's army here is composed on, and whether your Northern men will not grow sensible of their friends being deserted as likewise that many now in the King's army have their fathers, wives, friends and estates in the enemies' possession who now being forced to make their peace with the enemy may not be a means to draw their friends from the King's service to their own homes . . . I beseech your Highness let not our countrymen upbraid us with ungratefulness in deserting them, but rather give us leave to try what we can do.

No such startling cleavage between natural local concerns and overall allegiance can be found on the parliament's side; nor is such practical illogicality demonstrated in parliament's juggling of rival local and general military priorities. This is not, of course, to argue that parliament could always, or easily, reconcile the local and the national. The Northern Horse are as remarkable for their commitment as for their misfortunes. Throughout their trials they protested their loyalty and obeyed their orders; it will be argued below that the narrow possibilities for disobedience were a further weakness of royalism.

It is here suggested, then, that local loyalties were easier to harmonize with parliamentarianism than with royalism and, further, that this worked to parliament's practical advantage in producing a more resilient and broadly based war effort. This latter aspect can be demonstrated further through brief examination of local disputes within both sides. Conflicts between military and civilian authorities or among national, regional, and county bodies are often seen as 'bedevilling' both war efforts; but many such disputes in parliamentarian areas seem to have worked in fact to draw the contestants closer to the parliamentary cause. Conflicts in the town of Nottingham under the command of Colonel John Hutchinson are one example. Lucy Hutchinson described the situation in Nottingham in the 1640s as 'a sad confusion and thwarting of powers,' her husband's valiant attempts to strengthen the garrison and use its forces to contribute to the wider war effort being continually sabotaged by the corporation and inhabitants of the town, 'a close, hypocritical, false-hearted people,' and by most of the local committee, a body largely composed in Mrs. Hutchinson's account of jumped-up habitués of taverns and brothels, fainthearted or even traitorous parliamentarians.[29] Colonel Hutchinson's appointment as governor of the town as well as the castle of Nottingham was challenged by the committee, which procured a parallel commission for two of their own members from Lord Fairfax, the northern commander in chief, and the committee consistently denied Hutchinson's right to command the horse regiments in Nottingham.[30] It is clear that behind the uneasy relationship between Hutchinson and the corporation lay the common tension between urban elites and neighbouring county gentry, naturally enough intensified during the 1640s, when the local gentleman was a hot-tempered governor eager to destroy urban property to fortify the town yet prepared to abandon all but the castle in emergencies.[31] But the complexity of parliamentarian wartime administration gave the corporation more allies against outside interference than in the years of peace because of the presence of committeemen equally resentful of Hutchinson. On the other hand, the existence of a common enemy in the person of the governor brought a closer alliance between committee and corporation. After disagreements between these two bodies in early 1643, a joint subcommittee was established to sort out misunderstandings, and cooperation culminated in November 1644 with a notable exercise in horse trading at a semiclandestine night-time meeting at which the corporation supported a critical petition to the Committee of Both Kingdoms against Hutchinson in exchange for the committee's intercession with parliament over the town's arrears of sequestered royal rents.[32]

Similarly in parliamentarian Warwickshire, widespread resentment at harsh military rule by socially obscure committeemen did not lead to alienated neutralist or moderate gentry turning to neighbouring royalists. Again, discontent could be channeled through alternative parliamentarian structures, in this case through the moderate regional commander of the West Midlands Associations, the earl of Denbigh, appointed in December 1643. From the start there was fierce competition between the committee and Denbigh for dominance in Warwickshire. In the struggle for military resources, Denbigh suffered a humiliating defeat, but politically he gained great support from Warwickshire gentry who had hitherto been uninvolved in the war as well as from some who had given support to parliament in 1642 but had subsequently withdrawn from cooperation with the committee. Through practical support for the West Midlands Association and through a broad petitioning campaign in Denbigh's favour, men who were by no means wholehearted parliamentarians became, in the course of 1644, integrated into the parliamentarian cause.[33] This process continued long after Denbigh's association had withered away. Moderate opinion won the 'Recruiter' election for the county against all the military pressure the county committee could bring to bear, and moderates in Warwickshire, as in Lincolnshire, Somerset, and elsewhere, controlled the local subcommittees for accounts set up in late 1644. Attempts at local supervision and criticism of parliament's own war effort were thus possible *within* a parliamentarian framework.[34]

More important than local flexibility on parliament's side was the existence of a number of outside agencies as courts of appeal, each encompassing a variety of opinions. This ensured that local disputes could become long drawn out and that local rivals rarely faced final defeat. At Nottingham, Hutchinson's opponents conducted long campaigns against him through the house of commons and the Committee of both Kingdoms.[35] Denbigh and his supporters in Warwickshire concentrated on the house of lords, his enemies on the earl of Essex and then the house of commons. After Denbigh's failure locally, moderates in the county aired their grievances through the Recruiter knights of the shire in parliament, the national accounts committee, and the London press.[36] Clearly such local wrangling did little for military efficiency in the short term, but more vital politically was the availability of mechanisms for conducting such disputes within a parliamentarian framework. This worked to broaden the local base of parliament's support and to increase the resilience of its war effort. Until the very eve of Pride's Purge, alignments within parliament were fluid, and whenever a local committee or commander lost one round of a local faction fight there was always some other central body that offered some chance of redress.[37] The earl of Denbigh, apparently defeated locally, could continue to hope for revenge through the house of lords and could continue to play an influential role in national politics. Even in Warwickshire he could point to gains: by acting as a focus for moderate opposition to the county committee he had acquired a lasting influence in his native county that his family had hitherto lacked. Denbigh, and others like him, did not see one local setback as a reason for defection from parliament.[38]

There are, in any case, qualifications to be made to the view that local infighting necessarily had a debilitating military impact. To have any hope of gaining outside support in local disputes, participants had to establish themselves as credible parliamentarians by making some efforts to raise men and money. This process contributed to parliament's success in maintaining footholds in the royalist heartlands, ensuring those heartlands remained battlegrounds. Thus, despite short-term setbacks, Nottingham's position as a parliamentarian garrison in a largely royalist area was gradually strengthened.[39] In Warwickshire the committee was stimulated by Denbigh's rivalry to improve its military control of a vulnerable area, while a generous assessment would conclude that Denbigh's military activities did more good than harm in Shropshire and Staffordshire.[40]

Many local disputes in parliamentarian areas, articulated through a number of outside bodies, seem therefore to have left contestants either satisfied or with hopes of satisfaction and thus served to integrate a variety of interests into the general parliamentary cause. The local and central royalist organization was much less conducive to such a process. On a local level, despite the well-known royalist device of using open meetings of gentlemen and freeholders to sanction initial or ad hoc levies of troops or taxation, permanent royalist organization was in many ways less complex and more rigid than in parliamentarian areas. The contrast was particularly marked in frontier areas. There was, for instance, the very noticeable reliance on the individual sheriff, often because of an overt belief that 'public business' was better supervised by 'someone in particular' than left to the 'care of a committee.'[41] Also important is the fact that royalist committees for a variety of purposes tended to consist of the same personnel; even royalist accounts committees were made up of men already involved in administration. This last phenomenon has been seen as a deliberate and sensible policy intended to minimize friction, but the experience of several parliamentarian counties suggests it was a mistake.[42] Throughout the 1640s, local civilian bodies in general had a more real and lasting influence on the parliamentarian side. The contrast can be seen in divided Wiltshire from the summer of 1644. Parliament's military initiatives were hampered in the short term by many divisions between the military commanders, Massey and Waller, and their subordinates and between the military and the civilian county committee. The military drawbacks were more than counterbalanced, however, by the political advantages of having a local body that was seen to be keeping the more ruthless military figures, notably Colonel Nicholas Devereux, governor of Malmesbury, in check. Devereux's royalist counterpart, Sir Charles Lloyd, commander at Devizes, suffered no such irritations, for royalists in Wiltshire had never established a strong civilian organization. Lloyd's military successes were consequently won at the cost of political alienation of outraged moderates and proved fragile and superficial.[43]

But, of course, royalist areas were often as prone as parliamentarian strongholds were to conflicts of authority between civilians and military commanders, between rival military figures, or between county and regional bodies. The crucial royalist weaknesses were that the outside bodies to which local combatants could appeal were less various and less institutionalized than were those of parliament's side. Local royalist disputes were less likely to become extended and were more likely to lead to outright success for one individual or faction and to widespread dissatisfaction and defection. Examples are found in royalist Gloucestershire and Herefordshire. The surrender of Hereford to Waller in April 1643 was preceded by complex local disputes: among local royalists; between Herefordshire men and outside commanders; and between the regional commander, Lord Herbert, and everybody else. In the recriminations following Waller's victory, all but the powerful courtier Herbert, who was probably the most to blame for the disaster, felt the displeasure of the king. Thereafter the personnel of the royalist leadership in Herefordshire completely changed, with only a small minority of the activists of 1642–43 appearing in the county again. Yet in military terms Waller's advance was simply a 'smash and grab raid'.[44]

Conflicts in Gloucestershire between the summer of 1643 and the spring of 1644 were equally complex. The military commander, Sir William Vavasour, was resented both by the local commissioners and by his nominal superior, Herbert again, who was militarily inactive but conspired against Vavasour at court. To try to improve his position Vavasour sought the support of Prince Rupert and promoted Rupert's attempts to acquire the presidency of Wales against Herbert's claims, hoping this would bring him an unchallenged command in Gloucestershire, a command that was also sought by the prominent local royalists Viscount Conway and Lord Chandos. Rupert was appointed to overall command in Wales, but in order to harmonize central interests the king placated Herbert by dismissing Vavasour. This did nothing to benefit Vavasour's local rivals, however, for Rupert and the king preferred a professional soldier, Nicholas Mynne, to the Gloucestershire command. Against the decision of the king and his nephew there could be no redress, and the resolution of this dispute led to significant defection from the royalist cause: before the summer of 1644, Lords Conway and Chandos had both made their peace with parliament, as had Sir Humphrey Tracy, another leading Gloucestershire royalist who had been an ally first of Conway, then of Vavasour.[45]

There were exceptions to the pattern illustrated by these examples. There was 'disfunctional' local conflict in some parliamentarian areas on occasions and creative or integrative conflict among royalists. In Staffordshire, for example, the interlocking rivalries between the royalist commanders Leveson, Bagot and Loughborough spurred each commander to greater efforts, but these disputes were largely confined to military figures and did little to broaden the civilian support for royalism in the county.[46] More subtlety could be added to the argument with further research, but the general trend seems clear. A lack of flexibility in royalist organization often prevented the kind of extended local dispute that functioned among parliamentarians to draw participants closer to the cause. At Shrewsbury in 1643–44 there was tension between the governor, Sir Francis Ottley, and the corporation, while both were suspicious of the regional commander, Capel, and apprehensive of the implications of Rupert's reforms in early 1644.[47] Superficially this situation offered potential similar to that realized at Nottingham except that there were not the varieties of outside courts of appeal through which local disputes could be prolonged. Through the work of Hutton we know that in the spring of 1644 and, again, even in the early months of 1645 Prince Rupert established a rational balance between military and civilian authority in the areas under his control.[48] In favourable circumstances this organization functioned adequately, but if it broke down or led to conflict, Rupert was the only arbitrator. In this situation someone was bound to be finally defeated; the royalists rarely acquired any political benefits from extended disputes, and success was very dependent on brittle military foundations.[49]

On the evidence of surviving correspondence it seems that royalist military commanders were generally more contemptuous of civilian participation than their parliamentarian counterparts were. Notable examples include John Byron's comments on Shrewsbury, 'a garrison of burgesses ... ready enough to betray it,' under the command of Ottley, 'an old doting fool'; or Thomas Dabridgecourt's outburst to Rupert against the Welsh: 'If your Highness shall be pleased to command me to the Turk, or Jew, or Gentile, I will go on my bare feet to serve you, but from the Welsh, good Lord deliver me; and I shall beseech you to send me no more into this country, if you intend I shall do you any service, without a strong party to compel them, not to entreat them.' These expressions are typical of royalist opinions that could not be so openly expressed within parliamentarianism.[50] The decisive political difference, however, was that parliamentarian critics of Colonel Hutchinson or the unsavoury Warwickshire commanders could see possibilities of obtaining redress through local bodies, or central allies, until December 1648. This was less and less true of royalist organization.

This is to say not that there were no means by which local rivals on the royalist side could attempt to obtain central backing but that the process was more fraught and contradictory. Probably the most effective means was through private and personal influence at the court in Oxford – appeals to the king or to those believed to be close to him. Petitions from Oxfordshire villages complaining to the king of excessive contribution received prompt if not necessarily effective attention in spring 1645.[51] Warwickshire tenants of the earl of Northampton were able to use their landlord as a conduit for grievances against military exactions, while Northampton himself had an agent at Oxford to protect his own interests as military commander.[52] These private processes had serious drawbacks when compared to the regular and institutionalized references of disputes to committees by parliament. It was much more important for royalists to be present in person to argue their cases, as Sir Arthur Gorges emphasized to Hastings in his dispute with Leveson: 'Your own person though you stay but three days will satisfy more ten times than any other body can do for you.'[53] If leading military commanders felt vulnerable when not on the spot, the situation was more difficult for aggrieved civilians, especially in areas distant from Oxford. Decisions made in private as a result of personal influence often were or seemed capricious. An essential problem was that it was almost impossible to challenge an unfavourable decision by the king or Rupert, while it was frequently possible for someone else to reverse a favourable one. Hence Nicholas's apology to Hastings in May 1643 for the king's reversal of an order promising an arms supply.[54] The king was 'much troubled': 'But, sir, the truth is my Lord general and all the Colonels here came clamouring to his Majesty . . . in truth these officers were ready to mutiny at it which was the cause his Majesty did unwillingly revoke that warrant.' Indeed, one reason for the atmosphere of ill-tempered frustration that abounds in royalist sources was that royalist commanders were too close to the king to fall back on the comforting early parliamentarian ideology of evil counsellors but were only too well aware that they were dealing with a fallible individual leader.[55]

On a more institutionalized level, much of the business of the royalist Council of War concerned local military administration, and in 1643 the council acted as a reasonably effective court of appeal for local grievances.[56] But it became increasingly peripheral as the king relied more and more on small court cliques, and it had in any case little authority independent of Charles I.[57] The assembly of members of the Lords and Commons at Oxford, especially in its first spring 1644 session, acted as a forum for moderate critiques of courtiers and civilian attacks on the military and as an outlet for local disputes in Wiltshire, Staffordshire, and Chester, for example. Sir Francis Gamull, M.P., the 'localist' rival of the military Byrons in Chester, wrote home to the corporation: 'Though I be in obedience to his Majesty's commands at Oxford, yet the happiness and security of the city is ever in my thoughts and prayers, and I shall on all occasions be as ready to testify my service as the City shall expect or desire.'[58] Again, though, there were problems that limited the capacity of the assembly to blend together local and central concerns in the way indicated by Gamull's remarks. The assembly's sessions were short and irregular; its main function was propagandist: to validate the king's pacific intentions, to highlight the incompleteness of the Westminster gathering and thus challenge its legitimacy, and (in the first session) to publicize the Scots' invasion.[59] It was not intended as an arena for airing disagreement or local grievances, and all royalist accounts lay great emphasis on its unanimity. Nicholas wrote to Ormonde that the assembly 'proceed very unanimously and prudently'; Clarendon later declared that his aim had been 'to prevent the running into any excesses of discourse which so great assemblies can very hardly be kept from'; while Arthur Trevor lamented to Rupert: 'Yesterday the house of lords was divided, which though it were a small matter, yet was an occasion of siding and taking parts, and troubles many lookers-on that were in hopes they would never have found the way to turn their backs one upon another.'[60] In the extraordinarily brief mentions of the assembly's proceedings in *Mercurius Aulicus*, the general agreement among participants is again the main concern.[61] The contrast with parliament is again instructive: there political division was increasingly accepted, while both local and national disputes were vigorously prosecuted in the London newssheets.[62]

In February 1644 Charles disingenuously promised Gamull the governorship of Chester, while Digby assured Rupert that 'his Majesty is induced to give him that recommendation only for his satisfaction's sake.'[63] In March 1645 he repudiated his parallel parliament, rejoicing to Henrietta Maria that he was 'freed from the place of base and mutinous motions – that is to say, our mongrel Parliament here.'[64] Such events bring us close to the inevitable and obvious weakness royalists faced in trying to deal with local grievances or disputes. On the ground royalist areas may have been as 'bedevilled' or, as is argued here, as blessed by complex local disputes as parliamentarian areas were, but at the top there was no question about where ultimate authority lay. Hutton has perceptively remarked that 'parliament was a huge committee of theoretically equal members, anxious to avoid entrusting power to any one man or group of men.'[65] Parliamentarianism could thus be open, self-critical, and resilient; it was possible to reopen disputes, to challenge decisions, to find another committee to work through. For the royalists, the king's decision was final. He rarely tolerated defiance and it was difficult for those who had become royalists because of their belief in obedience to contemplate challenging the king. More likely they obeyed, or they gave up. The foolish, poignant loyalty of the Northern Horse or the defections in Gloucestershire, like the dramatic and rapid disgrace of loyal servants such as Wilmot or Percy, all illustrate these aspects of royalism.[66] The problem was not a contingent aspect of Charles's personality but implicit in the ultimate character of royalism – the acceptance of personal and, if necessary, arbitrary monarchy. An examination of the nature of local–central relationships on either side suggests therefore a fundamental contrast in the political processes of royalists and parliamentarians, a contrast beween an ordered, institutionalized, yet flexible parliamentarianism and a capricious, individualized, and private royalism.

Similar contrasts are revealed in the rhetoric of local disputes and in the directives to the localities issued by each side. Although the important topic of political languages has been neglected, a few features can be highlighted.[67] Royal proclamations ordering the levy of troops or money emphasized the duty of 'our subjects' to defend 'our rights' and 'our person' before the responsibility to protect the laws, the Protestant religion, or the liberties of the subject. Anyone who disobeyed would become 'a person disaffected to us' as well as 'an enemy to the public peace.'[68] Parliament's ordinances were justified with reference to general, public dangers: 'Forasmuch as the true Protestant Religion, the Laws and Liberties of the subject, and the Parliament are in danger to be subverted, idolatry and tyranny like to be introduced.' Either disobedience was treated in a low-key manner with set penalties ascribed to particular offenses, or else offenders were to be 'proceeded against as contemners of the orders of Parliament, and Abusers of the country and disturbers of the Peace thereof.'[69] The implications of such rhetoric, as of many of the practical matters already discussed, were that royalism involved loyalty to a cause and that parliamentarianism meant being part of a cause.[70] The latter stance was much more open to debate and dispute and much less likely to involve the abandoning of home and neighbourhood. Consequently, parliamentarianism allowed for a better balance between local and central interests.

The personalized, individualized conceptions of loyalty and honour among royalists are seen vividly in the rhetoric in which they expressed their grievances or described their disputes. 'I am resolved with your highness' leave rather to quit all than to go less in what you honoured me with from his Majesty,' declared Sir John Wintour to Rupert, while Sir Robert Howard more dramatically demanded: 'What horrid crime have I committed, or what brand of cowardice lies upon me and my men that we are not thought worthy of a subsistence . . . at the sight of this order of your highness', I resolved to disband them and come up to Oxford, where I'll starve in more security.'[71] Such a rhetoric seems to have influenced or made possible two very different patterns of behaviour. It underlay the sacrifices of the 'madmen or heroes' of the royalist last stand, but it could also justify desertion of the cause when failure or rejection by the king threatened personal disgrace: the exile of Newcastle after Marston Moor or the petulance of Rupert after Bristol are but the best-known examples.[72] The hierarchical chains of command between individuals implicit in royalism are revealed in the virulent complaints against subordinates and rivals, particularly civilian or corporate bodies, discussed above. The fierce determination to do the king honourable personal service naturally led to bitter execration of those whose rivalry seemed to obstruct success.

Among parliamentarians, individual pique and concern for personal reputation are also present in the rhetoric of conflict, but they are qualified by an equally prevalent discourse of 'public service' to the state, contrasted with disaffection or malignancy. The earl of Denbigh in December 1643 protested, 'I thought it did not become me to dispute of powers and points of honour when I was called upon to do real service to the state,' and although he promptly went on to complain that his lack of power meant 'I shall be looked upon in an inferior way and disadvantage to myself in point of honour and trust,' he added that this would bring 'prejudice to the public service.'[73] Hutchinson's Nottingham rivals complained of the personal attacks on them tending to 'blemish their reputations,' but again they emphasized also 'the great dishonour of the Parliament,' the danger to the 'public service in this county,' and the respect due to them from 'the state.'[74] Such language had a practical importance, making it more difficult for participants in quarrels to abandon their allegiance because of personal setbacks. It prompted instead the development of generalized political debate and mobilization around different conceptions of the ambiguous ideas of the state or the public service.[75] In sum, it is as if the complexity of private and public ideologies and processes that made up early modern government had been shattered by civil war, with parliament inheriting a public image, the royalists a private one.

By 1645, at the latest, all these issues became irrelevant to the royalists as the vicious cycle of war weariness in their heartlands and military defeat overcame them. By then, too, the victory of more extreme views in the royalist party was total.[76] The elimination of royalism as a viable alternative, except in 1648, meant that parliament's control could rely in a much more straightforward fashion on military strength. Nonetheless, it remained vital for parliament to harmonize local and central concerns and to provide a forum for the expression of local conflict in the years of disillusion following victory. In many counties, critics of county committees or military rule were active in accounts committees or on the commissions of the peace and had access to national arenas through sympathetic M.P.s or editors of the London press. National alignments in parliament continued to fluctuate, and a variety of interests and opinion remained within a parliamentarian framework, satisfied or hoping for satisfaction.[77] The challenge of 1648 was remarkably limited, given the heavy taxation and military rule imposed by parliament, and defection from parliament was often more serious in areas that had been most secure (and most monolithic in an organizational sense) during the first civil war. Frontier counties like Warwickshire and Somerset, where local conflict had been serious and consequently a broader range of opinion had been drawn into the parliamentarian war effort, tended to be quiescent. The continued flexibility of the political process, as well as simple military power, thus made possible the victory of zealous parliamentarians in 1648.

It has recently been argued that Charles I's defeat was providential, arising from 'chance weaknesses in the nature of the royalist party.'[78] Here the opposite is suggested: royalist weaknesses, revealed through a study of central–local relationships, were in no sense the product of chance but implicit in the very structure and character of personal monarchical rule in the context of previous political processes in England. Parliament's strengths, again illustrated through the nature of local and central connections, were equally integral. Military strength in isolation was not adequate to waging and winning a civil war in seventeenth-century England. Without the cooperation and the political acquiescence, at least, of sufficient numbers in the localities, neither king nor parliament could raise military forces, still less maintain or recruit them in difficult times. Superficially, and in the short term, the overriding of local interests may have served military efficiency. In the long run, however, political resilience depended on some actual or potential balance between local and national concerns. On the royalist side there was an implicit tension between individual loyalty to the person of the king and communal attachment to a particular locality, whereas a parliament was, in fact, a gathering together of local elites in a national institution. Throughout the war, parliament's administration, whether local or national, was more complex than the king's and thus allowed for the expression of a greater variety of interests and opinions. Disputes among local factions or between local, regional, and central figures could be pursued for an extended period within the parliament's administrative and political structures. Among royalists, greater institutional inflexibility meant that outright domination by one group was much more frequent. Royalist political processes and rhetoric both tended to reduce local or local–central disputes to personal conflicts and matters of honour. Such conflicts were commonly resolved by the private, once-and-for-all decisions of the individuals who headed the royalist hierarchy, notably the king or Rupert. Parliamentarian disputes were conducted in a more public manner, referred to committees, discussed in the press, and debated in the houses of parliament. Parliamentarian rhetoric emphasized ideological differences between rivals and indeed made it difficult to present conflicts in terms of private interests. For all these reasons, parliamentarian disputes were much less likely to result in complete despair with the parliamentary cause. It is thus argued that local and national loyalties were easier, or less difficult, to reconcile with parliamentarianism than they were with royalism. Parliament undoubtedly did offend localist susceptibilities with its fiscal and military policies, but throughout the war local critics of an all-out war effort had a place within parliament's administration and grounds for optimism that policies might be modified. For royalists it was harder to conceive of means through which local interests might receive more protection, and consequently local defection was a more common response.

Parliament's resilience and ultimate success is thus in large part attributable to its capacity to uphold the integration of the local and the central, characteristic of the English political process before 1642, and to its capacity to consolidate and refine a long-developing body of political discourse based on the 'country,' the commonwealth, or the state, a complex mix of legalism, conscientious Protestantism, and adherence to parliament as an important element in the English 'constitution.'[79] Parliament won because its cause represented the more logical development of both the ideological and the institutional aspects of the English political system as it had been emerging since the mid-sixteenth century. Lest this be taken to imply that parliament thereby represented the more 'conservative' side in the civil war, it should be remembered that it is in the slow working out of a 'public,' formalized, and abstract politics again in the realm of both institutions and ideas that the most 'modern' aspects of parliamentarianism lie. It may even be that the consolidation of a specialized, public realm of politics provides one of the best justifications for seeing the English Civil War as a 'bourgeois revolution.'[80]

Notes

1 Alan Everitt, *The Community of Kent and the Great Rebellion* (Leicester, 1966); Anthony Fletcher, *A County Community in Peace and War: Sussex, 1600–1660* (London, 1975); J.S. Morrill, *Cheshire, 1630–1660: County Government and Society during the 'English Revolution'* (Oxford, 1974), and *The Revolt of the Provinces: Conservatives and Radicals in the English Civil War, 1630–1650* (London, 1976); Ronald Hutton, *The Royalist War Effort, 1642–1646* (London, 1982).

2 J.S. Morrill, 'The Northern Gentry and the Great Rebellion,' *NH*, 15 (1979), pp. 66–87.

3 Ronald Hutton, 'The Royalist War Effort,' in *Reactions to the English Civil War, 1642–1649*, ed. John Morrill (London, 1982), p. 51.

4 Everitt, *Community of Kent*, pp. 190–93, 230–41; Morrill, *The Revolt of the Provinces*, pp. 98–111, 125–31.

5 John Morrill, introduction to Morrill (ed.), *Reactions*, pp. 17–19.

6 Clive Holmes, 'The County Community in Stuart Historiography' (Chapter 8 above); David Underdown, 'Community and Class: Theories of Local Politics in the English Revolution,' in *After the Reformation*, ed. Barbara Malament (Manchester, 1980), pp. 147–65; Ann Hughes, 'Warwickshire on the Eve of the Civil War: A "County Community"?'. *MH*, 7 (1982), pp. 42–72.

7 See Holmes, 'County Community', Underdown, 'Community and Class', Hughes, 'Warwickshire'; and also Derek Hirst, 'Court, Country and Politics before 1629,' in *Faction and Parliament: Essays on Early Stuart History*, ed. Kevin Sharpe (Oxford, 1978), pp. 105–37.

8 Derek Hirst, *The Representative of the People?* (Cambridge, 1975), esp. chs 8, 9; Anthony Fletcher, *The Outbreak of the English Civil War* (London, 1981), pp. 194–99.

9 Fletcher, *The Outbreak of the English Civil War*, p. 400.

10 See, e.g., David Underdown, *Pride's Purge: Politics in the Puritan Revolution* (Oxford, 1971); Clive Holmes, *The Eastern Association in the English Civil War* (Cambridge, 1974); Ann Hughes, 'Militancy and Localism: Warwickshire Politics and Westminster Politics,' *TRHS*, 5th ser., 31 (1981), pp. 51–68; Clive Holmes, 'Colonel King and Lincolnshire Politics,' *HJ*, 16 (1973), pp. 451–84.

11 Hughes, 'Militancy and Localism,' gives insufficient weight to local concerns; see Holmes, *The Eastern Association in the English Civil War*, pp. 1–2, for the view that parliament had to overcome localism. It could be argued that the major difference between Morrill and Hutton, on the one hand, and Holmes and Hughes, on the other, is that the former believe that the overcoming of localism – the dogged, legalistic integrity of provincial communities – was a more difficult and more transient process than do the latter with their denial that localism encompassed an extended legitimating ideology and their belief that national developments determined the outcome of events.

12 For this view of the English state, see, e.g., Penry Williams, *The Tudor Regime* (reprint, Oxford, 1981). It is clear that the approach of Peter Lake, 'The Collection of Ship Money in Cheshire: A Case Study of the Relations between Central and Local Government,' *NH*, 17 (1981), pp. 44–71; or Cynthia Herrup, 'The Counties and the Country: Some Thoughts on Seventeenth Century Historiography,' *Social History*, 8 (1983), pp. 169–81, has here been preferred to that of Derek Hirst, 'The Privy Council and Problems of Enforcement in the 1620s,' *JBS*, 18, no. 1 (1978), pp 46–66. See esp. Herrup's comment that ruling was 'a repeated exercise in compromise, co-operation, cooptation and resistance' (pp. 170–1).

13 Ian Roy, 'The Royalist Army in the First Civil War' (D. Phil. thesis, Oxford University, 1963), pp. 247, 342–50; M.D.G. Wanklyn, 'The King's Armies in the West of England, 1642–1646' (M.A. thesis, Manchester University, 1966), pp. 270–3; Hutton, *The Royalist War Effort, passim*, but esp. p. 178.

14 For a comparable argument in an earlier context, see Lake, 'The Collection of Ship Money in Cheshire', pp 54–58, where it is suggested that long-running intracounty disputes over ship money facilitated the collection of the levy. This present argument is perhaps controversial, and it must be emphasized that a very different judgment of royalist weaknesses can be found in M.D.G. Wanklyn, 'Royalist Strategy in the South of England, 1642–1646,' *Southern History*, 3 (1981), pp. 55–79, where it is argued that royalists were too divided and that local interests were given too much weight; see also Roy, 'The Royalist Army in the First Civil War', p. 349, for similar views.

15 The general aspects of the following discussion concentrate rather more on the relationship between the centre and the localities on the royalist side. This would seem to redress a balance in the existing literature, which includes many substantial works dealing with such issues for the parliamentarians; Holmes, *The Eastern Association in the English Civil War*; and Underdown, *Pride's Purge*, are the most notable examples.

16 Conrad Russell, *Parliaments and English Politics* (Oxford, 1979), pt. 1; Richard Cust and Peter Lake, 'Sir Richard Grosvenor and the Rhetoric of Magistracy,' *BIHR*, 54 (1981), pp. 40–53; Hirst, *The Representative of the People?*

17 Fletcher, *The Outbreak of the English Civil War*, pp. 348–50, 356–57.

18 J.S. Morrill, 'Mutiny and Discontent in English Provincial Armies, 1645–1647,' *P & P*, 56 (1972), pp. 49–50.

19 Ronald Hutton, 'The Structure of the Royalist Party, 1642–1646,' *HJ*, 24 (1983), pp. 553–69; *Proclamations*, vol. 2, no. 339, p. 774; William Phillips (ed.), *Sir Francis Ottley's Papers, Transactions of the Shropshire Archaeological and Natural History Society*, 2d ser., vol. 7 (Shrewsbury, 1895), p. 242; John Rushworth (ed.), *Historical Collections* (London, 1721), 5, p. 592. The proclamation of September 1644 declaring Charles's desire for peace and launching the 'association' movement in Somerset is a partial exception with more emphasis on the Protestant religion and the laws of the land than on the royal person and royal rights (*Proclamations*, vol. 2, no. 503, pp. 1047–48).

20 For one of the most famous manifestations of the parliamentarian separation of the personal and public aspects of kingship, see the 'Remonstrance of both Houses . . . concerning Hull, 26 May 1642,' in *The Stuart Constitution*, ed. J.P. Kenyon (Cambridge, 1966), pp. 242–44. Parliament was drawing on much earlier ideas; see, e.g., the discussions in Marie Axton, *The Queen's Two Bodies*, Royal Historical Society Studies in History (London, 1977); Richard P. Cust, 'The Forced Loan and English Politics, 1626–1628' (Ph.D. thesis, University of London, 1984), pp. 284–86; Conrad Russell, 'The Theory of Treason in the Trial of Strafford,' *EHR*, 80 (1965), pp. 30–50.

21 Ann Hughes, 'Warwickshire on the Eve of the Civil War', p. 60; B.G. Blackwood, *The Lancashire Gentry and the Great Rebellion, 1640–1660*, Chetham Society, 3d ser., vol. 25 (Manchester, 1978), pp. 50–1; G.A. Harrison, 'Royalist Organisation in Gloucestershire and Bristol, 1642–1645' (M.A. thesis, Manchester University, 1961), pp. 41, 55, and 'Royalist Organisation in Wiltshire, 1642–1646' (Ph.D. thesis, University of London, 1963), pp. 88–95; Fletcher, *The Outbreak of the English Civil War*, p. 394.

22 C.B. Phillips, 'The Royalist North: The Cumberland and Westmoreland Gentry, 1642–1660,' *NH*, 14 (1978), pp. 170–1; P.R. Newman, 'The Royalist Army in Northern England, 1642–1645' (D.Phil. thesis, Univesity of York, 1978), 1, pp. 25–6, 56, 83, 178; 2, pp. 12, 144, 208, 337, 397–8.

23 Roy, 'The Royalist Army in the First Civil War', pp. 189–91; BL, Harl. MS 6852, fos. 37–8, and Harl. MS 6802, fos. 88–9 (auxiliaries in Reading, Bristol and Oxford). For the association movement, see Hutton, *The Royalist War Effort*, pp. 157–71; and for a sample of royalist military commanders' reactions, see Bodl. L., Firth MS C6, fo. 332; BL, Add. MS 18982, fos. 16–17; B.E.G. Warburton (ed.), *Memoirs of Prince Rupert and the Cavaliers* (London, 1849), 3, p. 54. Wanklyn, 'The King's Armies in the West of England', pp. 183–84, quotes and endorses Clarendon's equally critical opinion, but David Underdown, *Somerset in the Civil War and Interregnum* (Newton Abbot, 1973), pp. 79–82, is suggestive of the potential of such movements, as are the Shropshire declarations in Phillips (ed.), *Sir Francis Ottley's Papers*, pp. 272, 284–85.

24 For Hopton, see Mary Coate, *Cornwall in the Great Civil War and Interregnum* (reprint, Truro, 1963), pp. 36–38, 58–59; for Astley, see Bodl. L., Firth MS C6, fos. 44–6, 48. By 1644, however, there were problems in satisfying local

demands in Cornwall (Ian Roy (ed.), *The Royalist Ordnance Papers, 1642–1646*, Oxfordshire Record Society, vols 43, 49 [Oxford, 1964, 1975], p. 380).

25 Fletcher, *The Outbreak of the English Civil War*, p. 327.

26 BL, Add. MS 18981, fo. 97^{r-v}, spring 1644. Compare Hopton's explanation to Rupert of the value of a local man as commander at Bristol, September 1643, and the Devonian John Greville's request to Maurice for the governorship of Barnstable, December 1644, where the obvious advantages have to be spelled out (Warburton (ed.), 2, p. 291; BL, Add. MS 18981, fo. 340^r).

27 Warburton, (ed.) *Memoirs of Prince Rupert and the Cavaliers*, 2, pp. 188–90; Harrison, 'Royalist Organisation in Wiltshire,' pp. 265, 284. Ten of the thirty-seven nominated commissioners of array, including Hyde and Nicholas, were active only outside Wiltshire.

28 Hutton, *The Royalist War Effort*, pp. 149–51, 155–56 (the telling phrase is at p. 151); Roy, 'The Royalist Army in the First Civil War', pp. 134–38; Newman, 'The Royalist Army in Northern England, 1642–1645', 1, pp. 381–83, 418–20, 455–62; BL, Add. MS 18981, fos. 227^v, 259, 261–62 (for the Northern Horse in general); Bodl. L., Firth MS C6, fo. 312 (For the appeal to Rupert); cf. also Warburton (ed.), *Memoirs of Prince Rupert and the Cavaliers*, 3, pp. 70–1.

29 Lucy Hutchinson, *Memoirs of the Life of Colonel Hutchinson*, ed. James Sutherland (Oxford, 1973), pp. 83–90, 104–25, 129–58, gives a partisan account of these disputes, but they are more soberly documented in W.T. Baker (ed.), *Records of the Borough of Nottingham* (Nottingham, 1900), vol. 5; and in the journals of the houses of parliament and the State Papers. Quotations are from Hutchinson, *Memoirs of the Life of Colonel Hutchinson*, pp. 122, 106, 146.

30 *CJ*, 3, p. 315. Hutchinson, *Memoirs of the Life of Colonel Hutchinson*, pp. 104–6, 116–17, 128–30, 139–40.

31 See, e.g., Hutchinson, p. 89, for Colonel Hutchinson's comment, 'It must not move them to see their houses flaming and, if need be, themselves firing them for the public advantage.'

32 Baker (ed.), 5, pp. 208–9, 221–22, 226–27. Hutchinson, *Memoirs of the Life of Colonel Hutchinson*, pp. 147–9.

33 Hughes, 'Militancy and Localism', pp. 51–64.

34 Ann Hughes, 'Politics, Society and Civil War in Warwickshire, 1620–1650' (Ph.D. thesis, University of Liverpool, 1980), pp. 380–98; Holmes, 'Colonel King and Lincolnshire Politics', pp. 471–75; Underdown, *Somerset in the Civil War and Interregnum*, pp. 141–2; Morrill, *The Revolt of the Provinces*, pp. 69–70; cf. Holmes, *The Eastern Association in the English Civil War*, pp. 216–23, for examples of criticism of the supercession of the association, again conducted through parliamentarian committees.

35 See *CSPD, 1644*, p. 368, and *1644–45*, pp. 111–12, 276, 305, 383, for the dealings of the Committee of Both Kingdoms with Nottingham, *CJ*, 3, p. 689; 4, pp. 75, 110, 118. An important role was played in these disputes by Gilbert Millington, the M.P. for Nottingham, who was seen as a mediator by parliament but regarded as an enemy by Mrs. Hutchinson. A compromise was patched up only in April 1645. Colonel Hutchinson preferred to appeal to his military superiors, Lord Fairfax or the earl of Essex, while believing it was 'ridiculous to send for satisfaction in unquestionable things.' Mrs. Hutchinson's sardonic view was that 'Generals understood not so well the power of a committee as the Parliament' (pp. 117–18).

36 Hughes, 'Militancy and Localism,' pp. 61–8; see Holmes, 'Colonel King and Lincolnshire Politics,' pp. 478–9, for the ways rivals in the complex Lincolnshire

disputes appealed to a multitude of outside bodies – the two houses of parliament, the committees of accounts, the army and the excise – and also used the London press.

37 This argument seems to me to hold whatever view is taken of national alignments. For a range of recent work, see Underdown, *Pride's Purge*; M.A. Kishlansky, *The Rise of the New Model Army* (Cambridge, 1979).

38 Denbigh's family had risen to preeminence through their links with the duke of Buckingham, a process with few local benefits. After the loss of his military command, Denbigh continued to play a significant political role through the house of lords; he was one of parliament's representatives at Uxbridge and sat on the early Commonwealth councils of state (see Hughes, 'Politics, Society and Civil War in Warwickshire,' pp. 44–45, 355–56, 380). Compare the career of Lord Willoughby of Parham, who lost command in Lincolnshire after a bitter dispute with the earl of Manchester and Colonel King. He too remained active on the parliament's side, sitting on Lords' committees and using the Lords to attack King. His ultimate defection to the royalists followed impeachment by the Commons and four months imprisonment in 1647 (see Holmes, 'Colonel King and Lincolnshire Politics,' pp. 454–61; *DNB*, s.v. 'Francis Willoughby, fifth Baron Willoughby of Parham').

39 In December 1643, in Newman's account, Nottingham was 'an isolated panicking town,' but in 1644 it was a force to be reckoned with, a factor in the royalists' confused strategic considerations, which culminated in disaster at Marston Moor (Newman, 'The Royalist Army in Northern England, 1642–1645', pp. 232, 294).

40 Hughes, 'Politics, Society and Civil War in Warwickshire,' pp. 308, 327–35; R.N. Dore (ed.), *The Letter Books of Sir William Brereton*, Record Society of Lancashire and Cheshire, vol. 123 (Gloucester, 1984), 1, pp. 18–20.

41 Hutton, *The Royalist War Effort*, esp. pp. 85–104, gives a general survey of Royalist organization. For the reliance on sheriffs, see, e.g., Newcastle to the sheriff of Derbyshire, January 14, 1644, HMC, *Hastings MS* (London, 1930), 2, p. 115 (From where the quotation is taken); *Proclamations*, vol. 2, no. 442, p. 945 (Gloucestershire); Harrison, 'Royalist Organisation in Wiltshire', pp. 213, 333–4, 342; Anthony Fletcher, 'The Coming of War,' in Morrill (ed.), *Reactions to the English Civil War*, p. 45; Bodl. L., Firth MS C6, fo. 337 (Rupert's reliance on sheriffs for the coordination of administrative reform in Wales, February 1644). Suggestive also are Charles's remarks when he knighted Francis Bassett, sheriff of Cornwall, in 1644; 'Now Mr. Sheriff I leave Cornwall to you safe and sound' (Coate, *Cornwall in the Great Civil War and Interregnum*, p. 155).

42 Hutton, *The Royalist War Effort*, pp. 93–94.

43 Harrison, 'Royalist Organisation in Wiltshire,' pp. 294–303, 320, 363–7, 376–7, 484–7, where the contrasts are explicitly drawn and royalists are described as showing 'total' disrespect for local susceptibilities. A quarter of the commissioners of array had abandoned the royalist cause in Wiltshire before the parliamentary military advance in summer 1644.

44 Hutton, *The Royalist War Effort*, pp. 53–8; the quotation is from p. 58.

45 Hutton, *The Royalist War Effort*, pp. 117–19; Harrison, 'Royalist Organisation in Gloucestershire and Bristol', pp. 140–41, 186–214, 251; BL, Add. MS 18980, fos. 91, 97, 155, and Add. MS 18981, fos. 16^r, 105^r. The naive comment of Sir Edward Walker's suggests something of the royalist incomprehension of the dynamics of local conflicts: 'Lord Chandos, who had with very much courage and seeming fidelity the two preceding years, served his Majesty . . . carried

away with some needless discontent, quitted his commands' (quoted in Harrison, 'Royalist Organisation in Gloucestershire and Bristol,' p. 214).

46 Hutton, *The Royalist War Effort*, pp. 100–4.

47 Phillips (ed.), *Sir Francis Ottley's Papers*, pp. 56–57; vol. 7, pp. 311–12, 321–23; vol. 8, pp. 212–13, 223–25, 240–46. As in Wiltshire there is a clear contrast between royalist problems when in an apparently strong position and parliamentarian resilience in difficult times (see Dore (ed.), *The Letter Books of Sir William Brereton*, pp. 19–21).

48 Hutton, *The Royalist War Effort*, pp. 129–32, 142, 170–5.

49 Besides the political disadvantages deriving from Rupert's prominence it seems that, in practical terms, he simply had too much to do to be efficient. For some of the innumerable appeals to Rupert to sort out local problems, see BL, Add. MS 18981, fo. 222–37 (Cheshire, Wales, and the Marches, August–September 1644); Bodl. L., Firth MS C7, fos. 241–80 (Staffordshire, Oxfordshire, Gloucestershire, and Wiltshire, November–December 1644). On parliament's side, the responsibility for such problems was shared among committees.

50 BL, Add. MS 18981, fo. 8^r; Warburton (ed.), *Memoirs of Prince Rupert and the Cavaliers*, 2, p. 386. Compare Byron on the corporation of Chester (BL, Add. MS 18981, fo. 53^r), Sir John Mennes's famous diatribe against the 'insulting' powers of the commissioners of array in Shropshire (BL, Add. MS 18981, fo. 25^r), and a remarkable petition to the king in May 1644 from Paul Wymond, asking for a personal command in the town of Dover, which argued that corporate organizations were inevitably factious and rebellious (PRO, PRO 30/5/6, pp. 339–40). On the parliamentary side, in any case, Fairfax, Cromwell, or Brereton as much as Essex, Manchester, or Waller surely did not see themselves simply as military leaders, in opposition to civilian interests, although they fretted at short term obstruction by civilian bodies.

51 PRO 30/5/6, pp. 359, 361, 365, 367.

52 For appeals to Northampton, see BL, Add. MS 18980, fo. 58; Manuscripts of the Marquess of Northampton at Castle Ashby, 1083/22. For Northampton's agent, see Roy, 'The Royalist Army in the First Civil War', p. 68.

53 HMC, *Hastings MS*, 2, p. 121 (February 1644); cf. Rupert to Legge, March 1645, Warburton (ed.), *Memoirs of Prince Rupert and the Cavaliers*, 3, p. 73: 'I would give anything to be but one day at Oxford.' Sir William Russell's absence from Oxford in early 1643 meant that his complaints against an unruly subordinate in Worcester went unpunished (see Robin Silcock, 'County Government in Worcestershire, 1603–1660' [Ph.D. thesis, University of London, 1974], p. 254); Sir Jacob Astley in December 1644 asked Rupert for leave to come to Oxford to promote his case for additional supplies for Cirencester better; while Richard Bagot complained that Rupert's decision in Leveson's favour in November 1644 was unfair: 'Had I been so happy to have been present when your Highness received information concerning the contribution, I should have been able to have given your highness clearer satisfaction concerning the equity of my pretensions, than I persuade myself you have yet received.' (Bodl. L., Firth MS C7, fos. 258^r, 233^r).

54 HMC, *Hastings MS*, 2, p. 101. Compare Goring's complaint to Rupert in June 1644: 'I have no manner of certainty in anything is promised me from court . . . what assurances can I ever have of his Majesty's favour when it is in the power of these people to carry him point blank against his former orders' (Bodl. L., Firth MS C7, fo. 128^r). See Roy, 'The Royalist Army in the First Civil War', pp. 68–70, for the king's habit of making decisions in private.

55 Examples of the bewilderment that Charles's decisions caused include Jermyn's comment to Rupert that 'the King was *ashamed* today of two particulars of the commission for pressing in Worcestershire and the compounding by his officers with the delinquents' (BL, Add. MS 18981, fo. 86^r, March 1644; my emphasis); Byron on the proposal to make Sir Francis Gamull governor of Chester: 'Certainly [the king] is persuaded much against his own judgment' (BL, Add. MS 18981, fo. 53^r, February 1644); and Edmund Wyndham's complaint at being subordinate to Hopton in Somerset: 'It seems strange to me that his Majesty, unless he had mind to disturb his own business, should thrust his Lordship upon me . . . No usage whatsoever shall make me less humbly and faithfully to serve him, but I cannot serve him against my own reason, nor place the affection of all my friends where he will dispose them' (Warburton (ed.), *Memoirs of Prince Rupert and the Cavaliers*, 3, p. 48, January 1645). The Worcestershire and Cheshire examples refer to opportunist concessions made by Charles to the Oxford Assembly (see the quotation of Goring in n. 54 above).

56 For a general assessment of the council, see Ian Roy, 'The Royalist Council of War, 1642–1646,' *BIHR*, 35 (1962), pp. 150–68. For examples of its dealings with local civilian grievances against military figures, see BL, Harl. MS 6802, no. 55 (Warwickshire, April 1644) and fo. 40^r (Berkshire, March 1643). For more general supervision of local affairs, see Harl. MS 6851, fos. 79–94 (Worcestershire, January 1643), 133–4 (Gloucestershire, March 1643); Harl. MS 6802, fo. 86^r (Gloucestershire, April 1644); Harrison, 'Royalist Organisation in Wiltshire', pp. 221–9 (August 1643–January 1644); and the provisions laid down in royal proclamations (*Proclamations*, vol. 2, nos. 445, 471 [Oxfordshire, September 1643, February 1644], 453 [Berkshire, October 1643], 463 [Wiltshire, December 1643], 466 [Berkeley division of Gloucestershire, December 1643]). As with informal channels, areas nearest to Oxford found appeals easiest.

57 Roy, 'The Royalist Army in the First Civil War,' p. 51; 'Latterly, individuals – from the king downwards – rather than councils made the important decisions.'

58 One focus for serious criticism was Henry Percy as general of artillery (see Roy (ed.), *The Royalist Ordnance Papers, 1642–1646*, pp. 30–1, 51; BL, Add. MS 18981, fos. 57^r, 73^r). For general attempts at military and administrative reform, see BL, Add. MS 18981, fos. 55^r, 57^v–58^r, 72^r, and Harl. MS 6804, fos. 156^{r-v}; Bodl. L., Firth MS C6, fo. 155; T. Carte (ed.), *The Life of James, Duke of Ormonde* (Oxford, 1851), 6, pp. 15–16; Roy, 'The Royalist Army in the First Civil War,' pp. 238–9; and the references to local auxiliaries in n. 23 above. For disputes in Wiltshire, see Harrison, 'Royalist Organisation in Wiltshire,' p. 229; BL, Harl. MS 6802, fos. 46^{r-v}; in Staffordshire, see HMC, *Hastings MS*, 2, pp. 121–24; in Chester, see BL, Add. MS 18981, fo. 53^r; Warburton (ed.), *Memoirs of Prince Rupert and the Cavaliers*, 2, p. 276; Bodl. L., Firth MS C6, fos. 81–82; BL, Harl. MS 2135, fo. 46^r (Gamull's letter).

59 The first session ran from January 22–April 16, 1644. A record of its public declarations is found in Rushworth, 5, pp. 559–600. The second session, from November 1644–March 10, 1645, was overshadowed by the Uxbridge negotiations and the peace intrigues of Percy, Andover, and Sussex (see Hutton, 'The Structure of the Royalist Party', p. 563). There is little mention of this session in royalist sources, contemporary or retrospective; see, for instance, Clarendon, 3, p. 460. There were also brief meetings in 1646, and on May 15, 1646, the

Lords at Oxford burned all records of its proceedings before the surrender of the city (see *Proclamations*, vol. 2, p. 1045n.).

60 Carte (ed.), *Life of James, Duke of Ormonde*, 3, p. 293n.; BL, Add. MS 18981, fo. 74. Compare Sir Francis Gamull to the Mayor of Chester, February 13, 1644, BL, Harl. MS 2135, fo. 46^r: 'I cannot send you any news but what is the joy of many. The Lords and Commons at Oxford are very unanimous.'

61 *Mercurius Aulicus* (January 28–April 27, 1644). On an admittedly brief survey of the royalist press it seems that royalist divisions in general were rarely aired.

62 M.A. Kishlansky, 'The Emergence of Adversary Politics in the Long Parliament,' (Chapter 2 in this volume). For the use of the press, see Hughes, 'Militancy and Localism', p. 657; Holmes, 'Colonel King and Lincolnshire Politics', pp. 455, n. 20; 457.

63 BL, Harl. MS 2135, fo. 52^r; Warburton (ed.), *Memoirs of Prince Rupert and the Cavaliers*, 2, p. 376.

64 S.R. Gardiner, *History of the Great Civil War, 1642–49* (New York, 1965), 2, p. 181.

65 Hutton, *The Royalist War Effort*, p. 105.

66 For Wilmot and Percy, see Hutton, 'The Structure of the Royalist Party,' pp. 562–3; Carte (ed.), 6, p. 190.

67 Connections between political language and political activity are obviously extremely complex; here I want only to suggest that the range of rhetoric and polemic open to royalists and to parliamentarians was so different and helped to construct different modes of political action. I have found J.G.A. Pocock, *Politics, Language and Time* (London, 1971), ch. 1, helpful; see p. 38 for the comment, 'The paradigms which order reality are part of the reality they order.' For discussion of similar issues in another context, see Lynn Hunt, 'The Rhetoric of Revolution in France,' *History Workshop Journal*, 15 (Spring 1983), pp. 78–94

68 *Proclamations*, vol. 2, nos. 351, 384–85, 387, 401, 407, 410–11, 430, 435, etc. See also the discussion above and n. 19 above.

69 C.H. Firth and R.S. Rait (ed.), *Acts and Ordinances of the Interregnum* (Abingdon, 1982), 1, pp. 241, 85–99, 192.

70 One noticeable way in which parliamentarian rhetoric and practice served to draw individuals into a general cause was through the use of oaths. The National Covenant of June 1643, e.g., holding that 'many ways of force and treachery are continually attempted, to bring to utter ruin and destruction the Parliament and Kingdom, and which is dearest, the true Protestant religion,' was not an oath of loyalty *to* parliament but a means by which 'all who are true-hearted and lovers of their country should bind themselves each to other in a sacred vow and convenant.' The first step was for each individual to 'declare my hearty sorrow for my own sins, and the sins of this nation,' and then 'to endeavour the amendment of my own ways' (Firth and Rait (eds), *Acts and Ordnances of the Interregnum*, 1, p. 175). The contrast between such inclusive oaths and the oaths of obedience, loyalty, and allegiance *to* the king is important.

71 Bodl. L., Firth MS C7, fo. 232^v (November 1644); Warburton (ed.), *Memoirs of Prince Rupert and the Cavaliers*, 3, p. 57 (January 1645). Royalist starvation rhetoric may be a topic in itself; for other examples, see Astley and Charles Lloyd to Rupert, November and December 1644, Bodl. L., Firth MS C7, fos. 243, 270. Other good examples of piqued royalist honour include John Byron to Rupert, October 1644, BL, Add. MS 18981, fos. 287–88; Belasyse to Rupert, March 1644, Bodl. L., Firth MS C7, fo. 7. See Jerrilyn Greene Marston,

'Gentry Honor and Royalism in Early Stuart England,' *JBS*, 13, no. 1 (1973), pp. 21–43, for a preliminary study of a neglected topic.

72 Hutton, *The Royalist War Effort*, p. 199, for the quotation. See, e.g., the defiant response of the governor of Pontefract to his parliamentarian besiegers, January 1645: 'According to my allegiance to which I am sworn and in pursuance of the trust reposed in me by his Majesty, I will defend this castle to the uttermost of my power, and I doubt not be God's assistance, the justness of his Majesty's cause, and the virtue of my comrades to quell all those that shall oppose me in the defence thereof for his Majesty's service' (quoted in Newman, 'The Royalist Army in Northern England, 1642–1645', 1, p. 452). For the defeatism of Newcastle and Rupert, see Newman, 'The Royalist Army in Northern England, 1642–1645', pp. 373–77; Warburton (ed.), *Memoirs of Prince Rupert and the Cavaliers*, 3, pp. 185–8, 200–7.

73 Bodl. L., Tanner MS 62, fo. 402.

74 Baker (ed.), *Records of the Borough of Nottingham*, 5, pp. 228–9. For other illustrations of local conflicts seen in terms of disgrace to parliament rather than personal dishonour, see PRO, SP 28/254/5, fo. 130^r (the Coventry sub-committee for accounts on the county committee, May 1647); Alan Everitt (ed.), *Suffolk and the Great Rebellion*, Suffolk Record Society, vol. 3 (Ipswich, 1960), pp. 87–88 (the Eastern Association's objections to the New Model Army, discussed by the Bury Conference, January 1645). A final contrast can be seen in royalist and parliamentarian resignations and dismissals (or the threats thereof). When Richard Byron lost the governorship of Newark, his protest to the king concentrated on the necessity for personal vindication, 'concerning myself much blemished in my reputation' (Bodl. L., Firth MS C7, fo. 287^r). The earl of Warwick's resignation after the Self-denying Ordinance could surely not have been written by any royalist: 'I do with all humility and cheerfulness, resign and surrender into their hands the office of Lord Admiral, wherewith they were pleased formerly to entrust me. And shall value it as my highest honour and contentment, next to my God, to be serviceable to them and my country in any other condition wherewith his Providence shall cast me; not counting my person, nor dearest interests, too precious to be laid out in maintenance of that great cause of religion and liberty, wherein they are so justly engaged' (*CJ*, 4, pp. 107–8 [April, 1645]).

75 This is perhaps assimilable to a view of parliamentarian discourse as a consensus politics if this is taken to mean a multifaceted, ambiguous rhetoric focusing on the commonwealth, the country, and the public service, a discourse that permitted significant differences of approach and ideas within a shared emphasis on unity; cf. Kishlansky, 'The Emergence of Adversary Politics in the Long Parliament'; Peter Lake, 'Constitutional consensus and Puritan Opposition in the 1620s: Thomas Scott and the Spanish Match,' *HJ*, 25 (1982), 805–25. The latter article lays more stress on the opportunity for conflict within a supposed consensus.

76 Hutton, *The Royalist War Effort*, pp. 178–200, and 'The Structure of the Royalist Party', pp. 563–67.

77 See references in nn. 34 and 37 above; Underdown, *Somerset in the Civil War and Interregnum*, pp. 129–33; and Morrill, *Cheshire*, p. 182: 'The moderates under Sir George Booth enjoyed in the years 1646–8 a greater degree of power than at any other time beween 1642 and 1659.' Ian Gentles, 'The Struggle for London in the Second Civil War,' *HJ*, 26 (1983), pp. 277–305, emphasizes parliament's military coercion as a reason for London's acquiescence in 1648 but also points to the importance of the existence of allies for the moderate

city authorities in the house of lords and the recovering 'Presbyterian' interest in the Commons. Ultimately parliament was able to withdraw much of its military strength from London to meet the threat from Kent without serious consequences.

78 Hutton, 'The Structure of the Royalist Party,' p. 569.

79 For various aspects of earlier development, see Russell, 'The Theory of Treason in the Trial of Strafford'; Cust and Lake, 'Sir Richard Grosvenor and the Rhetoric of Magistracy'; Lake, 'Constitutional Consensus and Puritan Opposition in the 1620s'; Patrick Collinson, *The Religion of Protestants* (Oxford, 1982), ch. 4.

80 For a recent analysis that argues that an essential characteristic of a 'bourgeois state' is the separation of the 'public' and 'private,' see Göran Therborn, *What Does the Ruling Class Do When It Rules?* (London, 1980), pp. 62–6.

11

The chalk and the cheese: contrasts among the English Clubmen

DAVID UNDERDOWN

I

Popular politics in general, and peasant uprisings in particular, are now receiving much attention from historians of early modern Europe. In this discussion the question of allegiance in the English Civil War ought to be an important one, near the top of the agenda. Did people in the lower orders of society really take sides? If so, what explains the variations between different regions in the support obtained by Charles I and parliament respectively? These regional variations used to be simply presented: a parliamentarian south-east against a royalist north and west. For religious and political or social and economic reasons, according to taste, the Puritan, progressive and economically developed southern and eastern counties were ranged against the semi-feudal 'dark corners of the land'.[1] In both versions active popular involvement was confined to the towns and the parliamentarian districts, exemplified in the familiar legend of the East Anglian freeholders who comprised the core of Cromwell's Ironsides. In royalist England, on the other hand, the common people blindly obeyed their betters: deference, rather than any real preference for king or parliament, was the determinant.

I am grateful to Dr. J.S. Morrill, Professor Clive Holmes and Dr. Joyce Lee Malcolm for their helpful comments on an earlier version of this paper.

Local studies have proliferated in recent years, and a more sophisticated range of explanations of regional behaviour is now available. The 'deference' thesis has been extended to parliamentarian as well as royalist areas, on the assumption that the nature of rural society everywhere ruled out active initiative by people below the gentry rank.[2] In a refinement of this socio-political model the rural lower orders are conceded to have had political attitudes, but they are defined as essentially parochial ones, visible only as reactions to external threats to the integrity of their communities. When the common people reacted to the civil war, in other words, it was only in local terms, in the cause of neutrality.[3]

Deference and neutralism have not, however, found universal acceptance. The case for the civil war as a class conflict, pitting the godly 'middle sort' against the defenders of traditional 'feudal' society, has recently been vigorously restated.[4] Here we encounter a different pattern of allegiance, with industrial districts of independent craftsmen and clothworkers – the West Riding, south Lancashire, the Birmingham area – demonstrating a passionate support for parliament, a support based on class feeling. Other historians, while rejecting the explicit class model, have nevertheless seen in the contrasting social structures of different agricultural regions a useful analytical approach. The typology of rural communities based on the 'field: forest-pasture' antithesis has never been systematically applied to civil war allegiances, but it is clearly visible in some recent local studies.[5] When they had any practical choice (which they did not in districts like East Anglia, firmly under parliament's military control), the arable 'field' areas, with their nucleated villages, tight bonds of kinship and neighbourhood, and firm mechanisms of social control from church and manor, might well see the best defence of their traditional society in the royalist 'party of order'. When they had any practical choice, the looser, more independent forest and pasture regions, with their scattered settlements, larger parishes and laxer manorial control, might well be attracted to parliament and the cause of 'liberty and property'.

There are many obstacles to testing these various hypotheses about popular allegiance, among them the total absence of really quantifiable evidence about the actual behaviour of the common people in the civil war. Another difficulty is that the peers and gentry so often get in the way. Rarely indeed can we confidently assess the relative importance of élite leadership and popular initiative. Was the parliamentarianism of wealden and east Sussex (compared with the tepid royalism of downland and west Sussex) merely the result of the authority of an entrenched Puritan oligarchy? Or did the Puritanism of the east Sussex gentry in some sense depend on more deeply rooted popular attitudes in their region? Was the massive turn-out against the marquis of Hertford in Somerset in August 1642 a genuine expression of popular enthusiasm, or simply a product of the territorial influence of Puritan magnates like the Pophams and the

Horners?[26] To clarify popular attitudes we need a case-study in which the role of the magnate gentry was, if not eliminated (that would be impossible), at least minimal. Such a case-study, fortunately, is available in the episode of the Clubmen.

II

The risings of the Clubmen – neutralist outbreaks which in 1645 engulfed large areas of southern and western England – have recently received long overdue attention, notably in J.S. Morrill's important study of English provincialism, *The Revolt of the Provinces*.[7] On Morrill's showing, the Clubmen appear to resemble very closely French peasant groups of the same period. Like the *Croquants* and the *Nu-Pieds* they are vertically organized, uniting all segments of local society from minor gentry and clergy to poorer farmers. They show the same fierce localism, make the same appeal to community traditions, to ancient rights and customs against external, centralizing innovations.[8]

Such characteristics determined the neutralist pattern of the Clubmen's behaviour. There were, to be sure, superficial differences between various groups of Clubmen. The Wiltshire and Dorset men, for example, tended to resist Fairfax's parliamentarian army, while those of central and north Somerset were more inclined to co-operate. However, Morrill quite reasonably dismisses these alliances as merely tactical: the result of the better discipline of Fairfax's troops, which made their presence preferable to that of Goring's brutal rabble, or of a simple desire to end the war quickly by supporting the strongest side.[9] Some of the Clubmen, he concedes, may have had faint preferences for one side or the other, but these preferences were subordinate to their attachment to neutrality and peace, to 'the traditional values of provincial society'. The whole book impressively demonstrates the strength of these traditional values, and the endurance of a 'pure Country' outlook through all the divisions of the civil war.

This does not mean, however, that the last word about the Clubmen has now been said. Morrill's analysis generally stresses the characteristics common to all the various local groups, and rests on a more or less unitary conception of English local societies. At a time when other historians are increasingly insisting on the diversity of these societies, it seems appropriate to ask whether in fact the contrasting behaviour of different groups of Clubmen reflected the real preferences, however vague, of different community types for either king or parliament. Do the Clubmen, in other words, tell us anything about regional patterns of allegiance? It will be argued in this paper that they do, and that the 'field : forest-pasture' typology provides a useful general explanation of the regional differences that we shall encounter.

Before we proceed, however, a few preliminaries must be disposed of. First, Morrill's contention that the apparent preferences of the Clubmen were in fact merely tactical responses to military situations can be accepted as valid for those outbreaks which supported parliament in the final stages of the war. The advantages of a swift parliamentarian victory rather than a hopeless prolongation of the war were by then sufficiently obvious, even to populations which had hitherto acquiesced in royalist rule. We can therefore exclude from consideration Club outbreaks favouring parliament after the fall of Bristol to Fairfax on 10 September 1645, choosing that, perhaps arbitrarily, as the date after which it was obvious that parliament was going to win. This disposes of the risings in Devon and Cornwall in the ensuing months, and the revival of activity in Worcestershire in November. The risings in south Wales preceded the fall of Bristol, but are also excluded because the differences in Welsh society make comparisons with English counties of perilously limited value.[10] The September risings in Hampshire and Sussex, on the other hand, are germane to our purpose, because they were in opposition to the now triumphant parliament. The Hampshire and Sussex men were not trying to end the war by supporting the winning side: they were doing the opposite.

Next, some problems of evidence. It is perplexingly difficult to identify precisely the villages from which the members of the Club associations were drawn. The Clubmen's own manifestoes usually describe themselves in very general terms: 'the Club-Men of the Counties of Dorset and Wilts.' or 'the inhabitants of all the north-west part of the County of Worcester', for example.[11] The newsbooks and the letters of military commanders are no more helpful. We can identify the villages from which some of the leaders came, but a list of leaders contains both a social and a political bias. Leaders tend to be more socially prominent and better educated than their followers. And it happens that virtually all the names that survive are those of 'royalist' Clubmen — men who were punished by the parliamentarian authorities.[12] On the other side the sources are sparse. We have the names of Jeremy Powell of Clun and a few others in Shropshire, of Humphrey Willis of Woolavington in Somerset. We can identify a few ringleaders whose arrest was ordered by the royalist governor of Hereford in March 1645, half a dozen who signed a declaration favourable to parliament in the New Forest in August, and a scattering of gentry adherents elsewhere.[13] But this scarcely redresses a bias in the evidence heavily weighted to the 'royalist' side.

There are, however, enough clues remaining to enable us to depict, at least in some areas, the general distribution of Club allegiance. Occasionally the Clubmen were a bit more precise in their descriptions.[14] Their places of rendezvous, mostly ancient hill-forts, are also helpful, for normally they are unlikely to have attracted people from more than ten or twelve miles away. A warrant of the Wiltshire Clubmen calls on the inhabitants of Dinton to appear at Buxbury, less than four miles to the south, by nine o'clock on 26 May, 'to confer with your neighbouring parishes about matters concerning your and their defence and safety'.[15] In September a letter of the Hampshire County Committee and a pamphlet describing the Sussex rising define the areas affected fairly closely.[16] Even the names of the arrested leaders provide a rough guide to the geographical distribution of the outbreaks. Where there were leaders there must have been followers, and just occasionally we get a glimpse of them in the record.

Most of this evidence, all too variable and imperfect in quality, comes from the three south-western counties – Dorset, Wiltshire and Somerset – in which the Club risings were most widespread and prolonged. It seems reasonable, therefore, to concentrate our attention on these western Clubmen, and on those in Berkshire, Hampshire and Sussex who were briefly associated with them.

III

The region we are considering offers ample opportunity to test the hypothesis that civil war behaviour was related to differences in regional economies and settlement patterns. Across the area runs the great stretch of chalk downland, from the South Downs in the east, through Salisbury Plain, to the Dorset Downs in the west. Here we have our 'field' area, with its nucleated villages and traditional sheep-corn husbandry. But the region also contains the other necessary component, in the shape of extensive tracts of forest and grassland. When we plot on the map the main centres of Club activity, distinguishing those groups which showed royalist and parliamentarian sympathies respectively, a rough but striking correspondence becomes clear. The Clubmen most friendly to the royalist forces were those from the 'chalk' – the nucleated settlements of the downlands. Those most friendly to the parliamentarians were from the fen-edge villages of the Somerset levels, from the clothing parishes of the wood-pasture region in the north of that county, and from the 'cheese' area of Wiltshire around Melksham and Chippenham.[17] The customary distinction between Wiltshire's chalk and cheese regions can thus be extended to other counties, with important socio-political implications.

The pattern is less clear in the earliest of the Club risings than in the later ones. The first outbreaks in Dorset coincided with the westward passage of Goring's turbulent army. On 29 February 1645 some royalist soldiers were killed by the villagers at Godmanstone, and the next day it was reported that nearly a thousand countrymen were in arms 'with guns and clubs to resist the French and Irish amongst the Cavaliers'.[18] The newsbooks are regrettably vague about the area affected, but even if they were more precise it would be unsafe to deduce parliamentarian sympathies merely from resistance to Goring's plunderers. Rumours that the

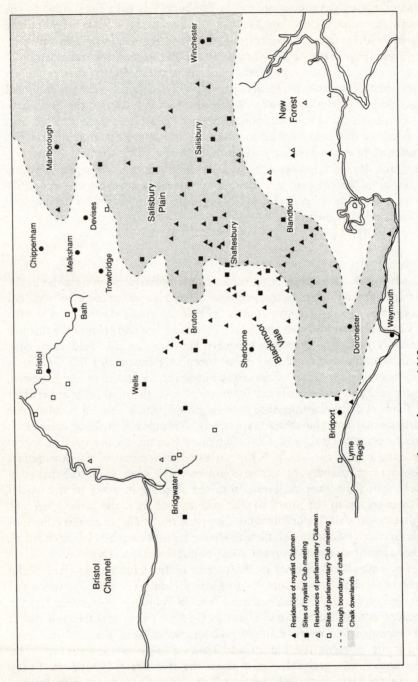

Fig. 11.1 Centres of Club activity in the south-west, 1645

Residences of royalist Clubmen
Sites of royalist Club meeting
Residences of parliamentary Clubmen
Sites of parliamentary Club meeting
Rough boundary of chalk
Chalk downlands

Bristol Channel

New Forest

Marlborough
Chippenham
Melksham
Devises
Trowbridge
Bath
Bristol
Wells
Bridgwater

Winchester
Salisbury
Salisbury Plain
Shaftesbury
Blandford
Bruton
Sherborne
Blackmoor Vale
Dorchester
Weymouth
Bridport
Lyme Regis

Clubmen were committing themselves to parliament both in south Dorset and on the other side of the downs, where attacks on Sir Lewis Dyve's Sherborne forces were also noted, proved to be inaccurate. Waller and Cromwell, who were shadowing Goring, seem to have made some effort to win over this 'Country party' (as a newsbook described them), but without much success. By the end of March the Dorset Committee had disbanded the few who were still in arms.[19] These early outbreaks seem to support Morrill's picture of unrelieved neutralism, in which an apparent swing to one side was simply the product of circumstances, in this case the devastating march of Goring's troops through the county.

But the pattern becomes clearer when we consider the events that followed the reappearance of the Clubmen two months later. They surfaced again on 12 May, when a group said to be three thousand strong assembled between Shaftesbury and Blandford.[20] During the next fortnight the movement spread rapidly. On 25 May a great meeting at Gussage Corner, Dorset, about five miles from the Wiltshire border, was attended by men from both counties, who adopted articles of association and other 'directions for present behaviour'.[21] Within the next few days and weeks there were further gatherings at Badbury Rings, a few miles south of Gussage; at Buxbury to the north; at Groveley and Harnham Hills near Salisbury; at Stonehenge; at Upavon, on the northern edge of Salisbury Plain; and at Whiteparish, near the Wiltshire-Hampshire border.[22] In July there was a meeting at Mere Beacon, and others at less easily identifiable places. Finally, on 4 August, came the great assemblies at Doncliff, west of Shaftesbury (which Cromwell persuaded to disperse), and at Hambledon Hill towards Blandford (which resisted him and was dispersed by force). Besides these mass meetings there were several smaller ones attended only by delegates: the one at Shaftesbury, for example, which precipitated the Hambledon Hill affair, and an earlier one of the 'chosen and able men' from each division of Dorset, at Sturminster Newton on 24 June.[23]

All these meeting-places lie upon, or on the edge of, the chalk. With the exception of the Shaftesbury and Hambledon Hill meetings, which included men from Blackmoor Vale and south-east Somerset, all were attended by Clubmen from downland parishes or from places a few miles away. The residential distribution of the leaders is equally striking. Again with few exceptions they were from the downland. There is a heavy concentration west and south-west of Salisbury: men from Linton, Chicksgrove, Combe Bisset, Alvediston, and other villages towards Shaftesbury. There is another cluster near Blandford, from Durweston to the north-west down the Stour Valley through Spetisbury and Shapwick to Sturminster Marshall. Further west, a triangle bounded by Bere Regis, Cerne Abbas and Ibberton includes another, looser cluster. All these are downland villages, but west of Shaftesbury we find scattered Clubmen from the pasture country of Blackmoor Vale: from Lyndlinch, the Stowers,

Fifehead Magdalen and Marnhull. These in turn link up with those from the wood-pasture region across the Somerset border, around Wincanton and Castle Cary. But apart from this last group the 'royalist' Clubmen were concentrated overwhelmingly in the downlands.

Were these Clubmen of the chalk downs in fact more friendly to the royalist cause than to parliament? They did, after all, negotiate with and agree to pay contributions to both sides. It is also true that royalist commanders like Dyve at Sherborne sometimes found their behaviour distinctly unsatisfactory. Among their leaders were men like Robert Culliford of Encomb, who had supported parliament at one time or another.[24] We need not swallow London's routine propaganda line that the risings stemmed from 'a Jesuitical plot of the enemy'.[25] But when all due allowance is made for their originally neutralist intentions, it remains true that the Wiltshire and Dorset Clubmen tended ever more strongly towards the royalist side.

This became particularly clear during the summer of 1645, when Fairfax had to arrest the 'peremptory and insolent' Dorset leader, George Hawles, just before the battle of Langport.[26] Few clashes are recorded between the Clubmen and royalist troops in this area, though there may have been some in the northern part of Salisbury Plain in June, involving forces from Devizes.[27] But far more serious were the battles with Massey's troops at Sturminster Newton on 19 June, with Ceely's men near Bridport on 3 July, and the final encounter at Hambledon Hill a month later. In all these there were fatalities: half a dozen at Sturminster Newton, an indeterminate number at Bridport, a dozen or so at Hambledon Hill.[28] The downland Clubmen were prepared to fight, and die for their localist beliefs – but against parliamentarians, not against royalists.

Some, but not all, of this hostility to parliament can be attributed to leadership. Granting all that Morrill has wisely said on the difficulty of distinguishing 'real' from merely apparent or accidental allegiance, it is still striking how many of the downland Clubmen had been in arms for, or had otherwise supported, the royalist side. John Fussell had been deputy-governor of Weymouth, Thomas Thornhurst of Winfrith in arms at the taking of Wareham, John Bennet of Pythouse an officer under Colonel Strangways. Others, like Bennet's father Thomas and the lawyer Thomas Young (a prominent figure at several rendezvous), had been royalist commissioners.[29] Not all the clergy were the 'Bishop-would-be's' of whom parliamentarian writers often complained. But they included a few Laudian hard-liners, like Thomas Hickman of Upton Lovell, and others, like Thomas Jay of Fittleton and Edmund Knevett of Calstone Wellington, who had given thanks for royalist victories and pressed oaths of association on their parishioners. William Layford, curate of Ockford Shilling, was among the most refractory of those at Hambledon Hill; it is interesting that he had been one of the few non-Catholic refusers of the

Protestation in 1641.[30] Although a handful of the leading Clubmen had given equivocal support to parliament, none had shown much zeal for their side.

Not only were many of the leaders royalist, so too were many of the policies advanced in the Clubmen's petitions and declarations. Their fundamentally conservative, localist character has been admirably described by Morrill. Such conservatism was not necessarily royalist. But in tone and content the Club petitions closely resemble the 'One-and-All' petitions of the previous autumn, by which the royalists had tried to provoke a popular rising against parliament. It must have been obvious, at least to the more politically educated leaders, that the impartiality professed in appealing to both king and parliament was a sham. Like their 'One-and-All' models, the Club petitions in effect called for peace on royalist terms, beyond that proposing nothing more specific than the four points of the 1641 Protestation; they were designed to be favourably received by Charles I but rejected by parliament. Their language often smacks of the parsonage. A Dorset declaration, for example, gives high priority to tithes and security of tenure for the clergy, and we get a glimpse of clerical intervention in Thomas Aylesbury's excited cry on Mere Beacon: 'Let not the Book of Common Prayer be forgotten'.[31]

From all this we might conclude that it was the influence of the gentry and clergy that gave the western Club movement its tincture of royalism. Yet it seems unlikely that in the disturbed conditions of 1645 the villagers could have been dragooned into action against their wills. On the contrary it is clear that the countrymen shared their leaders' general outlook. A speech to the men of Alderbury hundred by the royalist Sir Bartholomew Pell shows the kind of argument to which they were thought susceptible. 'If the Parliament prevail', Pell told them, 'your religion is lost, your marriages, your christenings, your burials be all lost, as appeared by the Directory which they have set forth'. It was well known, a hostile critic observed, what the Clubmen meant when they demanded the old laws: 'the old vanities and superstitions of their forefathers, the old necromantic order of prelacy, and the wondrous old heathen customs of Sunday-pipings and dancings, with the meritorious maypoles, garlands, galliards, and jolly Whitsun-Ales'.[32] Village festivals had survived in the cheese country too. But there Puritanism was a more indigenous growth, its sabbatarianism and rejection of Laudian ritual attracting a greater popular support. The old religion was more deeply rooted in the prevailing cultural matrix of the traditionalist downland communities.[33]

So it was something more basic than theories about monarchy and episcopacy which drew the Clubmen into the royalist camp. Their leaders fitted more comfortably into their communities than did the zealous reformers who were at least a vocal minority among the parliamentarians, and whose beliefs seemed dangerously disruptive of the old ways. The Club leader John Fussell is a good example. He had been appointed deputy-steward of the earl of Salisbury's western estates in 1624 when his predecessor Richard Sherfield, brother to the militantly Puritan recorder of Salisbury, was dismissed for alienating the tenantry by his harshness. Fussell, clearly, was more acceptable to local opinion than were the efficient, reforming Sherfields. It is not known what part he played in the plundering of Cranborne House in 1643, when Salisbury's court rolls were thrown away or sold to marauding tenants by Maurice's soldiers. But he was already openly disloyal to his employer, boasting that he had been asked to handle local lawsuits against the earl, and refusing to give up records in his custody. Fussell may not have been a particularly committed royalist – in 1646 he was said to have 'many times declared himself to be neither for King nor Parliament'. But whatever his motives, the Cranborne tenants might well perceive him and the side he had outwardly espoused as preferable to the kind of religious and tenurial reforms that the Sherfields represented. From the other side, an official more loyal to the earl contemptuously dismissed the tenants as 'a company of atheistical clowns, and all malignants or neuters'.[34]

The connection between Club royalism and anti-Puritan traditionalism is clearly apparent in the city of Salisbury, the one urban centre involved in the movement. Once again, a good many of the Clubmen there had assisted the royalist side in the war. Shortly before the rising, several had been summoned before the county committee at Falstone and fined for delinquency: they would have had good reason to turn Clubmen.[35] What is most remarkable at Salisbury, however, is the way the Club leadership perpetuated a longstanding local opposition to the clique of Puritan reformers in the corporation. In the 1620s, allied with Recorder Sherfield, the Puritans had promoted an ambitious scheme of poor relief, including the establishment of a municipal brewery, thus antagonizing a coalition of the brewing and victualling interest, the cathedral clergy, and what a reformer called 'all the loose unruly rabble of the town'. As Paul Slack puts it: 'A highly motivated group of Puritan aldermen . . . had tried to dragoon the whole community into employing and relieving the poor, to create a "godly commonwealth" by direction from above'.[36]

The continuity between the earlier anti-Puritan group and the Clubmen in Salisbury is unmistakable. 'Our singing-men and others depending in that nature upon the prelatical party are among the chief instigators', it was reported on 9 June. Three of the vicars-choral (Clark, London and Wenslow) were seen marching with the Clubmen and were present at the Groveley rendezvous. One of the town clergy, John King, was at the Harnham Hill meeting; he and Clark were arrested at Shaftesbury in August.[37] Two of the other leaders appear to have had cathedral connections: Thomas Hawles, a prominent activist in Wiltshire and brother of the Dorset leader, lived in the Close, while Thomas Lawes, a former mayor, may have been related to the composer Henry Lawes whose father (another

Thomas) had been a vicar-choral. The brewers were equally prominent. Maurice Greene, Thomas Hancock and Robert Jole had all fought the Puritan brewhouse scheme: they or their sons were all among the Club leadership in 1645.[38] So the Clubmen expressed a deep-rooted opposition to Puritanism, an opposition compounded by the severity of the Falstone House Committee. To episcopal Salisbury, as to the rural communities of the downlands, a Puritan parliament threatened the bonds of the traditional community.

IV

The Clubmen of the pasture and woodland regions also, though less dramatically, support the hypothesis that their support for king or parliament was influenced by the type of community in which they lived. According to this hypothesis we should expect to find a greater tendency towards parliament in these more independent, more egalitarian, less custom-bound communities. With some important exceptions, that is what we do indeed find.

I have written about the Somerset Clubmen elsewhere, and it is necessary here only to recall a few salient points about them.[39] The parliamentarian Clubmen in Somerset came from two areas: the levels south-east of Bridgwater and along the Poldens, and the wood-pasture region of the north-east, with its many clothing villages. The former group, of which Humphrey Willis was the leader, first gathered on Sedgemoor on 30 June. After overcoming attempted infiltration by royalist lawyers and clergy from Wells they moved decisively into the parliamentarian camp, and co-operated with Fairfax's army during the siege of Bridgwater. The north Somerset group resisted the landing of royalist reinforcements at Portishead and rebuffed Rupert's attempts to win them over, but responded with enthusiasm to Cromwell's call for aid in the attack on Bristol. They were then organized as auxiliary troops under the command of Alexander Popham.

It is worth noting that it was in this area, northward from the Mendips, that occurred the massive rising against the royalists in August 1642. Near Bath, where the three counties of Somerset, Gloucestershire and Wiltshire converge, lay what Clarendon called 'the most absolute disaffected parts of all three'. John Aubrey blamed much of the area's Puritanism on the vegetation. North Wiltshire, he observed, abounded in 'sour and austere plants, as sorrell, etc. which makes their humours sour'. But he also had an economic explanation. In the arable regions people had to work too hard following the plough to bother about religion or politics. In the cheese country they had time for such diversions: 'the Bible, and ease, for it is now all upon dairy-grassing and clothing, set their wits a-running and reforming'. The clothing villages, especially, were 'nurseries of sedition and rebellion'.[40]

We can reject Aubrey's botanical behaviourism and still concur in his assessment of the distinctly Puritan tone of this region. It had been strongly parliamentarian at the outset of the war, and three years of royalist occupation had not changed its basic character. John Corbet's description of the Gloucestershire farmers and clothworkers is well known: 'a generation of men truly laborious, jealous of their properties, whose principal aim is liberty and plenty'.[41] The turbulent inhabitants of the Forest of Dean were especially regarded as 'constant friends of the Parliament', and had stoutly resisted royalist forces under their own special enemy, Sir John Wintour.[42] The Gloucestershire Clubmen were slower than those of Somerset to support the New Model, but by the time Bristol fell, upwards of two thousand had appeared, under the leadership of Sir John Seymour and other local gentlemen.[43] The gentry's presence might raise doubts about the movement's spontaneity, but it is likely that Seymour and his friends played the same role as Sir John Horner and the Pophams in Somerset, taking charge of a rising that was already afoot. Their belated appearance might also indicate the sort of opportunism that Morrill argues for: a case of neutrals waiting until the issue was decided before committing themselves. However, the earlier record of the Gloucestershire populace suggests a greater degree of parliamentarian feeling.

The parliamentarian outlook of the Wiltshire cheese country – the dairying parishes around Chippenham and Melksham – might also be put down to magnate influence (by Sir Edward Baynton of Bromham, for example) if we knew nothing of the riots of 1630–1 and other turbulent events in the area's recent history. When the Club outbreaks erupted in the summer of 1645 this part of Wiltshire behaved very differently from the downlands. Like the chalk country, the cheese had suffered military incursions from both sides; by parliamentarians from Malmesbury and Great Chalfield, royalists from Devizes and Lacock. But there was a marked contrast in local attitudes to these garrisons. There was no serious conflict with the parliamentarians at Malmesbury. People complained about the garrison's oppressions, but their main grievances were that it did not properly protect them from the enemy, and that some of the officers were dishonest and probably disloyal. These are typical local complaints, but they are those of parliament's friends, who wanted a more effective war effort.[44]

The real enemies of the north-west Wiltshire men were the plundering royalists from Devizes. Even the more royalist-inclined Salisbury Plain Clubmen fought them on a number of occasions in June 1645. Early in July there was a major incident at Market Lavington, on the edge of the dairy country. When troops came to collect contributions, a local man named Merryweather roused the village by beating a 'pestle and pan' together. The market bell was rung to warn adjoining parishes, 'and so one town to another' until nearly a thousand Clubmen gathered and advanced on Devizes.[45] Merryweather was a tenant of the parliamentarian Sir John Danvers, which might imply some gentry influence, but this does not alter the fact that the Clubmen from this area north of Salisbury Plain, extending into the Vale of Pewsey, were more inclined to resist royalists than parliamentarians. They were unable to do so more effectively, a newsbook suggested, because of their remoteness from the New Model and its Club allies further west. Those who were able to do so joined the Somerset men, for Wiltshire Clubmen were present at the meetings on Lansdown at which Rupert's overtures were rejected. And skirmishing on the northern edge of Salisbury Plain continued into September, when a party of horse from Devizes came under attack at Collingbourne, with casualties on both sides.[46]

The behaviour of the Clubmen in the Devizes area is perhaps explicable in terms of resentment against a particularly predatory garrison. The best evidence for the different character of this part of Wiltshire is the almost total absence of any record of 'royalist' Club activity there. North of the Salisbury Plain escarpment there are only two recorded instances: at Calstone Wellington, near the western end of the Marlborough Downs, and at Wootton Rivers in the Vale of Pewsey. The parson of this latter village was alleged to have raised a party of Clubmen, 'all that he could get to join with him'. He later asserted that he and his son-in-law were isolated in the village: clearly it was no royalist community.[47] But perhaps conclusions about the geographical distribution of the Clubmen are unsafe because they rest so heavily on the leaders taken at Shaftesbury? This, after all, was too far away for many people from north Wiltshire to have attended. It is probably true that the Shaftesbury list distorts the picture for Dorset: out of forty-four Dorset Clubmen whose places of residence are known, only twenty would be known as Clubmen from other sources. For Wiltshire, however, the danger is reduced because the other sources are more plentiful. Only eight Wiltshire men whose places of residence are known were taken at Shaftesbury, and there is independent evidence of Club activity in every case.[48] So the absence of north Wiltshire names in these other sources – notably the papers of the Falstone House Committee – is highly significant. The royalist Clubmen in Wiltshire came from the chalk, not the cheese country.

V

Before we examine the difficult areas that remain – pastoral Dorset, south-east and west Somerset – a brief survey of the Club affair in the outlying counties of Berkshire, Hampshire and Sussex is in order. All three counties sustain the general hypothesis: royalist Clubmen in the downlands, parliamentarian Clubmen in forest and pasture regions. Berkshire can be quickly dealt with. In August there were several assemblies on the downs north of Newbury – typical chalk country. These Clubmen were clearly unfriendly to parliament. They obstructed the collection of contributions, and adopted a declaration similar to those of Dorset and Wiltshire, promising the usual peace petitions to king and parliament. After arresting a high constable who had been circulating the Clubmen's warrants, the Berkshire Committee prevented further meetings, backed by the Commons' prohibition against unlawful assemblies.[49]

In Hampshire two distinct groups can be identified: royalist Clubmen in the downs near Winchester, and more parliamentarian Clubmen in the New Forest. Again this is precisely what we should expect. The former group emerged before the end of June, when over five hundred men were in arms. It had some ties with the Wiltshire association: in July several Hampshire Clubmen attended a banquet at Salisbury. There was the usual clerical influence, with men like John Heath of Clanfield, Philip Oldfield of Lasham, and the notably royalist Edward Stanley of Mottisfont to the fore.[50] By the end of July a committee had been established at Petersfield, near the Sussex border: the Sussex authorities denounced them as 'traitors, . . . neuters, enemies to the Commonwealth'. In September there were clashes with parliamentarian troops besieging Winchester, in which four or five Clubmen were killed. Most of these people came, the Hampshire Committee noted, from 'eastward of Winton from the borders of Sussex, that part of this county being many of them Papists and many others the Bishop of Winton's tenants'.[51] The association of the downland with traditional religious and political views is again apparent.

In the New Forest it was a different story. When a trio of Hampshire committee men met the 'Club Commissioners' on 23 July they found them co-operative, and expected to 'rather have advantage than hindrance by them'. People in the Lymington area spoke of the royalists as 'the common enemy' and agreed to hand over plundering soldiers to the committee; the men of Fordingbridge hundred promised to keep watch and ward against royalists in return for exemption from impressment. A few weeks later a declaration of the New Forest inhabitants protested their loyalty to parliament, explained that their sole intention was to protect themselves from plunder, and denied 'any intention or design to prescribe rules to the Parliament, in the government of either church or commonwealth'.[52] The contrast with the downland men could scarcely be clearer.

The contrast in Sussex is equally clear. Wealden east Sussex had long been a parliamentarian stronghold, downland west Sussex much less so. The Club rising was confined, not surprisingly, to the west. It had both internal and external origins. Chichester and Arundel rapes had suffered badly in the war, and had complained about free quarter by parliamentarian troops in January 1645. Rural opinion was further upset in the summer when the county J.P.s issued one of their many decrees against church-ales.[53] The oppressive actions of the Chichester Committee's officials made the earl of Northumberland conclude that they wanted to provoke a rebellion, and profit from the resulting sequestrations.[54] On top of this came Westminster's demand for the impressment of four hundred Sussex men for the New Model; two M.P.s were sent to take charge. Meanwhile the proximity of the Hampshire Clubmen at Petersfield encouraged the Sussex men to resist.[55]

The Sussex rising occurred in a downland area bounded by Chichester, Midhurst, Petworth and Arundel. The first rendezvous was on Duncton Hill, south of Petworth, on 17 September, organized by parish gentry and yeomen 'in a confederacy with the vulgar multitude'. Warrants had been sent to the villages towards the Hampshire border. About six hundred men attended; they rescued some conscripts on their way to Chichester. But troops soon dispersed the main group of Clubmen at Mabberton, killing a man who tried to give the alarm, and taking two ministers prisoner.[56] Even after this set-back and the discouraging news from Hampshire a few days later, Clubmen remained active in the two western rapes. In October William Cawley was still lamenting their violence: 'sending sometimes a constable or tithingman with the blood running about his ears . . . no collector daring to distrain for fear of having his brains dashed out, forty servants and women rising together with prongs and other weapons'.[57]

When the Clubmen presented their demands to the committee at Lewes on 26 September they wisely avoided royalist statements. Their remonstrance had wider backing than the original movement, coming from 'the not ingaged as well as the ingaged party'. They acknowledged the authority of the M.P.s and 'other gents.' and asked them to transmit their grievances to parliament or (showing the deferential outlook of the area) to the earl of Northumberland. Still, the remonstrance loudly protested at parliamentarian interference with local customs. Besides the usual complaints about free quarter, impressment and taxation, the Sussex Clubmen voiced the same religious orthodoxy as their western counterparts. 'Mechanics and unknown persons' had replaced orthodox clergy at the whim of a single committee-man: the Clubmen insisted on proper hearings before the whole committee. In words similar to Northumberland's a few weeks earlier, they denounced the committee's employment of 'men of sordid condition' who had 'overthrown all our English liberties and have endeavoured to make us desperate'. Instead of these upstarts, they asked to be governed by 'gentlemen of worth, birth and integrity, and known amongst us'.[58] Their language goes far beyond the respectful obsequiousness shown by the New Forest men. Having already suffered military defeat, the Sussex Clubmen did not endorse the usual peace petitions, but in all other respects their programme was typical of the downlands.

What little is known about the Sussex leaders confirms this general impression. They included relatives of the royalist Sir Edward Ford of Harting, as well as people of less obvious allegiance such as the Peckhams of Chichester and the Aylwins of Goring. Richard Shallott, described as 'one of the chief ringleaders', was a son of the Chichester royalist Francis Shallott; his estate was at West Harting, close to Ford's territory.[59] The evidence suggests that royalist-inclined gentry and clergy played the same role in Sussex as in Wiltshire and Dorset. In Sussex as elsewhere, the fielden villages of the downlands resisted parliament; forest and pasture villages did not.

VI

In all the areas surveyed so far, the distribution of 'royalist' and 'parliamentarian' Clubmen corresponds closely with the distribution of field and pasture. But no model as simple as this one can conform completely to the complex variety of real historical experience. There are in fact three regions which were caught up in the west-country Club movement in which the hypothesis we have been pursuing seems less useful: the pasturelands of Dorset, south-east Somerset, and the western hills of Somerset.

One part of pastoral Dorset – the region inland from Lyme Regis and Bridport towards Beaminster – does perhaps fit the pattern tolerably well. An area of scattered farms rather than villages, its dairy farms and medium-sized holdings made it a stronghold of the independent yeoman.[60] Evidence of Club activity in this part of Dorset is unfortunately not very plentiful. In April 1645 Thomas Ceely, governor of Lyme Regis, administered the Covenant to a group of about five hundred who were choosing officers and asking to be supplied with arms.[61] The region was thought to be generally parliamentarian, and this was still evident on 2nd July, when Ceely enlisted a hundred and fifty of the countrymen in case his own troops were drawn away to fight Goring. The next day, however, the situation changed dramatically. A large crowd of Clubmen collected near Bridport; when Ceely sent to ask their intentions they arrested the messenger and tore up his papers. Ceely promptly brought troops to disperse them. A number of Clubmen were killed, and Ceely himself was slightly wounded.[62] At about the same time the governor of Weymouth had difficulty raising contributions and supplies because of obstruction by Clubmen, and nearby fishermen of parliamentarian loyalties also suffered at their hands.[63]

Before we dismiss the validity of the hypothesis for west Dorset, however, it should be noted that none of these outbreaks occurred further west than Bridport, where the downs approach the sea. The men who fought with Ceely's troops may well have come from the downs, not the pasturelands. Even after the fight it was reported that the Dorset men were not universally hostile to parliament; a small group of them had sent a message to Fairfax, 'declaring their affections'.[64] There is no evidence one way or the other, but again it is not impossible that these were from the dairy country inland from Lyme Regis. West Dorset does not necessarily negate the hypothesis.

The other main pasture region of Dorset, the grasslands of Blackmoor Vale, presents the real difficulties. The Blackmoor Clubmen seem to have been as firmly royalist as those from the chalk country. Among their leaders were men from villages throughout the vale, from Lydlinch and Manston in the south by way of Marnhull and Fifehead Magdalen to Gillingham in the north. Across the Somerset border the pattern continues, with Clubmen from Henstridge, Horsington and Wincanton, north to Bruton, Lamyatt, Evercreech and Milton Clevedon. There were great meetings of the Somerset men at Castle Cary and on Cattal Hill.[65]

This is a hard area to explain. One would expect it to be moderately sympathetic to parliament, at least as much so as central and north Somerset. It was not. The Bruton area had been royalist in the early part of the war, and evidently remained so. The whole region suffered badly during the skirmishing between Waller and Goring in the spring of 1645; a newsbook noted wholesale plundering and impressment by the royalists 'about Gillingham, the Stowers and parishes about, and in all Blackmore'.[66] The initial outbreaks were not surprisingly directed against Goring, and there were some violent clashes with royalist troops between Castle Cary and Cadbury. On the royalists' own admission, people were refusing to pay contributions, obstructing impressment, and forcibly rescuing conscripts. The meeting at Castle Cary adopted a petition that was presented to Prince Charles at Wells on 2 June. After thus announcing their grievances, however, the Clubmen of south-east Somerset made no further moves against the royalists. Some of their leaders indeed attended the meeting at Shaftesbury on 2 August.[67]

West Somerset, from the Quantocks to the Devon border, is another area of pastureland which exhibited few traces of popular support for parliament. With the exception of the towns and the Vale of Taunton, the area had taken little part in the mass movement of August 1642, and throughout the war placidly acquiesced in royalist rule. In the summer of 1645 there were complaints of Goring's 'insolencies and injuries' in these parts, as Prince Charles found at Dunster in June; a month later royalist troops were rounding up hostile Clubmen in the woods near Dulverton. Yet when on 30 July the local parliamentarian bosses wooed the Clubmen at a rendezvous in the Quantocks, they were firmly rebuffed. The meeting affirmed the same conservative, neutralist principles as the Wiltshire and Dorset men.[68] Reports of later anti-royalist Club outbreaks in west Somerset seem to relate either to the parliamentarian district near Taunton, to the activities of the auxiliaries from central and north

Somerset who went there after the fall of Bristol, or can be explained as the usual opportunism now that the war was virtually won.[69]

Why were these regions so different? A final answer would require a comparative economic, social and political analysis on a scale far beyond the scope of this essay. Obviously there were other variables that influenced a community's behaviour besides its place in the field-pasture spectrum. Economic development clearly had something to do with it. North Somerset was a wood-pasture region, but also had an extensive clothing industry: west Somerset, outside the towns, did not. Yet the presence or absence of a clothing industry is not by itself a sufficient explanation of allegiance. The Polden villages and the levels were parliamentarian without a cloth industry; there was cloth in places like Bruton and Castle Cary which were predominantly royalist. A possible explanation of west Somerset's royalism may be the relative poverty of the area – the upland parishes were thinly populated with a literacy rate lower than that of other parts of the county.[70] But this suggestion in turn is of little help for the Bruton area and Blackmoor Vale. In this region royalist landlords like the Berkeleys and the clergy they patronized had, for one reason or another, more control over their villagers. Among much else, the district's landlord–tenant relationships clearly demand further study.

VII

The behaviour of the western Clubmen at least partly vindicates the field-pasture antithesis as a useful analytical model of popular allegiance in the civil war. The model seems most applicable to the sheep-corn downland regions, with their nucleated villages, where the Clubmen were consistently royalist in their sympathies. It holds equally well for many of the woodland and pasture districts, especially (though not exclusively) those containing a significant cloth industry. For reasons that are not entirely clear, it is less useful in some other pasture regions, for example those surveyed in the previous section of this paper.

Whether the model is applicable to popular behaviour in the rest of England remains to be investigated. A glance at the distribution of Clubmen in the west midlands suggests that it may have some general validity. The three counties of Herefordshire, Worcestershire and Shropshire were all royalist throughout the war. There were extensive tracts of arable farming in all three, especially in Herefordshire, but for the most part these were pastoral counties. However, what little evidence there is about the Clubmen does not directly contradict the hypothesis. In Shropshire there is a marked contrast between the lowland eastern part of the county, where the Clubmen merely resisted royalist taxation, and Clun Forest in the west, where Jeremy Powell's followers were openly parliamentarian.[71] In Worcestershire the Clubmen were more active in the hilly western parishes, especially in the Malvern area, than in the arable parts of the Severn Valley and the Vale of Evesham.[72] In Herefordshire there were Clubmen near Leintwardine, close to Clun Forest, but the main rising occurred in Broxash hundred, north-east of Hereford, adjoining the part of Worcestershire most affected. It may be significant that Broxash contained a higher proportion of small landholders than other Herefordshire hundreds.[73]

The behaviour of the Clubmen in both the Welsh border region and the south-western counties confirms the truth that rural communities in the civil war were almost invariably localist and conservative. On this point Morrill's study needs no revision. Parliamentarian Clubmen no less than royalist ones retained traditional notions of community. When those notions were threatened after the war by parliament's local agents the Somerset men, for example, reacted almost as fiercely as they had against the royalists.[74] The Clubmen of all areas, royalist or parliamentarian, had much in common: a firm attachment to ancient rights and customs, a vague nostalgia for the good old days of Queen Elizabeth, an unquestioning acceptance of the social order. But, as in 1642, marginal differences over whether community values were more endangered by court and bishops, or by parliament and Puritans, were crucial. Men united by much else were divided over such matters: hence the civil war. In that war the leadership of the élite was important, but it was not the sole determinant of popular action. The contrasts among the Clubmen help us to understand this. They also confirm the supposition that the arable, fielden areas were more likely to be royalist, and the forests and pasturelands parliamentarian.

Popular behaviour in the civil war has been charted only very sketchily for many parts of England. Much detailed work remains to be done on such matters as settlement patterns, tenurial relations, literacy rates, popular culture, and other possible variables, before we can reach a full understanding of the geographical distribution of allegiance. The parliamentarian character of the fielden areas of East Anglia is sufficient to show that the model proposed in this essay cannot provide a total explanation of regional contrasts in the civil war. But the chalk and the cheese may be of some help as we work painfully towards such an explanation.

Notes

1 The continuing appeal of this form of analysis is evident in what is still the best general survey of the period: Christopher Hill, *The Century of Revolution, 1603–1714* (Edinburgh, 1961), pp. 121–2.

2 For the general argument, see Peter Laslett, *The World We Have Lost* (London, 1965). For applications to particular counties, see A.M. Everitt, *The Community of Kent and the Great Rebellion* (Leicester, 1966), esp. pp. 70, 83; Clive Holmes,

The Eastern Association in the English Civil War (Cambridge, 1974), pp. 19–22, 26, 34–48.

3 The outstanding example is J.S. Morrill, The Revolt of the Provinces (London, 1976).

4 Brian Manning, The English People and the English Revolution (London, 1976).

5 For example, Anthony Fletcher, A County Community in Peace and War: Sussex, 1600–1660 (London, 1975). The typology is defined in Joan Thirsk, 'The Farming Regions of England', in H.P.R. Finberg (ed.), The Agrarian History of England and Wales, IV, 1500–1640, ed. Joan Thirsk (Cambridge, 1967), ch. 1.

6 Fletcher, A County Community in Peace and War, chs. 3, 13.; David Underdown, Somerset in the Civil War and Interregnum (Newton Abbot, 1973), pp. 32–8.

7 Morrill, Revolt of the Provinces. Morrill provides full references for other recent work on the Clubmen.

8 Roland Mousnier, Peasant Uprisings in Seventeenth-Century France, Russia and China, trans. Brian Pearce (London, 1972), chs. 1–5; C.S.L. Davies, Peasant Revolt in France and England: A Comparison', AHR, 21 (1973), pp. 122–34.

9 Morrill, Revolt of the Provinces, pp. 99–100.

10 Both the similarities and the differences are evident in A.H. Dodd, Studies in Stuart Wales (Cardiff, 1952), ch. I.

11 A.R. Bayley, The Great Civil War in Dorset (Taunton, 1910), p. 472; Diary of Henry Townshend of Elmley Lovett, 1640–1663, ed. J.W. Willis Bund, 2 vols (London, 1920), II, p. 221.

12 The main sources for the leaders' names are the lists in Zachary Grey, Impartial Examination of the Third Volume of Mr. Daniel Neal's History of the Puritans (London, 1737), Appendix, p. 60; and Anon., The Kings Answer to the Propositions for Peace (25 July 1645): BL., Thomason Tracts (hereafter E.), E. 296(12). All dates supplied for works in this collection are as given in the Catalogue of the Pamphlets, Books, Newspapers and Manuscripts Relating to the Civil War, the Commonwealth and Restoration, Collected by George Thomason, 1640–1661, 2 vols (London, 1908). Other names can be retrieved from CCC; and from BL., Add. MSS 22084–5 (Register of Wilts. Committee), printed in part in 'The Falstone Day-Book', ed. J. Waylen, Wilts Archaeol. and Nat Hist. Mag., XXVI (1892), pp. 343–91.

13 The Letter Books, 1644–45, of Sir Samuel Luke, Parliamentary Governor of Newport Pagnell, ed. H.G. Tibbutt (Bedfordshire Hist. Rec. Soc., XLII, London, 1963), p. 490; Underdown, Somerset in the Civil War and Interregnum, p. 107; 'Declaration of Col. B. Scudamore', 19 Mar. 1644/5: BL., Add. MS. 11043, fos. 19–20; Heads of Some Notes of the Citie Scout, no. 4 (19 Aug. 1645): E. 297(4); Perfect Passages, no. 44 (26 Aug. 1645): E. 262(51); True Informer, no. 22 (20 Sept. 1645): E. 302(9); Bulstrode Whitelocke, Memorials of the English Affairs, 4 vols (Oxford, 1853), I, pp. 540, 544.

14 For example, those of the Malvern area, who spoke for the inhabitants of Leigh, Cradley, Suckley and other villages: Kingdomes Weekly Intelligencer, no. 92 (25 Mar. 1645): E. 274 (24).

15 True Informer, no. 8 (14 June 1645): E. 288 (18).

16 [Hants. Committee] to Committee of Both Kingdoms, Sept. 1645: BL., Add. MS. 24860, fo. 137; Anon., A True Relation of the Rising of the Club-Men in Sussex (23 Sept. 1645): E. 302 (18).

17 See Fig 11.1, p. 292. For Wiltshire agricultural districts, see E. Kerridge,

'Agriculture, *c.* 1500–*c.* 1793', in VCH, *Wiltshire*, IV (London, 1959), pp. 43–64. For Somerset and Dorset, see *Agrarian History of England and Wales*, IV, pp. 67–80; Barbara Kerr, *Bound to the Soil: A Social History of Dorset, 1750–1918* (London, 1968), pp. 8–11.

18 Bayley, *The Great Civil War in Dorset*, pp. 248, 260.

19 *Moderate Intelligencer*, nos 2, 4 (13 Mar. 1644/5, and 27 Mar. 1645): E. 273 (7), and E. 274 (27); *Kingdomes Weekly Intelligencer*, no. 90 (11 Mar. 1644/5): E. 273 (2); *Perfect Diurnall*, no. 85 (17 Mar. 1644/5): E. 258 (36); *Perfect Passages*, no. 21 (19 Mar. 1644/5): E. 258 (38); *Perfect Occurrences* (14–21 Mar. 1644/5): E. 260 (I); *Weekly Account* (19–25 Mar. 1644/5, and 26 Mar.–2 Apr. 1645): E. 274 (23), and E. 276 (6); *The Generall Account of the Proceedings in Parliament* (31 Mar. 1645): E. 260 (6).

20 *Weekly Account* (14–21 May 1645): E. 284 (25).

21 Anon., *The Desires and Resolutions of the Club-Men of the Counties of Dorset and Wilts.* (25 May 1645): E. 292 (24); also in Bayley, *The Great Civil War in Dorset*, pp. 472–5. The place of meeting is spelt 'Gorehedge': Gussage seems the only possible identification.

22 The Badbury meeting is recorded in Anon., *The Desires and Resolutions of the Club-Men of the Counties of Dorset and Wilts.* (25 May 1645): E. 292 (24). For Buxbury, see note 15 above. For the others, see *Kingdomes Weekly Intelligencer*, no. 104 (17 June 1645): E. 288 (31); *LJ, VII*, p. 485; BL, Add. MS. 22084, fo. 13ᵛ.

23 Morrill, *Revolt of the Provinces*, pp. 92–3; Joshua Sprigge, *Anglia Rediviva* (London, 1647), ed. H.T. Moore (Gainseville, Fla., 1960), pp. 77–81; Bodl. L., Oxford, Tanner MS. 60, fos. 163–4.

24 Morrill, *Revolt of the Provinces*, p. 101; *Minute Books of the Dorset Standing Committee*, ed. C.H. Mayo (Exeter, 1902), p. 16.

25 Anon., *The Kings Answer to the Propositions for Peace* (25 July 1645): E. 296 (12).

26 Sprigge, *Anglia Rediviva.*, p. 67; Anon., *A Letter Sent to the Speaker of the House of Commons* (7 July 1645): E. 292 (22).

27 *True Informer*, no. 8 (14 June 1645): E. 288 (18); *Mercurius Veridicus*, no. 9 (14 June 1645): E. 288 (19); *Perfect Occurrences* (20–7 June 1645): E. 262 (13).

28 *Perfect Occurrences* (27 June-4 July 1645): E. 292 (22); Whitelocke *Memorials of the English Affairs*, I, p. 468; *The Writings and Speeches of Oliver Cromwell*, ed. W.C. Abbott, 4 vols (Cambridge, Mass., 1937–47), I, p. 369. Estimates of the number killed near Bridport (between fifty and eighty) are obviously exaggerated.

29 HMC, *Salisbury MSS*, XXII p. 389; *Perfect Diurnall*, no. 107 (18 Aug. 1645): E. 262 (45); *Calendar of the Committee for Advance of Money*, ed. M.A.E. Green, 3 vols (London, 1888), II, pp. 986–8, 1026, 1064; CCC, II, pp. 941, 1412.

30 *Moderate Intelligencer*, no. 17 (26 June 1645): E. 289 (17); A.G. Matthews, *Walker Revised* (Oxford, 1948), pp. 373–5; *The Dorset Protestation Returns*, ed. E.A. Fry (Dorset Records, XII, London, 1912), p. 133.

31 *Kingdomes Weekly Intelligencer*, no. 103 (10 June 1645): E. 287 (7); Morrill, *Revolt of the Provinces*, pp. 93, 112. For examples of 'One-and-All' petitions, see Rushworth, 2nd edn, 8 vols (London, 1721–2), V, pp. 717–18.

32 *Heads of Some Notes of the Citie Scout*, no. 4 (19 Aug. 1645): E. 297 (4); *Mercurius Britannicus*, no. 95 (1 Sept. 1645): E. 298 (24).

33 The survival or disappearance of church-ales and other popular festivals in different regions is a subject that would repay further study. My impression, from admittedly imperfect evidence, is that by the early seventeenth century they were becoming less common in Puritan north-east Somerset than in other

parts of the county. However, after the Restoration Aubrey noted a good many surviving revels in the villages of north Wiltshire. See *Wiltshire: The Topographical Collections of John Aubrey*, ed. J.E. Jackson (Devizes, 1862), pp. 125, 139, 146, 185, 198, 272–4.

34 HMC, *Salisbury MSS, XXII, pp. 200–1, 374–5, 386, 389; Lawrence Stone, Family and Fortune* (Oxford, 1973), pp. 126–7, 148–9.

35 'The Falstone Day-Book', ed. Waylen, pp. 346–8, 363; *LJ*, VII, p. 485.

36 Paul Slack, 'Poverty and Politics in Salisbury, 1597–1666', in P. Clark and P. Slack (eds), *Crisis and Order in English Towns, 1500–1700* (London, 1972), ch. 5, esp. pp. 181–94. See also Paul Slack, 'An Election to the Short Parliament', *BIHR*, 46 (1973), pp. 108–14.

37 *Kingdomes Weekly Intelligencer*, no. 104 (17 June 1645): E. 288 (31); BL., Add. MS. 22084, fos. 7, 13ᵛ; Matthews, *Walker Revised*, pp. 15, 375–6.

38 *LJ*, VII, p. 485; *DNB*, under 'Hawles, Sir John (1645–1716)'; D.H. Robertson, *Sarum Close* (London, 1938), p. 171; Slack, 'Poverty and Politics in Salisbury', pp. 186, 191–3, and 201 note 67.

39 Underdown, *Somerset in the Civil War and Interregnum*, pp. 89, 98–100, 105–8, 111–18.

40 Clarendon, III, p. 94; *Wiltshire: The Topographical Collections of John Aubrey*, ed. Jackson, p. 266 and note; John Aubrey, *The Natural History of Wiltshire*, ed. J. Britton (London, 1847), pp. 11–12; E. Kerridge, 'Revolts in Wiltshire against Charles I', *Wilts. Archaeol. Mag.*, 57 (1958–60), pp. 70–1.

41 John Corbet, 'A True and Impartial History of the Military Government of the City of Gloucester' (London, 1647), in *Somers Tracts*, V, p. 303. For popular opinion in Gloucestershire, see also Ian Roy, 'The English Civil War and English Society', in Brian Bond and Ian Roy (eds), *War and Society* (London, 1975), pp. 35–42.

42 *Mercurius Aulicus* (29 Dec. 1644–5 Jan. 1644/5): E. 26 (5); *Scottish Dove*, no. 73 (14 Mar. 1644/5): E. 273 (10); *Moderate Intelligencer*, no. 6 (10 Apr. 1645): E. 277 (14); *Mercurius Veridicus*, no. 1 (19 Apr. 1645): E. 279 (18).

43 Sprigge, *Anglia Rediviva*, pp. 110–11; *True Informer*, no. 22 (20 Sept. 1645): E. 302 (9); *Parliaments Post*, no. 19 (23 Sept. 1645): E. 302 (22).

44 Morrill, *Revolt of the Provinces*, pp. 178–9. On 11 July 1645, apparently in response to this petition, the Committee of the West removed a number of the Malmesbury officers: BL., Add. MS. 22084, fo. 25.

45 *Perfect Occurrences* (4–11 July 1645): E. 262 (20). For the incidents on Salisbury Plain, see sources cited in note 27 above.

46 *Perfect Occurrences* (11–18 July 1645): E. 262 (25); *Perfect Diurnall*, no. 105 (4 Aug. 1645): E. 262 (37); *Kingdomes Weekly Intelligencer*, no. 117 (16 Sept. 1645): E. 301 (13).

47 Matthews, *Walker Revised*, pp. 375, 381; BL., Add. MS. 22084, fos. 12, 14ᵛ, 22ᵛ, *True Informer*, no. 11 (5 July 1645): E. 292 (9).

48 These calculations are based on the sources cited in notes 12 and 29 above.

49 *Mercurius Civicus*, no. 116 (14 Aug. 1645): E. 296 (23); H.M.C., *Portland MSS*, I, pp. 246–7; *CJ*, IV, p. 247.

50 Eliot Warburton, *Memoirs of Prince Rupert and the Cavaliers*, 3 vols (London, 1849), III, p. 124; *True Informer*, no. 14 (26 July 1645): E. 293 (35); Matthews, *Walker Revised*, pp. 184, 188, 190.

51 *Mercurius Aulicus* (10–17 Aug. 1645): E. 298 (23); *Perfect Passages*, no. 42 (13 Aug. 1645): E. 262 (42); *A Diary, or an Exact Journall*, no. 3 (9 Oct. 1645): E. 304 (13); *Perfect Occurrences* (3–10 Oct. 1645): E. 264 (25); [Hants. Committee] to Committee of Both Kingdoms, Sept. 1645: BL, Add. MS. 24860, fo. 137.

52 [R. Major] to [Committee of Both Kingdoms?], 25 July 1645: BL, Add. MS. 24860, fo. 133; documents from Fordingbridge hundred and the liberty of New Lymington [July 1645?]: BL, Add. MS. 24861, fos. 33–4; *Heads of Some Notes of the Citie Scout*, no. 4 (19 Aug. 1645): E. 297 (4).

53 Whitelocke, *Memorials of the English Affairs*, I, p. 372; *Perfect Passages*, no. 14 (28 Jan. 1644/5): E. 26 (9); *Quarter Sessions Order Book, 1642–1649*, ed. B.C. Redwood (Sussex Rec. Soc., LIV, Lewes, 1954), p. 76. See also Fletcher, *A County Community in Peace and War*, pp. 270–5.

54 Earl of Northumberland to Sussex deputy-lieutenants, 14 Aug. 1645: BL, Add. MS. 33058, fo. 71.

55 Committee of Both Kingdoms to Sussex Committee, 20 Aug. 1645: BL, Add. MS. 33058, fo. 73; *CJ*, IV, p. 267; Anon., *A True Relation of the Rising of the Club-Men in Sussex* (23 Sept. 1645): E. 302 (18).

56 *True Informer* no. 22 (20 Sept. 1645): E. 302 (9); Anon., *A True Relation of the Rising of the Club-Men in Sussex* (23 Sept. 1645): E. 302 (18). See also C. Thomas-Stanford, *Sussex in the Great Civil War and the Interregnum* (London, 1910), pp. 169–172.

57 H.M.C., *Portland MSS.*, I, p. 289. There are frequent reports of continuing Club activities in Sussex in newsbooks for late September.

58 Sussex Committee to the earl of Northumberland, 26 Sept. 1645: Bodl. L. Tanner MS. 60, fos. 251–5.

59 Anon., *A True Relation of the Rising of the Club-Men in Sussex* (23 Sept. 1645): E. 302 (18); *CCC*, II, pp. 921, 983–4; Fletcher, *A County Community in Peace and War*, pp. 272, 277; Thomas-Stanford, *Sussex in the Great Civil War*, p. 44.

60 Kerr, *Bound to the Soil*, pp. 9–10, 50–1, and Plate 22.

61 Bayley, *The Great Civil War in Dorset*, p. 255; *Weekly Account* (23–9 Apr. 1645): E. 279 (12).

62 *Perfect Occurrences* (4–11 July 1645): E. 262 (20); Anon., *The Proceedings of the Army under the Command of Sir Thomas Fairfax, Containing the Story of the Club Men and Relief of Taunton* (7 July 1645): E. 292 (16); *Mercurius Civicus*, no. 111 (10 July 1645): E. 292 (18); Anon., *A Letter sent to the Speaker to the House of Commons* (7 July 1645): E. 292 (22); Sprigge, *Anglia Rediviva*, p. 57.

63 Whitelocke, *Memorials of the English Affairs*, I, p. 470; Sprigge, *Anglia Rediviva*, p. 56; *Perfect Diurnall*, no. 102 (14 July 1645): E. 262 (21).

64 *Kingdomes Weekly Intelligencer*, no. 107 (8 July 1645): E. 292 (15). The only individual Clubman I can find in this area is William Derby, of Sturthill, at the western end of the downs. The charge that he took part in the fight was eventually dismissed: *Minute Books of the Dorset Standing Committee*, ed. Mayo, p. 566.

65 T.H. Lister, *Life and Administration of Edward, First Earl of Clarendon*, 3 vols (London, 1837–8), III, pp. 14–18; *Perfect Passages*, no. 37 (9 July 1645): E. 262 (19).

66 *Moderate Intelligencer*, no. 2 (13 Mar. 1644/5): E. 273 (7). See also *The Generall Account of the Proceedings in Parliament* (31 Mar. 1645): E. 260 (6).

67 J. Batten, 'Somersetshire Sequestrations during the Civil War', *Somerset Archaeol. and Nat. Hist. Soc. Proc.*, XVI pt. II (1870), pp. 23–4; Underdown, *Somerset in the Civil War and Interregnum* pp. 89, 96, 99.

68 HMC, *Portland MSS, I, pp. 227–8*; *Perfect Passages*, no. 40 (29 July 1645): E. 262 (34).

69 *Perfect Passages*, no. 44 (26 Aug. 1645): E. 262 (51); proclamation by Goring (20 Sept. 1645): BL, 669 fo. 10 (36); *Kingdomes Weekly Intelligencer*, no. 120 (7 Oct. 1645): E. 304 (7); *Perfect Occurrences* (24–31 Oct. 1645): E. 266 (10); *CSPD 1645–7*, pp. 200–1.

70 There were no schools in this area in the early seventeenth century, whereas in the rest of Somerset they were plentiful: W.K. Jordan, *The Forming of the Charitable Institutions of the West of England* (Amer. Philos. Soc. Trans., new ser., 1, pt. VIII, Philadelphia, 1960), p. 65.

71 *Weekly Account*, no. 76 (1 Jan. 1644/5): E. 23 (8); *ibid.* (4–11 June 1645): E. 288 (2); *Kingdomes Weekly Intelligencer*, no. 93 (1 Apr. 1645): E. 276 (3); *Letter Books of Sir Samuel Luke*, ed. Tibbutt, p. 490; Morrill, *Revolt of the Provinces*, p. 194.

72 *Letter Books of Sir Samuel Luke*, ed. Tibbutt, p. 689 (where 'Lycott' must mean Leigh Court, Worcs., not Lacock, Wilts.); *Diary of Henry Townshend of Elmley Lovett*, ed. Willis Bund, II, pp. 221–3; *A Diary, or an Exact Journall*, no. 43 (13 Mar. 1644/5): E. 273 (6); *Kingdomes Weekly Intelligencer*, nos. 91, 92 (18 Mar. 1644/5): E. 273 (6); *Kingdomes Weekly Intelligencer*, nos. 91, 92 (18 Mar. 1644/5, and 25 Mar. 1645): E. 274 (2), and E. 274 (24).

73 Corbet, 'A True and Impartial History of the Military Government of the City of Gloucester', in *Somers Tracts*, p. 367; 'Declaration of Col. B. Scudamore', 19 Mar. 1644/5; BL, Add. MS. 11043, fos. 19–20; *Heads of Some Notes of the Citie Scout*, no. 4 (19 Aug. 1645): E. 297 (4): *Herefordshire Militia Assessments of 1663*, ed. M.A. Faraday (Camden Soc., 4th ser., X, London, 1972), p. 19.

74 Underdown, *Somerset in the Civil War and Interregnum*, pp. 132–6. See also Morrill, *Revolt of the Provinces*, pp. 125–6.

12

Order and disorder in the English Revolution

JOHN MORRILL AND JOHN WALTER

Despite the hopes of a few (like the Somerset man who declared that there was now no law in force) and the fears of many more, Charles I's execution was not to be the signal for the collapse of that social order whose keystone he had claimed to be. Previous 'interregnums' had seen an outbreak of rioting prompted by the belief that the law died with the monarch, but the 'year of intended parity' saw no popular rising emerge to take advantage of such beliefs; the intention remained unrealised.[1] Indeed, an examination of disorder in the 1640s and 1650s might suggest that the possibilities of an 'intended parity' were greater in the fantasies projected by the fears of the propertied classes than in the reality of popular disorder in the period. There exists a notable discrepancy between both the character and level of disorder generated by the 'moral panic' that gripped propertied contemporaries and the evidence recoverable in the historical record. While the Revolution imposed new sources of conflict on pre-existing social and economic tensions, it failed to produce that popular explosion, fear of which ran like a red thread through the political history of the period.

Measuring disorder is at the best of times a difficult (and even questionable) exercise. To the familiar problems of the under-reporting of riot and patchy record survival, the Revolution added its own obstacles. That what the people said and did continued to be less often witnessed to by themselves, than reported by men of property who 'talked of the danger of a popular uprising in order to discourage each other from taking up arms',[2] makes even harder the Solomon-like task of disentangling reality from rumour and the paranoia of the propertied. The cessation of judicial activity for a time in some areas and at the centre the collapse of those prerogative courts preoccupied with the punishment of riot compounds the problem.[3] While this might have had the effect of understating the level of disorder, the switch to other courts, and notably parliament, probably had the opposite effect. Both as the focus of contemporary concern with civil conflict and as an institution that has left full documentation, parliament's assumption of the prosecution of various forms of riot may have served to inflate both contemporary and historical perceptions of the scale of disorder in the Revolution.[4] At the same time, the collapse of censorship and the emergence of unprecedented forms of communication reporting riot – pamphlet, broadsheet and newspaper – would have had the same effect.[5] The immediacy of this reporting was in stark contrast to the muffled, delayed and confused reports by which one region had heard of disturbances in other regions in preceding decades. Furthermore, there was an extensive correspondence between MPs and others in London and their families and friends in the provinces in which reports and rumours of disorder featured prominently.[6] Even if there had not been an actual increase in the incidence of disorder, these changes in the manner of reporting and recording riot would have inflated contemporaries' perceptions.

All this, we would wish to argue, has contributed to a tendency by some historians to misread the trajectory of disorder in the 1640s and 1650s. While this period witnessed an undoubted increase in disorder, it also registered important discontinuities with an earlier pattern of disorder and in the forms and levels of riot within the Revolution itself. The potential for some important forms of popular disorder (enclosure and grain riots) had been removed from some areas before 1640; within the Revolution there were two separate peaks of disorder, the early and late 1640s, with little continuity, and some surprising breaks, in the forms of riot. These discontinuities challenge the accepted wisdom of an interpretation that sees popular disorder growing throughout the period.

Disturbances were undoubtedly at their greatest in the first peak of disorder in the early 1640s. Enclosures were thrown down, altar rails torn out. Elections, both municipal and parliamentary, had seen the unwelcome and sometimes tumultuous intrusion of 'fellowes without shirts'. In the provinces, crowds attacked and pillaged the houses of recusants and malignants; in London, they pressed round parliament. And all this took place against a clamour of unemployed clothworkers and multiplying evidence of a breakdown of the traditional bulwarks of church and state.[7] Aggregating the various disturbances thus catches comtemporaries' uneasy perception of what seemed to them a social order in dissolution. But to disaggregate these various disturbances is to question the accuracy of that contemporary perception upon which historians have sometimes placed overmuch reliance as evidence of the *actuality* of disorder.

As MPs nervously debated and argued, it could indeed appear that their disagreement with the king might let loose a popular movement for 'Lex Graria', the confiscation and redistribution of their estates.[8] There was a notable increase in the number of agrarian riots in the early 1640s. To see these as the culmination of a *rising* trend of agrarian protest is to ignore the contradictory evidence of the changing geography of disorder. The classic locus of earlier enclosure riot and rebellion, the fielden midlands, remained remarkably still. For the most part, enclosure riots were restricted to areas where the radical challenge of enclosure to local economies prompted, and local social and economic structures permitted, the persistence of active, collective resistance. It was in the western forests and eastern fens and the larger estates whose royal, aristocratic and episcopal owners were associated with a discredited regime that most riots were to be found.[9]

In the charged political atmosphere of the 1640s, the tendency to equate the levelling of enclosures with the threat of levelling in society became more pronounced. As a description of the politics of agrarian disorder this reveals more about the propertied classes' fears than the rioters' intent. While recent assessments of agrarian disorder as non-ideological or apolitical are too cut and dried (it is possible to reconstruct the politics of enclosure rioters in contexts other than those of class or party allegiance),[10] it remains the case that agrarian crowds were intent on a recovery of rights that involved the righting, not the transformation, of a world turned upside-down. The not unsurprising decision of the house of commons (whose earlier attack on enclosure in the Grand Remonstrance had raised popular hopes) to throw their weight behind enclosers after 1643 ensured that enclosure rioters did not form a radical agrarian wing of the parliamentarian cause. Land and liberty was not to be the cry of the English Revolution. But this failure to meet popular expectations did not lead to a radicalisation of agrarian disorder. At its greatest in the early 1640s, agrarian disorder became progressively restricted. It remained a problem in forest and fen or flared up when new owners of confiscated estates attempted to enclose. There was, however, to be no revolution in the countryside. The passivity of the midlands (outside of its forests) suggests that the possibilities of a revolt of the fields may already have been undermined by the very changes in social and economic relationships which provoked popular discontent, an important point to which we later return.

What made agrarian disorder more threatening was the simultaneous occurrence of other disturbances. Popular iconoclasm was probably more common than the destruction of hedges; in Essex, for example, the authorities needed to hold a special court to deal with those who broke down altar rails.[11] A reaction to Laud's 'beauty of holiness', such riots nevertheless could seem to presage a more general toppling of traditional structures. Some contemporaries saw iconoclasm as 'abolishing superstition with sedition'.[12] It might involve the riotous destruction of altar rails and images, but iconoclasm had its own sources of legitimacy (parliamentary declarations and preaching) and discipline. Not infrequently, it involved the tacit co-operation of local elites.[13] Events like those at Chelmsford in which the royalist clergyman and polemicist, Bruno Ryves, drew a direct link between religious and social radicalism were, if true, an exception.[14] Popular iconoclasm was at its height in the early 1640s; after 1643 it became the prerogative of reforming parliamentary troops at whose hands many cathedrals suffered.[15]

More alarming were the attacks on recusants and malignants. Here could be seen more direct evidence of the people taking advantage of the times to challenge their 'betters'. According to Clarendon, malignants' goods were seized 'by the fury and license of the common people, who were in all places grown to that barbarity and rage against the nobility and gentry (under the style of Cavaliers) that it was not safe for any to live at their houses who were taken notice of as no votaries to the parliament'.[16] The focus on the riots in the Stour Valley in 1642 (on whose example Clarendon drew) in which crowds looted gentry households has, however, obscured the more general point that only a tiny minority of recusants were attacked. Even in the Stour Valley riots local evidence suggests that some victims owed their selection to a previous history of conflict with their local community; at Colchester, Sir John Lucas was in conflict with the corporation and popularly detested for his enclosures.[17] Attacks were concentrated in the period before the onset of armed conflict when official licence, rather than the collapse of political authority, made catholic and 'malignant' gentry legitimate targets. With the exception of those catholic officers murdered by troops raised to fight the Scots, violence when it did occur was directed against property and not persons. The outbreak of war saw a decline in this form of disorder which coincided with an end to the panics and alarums over supposed 'Popish plots'.[18] Where such attacks persisted it was the work of parliamentary troops who had been often at the heart of earlier crowds. But the English Revolution was not to be stained by the bloody violence that marked religious conflict on the continent.

What gave these generally distinct forms of disorder in the early 1640s their menace was the political context in which they took place. In London, sullen crowds jostled members of both Houses and prevented them from taking their seats in parliament, while the lord mayor found his authority flouted.[19] The worst actual violence occurred in May 1640 when rioters swarmed around the archbishop's palace at Westminster but failed to carry out their threat to burn it down. When some of the leaders were seized and imprisoned, rioters broke open the gaol and delivered the prisoners, for which they were tried for treason.[20] Thereafter the London crowd demonstrated against and intimidated churchmen, politicians and the royal family.[21] These examples in the capital of crowds who showed scant regard for established authority and of the coercive petitioning of parliament gave provincial disorders a threatening and unfolding unity they perhaps did not merit seen in isolation and in their local context. In the provinces, exaggerated reports of events in London had the same effect.

In reality, however, there was a failure to link radical ideas with popular grievances in the collective action of the early 1640s. Even in London the crowds often embraced substantial citizens and were well disciplined; there were few attacks on property or persons. As Valerie Pearl has written of events in the capital, here was 'a striking phenomenon . . . unknown in the rest of Europe: the rise of mass political activity of a new kind, accompanied by demonstrations in the streets and petitions . . . the absence of attacks on private property contrasts sharply with the behaviour of eighteenth-century city mobs . . . London remained without a popular uprising, even without significant bloodshed, during some of the most disturbed years in English history. . . The point was not lost on the French ambassador: blood would certainly have flowed in the streets of Paris, he wrote in 1642, if similar events had happened there.'[22] A third, popular force did not emerge from the widespread disorders of the early 1640s. There was, in fact, discontinuity in the patterns of disorder carried into the civil war. Much of the force of this earlier popular political initiative had been dissipated. It had been alienated by the failure of parliament, a body of landowners, to respond to their appeals, sublimated in the wider military conflict between crown and parliament or ultimately turned against both by the costs of the war.

It was the strains of the civil war and the politico-religious conflicts accompanying it that explain the second peak of disturbances in the later 1640s. The armies became the major direct and indirect source of disorder. Plundering troops prompted conflicts between civilians and the military that culminated in the Club risings in south and south-west England.[23] Ill-paid troops became themselves a source of disorder, staging mutinies in at least thirty-four English counties and in most of Wales in the years 1645 to 1647.[24] The excise, a new form of indirect taxation introduced to meet the costs of war, occasioned riots in both the larger cities (London, Norwich) and smaller communities. Though we lack a full study of excise riots, this form of disorder seems to have been at its height when the harvest failures of the later 1640s made the collection of a tax imposed on the consumption of basic commodities (but not bread) especially resented. While some areas may have been relatively untroubled by such riots, others might experience considerable disorder.[25] In 1647 there was a further outbreak of religious disorder, but this time associated with counter-revolution. In the Revolt of the Prayer Book, large crowds reinstated ejected ministers or compelled the use of the book of common prayer. These disturbances, spontaneously occurring in different regions, were linked to rumours that the army was negotiating with the king for the restoration of the old church.[26]

But while the pressures of civil war conflict produced a second peak of disorders in the later 1640s, these riots against specific grievances did not become the occasion for rebellion. Conflict over the tithe resulted in some riots for example (but how many precisely we have yet to discover) and more tithe-strikes probably, but the politics of the tithe never initiated disorder on the scale that it did in continental Europe.[27] And if the riots of the later 1640s challenged the exercise of authority, they did not automatically signal popular support for a radical attack on the social bases of authority. The largest popular movement of these years, the Clubmen, did not seek to threaten that social order whose hierarchies were seemingly well observed within its ranks.

Ironically the discontinuities between the two peaks of disorder in the early and late 1640s suggest that the emergence of more organised radical groupings, like the Levellers and Diggers, coincided with a decline in those forms of disorder which should have provided them with potentially their best opportunities for proselytising. By the later 1640s agrarian disorder had become even more confined to specific areas. The earlier attacks on recusants and malignants had not developed into the feared attack on 'Protestants as well as Papists'. There are isolated examples of attacks by tenants on manor houses and detailed local research may provide more, but the frequency with which a few familiar examples are cited raises doubts as to how common these were.[28] Sequestration and confiscation may have tilted the balance of power in favour of tenants (as incomplete evidence on rent-strikes and arrears suggests) and afforded the odd opportunity for riot, but they did not provide the legitimation nor pretext for wholesale popular plunder.[29] In the English Revolution (some) manorial records were burnt, but not châteaux. For reasons that we look at more fully later, this period did not witness an English rising against seigneurialism.

In the towns, economic discontent provoked tax riots and prompted some to support the radical groups, but harvest failure and popular chafing at the attempted puritan 'reformation of manners' persuaded others to join in the counter-revolutionary political demonstrations that took place in London and other cities.[30] As Peter Clark and Paul Slack note, political upheaval at the centre, popular opposition to high taxation and extreme religious radicalism in many towns meant that the new civil rulers, often differing but in degree from the social composition of their predecessors, were as anxious as their predecessors to exert their authority over the 'meaner sort'.[31]

And despite the tensions and sufferings caused by successive poor harvests in the later 1640s, the urban poor were not brought to the barricades by the demand for Bread and Justice. In fact, grain riots were not only noticeable by their continued absence from the capital; sensitive and previously much troubled areas, like Kent and Essex, also escaped the food riot. While the clothing districts of the West Country continued to experience grain riots, there seems to have been a contraction in the geography of the food riot.[32] Famine, even in the conditions of the later 1640s, never became the spur to popular risings.

After the king's execution, social hierarchies trembled but ultimately held firm. Charles's execution had coincided with a third year of harvest failure. Wildman, for the Levellers, had tried to draw on the evidence of food riots in Wiltshire to urge on a reluctant parliament the necessity for reforms to stave-off 'the many-headed monster'.[33] But after 1649 the harvest improved and, despite fears that military provisioning might provoke further disorder, grain riots faded away. Opposition to enclosure continued to flare up in those areas of forest and fen where disorder had been previously pronounced. In parts of the fens, notably Hatfield Chase, running warfare continued between drainers and commoners.[34] There were occasional riots in the western forests where communities of commoners continued the defence of their rights. Where a financially hard-pressed republic attempted to continue the royal policy of disafforestation on former crown lands, their efforts met similar resistance: there were riots in the later 1650s in the forests of Needwood and Sherwood and at Enfield Chase.[35] Elsewhere, attempts at piecemeal enclosure continued to prompt minor disorders.[36] But the overall impression is that the Interregnum witnessed a contraction in the pattern of disorder prompted by traditional popular grievances. Even in forest and fen, riots were less frequent, a silent testimony perhaps to the temporary victory of the commoners. Similarly, what is so far known about the collection of the excise suggests that it occasioned fewer confrontations in the 1650s than in the period 1645–9.[37]

In the 1640s, the army had been both source and focus of disorder because of its indiscipline: in the 1650s it became a cause of resentment and complaint but rarely of disorder, for it was ordered and effective.

There were at most times between 10,000 and 14,000 men in active service in England, scattered in garrisons mainly in London and around the coast and the Scots border.[38] Garrisoned troops were irritants in various ways: they asserted themselves over and against local governors, demanding custody of the town keys or insisting that senior officers be allowed to attend meetings of the corporation[39]; they frequently set up their own gathered church and welcomed citizens to it[40]; or they protected local separatist groups in the face of civilian hostility – one notable example being the Bristol garrison's succour of the Quakers in 1654–5.[41] Sometimes they intervened to carry out the suppression of popular festivities that the reformation of manners demanded.[42] Occasionally garrisons intervened in local elections.[43] But, despite the barrage of complaints against troops, there is little evidence of street fighting or other violent clashes between soldiers and civilians. Those that did occur, like the events at Enfield Chase, were well reported.[44]

In fact, the existence of well-disciplined and professionally led troops gave governments of the 1650s the opportunity to deal with riotous expressions of dissent by brute force. Agrarian rioters felt the full weight of a military presence when government desired it. Thus troops were used to put down disturbances in the Forest of Dean and Lincolnshire and Cambridgeshire fens.[45] They were called in by the corporation of Newcastle to break a strike by the keelmen;[46] and they enforced sequestration orders.[47] In the summer of 1649, one troop was quartered in each of the five lathes of Kent as direct response to the reports of the meeting of 'disaffected persons'.[48] It established a pattern. Occasionally, insufficient force was applied and disturbances continued, especially where there was considerable community support for the rioters and a difficult terrain for the troops. At Swaffham Bulbeck in 1653, the failure of stationed troops to prevent rioters from destroying the drainage works led a frustrated commander to recommend that a hundred or so inhabitants be pressed for naval service *in terrorem*.[49] But in general, the arrogant order represented by the army inhibited popular resistance as it did royalist resistance. It was not used all the time; that would have strained resources. Troops could maintain order but only while they remained on permanent standby. This probably explains why many scandalous ministers remained in their parsonages despite streams of orders from local and national committees dismissing them. Where they had the support of their congregations, it would have taken a permanent military presence to evict them and to sustain a successor. Only in 1659, as a lack of pay again began to lead to a collapse of discipline, did the army become again a force of disorder rather than of resentment.[50]

If the 1650s saw a contraction in the scale and scope of popular disorder, the government's sense of its own insecurities encouraged it to read into reports of often minor disorders 'the beginnings of insurrection'.

To the hyperbolic language of its predecessors, the republic added a new political vocabulary which spoke of often minor riots as evidence of 'designs against the Commonwealth'.[51] Men of property continued to fear 'an intended parity' that hurried them into a *de facto* acceptance of republican government. Their fear was less an accurate pointer to the possibilities of popular revolution from below than a reflection of the continuing failure to achieve a political settlement and the emergence of more organised forms of popular radicalism. Caught in a 'moral panic' and witness to many petty acts of insubordination,[52] they could only regard any evidence of disorder as the preliminary rites to the popular rising they had always feared.

From the very outset this 'moral panic' had been fuelled by the unprecedented availability of information about the activities of the 'many-headed monster'. The collapse of censorship and the rapid growth of newspapers and pamphlets at a time of political uncertainty would by themselves have fed this panic. That much of the reporting was just good copy directed at an anxious public fearfully greedy to learn about new disturbances only exacerbated the situation. Never hitherto could gentlemen buy hot from the presses tracts with such titles as *The Last Tumult in Fleet Street Raised by the Disorderly Preachment, Pratings and Pratlings of Mr Barbones the Leatherseller and Mr Greene the Feltmaker.*[53] Such alarmist writings could colour responses to more sober accounts of the marches of thousands of countrymen to present petitions at Westminster, or of disturbances in the provinces. In late 1641 and 1642, the tempo of such publications quickened,[54] with lurid accounts of atrocities in Ulster spilling over into circumstantial accounts of plots in England and even into plausible but fabricated narratives of popish uprisings.[55] The reality of the early 1640s was bad enough; rumour made it worse. One prebend of Hereford, preaching on 17 April 1642, solemnly told his congregation that he had certain knowledge that sectaries now controlled London and had forced the king to flee to the north.[56]

Both sides in the developing political conflict made deliberate and propagandist use of this alarmist literature. The royalists had the easier task, indicting the house of commons of 'traitorously endeavouring to subvert the fundamental laws and . . . to deprive the king of his royal power',[57] and claiming that this occasioned a breakdown of order. The royalists specifically accused the Commons of wilful encouragement of popular violence and iconoclasm, or more generally of wilful indulgence of them. Only the restoration of royal authority could lead to a restoration of order. It became a central prop of royal propaganda in 1642, most famously in the *Reply to the Nineteen Propositions*,[58] but even more pointedly elsewhere:

We complained . . . of the multitudes of seditious pamphlets and sermons. And the declaration tells us, they know we have ways enough in our ordinary courts of justice to punish those: so we have to punish tumults and riots, and yet they will not serve our turn to keep our towns, our forests and parks from violence. And it may be, those courts have still the power to punish, they have lost the skill to define what riots and tumults are: otherwise a jury in Southwark legally impanelled to examine a riot there, would not have been superceded, and the sheriff enjoyned not to proceed, by vertue of an order from the House of Commons.[59]

Equally, however, the managers of the Long Parliament were using the very threat of a collapse of order to advance the case for an imposed political settlement. Throughout the winter of 1641–2, the managers whipped up the hysteria about the massacres in Ireland, and the plans of the papists to spread their campaign to the mainland. They have been shown to have distorted the information flowing into them to that end.[60] Besmirching the king as deranged, incapable of governing, and arguing that anarchy was developing from the king's incapacity,[61] Pym and his colleagues used the existence of popular disturbances to illustrate the results of misgovernment and to justify further remedial legislation. Thus on 25 January 1642 Pym picked up a theme from a petition of the clothworkers of Essex, which had included the failure to crush popery amongst the causes of the depression,[62] when he predicted an insurrection of the poor if there was no political reform or religious renewal.[63] Five months later, crowds of clothiers sacked the houses of 'papists' and 'malignants', accusing them of being 'the cause of the present troubles and distractions'.[64] Here and elsewhere – in their response to iconoclasm, to lay preaching, even to enclosure riots – there was an ambivalence in parliamentarian attitudes to popular disturbances: they were understandable if reprehensible, to be met not by repression but by the prospect of reform.[65]

That parliament was aware of the damage royalist propaganda could inflict can be seen in the Houses' attempt on 19 May 1642 to vindicate the intimidation of MPs the previous December. Its speciousness stands out:

We do not conceive that Numbers do make an assembly unlawful, but when either the end or manner of their carriage shall be unlawful. Divers just occasions might draw the citizens to Westminster, and other causes were depending in Parliament, and why that should be found more faulty in the citizens than the resort of great numbers every day in the term to the ordinary courts of Justice we know not . . . [66]

Throughout the 1640s and the 1650s the same pattern was to recur. It was always in the interests of newsmen to report in exaggerated detail all manifestations of disorder; and it always suited the polemical purposes of government to exaggerate and to draw lessons from threats to the peace. The manipulation of 'Leveller' plots, of army mutinies, of Quaker plots are the most obvious examples. Historians who rely entirely or principally upon the press give us a reliable guide as to how contemporaries were led to believe in the imminent disintegration of the rule of law. But reality was only in part as it was portrayed at the time.

Propaganda was all the more readily believed, since it not only confirmed gentlemen's beliefs about the real nature of the many-headed monster, but because it also spoke to the deepening social divisions that pre-dated the Revolution. D'Ewes touched on a common fear amongst the propertied classes when he reminded his fellow MPs that, 'all right and property, meum et tuum, must cease in a civil war and they knew not what advantage the meaner sort also may take to divide the spoils of the rich and noble amongst them, who begin already to alledge that all being of one mould they saw no reason why some should have so much and others so little'. This was a common theme, given a popular (and deliberate) echo in petitions to parliament: 'Necessity dissolves all laws and government, and hunger will break through stone walls', asserted one such petition.[67] In the conditions of the 1640s, the gentry needed little reminding of such proverbial lore.

The real threat of the political conflict was, as D'Ewes observed, that it threatened to explode the deeper tensions latent within a situation of accelerating social and economic differentiation. But, as we have seen, in reality there was a notable discrepancy between actual and projected levels of disorder. This discrepancy suggests the need for a re-evaluation of the traditional view of the civil war period as one which saw a paralysis of political order permitting latent social conflicts to become manifest. We would wish to argue that the breakdown in order was less marked at the level of the local community than at Westminster and that the potential for widespread popular mobilisation in the social and economic changes preceding the Revolution was less great than has been assumed. This resilience of local structures of authority and the containment of disorder have common roots in the pattern of shifting social relationships. Economic change undoubtedly prompted greater popular discontent, but ultimately it created new structures which made possible the containment and even appeasement of that discontent.

If economic changes led to growing popular discontent, it did not of itself create a revolutionary potential. England's earlier omission from the roll-call of European rebellions in the extremely difficult conditions of the 1590s should caution against too facile an equation of economic distress with disorder.[68] A more sensitive assessment of the process and progress of economic change would suggest that there were limits (geographical as much as ideological) to the disorder that popular grievances might prompt.

Enclosure could promote riots which in areas with common grievances might achieve extensive coverage, but its ability to prompt a revolt of the countryside was questionable. England remained a society that was local and regional; there seems little evidence to suggest that rural rioters any more than sixteenth-century rebels could have burst the 'natural' boundaries to collective action that this imposed. Moreover, to the extent that agrarian grievances seem to have needed the physical evidence of hedges as a goad to riot, then enclosure's patchwork geography and piecemeal timing imposed further limits.

This is not to argue that these limitations were insurmountable. Famine, an effective collapse of local order which permitted the wider dissemination of destabilising rumours, a growing belief in the imminence of a radical millennium or an effective political lead by radical 'vanguard' parties – any of these might have broken down the ideological and physical restraints on wider popular political action. But the fear of popish plots never became the Great Fear of the French Revolution[69] and a radical millenarianism (for reasons which cry out for investigation) never mobilised the rural poor.[70] The bad harvests of the later 1640s led to a heightening of tensions but not to a breakdown of social order. The demographic evidence suggests that by the 1640s England (including previously vulnerable regions like the north-west) had slipped the shadow of a crisis of subsistence.[71] Increased agricultural output, achieved at the cost of heightened potential conflict where it required enclosure and engrossing for its achievement, not only prevented widespread famine but also made possible the continuing effectiveness of crisis relief which made grain available to the poor. These policies seem to have held up well in the later 1640s.[72] As we have already noted, there was a contraction in the areas scarred by food riots at the end of the decade. Despite worries expressed in the economic crisis of the early 1640s, necessity never became great enough in the English Revolution to impel the poor to break *en masse* through the walls of society.

Nor was there a breakdown of order at the level of the local community. There was within seventeenth-century England a process of growing social differentiation.[73] At one extreme this saw the growth in poverty that so alarmed contemporaries (though there is evidence to suggest that historians have perhaps exaggerated its depth and character).[74] But the corollary of this was the consolidation of the smaller but more significant growth of the 'middling sort', the yeomen and richer husbandmen in the countryside. The effect of this growing differentiation was to question the validity of the unitary description of those below the level of the gentry as 'the people'. For as a counterpart to the better-known political conflict between royalist and parliamentarian, there was a developing conflict at a lower level between the beneficiaries and victims of economic change.

As a consequence of this conflict there was a subtle shifting of alliances in the countryside which pre-dated the Revolution. Those groups whose combination of wealth, status and local parish or manorial office allowed them to dominate local communities had provided the backbone of many earlier rebellions.[75] But potential conflict with their poorer neighbours had encouraged them to align themselves with the state in a common attack on a developing 'culture of poverty'. Denied the earlier use of more informal ties of patron and client by their growing pursuit of 'possessive individualism',[76] they turned to local office and an alliance with the gentry as magistrates. This was an alliance eased by an identity of economic interests in service of the market, facilitated by the trend towards enclosure by agreement and cemented where there occurred a shared religion and literate culture. Increasing mobility from the ranks of the yeomen over time and through the avenue of university education had helped to blur the social distinction between parish gentry and wealthy farmers.[77]

Developing political and religious conflict between crown and political nation, therefore, placed the 'middling sort' in something of a dilemma. Like their betters, they resented royalist policies in the 1630s, especially where these seemed to endanger their attempts to impose greater controls over the poor. In the early stages of the Revolution they probably found some forms of crowd action (for example iconoclasm) not unwelcome. But, since the broader political conflict might offer the occasion for the popular attacks on them,[78] they offered only reluctant endorsement. Those who sided with parliament (and we should not assume that there was a natural identity between the 'middling sort' and support for parliament) wished for political and religious reform, not least to strengthen their position over their poorer neighbours. But they did not seek the radical social and economic reforms that the poorer sort might have sought. To challenge the drift of agrarian capitalism would have been to bite the hand that fed them their profits.

In the English Revolution, therefore, the yeomanry and richer husbandmen were not to play the vital role they had in sixteenth-century rebellions. Rather than use their considerable local power to mobilise a popular movement, they were more likely to use their power to stifle local grievance. Only where these local elites continued to find themselves in conflict with their landlord (or in the Revolution, with army or regime) would they be likely to organise popular action. Thus, the one major area where the 'middling sort' continued to give a lead to popular opposition to enclosure was that of forest and fen. Here imposed enclosure continued to challenge their interests. This was the more so, since the proposed conversion from pastoral to arable economies struck at the pursuit of their market interests which were best served within the context of regional specialisation by their ability to over-exploit the waste and commons. It is their willingness to continue to oppose enclosure that helps to explain the persistence of agrarian disorder in these areas.[79] Some historians have argued that the immediate decades before the Revolution saw a deterioration in the position of the yeomanry that gave them a common interest with the poorer tenants. Much of the evidence for this comes from regions with a history of poor landlord/tenant relationships.[80] But in southern and eastern England the evidence seems to point to growing co-operation between landlord and yeomen.[81]

The incorporation of the 'middling sort' into a state whose presence was becoming more effective at the level of the local community ensured the maintenance of order at a local level. Their presence served not only to suppress disorder but also to ensure that the traditional policies for coping with the problem of the poor did not collapse. In the English Revolution they, not the gentry, became the garrisons of good order. Where local elites succeeded in imposing tighter controls (and we have as yet an incomplete knowledge of the geography of these new patterns of order)[82] they doubtless denied radical groups, if not radical ideas, a toehold in their local communities. Thus, though there is sufficient evidence of popular grievances in outbursts of sedition to give some credence to the threats made in radical petitioning,[83] the possibilities for the collective expression of that discontent in riot were being narrowed rather than extended by social and economic change. Roger Crab's 'labouring poor Men, which in Times of Scarcity pine and murmur for Want of Bread, cursing the Rich behind his Back; and before his Face, Cap and Knee and a whining countenance' were those who had had to accommodate themselves to these changed realities.[84]

Not enough is known about the impact of the Revolution on social and economic relations at a village level to make generalisations safe or secure. But what is known suggests that it might be the case that increases in levels of disorder arose less from conflict within local communities than from pressure from without. While we would emphatically reject the view that the English village 'was a place filled with malice and hatred, its only unifying bond being the occasional episode of mass hysteria, which temporarily bound together the majority in order to harry and persecute the local witch',[85] we would not want to go to the other extreme. As other essays in this volume demonstrate, divisions of many kinds could create tensions and create disorder within particular communities. Disputes over land, over common rights, over local rates, over religion, over the performance of social duties could create brief or prolonged disagreements and conflict. Our concern is not with the existence of such tensions so much as with their prevalence during the 1640s and 1650s in comparison with the previous period. This, above all, is impossible to quantify. But despite the existence of new potential sources of internal conflict, our impression is that communal life was not generally more torn by dissension and disorder in the mid-century.

There were three potential new sources of conflict. The first was a direct result of the 'puritan' victory, which brought a renewed drive towards a 'reformation of manners', the imposition of more sober and self-disciplined ways of life: the regulation of alehouses and gaming, of sabbath observance and sexual relations. Pressure for the enforcement of existing legislation and for the introduction of additional ordinances in all of these areas was a constant feature of the period 1640–60, and was dear to the heart of Oliver Cromwell himself. Court records suggest patchy increases in prosecutions and magisterial initiatives. This was not merely an imposition from outside. In this instance, the survival of petitions from parishes calling for magisterial action is clear evidence of divided attitudes which led to the godly seeking external assistance. But we must beware of making too much even of this evidence. Concern for 'the reformation of manners' was nothing new; most of the specific demands of its proponents derive from legislation unanimously agreed in parliament and consonant with, growing out of, the canon law of the church; pleas for enforcement were characteristic of puritanism, but not their preserve alone; the apparent increase in secular court business may in large part reflect a transfer of business from the defunct church courts.[86]

The second and connected source of additional strain on parishes was the stillborn puritan church order.[87] The old church – its government, liturgy, even the rhythms of its calendar (the celebrations of the great Feasts) – was abolished and proscribed, but nothing was put in its place. A new system, replete with disciplinary procedures, service books, catechisms etc. was legislated for, but the political will at the centre to enforce it crumbled. In the 1650s, successive regimes in practice allowed local self-determination in matters of worship.[88] This led in many – probably most – parishes to the restoration of a watered-down Anglican worship, built around parts of the Prayer Book and Christmas and Easter communions. But in many parishes, godly minorities fought to impose the new order or at least to resist the (illegal) restoration of the old order. Yet all the signs are that violent confrontation between 'anglican' and 'puritan' parties were concentrated in the years 1646–8 when there was some political will at Westminster to introduce the new system. Thereafter, accommodation and compromises were reached: in market towns, the minister in one church would use the Prayer Book and in another the new services;[89] in the countryside, ministers would hold no holy communions at all, an unpopular decision but less inflammatory to the conservatives than of following puritan prescription and opening the communion table only to the godly, and less inflammatory to the godly than a 'promiscuous' communion of all but notorious sinners on the Anglican pattern.[90]

The third new source of conflict arose from the sequestration of the estates of many – perhaps a quarter – of the gentry for having served the king during the wars. This potentially gave an ideal opportunity to tenants and neighbours to settle scores, by denouncing them to parliamentary authority, uncovering lands which the delinquents were seeking to conceal, spoliating their homes and demesnes. Yet this happened remarkably rarely. Committeemen seem to have relied far more on professional informers than on tenants; looting and mean acts of vandalism cannot be found on any scale. There is plenty of evidence to suggest that successive regimes were concerned to minimise the degree of political ostracism and social humiliation of their defeated opponents. Although ex-royalists were, at least in theory, disfranchised and barred from public office, there was no wider proscription: ex-royalists continued to sit on juries, serve as churchwardens, overseers, constables. Nor is there evidence of political discrimination against ex-royalists in the administration of the poor laws (except that maimed royalist soldiers could not receive state pensions).[91]

In general, these potential new sources of conflict were most likely to divide the 'parish aristocracies' – literate, schooled in Christian teaching, independent proprietors – from labourers, artificers, the poor. In the 1640s and 1650s, as before, relations between the two were uneasy, ambivalent. On the one hand, the latter were dependent upon the former for employment, credit, relief, mediation with county or national authorities; on the other hand, they might find themselves the victims of the former's strengthening relations with the gentry in the extension of agrarian capitalism. Here we would stress that if in the 1640s and 1650s some magistrates and parish notables were increasing the pressure on the poor to conform to their idea of Christian duty, these same magistrates and parish notables were increasing their efforts to provide relief and succour in times of hardship. During the years 1647–9 when grain deficiencies were probably the worst of the century, the full battery of controls on the grain market were employed and a forthcoming study will argue for significant changes in the administration of poor relief in these years.[92] What evidence has been looked at makes the point just as clearly for the towns.[93] While the poor had grounds to be more in conflict with parish elites, they were also becoming ever more dependent upon them; and paradoxically while parish aristocracies felt more vulnerable, it increased their vested interest in the maintenance of order and it may well have increased their solidarity against outside pressures and demands. In stark contrast to the findings of historians of the French, the Russian, the Chinese Revolutions, in England the impression is that the civil war neither created nor fuelled vendettas or blood feuds. We are not aware of more than a handful of cases of inhabitants fighting one another over the issues dividing king and parliament, though many communities sent forth men to opposing armies; and after 1642 divisive actions such as the ejection of a minister most usually followed the arrival of 'foreign' commissioners with interrogatories rather than an initiative from within.

It is our impression, then, that increased levels of disorder owed less to intra-communal strife than to the intrusion of 'outsiders'. The most obvious flashpoints were the arrival of garrisons or the passage of troops; the impositions of new types of taxation; and externally imposed religious change. These were often linked: it was the use of troops to destroy religious images, stained-glass windows, altar rails, service books, or to requisition horses and supplies or to support tax-gatherers, which provoked some of the greatest scenes of violence.[94] Such interventions were especially likely to reinforce local solidarity against the intruders rather than to polarise the community.

Such demands varied, of course, from place to place and from time to time, and there is no simple relationship between the scale of demands and the likelihood of violent resistance. In part this was because the proximity of overwhelming physical force would act as a deterrent. The remarkably low level of violence in London in the 1650s probably owed much to the constant quartering of 3,000 or more troops in the centre.[95] But here and elsewhere it also owed something to the ability of 'passive resistance' to limit or to avoid the burdens. Local courts could be used to uphold religious practices banned by the Long Parliament; to indict soldiers for requisitioning horses and supplies and to secure recompense; to undo the work of excisemen.[96] The explicit orders of county committees or parliamentary committees could be flagrantly ignored in the knowledge that there was insufficient political will or physical force available to implement the original order.[97] Although the civil wars and Interregnum threw up new bureaucratic bodies with wide powers, most of the fiscal demands were enforced by existing local officials. Such men could get caught in the middle, but they could also mediate or mitigate the burdens, or negotiate distributions of taxation in ways felt to be as equitable as possible. It is surely no accident that there are many more reports of disturbances involving excise (assessed by itinerant agents) than assessment (handled by village constables). Once again, it may be noteworthy that those disorders which produced violence against persons and property were those in which there was direct conflict between local communities and outsiders where the scope for local mediation was very limited – in particular military/civilian skirmishes, excise riots, the imposition of a minister in place of one forcibly sequestered. The apparent decline of these disorders in the 1650s may be related to the state's relaxation of earlier burdens, and willingness to work through local elites: for example, in at least some areas, parishes 'compounded' with the excisemen and paid a local rate in lieu of the previous assessments backed up by house-searches and distraint; while Cromwell preferred to fill vacant livings in the church with men chosen by the parishioners themselves.[98]

We must not, therefore, exaggerate the extent to which government broke down at a local level. After the war years, when county institutions were suspended for up to four years, there was a return to the old ways and old officers: assizes, quarter sessions, grand juries, churchwardens, overseers. But on top of these familiar institutions and practices were laid new layers of bureaucracy and new forms of control: sequestration committees, assessment committees, commissioners for ejecting scandalous ministers, excisemen.[99] In general, the rhythms of administration at a village level were quickened rather than transformed, reinforced rather than abandoned. Successive regimes from 1646 to 1660 worked through existing structures in their concern with markets and with the poor; they created new structures when they made new demands. It is not surprising that provincial reaction was to cling to the familiar and to reject the unfamiliar which offered nothing and took much.

The resilience of local relationships of authority imposed constraints on the poor's ability to combine which perhaps only leadership from outside would have broken. But effective leadership was not available. Hugh Peter's wish that the army be used to teach the peasants liberty was never realised.[100] The radical sects made too little headway, though exaggerated estimates of their size and militancy created great fear of disaster. Despite the attention paid to them at the time, they constituted a tiny minority of the population. Probably less than 5 per cent attended religious assemblies other than those in their parish church.[101] The flamboyant evangelism of some of the tiny fringe groups provoked responses from their orthodox neighbours.

It is not clear how far the subversive ideas advanced by the sects and taken up, at different times, by groups within the army were responses to the events of the 1640s or the surfacing of subterranean traditions from previous decades and centuries, and irretrievable by us for lack of surviving evidence.[102] It hardly matters. It is hard to be evangelical and secretive. Clearly there was considerable momentum behind the radical ideas during the Revolution. Most striking is the rejection of Calvinist notions of Man and Grace, an insistence on the dignity rather than on the degradation of Man, of universal access to Grace, and of the need for all men to be free to seek out that Grace without the intervention of church or state; and the political and economic extensions of that liberated doctrine of Man. Yet, powerful and moving as the polemics of the new creeds were, they had very limited impact. In terms of membership, organisation, integration and ability to implement their ideas, they were much less impressive. Violence played little part in their history.

In the 1640s and 1650s, of course, many groups formulated, articulated, disseminated ideas which were profoundly subversive of the social, political and religious order. But those who had subversive *ideas* were not necessarily committed to the use of subversive *means* to impose those ideas. In general, the more subversive the ideas, the less violent the attempt to impose them. Tiny splinter groups like the Ranters and Muggletonians whose ideas were religious and/or individualistic showed little concern with the political implications of their beliefs or for their political implementation.[103] The Fifth Monarchists generally eschewed violent preparations for the Second Coming of Christ, and the breakaway group under Venner who tired of waiting passively and planned an insurrection in April 1657 appear to have numbered no more than twenty (Venner did only slightly better in 1661).[104]

The Diggers, too, had only a sketchy organization and hence little ability to proselytise their programme for the communal cultivation of the wastes and commons. The programme, in any case, while it might appeal to the rural poor (cottagers and landless labourers) jarred with an earlier tradition of agrarian protest in which the defence of the commons had been undertaken in support of diminishing individual holdings whose viability only common rights guaranteed. This had led to a growing clash between indigenous communities and squatters. Where the Diggers appeared as outsiders to a community (as in Surrey and Northamptonshire, though not at Iver in Buckinghamshire) they risked incurring the traditional hostility towards strangers. The Diggers' natural allies, the labourers and cottagers, were the groups with least scope for independent action, and therefore the most difficult to mobilise.[105]

These groups all derived their unity from the labelling of opponents, but even so, should be numbered in scores or hundreds rather than thousands. The most highly 'politicised' of the radicals were, of course, the Levellers. Growing out of the campaign for religious freedom, and coming to believe that there would be no religious liberty until there was political liberty, the Levellers articulated a radical doctrine of political obligation which held that moral authority had been forfeit by all existing political and ecclesiastical institutions. The three leaders at some point in 1646–7 declared the social contract null and void and the nation returned to a state of nature.[106] What was needed was a new social contract, an Agreement of all the People, to put themselves under a new, just and accountable government. This was heady stuff, movingly and extensively canvassed in several hundred tracts, and there was some ability to gather together thousands of supporters and a penumbra of sympathisers willing to petition and to lobby parliament.[107] In London, much of the activity seems to have been organised through (until 1649) sympathetic Baptist churches, although on occasion they canvassed through ad hoc and ephemeral committees in the wards of the city.[108] But they never appear to have contemplated raising their supporters in armed insurrections; their 'crowds' above all others seem to have been disciplined and orderly; and even their campaigns of civil disobedience may have been limited to encouragement of those who obstructed the collectors of the excise.[109] For the critical periods of mid- to late 1647 and late 1648 there is no indication that they appealed to the rank and file against the officers, rather than attempting to persuade both of the justice of their programme. They called upon the rank and file to disarm the Grandees in 1649, but they did not explain how they should do so; the agitators had long since lost their power; and there is little evidence that either the so-called Ware mutiny (which was not a mutiny) or the Burford mutiny (which was a mutiny but one disowned by Leveller leaders) were attempts to overthrow the authority of the officers, let alone of the state.[110] There was certainly a rhetoric of violence at times, but the principal thrust of all the leaders (and so unstructured a movement depended upon the decisions of the handful of leaders) was to emphasise 'moral force' rather than 'physical force'. They believed in the self-evident justice of their cause, and assumed that it would capture the hearts and minds of all whose attention could be attracted. There was a potentiality for violence in Leveller determination, but it was never realised. The only exception to this general point is the involvement of Lilburne and Wildman in the fenland disturbances in and around the Isle of Axholme in the early 1650s. As Clive Holmes shows elsewhere in this volume, Lilburne was certainly not averse to breaking the heads or burning the houses of hapless foreign settlers on drained fen. But *pace* Professor Holmes, their role remains mysterious. The fenmen may have paid (and paid lavishly) for the expertise of the Levellers in taking on the enclosers and the law courts, but the ex-Leveller leaders appear neither to have used their presence in Axholme to organise a rural campaign for the Agreement of the People, nor to raise the whole of the fens, and their lasting contribution to the shaping of fenmen's understanding of their plights appears, on present evidence, to be very slight.[111]

Because their organisation was ephemeral, the disillusion and disarray of the leadership in 1649 led to the evaporation of the 'Levellers' as a visible force. Unlike revolutionary movements in sixteenth-century Europe, they never evolved a cellular structure that could take on a will of its own. So far as our present state of knowledge allows us to determine, the Levellers made little impact beyond London, except in small patches, notably in the home counties, and where army garrisons acted as carriers to separatist congregations. It would seem that they failed to make headway in the countryside. Perhaps they never found a way of making their tracts available there; perhaps countervailing propaganda inoculated their natural constituency against their ideas; perhaps they failed adequately to integrate their agrarian programme into their political and religious eschatologies, and into their moving vision of restored human dignity. Their pamphlets do make reference to enclosure, but they never give this important issue the attention it deserved if they were to have hopes of mobilising the rural poor.[112]

The Levellers were a phenomenon of the late 1640s. Although their name and some of their ideas flickered on through the 1650s, it was then much more as a bogey, a phantom menace, than as an actual force.

However, the most substantial and, as it turned out, the most enduring of the sects, the Quakers, only emerged in 1652–3. Although, like the other sects (other than the Baptists), their membership was amorphous, casual, it has been plausibly suggested that there were about 40,000 active Quakers by 1660. Once more their ideas were more subversive than their actions, but there was nothing quietist about the early Quaker leaders. Their calculated disrespect for rank and degree, their disturbance of the worship of 'steeple houses' and of the preaching of 'hireling priests', their encouragement of tithe-strikes aroused fear and bewilderment. Amongst orthodox puritans, their dethronement of scripture and proclamation of the universality of grace created bitterness and resentment. But they did not burn down steeple houses, assault hireling priests, organise themselves nationally either in self-defence or to confront the Commonwealth. In fact they were more the victims of violence than the source of it. They were prosecuted under a wide variety of statutes, notably the late Elizabethan vagrancy laws and (ironically) under Marian legislation against field conventicles.[113] But many individual Quakers were set upon and beaten up and some of their larger meetings were broken up by angry crowds, as in Bristol by armed apprentices in 1654.[114] As James Powell told Secretary of State Thurloe on 24 February 1655:

> The other cause [of tension] is the comeinge of the Quakers, who with their franticke doctrines have made such an impression on the mindes of the people of this cittie and places adjacent that it is wonderfull to imagin, and hath also made such a rent in all societies and relations, which, with a publique affront offered to ministers and magistrates, hath caused a devision . . . and consequently many broyles and affronts; these quakers being countenanced by the officers of the garrison . . . [115]

Nothing illustrates better the principal theme of this paper: if we must beware of exaggerating the scale of disorder, we must also beware of underestimating how the fear of disorder filled the minds and affected the actions of those in authority. By 1659, the Quakers had become, in Barry Reay's words, 'the apotheosis of the ecclesiastical and social upheaval that was anathema to the provincial traditionalists who hearkened back to the old order'.[116]

The regimes of the 1650s survived because they had the perceived power to maintain order. Disheartened, divided, unconfident, the royalists licked their wounds and sought to restore their shattered finances. The lesson of the Penruddock rising was that thousands of royalists could have foreknowledge of a royalist rebellion without disclosing it to the authorities, but only a few hundred would take to arms. Royalist plotters in the 1650s made no effort to harness social and economic ills as part of a broad insurgency.[117] But such acceptance of the Commonwealth and Protectorate *de facto* rested upon a perception of the unity and purpose of the army. In 1659 army unity crumbled. This was in part due to the failure of the late Protectorate to keep expenditure under control: for the first time since 1646–9 army pay was falling seriously into arrears creating indiscipline and rank-and-file restiveness.[118] But it was also due to a bankruptcy of ideas once Richard Cromwell had fallen. From May 1659 on, there was an inexorable withdrawal of co-operation by the gentry as JPs, commissioners etc. With taxes unpaid and orders from Whitehall unheeded, government fell to pieces. Yet still, in the vacuum of power in the winter of 1659–60, there was astonishingly little disorder. Booth's rising was on a bigger scale than Penruddock's but it was still localised and quickly snuffed out by Lambert. In London, apprentices 'did very much affront the soulders as they went up and down the street'[119] and greeted a proclamation on 5 December by pelting the soldiers accompanying the serjeant-at-arms with tiles and lumps of ice.[120]

Yet again, however, the actual disorder and the perceived imminence of the total collapse of order are quite different. The political vacuum, the yearning for a restoration of 'the old parliament and a new king' tantalisingly just out of reach, the machinations of a divided and mean army leadership, all made for a total sense of insecurity. In 1640–2 this sense of dread, of the overturning of the natural order, led to the widespread 'catholic' panics and fears. There was no 'papist' conspiracy to slaughter protestants in their beds, despite all the apprehensions of the gentry and others. In 1659–60 there was a precisely similar Quaker panic. Across the country there were rumours of huge marauding bands of Quakers and fears of a God punishing the nation by allowing England 'to be transformed into a Munster'.[121] A central feature of Booth's rising was his proclamation that he was organising a pre-emptive strike against Quakers and Anabaptists.[122] As Barry Reay says, 'The king came back on the crest of a wave of reaction against the "immense and boundless liberty" of 1659'.[123]

This essay should not be read as arguing that the English Revolution produced little disorder. We are concerned only to suggest that a number of easy assumptions have been made by many scholars, and a number of false claims made. As we said at the outset, the disappearance of familiar sources, and their problematical replacement by new types of evidence makes the whole question a treacherous one. No two scholars can claim to have looked at more than a fragment of the sources, certainly not in the light of the conceptual framework developed here. No careful, analytical studies have been attempted of landlord–tenant relations in the wake of the abolition of the prerogative courts and the humiliating sequestration of a quarter of the landlords; of the nature and extent of tithe disputes; of the impact of military service and discipline on one in five of the adult male population; and many similar questions. In an overambitious and doubtless

overschematic essay, we have attempted to record our impressions based on
independent research which has led us to look at different aspects of these
problems from very different angles and for different regions.

But if the violence of civil war led on to an uneasy but far less violent
peace, there was no easy return to 'normality'. If scholars have assumed
too readily that the English Revolution saw a collapse of order, it is
because they have believed the testimony of the governors who were caught
up in it. Christopher Hill has rebuked historians of order for falling for the
'illusion of the epoch . . . accepting the standards of the articulate and
uncensored classes as though they represented "truth"'.[124] It is a warning
which historians of disorder must also beware. We have seen that there
were good reasons why contemporaries persuaded themselves that they
lived on the brink of anarchy, in the face of a disintegrating social and legal
order. Back in 1641, Sir Thomas Aston wrote that he

> looked upon the nobilitie and gentry of this Isle . . . situate as the
> Low Countries, in a flat, under the banks and bounds of the Lawes,
> secured from that ocean, the Vulgar, which by the breach of those
> bounds would quickly overwhelme us, and deface all distinctions of
> degrees and persons.[125]

The political elite was unsure of itself, unbelieving in the strength of
ubiquitous and formalised arbitration procedures, unrecognising the
decline of public violence, unaware how deeply (though not universally)
ideologies of acquiescence and order had penetrated. Over the next decade
they saw most of the landmarks of an ordered society destroyed: monarchy,
house of lords, the *ecclesia anglicana*. It seemed inconceivable that there
would not be a descent into chaos. Their preachers anticipated it; their
newspapers reported manifestations of disorder (but not of order). Minorities whose rhetoric and inspiration was indeed subversive talked openly
about their dreams. Men steeped in classical literature knew that great
empires could fall to the vandals; men steeped in the Old Testament knew
that God's chosen people were not only led to the land of Canaan but were
also made bondmen in Egypt, made captive in Babylon, scattered to the
corners of the earth. Such fears prospered, even in the 1650s when Oliver
Cromwell, seeing himself as a 'good constable set to keep the peace of the
parish',[126] maintained an order more abrasive than, but as effective as, that
of the 1630s.

The 'moral panic' of political elites was, in the event, one of the most
enduring legacies of the Revolution. It is a generalisation worth pondering
that the later a memoir of the Revolution was written by someone living
through it, the greater its memory of the disorders. Just as Sir John
Oglander, Richard Baxter, Edward Hyde, Denzil Holles retrospectively
got it wrong when they spoke of those who ruled as being drawn from
the dregs of the people, so they remembered in exaggerated fashion their

own anxieties and terrors as the familiar landmarks of their ordered universe were knocked away. Fear of impending anarchy made them give glum recognition to the Interregnum as *de facto* government forestalling chaos, and later inhibited them from a return to arms against their kings and encouraged them to vindictive repression of groups who disturbed their peace of mind. There was disorder in revolutionary England. But there was less than contemporaries anticipated and less than they led themselves and us to believe to have taken place.

Notes

1 Somerset RO, Q/SR 81/47; *The Souldiers Demand Shewing the Present Misery, And Prescribing a Perfect Remedy, Printed at Bristoll in the yeare of intended Parity*, BL, Thomason Tract E555 (29), a reference we owe to the kindness of Margaret Sampson.

2 L. Stone, *The Causes of the English Revolution 1529–1642* (London: Routledge, 1972), p. 77.

3 J. Mather, 'Parliamentary Committees and the Justices of the Peace, 1642–60', *American Journal of Legal History*, 23 (1979), pp. 122–3, 133n.

4 That the house of lords assumed the judicial business of Star Chamber (whose records exist mainly in manuscript and are largely missing, reports excepted, for the reign of Charles I) not only assured that evidence of disorder would be easier to recover by historians, but also that MPs would be made continuously aware of riots in the provinces and reflect this awareness in letters to friends and family.

5 J. Frank, *The Beginnings of the English Newspaper* (Cambridge, Mass.: Harvard University Press, 1961), pp. 19–31. For general comments on the astonishing growth of publications at this time, see P. Zagorin, *The Court and the Country* (London: Routledge, 1969), pp. 203–5; G.K. Fortescue, *Catalogue of the Pamphlets of George Thomason* (2 vols, London, 1908), vol. 1, pp. xx–xxiv. The total number of known publications between 1640 and 1660 exceeded the total number from 1485 to 1640. Thomason collected 721 items in 1641 and 2,104 in 1642. S. Lambert, 'The Beginnings of Printing for the House of Commons', *The Library*, 6th ser., 3 (1981), p. 45n., suggests that in these years, Thomason may have collected less than half the items actually published. We know that these publications were distributed very widely and passed from hand to hand: R. Cust, 'News and politics in early-seventeenth-century England' (Chapter 9 in this volume); J.S. Morrill, *Cheshire 1630–1660* (OUP, 1974), pp. 39–42.

6 For some examples, see D. Hirst, 'The Defection of Sir Edward Dering 1640–41', *HJ* 15 (1972), pp. 193–208; D. Gardiner (ed.), *The Oxinden Letters, 1607–1642* (London: Constable, 1933).

7 B. Manning, *The English People and the English Revolution 1640–1649* (London: Heinemann, 1976) gives a vivid sense of these years.

8 Manning, *English People*, p. 58.

9 The discussion of agrarian disorder is based on systematic research on a wide variety of sources, including *State Papers*; *Journals of the Lords and Commons*; Main Papers, HLRO; PRO, King's Bench; HMC and Quarter Sessions Records for a large number of counties. Further discussion of, and further reference for,

the points raised in the following discussion will be found in J. Walter, 'The Poor Man's Friend and the Gentleman's Plague: Agrarian Disorder in Early Modern England' (forthcoming paper). A. Charlesworth (ed.), *An Atlas of Rural Protest in Britain, 1548–1900* (London: Croom Helm, 1983), pp. 16–22, 39–42, provides a good, concise discussion.

10 Some preliminary comments on the politics of riot in early modern England are to be found in J. Walter, 'Reconstructing Popular Political Culture in Early Modern England' (forthcoming).

11 J.R. Phillips, *The Reformation of Images* (Berkeley: University of California, 1973); J. Morrill, 'The Church in England, 1642–9' in J. Morrill (ed.), *Reactions to the English Civil War 1642–1649* (London: Macmillan, 1982), pp. 94–5, 231–2 nn. 16–17; Morrill, *Cheshire*, pp. 36–7; D. Underdown, *Somerset in the Civil War and Interregnum* (Newton Abbot: David and Charles, 1973), pp. 27, 38, 44, 78; W. Hunt, *The Puritan Moment: The Coming of Revolution in an English County* (Cambridge, Mass.: Harvard University Press, 1983), pp. 285–6; B. Sharp. *In Contempt of All Authority* (Berkeley, Calif., 1980), pp. 84–6; [Bruno Ryves], *Mercurius Rusticus, or the Countries Complaint of the Sacriledges Prophanations and Plunderings.*

12 Manning, *English People*, pp. 32–45.

13 See, for example, J.T. Evans, *Seventeenth-Century Norwich: Politics, Religion, and Government, 1620–1690* (OUP, 1979), pp. 128–9; HLRO, Main Papers, 30 June 1641; HMC, *Buccleuch Mss.*, III, pp. 415–16; PRO, SP 16/460/31.

14 [B. Ryves], *Mercurius Rusticus* no. 3, pp. 17–21.

15 Morrill in *Reactions to the English Civil War*, p. 95; I. Gentles, 'Conflict between Soldiers and Civilians in the English Revolution, 1640–1655'. We are grateful to Professor Gentles for allowing us to read this valuable unpublished paper.

16 Clarendon, II, pp. 318–19.

17 C. Holmes, *The Eastern Association in the English Civil War* (CUP, 1974), pp. 35–6, 43–4; CUL, Add. MS 33, fols. 19–21; HMC, *Braye Mss.*, pp. 147–8; PRO, SP 16/458/12 and 13; HLRO, Main Papers, 5 August 1641; R. Clifton, 'The Popular Fear of Catholics during the English Revolution', *P&P*, 52 (1971), pp. 23–55, reprinted in P. Slack (ed.), *Rebellion, Popular Protest and the Social Order in Early Modern England* (CUP, 1984), pp. 129–61.

18 Clifton, 'Catholics'; pp. 32ff. A Hughes, 'Politics, Society and Civil War in Warwickshire 1620–50' (Ph.D. thesis, University of Liverpool, 1980) p. 265; Manning, *English People*, pp. 165–6; PRO, SP 16/491/119, 133, 138; 492/2, 11; *LJ*, v, 294–5; N.Z. Davies, 'The Rites of Violence: Religious Riot in Sixteenth-Century France', *P&P*, 49 (1973), pp. 51–91.

19 V. Pearl, *London and the Outbreak of the Puritan Revolution* (OUP, 1962), pp. 212–16 and *passim*.

20 Gardiner, *History*, IX, pp. 133–5.

21 Manning, *English People*, pp. 71–98.

22 V. Pearl, 'Change and Stability in Seventeenth Century London', *London Journal*, 4 (1979), p. 5.

23 J.S. Morrill, *The Revolt of the Provinces: Conservatives and Radicals in the English Civil War 1630–1650* (London: Allen and Unwin, 1976), pp. 98–111; J.S. Morrill, 'Mutiny and Discontent in English Provincial Armies 1645–1647', *P&P*, 56 (1972), pp. 49–74; D. Underdown, 'The Chalk and the Cheese: Contrasts among the English Clubmen' (Chapter 11 above); R. Hutton, 'The Worcestershire Clubmen in the English Civil War', *MH*, 5 (1979–80), pp. 39–49.

24 Morrill, 'Mutiny and discontent'.

25 C.H. Firth and R.S. Rait (eds), *Acts and Ordinances of the Interregnum 1642–1600* (3 vols, London, 1911), vol. 1, pp. 916–19, 1004–6; D. Underdown, *Pride's Purge: Politics in the Puritan Revolution* (OUP, 1971), pp. 90, 298; Evans, *Norwich*, pp. 170–1; Morrill, *Cheshire*, pp. 195–6. The geography of the excise riot awaits systematic study. While a large number of counties experienced disorder and opposition could be a particular problem in an area like the West Country, some counties seem to have been largely untroubled: J.S. Cockburn (ed.), *Western Circuit Assize Orders, 1629–1648: A Calendar* (Camden Society, 4th series, xvii, 1976), pp. 254, 276, 280; PRO SP 25/169, fos. 5–6; Wiltshire RO, Q/S Gt. Roll, Michaelmas 1659, 10 May 1659; Sharpe, p. 79.

26 Morrill in *Reactions to the English Civil War*, pp. 111–12.

27 Morrill in *Reactions to the English Civil War*, p. 110; cf. H. Kamen, *The Iron Century* (London: Weidenfeld, 1971), ch. 10.

28 See, for example, I. Roy, 'The English Civil War and English Society', B. Bond and I. Roy (eds), *A Yearbook of Military History*, 1 (1977), pp. 34–5. This is a subject crying out for systematic study. Most of the known attacks on muniment rooms seem to have occurred just after a fortified manor house was taken over by besieging parliamentary troops.

29 Charlesworth (ed.), *Atlas of Rural Protest*, p. 41; L. Stone, *Family and Fortune: Studies in Aristocratic Finance in the Sixteenth and Seventeenth Centuries* (OUP, 1973), p. 151; Hughes, 'Politics, Society and Civil War in Warwickshire, 1620–1650', pp. 220, 421–2; Manning, *English People*, p. 194; Gardiner (ed.), *Oxinden Letters*, pp. 67–8; B. Schofield (ed.), *The Knyvett Letters, 1620–1644* (Norfolk Record Society, XX, 1949), pp. 134, 137; HMC, *5th Report*, MSS E. Field, p. 388.

30 P. Clark and P. Slack, *English Towns in Transition 1500–1700* (OUP, 1976), pp. 99, 135–6; V. Pearl, 'London's Counter-Revolution' in G.E. Aylmer (ed.), *The Interregnum: The Quest for Settlement 1646–1660* (London: Macmillan, 1972); Underdown, *Pride's Purge*, pp. 323–4; Manning, *English People*, ch. 10; Gentles, 'Conflict between Soldiers and Civilians'; A. Everitt, *The Community of Kent and the Great Rebellion 1640–1660* (Leicester University Press, 1966), pp. 231–59; VCH, *Suffolk*, II, p. 192.

31 Clark and Slack, *English Towns*, p. 136.

32 J. Walter, 'The geography of food riots, 1585–1649' in Charlesworth (ed.), *Atlas of Rural Protest*, pp. 72–80.

33 J. Wildman, *Truth's Triumph or Treachery Anatomized* (London, 1648), pp. 3–4.

34 K. Lindley, *Fenland Riots and the English Revolution* (1982), chs. 4–6; C. Holmes, 'Drainers and Fenmen: the Problem of Popular Political Consciousness in the Seventeenth Century', in A. Fletcher and J. Stevenson, *Order and Disorder in Early Modern England* (Cambridge, 1985), pp. 166–95.

35 CSPD 1658–9, pp. 152, 328; VCH, *Staffordshire*, II, p. 353; D.O. Pam, *The Rude Multitude: Enfield and the Civil War* (Edmonton Hundred Historical Society, Occasional Papers, NS, 33, 1977); Sharp, *In Contempt of All Authority*, ch. ix.

36 For examples of minor riots prompted by enclosure in the 1650s, see Somerset RO, Q/SR 90/67, 93.2/72; Coventry RO, City Annals F, fo. 46^v.

37 G.E. Aylmer, *The State's Servants* (London: Routledge, 1973), p. 299.

38 H. Reece, 'The Military Presence in England, 1649–60' (D. Phil. thesis, University of Oxford, 1981), p. 287.

39 Reece, 'Military Presence', pp. 126–76.

40 At Hull, the parish church was divided by a wall, the garrison worshipping on one side and the citizens on the other: *CSPD 1650*, p. 452.

41 T. Birch (ed.), *Thurloe State Papers* (7 vols, London, 1742), III, pp. 170–2.

42 Gentles, 'Conflict between Soldiers and Civilians'.

43 *CSPD 1654*, pp. 331–2.

44 Pam, *The Rude Multitude*, pp. 10–11.

45 *CSPD 1649–50*, p. 316; *1651*, p. 286 (and cf. *1656–7*, p. 80); *1650*, p. 218.

46 *Weekly Intelligencer* for 22 August 1654, cited in Reece, 'Military Presence', p. 182.

47 *CCC*, vol. I, pp. 186, 222, 361, 366.

48 *CSPD 1649–50*, pp. 253–4.

49 PRO, SP 18/39/96.

50 See above pp. 330–1.

51 See, for example, the attitudes to disorder expressed in PRO, SP 25/194, fos. 43–4; 195, fo. 11/196, fo. 287.

52 What probably alarmed gentlemen as much as evidence of collective action by the poor was the growing evidence of plebeian disregard for the niceties of social and religious hierarchies, of which the Quakers' use of 'thou' to address superiors is only the best-known example. This is a subject calling for more investigation; see K.V. Thomas, 'The Place of Laughter in Tudor and Stuart England', *TLS*, 21 Jan. 1977, pp. 77–81.

53 BL, Thomason Tracts, E 180 (26).

54 See n. 6 above.

55 Rushworth, IV, pp. [398]–[416], 385–421 (page numbers 385–416 are used twice in this edition); K.J. Lindley, 'The Impact of the Irish Rebellion in England and Wales', *Irish Historical Studies*, 18 (1972–3), pp. 143–76; Clifton, 'Catholics', pp. 25–55; R. Clifton, 'Fear of Popery' in C.S.R. Russell (ed.), *The Origins of the English Civil War* (London: Macmillan, 1973), pp. 144–67. For an example of a fabricated papist rising, see 'A True Relation of a Bloody Conspiracy in Cheshire Intended for the Destruction of the Whole County' in J. Atkinson (ed.), *Civil War Tracts of Cheshire* (Chetham Society, 2nd series, 65, 1909), pp. 2–4.

56 BL, Loan MS 29, 173, fos. 237–8.

57 Rushworth, IV, p. 473.

58 J.P. Kenyon, *The Stuart Constitution* (CUP, 1962), pp. 21–3.

59 Rushworth, IV, p. 711.

60 M. Mendle, 'Mixed Government, The Estates and the Bishops' (Ph.D. thesis, Washington University, St Louis, 1977), pp. 396–432.

61 J.S. Morrill, 'The Religious Context of the English Civil War' (Chapter 6 above).

62 Hunt, *Puritan Moment*, pp. 293–4.

63 BL, Thomason Tract 200 (21).

64 See note 17 for sources.

65 J.S. Morrill, 'The Attack on the Church of England in the Long Parliament, 1640–1642' in D. Beales and G. Best, *History, Society and the Churches* (CUP, 1985), pp. 105–24.

66 Rushworth, IV, p. 695.

67 BL, Harleian MS 163, fo. 541; 'The mournfull Cryes of many thousand poor Tradesmen, who are ready to famish through decay of Trade' in D.M. Wolfe (ed.), *Leveller Manifestoes of the Puritan Revolution* (New York: Thomas Nelson, 1944), p. 278.

68 J. Walter, 'A Rising of the People? The Oxfordshire Rising and the Crisis of 1590s', *P&P*, 107 (1985).

69 Clifton, 'Catholics', pp. 159–60; G. Lefebvre, *The Great Fear of 1789* (London: NLB, 1973).

70 The Fifth Monarchists were predominantly an urban movement dominated by London: B.S. Capp, *The Fifth Monarchy Men: A Study in Seventeenth-Century English Millenarianism* (London: Faber, 1972), ch. 4.

71 E.A. Wrigley and R.S. Schofield, *The Population History of England 1541– 1871: A Reconstruction* (London: Edward Arnold, 1981), pp. 332–55 and appendix 10; R.S. Schofield, 'The Impact of Scarcity and Plenty on Population Change in England, 1541–1871', *Journal of Interdisciplinary History*, 14 (1983), 265–91; A. Appleby, *Famine in Tudor and Stuart England* (Liverpool University Press, 1978), ch. 10; A. Appleby, 'Grain Prices and Subsistence Crises in England and France', *Journal of Economic History*, 39 (1979), pp. 865–87.

72 J. Walter and K. Wrightson, 'Dearth and the Social Order in Early Modern England', *P&P*, 71 (1976), reprinted in Slack (ed.), *Rebellion, Popular Protest and Social Order*, pp. 124–6.

73 W.G. Hoskins, *The Midland Peasant* (London: Macmillan, 1957), chs. VI–VIII; M. Spufford, *Contrasting Communities* (Cambridge, 1974), pp. 46–167; J. Thirsk (ed.), *The Agrarian History of England and Wales*, IV (CUP, 1967), pp. 301–6, 396–465; F. Hull, 'Agriculture and Rural Society in Essex, 1500– 1640' (Ph.D. thesis, University of London, 1950), pp. 74–81.

74 J. Walter, 'Social Responses to Dearth in Early Modern England', in R.S. Schofield and J. Walter (eds), *Dearth and the Social Order* (CUP, 1985).

75 C.S.L. Davies, 'Peasant Revolt in France and England: a Comparison', *AHR*, 21 (1973), 130–2.

76 For the concept of 'possessive individualism', see C.B. Macpherson, *The Political Theory of Possessive Individualism: Hobbes to Locke* (OUP, 1964), pp. 52–61.

77 The best general discussion of this process is to be found in K. Wrightson, *English Society 1580–1680* (1982), chs. 6 and 7; for a detailed local study, K. Wrightson and D. Levine, *Poverty and Piety in an English Village: Terling 1525– 1700* (New York, 1979), chs 5–7; see also Walter, 'Oxfordshire rising'; M. Ingram, 'Religion, Communities, and Moral Discipline in Late Sixteenth and Early Seventeenth Century England' (forthcoming). We are very grateful to Dr Ingram for allowing us to see this paper. R. Smith, '"Modernisation" and the Corporate Medieval Village Community in England: Some Sceptical Reflections' (forthcoming).

78 See, for example, the comments of Thomas May in his *History of the Parliament of England* (London, 1647, repr. Oxford, 1854), p. 112. For popular attacks on puritans in response to their attempt to discipline the poor, see B. Manning, 'Religion and Politics: The Godly People' in Manning (ed.), *Politics, Religion and the English Civil War* (London, Edward Arnold, 1973), pp. 92–3, 102–3.

79 Historians have perhaps been too ready to accept the argument of Buchanan Sharp, based on a simple counting of heads from lists of rioters known to authority, which downplays the role of the yeomen in the western forests, ch. 5. For evidence of the 'middling sort's' role in the fens, see Lindley, p. 256; Holmes, 'Drainers and fenmen', p. 184.

80 B. Manning, 'The Peasantry and the English Revolution', *Journal of Peasant Studies*, 2 (1975), pp. 134–8, where much of the evidence comes from the north of England.

81 Charlesworth (ed.), *Atlas of Rural Protest*, p. 17.

82 Much of the best evidence for this pattern of changing relationships of authority

in the local community comes from a relatively few (and mostly southern) counties.

83 For some examples of popular discontent, see Wiltshire RO, Q/S Gt Roll Hilary 1647/8, petition of the inhabitants of Westbury; Essex RO, Q/SR 332/106.

84 Roger Crab, *Dagon's Downfall*, quoted in C. Hill, *Puritanism and Revolution: Studies in Interpretation of the English Revolution of the 17th Century* (London: Secker and Warburg, 1958), p. 307.

85 L. Stone, *The Family, Sex and Marriage in England, 1500–1800* (London: Weidenfeld and Nicolson, 1977), p. 98.

86 The fullest study is in K. Wrightson, 'The Puritan Reformation of Manners' (Ph.D. thesis, University of Cambridge 1973), *passim*; the main points are taken up in Wrightson, *English Society*, pp. 168–170. 181–2, 199–219.

87 Morrill in *Reactions to the English Civil War*, pp. 103–14.

88 C. Cross, 'The Church in England, 1646–1660' in Aylmer (ed.), *The Interregnum*, pp. 99–120.

89 For an example, see A.E. Preston, *The Church and Parish of St Nicholas, Abingdon* (Abingdon, 1909), p. 97. It is widely true of the towns in at least the south-west and the Welsh borders. We are grateful to Paul Gladwish, Patrick Higgins and Nick Marlowe for advice on this point.

90 Morrill in *Reactions to the English Civil War*, pp. 105–9.

91 This is based on a reading of printed quarter sessions records and committee papers and of several unpublished dissertations, as listed in G.E. Aylmer and J.S. Morrill, *The Civil Wars and Interregnum: Sources for Local Historians* (London: Bedford Square Press, 1979), appendices 4, 5, 7. See particularly S.K. Roberts, 'Participation and Performance in Devon Local Administration 1649–1670' (Ph.D. thesis, University of Exeter 1980), chs. 4–5; J.S. Morrill, *The Cheshire Grand Jury* (Leicester University Press, 1976), *passim*.

92 T. Wales, 'The Structure of Poverty in Seventeenth-Century Norfolk' (University of Cambridge Ph.D. thesis, forthcoming) and his important article, 'Poverty, Poor Relief and the Life-Cycle: Some Evidence from Seventeenth-Century Norfolk' in R.M. Smith (ed.), *Land, Kinship and Life-Cycle* (CUP, 1985), pp. 351–404; Morrill, *Cheshire*, pp. 247–52; J.P. Cooper, 'Social and Economic Policies under the Commonwealth' in Aylmer (ed.), *The Interregnum*, pp. 125–9.

93 V. Pearl, 'Puritans and the Poor: The London Workhouse 1649–1660' in D. Pennington and K. Thomas (eds), *Puritans and Revolutionaries* (OUP, 1978), pp. 206–32; see also R.W. Herlan's various articles on poor relief in London parishes during the English Revolution, *Guildhall Studies in London History*, II (1976), 45–53; III (1977), 13–36, 179–99.

94 For iconoclasm, see n. 11 above.

95 Reece, 'Military Presence', ch. I.

96 Aylmer, *State's Servants*, pp. 13–14, 299–302; J.S. Morrill, 'The Army Revolt of 1647' in A. Duke and C. Tamse (eds), *Britain and the Netherlands*, VI (1977), pp. 59–64. We are grateful to Bill Cliftlands for help with this and many other questions, and for allowing us to see his valuable unpublished paper on the working of indemnity commissioners who investigated these cases.

97 E.g. W.A. Shaw (ed.), 'Manchester Classis Minutes' (Chetham Society, 2nd series, XXII, 1891), pp. 375–95, supplemented by the *CSPD 1650*, p. 442; and W.A. Shaw (ed.), 'Plundered Ministers Accounts' (Lancashire and Cheshire Record Society, XXVII, 1894), pp. 185–7. This is not inconsistent with the point about 'overwhelming physical force'. To be effective, the force had to be at hand and in strength. In many parts of the country it was neither.

98 E.g. PRO, Chester 24/129 no. 2, grand jury petitions of 27 October 1651, speaking of a 'compositions' for ale made by the jury.

99 Mather, 'Parliamentary Committees', pp. 122–3, 133n. For the 1640s, Morrill, *Revolt of the Provinces*, pp. 52–72; for the 1650s, Aylmer, *State's Servants*, pp. 9–17, 305–16.

100 Quoted in C. Hill, *The Century of The Revolution 1603–1714*, 2nd edn (London: Nelson, 1980), p. 161.

101 A figure proposed by Morrill in *Reactions to the English Civil War*, p. 90.

102 B. Reay, 'Early Quaker Activity and Reactions to It' (D.Phil. thesis, University of Oxford, 1979), pp. 8–112. C. Hill, 'From Lollards to Levellers' in M. Cornforth (ed.), *Rebels and Their Causes* (London: Lawrence and Wishart, 1978), pp. 49–67.

103 J.F. Macgregor, 'Seekers and Ranters' in B. Reay and J.F. Macgregor (eds), *Radical Religion in the English Revolutions* (OUP, 1984), pp. 121–39; C. Hill, W. Lamont, B. Reay, *The World of the Muggletonians* (London: Temple Smith, 1982), *passim*.

104 Capp, *Fifth Monarchy Men*, *passim*; C.H. Firth, *The Last Years of the Protectorate* (2 vols, London: Longmans Green, 1909), II, pp. 208–18. While only twenty took part, over 4,700 Quakers were arrested in the wake of the rising.

105 C. Hill (ed.), *Gerrard Winstanley: The Law of Freedom and Other Writings* (Harmondsworth: Penguin, 1973), pp. 26–31; K. Thomas, 'Another Digger Broadside', *Past and Present*, 42 (1969), pp. 57–68; J. Walter, 'The Poor Man's Friend and the Gentleman's Plague' (forthcoming).

106 For example, see J. Lilburne, *Jonah's Cry from the Whale's Belly* (London, 1647); R. Overton, *Rash Oaths Unwarrantable* (London, 1647); W. Walwyn, *Outcryes of the Oppressed Citizens* (London, 1647).

107 The best of many books remains J. Frank, *The Levellers* (Cambridge, Mass.: Harvard University Press, 1958); G.E. Aylmer, *The Levellers in the English Revolution* (London: Thames and Hudson, 1975) is an excellent introduction and collection of key texts.

108 M. Tolmie, *The Triumph of the Saints* (CUP, 1977), pp. 138–55, 169–72, 181–4; N. Carlin, 'Leveller Organisation in London', *HJ*, 27 (1984), pp. 955-60.

109 See e.g. J. Lilburne, *England's Birthright Justified* (London, 1645).

110 M. Kishlansky, 'What Happened at Ware?' *HJ*, 25 (1982), pp. 827–40, sorts out that episode. The traditional view of the Burford mutiny was challenged in a paper by Brian Manning at a seminar in Cambridge in 1980.

111 C. Holmes, *Seventeenth Century Lincolnshire* (Lincoln, History of Lincoln Committee, 1980), pp. 198–9, 210–13; PRO, SP 18/37/11.

112 Morrill, 'Mutiny and Discontent', pp. 68–71; BL, Stowe MS 189, fos. 52–5; C. Hill, *The World Turned Upside Down* (London: Temple Smith, 1972), p. 96.

113 Reay, 'Early Quaker Activity', ch. 3.

114 Reece, 'Military Presence', p. 152.

115 Birch (ed.), *Thurloe State Papers*, III, p. 170.

116 B. Reay, 'The Quakers, 1659 and the Restoration of the Monarchy', *Hist.* 63 (1978), pp. 212–13.

117 D.E. Underdown, *Royalist Conspiracy in England* (New Haven: Yale University Press, 1962); P. Hardacre, *The Royalists in the Puritan Revolution* (The Hague, Nijhoff, 1955); A. Woolrych, *Penruddock's Rising* (Historical Association Pamphlet G.29).

118 Reece, 'Army Presence', pp. 45–8.

119 W.L. Sachse (ed.), 'The Diurnall of Thomas Rugg' (Camden Society, 3rd series, XCI, 1961), pp. 13, 16, 34–5.

120 A. Woolrych, introduction to R.W. Ayres (ed.), *The Complete Prose Works of John Milton* (8 vols, 1955–82), VII, p. 145.
121 Reay, 'Quakers, 1659 and the Restoration', p. 205.
122 Reay, 'Quakers, 1659 and the Restoration', pp. 198–201, 206–9; 'The Life of Adam Martindale' (Chetham Society, IV, 1845), pp. 135–9.
123 Reay, 'Quakers, 1659 and the Restoration', p. 212.
124 C. Hill in a review article in *Analytical and Enumerative Bibliography*, IV (1980), p. 270.
125 Sir Thomas Aston, *A Remonstrance Against Presbytery* (London, 1641), sig. A13.
126 A phrase from Oliver Cromwell's speech of 13 April 1657: T. Carlyle (ed.), *Letters and Speeches of Oliver Cromwell*, vol. III (1871), p. 248.

13

From rebellion to revolution: the crisis of the winter of 1642/3 and the origins of civil war radicalism

DAVID WOOTTON

Recent historical debates on the origins and nature of the civil war have been dominated by the work of the 'revisionists'.[1] The revisionist account of 1642 insists that the civil war began in a society where there was widespread consensus on constitutional principles and where there was general agreement that precedent, custom, and tradition were to be respected. This consensus shaped the terms in which both royalists and parliamentarians defined their objectives at the outbreak of the war. The community of values which united the political elite, at the same time as it was divided on religious principles, was only broken down by prolonged conflict. Only gradually did the rebellion slide into the maelstrom of revolution. The key moment in this transition, it has been suggested, is the emergence of 'adversary politics' in 1646.[2] Against this view I would maintain that both royalists and parliamentarians considered the possibility of revolution from an early date.[3] In this article I will argue that it was soon clear that a significant group on the parliamentary side would not settle for anything less.

Both the revisionists and their opponents have tended to halt their enquiries at the moment when the fighting began. An examination of debate in the following months presents problems for incautious formulations of the revisionist position, for the last months of 1642 saw the emergence of an uncompromising political radicalism. But it also presents problems for accounts of the radicalism which developed after the king's defeat: these usually maintain that it emerged either 'from below' or from the religious sects, and in doing so fail to recognize that the ground for it had been prepared in the early stages of the civil war by men immersed in the constitutionalist debate over the right of resistance. Radicalism appeared almost as soon as the war began, not because, as royalists argued and some parliamentarians recognized, it was a logical consequence of parliament's claims, but because in practice it became doubtful whether parliament was prepared to stand firm, and the choice appeared to lie between the adoption of more radical principles or rapid defeat.

It would, of course, be foolish to deny that the public pronouncements of parliamentarians in the period before 1646 were for the most part constitutionally conservative. It may even be the case that throughout this period the main differences between the parties were over religion, not the constitution, as the author of *A Short Discourse* (February, 1643) perceptively maintained.[4] But it is easy to go too far in this line of argument, and to maintain, as John Morrill has done, that no one in 1642 foresaw the radical implications of the arguments that parliament adopted in favour of resistance to the existing monarch:

> It is worth stressing that although all these arguments were advanced in 1642 to justify limited resistance to the existing monarch, all of them could as easily be employed to advance far more radical remedies: deposition and/or regicide. There is not a shred of evidence that this was recognised at the time. Instead their use in 1642 confirms that the objective on all sides was to preserve the constitution and not to change it . . . The Levellers were amongst the first to claim that all existing contracts between government and governed were null and void, and that a fresh start had to be made. The starting point for Leveller political thought was this . . . [5]

Yet, as 1642 drew to an end, many of the arguments that the Levellers were going to employ were beginning to echo through the pamphlets of the day. When, after the Restoration, Baxter looked back and asked himself at what moment a constitutional conflict in which the sacrosanctity of the king's person and the ancient constitution were accepted had degenerated into a revolution which culminated in the execution of the king and the declaration of a republic, he answered that the transition had begun early, not in 1645 or 1646, but in January of 1643, with the publication of an anonymous tract entitled *Plaine English*, a work generally attributed to the earl of Manchester's chaplain, Edward Bowles.[6] If it is anachronistic to imagine that revolution was in prospect from 1629 or 1640, it is equally dangerous to pretend that it could not be foreseen in 1642.[7]

My first argument, then, is that Baxter was right to look to the winter of 1642/3 to find the origins of the transition from rebellion to revolution, and that recognition of this fact casts in doubt the revisionist view that the causes of the civil war were essentially adventitious, that rebellion took place within a society dominated by unquestioning respect for hierarchy and tradition, and that revolution was an improbable outcome of rebellion. Since sensible revisionists are prepared to admit that their explanations of 1642 make 1649 harder to understand, they ought to be prepared to agree that if Baxter was right their task becomes even more difficult, for they lose the time they need to account for the process by which a solidly founded ancien regime crumbled, if only temporarily, into dust.[8]

My second argument, however, is that Baxter's analysis (which I share) presents difficulties for those opposed to revisionism. For the debate about revolution which broke out in 1642/3 was a debate conducted on terms established by royalist polemicists and parliamentary spokesmen. Popular radicalism and religious sectarianism were of only indirect relevance to it.[9] The revisionist view of 1642 in fact joins up with the Christian socialist and Marxist accounts of the Levellers, accounts which attribute much of their importance to the novelty of the positions they adopted in 1646. Taking for granted the novelty of the Levellers' views, historians as radically divergent in their approaches as Christopher Hill and J.C. Davis have been able to agree that their origin must lie in Christian heresy.[10] The question of their prehistory can then only be pursued through the records of heresy trials: the question is presented as lying in a choice between an account of their views as having 'an underground existence before 1640, so that the novelty is only in the freedom to express them', or seeing them as 'novel ideas, the product of novel circumstances'.[11] I want to suggest that there is an alternative: that the Levellers learnt their position, as Lilburne claimed, from the parliamentary *Book of Declarations*, and, more generally, from the pamphlet debates of the earliest stages of the civil war.[12] These debates involved 'novel ideas, the product of novel circumstances'. But they were the novel ideas of those close to the hardliners in the parliamentary leadership during the first crisis of the civil war, not of a social class or a religious movement that had previously had no voice. More important as a model for the Levellers' arguments than a folk memory of Jack Cade and Wat Tyler, or even than the king's dire foreboding of 'a dark equal chaos of confusion', were the pamphleteers I will be discussing here, men who had been prepared to make no concessions in their replies to parliament's royalist critics. Perhaps their ideas, too, had had an underground existence before 1642: but if so, I would suggest, they are as likely to be found amongst readers of Junius Brutus, Buchanan and Althusius as amongst Lollards and anti-enclosure rioters. If the educated in early Stuart England accepted divine right monarchy it was by choice, not for lack of alternatives (although none of those alternatives went, I think, as far as the radicals were prepared to go in 1642).

In arguing that the Levellers' views had been foreshadowed in 1642/3, I am presenting a view that did not impose itself upon contemporaries. Edwards, for example, believed that the views the future Levellers were expressing towards the end of 1646 were without parallel.[13] His natural reference points were theological, for he believed he was dealing with a by-product of heresy. Even the Anabaptists, however, he acknowledged, had never been recorded as showing as systematic a contempt for duly con-stitued authorities as John Lilburne, who refused to bare his head in the presence of the Lords. But it is not a view which is without precedent in the historical literature. Allen, for example, stressed the importance of the radical arguments of 1642/3, and Sirluck, in his study of Milton, saw that they foreshadowed those of the Levellers.[14] My view is that the revisionists and their opponents have been wrong to pass over this work, and that Baxter's judgement was as astute as Edwards'.

I do not mean to suggest that religion did not have a central role to play in the transition from rebellion to revolution (just as it had in the origins of the rebellion itself): it was in part their religious background that made the Levellers ready to put the radical arguments of 1642/3 to work.[15] Nor do I mean to suggest that we do not need a social explanation of the English revolution: on the contrary I think it was because English society in 1642 was already different from that of other ancien regimes that the issue of radic-alism came so quickly to the fore. It will not be possible, however, within the scope of the present article, for me to address these wider questions.

Were the Levellers' views as novel as Edwards believed? Most historical accounts of the Levellers' political views begin not in mid-1646, as he did, but in October of 1645, when Lilburne, at that point imprisoned by order of the house of commons for refusing to answer questions on a charge of slandering the Speaker, published *England's Birth-Right Justified*, which maintained that equity must take precedence over the letter of the law, that no man could be required to incriminate himself, and that Magna Carta guaranteed trial by jury under due process of law.[16] Lilburne's argument provoked William Walwyn to publish *England's Lamentable Slavery*, in which he rejected Magna Carta as a contemptible inheritance, a mess of pottage, and argued that Lilburne should appeal, not to his historical rights as an Englishman, but to universal principles of equity and justice which were binding on parliament as on any legal authority.[17] Parliament could have no claim to exercise an absolute jurisdiction, for it was obliged to maintain the safety and freedom of the people, and was, like all authorities, accountable to those it governed.

Walwyn's pamphlet is often taken to be the origin of the Leveller theory of popular sovereignty, which stressed the right of the people to rebel even against their representatives, and to have been a factor in Lilburn's increas-ing radicalization. In fact an even clearer and more systematic account of

Lilburne's right to appeal to the people against the tyranny of parliament, and of his right to call for revolution, had been published the month before: *England's Miserie and Remedie*, an anonymous work variously attributed to almost every prominent future Leveller.[18]

The radical arguments of the autumn of 1645 were of only passing significance, although for the first time they united the future Levellers in a common cause: Lilburne was soon released from prison, and the radicals were bound to support parliament as long as the war with the king continued. It was the prospect of that war ending and parliament reaching a settlement with the king which opened the way to a radical assault upon the constitution. Conventionally, then, 1645 is seen as the prehistory of the Leveller movement, whose origins are dated to the *Remonstrance of Many Thousand Citizens* of July 1646, the first pamphlet claiming to speak on behalf of a mass movement.[19] This approach, however, conceals the extent to which the arguments of the Levellers were not newly invented, but represented merely an attempt to apply lines of thought of which radicals had been aware since early in the civil war.

Conventionally, the Levellers are said to have drawn upon the arguments of Henry Parker, who was parliament's leading spokesman in 1642, and who had come close to arguing for the sovereignty of the Commons as the representative of the people, although he had denied that the people could act in their own behalf or put in question the decisions of their representatives; and on those of Samuel Rutherford, whose *Lex Rex* of 1644 had implied that the king could be deposed, that the people could act independently of constituted authority, as in a hue and cry after a thief, and that representatives who betrayed their trust could be disowned.[20] Neither Parker nor Rutherford, however, had directly addressed the possibility of a constitutional revolution: both had assumed that government by kings, lords and commons must be sustained whatever momentary crisis might disrupt its proper functioning. Thus when I first tackled this problem a few years ago I felt safe in offering only a modest modification of the conventional periodization: 1645 saw the birth of civil war radicalism, 1646 its consolidation.[21]

In fact the winter of 1642/3 saw something of a dress rehearsal for the arguments of 1646, not, this first time round, because parliament had won the war, but because it seemed in danger of defeat.[22] At Edgehill, Brentford and Turnham Green the king had repeatedly come close to outright victory. In December negotiations were taking place, and many feared that parliament would cut its losses, hand the Five Members over to the king, and settle on his terms.[23] According to Hexter, the peace party held the upper hand in the house of commons from 21 November 1642 until 11 February 1643.[24] It was in the light of this crisis in their political influence, a crisis which was not finally over until negotiations broke down on 17 April, that supporters of the war party had to ask themselves, as they asked themselves again in 1646, what the people were entitled to do if the Commons betrayed them. Once the immediate threat of a settlement drifted into the background the issues were buried once more until the Levellers resurrected them in 1646.

Let us take first the question of parliament's right to depose the king.[25] Henry Marten was apparently in favour of the king's deposition as early as 1641.[26] Numerous authors showed their awareness of arguments that would legitimate deposition of a tyrannical ruler by the Estates. Generally they dissociated themselves from such arguments by calling them papist.[27] Sometimes however they attributed them to respectable Protestant scholars such as Keckerman.[28] In any case, *An Answer to Mis'Led Dr. Ferne*, of January 1643, went the whole hog.[29] The deposition of Richard II had been justified, and those such as Ferne who argued that elective rulers could be deposed but hereditary ones could not were mistaken: all royal authority was essentially elective, and indeed government should be based on the principle that the most numerous voices should prevail. In March a Puritan minister preaching a sermon before the Lord Mayor seemed to regret the limits parliament had imposed upon itself:

> Yea, I hope it will not be distastefull, I know it is seasonable at this time to say even *unto the King and unto the Queene*, as the prophet *Jeremiah* directs in the 13 of his Prophesie 18. *Say unto the King and unto the Queene, sit downe, humble your selves*: I will not adde that which followes, I have no Commission for it, *for your Principalities shall come downe, even the Crowne of your glory.*[30]

When Marten was imprisoned by parliament in August of 1643 for supporting John Saltmarsh, who had said the destruction of the Stuart family was preferable to the destruction of the nation, he was uttering sentiments that were not new amongst the radicals:[31] royalist complaints on this score have been too casually rejected by historians.[32]

A striking example of the evolution of opinion on the subject of deposition is provided by William Prynne's *The Treachery and Disloyalty of Papists to their Soveraignes* of March 1643. In this, the first part of *The Soveraigne Power of Parliaments and Kingdomes*, Prynne gave numerous examples of the deposition of kings in pre-Reformation England. He seemed reluctant to declare whether such precedents were still to be followed, but he did declare that he felt that there was a danger that the king might provoke parliament 'to use the extremity of their power and revive dead sleeping precedents for their relief.'[33] By the time part four appeared in August, his attitude had shifted, and he devoted a two hundred page 'appendix' to arguments for deposition and regicide, the first two-thirds consisting of precedents from countries other than England (including the kingdom of Israel), and the last third consisting very largely of extracts from the *Vindiciae contra tyrannos*, a work of indubitably Protestant origins.[34] The first complete English translation of the *Vindiciae* appeared, as one would expect, in 1648. What conventional histories would not prepare one for is the appearance of a translation of all the book's key secular arguments for tyrannicide in 1643.[35] My own account may make one wonder why it should appear so late as August, but it seems to have been written before May, for Prynne refers to the appendix in the 'expanded' edition of *The Treachery and Disloyalty of Papists*.[36]

Other authors were, like Prynne, unwilling to acknowledge any constitutional balance of power between king and parliament. The *Discourse between a Resolved and Doubtful Englishman* of December 1642 had already denied that the king could reject parliamentary legislation: his role was purely executive, and he was answerable to parliament for his fulfilment of that role. Parliament for its part was free to set aside all pre-existing precedents or constitutional practices. Why had parliament not made clear its true constitutional supremacy?

> I have observed the parliament have revealed their power but by degrees, and only upon necessity, that necessity might make the people know that that power was just and reasonable, as fearing the people's weakness could not digest those strong and sinewy truths, whereunto their stomachs had not of long time been accustomed, though indeed it be the only food that makes us firm, and resolute, and true Englishmen.[37]

Similarly, *The Priviledges of Parliament* of February 1643 maintained that parliament had the right to impose legislation on a dissenting king by force and to change the constitution as it saw fit:

> This Parliament hath changed the continued Order of divers Parliaments, by expelling the Lords Spirituall out of the upper House, and taking away their Votes, and the Votes of Popish Lords: upon which I conclude, that a Parliament hath power to alter government, if the diversity of times, and necessity of the State, for the safety and preservation thereof, so require, of which a Parliament is the sole Judge.[38]

A Sovereign Salve to Cure the Blind, of April, also felt that parliament's true supremacy, once properly concealed, must now be revealed.[39] All that was needed to complete the Leveller position of mid-1646 was an argument for the supremacy of the Commons over the Lords, an argument that was gestured at, although scarcely formulated, in *The Privileges of the Commons* of December 1642.[40]

Both king and parliament claimed to be fighting in defence of the ancient constitution. But those few radicals who adopted the view that parliament was sovereign and bound by no precedents were able to dismiss the ancient constitution as an irrelevance. Thus the author of *A Disclaimer and Answer* (May 1643) maintained that the 'Knowne Lawe of this Land', to which royalists and moderates appealed, was 'a Snake hid under this greene Grasse': only parliament could judge what the law was, and no one should seek to limit parliament to their private conception of the law.[41]

Such arguments in favour of parliamentary sovereignty made, as their authors recognized, parliament an absolute and unchecked authority, bound neither by Magna Carta nor the Petition of Right.[42] The royal prerogative had thus reappeared in a new, and some felt a more menacing, form.[43] It was against this view that Walwyn was to protest in *England's Lamentable Slavery*, where he insisted that neither historical rights nor parliamentary supremacy provided an adequate protection for the liberties of Englishmen: only universal principles of justice and equity and the accountability of governors to the governed could do that.

These views too had been expounded in the crisis of 1642/3. *Touching the Fundamental Laws* (February 1643) had insisted that 'the Fundamental Laws of England are nothing but the Common laws of Equity and Nature reduced into a particular way of policy'.[44] Particular laws were subordinate to this fundamental law, and in the name of it parliament could override the Petition of Right or depose the king. Even oaths of obedience could be set aside when the people's safety was at stake. 'God calls to have the wicked removed from the Throne, and whom doth he call upon to doe it but upon the people, . . . or their trustees . . .'. For this author the ultimate authority was not parliament but the people themselves: 'that universall and popular authority, that is in the body of the people, and which (for the publike good, and preservation) is above every man and all Laws . . .'.[45]

What then if parliament should betray its trust and join forces with the king to tyrannize over the people? A few authors faced this question squarely and concluded that the people would have the right to resist all the constituted authorities. Thus the puritan ministers who wrote *Scripture and Reason Pleaded for Defensive Arms*, published by authority of parliament in April 1643, maintained that the body of the people could act even against the three estates if necessary.[46] This had been the conclusion – however reluctantly expressed – of *Plaine English*, the work which, in Baxter's eyes, marked the demise of constitutionalism:

> But suppose (if it be lawfull to be supposed) that the Parliament, through the absence of many resolved men, now imployed in particular services for their owne Countries, out of an intolerable wearinesse of this present condition, and feare of the event, agree to the making up of an unsafe unsatisfying Accommodation. This would beget a question, which I hope I shall never have occasion to dispute, whether in case the representative body cannot, or will not, discharge

their trust to the satisfaction, not of fancy, but of reason in the
people, they may resume (if ever yet they parted with a power to
their manifest undoing) and use their power so farr as conduces to
their safety; And if this doubt cannot be resolved ᴏ the advantage of
the people but be found either unlawfull or otherwise impossible, I
know but two waies more betwixt which the choice is very hard: hang
or flye. As for hanging I should not much like it, though it were in a
blue ribband; but for flying you will say the way is open, I would it
were as I could wish it, if ever God bring us to such a strait . . . [47]

Bowles (if he was indeed the author) was unwilling to be bound by
constitutional precedents and hostile to 'a cold Accommodation: Doubt-
lesse the period of this businesse will be some great alteration, liberty or
tyranny, Popery or true piety.'[48] His puritan enthusiasm was accompanied
by a Machiavellian analysis of the political forces at work. He proposed to
form a bond or association of those willing to fight on should parliament
come to terms with the king, committed 'To the maintainance of our
establish'd Religion and Law *with all possible improvement*'.[49] He was
no proto-Leveller however, in that he insisted he was 'farre from the
Monster of a *Democracy*.[50] All that he was asking of the people was
that they should 'out-run' the commands they had received from parliament. Above all, he sought to concentrate the radicals' minds on the
alternatives they were likely eventually to face: exile, execution, or the
resumption of the power entrusted to parliament.

It is not surprising that Baxter should have looked back to *Plaine
English* as a turning point. Here was a clear threat of a war not for
constitutional but revolutionary ends, and of a settlement finally imposed
against the wishes not only of king, but also of parliament. Moreover the
tract caused a stir at the time. Royalists argued that they for their part
could resume the authority they had entrusted to their parliamentary
representatives, who had betrayed them by opposing the king.[51] Parliamentarians insisted that such arguments in favour of a resumption of powers
could only be tolerated by royalists and, they protested, despite the evidence, were held by no one on their side.[52] *A Second Plain English* and *An
Answer to Plain English* presented the orthodox parliamentary case, as did
A Plain Fault in Plain English, which chose to conclude that if the people
were to resume the authority they had entrusted to their representatives
decisions would have to be taken by the majority of the nation at large.
But where would they meet? And who would be allowed to vote? Would
it be only forty-shilling freeholders, or the population at large, including
almstakers?[53] Thus the willingness of the radicals to appeal to 'that
universal and popular authority that is in the body of the people' had
raised as early as the spring of 1643 the central issues which were to be
debated at Putney.

Perhaps the most important of these radical texts of 1642/3 was Jeremiah Burroughs' sermon on *The Glorious Name of God, the Lord of Hosts* of December 1642, a work which, royalists protested, blasphemously compared Essex, commander-in-chief of the parliamentary forces, to God himself, and to which was appended *A Brief Answer* to the royalist Henry Ferne.[54] Already in 1642 Burroughs was struggling with the key question which the Levellers were pressing home in 1646–7. It was a question that had been asked by Ferne: 'But if Parliaments should degenerate and grow tyrannical, what means of safety could there be for such a State?'[55] Most parliamentarians had been happy to argue, with Parker, that parliaments embodied the wisdom of the nation, and thus would never act wickedly; they had no time for the royalist claim that the Commons might become an agent of tyranny (a claim that the Levellers were later to endorse). But Burroughs, faced with a house of commons that seemed capable of settling with the king, felt obliged to answer the question without evasion, for he had to consider the possibility that the Commons might allow themselves to be corrupted by the king:

> I confesse the condition of such a State would bee very dangerous and like to come to confusion; particular men could not help themselves, and the whole State ought to suffer much before it should helpe it selfe by any wayes of resisting; but if you can suppose a Parliament so far to degenerate, as they should all conspire together with the King to destroy the Kingdome and to possesse the lands and riches of the Kingdome themselves, in this case whether a Law of Nature would not allow of standing up to defend our selves, yea to re-assume the power given to them, to discharge them of that power they had, and set up some other, I leave to the light of nature to judge.
>
> You will say, This cannot be, because the higher powers must not be resisted by any.
>
> This is not properly to resist the power, but to discharge the power, to set the power elsewhere. The servant does not resist the power of his master, when he upon just grounds leaves him, and goes to another, if he be such a master, as is his master by his owne choice, for such and such ends and purposes, and had his power limited by agreement.
>
> I know this will be cried out as of dangerous consequence, wherefore God deliver us (as I hope he will) for ever making use of such a principle.
>
> It is hard to conceive it possible that a Parliament can so degenerate, as to make our condition more grievous by unjust acts, then it would be if the power in a Kingdome should returne to the law of nature, from whence at first it rose.[56]

It was a long step from this cautious statement to the conclusion the Levellers reached in 1647, that the constitution had been dissolved and the state of nature restored. But the step was a political one; for at least four years there had been no intellectual barriers standing in the way.[57] It is not surprising that the Levellers found the issue straightforward:

> *for tyrannie is tyrannie*, exercised by whom soever; yea, though it be by members of Parliament, as well as by the King, and they themselves have taught us by their Declarations and practises, that tyrannie is resistable.[58]

The arguments the Levellers employed were thus not their own invention. They had been in the air since the crisis of 1642/3 and had, indeed, been expounded not only by a small number of obscure radicals, but by the most prominent royalist theorists. Ferne had argued in 1642 that if the parliamentarians were consistent they would accept that the people could as legitimately resume the authority they had entrusted to parliament as the nation could resume the power it had entrusted to the king, and John Maxwell argued in 1644 that the logical implication of parliament's insistence on consent was some form of democratic government, unchecked by constitutional precedent.[59] Maxwell thought that no parliamentarian had been willing to admit this: like Edwards, and most modern historians, he seems not to have realized quite how far some parliamentarians had been willing to go during the winter of 1642/3. The future Leveller leaders, however, are likely to have been much more directly aware of the positions a few radicals had been willing to adopt during those months; if not they could have derived similar arguments from the best known of the royalist propagandists.[60]

The originality of the Levellers thus lay not so much in their ideas, but in the steps they took to put those ideas into practice, creating a political platform appropriate for the reconstruction of political society after the existing constitution had been dissolved, and a political movement capable of acting outside the parliamentary arena. Political movements, however, can only gain a foothold where they reflect the wider values of society. To diminish the novelty of the Leveller position in 1646 is not to dissolve the problem presented by their conviction that it represented practical politics. In this context it is of some interest that at least one of the participants in the debate of 1642/3 thought that English politics was different from that of other countries because English society was different.

In his sermon on *The Glorious Name of God*, Burroughs set out to celebrate traditional English freedoms by contrasting them with the slavery of absolutist government on the continent:

> There is no Countrey in the world where countrey men, such as we call the yeomandry, yea, and their Farmers and workmen under them, doe live in that fashion and freedome as they doe in *England*; in all other places they are slaves in comparison, their lives are so miserable

as they are not worth the enjoying, they have no influence at all into the government they are under, nothing to doe in the making of Laws, or any way consenting to them, but must receive them from others, according to their pleasure; but in *England* every Free-holder hath an influence into the making and consenting every Law he is under, and enjoyes his owne with as true a title as the Nobleman enjoys whatsoever is his.[61]

And he went on to defend four basic freedoms to which everyone (and not merely freeholders) should lay claim: the rights to property, to government by consent, to freedom of conscience, and to reliable justice in peace of grace and favour.

Burroughs himself took it for granted that his political objectives had been shaped by the society in which he lived, and that it was the social and political differences between England and the absolutisms of the Continent which partly explained the revolution that was currently taking place. Burroughs' view of an egalitarian society, along with the basic freedoms he aspired to defend, corresponds very closely to that of the Levellers – and in 1646 Edwards was to see him as a sectarian of the same stripe as the future Levellers. It is in the light of Burroughs' political egalitarianism that one should read the complaints of *The Moderator*:

It hath been observed, the Parliament hath made little difference, (or not the right) between the Gentry and Yeomanry, rather complying and winning upon the latter, then regarding or applying themselves at all to the former. And they may be thus excused; they did not thinke it justice to looke upon any man according to his quality, but as hee was a subject; I hope this was all the reason . . . [62]

for (he maintained) military victory would be impossible unless a systematic attempt was made to win gentry support. The royalist *True Informer* similarly protested that what was now at stake was the social hierarchy itself: 'the securitie of the Nobilitie and Gentrie depends upon the strength of the Crowne, otherwise popular government would rush in like a torrent upon them.'[63]

If we are to understand why rebellion turned into revolution we cannot simply trace the debates about sovereignty that run through the Thomason tracts; nor is it sufficient to amplify such an account by stressing the religious commitments of the authors of *Plaine English* and *The Glorious Name of God*. We must also note Burroughs' references to farmers and workmen, and listen to *The Moderator* and *The True Informer* on the threat that parliament posed to the traditional distinctions between gentlemen and yeomen. If the issues regarding political accountability faced by the radicals in 1642 were in large part new ones, there was nothing new about the fear of egalitarianism and popular power. In 1640 Lord Maynard had declared his abhorrence of elections which took the form of 'popular assemblies where fellowes without shirts challenge as good a voice as myselfe', and fears of 'popularity' had long been expressed by king and court.[64] The rapid emergence of radicalism at the beginning of the civil war casts in doubt the revisionist thesis that there was unquestioning agreement amongst the educated in early Stuart England on the need to preserve hierarchy and tradition, and suggests that earlier royalist fears of 'popularity' were not entirely misplaced.[65] To explore this question would be to re-open the vexed problem of ideas which have 'an underground existence'. For the moment I hope to have shown, firstly, that it is not the case that 'the objective on all sides' as 1642 came to an end 'was to preserve the constitution and not to change it.' Secondly, that arguments for revolution were first presented by an educated elite in terms of parliamentary and popular sovereignty, and did not arise directly out of sectarian theology or of aspirations towards social levelling (although both the sects and social levellers stood to benefit by them). If they were in circulation before 1642, then we should look for them, not only amongst the sects and amongst anti-enclosure rioters but also amongst members of the political elite.

Perhaps there was no 'high road to civil war'; but there evidently was one from rebellion to revolution. It was, as Baxter remembered, mapped out by the author of *Plaine English* long before the Leveller movement came into existence. The willingness of English pamphleteers in 1642 to contemplate the destruction of the ancient constitution must be part of any explanation of why there is no parallel to the Putney debates to be found elsewhere in seventeenth century Europe, of why no other contemporary rebellion culminated in the trial and execution of a king. According to an inscription on the British Library copy of the first complete English translation of the *Vindiciae contra tyrannos* the translator was later employed to cut off the king's head. The identity of the executioner has always been something of a mystery, so perhaps there is truth in the story: who would claim to be better qualified for the task? My suggestion is that if William Walker wielded the axe, Bowles, Burroughs and Prynne (no matter how far their views had changed by 1649) had sharpened it.

Notes

1 See R. Cust and A. Hughes, 'Introduction: after Revisionism', in Cust and Hughes (eds), *Conflict in Early Stuart England* (London, 1989), pp. 1–46. J.C.D. Clark, *Revolution and Rebellion* (Cambridge, 1986) provides a revisionist account of the seventeenth and eighteenth centuries as a whole.
2 M. Kishlansky, 'The Emergence of Adversary Politics in the Long Parliament', (chapter 2 above).
3 P. Williams, 'Rebellion and Revolution in Early Modern England', in M.R.D.

Foot (ed.), *War and Society* (London, 1973), pp. 225–40, 328–30, rightly stresses the differences between the civil war and earlier rebellions. He sees 'a decisive break with the past' in the new constitutional doctrines employed to justify the impeachment of Strafford.

4 BL, E88(28). (Where possible I give, as here, catalogue numbers from G.K. Fortescue (ed.), *Catalogue of the Pamphlets . . . Collected by George Thomason, 1640–1661* (2 vols, London, 1908).)

5 J. Morrill, 'Introduction' to Morrill (ed.), *Reactions to the English Civil War, 1642–1649* (London, 1982), pp. 1–27, at pp. 7, 22.

6 BL, E84(42). R. Baxter, *Reliquiae Baxterianae* (London, 1696), p. 49. For differing interpretations of *Plaine English* see B.S. Manning, 'Religion and Politics: The Godly People', in Manning (ed.), *Politics, Religion, and the English Civil War* (London, 1973), pp. 83–123, at pp. 121–2; and W.M. Lamont, *Richard Baxter and the Millennium* (London, 1979), pp. 76–8.

7 J. Sommerville, *Politics and Ideology in England, 1603–1640* (London, 1986), p. 74.

8 Morrill, *Reactions*, 'Introduction', p. 1.

9 Useful here is a distinction between 'motive' and 'intention' much stressed by Quentin Skinner (e.g. 'Motives, intentions and the interpretation of texts' (1972), in J. Tully (ed.), *Meaning and Context: Quentin Skinner and his Critics* (Princeton, 1988), pp. 68–78). My claim is that even if the motives of authors such as Bowles and Burroughs were religious, their intention was to solve a problem in constitutional theory. Moreover they intended to solve that problem, not by applying the religious principles of a minority, but by drawing novel conclusions from political and religious principles which they shared with their parliamentary allies.

10 J.C. Davis, 'The Levellers and Christianity', in Manning (ed.), *Politics, Religion and the English Civil War*, pp. 225–50. I have criticized Davis's account of the Levellers' theology in 'Leveller Democracy and Puritan Revolution', forthcoming in J.H. Burns (ed.), *The Cambridge History of Political Thought*, ii (Cambridge 1990). The Levellers did share certain peculiar theological premises: but I would argue these were directly relevant to their position on toleration, and only indirectly relevant to their position on popular sovereignty. Once toleration became a central issue it was bound to create divisions between supporters of parliament who had held similar views on the question of sovereignty in 1642/3.

11 C. Hill, 'From Lollards to Levellers', in M. Cornforth (ed.), *Rebels and their Causes* (London, 1978), pp. 49–68, at p. 49.

12 A. Sharp, 'John Lilburne and the Long Parliament's *Book of Declarations*', *History of Political Thought*, 9 (1988), pp. 19–44.

13 T. Edwards, *The Third Part of Gangraena* (28 December 1646; E368(5)), reprinted with parts One and Two, eds M.M. Goldsmith and I. Roots (Exeter, 1977).

14 J.W. Allen, *English Political Thought, 1603–1660*, vol. i (no further vols. published; London, 1938); E. Sirluck, introduction to *idem* (ed.), *Complete Prose Works of John Milton*, vol. ii (New Haven, 1959).

15 Valuable on this subject is M. Tolmie, *The Triumph of the Saints* (Cambridge, 1977).

16 W. Haller (ed.), *Tracts on Liberty in the Puritan Revolution, 1638–47* (3 vols, New York, 1934), vol. iii, 257–307.

17 Haller (ed.), *Tracts on Liberty in the Puritan Revolution*, vol. iii, 309–18.

18 D. Wootton (ed.), *Divine Right and Democracy* (Harmondsworth, 1986), pp. 276–82.
19 E.g. D.M. Wolfe (ed.), *Leveller Manifestoes of the Puritan Revolution* (New York, 1944); J. Frank, *The Levellers: A History of the Writings of Three Seventeenth-Century Social Democrats* (Cambridge, Mass., 1955).
20 P. Zagorin, *A History of Political Thought in the English Revolution* (London, 1954).
21 D. Wootton, 'Democracy: the People and the Multitude', in *idem* (ed.), *Divine Right and Democracy*, pp. 35–38.
22 Apart from Allen and Sirluck (*supra* p. 657, n. 3), see B.S. Manning, 'Puritanism and Democracy, 1640–1642', in D. Pennington and K. Thomas (eds), *Puritans and Revolutionaries* (Oxford, 1978), pp. 139–60, and B.S. Manning, *The English People and the English Revolution* (London, 1976).
23 The two books which give the clearest account of the crisis of the winter of 1642/3 are J.H. Hexter, *The Reign of King Pym* (Cambridge, Mass., 1941) and C.V. Wedgwood's chapter on 'The Winter of Discontent' in *The King's War, 1641–1647* (London, 1958). Hexter rightly complains (pp. 51–2) that Clarendon and Gardiner are below their usual standard on this topic.
24 Hexter, *Reign of King Pym*, pp. 49–51, 67–72.
25 For further examples other than those discussed here, Hexter, *Reign of King Pym*, pp. 105–7.
26 C.M. Williams, 'The Anatomy of a Radical Gentleman: Henry Marten', in Pennington and Thomas (eds), *Puritans and Revolutionaries*, pp. 118–38.
27 E.g., W. Bridge, *The Wounded Conscience Cured. By Way of Answer to Dr. Fearne* (Feb. 1643, E89(8)); *idem, The Truth of the Times vindicated . . . and Doctor Fernes Reply answered* (24 July 1643; E61(20)).
28 J.S., *Some New Observations and Considerations* (16 Mar. 1643; E93(14)), p. 4.
29 E245(1); cf. also *The Power of the Lawes of a Kingdome over the Will of a Misled King* (26 Jan. 1643; E86(11)); *Touching the Fundamentall Lawes of this Kingdome* (24 Feb. 1643; E90(21)); J.M., *A Sovereign Salve to Cure the Blind* (27 Apr. 1643, E99(23)).
30 J. Caryl, *Davids Prayer for Solomon* (27 Mar. 1643; E97(12)), p. 37.
31 M. Ashley, *John Wildman, Plotter and Postmaster* (London, 1947), p. 22.
32 E.g., *A Complaint to the House of Commons* (2 Jan. 1643; E244(31)), p. 10 (a pamphlet so successful that within ten days the parliamentarians were forced to produce a fraudulent version, with the same title but quite different arguments (E245(5)); also *A Warning-Piece to all His Majesties Subjects* (20 Feb. 1643; E90(4)).
33 BL, E248(1), p. 88. A second, expanded, edition was printed by order of the Commons, 2 May, 1643 (the chief additions being on pp. 78–86, 89–92, 102–4, 108–9, 111). For a study of this work, see W.M. Lamont, *Marginal Prynne* (London, 1963), pp. 85–118.
34 BL, E248(4). Lamont makes no mention of this second part of the 'appendix'. Lilburne drew on Prynne's 'appendix' in *Innocency and Truth Justified* (6 Jan. 1646; E314(21)), p. 11.
35 J.H.M. Salmon's statement that 'Those sections of the work which had been written to justify resistance to absolute monarchy . . . were not published in English until 1648' scarcely takes account of his own recognition that 'Most of the third question of the *Vindiciae* . . . [was] translated and reproduced in long extracts in the appendix to . . . *Soveraigne Power* (*The French Religious Wars in English Political Thought* (Oxford, 1959), pp. 17, 84–5), for the third question is over half the book, and the whole of its secular resistance theory.

36 At p. 91.

37 BL, E128(41), fos. A2vA3r.

38 *Englands State Policy, or The Priviledges of Parliaments* (E89(19)), p. 3 .

39 BL, E99(23). Similar views were expressed by others: *The Grand Case of England* (8 Feb. 1643. E88(27)); *The Priviledges of Parliament; Touching the Fundamentall Lawes.*

40 BL, E83(39). See also Hexter, *Reign of King Pym*, p. 58.

41 BL, E100(23), pp. 5–6. A similar view had been presented in *A Sovereign Salve to Cure the Blind* in April.

42 See Prynne, *The Soveraigne Power of Parliament*, part 4, p. 15 (quoted in Lamont, *Marginal Prynne*, p. 97).

43 See, for example, *A Discourse, or Parly* (July 1643; E61(14)).

44 BL, E90(21), p. 5. The same stress on equity had appeared as early as April 1642 in an isolated pamphlet entitled *A Question Answered* (669 f. 6(7)), reprinted in parliament's *Book of Declarations* (21 Mar. 1643, E241(1)), p. 150 because it had attracted the attention of the king. The publication of the *Book of Declarations* marks the beginning of the end of the crisis of 1642/3.

45 At p. 13.

46 BL, E247(22), p. 53. Prynne regarded this as the 'best and acutest' of the defences of resistance: 3rd part of *Soveraignty of Parliament* (23 June 1643; E248(3)), p. 61.

47 BL, E84(42), p. 20.

48 At p. 19.

49 At p. 27; my italics. The bond and association directed against Mary Queen of Scots in July 1584 was the model for an organization committed to a just but illegal activity. For discussion of the theme of 'association' during the Exclusion Crisis and its aftermath, R. Ashcraft, *Revolutionary Politics and Locke's 'Two Treatises of Government'* (Princeton, 1986), pp. 327–9. Our author may have inspired the 'Association' sworn after Pym's decisive attack on the peace party delivered at the Guildhall on 13 January (see *Book of Declarations*, vol. 2 (E243(1)), p. 848): if not, he wrote within hours of the event. The association was a particular project of Pym's at this time: see Hexter, *Reign of King Pym*, pp. 28–30. It was supported by *Scripture and Reason* (*supra*, n.46), p. 11.

50 At p. 25.

51 *A Present Answer to the Late Complaint unto the House of Commons* (11 Feb. 1643; E89(6)); E244(31) (*supra*, p. 660, n. 8), p. 23.

52 *A Just Complaint . . . against A Complaint to the House of Commons* (31 Jan. 1643; E245(27); the same claim is made in a work which just predates *Plaine English*: [C. Herle], *A Fuller Answer to a Treatise by Doctor Ferne* (29 Dec. 1642; E245(3)).

53 *A Plain Fault in Plain English, and the same in Doctor Fearne* (9 Feb. 1643; E88(30). Something close to a statement of democratic principles is also to be found in *An Answer to Mis-Led Dr. Ferne*, p. 19: 'I do wonder what government this objector would have in the world, if that most voices might not prevail . . . ?'

54 For the date of publication, Sirluck (ed.), *Complete Prose Works of John Milton*, ii. 46.

55 H. Ferne, *The Resolving of Conscience* (Cambridge, 1642), p. 25 (not in the Thomason collection). Ferne had also been refuted by Herle (*supra*, p. 664, n. 4) and was attacked in *Scripture and Reason Pleaded*. He restated his case in *Conscience Satisfied that there is no Warrant for the Arms now taken up by Subjects* (18 April 1643; E97(7)).

56 At pp. 133–4 of the 4° ed., 1643 (there being also an 8° edition). The *Brief Answer* was also published separately in 1643 (pp. 9–10 of that edition). The *postscript* to *The Glorious Name of God* shows that its separate publication came later. There is no copy of any of these editions in the Thomason collection.

57 On 20 May 1642 parliament had protested that the king's actions threatened the dissolution of the government: *Book of Declarations* vol. i (E24(1)), 259. On the theme of the dissolution of government, J.H. Franklin, *John Locke and the Theory of Sovereignty* (Cambridge, 1978).

58 J. Lilburne, *The Oppressed Mans Oppressions Declared* (30 Jan. 1647; E373(1)), p. 34.

59 *Sacro-sancta Regum Majestas* (30 Jan. 1644; E30(2)).

60 Sirluck (ed.), *Complete Prose Works of John Milton*, ii. 26–9, 133.

61 At p. 51.

62 BL, E89(21), p. 15.

63 BL, E96(10), p. 39.

64 R. Cust, 'Politics and the Electorate in the 1620s', in Cust and Hughes (eds), *Conflict in Early Stuart England*, pp. 134–67, at p. 139. For further discussion of fears of 'popularity' see the introduction by Cust and Hughes, and P. Lake's chapter, 'Anti-popery: The Structure of a Prejudice' (also chapter 7 above. Catholic and Protestant theories of 'popularity', meaning popular sovereignty, are attacked in [H. Constable], *A Discovery of a Counterfecte Conference* (Collen, 1600).

65 See A. Patterson, *Shakespeare and the Popular Voice* (Oxford, 1989), pp. 135–46.

Suggestions for further reading

It is impossible to give a comprehensive bibliography for this, one of the most studied periods of British history, so the following concentrates on books and articles which are representative of recent work and which supplement the themes explored in the Introduction and the articles we have selected. Additional material will be found in the notes.

A brief account of some recent divergent interpretations of the civil war is J.S. Morrill, B. Manning and D.E. Underdown, 'What was the English Revolution?', *History Today* (March, 1984). More wide-ranging guides to the historiography are R.P. Cust and A.L. Hughes, 'Introduction: After Revisionism', in R.P. Cust and A.L. Hughes (eds), *Conflict in Early Stuart England* (Harlow, Longman, 1989) and P.G. Lake, 'Wentworth's Political World in Revisionist and Post-revisionist Perspective', in J.F. Merritt (ed.), *The Political World of Thomas Wentworth, Earl of Strafford, 1621–1641* (Cambridge, Cambridge University Press, 1996). The most comprehensive guide is R.C. Richardson, *The Debate on the English Revolution Revisited* (London, Routledge, 1988).

Up-to-date textbooks combining analysis and narrative are B. Coward, *The Stuart Age* (2nd edn, Harlow, Longman, 1994) and D. Hirst, *Authority and Conflict, 1603–1658* (London, Arnold, 1986). For contrasting general interpretations, see C.S.R. Russell, *The Causes of the English Civil War* (Oxford, Oxford University Press, 1990) and A.L. Hughes, *The Causes of the English Civil War* (Basingstoke, Macmillan, 1991).

Parliament and politics

The main political events of the period from the beginning of the 1620s to the end of the 1640s – with the exception of the civil war years – are covered in a series of large monographs which combine analysis and narrative: C.S.R. Russell, *Parliaments and English Politics, 1621–1629*

(Oxford, Oxford University Press, 1979); K. Sharpe, *The Personal Rule of Charles I* (London, Yale University Press, 1992); C.S.R. Russell, *The Fall of the British Monarchies, 1637–1642* (Oxford, Oxford University Press, 1991); R. Ashton, *Counter Revolution: The Second Civil War and its Origins, 1646–1648* (London, Yale University Press, 1994); D. Underdown, *Pride's Purge: Politics in the Puritan Revolution* (Oxford, Oxford University Press, 1971).

For interpretations of the 1620s and 1630s which are critical of Russell's account of parliaments and revisionist approaches more generally, see J.P. Sommerville, *Politics and Ideology in England, 1603–1640* (Harlow, Longman, 1986); T.E. Cogswell, *The Blessed Revolution* (Cambridge, Cambridge University Press, 1989); R.P. Cust, *The Forced Loan and English Politics, 1626–1628* (Oxford, Oxford University Press, 1987); T.E. Cogswell, 'A Low Road to Extinction? Supply and Redress of Grievances in the Parliaments of the 1620s', *HJ*, 33 (1990) and the essays published in Cust and Hughes (eds), *Conflict in Early Stuart England* (1989). For a different emphasis, see K. Sharpe, 'Crown, Parliament and Locality: Government and Communication in Early Stuart England', *EHR*, 399 (1986) and G. Burgess, *The Politics of the Ancient Constitution* (Basingstoke, Macmillan, 1992).

Adamson's work on the baronial context of the 1640s is developed in his 'Parliamentary Management, Men of Business and the House of Lords, 1640–9', in C. Jones (ed.), *A Pillar of the Constitution: The House of Lords in British Politics, 1640–1784* (London, Hambledon, 1989) and 'The English Nobility and the Projected Settlement of 1647', *HJ*, 30 (1987). Kishlansky's arguments on the 1640s are further explored in his book *The Rise of the New Model Army* (Cambridge, Cambridge University Press, 1979) and his interpretation of seventeenth-century politics more generally in *Parliamentary Selection* (Cambridge, Cambridge University Press, 1986). Alternative interpretations of the New Model Army's role in politics are provided by I.J. Gentles, *The New Model Army in England, Ireland and Scotland, 1645–1653* (Oxford, Blackwell, 1992) and A. Woolrych, *Soldiers and Statesmen: The General Council of the Army and its Debates, 1647–8* (Oxford, Oxford University Press, 1987).

The British Problem

New work on the British Problem is being published all the time. For two valuable recent collections of essays, see S.G. Ellis and S. Barber (eds), *Conquest and Union: Fashioning a British State, 1485–1725* (Harlow, Longman, 1995) and A.J. Grant and K.J. Stringer (eds), *Uniting the Kingdom? The Making of British History* (London, Routledge, 1995). For Scotland, see also J.S. Morrill (ed.), *The Scottish National Covenant in* its British Context, 1638–1651 (Edinburgh, Edinburgh University Press, 1990) and C.S.R. Russell, 'The Anglo-Scottish Union 1603–1643: A Success?, in A. Fletcher and P. Roberts (eds), *Religion, Culture and Society in Early Modern Britain: Essays in Honour of Patrick Collinson* (Cambridge, Cambridge University Press, 1994); for Ireland, N. Canny, 'The Attempted Anglicization of Ireland in the Seventeenth Century: An Exemplar of "British History"', in Merritt (ed.), *The Political World of Thomas Wentworth, Earl of Strafford, 1621–1641* and the essays in J.H. Ohlmeyer (ed.), *Ireland From Independence to Occupation, 1641–1660* (Cambridge, Cambridge University Press, 1995).

Religion

Tyacke's interpretation of the impact of Arminianism on politics in this period is more fully developed in his *Anti-Calvinists: The Rise of English Arminianism, c. 1590–1640* (Oxford, Oxford University Press, 1987) and is also explored in the essays in K. Fincham (ed.), *The Early Stuart Church* (Basingstoke, Macmillan, 1993). Julian Davies, *The Caroline Captivity of the Church: Charles 1 and the Remoulding of Anglicanism* (Oxford, Oxford University Press, 1992), emphasizes the role of the king, while Peter White, *Predestination, Policy and Polemic* (Cambridge, Cambridge University Press, 1992) stresses the moderation of the Arminians. On the other hand P.G. Lake, 'Calvinism and the English Church, 1570–1635', *P&P*, 114 (1987), and A. Milton, *Catholic and Reformed: The Roman and Protestant Church in English Protestant Thought, 1600–1640* (Cambridge, Cambridge University Press, 1995) emphasize the Arminians' divisiveness.

The nature of Puritanism is discussed in P. Collinson, *The Religion of Protestants: The Church in English Society, 1559–1625* (Oxford, Oxford University Press, 1982); P.G. Lake, 'Defining Puritanism – Again?', in F. Bremer (ed.), *Puritanism: Transatlantic Perspectives on a Seventeenth-Century Anglo-American Faith* (Boston, MA, Massachusetts Historical Society 1993); N.R.N. Tyacke, *The Fortunes of English Puritanism, 1603–1640* (Dr Williams's Library Lecture, London, 1990); P.G. Lake, 'Deeds Against Nature: Cheap Print, Protestantism and Murder in Early-Seventeenth-Century England', in P.G. Lake and K. Sharpe (eds), *Culture and Politics in Early Stuart England* (Basingstoke, Macmillan, 1994) and the essays in C. Durston and J. Eales (eds), *The Culture of English Puritanism, 1560–1700* (Basingstoke, Macmillan, 1996).

For 'parish anglicanism', see C. Haigh, *English Reformations: Religion, Politics and Society under the Tudors* (Oxford, Oxford University Press, 1993); J. Maltby '"By this Book": Parishioners, the Prayer Book and the Established Church', in Fincham (ed.), *The Early Stuart Church* and J.S.

Morrill, 'The Church in England', in J.S. Morrill (ed.), *Reactions to the English Civil War* (Basingstoke, Macmillan, 1982).

Localism

For interpretations of the period which emphasize localism and loyalty to the 'county community', see A. Everitt, *The Community of Kent and the Great Rebellion* (Leicester, Leicester University Press, 1966) and his *The Local Community and the Great Rebellion* (Historical Association pamphlet, 1969) and J.S. Morrill, *The Revolt of the Provinces* (London, George Allen and Unwin, 1976). Holmes's critique of this framework is further developed in A.L. Hughes, 'Warwickshire on the Eve of Civil War: A County Community?', *MH*, 7 (1982), her 'Local History and the Origins of the Civil War', in Cust and Hughes (eds), *Conflict in Early Stuart England* and R.P. Cust and P.G. Lake, 'Sir Richard Grosvenor and the Rhetoric of Magistracy', *BIHR*, 54 (1981). For local attitudes to national politics, see R.P. Cust, 'Politics and the Electorate in the 1620s', in Cust and Hughes (eds), *Conflict in Early Stuart England* and C.B. Herrup, 'The Counties and the Country: Some Thoughts on Seventeenth-Century Historiography', *Social History*, 8 (1993).

The impact of the civil war on local communities is discussed in C. Carlton, *Going to the Wars: The Experience of the English Civil Wars, 1638–1651* (London, Routledge, 1992) and I. Roy, 'England Turned Germany? The Aftermath of the Civil War in its European Context', *TRHS* (1986).

Society and culture

Interpretations of the civil war within a Marxist framework are provided by Christopher Hill, *Puritanism and Revolution* (London, Secker and Warburg, 1958; pbk edn, London, Panther History, 1968), and *Society and Puritanism* (London, Secker and Warburg, 1964; pbk edn, London, Panther History, 1969), and also B. Manning, *The English People and the English Revolution* (London, Heinemann, 1976). Christopher Hill, *The World Turned Upside Down* (London, Temple Smith, 1972) sets the radical ideas of the 1640s and 1650s within this context. For a discussion of the significance of 'class' in this period, see K. Wrightson, 'Estates, Degrees and Sorts: Changing Perceptions of Society in Tudor and Stuart England', in P. Corfield (ed.), *Language, History and Class* (Oxford, Blackwell, 1991); for a more 'conservative' interpretation of popular culture see the essays in T. Harris, *Popular Culture in England, c. 1500–1850* (Basingstoke, Macmillan, 1995).

K. Wrightson, *English Society, 1580–1680* (London, Hutchinson, 1982) and D. Underdown, *Revel, Riot and Rebellion: Popular Politics and Culture in England, 1603–1660* (Oxford, Oxford University Press, 1985) discuss religion and politics in their social and cultural context.

Political culture

Two recent collections of essays, P.G. Lake and K. Sharpe (eds), *Culture and Politics in Early Stuart England* (Basingstoke, Macmillan, 1994) and S.D. Amussen and M.A. Kishlansky (eds), *Political Culture and Cultural Politics in Early Modern England* (Manchester, Manchester University Press, 1995), offer some of the most important work on the political culture of the period; see, in particular, the introduction to Sharpe and Lake. R.P. Cust, 'Wentworth's "Change of Sides" in the 1620s' and A. Milton, 'Thomas Wentworth and the Political Thought of the Personal Rule', in Merritt (ed.), *The Political World of Thomas Wentworth* also discuss politics from a similar perspective.

Index